Dinosaurs Ever Evolving

Dinosaurs Ever Evolving

The Changing Face of Prehistoric Animals in Popular Culture

ALLEN A. DEBUS

Foreword by J.D. Lees

McFarland & Company, Inc., Publishers
Jefferson, North Carolina

Also of Interest
and from McFarland

Dinosaur Sculpting: A Complete Guide, 2d ed.,
by Allen A. Debus, Bob Morales *and* Diane E. Debus (2013)

Prehistoric Monsters: The Real and Imagined Creatures of the Past That We Love to Fear, by Allen A. Debus (2010)

Dinosaurs in Fantastic Fiction: A Thematic Survey,
by Allen A. Debus (2006; softcover 2013)

Paleoimagery: The Evolution of Dinosaurs in Art,
by Allen A. Debus *and* Diane E. Debus (2002; softcover 2011)

Library of Congress Cataloguing-in-Publication Data

Names: Debus, Allen A.
Title: Dinosaurs ever evolving : the changing face of prehistoric animals in popular culture / Allen A. Debus ; foreword by J.D. Lees.
Description: Jefferson, North Carolina : McFarland & Company, Inc., Publishers, 2016. | Includes bibliographical references and index.
Identifiers: LCCN 2016021667 | ISBN 9780786499519 (softcover : acid free paper) ∞
Subjects: LCSH: Dinosaurs in popular culture. | Dinosaurs in mass media.
Classification: LCC QE861.95 .D34 2016 | DDC 567.9—dc23
LC record available at https://lccn.loc.gov/2016021667

British Library cataloguing data are available

ISBN (print) 978-0-7864-9951-9
ISBN (ebook) 978-1-4766-2432-7

Front cover: "Dinosaurs in the Nuclear Age" by Todd Tennant/
Tennart Illustrations

Printed in the United States of America

McFarland & Company, Inc., Publishers
Box 611, Jefferson, North Carolina 28640
www.mcfarlandpub.com

To my grandson,
Tyler Dennis

Table of Contents

Foreword by J.D. Lees

As the saying goes, "Some men see things as they are and say why." I would suggest that most men, and most women, too, for that matter, may see things as they are, but never actually get to the "why."

At this point in human history, we live amidst an unprecedented flood of cultural offerings. From amateur YouTube uploads to quarter-billion-dollar major studio summer blockbuster movies, from self-recorded CDs to established "record" label releases that garner ten million on-line hits the day of release, from self-published, downloadable novels, comics and graphic novels to a bewildering blizzard of visual and literary media churned out by uncountable publishing houses, "culture" has never been easier and more accessible to create and market, and as a result, there's never been more of it.

Most of us are so busy consuming this cultural avalanche, is it any wonder that few even consider the "why"? Why does the culture we encounter every day exist in its peculiar forms at this particular time?

Just as the current diversity of life on our planet is the outcome of millions of years of related events, including catastrophes, mutations, competition, hybridization, and a myriad of other processes, so too must various aspects of current culture be the product of a similar synthesis. Since today's culture didn't appear fully formed from a theoretical Big Bang, what influences have caused it to take on the shape and content that it has?

For the few who would pause to even begin such a contemplation, it's obvious that this sort of question doesn't lend itself to a quick Google search or a brief browse through Wikipedia. Formulating any sort of coherent and credible answer, for any aspect of popular culture, would take a great deal of research and thoughtfulness. It would demand encyclopedic knowledge, a prodigious memory, a mind capable of recognizing and reconstructing patterns of the recent past, and a superior communication ability to express the findings in an engaging and accessible manner.

Fortunately for fans of those grand and glorious creatures, the dinosaurs (whether of the real or fanciful, literary or cinematic variety), there is an individual, perhaps a one-in-a-billion individual, possessing all the attributes listed above. His name is Allen A. Debus, and he's the author of the book currently resting in your talons.

In addition to previously having authored a small plethora of books on dino-related topics, Allen has been writing for my publication (*G-FAN*, devoted to Godzilla and his kindred kaiju) and a variety of other publications in different but related genres, for many years. His work consistently exhibits a depth and breadth of familiarity with all aspects of dinosaur/kaiju culture like no other author's. This includes not only the natural history aspect (itself an almost overwhelming field of knowledge), but also the history of the natural history, if I may call it that. (I'm referring to the bone-hunters and discoverers, the curators and organizers and theorists from Bakker to Cuvier and back again, the trends and topics, friendships and feuds, all the happenstance and circumstance that accompanied the unearthing of our present-day knowledge of the life of long, long ago.)

Allen also exhibits a commanding knowledge of dinosaurian literary history, from pulps to comics, from movie novelizations to the flights of fancy from the great sci-fi authors. He not only reads them but remembers them, analyzes them, tears them apart and puts them back together in an interwoven tapestry of enlightenment. He's an artist and accomplished sculptor, and an expert on the origins and evolution of what he calls "paleo-imagery." Life alone didn't change through time. The way artists depict the parade of life has undergone its own form of evolution, to match our dynamic understanding and perceptions of the ancient beasts.

So when it comes to selecting a guide for a time-traveling examination of the ever-changing role and meaning of the dinosaur in popular culture, there's literally no man on the planet better qualified for the job than Allen. Be prepared for an intricate yet orderly passage through the strata of cultural consciousness. Unearth the early paleo-novels and learn how they connected with the popular paradigms of their day. Thrill as the tensions of the Cold War create new and ever more bizarre cinematic dinosaurian horrors. Uncover the exotic links between life in the ancient past and the modern-day environmental movement. And witness the ultimate convergence of man with dinosaur, as the boundaries between science fiction and reality blur and meld.

If it all sounds like an epic "a million years in the making," I'd say you've got the general idea. Buckle up and enjoy your adventure. You're in the best of hands.

J. D. Lees, a retired educator who lives in Manitoba, is a devoted fan and researcher of Godzilla and kaiju films. He organizes and oversees the annual G-Fest in Chicago and has edited and published the popular magazine G-FAN *for a quarter of a century, more than 110 issues. He is a coauthor (with Marc Cerasini) of* The Official Godzilla Compendium *(1998).*

Introduction

Pop-Cultural Evolution of the Prehistoric Dino-Monster: Meaning and Metaphor

The dinosaurs evolved into "us." In a socio-cultural context, dinosaurs assumed early popular roles as ambassadors to discovering the geological past as it was being defined through contemporary "evolutionary epics," later giving way in the aftermath of World War II to more highly mutated forms framing society's fears of extinction. Throughout, dinosaurs as conveyed to the masses through the minds of writers and film producers have become increasingly *anthropomorphized*, especially in the wake of hydrogen bomb testing. In a nutshell, this is an alternate history to the "evolution" of dinosaurs as they've existed in popular culture. Rather than a simple twofold history as illustrated within a scientific realm (dinosaurs as cold-blooded creatures, bowing to their warmer-blooded, scientifically reinvented selves during the "Dinosaur Renaissance" of the 1970s), within popular culture dinosaurs (a term used loosely and more inclusively herein) enjoyed a tripartite history—one perhaps not fully addressed until now.

Accordingly, this book has threefold organization. First, origins of the dinosaur's prominence in popular culture stem from its didactic role in 19th century readings of life through time, also known as the "evolutionary epic." Although dinosaurs were not the only group of prehistoric animals encountered on this geological time tour by museum visitors and avid readers, they became prehistory's totemic figures. Secondly, by the mid–20th century, dinosaurs acquired a darker, grimmer symbolic countenance, mirroring mankind's fears of extinction, especially in light of the hydrogen bomb's invention. During this intermediate phase, dinosaurs in popular culture often served as warnings to mankind. Finally, during our self-inflicted Anthropocene age, as scientists contemplated other environmental and ecological hurdles faced by civilization that could lead to our demise, like never before, dinosaurs of popular culture increasingly became "relevant." They assumed outright human shape and intelligence, desperately or sometimes mockingly urging us from our destructive path.

A synopsis of this original topic, featuring several visual examples, appeared previously in Chapter Two of *Dinosaur Sculpting: A Complete Guide*, 2nd ed. (McFarland, 2013).[1] Here, in *Three Ages of the Dinosaur*, the topic is expanded, relying on considerably different examples, elaborating on the traditionalized life-through-time phase which became superseded as nuclear fears of the mid–20th century escalated, translating into increasingly anthropomorphized dino-monsters, then ultimately into dino-men (evolved in sci-fi guise from gill-men stock) or "dinosauroids" comprehending our inevitable shared fates.

Part I

As paleontologist Jose Luis Sanz noted, what became known as "dinomania" didn't originate with release of the phenomenal 1993 film, *Jurassic Park*. Rather, popular interest in prehistoric life and paleontology was stoked during the first half of the 19th century.[2] Among early popularized publications framing prehistoria with evolutionary concepts was Robert Chambers's *Vestiges of Natural History of Creation* (1st ed. 1844), which will be addressed in Chapter Two. *Vestiges* was among the earliest pseudoscientific life-through-time embellishments (incorporating dinosaurians), and most popular for its time. Through a variety of means and media, even before dinosaurs were scarcely known (e.g., before they became household names during the 20th century), there were other paleo-monsters for fertile minds and imaginations to feast upon. Yet for a century, the emphasis was usually on addressing the evolution of such creatures throughout geological time.

Quite apart from constantly relaying strict scientific impressions and interpretations, perhaps catalyzed by early influential works such as by Chambers, gradually the life-through-time theme as broadcast via paleoart and accompanying imagetext became borrowed into popular venues, including scores of popular books, and more commonly recruited into science-fictional or fantasy representations (e.g., novels, short stories and films). In Part I of this book we'll explore several unexpected extrapolations or unusual enhancements of the fossil life through geological time theme (usually without granting dinosaurs special emphasis or prominence, as was often the case then but which usually isn't the case today).

True, dinosaurs' popularity didn't become an item in popular literature—as in newspaper accounts—until after 1896.[3] Instead, for many decades, among the paleo-vertebrata there was a general emphasis on prehistoric mammals. But by the early 1900s through 1910s, dinosaurs (or rather their likenesses as restored by artists) were already ensconced within lavishly illustrated books of the time, such as those authored by Henry R. Knipe and Henry Fairfield Osborn, and their crumbly old bones were beginning to invade museums around the globe in the form of mounted displays, especially in America (thanks to Osborn's work at New York's American Museum of Natural History).

Charles Darwin's (1809–1882) grandfather, Erasmus Darwin (1731–1802), published one of the earliest life-through-time speculations in English, titled *Zoonomania; or the Laws of Organic Life* (between 1794 to 1796). And thereafter as the 19th century unfolded, dawning into the 20th, visual artists increasingly conveyed their impressions of life's progression from earliest geological eras and periods, leading to the present.[4] These paintings, murals and other restorations adorned museum displays situated aside reconstructed skeletons, and wended their way into popular books.

By mid–20th century, a host of such artistic renderings appearing in numerous venues and publications inculcated the salient life-through-time theme. In 1993, paleontologist Stephen Jay Gould noted four successive stages, or "waystations" in the developmental history of paleo-iconography, while in 1999, in the more general case of fannish paleoimagery, cultural historian W.J.T. Mitchell suggested a more abstract threefold synopsis.[5] Neither outlined paleoart history quite like I have organizationally addressed the overall dinosaurian "odyssey" herein, delving beyond (strictly) the visual arts into contemporary popular and scientific literature.[6] (Also see the Epilogue.) Perhaps owing largely to this earliest, foundational phase in "dinomania," Mitchell astutely claims that the generalized concept of the dinosaur is "not just 'a' totem animal of modernity, but *the* animal image that has, by a complex process of cultural selection, emerged as the globally popular symbol of modern humanity's relation to nature."[7]

Part II

However, for our purposes the central life-through-time example is Rudolph F. Zallinger's (1919–1995) *Age of Reptiles,* completed for Yale University's Peabody Museum in 1947, particularly the Late Cretaceous terminus of this mural, with its menacing smoldering volcanoes. One may contemplate as well in this painting what has been termed the feared "human volcano" of extinction.[8] Zallinger's vignette augurs the Cold War angst phase of dinosaurian reign—leading toward intricately refined mass extinction theories as they emerged three decades later, during the early Dinosaur Renaissance period.

During the 1950s, dinosaurs' utility as reminders, or as most emblematic and endearing "instructors" and symbolic guides directing perceptions of life's long history, was steadily becoming secondary to a newly adapted role and darker purpose in movies and novels. After all, as paleontologist Stephen L. Brusatte observed:

> The end–Cretaceous mass extinction is one of five such mass die-offs in the fossil record, and has undoubtedly been the most studied of the bunch. While great extinctions and global catastrophes will always arouse the interest of the general public, the true importance of understanding the dinosaur extinction really relates to comprehending our place in nature, and coming to grips with the causes and effects of periods of mass global devastation.... There is mounting evidence that human-induced pollution and overpopulation is actively causing a so-called 'sixth mass extinction,' whose effects, and perhaps very reality, are obscured by humanity's inability to comprehend long-term trends.[9]

Brusatte made his remarks in 2012, although prominent scientists were already pondering these weighty concerns throughout the 1950s and 1960s.

However, one still finds filmic references to dinosaurs conveying life-through-time imagery and perspective in filmic fare lingering into the Cold War period, such as the 1959 Americanized version of Toho's *Godzilla Raids Again* (i.e., *Gigantis, the Fire Monster*), and Karel Zeman's Czech masterpiece, *Journey to the Beginning of Time* (1955), to be addressed in Chapter Five. And although intrigue over the old life-through-time tale diminished during the Dinosaur Renaissance of the 1970s and beyond into the next, current millennium, yet a whimsical vestige of this former tradition persists every evening via a television theme song composed by the Barenaked Ladies to introduce one of television's most popular syndicated comedies, *The Big Bang Theory.*

For many decades, dinosaurs and a cohort of other popular prehistoric animals (e.g., mastodons, saber-toothed cats, pterodactyls, fin-backed Permian reptiles, plesiosaurs and even certain groupings of cavemen) were "intended" to symbolize American might, virility, and industriousness, man's superiority over nature, or were simply emblematic of "moral lessons" concerning evolutionary ideology (which most vertebrate paleontologists of today would no longer espouse), culminating in human civilization. But during the early years of the Cold War, thanks to motion picture studios and other media, the nature of lessons men were learning from prehistoria, whether subliminally or directly, such as these steered quite a different course. Dinosaurs were "evolving" in public view, becoming all too eerily familiar, taking on human guise as concerns about polluting volcanoes were giving way to fears over damaging effects of radioactivity, and how mankind might topple his precarious existence on Earth. Writer Jase Short aptly commented in 2013, "The strange beasts ... are more than frightening creatures, they are social hauntings embodying human history.... They are produced, in short, to exorcise the real monsters that haunt human history."[10]

By 1953, recognition of the metaphorical "human volcano"—atmospheric pollution caused by man—became translated into an equivalently destructive, yet human-caused manner of extinction. Giant dino-monsters invaded the silver screen warning of human folly. Many of these faux- or pseudo-dinosaurians strained belief, due to their impossible size, unnatural biology and invulnerability—let alone their very existence in modernity. And so film producers often resorted to visual sleight of hand in order to suspend disbelief in their implausibility.[11] Other "genera" of giant, radioactive monsters also appeared in drive-in movies and matinees (especially giant insects and spiders), but as we shall see, it was only the dinosaurian monster breed which persisted through the decades since, transforming into slighter varieties—dino-doppelgangers thereafter wielding intelligence capable of communicating our plight. As shall be discussed in Part II of this book, the most significant gigantic dino-monster revenant starred in Toho's 1954 *Gojira*. During this harrowing phase of their pop-cultural odyssey, Godzilla stole the show, enjoying accolades equally shared with real dinosaurs then known to science.

Coupled with Dr. Yamane's (played by actor Takashi Shimura) prophetic warning, the two Godzilla creatures appearing in, first, *Gojira* (1954) and then *Godzilla Raids Again* (1955) may possibly be considered symbolic of the two relatively low-yield atomic bombs detonated over Hiroshima and then Nagasaki in August 1945. But there is greater inspiration leading to the *Gojira* tale than two (horrific) atomic attacks, namely the *Lucky Dragon* incident of 1954, coincident with *Gojira*'s production.

It may be considered politically incorrect today for Americans to think this way. But in the aftermath of World War II, it must be (historically) understandable that, generally, the Japanese islanders were not thought highly of by many if not most Americans then, especially by those who defended our country in the Pacific theater. The pairing of atomic attacks was believed absolutely essential to end a brutal, bloody war. Applying political spin, the *Lucky Dragon* incident, likewise, was not considered to be our fault. (See Chapter Nine.) After all, politically and militarily, we had a right to develop and test our weapons and protect ourselves because the Russian Soviets had also deciphered how to build hydrogen bombs (or the H-bomb). And it was the Cold War (or as some have lately opined–Cold War I).

Atomic bombs could devastate most sectors of an industrial city, but it was becoming generally understood that hydrogen bombs were vastly more powerful, and capable of unleashing far more radioactivity. Prophetically so, for what can be imagined is always eventually done. If sufficient quantities of such bombs were detonated in a world war, radiation would be widespread and mankind would face extinction. Indeed, several contemporary prominent scientists even (analogously) proposed theories of mass extinction in the fossil record founded upon *radiation* emitted from supernova blasts. Understandably, when the

Soviets could deploy weapons 1000 times more powerful than the U.S. bombs detonated to truncate the brutal Pacific War in 1945, then it's a problem—*our* problem. So who really cares as much about life's magnificent journey through an abyss of time when our short reign on Earth seems on the verge of ending in undignified fashion? Placing matters further in perspective, you know the drill, as we then practiced—crouch down in the hall, head between your legs and kiss your ass goodbye.

However, apart from geopolitical matters, U.S. public concern and angst—as reflected "pop-culturally" in numerous B-grade and many monster movies of the time—rose after Russia wielded the H-Bomb too, thus greatly escalating America's Cold War fears (which weren't as heightened *before* Russia had the H-bomb). In time, nuclear fears of what never happened to Americans then must have (psychologically) escalated to the dread and painful memories of what actually had happened earlier in 1945 Japan and to the Japanese, only far worse.

And so, in short, while the Japanese dino-monsters of the 1950s are a reflection of the two World War II bombings, but more so resultant of the *Lucky Dragon* incident, America's giant filmic monsters (dinosaurs, colossal men and big bugs, etc.) are a creative metaphoric outcome and outpouring of our Cold War confrontation with Russia, although focused on the "what if" possibility that the two nations may attack each other with hydrogen bombs. Simply the *fear* that American cities were about to be assaulted by the Soviets with their hydrogen bombs launched from foreign soil or (later) even outer space proved all-consuming and prevalent.

Japanese and American giant monsters of the 1950s and early 1960s are both allegorical and metaphoric for contemporary nuclear tensions, but (in contrast to Japan's wartime and incidental circumstances) our giant monsters more closely mirror Cold War fears of H-bomb attacks from Russia, which increasingly became a conceivable, realistic concern circa post–1953. In Japanese monster movies, use of nuclear weapons is generally restrained, refrained or substituted for more palatable (i.e., to the Japanese) non-radioactive technology. Conversely, in a host of analogous U.S. period films and other public media such as the Charlton *Gorgo* comic book series of the early 1960s, we wield nuclear might with demonstrative impunity, winning success, while then unconvincingly resolving radioactive "outbreaks" in some satisfying, if not all-too-convenient manner.

Part III

In his *Evolution in the Past* (1912), Henry R. Knipe refers to the ancient Greek philosopher Plato's "special definition" of a man, namely a "biped without feathers. Dinosaurs, therefore, were not dreamt of in his philosophy."[12] With scientific revelations dating to 1996, now we know certain dinosaurs were feathered and bipedal. But even with or without feathery adornment, dinosaurians increasingly began (science fictionally) morphing into humans (and vice versa) decades ago, notably during the mid–1950s. By the late 1990s, an assortment of dino-people had become commonly encountered science fictional and fantasy characters. As we shall learn in Part III of this book, there were particular apocalyptical reasons for the emergence of such "dinosauroids" then and their profound establishment thereafter.

While the earliest apocalyptical dino-monsters of film were frightening in countenance, eventually during the mid–1960s through the early 1970s, even the most harrowing of these—Godzilla—became anthropomorphized in appearance, looking far less menacing and human-like.[13] Godzilla adopted a "son" tagged "Minya," whose annoying human-like characteristics definitively place it among the early dinosauroids. The overall effect across several Toho films is not unlike the pattern of "neoteny" in which organisms successively engender offspring across many generations that tend to increasingly bear juvenile qualities even on into adulthood. Stephen Jay Gould discussed the neotenous fifty-year evolution in the Disney character, Mickey Mouse, for example, in which the mouse's appearance became more expressively youthful.[14] During later stages of the Dinosaur Renaissance, film and television producers, and story writers quite resourcefully featured dinosaurian characters as reptilian-humans ... as if normal humans had awoken one morning in full dinosaurian suits and guises. Characters such as "Barney," the purple children's dinosaur (to adults, the scariest dino-monster of all!), extraterrestrial reptiloids in the television show and novel *V*, the "Sinclair" family featured in the early 1990s satire comedy program *Dinosaurs* and, thereafter, characters in steamy novels in which humans even engage in coitus with dinosaurs, count among the growing, wildly diversifying flock here. So since 1940, dino-anthropormorphism (here contrasted with the amphibioid gillmen of science fiction and fantasy—see Chapter Seventeen) took on a host of guises and in-your-face meaning.

At first, human actors wore dinosaurian suits for filmic roles—a symbolic melding of species personae, one which had experienced cataclysmic extinction 66 million years ago, the other facing extinction while suicidally possessing the means for self-extermination. Dinosaurs later "talked" to one another, not only in giant dino-monster movies of the 1950s or *Jurassic Park III* (2001), but also in children's cartoon films. And so we must decipher what is "a" dinosauroid, vs. *the* Dinosauroid of 1982, while comprehending the many other near varieties. Capable of intelligent conversation or spiteful mockery, such creatures can indeed warn mankind, or may simply be reduced to human caricatures living in structured societies meant to entertain or perhaps chide us into thinking more deeply about our folly and where it's all leading. (If only Jonathan Swift were alive today!)

U.S. citizens have experienced (or rather, weathered) two heightened phases of concern over potential nuclear attack from the (former) Soviet Union, first from 1953 through the Cuban Missile Crisis of 1962, and then two decades later during the early 1980s when scientists unveiled the apocalyptical nature of global "nuclear winter." Curiously if not coincidentally, it was during these times that dinosauroids of literature and art, respectively, originated and then began proliferating. Ultimately, conceivable extinction of the human race formed a basis for their creation. After all, as related by astrophysicist Neil deGrasse Tyson in the popular televised *Cosmos: A Spacetime Odyssey* (Episode 9, "The Lost Worlds of Planet Earth," first aired on May 4, 2014), "The dinosaurs never saw the asteroid coming. What's our excuse?"

Note that dino-anthropmoriphism hasn't entirely replaced life-through-time, although it has taken up an increasingly larger chunk of the pop-cultural paleo-pie. Understand that just as in organic evolution, one newly evolved form doesn't necessarily replace the previous ancestral line, newly conceptualized kinds of dinosaurians taking place in recent popular culture do not entirely wipe out the old lineage. (In nature, speciation is usually a "bush," not a "ladder," and sometimes newly sprouted twigs can eventually become more prominent and diverse than earlier branches.) The three ages of the dinosaur as outlined here aren't temporally exclusive. Hence, we will continue to see creative examples of traditional life-through-time paleoimagery alongside successively newer emblematic imaginings such as gigantic metaphorical dino-monsters and intelligent dinosauroids of the Cold War and Dinosaur Renaissance periods, respectively.[15]

I sincerely appreciate the artistic talents of my artists this go-around, each of whom contributed new portrayals—Mike Fredericks, Dougal Dixon, Jason Croghan, and my daughters Kristen L. Dennis and Lisa R. Szilagyi. Todd Tennant vividly captured the spirit of the book with his magnificent cover prepared especially for this volume. John D. Lees, editor of the illustrious *G-Fan* magazine—devoted to all things Godzilla—took time out from his ultra-busy schedule to pen a foreword. Thanks also for love and encouragement of my wife, Diane, and my mother Brunilda L. Debus. Hope lingers that harrowing events of this turmoil-stricken, rapidly environmentally-depredated century might eventually favor our planet upon which the up and coming generation, that to which my grandson Tyler E. Dennis (to whom this book is dedicated) belongs, must survive.

PART I

Perpetuating the Life Through Geological Time Paradigm

The first six chapters in this book address the traditional life through geological time tale, which is the basic bedrock backstory to that favored tale of the gradual unfolding of prehistoric life many of us are familiar with today. When one casually thought of prehistoric life a century or so ago, ideology of evolutionary forces majestically churning forth distinctive creatures from the earliest Cambrian Period (e.g., trilobites) leading to the Mesozoic dinosaurian ages, and onward through the exalted "Age of Mammals," with civilized man poised at the apotheosis—the topmost rung of the ladder of geological time—is the (erroneous, yet) highly popularized imagery which typically came to mind. All thanks to contemporary science popularizers of the 19th century.

But circumstances weren't always this way. For many years the "evolutionary epic" wasn't known or commonly understood by the public. Perhaps it's a little like challenging concepts in chemistry and physics. During the early to mid–20th century only a small student percentage became well acquainted with, for example, chemical thermodynamics, quantum mechanics, or Einstein's relativity principles. Not everyone took courses in calculus then. Today especially, physics classes are well attended, even in high school, and consequently, it would be rather challenging to follow popular science fiction, or popular documentaries on astronomy and cosmology, or to just be a "nerd," without being at least conversant with such fundamental concepts. Likewise, during the 19th century, the idea of a life through geological time tour must have seemed engagingly fresh and dazzlingly new to receptive minds, even if that marvelous journey could only occur in one's imagination, or stem from within the pages of a book.

This phase of popular excitement concerning dinosaurs and those other prehistoric animals and their mysterious, nearly impenetrable worlds of the past, is usually addressed by presenting a succession of imagery, visually illustrating how scientists and artists perceived sequential ages of remote prehistory. And thus, this is how the depiction of deep geological time was imprinted on the minds of an adoring public, museum-goers, amateur fossil hunters, avid readers, or aspiring science fiction authors, decades before. But this visual element has been thoroughly examined a number of times already, and so my goal here is to instead exemplify how the idea of life through geological time permeated into other popular venues—beyond museum murals, paintings and displays, or images authorized by contemporary paleontologists. For if a concept was popularized, then there must have been other markers and vestiges recording how such ideology proliferated and spread, encouraging while inculcating the masses toward its fuller contemporary meaning.

So in Part I, important and influential books will be emphasized, delving into philosophical, fictional and (from our perspective) not quite so fictional ideologies, as well as two once popular films. Of course it's difficult to talk about life through time *without* occasionally referring to contemporary static paleoart and cinematic paleoimagery, as addressed, respectively, in Chapters Three and Five.

And so I've corralled seven rare or unusual examples (in six chapters) proffering thematic perspective on this prevalent and prominent first phase. There are others, of course, stemming from this period. For instance, Jules Verne's 1864 (1867 revised ed.) novel *Journey to the Center of the Earth* (discussed in Chapter One of my book *Dinosaurs in Fantastic Fiction*) would be one example, while paleontologist Charles H. Sternberg's science fiction time travel story (discussed in Chapter Seven of my book *Prehistoric Monsters*) would be another. Here, I've chosen a rather unconventional means for outlining paleontology's most traditional tale! But the story must eventually lead somewhere (beyond cultural tradition—presenting further key stages in public perception of the divergently evolving cultural history of dinosaurs, coupled with their widely projected images and meaning—the gist of *my* story), and so accordingly Part I will be the shortest of the three.

In order for scientific ideas to be disseminated and cultivated within a popular vein, it helps if there are science popularizers around—science geeks, then and now!—who affably and dramatically convey, facilitate, infuse, or simply "wow" an adoring public with such knowledge. And when it came to early understanding of the ideology concerning life's long geohistory, two such rock stars emerged: Humphry Davy, who outlined an early view on life's changes through time; and Georges Cuvier, who propounded the idea of successive episodes of "revolutionary" mass extinctions in the fossil record (and who will further discussed in Part II). During the early 19th century, Cuvier convincingly established that distinctive life forms and organisms had appeared in a *succession* of former geological ages, punctuated by mass extinctions. It was then left to others, such as Davy, to debate, consider, modify and perpetuate Cuvier's dramatic and well-publicized conclusions, through many decades down to the present day.

Chapter One

Sir Humphry Davy's Volcanic Considerations of Life Through Geological Time

In the beginning, there was the volcano. Partly a metaphor, but far more than simply that. Mount Tambora in Indonesia exploded in 1815; although little is known of the eruption itself today, we know of its aftermath. Tambora, releasing perhaps as much as 100 cubic kilometers of ash ejected into the atmosphere, may have been even more explosive than Krakatoa's 1883 dramatic and well documented detonation. But for our purposes, Tambora's scattered atmospheric particulate caused widespread weather cooling, or what has been referred to as a persistently rainy "year without a summer"—1816, extending over Europe and Great Britain. For our purposes, however, thousands of miles away during that anomalous summer of 1816, Tambora's fiery outburst may have led to a foundational literary invention—*Frankenstein, or the Modern Prometheus*! As cited by Michael Allaby and James Lovelock, "We may owe the story of Frankenstein and his monster to a volcanic eruption, for quite possibly it is this that produced the poor weather of the summer of 1816, and it was that poor weather which kept Percy Bysshe Shelley, Mary Godwin, Claire Clairmont, and Lord Byron indoors during their visit to Geneva and provided the romantic circumstances that led Mary to write her novel...."[1]

Volcanoes and the cause of their eruptions were then a favored research area for one very popular and singular scientist of the day, one who also was clearly within Mary Godwin's (1797–1851, later Shelley's) father's (William Godwin) inner sanctum of associates—Humphry Davy, himself imbued with a "Romantic outlook."[2] From several sources we know that Davy visited the elder Godwin at his domicile in London, where Mary may have met him. Also it is documented that Mary consulted Davy's *Elements of Chemical Philosophy* (1812) during the time she was feverishly writing her *Frankenstein* tale in 1816. Years later, Mary even pondered writing work on geology, which surely would have addressed the nature of volcanoes, and perhaps the story of life through geological time—both topics tackled by Davy during his auspicious career. Mary's 1830 proposal was for an "elementary work on the science ... although she was unsure 'how far such a *history* [my italics] would be amusing.'"[3]

Not long after Mary died in 1851, another famed but then aspiring foundational author, Jules Verne, published 1864's *Journey to the Center of the Earth*, concerning representations of life through geological time encountered by intrepid scientists who descend within an Icelandic volcano; references to Davy's by then antiquated work on volcanoes are scattered throughout this imaginative novel. And here we note Davy's pop-cultural significance, whose chemical work facilitated Mary's envisioning of the metaphorical Frankenstein monster—reanimated spawn of volcanoes and electrochemistry—whose meaning and theme lives on today even in such modern monsters of the atomic age as Godzilla and Gorgo. Davy's life through geological time contemplations of 1830 were inextricably linked to his understanding of Earth's volcanic history, as envisioned within Verne's fascinating novel. And so much of this was fated during that shadowy Summer of the Volcano. Eventually, during the dawning nuclear age, volcanoes were to become symbolic of major disruptions in the flow and continuity of life through geological time, and perhaps even of man's coming extinction! But in time we'll come to all that.

Science popularizers are not far out of reach today. Quite often they must seem ubiquitously visible, instructing in televised documentaries, for example, on the NOVA, Smithsonian, Science or History Channels, or even seen doing television commercials. Besides astronomy and environmental topics, dinosaurs and paleontology are commonly sought-after and viewed themes. Therein, the life-through-time story is often assumed or replayed, although more often, lately, one may expect to view a paleontological episode concerning mass extinctions of prehistory—especially that of the dinosaurs 66 million years ago, or more ominously speculate on how man too may eventually become extinct, victimized by a catastrophe. Alternatively, if one tunes out the airwaves (or cable), a quick search at Amazon.com will conjure up a number of popular books concerning paleontology, dinosaurs, and of course their associated mass extinction.

Certain scientists (not all of them, by any means) have long been prone to inciting the public with their original ideas, enlightening interested audiences about science. Two centuries ago, one of the first to have scored successes in this venue was British chemist Humphry Davy (1778–1829). A chemist? Yes, and certainly a hallowed name—but he far more than merely dabbled in what today would be considered geological or even paleontological matters, as noted in a portion of a rare publication exposing his views on how life proceeded throughout geological history.

True, Davy's views on chemistry, coupled with historical geological events of 1816 as well as published results of his electrochemical experiments, certainly fueled young Mary Shelley's fertile mind, leading to her invention of history's most famous, fictional, yet metaphorical monster—the creation of Victor Frankenstein. And, as also stated, Davy's volcanic theories also proved pivotal toward suspending disbelief in Jules Verne's most famous novel, *Journey to the Center of the Earth*, which itself is an imaginative life-through-time extrapolation. As we shall note here, however, Davy also pondered life through geological time in a semi-fictionalized setting decades before Verne. But while both the names Mary Shelley and Jules Verne remain famous today, Davy is rarely mentioned anymore, except perhaps in history texts outlining early developments in chemistry or geology.

What then was Davy's little-known contribution to the understanding and popularization of life through time? It would be some time thereafter before such discerning matters would filter through to and beyond the middle-class reader, yet Davy's outline sets the stage for what would come. Here is our first rarely cited example of how prehistoric life was becoming imagined and ingrained in intellectual minds so long ago. One prominent geologist of the day, Charles Lyell (1797–1875), who favored a steady state "uniformitarian" view of Earth history (and for its organic inhabitants as well) through geological time, quoted "extensive passages" from Davy's *Consolations* in his own *Principles of Geology* (1830–1833). Lyell claimed that Davy "advanced some of the weightiest ... objections" to his own doctrine. As Robert Siegfried and Robert H. Dott, Jr., later opined in 1980, "Lyell's attempts to refute these [i.e., Davy's] views may be the best testimony to offer for Davy's contemporary reputation as a geologist."[4]

Few are aware of the eminent Davy's paleontological interests, interconnecting and straying into geological matters as well. So let's take this opportunity to outline Davy's little-known treasure, written following a stroke suffered in 1826 during a trip to Europe: *Consolations in Travel, or the Last Days of a Philosopher,* which went through several editions, each lacking printed figures or visual illustrations.[5] While Davy is revered by historians of science, usually counted among the ranks of pioneer chemists, this 1830 publication proves how difficult it can be to categorize early scientists by profession. For in this rarely cited work, Davy did indeed offer paleontological speculations, insights and personal views concerning Earth's history.

Davy as chemist

Before proceeding further, it would be appropriate to summarize Davy's importance to the field of early modern chemistry (very difficult to do in less than a hundred words or so, considering how extensive his overall scientific contributions were), while recognizing that his paleontological ideas will be emphasized here.

The best concise account of Davy's life is David M. Knight's article found in *Dictionary of Scientific Biography.*[6] Between 1807 and 1808, Davy discovered the chemical elements barium, strontium, calcium, magnesium, potassium and sodium (and later boron, although nine days after its discovery in France, and then went on to later identify chlorine and iodine as elements) by isolating the elements electrochemically. He is also credited with the discovery (in 1800) of the intoxicating "laughing gas"—nitrous oxide. Davy's extensive work on the evolution and testing of gases was caricatured humorously.[7] All this would have capped a highly distinguished career in itself, but Davy's early electrochemical experiments also showed how substances decompose or purify into elemental form in determinate proportions when subjected to electrical currents. This work in electricity paved the way for his protégé Michael Faraday (1791–1867), who eventually outshone Davy, and whose name is more familiar today.

Davy as a public figure

Described as a "born chemist ... with a penchant for explosions,"[8] Davy quickly became a star celebrity scientist of his day, largely due to his public lectures—entertainment for the elite and middle class. "Davy was an expert at public demonstrations, showing off his own extraordinary discoveries, and a flair for the theatrical that kept his audience riveted to their seats—and kept them talking about him long after they'd left the lecture hall.... Ladies in the audience twittered at Davy's fireworks and surreptitiously took notes. Aristocrats preened and even took turns standing in as Davy's assistant. He was revered by the audience as a scientific wunderkind. Davy was at the top of his game."[9] But despite his celebrity among the populace, his peers sometimes viewed him askance, for his humble beginnings and the rustic clothes he wore, or for pitching "theatrics to the women in his audience." He was criticized as a pretentious social climber by the "scientific elite," from whom he curried favor.[10] And indeed, despite his brilliancy, Davy, who had been largely self-educated through age fifteen, did feel as an outsider, a stranger in such circles. Yet as T.K. Kenyon suggests, "Davy's outsider status—the very fodder for criticism, gossip, and speculation—made him all the more noteworthy to an enraptured public. It may have been the very thing that made him a spectacular star."[11]

Eventually Davy's interest in the geological arena came to the fore, as documented in his series of ten lectures tailored for public audiences, given in 1805.[12] Siegfried and Dott stated in 1980, "In contrast to his fame in chemistry, Davy's contributions to the history of geology are virtually unknown. Though he was serious about geology ... he made no startling discovery in the field, and his few publications contained little of significance. But his popular lectures in geology, delivered before large and enthusiastic audiences at the Royal Institution in London, antedated by several years the appearance of the first English textbook in the field and may have had a greater influence on the development of geology than did his role in the founding of the Geological Society of London."[13]

Davy, a product of Britain's Romantic Age, also pioneered the field of agricultural chemistry; he refined the compositional theory of acids, investigated the nature of chlorine, performed early photosynthesis experiments, and in 1815 invented a safety lamp used by miners that lessened the potential for explosions in coal mines caused by seepage of explosive gases. He experimentally demonstrated that diamonds and charcoal were composed of elemental carbon. Along the course of his illustrious career, Davy overturned several of French chemist Antoine Lavoisier's (1743–1794) theories (who incidentally also made interesting geological contributions recounted by Stephen Jay Gould in his 2000 essay collection, *The Lying Stones of Marrakech*).[14] Shortly after Davy's death, physician John Ayrton Paris (1785–1856), who wrote a two-volume biography of Davy titled *The Life of Humphry Davy*,[15] offered high praise, elevating the significance of Davy's scientific contributions to a par with Isaac Newton's. (See Figure 1-1.)

Melding chemistry with earth science

But the hallowed Davy also far more than simply dabbled in the earth sciences—mineralogy and geology. In fact, one might classify him among the early geochemists, although there was no such specialty named or recognized then. Davy's enduring interest in geology led late in life to publications on the mineralogy of granitic veins and volcanoes, and another on his paleontological speculations. As a youth, Davy collected geological specimens and later contributed minerals to the cabinets of scientific institutions. His popular lectures, often embellished by the then novel aid of transparencies at the Royal Institution, given to very crowded audiences, focused on geological theses, probing Earth's (geo-) chemical history, linking chemistry with mineralogy while commenting on the nature of fossils.

Upon visiting the (basaltic) Giant's Causeway in Ireland, Davy commented in a September 1805 letter, "The arrangement of rocks ... appear to me to present facts equally irreconcilable upon either the Plutonic or Neptunic theory, and I am convinced that general fanciful theories will lose ground in proportion as minute observations are multiplied."[16]

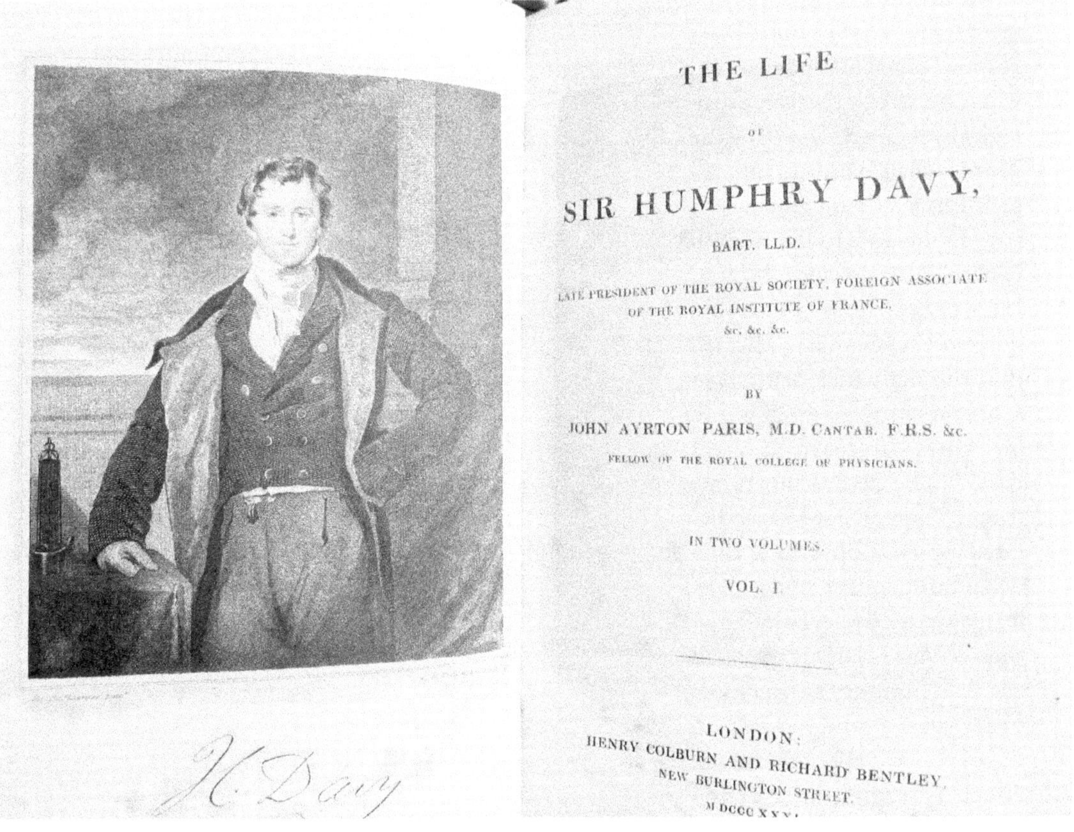

THE LIFE

OF

SIR HUMPHRY DAVY,

BART. LL.D.

LATE PRESIDENT OF THE ROYAL SOCIETY, FOREIGN ASSOCIATE
OF THE ROYAL INSTITUTE OF FRANCE,
&c. &c. &c.

BY

JOHN AYRTON PARIS, M.D. CANTAB. F.R.S. &c.

FELLOW OF THE ROYAL COLLEGE OF PHYSICIANS.

IN TWO VOLUMES.

VOL. I.

LONDON:
HENRY COLBURN AND RICHARD BENTLEY,
NEW BURLINGTON STREET.
M DCCC XXX.

Fig 1-1: Frontispiece showing Davy's likeness and the title page to his biography written by John Ayrton Paris in 1831 (Debus collection).

Furthermore, Davy determined experimentally that the air content of minerals in igneous rocks was more rarified (by 60 to 70 percent) than would be reasonably allowed by those favoring an aqueous origin for basalt (which today is known to be of igneous, "plutonic" origin). Thus, such rocks must have formed at high temperature; the water content of igneous rocks could be viewed as in combination with silica (bonded) at high temperatures, instead of reflecting an aqueous origin. Rather paradoxically, given his preference for explaining volcanic eruptions in terms of chemical processes rather than a central heat (which implied a cooler planetary core), Davy was more of a plutonist than neptunist.[17] Davy clarified his views on plutonism versus neptunism, contrasting two geological processes he had witnessed, in another paper prepared for the Geological Society of Cornwall in 1813.[18]

We'll return to these points later in the context of Davy's *Consolations*. (See Figure 1-2.)

Around this time, following a visit to the coast, Davy wrote verses in which he noted a "Majestic cliff! Thou birth of unknown Time," indicating Davy may have been partial to the uniformitarian idea of a geologically old Earth.[19] He comprehended the very gradual nature of weathering and was at least peripherally open-minded regarding the graduality if fossil forms leading to recent times.

As historian Charles Coulton Gillispie suggested in *Genesis and Geology*,[20] Davy only downsized his geological affairs following successes in electrochemistry which commanded attention and brought him the most fame. That is, until Davy acknowledged his end nearing, when he wrote the paleontologically themed "Dialogue the Third—the Unknown," pp. 114 to 161 in his *Consolations*.

In the note to the English edition, Davy's younger brother John (1790–1868), himself a noteworthy scientist, indicated that the dialogues printed in *Consolations* were intended to be "ideal, at least in great part."[21] The dedication to his friend Thomas Poole was dictated by Humphry at a time when he no longer could physically write. So, even though the account is largely founded upon Humphry's personal observations and travels in Europe especially, the overall effect is rather like Plato's ancient, instructive writings. There are several dialogues in *Consolations*, only one of which addresses paleontology.

CONSOLATIONS IN TRAVEL,

OR

THE LAST DAYS

OF

A PHILOSOPHER.

BY

SIR HUMPHRY DAVY, BART.

Late President of the Royal Society.

WITH A SKETCH OF THE AUTHOR'S LIFE, AND NOTES,

BY JACOB GREEN, M.D.

Professor of Chemistry in Jefferson Medical College.

Philadelphia:

JOHN GRIGG, No. 9, NORTH FOURTH STREET.

Clark & Raser, Printers.

1830.

Fig 1-2: The front cover to Humphry Davy's *Consolations in Travel* of 1830 (Debus collection).

Davy's life-through-time paleontological ideas, as expressed in Consolations

In "The Unknown," Davy begins with a journey set forth by three travelers to Roman ruins situated by the Bay of Sorento, where they encounter a "Stranger," with whom they hold discourse. Eventually discussion turns to the source of travertine among the ruins themselves. Soon they address carbonates, broaching the topic of subterranean fire giving rise to volcanic action, acting in turn upon the carbonate rocks and affected lake waters of southern Italy. The carbonates in one lake named the "lake of the Solfatara"—situated near Vesuvius—readily precipitate, coating objects therein. After acknowledging Athanasius Kircher's (1601–1680) *Mundus Subterraneus* (1664), which posited a central planetary fire, the Stranger (who may be identified with Davy himself), goes on to reflect on the processes of fossilization:

> I have passed many hours ... many days, in studying this wonderful lake; it has brought many trains of thought into my mind connected with the early changes of our globe, and I have sometimes reasoned from the forms of plants and animals preserved in marble in this warm source, to the grander depositions

> in the secondary rocks, where the zoophytes or coral insects have worked upon a grander scale, and where palms and vegetables now unknown, are preserved with the remains of crocodiles, turtles, and gigantic extinct animals of the sauri genus, and which might appear to have belonged to a period when the whole globe possessed a much higher temperature.[22] [See Figure 1-3.]

Now addressing the hydrological cycle and then the phenomenon of volcanic action, the Stranger is further encouraged: "[F]ew things would give us more pleasure than to know your opinion respecting the early changes and history of the globe, for I perceive you do not belong to the modern geological schools." And then for their "amusement and instruction," the Stranger orates his observations and speculations, while cautioning that they're "hardly worth communicating." Nevertheless, the Stranger goes on to relate how the Earth formed as a planet. "In the early age, 'there was no order of events similar to the present,' for the crust was thin and the central fire close to the surface. Only gradually, as the planet cooled, did the world approximate its modern state."[23]

After formation of the primary rocks, "which contain no vestiges of a former order of things ... upon ... further cooling, the water which more or less had covered it, contracted; depositions took place, shell fish and coral insects of the first creation began their labours; and islands appeared in the midst of the ocean raised from the deep by the productive energies of millions of zoophytes."[24]

Fig 1-3: Two marine paleo-monsters, *Ichthyosaurus* and *Plesiosaurus*, and a *Pterodactylus*, referred to as the members of the Secondary Period's (i.e., Mesozoic) "sauri" in Davy's *Consolations in Travel*. Although the term "dinosaur" wasn't coined until 1842 by Sir Richard Owen, technically, such creatures are not dinosaurs (image from David Page's *The Past and Present Life of the Globe* [1861], p. 137).

Next, Davy, or perhaps the Stranger, briefly describes how vegetation originated along shorelines, providing nourishment for fishes and invertebrates. The first fossiliferous secondary rocks then formed as cooling of watery carbonate-containing fluids deposited masses of crystallized, encrusted matter. Further cooling of the globe permitted the appearance of new species. "As the temperature of the globe became lower, species of the oviparous reptiles were created to inhabit it;—and the turtle, crocodile and various gigantic animals of the sauri kind seem to have haunted the bays and waters of the primitive lands."[25]

With the Earth's crust in a "slender" or thin condition,

internal fires were a relatively short distance from the surface of the globe. Hence, localized contractions permitted seawater to enter the Earth through crustal cavities, causing volcanic explosions. "Changes of this kind must have been extremely frequent in the early epochs of nature; and the only living forms of which the remains are found in the strata that are the monuments of these changes, are those of plants, fishes, birds, and oviparous reptiles, which seem most fitted to exist in such a war of the elements."[26]

But with dissipation of such volcanism, and continued global cooling (especially of the planetary interior and crust), "more perfect animals became its inhabitants." Here Davy cited extinct Ice Age species such as *Megatherium*, the woolly mammoth and "gigantic hyena" (the latter doubtless inspired by William Buckland's investigations of Kirkdale Cave in Yorkshire). Next, "when the system of things became so permanent, that the tremendous revolutions depending upon the destruction of equilibrium between the heating and cooling agencies were no longer to be dreaded, the creation of man took place."[27] All in all, a tidy little chemically founded life-through-time theory!

Ideas about volcanism

Next the Stranger relates the competing volcanic hypotheses which Davy wrestled with, scientifically: the central fire concept vs. the chemical oxidation process. During the 1820s, the causes of volcanic eruptions and the nature of the earth's interior were of great scientific interest. So, naturally, Davy applied his chemical expertise to the problem, suggesting that when fresh surface water infiltrated crustal cracks, contacting deposits of alkaline metals postulated to be present within the Earth, vigorous hydrogen-gas-evolving reactions would take place which observers would perceive as volcanic eruptions. Davy's biographer Paris suggested, "It is evident that the metals of the earth ... may constitute a part of its interior, and such an assumption would at once offer a plausible theory in explanation of the phenomena of volcanoes, the formation of lavas, and the excitement and effects of subterranean heat.... "[28]

Davy had even made what is perhaps the earliest model (artificial) volcano, exemplifying his principle using a reactive alkaline metal and water (instead of using baking soda and vinegar) as reactants. This experiment was footnoted in *Consolations*.

"A mountain had been modelled in clay, and a quantity of potassium introduced into its interior: on the addition of a little water, the potassium inflamed, successive explosions were produced, boiling lava was seen flowing down its sides from a crater around its summit. An eye witness observed 'that the tumultuous applause of the audience might in the dramatic illusion produced have been mistaken for the shouts of alarmed fugitives of Herculaneum or Pompeii.'"[29] Anyone who has ever witnessed the reactive effect of sodium metal exposed to water (evolving hydrogen gas) will appreciate the nature of Davy's miniature volcano.

During his 1813 tour of the Continent, Davy intended to test his chemical oxidation theory of volcanic eruptions. Besides the central fire hypothesis, Davy's hypothesis had two outstanding rivals. In Joseph Gay-Lussac's (1778–1850) chemical oxidation theory of 1823, volcanoes exploded when contacted by *salty* seawater—instead of Davy's fresh water—and therefore, gases evolved contained chlorine and sulfide (rather than highly flammable hydrogen). Davy had, in 1820, however, already suggested that eruptions along the coast might be initiated when seawater contacted metals within the Earth.[30] Because volcanoes often occurred within the vicinity of coastlines, and vast subterranean cavities were often found in association with these volcanic regions, as in Mount Vesuvius's case, wouldn't it be likely, Davy reasoned, for seawater to enter the Earth's interior and ignite metals existing within? This provenance now seems rather similar to that envisioned for origin of a "Central Sea," as it was known in English translations of Jules Verne's 1864 novel (referred to as the Lidenbrock Sea in the French original). Meanwhile, German geologist Leopold von Buch (1774–1853) explored the problem from a different angle. According to his theory of "elevation craters," laid out in publications of 1820 and 1825, he postulated that Davy's model of volcanic action could result in basaltic uplift.

Historian of science Rachel Laudan noted in *From Mineralogy to Geology: The Foundations of a Science 1650–1830*,[31] "As the physical account of the source of volcanic heat grew in popularity, the chemical theory declined. By the end of the 1820s, Davy had severe doubts about his chemical theory of volcanic action." For in his 1828 article, "On the phenomena of volcanoes," Davy stated that although there was "no other adequate source other than the oxidation of the metals which form the bases of the earths and alkalies ... it must not be denied that considerations derived from thermometrical experiments on the temperature of mines and on sources of hot water, render it probable that the interior of the globe possesses a very high temperature; and the hypothesis of the nucleus of the globe being composed of fluid matter, offers a still more simple solution of the phenomenon of volcanic fires than that which has just been developed."[32]

In other words, the "central fire" concept then seemed more convincing to Davy than did his own "cooler" chemical model, in which volcanoes were viewed as having reactive alkaline cores, albeit of lower temperature. Furthermore and significantly, chemical analyses of lava weren't consistent with Davy's volcanic theory. Apart from Davy's ruminations on paleontology and life through geological time as expressed later in *Consolations*, this admission seems to have downsized the active phase of Davy's career in geology.

In his *Consolations*, however, Davy struck a middle ground, as the Stranger confessed that while all observations are consistent with the central fire concept, "it is extremely probable" that combustible bases of the earths and alkalies exist within the Earth, and that these may fuse upon contact with air and water circulating from above. Following a digression on the length of geological time, the Stranger acknowledges his preference for the "refined plutonic view" of geological phenomena (as originated by James Hutton and elaborated by John Playfair and Sir James Hall—all of whom are named in *Consolations*). Evidently the Stranger is given to ideas which, peripherally, seem rather evolutionist in nature as he claims, "It is supposed that there are always the same types both of dead and living matter, that the remains of rocks, of vegetables and animals of one age are found imbedded in rocks raised from the bottom of the ocean in another. Now to support this view, not only the remains of living beings, which at present people the globe, might be expected to be found in the oldest sedimentary strata, but even those of the arts of man, the most powerful and populous of its inhabitants, which is well known not to be the case."[33]

So essentially, in his *Consolations* Davy framed a chemical model of Earth history (acknowledging the then resurgent central fire concept), incorporating contemporary paleontological findings while addressing organic succession in the fossil record!

Fossils and geological time

Therefore, considerable change is evident upon the Earth's surface. Traces of man aren't found in deep layers, while more primitive beings—such as the colossal "megalosauri" evident as fossils—aren't living on the surface of the globe. Then Davy—through the Stranger—goes on to say:

> *On the contrary* [my italics], each stratum of the secondary rocks contains remains of peculiar and mostly now unknown species of vegetables and animals. In those strata which are deepest and which must consequently be supposed to be the earliest deposited, forms even of vegetable life are rare; shells and vegetable remains are found in the next order; the bones of fishes and oviparous reptiles exist in the following class; the remains of birds, with those of the same genera mentioned before, in the next order; those of quadrupeds of extinct species in a still more recent class; and it is only in the loose and slightly consolidated strata of gravel and sand, and which are usually called diluvian formations, that the remains of animals, such as now people the globe, are found with others belonging to extinct species. But, in none of these formations, whether called secondary, tertiary or diluvial, have the remains of man or any of his works been discovered.[34]

Years earlier, when the skeleton of a human encased in solid limestone rock was disinterred from the island of Guadaloupe, and transferred for further study to London, Davy's chemical analysis of 1814 proved that the skeleton wasn't fossilized. In fact, the specimen represented a human who died in quite recent times, after the "general cataclysm" that "wiped out the truly fossil mammals."[35]

So now Davy, who speculated on the nature of prehistoric cave people in another section of his *Consolations*, drove home his main points. First, older stratigraphy records the existence of former organisms such as "the immense reptiles, the megalosauri with paddles instead of legs and clothed in mail, in size equal or even superior to the whale; and the great amphibian, plethiosauri [*sic*] with bodies like turtles, but furnished with necks longer than their bodies probably to enable them to feed on vegetables growing in the shallows of the primitive ocean,"[36] decidedly different from modern species. Secondly, these fauna (and flora) are not simply localized agglomerations, but represent global distributions which perished in a succession of universal (i.e., worldwide) catastrophes ("destructions" subsequently followed by "creations"), unwitnessed by man. Or as the Stranger phrases it, "In the oldest secondary strata, there are no remains of such animals as now belong to the surface, and in the rocks which may now be regarded as more recently deposited, these deposits occur but rarely and with abundance of extinct species—there seems ... a *gradual approach* [my italics] to the present system of things, and a succession of destructions and creations preparatory to the existence of man."[37]

This was an outline of his "refined plutonic view," in which the factor of heat in the formation of "secondary" (a term then loosely meaning "sedimentary") rocks and notion of steady-state terrestrial conditions could be rejected (counter to Lyell's uniformitarian theory), thus allowing a succession of life, as noted in the fossil record, to emerge and become deposited within subsequently formed strata.[38]

Not an evolutionist

A "gradual approach"? Davy, through the Stanger, however, isn't espousing pre–Darwinian evolutionist ideals. For while supportive of extinction as recorded in the fossil record, he vehemently opposes that "absurd, vague doctrine" which, as stated by one of the travelers, "supposes that living nature has undergone gradual changes ... that the fish has in millions of generations ripened into the quadruped, and the quadruped into the man ...."[39] Here, Davy is merely in tune with contemporary views. This is perhaps no real surprise, but given the obscurity of Davy's paleontological and geological writings today, it remains interesting as an early example of how life through geological time themes pervaded into one's daily philosophy then, that is—for those who possessed the faculties, means and luxury of time to contemplate it, even before the "invention" of dinosaurs, dinosaur books, vast paleontological museum displays teeming with evolutionary messages—varied as they may have been through the decades since Darwin, or streaming high-definition television documentaries on life's history.

Further proof of Davy's rather probable pious perception of the Grand Succession of Life may be found in the conclusion of an address he presented. Davy was lauding British geologist William Buckland (1784–1856) upon his receipt of a Royal Society medal in 1822 for researching Yorkshire's Kirkdale Cave, now known to be of the Pleistocene age, in which fossiliferous remains of an extinct Ice Age hyena had been discovered and reconstructed.[40] On an excursion, Davy and Buckland had explored the cave together. Davy wrote of Buckland's accomplishment: "[B]y these inquiries, a distinct epoch has, as it were, been established in the history of the revolutions of the globe: a point fixed, from which our researches may be pursued through the immensity of ages, and the records of animate nature, as it were, carried back to the time of the creation."[41]

As Siegfried and Dott noted in 1980, "Davy's providential theme, that all nature conspires to preserve the 'beautiful cycle of terrestrial events ... subservient to the permanency of life,'" was evident in his six additional public geology lectures of 1811.[42] Furthermore, Davy did not intend to "force his geology to conform to scripture," but rather to allow scientific findings to "independently confirm scriptural truth."[43] Davy, for example, had written how gratifying it was that the "progress of science, beyond all doubts," establishes "the great catastrophe described in the sacred history," which of course was in reference to Buckland's belief in a great universal Deluge that destroyed creatures once alive during the last epoch, in antediluvian times (i.e., before the presumed biblical deluge). And of course, his *Consolations* was "essentially a theologically based justification of a life spent in science."[44] So rather than branding Davy as a creation scientist, or attempting to elevate his possible objectively evolutionary ideas, instead refer to him as a "philosopher"—as noted in the subtitle to his *Consolations*.

Davy's geology has long been surpassed, and his name is virtually unknown to modern paleontologists in such a context. Curiously, Davy's interests in volcanism, mineralogy, deposition, stratigraphy, the succession of life, and even ancient men mirror French writer Jules Verne's intrigue as expressed in his classic novel *Journey to the Center of the Earth* (1864, 1867 eds.), which itself contains many fascinating paleontological life through geological time references.[45] Yet through Verne's references to Davy's geological work, published in *Journey*—which shall ring eternal through many printed editions down through the centuries—Davy won a marvelous, if not everlasting "Consolations" prize!

Davy's *Consolations*, while popular in tone, remains relatively obscure—even to today's historians. Yet it is clear that by 1830, scientists and early science-popularizers were warming to the idea of a progressionally phased planet, wherein distinctive life forms had appeared and adapted to a series of prior ages, leading sequentially, eventually to the advent of exalted, civilized man. So how did such ideology finally become effectively delivered and communicated to the masses (at least in English-speaking lands), oddly in a complete absence of visual illustrations and figures, thus promoting popularity of the grand evolutionary epic?

Alluding to Mary Shelley's creation, one contemporary critic suggested after reading another life-through-time outline appearing a decade later, *Vestiges of the Natural History of Creation,* parts of which were also presented in a grand evolutionary epic style, this new abomination was likewise a hybrid, whose author could "create worlds with a dash of his wizard pen ... animalise the dull lamp of inorganic matter—and spiritualize, like another Frankenstein, the animal to which his fancy had given birth."[46]

Chapter Two

Popularizing the Life-Through-Time "Paleo-Novel"

So much of paleontology is visual. But what about non-visual language ... *the words*, that is, *paleo*-words addressing the traditional life-through-time theme? We're so used to that story *now* that it's become cliché, but how about *then*?

Today there are loads of popular science books and magazines available, and we all know that dinosaurs and those "other" prehistoric animals have also reached a pinnacle of popularity. Nearly *everybody* knows what *Triceratops* and *Tyrannosaurus* are these days, which wasn't the case over half a century ago. But how did this "dino-adoration" originate? When and for what reasons did the masses first become enthralled with paleontology? More specifically, can we identify any particular publication where it all began, where things really got rolling—that is, for our present purposes, divulging how developing perceptions of life-through-time became so intriguing to nonspecialists? By the 1830s, geology had become *the* most popular science. Assuredly there are several historical factors, scientists, authors and popularizers in the mix. However, one possible key answer may surprise you.

Geology's popularity steadily heightened during the early 19th century, attaining status as the most popular science by the 1830s, dawning what has been referred to as the "golden age for the writing of earth history."[1] According to Susan Shatto, "Dinosaurs captured the nineteenth-century romantic imagination first as vestiges of the Creation, and later as representatives of a remote world whose one-time existence as rulers of the earth might shed light on man's own origins and future."[2] Baron Georges Cuvier's learned writings (and translations thereof) certainly alerted eclectic readers to awful cataclysms and revolutions recorded at various geological junctures, causing wholesale extinctions of life. However, more so than any rival, Robert Chambers's anonymously published book, *Vestiges of the Natural History of Creation* (1st ed., October 1844)[3] indelibly fueled popular interest in fossils via the written geological era-to-era "evolutionary epic." Like a great scientific paleo-novel, *Vestiges* stormed the collective consciousness of the Victorian reading public! (See Figure 2-1.)

Previously, French scholar Georges-Louis Leclerc Buffon (1707–1788) speculated about the globe's prehistory in 1778, essays titled *The Epochs of Nature*, a "synthesis of earth history from our solar system's beginning (e.g., involving a collision between a comet and the Sun), to the present including the origin and development of life and a numerical estimate of the duration of geologic time that was outrageously long for its day."[4] However, "cosmic romances" such as these were scoffed at by more serious-minded natural historians. (Terms like "scientist" and "paleontologist" didn't come along until much later.) Where's the scientific evidence for such stories, critics decried?

Meanwhile, other naturalists stoked fires of popular imagination by dramatically placing reconstructed skeletons, such as America's "Incognitum" (*Mastodon*) and "Great Claw" (*Megalonyx*), on touring public exhibition, or offering public lectures—especially those featuring British geologist William Buckland's showmanship—addressing the few fascinating ages of prehistory as revealed scientifically.

But it would be incorrect to suggest that fossils of animals and plants then thought to have lived at a time prior to man's existence, before the documentation of history (i.e., in a mind-boggling "pre"-historic age), were as popular and celebrated among the masses during the early 19th century as they would later become during the 20th. True—geological popularization was entering the mainstream through a variety of media, especially calling upon the imaginations of a reading public resorting to visualization of prehuman landscapes in their mind's eye. By the mid–1820s, a fresh crop of naturalists such as Gideon Mantell occasionally excited audiences with pictorial passages evoking images of, for instance, a Wealden Britain "witnessed" via the narrator during an Age of Reptiles. (Yet at this early time, specialist writers usually refrained from visualizing beyond a particular time period, key strata, or ranging throughout what would later be named the Phanerozoic Era). Poets of the period also waxed on about prehistoric time and its inhabitants in their writings, often adding an enchanting, mythical spin.

VESTIGES

OF

THE NATURAL HISTORY

OF

CREATION.

Fifth Edition.

LONDON:

JOHN CHURCHILL, PRINCES STREET, SOHO.

M DCCC XLVI.

Fig 2-1: Title page to the 5th edition of *Vestiges*.

Two influential works of the 1830s written by authorities addressed geological concepts, tailored for popular consumption. But these rather famed specialists, Buckland and Charles Lyell, didn't embark on what is now considered a "conventional" path in mapping a course of geological history, via life through time. In his *Geology and Mineralogy considered with reference to natural theology* (1836) contribution to the *Bridgewater Treatises,* Buckland described providential hallmarks of representative or extraordinary fossil specimens dating from strata chronologically arranged in regressive (backwards in time) order (most recent to oldest genus).[5] Several vivid, verbal passages highlight these descriptions. However, his book, a paleontological masterpiece for its time, is chopped into *two* conceptualized portions. Discussion of the geological column is outlined chronologically (ascending order) in chapters *before* presentation of the inverted (descending in time) sequence of fossils. (Conceptually, Chambers would eventually meld together these two sections, i.e., description of geological strata allied with fossils contained within respective layered deposits, upward through time).[6]

Conversely, in his *Principles of Geology, being an attempt to explain the former changes of the earth's surface, by reference to causes now in operation* (1830–1833), Lyell adopted a theoretical "uniformitarian," cyclical geological system which denied any sense of overall "progress" throughout geological history.[7] Counterintuitively to today's mindset, Lyell objected to any possibility of directional progress in life's history and geohistory. For, if environmental circumstances proved favorable, formerly extinct genera might even reappear. Lyell further conceived a futuristic geological period, when "the huge Iguanodon might reappear in the woods, and the ichthyosaur in the sea, while the pterodactyle might flit again through the umbrageous groves of tree-ferns." One of Lyell's colleagues, Henry De la Beche, satirized this nonprogressive view in a cartoon, named "Awful Changes."[8]

But while fossils and the deep, mysterious past could seem wildly enchanting, popularization required something *beyond* the learned intellect of focused, visionary men who investigated rock strata. Individuals who were skilled at relating Earth's prehistory, a succession of life through time, and how its organic forms manifested through time—or at least, a *good story weaving it all together*—could fill the void for nonspecialists yearning for such knowledge. Right or wrong, firsthand scientific or perhaps only armchair pseudoscientific perspective would even do. Would a writer sufficiently bold to reach for that broad, layman audience, risking reputation and the wrath of critics in producing another "cosmic romance," dare step forward? No single writer scored more success in this arena, in setting the fertile Victorian British public imagination agog and ablaze with fossils and fantastical evolutionary tales in the popular, life-through-time genre, than Robert Chambers (1802–1883). Chambers's stylistic "evolutionary epic"[9] composition became the talk of London and elsewhere, paving ground for over a century's later preoccupation with what became the "traditional" paleontological, life-through-time tour, rather science fictional or at least speculative in nature, or that to which we've become so accustomed. In this regard, Chambers broke the ice, so to speak.

Chambers was not an anatomist, a paleontologist or even what would have been considered then a "scientist," like Davy, Lyell or Buckland. At best, he was branded as a pseudoscientist (an old-time Victorian Velikovsky). Chambers believed his work to be the "first attempt to connect the natural sciences into a history of creation."[10] He accepted that prolonged periods of time must have been necessitated for "peopling" the earth through natural means. He challenged "fixity of species," even using the word "evolution" in another book, *Explanations,*[11] yet suggested that it was possible for one genus to wholly arise anew from the womb or ova of a predecessor or ancestral genus without many intermediate generations showing progressive variation. Moreover, Man would "ascend" further beyond his current state of being, from far humbler beginnings.

Another curious instance causing much fulmination was Chambers's fascinating suggestion in *Vestiges* that "Man had descended from a large frog, which had subsequently become extinct."[12] By the 5th edition of *Vestiges*, Chambers had indeed asserted the analogous resemblances between "batrachians" (e.g., frogs) and the mysterious *Cheirotherium* [*sic*], whose footprints had been discovered in the New Red Sandstone. And, almost ludicrously when considered today, he quoted another naturalist who claimed the "frog, though so low in the scale of vertebrate animals, should bear a striking resemblance to the human conformation in its organs of progressive motion."[13] (See Figure 2-2.) *Cheirotherium*'s five-fingered, batrachian "hand-like footsteps" (whose trackways were eventually assigned to fossils belonging to the amphibian *Labyrinthodon*, known from the same strata) were then regarded as the "ghost of anticipated humanity," perhaps explaining the fascination of the early naturalists with this ambiguous creature. (See Jane P. Davidson for a compilation of the old *Cheirotherium* restorations, although not including a more recent one by Z. Burian.[14])

So let's examine Chambers's influential life-through-time passages in *Vestiges*.

Whereas over a decade later, Charles Darwin concluded his *Origin* with a nod to the perpetual workings of celestial mechanics (i.e., astronomical motions), Chambers *began* his anomalously written treatise by outlining (then) current astronomical understanding. He

Fig 2-2: Restoration of the *Labyrinthodon* resembling a frog creating human-like handprints that would eventually fossilize. This illustration (Plate XIV) by Edouard Riou, prepared for an (undated) 1860s English translation of Louis Figuier's *The World Before the Deluge*, is one of three in that popular text showing the *Labyrinthodon* as part of a life-through-time sequence within a geohistorical panorama. In a relatively short time after Chambers's *Vestiges*, the revelation of life-through-time via the evolutionary epic (books which were sometimes theologically toned) had become traditionalized, maturing rapidly into (for their time) lavish publications such as this (illustration by Edouard Riou, from Louis Figuier's *The World Before the Deluge*, undated but possibly 1867 edition).

was particularly influenced by Sir John Herschel's and Sir William Herschel's discoveries as well as Pierre Simon LaPlace's nebular hypothesis of planetary formation. Then Chambers considered the elemental composition of planetary bodies, emphasizing, of course, Earth (its metallic components, carbon and oxygen content, etc.), composing itself from a "universal Fire Mist." How Earth's Primary crystalline, fused rock system forms from a molten primordial state was up next, leading to discussion of the first stratified rocks and, eventually, oceans. From here Chambers describes in subsequent chapters, life—as preserved in rocks dating from successive rock systems above (i.e., younger than) the Primary.

Subsequent, metaphorical "leaves" from the "Stone Book" to be described stemmed from the Lower and Upper Silurian (existing above the Primary rocks), for which there were abundant fossils. Referring to French anatomist Georges Cuvier, Chambers mentions numerous extinct invertebrates (emphasizing crinoids and trilobites) known from this time, remarking that coexisting plant life was also of a "very lowly grade." Life apparently flourished *suddenly*, originating from inorganic materials, conceivably when sparked by electricity in downright Frankensteinian fashion.

Chambers suggests that "there is much reason to suppose that life began before advent of the Lower Silurian, and in forms of a kind humbler than many of those found in that portion of the rock series." According to Chambers, fishes were "abundant" during the "Era of the Old Red Sandstone," equivalent to the Devonian facies in Britain.[15] Here, he relied on the researchers of luminaries Louis Agassiz and Hugh Miller. Armored fishes were "inferior" or "primitive," some even resembling invertebrate trilobites. Chambers attested to a variation or "gradual change of physical conditions ... constantly going on" as giving rise to "constant change of genera and species in the inhabitants of those seas to which the organic contents of the rocks bear witness."[16] Both animals and plants underwent an "advancing organization" through geological time, fostered by prevailing planetary atmospheric conditions.

Having surveyed what Chambers assigned to the Primary rock system, now he addressed "Secondary Rocks," beginning with the Carboniferous Formation and coal beds, an early age of diversified terrestrial plant life thriving in tropical conditions. The first impressions of landlubbing insects, arthropods and even reptilian footprints are noted from strata representing this age. The New Red Sandstone was an old term corresponding to "Permo-Triassic" strata of Europe. Obviously, there were still refinements to be made in the study of stratigraphy in ensuing decades. But this New Red presented abundant evidence of reptiles and vestiges of enormous birds, actually dinosaur footprints. There were also bony elements of "palaeosaurs, thecodonts, monitors.... *Rhynchosaurus*.... Labyrinthodonts" to revel in.[17] Chambers marveled at the fossil anatomies of strange *Plesiosaurus* and *Ichthyosaurus*.

And so with announcement of Jurassic strata, Chambers defers to the many fossils of fishes and land plants dating from this age, as well as the flourishing marine and bat-winged reptiles (pterosaurs). Crocodilians are discussed too, here including *Cetiosaurus* (as it was then regarded). But, most significantly, there were traces of the first (then) known paleo-mammals—this, a marsupial insectivorous creature from the Stonesfield slate, and another genus assigned by Richard Owen to the whale family. Of course, Chambers would have been remiss by not mentioning dinosauria recently described by Owen in 1842, as well as "first fossils referred to birds in the Wealden." (See Figure 2-3.) Thus, leading to discussion of the organic, marine origin of the Cretaceous chalk beds and bird remains belonging to this period

Fig 2-3: Life restorations of carnivorous *Megalosaurus* and spiny *Hylaeosaurus* categorized as dinosaurs by Sir Richard Owen in 1842. Both animals were mentioned in editions of Robert Chambers's *Vestiges*. The third saurian classified as "dinosaur" by Owen was *Iguanodon*. The megalosaur is how Charles Dickens may have envisioned his behemoth striding up Holburn Hill in *Bleak House*, as mentioned in Chapter Thirteen (image from David Page's *The Past and Present Life of the Globe* [1861], p. 138).

found at Maidstone, and a mosaesaurus [*sic*], "which seems to have an intermediate place between the monitor and iguana."[18]

The Tertiary formation, especially then known from Paris and London, indicated a time of abundant mammalian life, progressing since its recorded commencement during the Jurassic. Chambers noted the great extinction boundary, stating, "Between the close of the chalk age and the beginning of the tertiary, a greater gap occurs in the fossil history of the earth than at any other period. The species now presented are almost wholly new, as if a considerable time had elapsed, during which the usual progressive change of animals had been going on, but from geognostic causes, without the usual record having been kept."[19] Of course, we now know this transition interval was relatively brief. (However, see Chapter Sixteen.)

Charles Lyell had observed and recorded percentages of shelly organisms increasingly surviving to modernity from successive stages (which he named as "epochs"), indicative of the Tertiary. Chambers interpreted these statistics to mean that as recent time approached, ecologically, the biosphere began to gradually appear more like the present, increasingly tenanted with familiar, extant fauna. In a chapter that was taking on what would become conventional overtones for its scope, subtitled "Mammalia Abundant," Chambers discussed life that was prevalent, sequentially, in each of Lyell's epochs. On land, mammals were abundant throughout the Tertiary, to the exclusion of dinosaurs and other giant reptilians known from fossils. He cited extinct elephants "variously distinguished from the present by peculiarities in their dentition," and marveled how they enjoyed a more cosmopolitan existence during their heyday.[20] The mammoth specimen found frozen in Siberia in 1801, and a raft of other fossil mammalia, were also mentioned. The modern, egg-laying *Platypus* was viewed as an important transition type.

Skillfully outlining the oldest of "Superficial deposits" (an antiquated term for Pleistocene), Chambers noted absence of fossil man. Yet fauna of this more recent time closely resembled extant species. Also, "diluvium" deposits formed then, predominantly through emergence of land from the sea—geological history's great "concluding event."[21] It seemed there was a gradational progress evident in animal forms of the past leading to those of the present (with exalted European man poised at the pinnacle).

If the content of this geological tale sounds at least vaguely familiar to you, well it should. Chambers's widely distributed book was perhaps the very first to transparently describe in layman's terms, life common to each of the former eras, periods and epochs as known to science, sequentially, in context with and as recovered from the rock record, thus forming a template for many other popular writers to follow in ensuing decades. All in all, quite an epical, literary adventure for the early 1840s! And written in a popular vein; a perfect "wild ride" for armchair naturalists of the time.

What was the overall reaction to Robert Chambers's anonymously published yet highly seductive *Vestiges*? How had he won over his readers via *style*? After all, in the wake of *Vestiges*' success, so many well-received books written by a bevy of authors and popularizers concerning the evolutionary life-through-time epic of our planet, otherwise known as the panorama of life's history or Panorama of the Ages, were published during Victorian times. (None of them sold "wildfire" like a Stephen King paperback novel, although due to public demand, a few, like *Vestiges*, had the good fortune of making it through numerous copiously updated editions.) Today's generation of paleophiles revel in Robert Bakker's discoveries and writings, while individuals fascinated by astronomy can pull books by Carl Sagan or Neil deGrasse Tyson off the shelf. But circumstances then are rather more difficult to imagine for a number of reasons. To get us started, perhaps if you can picture a festive scene not unlike from that popular BBC show *Downton Abbey*, except reset during the mid–1840s, with partiers, penguin-suited gentlemen and gaily gowned ladies milling about chatting of monkeys from men and that odd, jolly old "Mr. Vestiges." Who was that fellow anyway? Why does he still remain ... unmasked? Peculiar, eh? What got them all talking about it and why?

Although among the sciences, geology had become most popular during the 1830s, thanks to a number of talented writers (such as Charles Lyell), after 1844, general public interest among the more educated classes flagged somewhat. This may be correlated to *Vestiges*' promotion of the controversial species transmutation theme. However, while idolatry of geology diminished somewhat, in polite circles *Vestiges* certainly became the talk of the town. (This was also a time, remember, when access to natural history museums and displays was generally restricted.) During the 1830s, the term "popular science" meant increasingly "science *effectively communicated*," rather than "science *widely* disseminated." Of course, this encouraged a literature of lively storytelling about the Earth.[22]

It might have facilitated matters if early editions had been illustrated pictorially, but then Darwin's later *The Origin of Species: By Means of Natural Selection or the Preservation of Favoured Races in the Struggle for Life* (1st ed. 1859) wasn't illustrated either. Both the 10th and 11th editions of *Vestiges* (1853 & 1860, respectively) were illustrated using woodcut engravings by William G.T. Bagg (mainly images of fossils and embryos). But during that day and age, pictures and visuals were less substantial in conjuring images in the mind's eye, relative to well-chosen words. Victorian readers were more adept at pictorially *imagining* the meaning and intent of written words, whereas today's readers tend to rely more on pictorial cues. Thus, selection of picturesque scenes, virtual tourism framed within vignettes describing appearances and habits of extinct creatures, adoption of a friendly, subdued, yet learned-sounding narrative voice throughout emphasizing the inclusive plural pronoun "we" (as in "*we're* on this amazing journey," not just an unnamed, pompous author lecturing monotonously), and the savvy know-how of publisher John Churchill, all conspired to make readings of *Vestiges* a grand, "viral" must-read water cooler affair for its time.[23]

Well, of course, during the Victorian period there eventually *were* several public displays such as Benjamin Waterhouse Hawkins's (and Richard Owen's) large constructions of dinosaurian antediluvia erected in 1853 on "prehistoric" islands at Sydenham, England, to feast one's eyes upon![24]

Also, through time and subsequent editions, Chambers's paleontological "romance" increased in accuracy and persuasiveness. One contemporary critic, Scottish physicist James Forbes, stated, for instance, that by the 4th edition its anonymous author/scholar had become "apt" and by removing traces of "ignorance and presumption" in earlier editions had become "more dangerous."[25] Indeed, Chambers's rhetorically seductive writing style, buttressed with sufficiently convincing factual accuracy, formed a template for many evolutionary epics to come, offering an absorbing means of public edification.

Ralph O'Connor, author of *The Earth on Show* (2007), refers to early examples of such writings as "poetics of geology," or "word-paintings of the past." (And if you find his "poetics" term quaint, recall that in a landmark 1962 paper, geologist Harry Hess referred to his discussion of plate tectonics as "an essay in geopoetry."[26]) While only a few experienced geologists were adept at employing such theatrical, metaphorical language in their more technically inclined books and monographs, renowned poets, contemporary amateur science popularizers, and those leaning toward the fictional realm offered startling imaginary "voyages" into primeval history. Writers typically availed themselves of any of four stylistic literary categories, or perspectives, exemplifying and embellishing the art of the written evolutionary life-through-time epic, including (1) the reader as "viewer" via a time portal; (2) the "authorial narrator" prone to "waking dreams"; (3) the scene imagined in one's mind's eye; and (4) the "face-to-face" encounter within a restored scene.[27] Any of these perspectives could be creatively adapted from a simpler geological vignette into a full-blown story. Idealized fact vs. fiction: would readers object?

Gideon Mantell—revered for discovery and description of the *Iguanodon*—for instance, was one whose vivid monographs and books (e.g., *Illustrations of the Geology of Sussex*, 1827; *The Wonders of Geology*, 1838; *The Medals of Creation*, 1844) presented a sumptuous serving of "the earth's physical drama," highlighting Britain during Wealden times.[28] Like Mantell, and contemporary Hugh Miller,[29] in life-through-time chapters and passages edited into *Vestiges'* sixth edition (1847), Chambers was also providing vivid commentary, wielding the science-fictional tone and perspective of an imagined "visitant" who observes the Oolitic dinosaurians.

As decades passed, more evolutionary epics were published, increasingly incorporating more prehistoric or "antediluvian" monster visual iconography. Projected authorial confidence and seriousness in such writings also escalated. Eventually, by the mid–1800s, writing strategies and presentation styles honed by amateur popularizers of the thought-provoking (sublime) evolutionary epic and imaginative yet often controversial theories of the Earth, merged with those of the more scientifically trained. Both professional and amateur writers alike sought to disseminate knowledge about paleontology among the reading laity, nonspecialists of the educated middle and upper classes. Such books offered a "rational amusement" catering to those seeking truths that "'far exceed the fictions of romance,' providing the thrill of sensational fiction without the stigma of falsehood."[30]

As O'Connor stated, use of literary techniques "anticipated the techniques of later science-fiction writers.... When surveying these passages, from cautious restorations to full-scale voyages back in time, it becomes impossible to draw a clear dividing line between popular science and science fiction."[31] But not only that, authors of the Victorian period—besides Chambers—were adopting and refining techniques and strategies anticipating those employed over a century later by, say, the familiar Tim Haines's BBC docudrama, *Walking with Dinosaurs* (1999). And yet the uninitiated Victorian reader was captivated by concepts to which we've become inured (or take for granted), such as startling (if not "poetic") ideas of repeated tragedy—apocalyptical mass extinctions; a panoramic *succession* of geological epochs and periods, each with its characteristic flora and fauna—rather than a single prehistoric time populated by all "antediluvians" living together. And as O'Connor suggests, the dizzying chronological vertigo resulting from attempts to read of and perceive an Earth aged many millions of years (as men like Lyell espoused)—a uniformitarian abyss of time—must have seemed simply mind-boggling. It was all so controversial, revolutionary—hard to swallow then, or at least truly *sensational* (coming at a time when that term was more loaded than in the present day)!

One such contemporary, imaginative voyage was written by Henry Morley (1822–1894), educator, apothecary, journalist and literary scholar, writing for Charles Dickens's *Household Words* magazine in 1851. This completely fleshed-out, life-through-time adventure was written even before Dickens's *Bleak House* (with its famous introductory remark about how "wonderful" it would be to greet a *Megalosaurus* lumbering up Holburn Hill), and more than a decade prior to Jules Verne's *Journey to the Center of the Earth.* Morley's "Our Phantom Ship on an Antediluvian Cruise"[32] contains all the core elements of dino-time travel fantasy, indicating how readily factual information concerning prehistoria then known to experts could be disseminated in popular, faux-scientific, yet edifying fashion. "So we ... sail out ... leaving man behind us; ... a thousand years roll back upon themselves with every syllable we utter, years, by millions and millions, will ... restore their dead before our ghostly voyage back into the past...." Morley's little-known tale anticipates the gist of Karel Zeman's film, *Journey to the Beginning of Time,* by a century. (See Chapter Five.) Hardly judged an evolutionary "epic" due to its brevity, Morley's tale still introduced life through time, though in reverse order.

Perhaps inspired by Mr. Wyld's huge globe, then on exhibition at Leicester Square, London, Morley invites readers to undertake an imaginative voyage, sailing around the planet, yet progressively further back into Earth's prehistory, resulting in face-to-face, harrowing encounters with extinct life forms. The first port of call becomes the Pleistocene of South America where readers "witness" a living glyptodont munching on foliage, *Mylodon* and "Megalotherium" [*sic*] overturning trees, and *Dinornis* and *Macrauchenia.* From here, after musing on geological causes of past glacial climates, Morley sweeps us along into what must have been intended to be a mashup of Plio-Pleistocene with Tertiary Period British fauna.

Here, readers are greeted by a grinning monkey, a mastodon, a cave bear, an Irish elk, a hyena, a *Paleotherium*, and other staunch Cenozoic representatives. Sight of a symbolic volcano (*non*-catastrophically, thanks to Lyell) divides Tertiary from older, "Secondary" fauna and rocks.

Referring to Thomas Malthus (1766–1834), Morley explains how chalk cliffs were deposited from a multitude of micro-skeletons raining down from the surface of the Cretaceous sea. Next, dinosaurs are encountered—*Megalosaurus* and *Iguanodon*, as well as other reptiles—a pterodactyl (regarded as a winged crocodile) eating a rat, and at sea there's *Ichthyosaurus*. In this setting there are also birds (yet *Archaeopteryx* was still eight years in Morley's real future). Going farther back in time, after the reader encounters an in-the-flesh "Cheirotherium" making its famous prints, another smoldering volcano marks the transition into the "remotest ages of the antediluvian world"—the Paleozoic Era. Morley's phantom ship sails past a Carboniferous forest, glides among Devonian "Old Red Sandstone" fishes, glimpses an Age of Trilobites (Silurian), and settles into a time of graptolites, whereupon the ship is docked on a primeval coral reef. Best not tread farther, for the "bounds of life" and knowledge would be surpassed (and Morley would be forced into serious speculation). Cautious readers then briskly "row" upward into the present. Morley may therefore be considered one of the many "disciples" of *Vestiges'* success, and a harbinger of Jules Verne.

Rather in contrast to his nurturing style in *Vestiges*, Robert Chambers's *Explanations: A Sequel to the Vestiges* (1846), also published anonymously, was intended as "forcible and argumentative" persuasion tailored for "convincing stern-minded men," especially such as Cambridge University's theologically minded geologist Adam Sedgwick.[33] Here, Chambers came out swinging, claiming that "organic creation ... [arose] in the manner of natural order," and "there is no real obstacle to the theory of a gradual natural development of life upon our planet."[34]

For example, owing to Richard Owen's interpretations, dinosauria, including the oolitic *Cetiosaur*, approached the (next "higher" and geologically younger) mammalian type, thus substantiating the theory of "progressive development." Chambers also deftly brushed off attacks concerning the general paucity of fossil "transitions" between animal classes and their first occurrences in the fossil record in relation to one another reflecting "advance from the lower to the higher classes of animals."[35] He precociously espoused a bushy tree of life (a "plurality of lines") to this progress through geologic time, as opposed to a metaphorical "ladder," claiming, for example, "[M]ight the giraffe be a changed *Sivatherium*, and yet the *Sivatherium* continue to exist."[36] Furthermore, he hinted at an understanding of convergent evolution.

Yet, Chambers's approach was rather risqué, for in the infancy of paleontology then there remained a genuine possibility that organisms of ever higher complexity and organization might yet be discovered in increasingly *older* deposits, thus bearing potential to falsify any theory of life's gradual succession and progression through geological time. After all, paleontologists had noted that prehistoric marine and terrestrial environments appeared to have already been acceptable for forms of life (that didn't evolve much later in time), even during earlier periods. So maybe those hypothetical, modern-aspect fossils dating from these early periods simply hadn't been discovered yet.

Chambers considered that species transmutation proceeded according to structured programming, infused within each being. This was the foundation of his theory of Progressive Development, "in short, a universal gestation of nature, analogous to that of the individual being."[37] In its 1st edition, Chambers stated, "The idea ... which I form of the progress of organic life upon the globe ... is, that the simplest and most primitive type, under a law to which that of like-production is subordinate, gave birth to the type next above it, that this again produced the next higher, and so on to the very highest, the stages of advance being in all cases small—namely from one species only to another; so that the phenomenon has always been of a simple and modest character."[38] But Chambers erroneously attributed the lack of mammalian life on the Galapagos Islands, which Charles Darwin had already visited while on his HMS *Beagle* expedition, as a result of life's having had insufficient time to develop its full potential, and hence was unable to culminate in "completion of the animal series" on a younger volcanic chain.[39]

Unlike the celebrated Lyell—champion of geological "uniformitarianism," who claimed there was no (organic) evolutionary progress and who had quashed the transformist ideas of Jean-Baptiste Lamarck—Chambers believed there was a mysterious internal "impulse" within species to "advance, in certain times through grades of organization terminating in the highest species representatives." Then a second, polishing or "perfecting impulse," imposed by the environment, modified biological structures for adaptability. (Exerting forces were thought to have sometimes manifested results quite rapidly.) Thus, through interaction of such impulses, one may observe "progress" and increasing complexity among biota trending upward through geological time. These were universal tendencies continually conspiring upon and conjuring varieties within species, even on other (hypothesized) life-bearing planets, producing a gradation of forms, or a natural "descent" through time decipherable through comparative anatomy.[40] (Chambers, following Lyell, did not support Lamarck's theory.)

Rather than appealing to divine origins for life, "fiat" origination of species through time, and even the curious development of mankind's civilization and consciousness, Chambers preferred rational explanations and physical analogies, founded in scientific evidence and experimentation, however rudimentary that evidence might have been. Here it's tempting (yet rather beguiling) to paint Chambers as a "modern," as did Henry F. Osborn in 1899.[41] True—*Vestiges* and his *Explanations* were as anti-miraculous in tone as could be tolerated for the time—yet highly contentious because both were indeed products of their age. (However, much of what was once deep and contentious, yet of complexly interwoven theological significance then, need not concern us here.) You may suggest Chambers rather presages Charles Darwin's (1809–1882) and Alfred Russell Wallace's (1823–1913) great idea. In fact, Darwin was already on the prowl, already a nonbeliever in species fixity (e.g., accentuated with intertwining concepts of Malthusian geometrical propagation tempered by natural selection), yet hesitant to move forward by publishing. According to Lynn Barber, Darwin may have penned the 35-page abstract of his theory in 1844, "probably prompted by the publication of *Vestiges*."[42] Much of Darwin's "intellectual turmoil" during the 1840s was due to the outcry and clamor over *Vestiges*.[43]

Vestiges' anonymous author was maddeningly viewed as a mere compiler of facts culled from numerous and various sources, and his dastardly deed was done at a time when amateur writers and popularizers were expected to write obsequiously, showing due respect to accepted expert theoreticians and field practitioners. But, many wondered, who was *Vestiges*' author?

Chambers allowed a few individuals within his inner sanctum, those who knew it was he who had written all the editions of *Vestiges*. One was his wife, Anne. Another interesting confidant was writer David Page, a geological popularizer who wrote several books including one evolutionary epic, a "Page"-turner titled *The Past and Present Life of the Globe* (1861), in which he lambasted *Vestiges*, "which stands bastardised by the moral cowardice that shrinks from avowing its paternity."[44] (For Page, any sense of evolution was "predetermined.") Although Chambers went to his grave in 1883 without ever having revealed he had authored *Vestiges* and *Explanations*, Page attempted to unmask him in 1854. However, despite this betrayal, few believed his accusation.

Perhaps, owing to Chambers, paleontology books written from an epical, omniscient life-through-time perspective (unlike more theoretically oriented treatises composed by men such as Lyell and Darwin, or decades later by Steven Stanley and David Raup, authors of *Principles of Paleontology*—the textbook used for the paleontology course I completed[45]), became more distinctively regarded as popular (or textbookish) in tone. Nevertheless, today some historical geology textbooks necessarily adopt or rely upon literary elements characterizing the evolutionary epical tradition as well.

Vestiges was written when scholarly study of natural theology reigned. Those who challenged scriptural authority could be branded as heretic or at least risked their social status and reputation. So much safer to remain anonymous! Furthermore, compared to over a century and a half later, Chambers and his contemporaries had far fewer fossils to reflect upon.

Chambers clearly wrestled with concepts such as inferior versus elevated character states, especially when their manifestation in species didn't nicely coincide with predictions of the species development theory, aligned with succession in geological time. Chambers lacked understanding of modern genetics and DNA, which virtually replaced reliance upon earlier comparative studies of embryological development among species—once brandished in early evolutionary studies. And his moralistic, preachy-toned, theological rationalizations adjoining mankind's neurological and behavioral tendencies to those exhibited within other mammals is in the ballpark, yet still archaic. (Readers are deferred to a popular account, Edward O. Wilson's *The Social Conquest of Earth* (2012) for a modern spin on such themes.[46]) Chambers also never could have anticipated modern understanding of biochemical equilibria and intricacies maintained in living tissues. But then again, neither could have Darwin at that time.

CHAPTER THREE

Henry Robert Knipe
A Forgotten Paleo-Popularizer

Since the dawn of the paleontological sciences, the ultimate story earth scientists yearn to tell is that of our planet's life through time, or historical geology's pageant of life. Arguably, for two centuries, this has been paleontology's shining saga, retold by numerous writers, especially on the popular level. As Stephen Jay Gould suggested in a preface to *The Book of Life*, elucidating the chronology of past eras, periods and epochs has been geology's "major triumph," yet such "a spectacular success had to be accompanied by a maturing iconography committed to representing the past as a series of successive stages ...."[1] The life-through-time theme, now cliché, is sometimes referred to as the evolutionary epic, which can take on cosmic (or even divine) proportions. Beyond museum displays, the most *traditional* and accessible, although not only, format for conveying the evolutionary succession of organisms has been through book and magazine hard copy publications. Vintage books lavishly or amply illustrated with depictions of how extinct organisms and landscapes appeared especially after the 1850s—chronologically arranged—tend to be most memorable and sought after.

During the past two decades there has been considerable interest in paleoart, particularly artistry portraying how prehistoric animals appeared in their respective ages. Everyone has his favorite illustrations; books like Charles R. Knight's *Before the Dawn of History* (1935) are exemplary. Certainly following completion of his 28 murals for the Chicago Natural History Museum (1926–1930), it is difficult to envision how we would imagine Earth's evolution as well as its prevailing life through time without "Knightian" spectacles and perspective. And yet there was a time early in the past century when Knight did not yet reign in this regard. In fact, chief practitioners who depicted life through time came from overseas; one of them was a woman. Oddly, given such intrigue focused on the history of paleoart today, two extraordinary volumes, *Nebula to Man* (1905) and *Evolution in the Past* (1912), written by Henry R. Knipe—of whom generally little is known—are rarely cited today. Herein, the artistry of Alice B. Woodward was featured, twofold; J. Smit's work appears prominently in Knipe's 1905 entry.

Two decades ago, while researching paleoartists of the past, I borrowed original reference library editions of Knipe's two books. *Nebula to Man* and *Evolution in the Past* characterized the popular life-through-time genre in the early years just before Charles R. Knight gained fame as the century's greatest paleoartist. The books were written by British geologist Henry R. Knipe. Neither volume was intended as a textbook of historical geology. Instead, Knipe was one in a long tradition of geological popularizers. I was especially struck by how lavish was the edition of *Nebula to Man*. While the library original had to be eventually returned to their respective rare book rooms, fortunately, today one may obtain inexpensive facsimile hard copies from publishing houses like Kessinger Publishing and Nabu Public Domain Reprints. Also, Knipe's books are available online.

So it remained to dig for biographical information on Knipe. Here's what the Library of Congress forwarded, originally published in a British publication, *The Geological Magazine*:

> Henry Robert Knipe, F.L.S., F.G.S. (Born 1855, died July 26, 1918); We regret to record the death of Mr. Henry R. Knipe, who devoted much time and labour to the popularization of the study of extinct animals in this country. With the aid especially of the Staff of the British Museum, and utilizing its collections and library, he attempted to portray the animals of the past as they appeared when living and, sparing no expense, he employed the most skilled artists to carry out his plans. Among those who produced his restorations may be mentioned Mr. John [*sic*] Smit and Miss Alice B. Woodward. His earliest efforts were published as a series of plates illustrating a long poem named *Nebula to Man* (London 1905). More recently a still finer series of illustrations, chiefly by Miss Woodward, was issued in his more systematic work in prose, *Evolution in the Past* (London, 1912). Apart from his scientific studies Mr. Knipe's interests were wide and varied, and by his death Tunbridge Wells loses one of its most esteemed citizens and most generous philanthropists.[2]

Of the two books mentioned in his obituary, Knipe's *Nebula to Man*[3] is the more encompassing of the two, as it focuses more on geological changes (besides organismal evolution). But what a strange bird it is! It's a book of rhyme, an epic, evolutionary ballad tracing from the Earth's cosmic origins through modernity. But the rhyme is terribly choppy and halfway through had me realizing that the tempo could be set to a rap song.[4] In his preface, Knipe confessed that this exercise is a "bold experiment ... but ... Geology is truly the most enchanting story in the world; and rhyme may well be regarded as an appropriate form in which to present it.... We may well hope that some day it will be taken in hand by some great poetic genius."[5] Reading *Nebula to Man* today is quite an experience.

In order to fit scientific descriptions and aspects of geological succession into a vast poetic—if not rather amazing—construct, Knipe was forced into spinning some truly odd or thick lines and twisted grammar. So, to further clarify what he meant, technically, within the poem, an extensive notes section was added to the book's end (before the bibliography and index), arranged by page and individual lines cited on respective pages. Here, individual species or genera of prehistoria or geological events that he was referring to (often metaphorically within the poem) would be clarified to readers; cited literature could also be consulted.

Even for its time, the book was old school, in the sense that it favored more of a natural history glimpse of past geological ages like popular writers of the mid to late 19th century often did. It is clearly not a *technical* treatise on historical geology. Due to its size and lavishly illustrated nature, it perhaps succeeded as a coffee (or tea) table picture book. And yet Knipe—to get things right—consulted with many colleagues and contemporary scientists, such as the Rev. H.N. Hutchinson, Baron Nopsca, C.W. Andrews, H.F. Osborn, Arthur Smith Woodward and Henry Woodward, former Keeper of Geology at London's British Museum *and* father of artist Alice B. Woodward—who did many prehistoric animal restorations for Knipe's two books. (In the case of marine life restorations, Henry Woodward offered technical suggestions to his daughter.)

Throughout, Knipe expresses a belief in evolutionary progress as nature's "supreme law." Although natural selection is a reckoning force, the word "Creation," appears at times within the text. Yet, as scholar Bernard Lightman suggests in the case of another early popularizer of the evolutionary epic, R.S. Ball, Knipe's sense of creation may have had "sublime" rather than "divine" connotations.[6] Evolution of the mammalian line and mankind's fateful, inevitable ascent is a recurrent motif. As recounted in *Nebula,* so much happened throughout countless ages "whilst Man still slumbered in the womb of Time."[7] The trials, tribulations and strides made by many of the former, extinct genera or species on the rise are often likened to historical events—conquerors and the vanquished. Such ideas and accompanying (verbal) imagery are more self-evident in Knipe's second book, *Evolution in the Past.* But in *Nebula,* there is considerably more poetic description of terrestrial crustal changes driven by a cooling (shrinking) Earth; there's also considerable discussion of more recent changes such as Ice Age episodes. In an original take on the Darwinian bushy tree of life, instead, diversification of ancestral species and lineages into life's evolutionary descendants is likened to a mighty flowing river, splitting into many rills and smaller streams. Knipe states many transition species or links have been obscured by incompleteness of the rock record.

Say what you will of Knipe's rhyming, but the book's value remains in those wonderful pictures outlining life through deep time as portrayed before Charles R. Knight really transformed (if not predominated over) the field of prehistoric animal image-making. Photos from the Yerkes and Lick Observatories, respectively, showed the Great Nebula in Orion and the Spiral Nebula in Canes Venatici. These photos significantly underscore the then popularly perceived union between astronomy and biology in the grand evolutionary epic—asserting how Earth's beginnings and Man's remote origins precipitated from the very dust of the cosmos. Here is the cosmic nebula connection, which when you think about it lingers even in modern popular tellings of the grand evolutionary epic. Think of Carl Sagan's "billions and billions of stars" phrase, for example. (Vernacular of our nebular origin has been replaced by the Big Bang theory, however.)

Although the artistry of Alice B. Woodward (1862–1951) and J. Smit (1836–1929) steals the show, other artists featured here are Ernest Bucknall, L. Speed, C. Whymper, E.A. Wilson and J. Charlton. Altogether, there are 14 colored restorations and 57 tinted illustrations and Speed's colored frontispiece. J. Smit had a long and successful career as a wildlife artist as well as in the paleo-genre. By 1905 he was already renown for illustrating editions of the Rev. Henry Neville Hutchinson's (1856–1927) popular books on prehistoric life, e.g., *Extinct Monsters* (1892 and later editions), and *Creatures of Other Days* (1894). Smit's new work for *Nebula* was to a large degree based on Knight's paintings for the American Museum and *Century Magazine. Nebula* is graced with 33 of Smit's paintings, two reproduced in color. For Woodward, who later became more acclaimed for illustrating children's books, *Nebula* was a marvelous opportunity to establish herself in the broadening field of popular paleontology. Besides *Nebula* and *Evolution,* Woodward's prehistoric animal art was also published in *Illustrated London News.* (See Figure 3-1.) Thirteen of her paintings adorn *Nebula*'s pages.

Knipe's second major entry, *Evolution in the Past* (London, 1912), was another life-through-time tour de force, *sans* (thankfully) rhyming. In outline, it's essentially the same book as *Nebula to Man,* although, more clearly stated, an easier read. *Evolution* is graced with 56 plate illustrations, 51 of which were prepared specifically for the newer book. This time Knipe relied principally on Alice B. Woodward's illustrations, with four by Bucknall. Certainly in retrospect, three key (if not eventually exciting) discoveries had transpired in the period intervening since *Nebula to Man*'s release: descriptions and restorations of North America's

Fig 3-1: *Stegosaurus* restoration by Alice B. Woodward, appearing as Plate facing p. 90 in Henry R. Knipe's *Evolution in the Past* (1912).

iconic *Tyrannosaurus rex*; publicizing of England's "Piltdown Man"; and discovery of Canada's Burgess Shale fauna. Release of Knipe's new book came too soon, apparently, to include references to these new citizens of the prehistoric world. (Decades later Piltdown Man was proven to be a fraud.)

Ultimately, *Evolution in the Past* was intended, and succeeds admirably, as a "sketch of life, founded on discoveries made in the geological strata."[8] Here, the emphasis is on *evolution* taking place in the geological past. Knipe's Introduction is a well-conceived summary of the state of knowledge, then, about organismal change through time and factors giving rise to such changes, including remarks on the Mutation Theory as espoused by contemporary geneticists. Knipe testifies his allegiance to the "doctrine of evolution."[9] He underscores Charles Darwin's contributions—the idea of natural selection, particularly—to modern understanding of organic evolution supported by paleontological facts.

Remarking on the "Foundational Ages," or the Precambrian, Knipe accepted that much evolutionary change must have occurred long before the sudden creation of metazoan life in the Cambrian Period. Yet he speculated on links that are missing from the rock record as, for instance, "fishes must certainly have had remote ancestors in pre–Cambrian seas, but the ancestral forms are quite unknown."[10] Knipe's Chronology of the Earth table indicates suggests Earth was well over 100 million years old.

Knipe's *Evolution in the Past* is organized according to chapters describing life that appeared in each successive period, as recorded in fossils. (Paleogene epochs are referred to as periods.) Headings printed in margins announce the various types of organisms under discussion on respective pages, such as "Jelly-fishes, Corals and Star Fishes" described in the Cambrian Period chapter. (Curiously, it seems that Knipe mistakenly believed ammonites crawled about the sea bottom, walking on their heads, not swimming.) Regularly, Knipe inserts one of Woodward's or Bucknall's illustrations showing how each of the ancient denizens appeared in life. As in the case of *Nebula to Man*, there are both idealized landscapes and underwater scenes including multiple life forms congregating and, as in later chapters, numerous restorations of individual species of vertebrate prehistoria. The organization was informative, especially given Knipe's flair for writing.

As in *Nebula*, Knipe's life-through-time general theme is wedded to belief in the exalted ascent of Man, as if mankind is the inevitable, inexorable outcome of evolutionary progress. In *Evolution in the Past*, mankind is seen as the ultimate goal toward which evolution persisted. Certainly in our special case, we are unquestionably one current outcome of Earth's geological history, but at earlier geological stages (as noted elsewhere and more recently by Stephen Jay Gould), any set of contingent factors *could have* prohibited our evolution in favor of something else. Knipe also takes stock in "orthogenesis," a since falsified evolutionary theory wherein certain successive species of organisms trended toward "over-specialization," and thus fateful extinction, or the "long sleep."[11] (See Chapter Four for more on this.) For example, in one flowery passage Knipe refers to saber-toothed feline *Smilodon*, or "creatures in such predicament, with palatable prey near but not negotiable, bring to mind the fate of Tantalus."[12]

Knipe recognizes certain major events such as the Permian/Triassic ("Permo-Triassic") transition. Nonetheless, "of waste and suffering, the main movement was distinctly onward. Nor were signs wanting at the close of the Permian of coming great developments."[13] But readers would probably find Knipe's description of dinosaurs, or "Earth's first bipeds," introduced in his Triassic chapter, most intriguing. Quite astutely, he observes, "they come ... within Plato's special definition of a man—'a biped without feathers.'"[14] (See Figure 3-2.) But ultimate planetary rule has yet to be settled, as the contemporaneous appearance of mammals is of highest significance. To Knipe, mammals had evolved from reptiles—those known as "Theromorphs"and "Theriodonts"—but he speculates as to what drove our primitive ancestors' destiny forward,[15] musing that it was "Morality in active evolution, breaking like sunbeams through clouds. Animals had appeared parts of whose bodies were designed, not for their own convenience and welfare, but for the use and benefit of their offspring. Altruism had passed to a higher stage; and many virtues, hitherto obscured or undeveloped, were coming forth as lights in the world."[16] Therefore, it well suited Knipe's scheme that most dinosaurs, especially those of grandest size, were egg-layers, unequipped for parental duties.

Knipe's century-old insights refresh, like *Triceratops*'s bony frill "suggestive of an Elizabethan collar." How unlikely it was that the head ornamentation of such dull-witted creatures would have aided their "ardour or discrimination in their love affairs."[17] The K/T boundary (now properly referred to as the "K/Pg," or Cretaceous/Paleogene), as known today, is referred to as the "great reptile slump ... one of the darkest epochs in Geology."[18] Plesiosaurs were "essentially creatures of old-fashioned type, and without sufficient elasticity to be effectively transformed."[19] And certain bivalves (e.g., rudists) "certainly kept up appearances for a long time; but towards the close of the Cretaceous ... they failed to meet the *demands of Evolution* ...."[20] (My italics.) Meanwhile, among fossil fishes, throughout the Cretaceous Period, "brisk progress continued."[21] Birds appeared, considerably advanced since *Archaeopteryx*'s heyday. Knipe believed birds were clearly derived from as yet unknown dinosaurian stock. Among plants, flowering angiosperms began to proliferate, much like "the northern barbarians moving down on the Roman Empire."[22]

So when the Eocene "dawned," following a "long night," it's as if "the lights in a playhouse had been abruptly extinguished, and after a lapse had been restored, disclosing a stage crowded with new characters."[23] Dinosaurs and their ilk had left the stage, never to return. Quite a serene ending contrasted with the cosmic jolt later realized as a means to their final bow! (See Chapter Sixteen.) To Knipe, historical geology was not unlike a Shakespearean play.

Knipe's theme hereon regards regions of the planet (Africa especially, despite missing strata) where evolution had been most "active," as in producing mammals along more familiar lines, converging linearly toward modern horses, rhinoceroses, whales and elephants. Throughout, Knipe's entertaining description of Cenozoic avian and mammalian lineages is masterful for its time. When the Oligocene Age is introduced, Knipe declared that due to the "decidedly closer resemblance"[24] of invertebrate life to modern forms, there was simply no further need to discuss it. So, with increasing vertebrate bias, attainment of intelligence is stressed as vital to further development of placentals, such as modern carnivora and man. Less intelligent lines, however, such as horned uintatheres, the later "titanotheres" and others, were "not on the active list of Evolution." "Brute force ... had long been a declining power in creation." Certain (doomed) genera already were "suffering from old age and consequential eccentricities."[25]

Fig 3-2: *Ceratosaurus* by J. Smit, one of "Earth's first bipeds," appearing as Plate XVII in Henry R. Knipe's *Nebula to Man* (1905).

Knipe had a flair for turning a humorous catch phrase or two, as in addressing the plight of paleo-swine (entelodont *Elotherium*, "heretical pigs"), when "towards the close of the Period they were roasted, one and all, in the inquisition-fires of Natural Selection."[26] A hellish pig roast indeed! Meanwhile, when the Isthmus of Panama was uplifted, South America's supposedly inferior "mammal-products were no longer 'protected'" because "the tariff wall ... had ceased to be."[27] Knipe likened these extinctions to that "experienced by the South American natives when the Spaniards invaded their dominions."[28] Analogous conditions prevailed in prehistoric Australia, where (he perceived, subjectively) inferior and more primitive marsupials prevailed, eventually succumbing during historical times to placentals. Yet, Knipe startlingly speculates that had "marsupialism continued free to develop, some pouched animals with resemblance to anthropoid apes, and even to human beings, might have appeared."

Perhaps the single most controversial subject for any popularizer of evolution writing a century ago would have been discussion of primeval man. While perhaps by then, many could accept evolution among the "lower ranks" of life, certainly Man wasn't a product of blind chance—or are we? Knipe supported the evolutionist side (although plainly his views of evolution were in themselves outmoded based on today's understanding). In *Evolution in the Past,* text is devoted to *Propliopithecus, Pithecanthropus,* and various types of *Neanderthal*—"Heidelberg Man," "Mousterian Man" and "Aurignacian Man." These hominids evolved from stock common to early apes. Such "progressive" creatures developed a taste for meat, gained higher brain power and, assuming an upright posture, no longer sought the safety of the trees. And while during interglacial times, Man was "destined to kingship," Knipe's commentary on the subject of prehistoric man is rather racist (a common tone for the time).[29] In spite of this, and looking toward our continued evolution, it is proclaimed, we would profit from mastery of those primitive and brute psychological impulses derived from our remote past.

In researching *Evolution in the Past,* Knipe relied on numerous technical references, most of them published during or after the mid–1890s, listed in an extensive bibliography ("Authors Consulted"). In short, this handy if not illustrious little tome covered all the bases. How peculiar that Knipe's offerings are seldom mentioned in recent discussions of early life-through-time presentations.

Knipe thanked Henry Neville Hutchinson (who became an ordained minister in 1885) for reading the manuscript of *Nebula to Man,* during which "many useful criticisms and suggestions" were offered. Hutchinson also "rendered ... much assistance in working out restorations of extinct animals."[30] While Knipe may have preferred Woodward's art over Smit's, Hutchinson clearly preferred Smit's (who illustrated three of Hutchinson's books). However, Hutchinson is rarely credited as the individual who revitalized the geological evolutionary epic, that is, by promoting its *visual* side. Noting how the 1st edition of his *Extinct Monsters* (1892) filled a void, given the "scarcity of popular works in Geology at the present time" (i.e., circa 1890), Hutchinson claimed that (Louis) Figuier's *World Before the Deluge* (1860s eds.)—the most recent lavishly illustrated book published prior—was by then "hardly a trustworthy book."[31] With publications such as *Autobiography of the Earth* (1890), *Extinct Monsters, Creatures of Other Days* (1894), *Prehistoric Man and Beast* (1896), and *Extinct Monsters and Creatures of Other Days: A Popular Account of Some of the Larger Forms of Ancient Animal Life* (1910), Hutchinson carved a niche for his popular, assiduously illustrated and well-received writings.[32]

In a preface printed in the latter, Hutchinson noted that Knipe's *Nebula to Man* "contains a large number of beautiful restorations and landscapes."[33] Despite such praise, Hutchinson did not include *Nebula to Man* in *Extinct Monsters and Creatures of Other Days'* bibliography. Perhaps Hutchinson wasn't into poetry, or maybe there were competitive reasons and/or differences of opinion for this slight. Hutchinson described how difficult was the task of conveying realistic portraits of the prehistoric life featured in his books, and his indebtedness to the artists involved—particularly Smit. Only four of Charles R. Knight's restorations appear in Hutchinson's 1910 volume.

That Hutchinson preferred the accuracy of Smit's portrayals over Alice B. Woodward's is apparent in a December 26, 1926, letter addressed to Dr. F.A. Bather (a crinoid expert), in which he critiqued several drafts of Woodward's dinosaur restorations. Here, Hutchinson declared, "*some of* the restorations of dinosaurs by Miss Woodward are not correct. She has not studied *their bones*—evidently—or she would give them more flesh—esp. *Ceratosaurus*. I don't like her *Cetiosaurus*—with all that loose flesh. Aquatic animals do *not* have loose flesh hanging about like that. Could you get her to do some of these *again*? I can give her a few hints if she cares to consult me. I think some of dear old Smit's restorations are more correct."[34]

In contrast to Knipe's open acceptance of evolution, Hutchinson was more devout yet subtle in his delivery. For instance, in *Prehistoric Man and Beast* (1896, illustrated by Cecil Aldin), Hutchinson reconciled theology with human evolution while refuting Darwinian natural selection (that is, preferring Lamarckian precepts). While addressing the theory of evolution in *Extinct Monsters and Creatures of Other Days* (1910), he did not discuss the touchy issue of prehistoric man. Hutchinson took his cue from prior popular natural history writers of the cosmic evolutionary epic, such as Hugh Miller, Arabella Buckley, and Peter Parley—spiritually minded evolutionists whom he admired. Overall, Knipe was more secular in his views on organic evolution than his contemporary Hutchinson. Both popularizers shared a belief in the inevitable ascendancy of Man—the self-proclaimed pinnacle of evolution. However, Knipe states in *Evolution in the Past,* "That Natural Selection applies and must always have applied to all forms of life was first recognized by Darwin and Wallace.... Natural Selection, therefore, ... may be said to originate species."[35]

In a letter dated October 26, 1928, Alice B. Woodward answered W.D. Lang's (a fossil sponge expert) query about her prehistoric animal restorations completed for Knipe's publications. She said, "Unfortunately Mr. Knipe died during wartime. I did not hear of his death for a considerable time. His people took no interest in science & all his books & collections, & with them all my original drawings were sold by auction. When I heard of Mr. Knipe's death I wrote to the trustees as did also Sir Arthur Smith Woodward but the drawings could not be traced.... I am quite willing to make any fresh drawings of these or other subjects for Mr. Maxwell Reed should he wish it. He has some nice things anyway with Mr. Knight's beautiful drawings."[36]

While astronomer W. Maxwell Reed (1871–1962) did have Knight's restorations to rely on, by July of 1928, he was already signing the preface to, perhaps, the definitive genre book of its time, *The Earth for Sam*. Reed essentially accomplished what so many popular authors had traditionally done, in capturing the Earth's geological history and its curious inhabitants in a delightful volume, although tailored for children. The book was not by any means lavish, although it was amply illustrated. Reed relied upon a splendid array of the finest paleoart (restorations and photos) available (reproduced in black and white). Woodward's, Smit's and Bucknall's artwork—drawn from *Nebula* and *Evolution* sources—was represented prominently therein, alongside several of Knight's restorations as well as a host of other artists' work. As far as popular paleontology goes, *Earth for Sam* (which ran through several editions) was not to be rivaled (or eclipsed) perhaps until publication of Knight's majestic *Before the Dawn of History*.[37]

Before the Dawn of History depicted the grandeur of life through time in a mystical, romantic way that only a master like Knight—reflecting prehistoric visions framed by his

Chicago Natural History Museum murals, completed less than a decade before—could visually convey. Like Reed's and Knipe's volumes before, Knight's was an elegant and welcome home bookshelf adornment.

Today, scholars note how popularization of the evolutionary epic encompasses far beyond Earth's life through geological time. This prevalent theme has remained popular at least since Robert Chambers (1802–1883) published his controversial book, *Vestiges of Creation,* anonymously in 1844–which, like Knipe's *Nebula to Man,* was also founded on the Nebular Hypothesis. More recently, however, while life through time remains ever popular and vital, this traditional theme now competes on a computer-fueled popular level with ideas born of the dinosaur renaissance. While organizing life through time for nonspecialists may seem old hat, scientist-specialists have instead emphasized thorny matters such as (1) hot vs. cold-blooded dinosaurs; (2) causes of mass extinctions in the fossil record; (3) cradle-to-grave paleobiology of individual genera of (especially) dinosaurs and other Mesozoic beasts; and (4) the feathered dinosaur phenomenon. Detailed dinosaur encyclopedias strive to capture the wealth of the ever-expanding dinosaur renaissance wave. Meanwhile, our love affair with life through time has been intriguingly modified at a popular level with considerations given to oxygen's history, as in Peter Ward's fascinating 2006 evolutionary epic alternative, *Out of Thin Air.*[38] We take it for granted that there was a succession of life, yet must rely on sophisticated biogeochemical computer modeling to understand what prior life conditions were really like and how such conditions tempered organic evolution ... *through the course of geological time.*

One last aspect worthy of note within and throughout Knipe's two masterpieces is how highly "anthropomorphized" are both (1) the creatures of those other long-ago days in their theatrical waxings and wanings, ebb and flow, or their leaving the metaphorical stage (of life) with fading lights, etc., as well as (2) the orchestrating force of evolution, having directional influence along the proper pathway leading to man's (evolutionarily ordained) arrival. Extinct organisms take on personalized character, described via more familiar human-like terms, recognizable feelings and qualities. Species behavior and fortunes are often likened to those of modern or historical human societies, cultures and empires. This was clearly done for ease of readership, but this instructional perspective and tone would be used later on, to significant degree.

Chapter Four

Dinosaur Extinctions I

When a "dinosaur book" Isn't: Henry Fairfield Osborn's Origin and Evolution of Life *(1917)*

"... in evolution law prevails over chance."[1]

My late father was an antiquarian specializing in rare, old chemistry and alchemy books pertaining to early advances in medicine, which was his professional field of study. Yet, avocationally, he loved paleontology; many old geological texts dotted shelves in his study. One book especially intrigued me: Henry Fairfield Osborn's sumptuous *The Origin and Evolution of Life* (New York: Charles Scribner's Sons, 1917). When I first paged through it three decades ago, *Origin and Evolution* seemed merely another one of those early pop-cultural texts capitalizing on dinosaurs and those "other" prehistoric animals presented through chapters sequentially moving from the Precambrian Era toward the Recent in life-through-time context. Like many others published between 1900 and the mid–1930s, its pages brandished Charles R. Knight's American Museum paintings. The aristocratic Osborn was a prolific author, an American Museum of Natural History scientific director, who wrote about fossil horses, elephants, titanotheres (now known as brontotheres), paleo-men and dinosaurs, on both scholarly as well as popular levels. He formally named and described the most famous real dinosaur—*Tyrannosaurus rex*. He was prone to theorize about evolution too, or rather his particular vision and version of it. (See Figure 4-1.)

Whereas for its time, Knipe's *Evolution in the Past* was fairly mainstream, Henry F. Osborn's *The Origin and Evolution of Life* (a popular lecture series published as a book) was far more peculiar and idiosyncratic. Yet in pondering the mysteries of evolution and eventual extinction, viewed in progressive life-through-time context, offering physicochemical reasoning for such events presented as a profound packaging of original biological "laws," Osborn produced a volume of distinctive, eclectic quality, just as outrageously peculiar as Knipe's *Nebula to Man*. Thus we may share another antiquated early view offering interpretations of how life's history, focusing on the evolution of *energy* (before DNA's discovery), was divulged to interested readership. To Osborn, the germ-plasm, as it was referred to then, seemed as mysterious as the energy emitted by recently discovered (radioactive) radium.

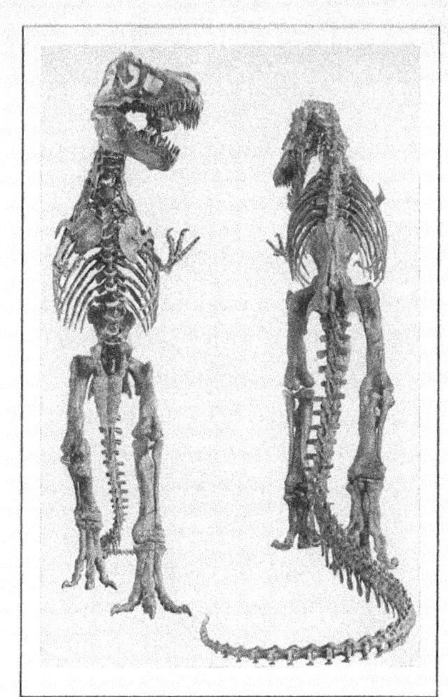

Tyrannosaurus rex, THE KING OF THE TYRANT SAURIANS.

The climax among carnivorous reptiles of a complex mechanism for the capture, storage, and release of energy. Contemporary with and destroyer of the large herbivorous dinosaurs. Compare p. 224.

THE ORIGIN AND EVOLUTION OF LIFE

ON THE THEORY OF ACTION
REACTION AND INTERACTION OF ENERGY

BY

HENRY FAIRFIELD OSBORN

SC.D. PRINCETON, HON. LL.D. TRINITY, PRINCETON, COLUMBIA, HON. D.SC. CAMBRIDGE
HON. PH.D. CHRISTIANIA
RESEARCH PROFESSOR OF ZOOLOGY, COLUMBIA UNIVERSITY
VERTEBRATE PALÆONTOLOGIST U. S. GEOLOGICAL SURVEY, CURATOR EMERITUS OF VERTEBRATE
PALÆONTOLOGY IN THE AMERICAN MUSEUM OF NATURAL HISTORY
AUTHOR OF "FROM THE GREEKS TO DARWIN"
"THE AGE OF MAMMALS," "MEN OF THE OLD STONE AGE"

WITH 136 ILLUSTRATIONS

NEW YORK
CHARLES SCRIBNER'S SONS
1918

Fig 4-1: Frontispiece showing American Museum of Natural History views of Osborn's *Tyrannosaurus rex* museum skeletal reconstruction and title page to his *Origin and Evolution of Life* (1917).

Upon initial, first-glance inspection, many images featured in *Origin and Evolution,* such as those showing microscopical photographs of chromosomal splitting and microbes, seemed rather peculiar for a run-of-the-mill prehistoric animal book. The first chapter dealt with subject matter that, at least on an introductory level, would be considered atypical of the genre as we embrace it today, or even when compared to contemporary, turn of the 20th century, popular, history of life accounts—tempting rarities such as H.N. Hutchinson's *Extinct Monsters,* E. Ray Lankester's *Extinct Animals,* H.R. Knipe's *Evolution in the Past,* Charles Schuchert's *Outlines of Historical Geology,* or B. Webster Smith's *The World in the Past.*[2] Instead, Osborn's *Origin and Evolution* appears to be a peculiar early treatise on thermodynamics and genetic principles as applied to the history of life. Why was Osborn's text, written at such a fruitful, pivotal period in the history of genetics and chemical understanding, evidently so different for its time, and where was he going with it? What inspired Osborn's 1910s interests in biophysical chemistry, interwoven throughout his life-through-geological-time treatise?

Osborn's book (I'm familiar with 1917, 1918 and 1923 editions, each straying into technical matters to be outlined here) carries the revealing subtitle, *On the Theory of Action, Reaction and Interaction of Energy* (offhand, suggesting a merging of Isaac Newton's and J. Willard Gibbs's ideologies[3]). Each of the individual eight chapters were part of a series of lectures dedicated to astronomer George Ellery Hale. Here, I would like to describe those chapters, emphasizing key contents divulging *Origin and Evolution* as a text quite apart from merely another early "dinosaur book" of the day. For Osborn steered away from the then conventional "outline of geology" into a biophysical chemistry (or perhaps "biogeochemical") basis of life, as *he believed* it fostered evolution. Osborn's *Origin and Evolution* would have seemed both as curious and novel then, as it is today.

Who was Osborn? Henry Fairfield Osborn (1857–1935) was an aristocratic paleontologist, mastermind and orchestrator behind many of the early great vertebrate paleontological displays at the American Museum of Natural History. He was also responsible for introducing Charles R. Knight's magnificent paleoart to those hallowed halls. Osborn's decisive tenure at the American Museum lasted from 1890 to 1935. Osborn, a Princeton graduate, became a protégé of the aging Edward D. Cope (1840–1897). (In 1931, Osborn even published a biography about Cope's career.[4]) During the early 20th century, dinosaurs and fossil mammals became popular largely due to Osborn's efforts. Yet few know about his more theoretical leanings.

In a sense, Osborn audaciously elevated himself to the ranks of the greatest scientists—Isaac Newton and Charles Darwin, particularly—by refining understanding of the law of evolution. In his preface, Osborn stated his purpose: "In these lectures we may take some of the initial steps toward an energy conception of Evolution and an energy conception of Heredity...."[5] Bear in mind that the structure and significance of DNA, now known to all high school freshmen and seemingly in everyday crime-related news, was not yet understood. That discovery would come four decades later. So instead we may marvel at his fascination over the unknown nature of the "germ plasm of heredity"; as he articulated with awe, "the germ evolution is the most incomprehensible phenomenon which has yet been discovered in the universe...."[6] Osborn offered explanations for *why* evolution happens, a weighty challenge then. Osborn wrestled with questions such as—was evolution driven from the outer environment, inward toward the germ plasm (essentially Lamarckian inheritance via acquired characteristics), or are biological changes that later become pronounced as evolutionary instigated within the germ plasm (i.e., a mutational construct)? Rather than examining organismal energy flow *into* evolved forms of matter, a cart-before-the-horse ideology, Osborn preferred considering how energy permeates from the cosmos, then outwardly from organisms throughout the biosphere, through time. In other words, in the first half of *Origin and Evolution*, in rudimentary fashion Osborn rather precociously pondered the thermodynamics of life.

But Osborn certainly challenged readers (both contemporary and modern) in his first chapter, culminating in a discussion of the four physicochemical "complexes of energy." Indeed, this is not the usual fare for a run-of-the-mill "prehistoric animal book." Osborn suggested that life chemistry represented recombination of cosmic (stellar) and inorganic chemistry, and that (most likely) there were no new forms of energy created by the principle of life. However, here Osborn hedged his bets, admitting that possibly someday he could be proved wrong, say, if scientists were to discover an element analogous to (then recently discovered) radium that was somehow enveloped, or "wrapped up in living matter but remain as yet undetected." Or there could conceivably be some "*unknown* chemical element, to which the hypothetical term *bion* might be given ... or an unknown source of energy may be active here."[7] Although not a new energy form, in modern parlance, figuratively, Osborn's "bion" would decades later became translatable into what we now call "DNA."

Could evolution somehow become genetically "wired" to inevitably lead through geological time to extinction of more derived genera, those (allegedly) "linearly" trending toward development of exaggerated, useless bodily features? Osborn thought so.

Osborn questioned whether evolutionary change resulted from the operations of sheer *chance*. Chance, or randomness—upon which selection operates, according to Darwin—was, to Osborn mere dogma, or a "hypothesis which has gained credence through constant reiteration, for I do not know that it has ever been demonstrated through the actual observation of any evolutionary series."[8] Was Osborn dissing Darwin? To a certain extent, evidently. Osborn fortified his arguments, borrowing a thesis from biochemist Lawrence J. Henderson's (1878–1942) widely read *The Fitness of the Environment.*[9] Henderson discovered human blood's buffering capacity, an acid-base equilibrium later articulated mathematically (and now known to freshman chemistry students as the Henderson-Hasselbach equation). Henderson found it inconceivable that compounds such as carbonic acid, metabolically keyed to physiological processes, were (chiefly) resultant of adaptation.[10]

Henderson was deeply impressed by the perfection of the terrestrial environment's capacity for supporting life. Much of his case and sense of wonder rested on physical chemistry properties of water, carbon dioxide, oxygen and other elements and compounds fostering forms of life then known to science, as found in the natural environment. It seemed that a correspondence between organismal "fitness" and Earth's environmental chemistry could not have arisen through chance alone. Today, such arguments would be regarded as "teleological" in nature, although Henderson was agnostic. Henderson's "lasting contribution was to make it clear that the inorganic world has placed certain restrictions on the direction that organic evolution can take."[11]

Evidently in 1913, Henderson was preaching to the choir, as Osborn frequently referenced the former in *Origin and Evolution*, stating that a "modern chemist (i.e., Henderson) ... questions the probability of the environmental fitness of the earth for life being a mere chance process...."[12] Osborn then described the energy concept of life, introducing Newton's laws and the laws of thermodynamics. Applying such concepts to living matter, Osborn suggested that every physicochemical action and reaction that transforms, conserves or dissipates energy in an organism must produce a physicochemical "agent of interaction" affecting the organism. Ultimately, coordinated reactions and actions would evolve in nature, and the "corresponding evolution of interaction" would allow organisms to evolve "harmoniously."[13] Admittedly, today, Osborn's chemical views on biochemistry of evolution seem either prematurely, or simplistically, represented. He dared to proclaim much in the absence of detail.

Osborn then articulated his manifesto, an overarching view of all factors and agents of evolution, focusing on those involving energy interactions, while (not denying but) relegating Darwin's emphasis on natural selection to the sideline: "*Selection* is not a form of energy nor a part of the energy complex; it is an arbiter between different complexes and forms of energy; it antedates the origin of life just as adaptation or fitness antedates the origin of life, as remarked by Henderson.... Selection merely determines which one of a combination of energies shall survive and which shall perish."[14] It is tempting to dismiss Osborn's thesis as mumbo-jumbo, but as we'll soon see, there is a specter of reasoning behind it all.

Osborn was mystified as well as fascinated by the heredity germ (or "Heredity-chromatin," i.e., DNA) energy "complex," then undecipherable in its nature and operations. But this was only one of the four energy complexes, which he also referred to as "four simultaneous evolutions," or the fundamental biological law.[15] Osborn stated the interrelationship between these: "In each organism the phenomena of life represent the action, reaction, and interaction of four complexes of physicochemical energy, namely those of (1) the Inorganic Environment, (2) the developing Organism (protoplasm and body-chromatin), (3) the germ or Heredity-chromatin, (4) the Life Environment. Upon the resultant actions, reactions, and interactions of potential and kinetic energy in each organism Selection is constantly operating wherever there is competition with the competition actions, reactions and interactions of other organisms."[16] To Osborn, the third energy "evolution" (i.e., Heredity-chromatin) surpassed the others in terms of complexity and infinitude. As he was prone to do, by 1912, he had even bestowed an abstruse name to the interrelationship, tetrakinetic theory, explaining the tetra-*plastic* nature of organisms molded plastically in relation to the aforementioned four omnipresent sets of energies.

Osborn's tetrakinetic theory may have sounded like a brilliant extrapolation of Newton's and Darwin's theories. Why do we not then regard the tetrakinetic theory today at the same exalted level in the scientific pantheon, as Newton's physical force laws or Darwin's law of evolution? How far was Osborn off the mark?

The remainder of Osborn's "dinosaur book" outlines how these four energy complexes have manifested themselves in the origin and subsequent evolution of life on Earth through the dim corridors of geological time. Osborn may have proclaimed he was an evolutionist, yet throughout his career he took pains to show where and how he differed from (or even exceeded) Charles Darwin, so that his own brilliance would shine. Here, he wielded powerful "energy complexes." Yet in the arena of elucidating evolutionary tendencies, history has shown that an ounce of sound inference is worth far more than a pound of utter speculation.

Citing Henderson's thoughtful reflections, Osborn was confident that life originated in water, owing to its unique chemical properties and because the "fitness of water to life is maximal."[17] Colloids and enzymes (which catalyze biochemical, cellular reactions) had recently been discovered in organisms, and Osborn discussed their nature as the basis of how early organisms interacted with the primordial environment. Then Osborn outlined key sections of Henderson's book in his treatment of the essentiality and "fitness" of the life elements.

Osborn had acquired knowledge of the latest developments in contemporary genetics and biochemistry. He sought to apply such knowledge to the mystery of evolution, albeit his own special (non-Darwinian) brand of evolution (largely shaped by the late Edward Cope's concepts). And Osborn wrote of primordial bacterial populations acquiring "physicochemical powers" (such as enzymes), then radiating adaptively, profiting from the ability to synthesize needed chemicals from each newly exploited energy source. Theirs was an important role in early phases of planetary history—as it remains today. Here, it is readily apparent that Osborn had vast appreciation for the work of early modern bacteriologists, as well as biophysicists and biochemists who studied and analyzed plant and animal tissues both in the test tube as well as through the microscope lens. Yet throughout, he appealed to his fundamental biologic law.[18]

Osborn spun complicated theoretical evolutionary ideas throughout his life-through-time *opus*, few of which would pass muster today. In fact, he's been regarded as a third-rate scientist. Appealing to the (then) latest developments in "hard sciences" such as chemistry and physics would not be enough to salvage his evolutionary views, ideals which may seem odd today yet were not as peculiar in Osborn's heyday.

Osborn ended the fourth chapter of his book, *The Origin and Evolution of Life*, concerning the rise of early Paleozoic invertebrate life, profoundly, with several claims concerning the laws of evolution, as he perceived them. This became a twofold attack on Charles Darwin and geneticist Hugo de Vries. Osborn believed the common problem with Darwin and, later, de Vries was that they both perceived evolutionary changes as initiated through fortuitous (random) changes in organismal phenotype (i.e., form), upon which natural selection would preferentially "select," therefore, the most "successful" types to pass along inheritance in a further generation. Osborn did not believe that evolution proceeded from one species or form into another, that is—*fortuitously*. Mutations (i.e., "saltations"), as noted by Hugo de Vries in laboratory experimentation, were *not* observed in the fossil record. Nor were randomly distributed phenotypes observed to become phylogenetic "links."

Fortifying his evolutionary alternative, Osborn referred to the work of Austrian paleontologist Wilhelm Heinrich Waagen, who had investigated a series of Jurassic ammonites in 1869. Osborn essentially hitched his wagon to Waagen, claiming Waagen's evidence noted in the genus *Ammonites* established "the law of minute and inconspicuous changes of form which accumulate so gradually that they are observable only after a considerable passage of time ... a true evolution of the heredity-chromatin."[19] But while, superficially, a linking of infinitesimal changes might seem consistent with Darwin's evolutionary ideas, instead Osborn attributed a sense of continuously, "*definitely directed* (adaptive) evolution"[20] to each inconspicuous link. Although this *Ammonites* series illustration became known as the "mutations of Waagen," here there was no "saltation" (per de Vries) and no randomness (per Charles Darwin) assigned to its phylogenetic unfolding through geological time. In subsequent chapters of his *Origin and Evolution*, Osborn's evolutionary views of invertebrate life would be carried over into vertebrate terrain.

Adhering to Waagen's and fellow paleo-mammalogist William Berryman Scott's views, Osborn noted both ontogenetic and phylogenetic variations in form. The first occurred (i.e., ontogenetically) during the individual lifetime of an organism; the second (phylogenetically) over the course of many generations. Therefore, ontogenetic changes, driven by the heredity germ-plasm (or "heredity chromatin"), ultimately precipitated changes that became evolutionary, or phylogenetic. However, to Osborn, phylogenetic changes were also "predetermined," adding a teleological sense to his views on life's history. A complex admixture of factors—or energies—was involved. Environmental factors as well as habitual, adaptational patterns established in an ancestral organism would stimulate ontogenetic responses, which would in turn produce a pronounced, corresponding "heredity potential" in its germ-plasm. This heredity potential would subsequently manifest itself through many genera of evolutionary descendants. So, for instance, it was under the right mix of circumstances (i.e., interacting "energy complexes") that the heredity potential in the germ plasm of, say, an Eocene ancestral titanothere genus (e.g., *Eotitanops*) would over millions of years later give rise to magnificently twin-horned genera, such as *Brontops*. So, Osborn stated, ontogenetic variations "may extend over an enormously long period of time ... and predetermine the course of evolution. They set a groove, as it were, along which evolution must take its course."[21] (See Figure 4-2.)

Leading off a subsequent chapter of *Origin and Evolution* that dealt with the vertebrate form, Osborn lectured on Lamarckianism vs. Darwinism—then outlined his own confounding explanations for evolution, the crux of his book.

Osborn contrasted the views of French naturalist (Jean Baptiste) Chevalier de Lamarck (1744–1829), and the later "Neo-Lamarckian" American paleontologist Edward D. Cope, with the then generally prevailing idea–Darwinian evolution. As noted by Osborn, during the early 1800s, Lamarck theorized that evolutionary changes proceeded from the "genesis of new form and function" influenced or stimulated by the environment interacting with body cells. Osborn noted that alterations of the effected body cells then *caused* corresponding physicochemical changes expressed within the heredity-chromatin: "According to this ... explanation a change of environment, of habit, and of function should always be antecedent to changes of form in succeeding generations."[22] Decades later, Cope noted that bodily parts also were subjected to disuse and consequent degeneration, that is, besides additive changes tacked on to later growth stages of the developing organism, caused through heightened utility. On the surface, Cope's ideas (known as "kinetogenesis," or "mechanical use of parts creating change," and "bathmism"–growth force) were rather analogous to Lamarck's. Ronald Rainger has defined Cope's theory as the (Lamarckian) "inheritance of those choices, habits, and acquired characteristics [that] constituted evolution."[23]

Of course, Darwinian genetic modifications (as supported and restated by early geneticists August Weismann, William Bateson, Hugo de Vries and the "rediscovered" Gregor Mendel), more or less worked the other way around, in *anti*–Lamarckian fashion. Instead, the germ heredity-chromatin (as Osborn referred to it) is responsible for producing morphotypes from which the environment could subsequently "select" for relative fitness, and therefore procreation. But rather than conjuring new forms according to some unknown, mystically aligned (i.e., predestined), internal adaptive law, the heredity-chromatin incessantly "experiments," fortuitously.

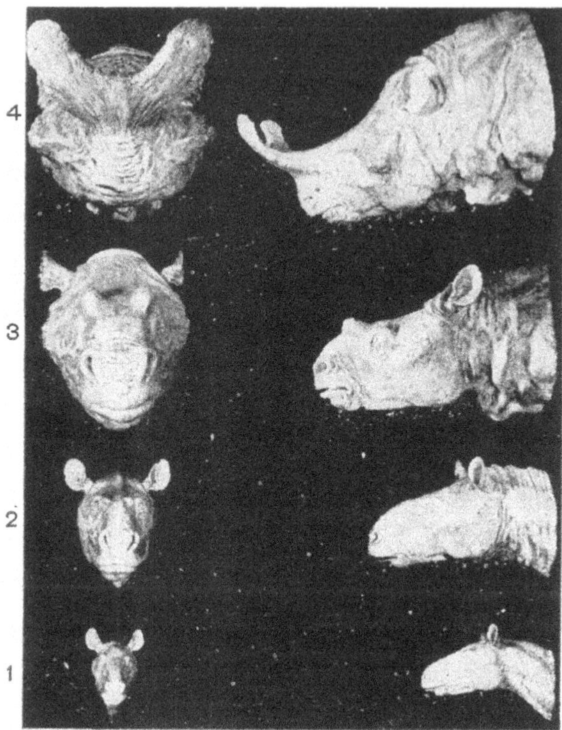

FIG. 128. STAGES IN THE EVOLUTION OF THE HORN IN THE TITANOTHERES.

This shows that these important weapons arise as rectigradations, *i. e.*, orthogenetically and not as the result of the selection of chance or fortuitous variations. Horns, large, 4, *Brontotherium platyceras*, Lower Oligocene; horns, small, 3, *Protitanotherium emarginatum*, Upper Eocene; horns, rudimentary, 2, *Manteoceras manteoceras*, Middle Eocene; hornless stage, 1, *Eotitanops borealis*, Lower Eocene.

Models in the American Museum of Natural History, prepared for the author by Erwin S. Christman.

Fig 4-2: Erwin S. Christman's sculpted evolutionary sequence in geologically successive genera of "Titanothere" heads and horns, illustrating "orthogenesis," a predestined tendency to create enlarged or enhanced structures in organisms, "and not as the result of selection of chance," thus leading ultimately to their extinction (image from Osborn's *Origin and Evolution of Life*, 1917, p. 264).

In formulating his own physicochemical laws of evolution, Osborn didn't wholly reject these opposing ideas outright. Appealing to truth evident in the fossil record, Osborn stated that Lamarck's, Darwin's and de Vries's views were flawed. Rather, "continuity and law in chromatin evolution prevails over the evidence either of fortuity or of sudden leaps or mutations, that in the genesis of many characters there is a slow and prolonged rectigradation or direct evolution of the chromatin toward adaptive ends."[24] While it is easy to proclaim that maybe he just didn't know better, as we'll see, much of this was founded on faith, deliberately contrived.

Osborn marveled at how the expression of individual characters noted in certain species (such as the sizes of titanothere horns) seemed to accelerate in expression through geological time. For explanation, he mentioned analogous factors driving chemical reaction rates, such as catalysis, enzymes or hormonal compounds. If chemicals such as bodily enzymes could accelerate the growth of titanothere horns, somehow mysteriously predisposed to such growth, over an individual's lifetime, then as time marched methodically on, through adaptive pathways such chemical catalysis would also reinforce tendencies in the genetic (germ plasm) material—thus further enhancing horn sizes, sequentially, in subsequent generations. Through such "accelerative" processes, individuals would become increasingly fit to meet "emergencies of the present."[25]

In characteristic grandiose style, Osborn discussed the law of convergence, e.g., "which escaped the keen observation of (Thomas Henry) Huxley" in 1880,[26] describing tendencies of vertebrate forms in unrelated species to converge analogously (such as the fins of sharks and ichthyosaurs, or wings of bats and birds). Then he pompously introduced his great principles of convergence and divergence ("perceived by Lamarck and rediscovered by Darwin ... " although, of course "... expanded by Osborn"). Because of the irreversible nature of evolution and "non-revival of characters once lost by the chromatin," Osborn noted species that are most harmoniously adapted to special environments and which are the most highly *specialized*, become extinct. Conversely, relatively conservative or unspecialized forms "invariably become the centers of new adaptive radiations."[27]

Next, Osborn further expounded on what he referred to as the law of reversal of adaptation in the case of the aquatic reptiles. Acknowledging that reptilian fauna, which had returned to aquatic habitat (such as plesiosaurs, ichthyosaurs, and crocodilians), cannot regenerate an amputated limb like some amphibia can do, accordingly, this characteristic must be attributable to fundamental (heredity-chromatin) differences between reptiles and amphibians. Therefore, when certain reptilians became readapted for an aquatic existence, they were only able to do so without tapping into amphibian mechanisms of the heredity-chromatin—which by then had been lost. Here we are broaching facets of another famous "law" often referred to as "Dollo's Law."[28] But while it is highly unlikely that any reptile returning to the seas would follow an evolutionary, genetic pathway leading *exactly* in reverse back to an ancestral amphibian stage, still, we do have examples of animals like turtles, ichthyosaurs and mosasaurs, which Osborn appreciated and attempted to explain the origins of in *Origin and Evolution*. (And yet Osborn never refers specifically to "Dollo's Law," as such, perhaps preferring his own spin on it.)

During the 19th century (especially from 1865 to 1895), paleo-minded naturalists such as Louis Agassiz, Ernst Haeckel, and Alpheus Hyatt, seeking explanation for the succession of genera observed in the fossil record, turned to the subject of embryology, or "recapitulation," also known as the "biogenetic law," stating that "ontogeny recapitulates phylogeny." In particular, the life cycle of any individual organism appeared to transform through various ancestral embryological life stages known in geological history. On page 152 of *Origin and Evolution*, Osborn referred to this as the "law of ancestral repetition." Osborn was a convert to this "law."

Life circumstances sometimes led to biological arms races, referred to as the "*counteracting evolution* of offensive and defensive adaptations." A vivid example may be observed in Late Cretaceous dinosaurs; super-predator *Tyrannosaurus* (which Osborn described in 1905) *versus* its three-horned nemesis, *Triceratops*. Such arms races were repeated throughout the Cenozoic Era as well. Osborn explained, acknowledging Darwin, that "the struggle for existence is very severe at every stage of development and where advantageous or disadvantageous chromatin dispositions in evolution come constantly under the operation of the *law of selection*."[29] (See Figure 4-3.)

Osborn concluded his summary of the history of reptilian lineages with speculations about their evolutionary inertia, or an arrested development. Quite conveniently, whereas four physicochemical energy complex interactions exert influence throughout the biosphere, during all geological ages, they do not seem to have factored in fully to more primitive (reptilian) stages (i.e., relative to the mammals). Before one could wonder why a "law" of nature should apply to one major branching of vertebrates, but not to another, Osborn offered a feeble "save-face" explanation. After rejecting properties of the physical and life environment as being responsible, *as well as* Darwinian fitness and natural selection, Osborn blamed the heredity-chromatin. Reptiles suffered "due to a slowing down of physico-chemical interactions, to a reduced activity of the chemical messengers which theoretically are among the causes of rapid evolution."[30] If evolution can be viewed (as Osborn saw it) as the net sum of the acceleration or retardation in velocity of development across many generations in single characters (e.g., ceratopsian horns, long hind legs and necks, etc.), then reptiles surviving into modernity were those in which such velocities *diminished* the most. Conversely, those reptilian (e.g., dinosaurian) genera undergoing extinction in the Late Cretaceous were those in which single character velocity was *maximal*. Here was an example of the "orthogenetic" view.

However, as opposed to marine reptiles and dinosaurs, Osborn's greatest expertise, wielded confidently in the concluding chapters of *Origin and Evolution*, resided in the

Fig 4-3: Charles R. Knight's classic restoration of *Tyrannosaurus* and *Triceratops*, viewed as an evolutionarily locked-in arms race waged between such genera in Osborn's *Origin and Evolution of Life* (1917). Knight's paleoart careeer was highly nurtured by the eminent Osborn (image from p. 224).

consideration of fossil mammals. This material became a proving ground for his theoretical notions. First, in reviewing the nature of mammalian adaptations, then casting aside both Cuvier's by then outmoded "law of correlation of parts"[31] as well as Darwin's hypothesis of natural selection, Osborn took center stage with his views on "character complexes." Although Huxley had refuted Cuvier's law decades before, Osborn now claimed Cuvier's notions were flawed because each single character is *independently* associated through heredity-chromatin, and not so essentially with another body part. Thus there is no inherent correlation between, say, claws and teeth, like the illustrious Cuvier believed a century earlier. Meanwhile, Darwin erred in defining his natural selection principle because this would imply that "teeth, limbs and feet are varying fortuitously rather than evolving under certain definite although still unknown laws."[32] Then, to reinforce his ideas of directional predetermination of body characters, Osborn appealed to paleo-mammalian case histories.

Citing how certain genera of hornless mammals may (at differing geological periods) begin to acquire horny growths on their heads, radiating into a number of large-horned descendants, Osborn defined his hereditary "law of rectigradation."[33] In other words, there are invisible predispositions inherent in ancestral heredity-chromatin that, once made apparent, will assume additive, cumulative growth through subsequent phylogeny. Once formed, under the influence of the heredity-chromatin, those horns will just keep getting larger and larger, until reaching an "extreme."[34] However, natural selection operates incessantly upon these intermediate forms, thus only reinforcing the inherent, directional, hereditary, (physicochemically controlled) tendencies. Additionally, Osborn denied the prevalence of "saltation," although contradictorily professing that no more than one fifth of the causes of mammalian evolution may be attributed to sudden leaps or species discontinuities (such as the generation of an additional vertebra, the sudden addition of a new tooth, or rapid immunological changes). Instead, most evolutionary changes can be explained in terms of growth-relativistic acceleration or retardation of body parts.

Next, Osborn distinguished mammal species originating primarily through environmental causes, from those which he termed "chromatin species." The first category were those resulting from adaptational responses to secular geological, environmental shifts (such as the growth of fur in woolly mammoths and rhinoceroses during episodes of continental glaciation), while the latter kind originated through "altered hereditary characters."[35]

Osborn set many evolutionary "laws" in operation simultaneously and synchronously, waxing and waning in concert, conveniently (if not, at times, inconsistently applied in *ad hoc* fashion) producing the varieties of prehistoric fauna in the geological record that he needed to explain, all in a manner (as we shall see) matching his spiritual and aristocratic ideals. Yet, Osborn was perhaps a bit ahead of his time in assigning physicochemical (i.e., genetic) rationale as the basis for why, during embryological stages of individual development, mammals pass through formative growth stages divulging their ancestral tree. He noted H.S. Jenning's assertion that "it is highly probable that every inherited variation does involve a chemical change for there is no character change so slight that it may not be chemical in nature."[36] Even before the chemical structure of genes had been elucidated by biochemists, Osborn sensed how bodily chemical systems were mysteriously tied to genes, and how "heredity-chromatin" might conceivably influence the generation of new species.

The Origin and Evolution of Life was not a typical "dinosaur book," even for its time. Although considering life as recorded in the fossil record through geological time and how extinctions resulted, it illustrated Osborn's peculiar evolutionary notions, attacking reliance on "chance" as an evolutionary factor, while fortifying (since falsified) phylogenetic theories that modern paleontologists would not accept. In the concluding pages of *Origin and Evolution,* Osborn summed up arguments using genera of fossil mammalia as examples, such as *Brontotherium,* "the most imposing product of mammalian evolution, with exception of the Proboscidea."[37]

In regard to the evolutionary production leading to the Tertiary appearance of this magnificent horned titanothere, Osborn proclaimed, in defiance of Darwin's (and Alfred Russell Wallace's) theory: "Every known step in this transformation is determinate and definite, every additional character which has been observed arises according to a fixed law and not according to any principle of chance."[38] And in the case of fossil horses, which through time lost vestigial toes to emerge on a central enlarged single toe in modern *Equus,* such evolution was not resultant of chance, nor of saltation. Instead such changes arose as a harmonious orchestration of the laws of acceleration, balance and retardation of bodily parts, via "the universal law that the limb proportions of mammals are closely adjusted to provide for escape from enemies at each stage of development."[39] Osborn accepted that Darwinian natural selection would have operated on the intermediate forms that arose (although directionally) through physico-chemical, environmental factors and forces. But why did *Proboscidea* evolve more rapidly than rodents (mice and rats)? Such circumstances could not have arisen through blind chance alone, as elephants, horses and titanotheres were majestically yet mystically striding toward mechanical, organic perfection (yes, ironically *unlike* rats because they're still around, as opposed to "titanotheres"–but try explaining or rationalizing that with a pest exterminator).[40]

A recurrent motif throughout was Osborn's invocation of terms, or metaphors and analogies used or founded upon physics and chemistry. So, the "potential" to produce characters (such as titanothere horns in a phylogenetic trend) became manifested when the heredity germ plasm's "latent energy" is called on by "chemical messengers" to bring them forth. Further invoking physics terminology awkwardly, Osborn wondered whether the heredity germ plasm affects body cells through "centrifugal" actions, or if such interactions might be "centripetal" instead?[41]

What does all this inform modern paleoenthusiasts about the much vaunted, oft-revered Osborn?

My rite of passage with the strange term "orthogenesis," a tenet or basis of Osborn's theorizing, came as a youngster from books about evolution and museum exhibits, back in the mid–1960s. And what's more, I accepted the tenet—that is, until I read more, beginning with George Gaylord Simpson's popular *Life of the Past* (1968 ed.) Afterward, I read what Stephen Jay Gould had to say on the subject in the "Irish Elk" chapter of his 1977 bestseller, *Ever Since Darwin.* And when I returned to the classroom to take a university course on invertebrate paleontology in 1981, David M. Raup and Steven M. Stanley nailed it all down for me in chapter 11 of their excellent text, *Principles of Paleontology,* 2nd ed., (1978).[42] I hadn't, until then, fully comprehended Osborn's dedication to orthogenetic principles, or in fact, what a scientific scoundrel he was.

So, by way of illustration, this time let's outline what modern evolutionists have to say about orthogenesis, using time-honored examples of the bivalve *Gryphea,* saber-tooth cat *Smilodon,* the "Irish Elk," and those famous odd-toed ungulates known as brontotheres (formerly "titanotheres").[43] Then, we'll reconsider Osborn's motives for defying Darwinian evolution.

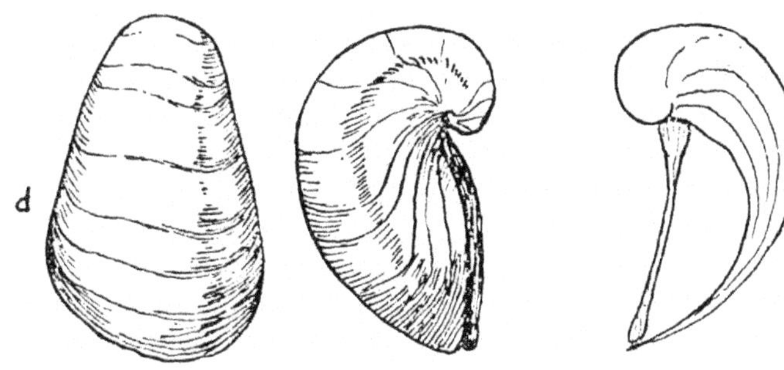

Fig 4-4: The Jurassic clam genus *Gryphaea*, showing its tight coiling which had become more exaggerated in species belonging to this genus throughout evolutionary history of the lineage. *Gryphaea* was also formerly thought to be resultant of a mystical orthogenetic process taking place within geologically successive species, as once espoused by paleontologists like Osborn. From "The Use of Gryphaea in the Correlation of the Lower Lias," by A.E. Trueman, in *The Geological Magazine* 59 (1922).

Stephen Jay Gould considered *Gryphaea*'s role in elucidation of orthogenetic principles in his massive 2002 tome, *The Structure of Evolutionary Theory*, and in a 1980 book he edited, *The Evolution of Gryphaea* (Arno Press).[44] For decades, the Liassic bivalve *Gryphaea* was considered one of the best examples of orthogenesis "in action," according to early 20th century proponents of that theory. (See Figure 4-4.) Besides Osborn, as exemplified through his orthogenetic "laws" of evolution, there were several prominent individuals espousing this late 19th century principle. The story often told about *Gryphaea* is that paleontologists claimed they had determined its evolutionary trend, or "ladder," leading to a terminal affliction of "overcoiling": hence, its demise. At a stage in its "declining" phylogeny ,when the larger valve clamped the smaller one shut, the poor living organism became locked inside, thus sealing *Gryphaea*'s fate! Poor *Gryphaea* was born and evolved, *programmed* for extinction!

What was the cause of this trend leading to inevitable, nonadaptive doom? According to geologist A.E. Trueman, who in 1922 "developed the empirical case for *Gryphaea*, ... 'Excessive development implies that the evolution was out of the control of the environment and it may be presumed that some internal factor was responsible.'"[45] At that time, Trueman had stated, "offshoots from the oyster family continued to progress in the characters named, particularly in the curving of the left valve, until a stage was reached when the coiled apical portion pressed against the opercular right valve. Thus in such advanced *Gryphaeas* the shell would be kept closed, and consequently this stage marks the limit of evolution in that direction.... Although it may be conceded that the earliest stages in such a lineage may have been of some advantage to the animal, it is obviously difficult to account for evolution in a direction that inevitably leads to the extinction of the lineage, if evolution is the result of the operation of natural selection."[46]

Later, in 1939 Trueman outlined the meaning of orthogenesis, citing *Gryphaea*'s extreme coiling tendency, apparently trending toward self-destruction in advanced species.[47] Extinction would have been inevitable if growth "acceleration" led to the sealed aperture condition at continually younger growth stages, *before* the main population attained reproductive stages.

During the early 1920s, vertebrate Richard Swann Lull, who was influenced by Hyatt, interpreted the twilight extinction of dinosaurs in terms of an orthogenetic theory of "racial senescence." According to Lull, throughout their 100-million-year reign, dinosaur genera underwent evolutionary phases of youth, followed by maturity, then ultimately "senility," leading toward death = extinction. The general increase in sizes toward natural physical constraints through geological time, and the more grotesque, baroque bodily shapes, and lengths of accouterments (e.g., horns), supposedly testified to this outmoded idea. Their rise and fall, although extended in time, seemed not unlike that of many great civilizations in human history.

As dinosaur paleontologist Michael Benton stated in 1990, dinosaurs' decline leading to extinction, perceived at the time as gradual, was a natural consequence of racial senility,

> the belief that certain long-lived groups of animals became old and their store of evolutionary novelty dried up. There was a parallel here between the life-span of an individual plant or animal and that of an evolutionary stock. Youth and early racial vigor were equated and seen to be just as inevitable as the old age and death of an individual and the racial senescence and eventual extinction of a major phylogenetic group. According to this view, the dinosaurs had been around for a long time, and they simply ran out of the genetic variability that was necessary to survive. The remarkable horns, frills, and spines of some late Cretaceous dinosaurs were occasionally cited as evidence for this racial senility, but in general the extinction of the dinosaurs remained a nonquestion.

Furthermore, although evolutionary biology has since moved on from the old orthogenetic ideals, "The lumbering dinosaur doomed to extinction is an insistent metaphor that refuses to die."[48]

Most of you are perhaps more familiar with analogous interpretations of *Smilodon*, the Pleistocene saber-tooth cat, and *Megaloceros*, the Pleistocene "Irish Elk." According to orthogenetic principles, extinction of these iconic former wildlife occurred when the bizarre enlarged canine "saber" teeth of the former, and the antlers of the latter, grew to excessive, possibly maladaptive sizes, thus sealing their respective fates. The conjured anti–Darwinian forces may have been mutational, yet of such an overwhelmingly powerful nature that natural selection couldn't hold the maladaptive tendencies and characters in check even as they became manifested in a trend of genera succeeding from the ancestral variety. Yet, no need for mystical forces here! For *Smilodon*'s canines certainly did not prevent the carnivore from biting or chewing its meat; Irish elk's antlers served an adaptive display function. Both sets of features, respectively, would have been subjected to (Darwinian) forces of natural selection selecting fittest variations (randomly) produced among populations of these species. As Kenneth J. McNamara commented on *Megaloceros* in his *Shapes of Time*, "The larger the body size, the stronger the animal ... the larger the antlers, the more attractive the male, or the more effective in actual male-male threat or combat."[49] (See Figure 4-5.)

Furthermore, especially in the fossil record of felines, species evolved larger and smaller canines through time. So there was no mad dash, out of control, absolute trend toward production of unusably large, nonfunctional canine teeth. In the mid–20th century, George Gaylord Simpson noted that in the case of *Smilodon*, "The earliest sabertooths had canines relatively about as large as the last survivors of the group. For some forty million years of great success the canines simply varied in size, partly at random and partly in accordance with individual advantage to species of various sizes and detailed habits. The famous trend for the sabers to become larger did not really occur at all."[50] (See Figure 4-6.)

According to Raup and Stanley (1978), "natural selection was rejected (i.e., by proponents of orthogenesis) as the process of evolutionary change ... this view reflected the somewhat bizarre morphology of advanced species in certain groups. We now recognize that the structures in question were probably adaptive, and no mysterious driving force seems to have been required for their evolution."[51] Note, however, that in his *Origin and Evolution of Life*, even though Osborn suggested that evolution led to predetermined goals, he was not rejecting

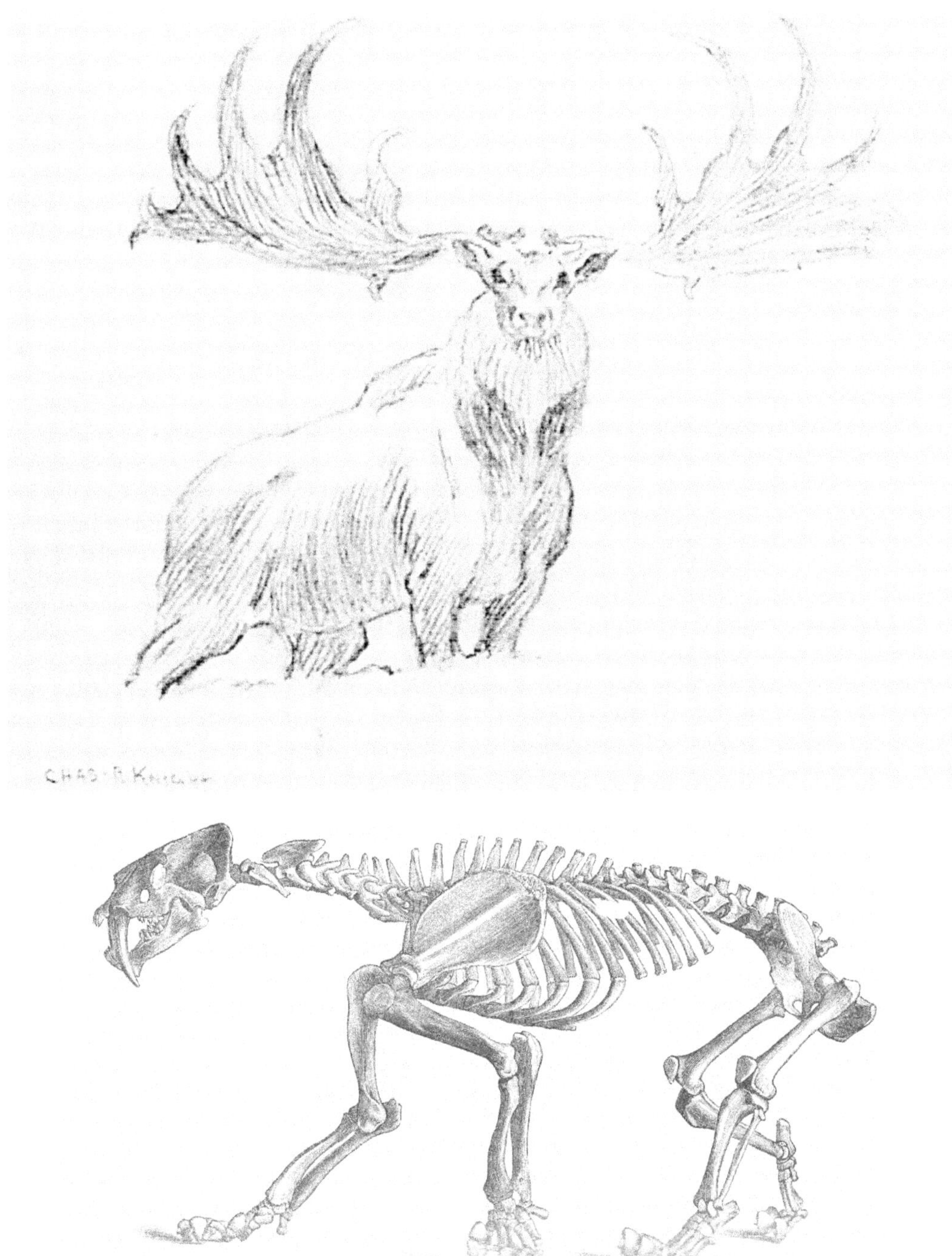

Top: **Fig 4-5: The Irish Elk (or deer), as restored by Charles R. Knight. Osborn and others who favored the prevalence of mystical, predestined (nonexistent) orthogenetic evolutionary forces believed the greatly elongated antlers eventually led to demise of the Late Pleistocene genus. However, this misguided notion was eventually falsified and discarded (from Osborn's *Origin and Evolution of Life* [1917], p. 224). *Bottom:* Fig 4-6: Skeletal reconstruction of the quintessential Pleistocene saber-toothed cat, *Smilodon*, brandishing its enlarged fangs, thought by Osborn to have resulted from orthogenetic growth, leading to eventual extinction of the saber-tooth lineage (i.e., analogous to physical structures evident in titanotheres, the Irish Elk, and *Gryphaea*) (from Joseph Le Conte's *Elements of Geology* [New York: D. Appleton and Company, 1903], p. 608).**

Charles Darwin's natural selection outright. Osborn reserved a special role for it, although therein natural selection was subsidiary to those mysterious driving forces. Therefore, to him, natural selection may have not operated upon species with full "Darwinian" vigor.

For decades, fossil horses and titanotheres (both perissodactyla, or odd-toed ungulates—like horses) were also figured as prime examples of orthogenetic law. Whereas there seemed to be running trends among the chief fossilized examples, viewed across the epochs of Cenozoic time, toward larger body sizes and related features (horns in titanotheres; teeth in horses, coupled with enhanced increasing reliance on the middle toe or hoof—as side toes reduced to vestigial significance, then disappeared), as additional fossils turned up, here was evidence of complex, totally functional phylogeny afoot.

So what ultimately killed the saber-tooths and presumably the dinosaurs? According to Osborn, suicidally their very own genes.

Besides displays of *Tyrannosaurus rex,* Osborn exhibited fossil horses and titanotheres at the American Museum of Natural History so that evolution's messages could be properly conveyed, if even on a subliminal plane. Rather like vertebrate paleontologist Othniel Marsh before him, Osborn interpreted the progression of linear trends evident in certain lineages of fossil horses arranged through geological time, orthogenetically. Titanothere displays offered further opportunities. Here, Osborn enlisted the museum's most talented and renowned artists from this stalwart period–Charles R. Knight and Erwin S. Christman—to paint and sculpt life restorations reflecting titanothere phylogeny, emphasizing its most magnificent culmination—*Brontotherium.* Osborn believed he was illustrating laws of nature occurring with systematic regularity among allied mammalian phyla, not attributable to sheer chance.

From such humble beginnings (e.g., small body and limb sizes, tiny horn nubs, and small teeth), titanothere linages irreversibly evolved massive biocharacters, as a result of "rectigradations [which] appear to indicate a germinal predisposition or predetermination to vary in the same direction...." According to historian of science Ronald Rainger, while other museum scientists objected to Osborn's evolutionary demonstrations, "Nevertheless, the museum's display and message remained intact and influenced public perceptions about evolution at least into the 1950s."[52] Rainger astutely added, "There, modeled in clay, was Osborn's view that evolution resulted in ever larger, more complex, and more baroque skull and horn structure. The display also embodied another and perhaps more important message ... that the evolution of those large, bizarre creatures had ended abruptly in the Miocene epoch; titanotheres, unlike horses, had become extinct. Extinction was, for Osborn, a natural law that had scientific as well as social meaning."[53] However, their horns weren't the ultimate cause of titanothere extinctions. Rather it was their specialized grinding teeth, disallowing *Brontotherium* opportunity to readapt when environmental conditions changed. Thus, organic *specialization*—when species found themselves trapped in evolutionary "cul de sacs"—often resulted in extinction.

Today, paleontologists have clearer comprehension of the genetic basis for production of (chance) variations in progeny, and realize that via the apparent fickleness of natural selection, only certain types will produce viable offspring. Indeed, thanks to J.D. Watson, F.H.C. Crick (and many others), since 1953 there's a molecular basis (DNA) for those variations and also for (prescribing) an individual's life ontogeny. Scientists have even extracted biomolecules from fossilized remains, such as dinosaur bone. As Osborn appreciated, surely there is mystery within the genes.

Rather than relying on 19th century–style "recapitulation" (i.e., Ernst Haeckel's Biogenetic Law) for explaining the apparent phylogenetic trend growth of titanothere horns, elongation in horses' middle toes, exaggerated coiling in *Gryphaea* shells, pronounced manifestations in Irish elk antlers (wherein added character growth phases were conceived as having been tacked onto the terminal adult phase of ancestral species), today, life scientists understand that such features resulted from relativistic changes in growth of parts due to genetic and hormonal changes. Such enlarged or "advanced" characters, evolved beyond those manifested in ancestral forms, are termed "peramorphic."[54]

Perhaps the chief dinosaurian example of peramorphosis has been North America's iconic, 66-million-year-old hypercarnivore, *Tyrannosaurus rex*. For many years, Osborn's famous dinosaur was considered the result of a "passive, allometric consequence of body size increase or the product of an extended (peramorphic) growth trajectory, sprouting from smaller ancestral carnosaur species."[55] In other words, those ancestral "rexes" just couldn't help themselves (or, rather, their hallmark body features—proportionally large skull, jaws, teeth, hind limb proportions, etc.) from getting bigger and bigger, in posthaste fashion! Such a phylogenetic pathway proved too favorable, and besides, wasn't it just programmed that way within their genes? But with discovery of the 125-million-year-old *Raptorex kriegsteini*, Paul Sereno, Lin Tan, Steve Brusatte (and others) note that the traditional view of *Tyrannosaurus* as "heterochronic 'peramorphs' ... which grew beyond the size and form of smaller-bodied ancestors via developmental acceleration" isn't quite correct.[56] So now the conventional view has been modified in ways that Osborn would have struggled to comprehend.

Yet, Osborn's "Just–So" explanation for why *Tyrannosaurus* grew to such large size was entrenched in orthogenetic idealism, invoking a Mesozoic arms race with the horned dinosaurs, such as *Triceratops*. Osborn referred to this as the "counteracting evolution of offensive and defensive adapatations."[57] Again, not denying natural selection's role, Osborn claimed this is a case where warring competition—such as illustrated so keenly on canvas by Charles R. Knight—between Rex and Tops (orthogenetically) irreversibly drove these genera simultaneously to the brink of extinction.

Osborn didn't invent the concept of orthogenesis, a term meaning "goal-directed evolution" coined in 1895 by the Swiss zoologist Theodor Eimer (1843–1898).[58] Although Osborn had become a convert by 1897, concocting his own allied theories, the term orthogenesis does not even appear in Osborn's *Origin and Evolution*. Both Eimer and the late 19th century American paleontologist Alpheus Hyatt viewed orthogenesis, founded on internal factors, as an evolutionary alternative to Darwin's reliance on natural selection. Certainly, there were different nuances and versions of the ideology rankling through the professional journals when orthogenesis was all the rage, each with differing implications for correcting or amending Darwin's evolutionary views.

A.E. Trueman, who in 1939 outlined the contemporary meaning of orthogenesis, differed with those who wedded the idea of orthogenetic trends to mystical/teleological ideologies, or even those steeped in predetermination. However, Trueman recused Eimer, claiming that the latter's reliance on internal causes of orthogenesis were not tied to mystical, vital forces, but instead genetically prescribed "physical and chemical processes." Trueman also recognized another form of orthogenesis, named "programme-driven," observed independently in allied species, wherein "once a lineage begins to undergo modification in a particular direction it continues to change in accordance with a 'programme.'"[59] Earlier, Osborn had indeed noted such "programmed" manifestations among related genera of fossil mammalia.[60]

Ronald Rainger has noted that Osborn's stylized laws and theories of evolution were infused with religious meaning. Here, he remained fundamentally at odds with Darwin. This overarching theological commitment arguably clouded Osborn's objectivity, as "he required a role for the creator as causal agent and guiding principle...."[61] Characteristically, Osborn theorized rather pompously without offering falsifiable statements designed to test his "laws."

Furthermore, Osborn employed exhibits at the American Museum of Natural History to illustrate his theories, which were neither objectively reasoned, nor inherently Darwinian. Sadly, as Rainger explains in his fascinating biographical account, when it came to considerations of prehistoric men, Osborn's true (racist) colors surfaced. The aristocratic Osborn believed miscegenation weakened the dominant race (which he believed, like his ancestry, were of white Scandinavian descent).[62] An implicit moralistic message was that if such societal trends didn't cease, then, like the mighty titanotheres and dinosaurs before, mankind's extinction would be inevitable, destined not as much from environmental or industrial factors, but from mysteriously programmed internal causes—much sooner than later. Osborn's opinions mirrored his time. It's unfortunate that Osborn was such an influential paleontological potentate, and a prolific writer besides, whose unattractive views permeated throughout American society for many decades, creating false impressions.

In an 1895 publication titled "The Hereditary Mechanism and the Search for the Unknown Factors of Evolution," Osborn expressed the view that "we are entering the threshold of the Evolution problem.... The hardest tasks lie before us, not behind us, and their solution will carry us well into the twentieth century."[63] In a sense, Osborn boldly tackled evolutionary problems that were then beyond comprehension, and which are only on the verge of being understood; paleontological evidence coupled with elucidating the mystery of the gene. As Jack Horner (with James Gorman) outlined in *How to Build a Dinosaur: Extinction Doesn't Have to Be Forever* (2009), it may someday be possible to retrace exact steps of evolutionary descent by unraveling genetically controlled mechanics of embryological development.[64] Can a dinosaur be recreated from a modern chicken embryo? Can we recreate *Gryphaea* from modern oyster stock? Osborn—who outright rejected evolutionary claims of contemporary geneticists—would both be amazed, and marvel how inapplicable his "laws" are to such matters. Despite the nature of his "wannabe" writings in *Origin and Evolution*, Osborn does not qualify as an early modern biogeochemist, like researchers working in conjunction with dinosaur hunter Horner.

While reading Osborn's *Origin and Evolution*, I found myself wondering whether his restricted, three-million-year view (as then known) of the 66-million-year expanse of geological time since the beginning of the Cenozoic Era[65] fostered Osborn's acceptance of orthogenesis? After all, unless something is guiding, or propelling, speciation along set, guided trends, in accelerated fashion, there wouldn't seem to have been sufficient time for all the happenings recorded in the fossil record to have occurred. If all the cool, gigantic paleomammals are to have originated and evolved, some becoming extinct—all within a mere 3-million-year interval—then there's too little time for Darwinian randomness to accomplish such phenomena. Osborn didn't quantify rates of evolutionary speciation in *Origin and Evolution*, yet he clearly lacked modern perspective on the length of geological time. So perhaps Osborn thought that Darwinian blind chance was obviated because there was insufficient time, geologically, for production of time-wasting variations and bushy evolutionary "sidebars" resulting from sheer randomness. True—geneticists could produce ontogenetic mutations more quickly in laboratory settings, but, to Osborn, such specimens and experimentation bore no evolutionary (phylogenetic) significance.

Eventually, during the early 1930s, Osborn reformulated his "rectigradations" as "aristogenesis," controlled by something extra—"aristogenes"—within the heredity germ-plasm. Aristogenesis guided organisms rapidly through evolutionary stages in the correct direction of future adaptation, and was not tied to natural selection. Ironically, the slow-breeding noble elephant lineage had evolved with remarkable rapidity (whereas fast-breeding rodent species hadn't evolved as noticeably within a similar interval). So, the proboscidea—lacking evidence of species competition—simply must have been equipped with aristogenes propelling them along their fated evolutionary pathways, or so Osborn believed. Such reasoning is consistent with my speculation about Osborn's delimited views of geological time.

Again, rather ironically, by the time Osborn had invented aristogenesis (a term derived from "aristocratic"[66]), the geological timetable was expanding (thanks to refined radiometric age-dating methods), permitting more time for Darwinian evolution of gigantic dinosaurs, mammals and other organisms—without impatient need of internally directed, falsifiable "let's just get on with it" processes.

In the race to comprehend nature's mysteries, abject objectivity was winning. In pondering the mysteries of evolution and eventual extinction, viewed in life-through-geological-time context, Osborn had produced a volume of distinctive, eclectic quality, presented as a profound, self-serving packaging of biological "laws," yet in its own way, when considered in retrospect, just as outrageously peculiar as Knipe's *Nebula to Man*.

With life through time fully memorialized in books (and museum displays[67]), the evolutionary epic would soon materialize in another favored popular medium—film!

Chapter Five

Filmic Illustrations of Life Through Geological Time

Evolution

It should be apparent in the early exposition of life through geological time, how prominent was the theme of evolution—so vital to writing an evolutionary epic. To many, "evolution" simply *means* life through geological time, although by the turn of the 20th century, these were terms that one usually only encountered in museums and books (both popular and textbooks). Of course, today, we're accustomed to being bombarded not only in televised nature and science documentaries with accounts about how life developed and changed throughout the Phanerozoic Era, but we're also exposed to this theme even in popular movies and television series. Counterintuitively, for example, the 2014 film *Noah* actually includes a CGI–animated evolutionary sequence. A Godzilla movie, Americanized as *Gigantis the Fire Monster* (1959), contains a recreated life-through-time element, incorporating several life-through-time stop-motion animated shots. Yes—and there are *numerous* other examples abounding!

By the early to mid–20th century, life-through-time explanations of prehistory had truly become irrevocably popular. This is perhaps, especially, because producers were able to incorporate knowledge and restorations of fossils, dinosaurs and other prehistoric and extinct animals into the traditionalized tale, as related in film. By the late 1910s, the then (new) stop-motion animation technique offered fresh and startling opportunities for portraying creatures as genuinely fascinating as dino-monsters!

So when did representations of *life-through-time* most prominently first appear for wider audiences, not simply in books, but on film? Possibly in 1923, in a silent 41-minute documentary titled *Evolution*, directed by Max Fleischer (1883–1972), with scientific supervision provided by Edward J. Foyles (American Museum of Natural History). Footage in this rather simple (and needless to say, black and white) silent film may seem far removed from the more sophisticated, analogously themed fare one views today (for example, contrasting the visually absorbing 2014 remake, *Cosmos: A Spacetime Odyssey*, hosted by Neil deGrasse Tyson). But in attempting to present the essence of the evolutionary, life-through-time *idea*, without becoming overly technical, *Evolution* scored mightily. Charles Darwin probably would have enjoyed viewing it, had he been alive then, without being overly critical of the effort.

Evolution also straddles the period in between release of two early significant silent dinosaur pictures, 1919's *Ghost of Slumber Mountain*, and *The Lost World* (1925). Perhaps for today's audiences and film historians, *Evolution* is most notable due to its incorporation of several stop-motion scenes swiped from *Ghost of Slumber Mountain*.

Evolution's fundamental question is, how did we come to be upon the Earth? Also, was man always man, or formerly a lower animal? To answer such queries, viewers are treated to quite a variety of visuals. In an extended opening segment, Fleischer outlines familiar geological processes, as well as techniques and the tool kit utilized by scientists in inferring what we've learned about prehistory from fossils. So we see the usual suspects, trilobites and ammonites, and are mesmerized by the results of fossil vertebrate restoration (spying Charles Knight's swamp-dwelling *Apatosaurus* American Museum painting, and his horned "Agathaumas" sculpture). Prehistoric cave paintings (Lascaux) and examples of ancient architecture (Aztec, Egyptian, Stonehenge and Roman ruins) are also shown. While interesting, this introductory, instructive (or table-setting) portion of the film is uneven in meaning and at best rather vague conceptually. Next, we delve into Earth's murky origins, quickly progressing to modern times, a visualized life-through-time sequence which is the main focus of the film.

Life's development on Earth is outlined, but only after visuals illustrate how the solar system originated from the near-collision of stellar bodies (still a popular astronomical theory then), followed by formation of the Earth and planetary system from swirling stardust. As a prerequisite to life's origin, we see examples of molten masses, steaming lakes, and then, as the surface cools, formation of oceans. The Moon finally becomes visible through vaporous clouds, volcanoes erupt and mountain ranges buckle. These effects are achieved with minimal use of model-making, live footage and props, yet they effectively convey ideas as read by audiences on intertitle cards. Chemical reactions give rise to aqueous, microscopic life, which rapidly proliferates from single-celled "shapeless protoplasms" into multicellular jellyfish and other invertebrates. Here, Fleischer spliced in footage of modern echinoderms, an octopus and then the first vertebrates—fish, all representing nature's struggle for existence in which, it is claimed, instinctual *fear* became instilled during primeval times. The next important marker is the arrival of lungfish sprawling onto shallow beachheads (gills making way for lungs), amidst the carpet of awaiting terrestrial vegetation. These biological "milestones" are achieved without indicating how much intervening geological time has passed (which wasn't accurately known then). We also sense the old "ladder" concept of evolutionary development in play here, leading somewhere—inevitably—to that fully anticipated, familiar biological culmination.

Of course, after life spreads onto land, reptiles dutifully evolve. Fleischer shows us several modern examples, and then more dramatically—restorations of prehistoric reptiles—dinosaurs! The dinosaurs' age as featured in this documentary comes from two main sources. Several of Josef Pallenberg's life-sized dinosaur statues displayed in Hamburg's Zoo Tiergarten, as well as footage from *The Ghost of Slumber Mountain* (not a documentary, but an early sci-fi/fantasy film released in June 1919) represent the Mesozoic Era. First we see Pallenberg's *Iguanodon* (misidentified as *Tyrannosaurus*), followed by *Allosaurus* biting *Stegosaurus*'s flank, and a *Triceratops* "family."[1]

Then several sequences from *Ghost* are spliced into the sequence: brief scenes showing Willis O'Brien's stop-motion animated "Brontosaurus," feeding and jousting *Triceratops*, and a tyrannosaur "Tyrant Lizard King" vs. *Triceratops* battle. Mark F. Berry notes in his *Dinosaur Filmography* that 9 of the original 17 stop-motion cuts in *Ghost* are represented in *Evolution*.

Berry also claims the 15-minute silent "*The Ghost of Slumber Mountain* is notable as more than just a stepping stone on [O'Brien's] progressive journey to *King Kong*; it is in fact the first movie to really begin to exploit the cinematic potential of dinosaurs."[2] There were two additional prehistoria animated by Herbert M. Dawley and O'Brien for *Ghost*; however, Fleischer chose to feature (i.e., borrow) only the most dramatic scenes.

O'Brien had a falling out with *Ghost of Slumber Mountain*'s producer, Dawley, following its release resulting from their woeful collaboration on stop-motion animation. Dawley had experimented with an alternate stop-motion technique, differing from O'Brien's, involving the sculpting and later casting for photographic purposes of flexible full-bodied miniature prehistoric animal puppets. As the pliant puppets were moved incrementally, photos could be taken of the models "moving." According to Jeff Rovin in *The Land Beyond Beyond*, Dawley "hadn't ... actually shot any film of these creations. He had simply taken still photographs and pasted them into a book. When the pages were flipped, the animals appeared to move."[3] Dawley hired O'Brien, who had some experience working with stop-motion animation. *Ghost* was ultimately successful, owing mainly to the special effects (not so much the story itself).

In the August 1919 issue of *Motion Picture Magazine*, a writer describes the exacting process Dawley allegedly went through to produce the startling effects, claiming: "Mr. Dawley wanted to film prehistoric mammoths in action, and he built huge models—of cloth, wire, and steel—of the dinosaurs and other monstrosities of the pre-stone ages. Placing these in front of the camera and slowly filming their movements—that is, by moving their head a bit and photographing, moving it again a bit more and again photographing—he attained the effect of prehistoric animals in action. Mr. Dawley was able to take something like twenty feet of film a day—that is, on days he worked hard and consistently. But the result! Astonishing, even to the fight to the death between huge creatures of the dim past."[4] Then in the November 1919 issue of *Illustrated World*, another writer states:

> Maj. Dawley ... laid in a supply of lumber, cloth, paint, clay and other materials.... He first prepared a rugged wooden skeleton ... with a covering of clay to express the muscles, tendons and bones ... and over this placed a skin-like covering of cloth painted a dark brown color. After building several animals—one of them was 17 feet high—he was ready to make them act for the camera.... In addition to placing the legs in the proper posture each time an exposure was made, he had to change the position of the neck, the trunk and the tail each time a new step was taken.... In one of Maj. Dawley's films, two animals are shown fighting ... twice as much effort as a film showing but one monster in action. Yet this sculptor did not stop with two in the same picture; he put in three and four, and the difficulty ... was quadrupled.[5]

Actually, Dawley hadn't built life-sized prehistoria for such a purpose. Like O'Brien's, his were scale miniatures.

Dawley went on to animate several dinosaurs for his own feature film, *Along the Moonbeam Trail* (1920). A recently "rediscovered" film (i.e., as of late 2009), *Moonbeam Trail* relied on footage of a duckbilled "Trachodon," a tyrannosaur, and a *Stegosaurus* menacing people in a cave. The film involved youngsters whisked off to outer space, where on another planet they see these creatures. (The film is retained within the collection of the Academy of Motion Picture Arts and Sciences.[6])

Eventually, O'Brien began his fruitful association with Watterson R. Rothacker. This led both to 1925's *The Lost World*, and a lawsuit brought by Dawley against Rothacker and Arthur Conan Doyle (author of *The Lost World*, serialized in 1912) for property and patent infringement. The case was settled out of court.[7]

Compared to the version of *Ghost of Slumber Mountain* featured in a recent DVD (appended as a special feature to Retromedia's 20th anniversary edition release of *Planet of Dinosaurs*), the visual clarity of the dinosaur scenes borrowed from *Ghost* and spliced into *Evolution* is clearer (and less "ghost-like"). According to Steve Archer, surviving prints of *Ghost* were derived from one poorly preserved 16 mm negative: "This is a big problem with viewing films from the silent period. Films were not expected to make any money after their initial release, so they were stored—not so future generations could see them, but to be forgotten and to disintegrate slowly to unviewable dust.... According to some sources, the original running time of *The Ghost of Slumber Mountain* was considerably longer than it is today."[8]

Fleischer, who went on later to create cartoon characters Betty Boop and Popeye and to be credited with an early classic *Superman* cartoon series, was evidently highly inspired by Willis O'Brien's animation of *The Ghost of Slumber Mountain* dinosaurs. However, as Neil Pettigrew suggests in his *The Stop-Motion Filmography*, he may have thought such avenue of trick photography too intricate (and costly) to perform routinely, thus moving toward the two-dimensional cartoon medium.[9]

Fleischer's evolutionary sequence continues in *Evolution*, with footage of modern birds and a new warm-blooded type—mammals! Curiously, no prehistoric paleomammals are indicated or shown in the film. Or even fossil birds. Where is *Archaeopteryx* in a documentary concerning evolution? And Fleischer missed an opportunity to borrow the *Diatryma* flightless bird also animated by O'Brien for *Ghost*. Interestingly, in *Ghost of Slumber Mountain*, the *Diatryma* bends to scratch its ear with its right leg, analogously to how Marcel Delgado's *Tyrannosaurus* in 1933's *King Kong* also scratches its ear upon making its startling appearance. This was a signature characterization inaugurated by O'Brien in his earlier film, *Prehistoric Poultry* (1917).

Climate change next ensues in Fleischer's *Evolution*, and a pervading glacial period results in widespread extinctions. In the wake of the great continental glaciers, after the ice sheets melt, we witness modern faunal assemblages, emphasizing organismal adaptations for survival. There is also an evolutionary trend noticeable, with successive shots of creatures on that supposedly inevitable branch leading to man. So we see not only lemurs and various primates, but also J. Howard McGregor's head restorations of prehistoric humans, including Java Man, Piltdown Man, Neanderthal Man and Cro-Magnon. (Relics then attributed to Piltdown Man, of course, planted in a rock stratum for unwary discoverers to find in 1915, fooled many. The Piltdown hoax wasn't proven until the 1950s.[10]) From there, various races spread worldwide leading to modern civilization, and we read of the voice of nature calling for "everlasting change." The film ends cautiously on a theological tone, not unlike the early 1960s Americanized version of Karel Zeman's *Journey to the Beginning of Time*, also another life-through-time extravaganza relying heavily on stop-motion animation, except with a fantasy plot moving backward into the geological past, from the present instead of forward from the beginning.

Certainly by today's standards, as a documentary concerning life's history, *Evolution* isn't visually captivating. Modern youthful audiences wouldn't appreciate it. And yet, even for its time, it would appear to be antiquated. It missed great opportunities for embellishment or to capitalize on other significant matters then known to science from the fossil record. *Evolution* is overly ambitious, yet superficial. In his *Prehistoric Humans in Film and Television*, Michael Klossner claims the subtitles in *Evolution* are "overwrought."[11] Berry adds, "[D]espite its drawbacks, this creaky but thankfully straightforward relic is actually more watchable—the dinosaur sequences notwithstanding—than Irwin Allen's similar but painfully smug 1956 entry, *The Animal World*" (which incorporated Ray Harryhausen's stop-motion dinosaur scenes).[12]

With that said, however, the life-through-time theme of portraying prehistoric times has also taken a back seat to more forward probing, state-of-the-art, variegated "dinosaur renaissance" scientific matters. True—despite its former heraldry during Victorian times (usually illustrated and outlined in an array of popular books), by the late 20th century, the life-through-time theme had become prosaic, if not mundane (nonexciting or noncontroversial). And *Ghost of Slumber Mountain*, rarely witnessed today, with its dramatic, pre–*Lost World* dino-monster stop-motion footage once central to a lawsuit, has quietly settled into the dust of yesteryear, projecting mere phantasms from a simpler, forgotten time.[13]

Time's River Metaphor

What's like four Huckleberry Finns boating upriver alongside prehistoric monsters out of time's abyss? What's one of the earliest edifying, walking-with-dinosaurs type, faux "documentaries" preaching the fossil record's majesty? Answer: *Journey to the Beginning of Time.* Never had the pleasure? Watch it on YouTube ... but *first* read this synopsis.

In popularizing theories and ideas about the deep past, scientists often appeal to the tempting and long traditional life-through-time theme. To paleontologists, *the* ultimate story is Earth's historical pageant of life, or in other words, change—the (Charles) Darwinian evolution of species through time, the ceaseless invention of organismic complexity. Through the past two centuries, scholars, researchers and artists alike have refined how we convey *this*—our triumphant story, such as with striking visual imagery or in words. (Often, in its most effective form, words and visual imagery are coupled, melded as "imagetext."[14]) Technological breakthroughs increasingly allow more "realistic" portrayal of idealized scenes, individual creatures and pivotal geological episodes in the magnificent, eons-long unfolding tale, of course, founded—as we like to say—on science.

Yet in reconstructing the dimly lit past, especially with such a fascinating slate as that involving magnificent creatures like dinosaurs, fiction inevitably works its way in! Individual, scientifically restored animals of the past necessarily live again in our hearts and imaginations. Then, science is woven with fantasy; metaphor is poetically relied upon where science cannot boldly go. In this day and age, few complain!

Besides marvelous mural restorations of the past showing long segments out of prehistory (such as Zallinger's *Age of Reptiles* and *Age of Mammals* murals displayed at Yale's Peabody Museum), and sci-fi novels offering dramatic life-through-time tours (such as Jules Verne's *Journey to the Center of the Earth* or Edgar Rice Burroughs's *The Land That Time Forgot*), *filmic* means of portraying life's history usually do satisfy and may even be more fondly recalled due to the visual element.[15] One of the most interesting movie examples that left strong impressions on me half a century ago is a Czech entry titled *Cesta do Pravěku*, or *Journey to the Beginning of Time*, directed by Karel Zeman (1910–1989). This isn't just another "dinosaur movie" afflicted with a rickety premise, riddled with cheesy effects. It's about the exploration of life's history, steeped with paleontological facts. While the chief intent was to entertain, it was also intended to be educational. *Journey to the Beginning of Time* was released in Czechoslovakia in 1954, later released in the U.S. in 1966. In the early 1960s it played as a serial on a Chicagoland children's show, *Garfield Goose and Friends.* Zeman employed no time machines, "time slips," or wormholes to project his impressions of paleohistory. The plot gimmick is metaphorical, namely a "river" of time. Well, that and a dream.

Given all the fuss lately concerning dinosaurs in movies or popular culture, the exemplary *Journey to the Beginning of Time* has been granted relatively little consideration. I think this is partially because the movie succeeds more as an educational device, as opposed to capitalizing on the prevalent bloody horror element. *Journey to the Beginning of Time* is anything but just another dinosaur-on-the-loose thriller. What can be gleaned from such a curious production? Was *Journey to the Beginning of Time* any less edifying in its day than, say, the television documentary *Walking with Dinosaurs* is in ours?[16]

In fantastic "time tours" made to accentuate scientific explanation or merely for entertainment purposes, time flows geologically from the lifeless Azoic to the Recent or, as in *Journey to the Beginning of Time*'s case, inversely from the Recent to the deep past. In the serialized format that I avidly watched several times so long ago (released by National Education Television), then American Museum paleontologist Edwin H. Colbert (1905–2001) introduced the approximately 5-minute segments. This was certainly not the first nor last time that a professional paleontologist would be recruited into service popularizing their famous extinct charges.

The American version of *Journey to the Beginning of Time* begins ominously, prophetically, foreshadowing: "If it was possible to Man to journey back into time, back millions and millions of years, back at last to the Creation itself, he would very probably see the Spectacle of Life largely as it is presented in this film." Indeed, *Journey to the Beginning of Time*'s prehistoric animal imagery is delightful.

Next, four youths visiting the American Museum's exhibits become mesmerized by wooden figures of a Haida Indian warrior posed in a war canoe. The youngest character, named "Jo-Jo," declares, "Look at that Medicine Man. It's as though he's trying to hypnotize us from out of the past!" And soon their adventure begins, initially, touring the museum's dinosaur halls, with scientifically minded "Doc" taking copious notes in his diary about each display. Next, they venture outside toward the shore of Central Park's lake. Discovering a rowboat, they set out upon the water, only to pass through the mouth of a mysterious cave—a portal from the modern-day world into time's recesses. Obviously something strange has occurred, for now they've exited the cave into frigid weather! Yes, they've plunged into the Ice Age! Doc deduces that they're floating upstream into the past on the River of Time. Yet this isn't a horror flick. Instead, as Gary Williams noted, the boys "are driven by a healthy fascination" with all that is about to transpire.[17] After all, this is about the grandeur of life's history.

From here onward, Zeman offers outstanding animated prehistoric animal recreations representing the main prehistoric ages. Their appearance is generally ordered oppositely to their occurrence in geological history. For the Pleistocene, they visit a prehistoric human's cave dwelling. We're treated to a roaring woolly mammoth, a prehistoric bison and two magnificent battling woolly rhinos. The "Age of Mammals" tableau is enriched in a variety of life as there's a herd of running (prehistoric) gazelles and flying, cawing birds (e.g., vultures). As the air grows warmer, we identify *Deinotherium*, a stealthy saber-toothed cat and galloping giraffes. Next stop is the Tertiary Period.

Journey to the Beginning of Time is marvelously enhanced with Cenozoic recreations, a shortcoming of most other "genre" films, which predictably feature a bloodthirsty tyrannosaur, while giving short shrift to paleo-mammals. Zeman's production continues in this vein with striking shots of a sensational *Uintatherium* and other related "-theres." A herd of prehistoric horses is spied galloping in the distance, and one of the boys has an exciting close encounter with a charging flightless "terror bird," *Phororhacos*. In this hair-raising segment, the big bird chases the boys into their rowboat, and down the river they go.

Entering the Mesozoic Era, a winged *Pteranodon* knocks Jo-Jo into the water. Convincingly restored cycads pepper the landscape! They're surrounded by "amphibious" dinosaurs (i.e., as they were formerly viewed during the early 1950s), a "Brontosaurus" and "Trachodon." Zeman rather blurs the Mesozoic, staging Cretaceous and Jurassic genera more or less together in the same setting. *Styracosaurus* ambles about. Doc continues to take notes and the boys photograph the swimming brontosaur with their camera. Their tour of Mesozoic time culminates dramatically at dusk as *Stegosaurus* battles its traditional adversary *Ceratosaurus*. The plated paragon expires after wounding the theropod. The next morning the boys cross the river to examine the dead stegosaur (a full-sized prop) up close.

Admittedly, after passing into the misty Paleozoic, all the really cool animals have been used up, exiting from the film. So to represent the Coal Age, Zeman resorts to the symbolic, large dragonfly *Meganeura*, a croaking amphibian (possibly *Eryops*), and a "walking fish" (possibly *Eusthenopteron*). Not the usual cast of prehistoric "monsters" populating sci-fi/horror flicks, but perhaps quite an understandable assortment if the film can instead be interpreted as a dramatic yet educational documentary tribute to organismic evolution and Earth history. Doc's diary falls into the swamp but, now quite soggy, is retrieved by Jo-Jo.

Zeman probes further still, while viewers catch themselves asking "what will come next?" and breathtakingly wondering what will really happen at time's beginning. They arrive at the point of further inaccessibility, finding themselves stranded along a rocky shore, confronted by a great Precambrian ocean presumably devoid of life, yet where life began. The American version adds kaleidoscopic imagery representing Earth's fiery origin, and, as Pettigrew notes, "the film ends with some unnecessary biblical musings ... it is unlikely that these would have been part of Zeman's [1954] original."[18] The boys awaken suddenly, surprised to find themselves situated next to that Haida warrior museum display. They never left the museum after all! So was it all just a shared dream. But if that's what happened, how did Doc's scientific journal become water damaged?

Journey to the Beginning of Time is like the American Museum having come to life in a dream collectively shared by the adventurers. Accordingly, the film plays out in part as a science presentation, half documentary—half fantasy. The first 5 minutes or so of the movie feature exhibits actually in the American Museum, including several dinosaur skeletons, a Charles R. Knight–painted restoration, a dinosaurian evolutionary family tree, and a geological time chart. Doc is our narrator as he is most science-minded. And so we are always lectured to, but never in a condescending or professorial manner. Doc's interesting geologic time data and musings about the animals they encounter—each in their proper Epoch, Period or Age—are the motif, giving the movie flair and continuity. He knows the animals' scientific names and introduces the periods in which they lived. Doc is also mindful about the "whole process of evolution" and how science is supposed to work, claiming, "A good scientist doesn't jump to conclusions." Doc is the one who encourages his companions to make meticulous measurements of the dead *Stegosaurus* specimen. Yet anecdotal information is sometimes mistaken, as when pterodactyls are erroneously referred to as "birds." Doc is mainly intrigued by how the farther one looks back into time, the simpler life becomes. Zeman strove to illustrate this point, although with only a modicum of success.

One of the interesting questions surrounding *Journey to the Beginning of Time*'s convincing prehistoric life recreations is to what extent the prehistoric vertebrates, mostly restored using stop-motion animation techniques, were founded upon famed Czech paleoartist Zdeněk Burian's (1905–1981) painted restorations. Most convincing connections to a filmed "Brontosaurus" standing on the shore, and also the *Phororhacos, Styracosaurus,* and *Uintatherium* animated puppets, are to Burian's highly similar restorations painted during the 1930s and 1940s, later appearing in paleontologist Josef Augusta's book *Prehistoric Animals* (1956).[19] (See Figure 5-3.) Clearly, Burian's paintings were used as a basis for these stop-motion puppets. Some film historians even suggest Burian was actively involved in this movie production, although a "Z. Burian" is not duly credited and there is no positive evidence supporting this claim. It also isn't clear, from American prints, who (besides Zeman himself) actually performed the miniature animation work. According to Thomas Kovacs, Zdeněk Burian's paintings inspired Zeman, but to stray beyond that assertion would be mere speculation.[20] Notably, Zdeněk Burian's artwork was already "out there," available in at least half a dozen Czech books published during the 1940s.

Karel Zeman didn't stop there, returning to prehistoric animal stop-motion recreations for his 1970 film, *On the Comet* (quite loosely based on H.G. Wells's novel, *In the Days of the Comet*). Prehistory isn't emphasized, however. Following the close approach of a comet,

Fig 5-3: A "Brontosaurus" scene as shown animated for Karel Zeman's *Journey to the Beginning of Time*, which was inspired by Zdeněk Burian's magnificent highly similar 1950 restoration, later published as Plate 24 in J. Augusta's *Prehistoric Animals* (1956).

landmasses of Earth bearing inhabitants are whisked away gravitationally to the comet's surface. There, several prehistoric forms thrive, resembling fauna long extinct on Earth. For select scenes Zeman animated *Edaphosaurus,* a sauropod herd and hungry theropod dinosaurs that charge through a human settlement. There are also *Styracosaurus,* a plesiosaur, pterodactyls, and in a comical nod to Charles Darwin, a strange primitive fish that before our eyes transforms (*evolves*) into a bipedal wild boar, demonstrating that "all life came from the sea." As in *Journey to the Beginning of Time,* in the end, events transpiring in *On the Comet* turn out to be just another dream. Special effects were attributed to Zeman and F. Pickhart.

While not truly a documentary on the evolution of life on planet Earth, *Journey to the Beginning of Time* stems from that vibrant tradition. This life through geological time portrayal of course was seized early on by paleontologists as their main story theme, which has been told time and again in a variety of inventive and artistic ways since the late 18th century, based on known science. In the early 20th century, movie producers saw opportunities to use the new technology of motion pictures to reframe the life-through-time tale. Accordingly, we can still watch antiquated, restored versions of silent pictures such as Max Fleischer's quaint *Evolution* (1923), in which the evolution of life from the Precambrian to the modern world was depicted. As noted, in the era of "Middle Life," there are even stop-motion dinosaurs at large, borrowed from other silent shorts such as *The Ghost of Slumber Mountain* (1919). And *Evolution* features life-sized dinosaurs too, statues erected by Josef Pallenberg for Carl Hagenbeck's Tiergarten in Stellingen, Germany, before World War I. In *Evolution*'s case, the narrator becomes the series of explanatory note cards (or captions) spliced in between footage.

BBC's *Walking with Dinosaurs* (1999), although purporting to be a factual wildlife documentary, relates interesting fictional stories about individual Mesozoic creatures. *Walking with Dinosaurs* retains much of the "wow factor" (stemming from its reliance on CGI special effects) while not relinquishing key data, instructing viewers about events and species inherent to each successive geological period. And yet *Walking with Dinosaurs* (and a host of other subsequent CGI–using documentary spinoffs) provoked considerable controversy. For instance, critics questioned whether science was sacrificed or usurped. Was only an illusion of reality conveyed by producers whose fabricated tales about personified dinosaurians given cutesy names were merely intended to gain favorable ratings?[21]

While CGI–using prehistoric park–type productions (to a certain extent inspired by 1993's fictional *Jurassic Park*) comprise the latest wildlife tradition, the roots of such programming are intertwined with the essence and heart of paleoimagery and paleontological imagetext, already established two centuries ago. Quite separated in time and production technology, 1923's *Evolution,* 1954's *Journey to the Beginning of Time,* and even 1999's *Walking with Dinosaurs* are all cast from the same pseudo-documentary mold.

And so we understand how books, at first lacking illustrations, later relying on numerous prehistoric animal restorations and "scenes from deep time,"[22] purporting to accurately frame the life through geological time evolutionary epic, eventually led in turn to filmic representations of this majestic paleontological tale. Yet as already hinted, via references to Jules Verne and Edgar Rice Burroughs, by the early 1930s, one of horror fiction's most revered writers just couldn't let this intoxicating theme rest either. And as we shall see, many readers "loved" his "craft"!

CHAPTER SIX

Lovecraft's Paleontological Time Travels

While most link the name Howard P. Lovecraft (1890–1937) with the ineffably macabre, the chilling Cthulhu Mythos, as well as several film releases based on his stories (e.g., *The Dunwich Horror*), my introduction to this esteemed writer of eldritch tales began in another direction—which I'll share with you now.[1] I've long been interested in paleontology, including its pop-cultural side, perhaps explaining my love of that most unusual "drago-dinosaurian," Godzilla. Over thirty years ago, while researching paleontology in science fiction tales, I came across Lovecraft's eminently atmospheric novella *At the Mountains of Madness,* a fusion of weird-*with*-science fiction, which quickly became a "can't-quite-put-it-down" page-turning experience. Lovecraft's early references to a curious fossil assemblage found in Antarctica lured me in, hooked. Later, his terror-stricken explorers confront a horrific relic surviving in an ice-slathered, once majestic ruined city of cyclopean dimensions, tens of millions of years old. Yet the expedition leader lives to tell the tale! In between, Lovecraft laid out a completely alternate and cosmic Earth history, far surpassing what geologists would proclaim is true.

From his copious writings, Lovecraft was clearly interested in science—especially astronomy. But while he wasn't so much a paleo-phile—a lover of things paleontological—he certainly appreciated and often appealed to prehistory, incorporating many paleontological and archaeological elements and references in his stories, perhaps inaugurated with his 1921 short story, "The Nameless City." *Mountains of Madness* may be viewed as yet another in the popular life-through-time saga tradition of storytelling (and visual reconstruction) harking back to the early 19th century, as first perfected in fiction by Jules Verne in his *Journey to the Center of the Earth. Mountains of Madness* is a well-crafted—perhaps *the* quintessential—melding of geological, archaeological and paleontological sciences gone wild, sprinkled with mad, febrile, yet non-supernatural doses of creepiness! A grand, veritable, yet highly "alternate" evolutionary epic!

And so here is a *new* way of looking at H.P. Lovecraft.

In order to avoid encountering horrors suffered by the ill-fated Miskatonic University expedition, the story's narrator, geologist Professor Dyer, issues his dire warning in guise of a pseudoscientific report, cautioning readers *not* to return to the Antarctic. Dyer, who led Miskatonic's expedition during 1930–31, feels utterly compelled to break his own call for reticence concerning the titular mountains and "that nameless thing beyond the mountains of madness,"[2] so that leaders of the next planned expedition, the Starkweather-Moore exploration party, might come to their senses and call off their pending mission. For to tread further within that "innermost nucleus of the Antarctic" may conjure "that which may end the world we know."[3] Dyer then summarizes their itinerary and events, leading to discovery of ancient fossils, as well as certain specimens of types unknown to science. Dyer also describes their firsthand investigation of mountainous ruins higher than the Himalayas within the cold continent.

During a survey mission to the foothills of the tallest mountains, biologist Professor Lake's team unearths peculiar fossils thought to be Precambrian in age and other remains, excitedly describing them to Dyer at the main station in a series of wireless reports. Lovecraft describes how Lake's party excavated through a particularly fossiliferous, continuous deposit ranging back from the Tertiary, late Cretaceous and Jurassic (dinosaurian) ages down into the early Paleozoic. Along the way they identify a host of incredible vertebrate artifacts, including pterodactyl and mosasaur fossils, and *Archaeopteryx* bones. In fact, Lake reports via radio that these discoveries mean "to biology what Einstein has meant to mathematics and physics.... [They] indicate ... that Earth has seen whole ... cycles of organic life before known one that begins with Archaeozoic cells. [Life] was evolved and specialized not later than a thousand million years ago, when planet was young and uninhabitable for any life forms or normal protoplasmic structure."[4] Yet far more dramatic if not eerie discoveries are pending.

Soon Professor Lake identifies a "monstrous barrel-shaped fossil of wholly unknown nature.... Tissue evidently preserved by mineral salts."[5] Additional specimens are found—14 in all, of which 8 are disinterred from icy tombs; their internal organs are immaculately preserved, surprisingly even after 40 million years! Here's where the trouble really begins! For as Lake dissects these cryogenically preserved, leathery specimens, essentially (as Dyer later reasons) they thaw, resuscitate, and then attack Lake's doomed party. The mysterious barrel-shaped creatures, referred to as "Elder" or "Old Ones," recall those "fabled Elder Things" described in that fictitious tome, the *Necronomicon*, as Lake recalls from his archival readings of Miskatonic University's copy. The Old Ones are eight-foot-long, pseudo-crinoidal organisms with pentagonal symmetry (not unlike echinoderms). They also have membranous wings each 7 feet long, sport a fivefold tentacular system of flexible arms (25 in all), and are gifted with 5-lobed brains. In rapture, Lake speculates on their "Fabulously early date of evolution, preceding even simplest Archaean protozoa hitherto known," baffling "all conjecture as to origin."[6] Perhaps most importantly, even the sled dogs do not like them!

Then communications with Lake's party mysteriously cease, prompting Dyer and a young graduate student named Danforth to fly an airplane out to Lake's site in the foothills of the beckoning mountains of madness. They appallingly discover that with the exception of a man named Gedney who is missing (but later found dissected within the cyclopean city), all of Lake's team has been slaughtered; the eight perfect "crinoidal"[7] specimens, and the sled dogs, have disappeared. Much of Lake's equipment was either tampered with, or is missing. So Dyer and Danforth fly their plane over the weirdly beckoning mountainous ranges, discovering that these are not volcanic, natural formations, but rather a "blasphemous" primordial city structure of incomprehensible magnitude, stretching for miles across the horizon, built eons ago by ... The Elder Things.

Their investigation of this "cosmic abnormality"[8] continues as they crawl through openings, descending into a labyrinth encapsulated by glacial debris. Much of what follows concerns Dyer's interpretations of pictorial bas-reliefs, hieroglyphics, murals and sculptures aligning the walls of tunnels they pass through. Accordingly, the intrepid explorers decipher the history of the Old Ones, tracing back hundreds of millions of years. Relying on such archaeological relics provides understanding of a vast, previously unknown civilization and geological history. Two curious findings emerge. First, it seems unlikely that such complex beings could have evolved so early on the forming, steaming Earth, so they must have "filtered down from the stars" when the sterile, lifeless Earth was young. Then the brainy, advanced extraterrestrials might themselves have "concocted Earth life as a joke or mistake,"[9] which thereafter evolved in uncontrolled fashion. Notice that, to Lovecraft, we're nothing more than a cosmic joke, or mistake!

Furthermore, as divulged by fossils and artwork adorning the cavern walls, younger versions of the Old or Elder Ones seem more primitive, atrophied or "decadent" than those found in the earliest layers. Like the rise and fall of the Roman Empire, as interpreted from artwork, Dyer and Danforth record the ascendancy and fate of the Old, or Elder Ones. However, as Robert M. Price noted, the geological history outlined in *Mountains of Madness* is inconsistent with and will not chronologically conform with Lovecraft's other unveilings of cosmic prehistory, as divulged in his other Cthulhu Mythos tales.[10]

In the long run, Earthly existence and an overwhelming reign of ice had been unkind to these celestial beings. While in appearance the Elder Ones would seem horrific to us, they're also essentially likened to humanity. Lovecraft even forgives them for what (perhaps understandably) they did to poor Gedney. For, like his Miskatonic team, Dyer empathizes, "Scientists to the last—what had they done that we would not have done in their place? ... Radiates, vegetables, monstrosities, star spawn—whatever they had been, they were men."[11] Later, we learn the true horror, or the slavish entities created by the Old Ones—Shoggoths, which proved their fateful undoing by waging war against their former masters.

Lovecraft's unveiling of life's alternative history may seem analogous as to how—65 years earlier—Jules Verne outlined Earth's life through time in his pivotal *Journey to the Center of the Earth*. By descending into a volcano (rather than a cyclopean city structure originally mistaken for volcanic in nature), Verne's explorers are able to "read" or interpret fossiliferous remains deposited along the walls of labyrinthine tunnels and ancient shorelines, in geological succession, much as Lovecraft's narrator is able to understand the detailed history of the Elder Ones and their impact on life—such as dinosaurs and other Mesozoic reptilians—from alien wall carvings and artwork. Furthermore, just as Verne offered a glimpse of a phantasmagoric, possibly real as opposed to imaginary, gigantic fossil man shepherding mastodons near *Journey*'s climax, prompting his explorers to flee in terror, likewise, Lovecraft projects a real, living ancient terror, a protoplasmic blob-ish Shoggoth, which has murdered the thawed Old Ones that devastated Lakes's encampment. Dyer and Danforth run for their lives. Neither knowing (nor here pronouncing) whether Lovecraft read Verne, I note that plotwise at least, their masterpieces do seem conceptually similar.

More likely, Lovecraft launched *Mountains of Madness* from his own predecessor tale, "The Nameless City" (1921), published in an amateur rag. Despite its numerous rejections elsewhere, Lovecraft always maintained an "inexplicable fondness" for this weird tale.[12] Here, an explorer combing the Egyptian desert enters a tunnel. Within, he encounters archaeological relics and mummified remains of a "palaeogean species" extending remotely in time to 10 million years. This was a race of "alligator people" (anticipated 4 decades prior to that titular

1959 B-movie starring Beverly Garland). Rather than in the case of fossils, as with Verne, Lovecraft relied on his device of having the narrator interpret millions of years of (pre-)history on the fly, from preserved bas-reliefs, carvings, sculptures and other artistic renderings, as later performed by Dyer-as-narrator in *At the Mountains of Madness.* In one of the later antediluvian "Nameless City" frescoes, the narrator sees a "poor primitive man torn to pieces." This is not unlike the *Mountains of Madness* scene in which Dyer and Danforth note a sculptural rendition of a primitive mammal relegated to insignificance, "whose vaguely simian and human foreshadowings were unmistakable." Whether imagined or less likely real, the archaeologist is trapped, either mentally or physically, within the bowels of this primordial city. In the end, has he gone stark raving mad, haunted by living "half-transparent devils" of the nameless city, or have they actually confronted him? Critics and scholars view "Nameless City" as one of Lovecraft's inferior works.

If you revere Lovecraft you might find it odd to learn that his now acknowledged classic *Mountains of Madness* was not by any means an immediate success. First, Lovecraft was dismayed when Farnsworth Wright, editor of *Weird Tales*—the pulp magazine where many of his stories had been published before—had the temerity to reject *Mountains of Madness.* Wright claimed it was too long and unconvincing. How demoralizing for Lovecraft, as he believed it was his best story. Eventually, it was accepted by *Astounding Stories* editor F. Orlin Tremaine, for serialization (February to April 1936), six years after it had been written, although riddled with numerous errors. Reception was at best mixed, including this scathing comment: "[W]hy in the name of science-fiction did you ever print such a story as *At the Mountains of Madness* by Lovecraft? Are you in such dire straits that you *must* print this kind of drivel?"[13]

Curiously, John W. Campbell, who became *Astounding*'s editor in late 1937, was himself no fan of Lovecraft, as he once remarked, "Don't give me any Lovecraft stuff."[14] Even today, Lovecraft scholars note that many readers of *Mountains of Madness* "find it very difficult to get through." It's rather long and "it tends to become a slog, especially in the middle."[15] And yet it is the quasi-scientific (fossils, paleontological, geological and archaeological) material within that middle, perhaps tedious "slog" which supremely suspends disbelief, garnering verisimilitude. This is how Lovecraft earns our respect as a realistic fantasy writer.

Where did he get the idea for this magnificent story? How was it inspired? Probably not from one, but several principal sources. "Nameless City" served as more or less a template, while other writers and scientific endeavors of the period also inspired his masterpiece. The most contemporary immediate trigger for the story may have been a short story written by Katharine Metcalf Roof, "A Million Years After," published in *Weird Tales* (November 1930). Roof's tale inspired the issue's cover art by C.C. Senf, showing an enormous brontosaur poised to flatten cars and a building under its massive front paws. In *The Dinosaur Scrapbook* (1980), Donald F. Glut referred to Roof's contribution as a "whimsical story," concerning burglars who steal a dinosaur egg from a museum, which later incubates and hatches. The soon monstrously sized dinosaur then goes on a rampage, only to die from gunfire wounds; its immense remains are lost in an ensuing fire.[16] While not the most enduring or exciting sort of "weird tale," one may well imagine that eighty years ago "A Million Years After" was certainly in vogue. For during the 1920s, Roy Chapman Andrews's expeditions to Mongolia's Flaming Cliffs site triumphantly brought back fossil dinosaur eggs to New York's American Museum. And the silent 1925 movie version of Arthur Conan Doyle's novel *The Lost World* thrilled movie audiences, especially with its climactic scene in which a large stop-motion animated sauropod smashes into the side of a London building—probably the inspiration for Senf's illustration. (Then in 1933, RKO released *King Kong* with its monstrous, aquatic brontosaur.)

But Lovecraft regarded Roof's seemingly unrelated "A Million Years After" rather jealously. Lovecraft scholars S.T. Joshi and David E. Schultz noted:

> It is possible to conjecture what led H.P. Lovecraft (HPL) to write the novel when he did. The lead story in the November 1930 *Weird Tales* was a poorly written and unimaginative tale by Katharine Metcalf Roof, "A Million Years After," that dealt with the hatching of ancient dinosaur eggs. HPL fumed when he read it, not only because he felt that H.G. Wells' "Aepyornis Island" had anticipated the idea. In mid October, after seeing the Roof tale in print, HPL wrote, "Rotten—cheap—puerile.... I've half a mind to write an egg story myself right now—though I fancy my primal ovoid would hatch out something infinitely more palaeogean and unrecognizable than the relatively commonplace dinosaur." ... HPL may have felt that the use of a viable dinosaur egg was impossible, so that the only solution would be the freezing of ancient living entities in the Arctic or Antarctic regions.... [In 1930, HPL wrote] "What hatches from primordial egg."[17]

Furthermore, as we know, Lovecraft incorporated several references to commonplace dinosaurs and pterodactyls within *Mountains of Madness*. Another possible (though as yet unverified) fictional influence could have been Frank MacKenzie Saville's 1901 novel, *Beyond the Great South Wall*, in which explorers seeking whereabouts of the ancient Mayan race in—of all places—Antarctica, also are terrorized by a monstrous brontosaur, the last dinosaur alive.

Other fictional works dwelling on the foreboding frozen continent had appeared prior to *Mountains of Madness* as well, with which Lovecraft had familiarity. Perhaps the most obvious, yet arguably not most influential of these was Edgar Allan Poe's 1838 novel, *The Narrative of Arthur Gordon Pym*. Another is John Taine's (pseudonym for mathematician Eric Temple Bell, 1883–1960) uncanny novel, *The Greatest Adventure* (1929), wherein prehistoric elements are vastly pronounced, much like in *Mountains of Madness*. However, Lovecraft did not perceive his *Madness of Madness* as a sequel to either.

Polar and South Sea exploration had been an increasingly intriguing ambition throughout the 19th century, seemingly then as difficult or as unattainable as reaching the Moon.[18] Furthermore, there *was* scant pseudoscientific rationale supporting the possibility of entering the Earth's interior through awful yet sublime "holes at the poles," as envisioned by Poe.[19] Lovecraft wasn't quite so gullible, having published an article titled "The Earth Not Hollow" in the *Providence Sunday Journal* (8/12/1906).[20] Other than *Mountains of Madness*'s Antarctic setting, however (which did not rely on a holes-at-the-poles gimmick), what tie is there to Poe? Well, Lovecraft incorporated direct references to Poe's *Narrative of Arthur Gordon Pym* in *Mountains of Madness*. Particularly, at the end, Lovecraft attributes strange piping sounds heard by Lake, Dyer and Danforth, as well as the "Tekeli-li, Tekeli-li" wailing, also mentioned verbatim by Poe near the end of his novel, to the menacing Shoggoth. Commercially, Poe's novel was a failure (and its direct "sequel"—Jules Verne's *Sphinx of the Ice Fields* (1897)—is clearly not the latter's best-known tale).

But John Taine's *The Greatest Adventure* is another matter indeed. Robert M. Price concludes that Taine was a "major influence on Lovecraft, and particularly that *The Greatest Adventure* was a major influence on *At the Mountains of Madness*.... Can we ignore ... the overt similarities?"[21] What are those similarities? Primarily they are evolutionary and paleontological themes, with interwoven archaeological elements.

In *The Greatest Adventure*, Dr. Eric Lane's expedition to Antarctica begins as a quest to seek the very origins of life. Upon their arrival, they find gigantic dinosaurian creatures—Godzilla-sized! These are found to be Frankensteinian monstrosities, though, because Lane's party determines they've evolved parallel to ordinary terrestrial life from spores created by an intelligent and technological prehistoric race that (like Lovecraft's Old Ones) perfected the science of bioengineering. Hence, unrelated to our ancestral tree, the Godzillean creatures are "bad copies, botched imitations if you like, of those huge brutes whose bones we chisel out of the rocks.... Every one of them is a freak."[22] Using modern terminology, they're resultant from alternate—if not alien—DNA. While the terrifying, "half natural" dinosaurians are on the prowl, danger lurking at every bend, expedition members decipher their origin and the ancient history of the extinct race who originally conceived them from artificial spores. And, as in *Mountains of Madness*, they manage this from interpreting the meaning of carvings, bas-reliefs and inscriptions preserved within subterranean cavern walls!

Yes, clearly there are connections between Taine and Lovecraft. First, there's a curious array of fossils for the scientists to ponder. There are ancient technological races, which created organisms pregnant with evolutionary possibilities (leading to prehistoric terrestrial life in Lovecraft's case; the alternate dinosaurian creatures in Taine's). And in both scenarios we have archaeological inscriptions and artistic renderings preserving a geological history record of the ancient races for modern interpretation by each scientific team, respectively. We also fear terrifying survivors from ancient days: Lovecraft's thawed Old Ones and the climactic, menacing Shoggoth, analogous to Taine's threatening dinosaurian abominations. We have also, in both stories, cycles of recorded evolution and ultimate demise of the once dominant, lost race.

Realizing their Frankensteinian blunder, Taine's ancient bioengineers long ago projected what abominations these spores would eventually evolve into—entities that would in turn annihilate their creators (much like Lovecraft's Shoggoths would turn rogue). But what they were able to create could not be destroyed. Taine's ancient race predicted its inevitable decline and extinction, resultant of their uncontrolled biogenetic oversight. And so, for millions of years, the dinosaurian monsters have been "living, multiplying and dying in the galleries and uncemented mines." Accordingly, "They decided to leave a record of the harsh science ... intended as a warning to their successors should intelligence ever again visit the Earth."[23] Will mankind heed the warning?

Later in Taine's tale, the explorers encounter a grayish-green dust, remnant spores which the prehistoric race tried to seal hermetically within an underground lair, using diamond-hard cement, when they realized their genetic experiments had gone awry. While, if left isolated, the strange dinosaurians may self-extinguish within a few million years, the spores threaten the rest of our planet. For (invoking panspermia theory) if the spores emerge or are exposed and carried by the atmosphere to other parts of the globe, the strange alternate evolutionary forces would eventually nullify Earth's natural life. Taine's Dr. Eric Lane realizes they're about to unleash a spore-driven plague upon the planet unless they act quickly. Likewise, Lovecraft's Professor Dyer warns the impending Starkweather-Moore mission, lest the world as we know it may come to an end. Inescapably, close analogies can be made linking *The Greatest Adventure* to *At the Mountains of Madness*.

Another likely influence on Lovecraft may have been Edgar Rice Burroughs, who has intrigued generations of readers with stories such as his Pellucidar and Caspak series.[24] Burroughs—in his Caspak trilogy of novels, beginning with *The Land That Time Forgot* (1918)—dealt with evolutionary, paleontological themes: an uncharted prehistoric island in the southern seas, influenced by strange evolutionary patterns.

Beyond organic remains, artwork is an important key to understanding ancient (alien, in the case of *Mountains of Madness*) prehistory. One particular artist is mentioned half a dozen times in *Mountains of Madness* by Lovecraft: the Russian painter Nicholas Roerich, who notably painted atmospheric scenes in the Himalayas. Not surprisingly, yet coincidentally, the Roerich Museum (at 317 West 107th St., New York) opened in the spring of 1930. Roerich's art undoubtedly served as muse, facilitating Lovecraft's sublime visions, if not the terrible aspect, of the planet's tallest mountains. (Examine Roerich's artistry online, at Wikipedia or other sites.)

Of course, beyond fictional tales, real polar expeditions proved the impetus for *Mountains of Madness*. Jason C. Eckardt outlined historical ties to polar exploration, citing Lovecraft's admission, "I think the Antarctic continent is really paramount in my geographico-fantastic imagination.... About 1900 I became a passionate devotee of geography and history, and an intense fanatic on the subject of Antarctic exploration.... Lost Arctic and Antarctic civilizations form a fascinating idea to me—I used it once in 'Polaris' and expect to use it again."[25] Eckhardt also reflects upon Lovecraft's pronounced aversion to extreme cold. According to Joshi, Lovecraft may have suffered from "poikilothermia," possibly caused by a damaged hypothalamus, causing him to have heightened sensitivity to cold.[26]

During Lovecraft's youth, several turn-of-the-century expeditions reached the southernmost continent, captivating his imagination, with Roald Amundsen attaining the Pole in 1911. Later, in the period from 1928 to 1931, four expeditions set out for the ice pack, one of which—the Byrd Expedition (1928–30)—proved most influential toward the "Lovecrafting" of *At the Mountains of Madness*. Byrd's team employed aircraft similar to those mentioned in Lovecraft's novella. Relying heavily on polar reports, Lovecraft was able to further suspend disbelief in his fictional account. Lovecraft certainly had access to Rear Admiral Richard E. Byrd's published accounts of the mission, including *National Geographic* (August 1930), newspaper articles, and Byrd's book, *Little America* (October 1930). Byrd—a most fitting name here—led the first flight over the South Pole, November 28–29, 1929. According to Eckhardt, Lovecraft wrote *Mountains of Madness* between February and March 22, 1931, and "so would have had plenty of time to read any of these stories and adapt the information to his own use."[27] Much of this material wended its way into the fictional account. Eckhardt concludes, "*At the Mountains of Madness* thus stands as a monument to Lovecraft's imagination, his ability to capture the real and to make us believe the unreal."[28]

Fossils and paleontology also shaped Lovecraft's fertile mind. Lovecraft avidly read Charles Darwin and Thomas Henry Huxley, and demonstrated expert armchair knowledge of geology, invoking drifting continents. Fossils indicating that Antarctica had a former *tropical past* had indeed been discovered during Byrd's Antarctic expedition, a fact which Lovecraft noted in April 1930.[29] Since the early 19th century, writers such as Poe and John Cleves Symmes—author of *Symzonia: A Voyage of Discovery* (1820)—had speculated in their fiction that the further south one traveled by sea, paradoxically, the warmer it would become.[30] Furthermore, by the early 20th century there came the startling revelation that *Precambrian* fossils (of the right sort of mind-bogglingly old age to buttress the idea of billion-year-old cities as well as Lake's fantastical evolutionary theories in *Mountains of Madness*) had been found—although in North America, not Antarctica. Three decades more would pass before important vertebrate fossils began turning up in Antarctica, as continues to be the case today.

Certainly authors of contemporary fantastic literature could take great artistic license in speculating on the southernmost continent, because through the mid–1930s its geography mystified. Even by the year of Lovecraft's death from cancer, 1937, the icy continent's interior remained relatively unknown. However, within a few years, this was no longer quite the case. Explorers and geographers had done their work well, revealing (a) that there were no Antarctic holes extending into the center of the Earth, (b) that temperatures within the barren continental confines did not (in the present day) mysteriously climb to tropical conditions, and (c) that mountain ranges higher than the Himalayas did not exist there.

Whereas John W. Campbell didn't revere Lovecraft's writing, *Astounding*, which he later helmed, did publish the latter's last major work, *The Shadow Out of Time*, published (with errors) in the June 1936 issue (the story was accepted by Tremaine). In *The Shadow Out of Time*, William Dyer makes a cameo, and Lovecraft relied on a similar plot device. The essence of this story is about a man named Peaslee, stricken with the realization that he—or rather his mind, transferred backward in time into the huge, conically-shaped body of a member of the superior "Great Race"—had written documents, 150 million years prior to evolution of mankind. These records remain preserved within cyclopean ruins buried in Australia!

During Peaslee's mind-exchange interval, lasting five human years, in our present he appears and behaves strangely, rather amnesic. But the 150-million-year-old body in which Peaslee's mind is occupied witnesses Earth's prehistoric life, including dinosaurs and other reptilians "made familiar through paleontology."[31] Peaslee even records when the Great Race battled the winged, star-headed Elder Ones (i.e., those described in *Mountains of Madness*) of the Antarctic, with "infinitely devastating" effects. When the time roving mind-exchange is terminated, Peaslee is haunted by nightmarish recollections. Ultimately, he descends within the labyrinthine Australian ruins, only to find "his" own ancient handwritten documents; clearly, this is one of science fiction's most sublime moments. Then he is chased by a horrid thing (analogous to *Mountains of Madness*'s Shoggoth) that emerges from the lowest catacombs.

Was *At the Mountains of Madness* a magnificent template for the even more cosmic *Shadow Out of Time*? This paleontologically themed topic surely was his forte! In this incredible time travel tale, Lovecraft spanned the range of time using mind transference as a time travel device, yet climatically relies on prehistoric relics to accentuate the mounting terror. And what is this ultimate terror? Essentially, as Peaslee realizes, man is but a trifle, a mere transient species in the overall cosmic shuffle. And because time is infinite, existence is meaningless.[32]

Comparisons have been aptly suggested between Lovecraft's seminal tales, *Shadow Out of Time* and *Mountains of Madness*—each magnificently melding horror with science fiction—in both of which cycles of evolution and the majestic rise and fall of alien civilizations are charted, and Olaf Stapledon's *Last and First Men* (1930) and *Star Maker* (1937).[33] Stapledon projected mankind's remote future history billions of years hence, highlighting our many and varied evolutionary changes along an intergalactic journey. However, according to Joshi, most likely Lovecraft didn't read *Last and First Men* until August 1935, or six months after he had finished *Shadow Out of Time*. But, remember, to Dyer, the Elder Things were also scientifically minded "men." So, rather than attempting to propose who influenced whom here (Lovecraft vs. Stapledon), that is, with regard to fictional futuristic renderings of the cosmos, it is more satisfying to identify the inspiration behind this crazed sense of establishing paleontological 'orderliness,' as outlined in Lovecraft's two seminal stories, particularly that middle "slog" in *Mountains of Madness*. Quite simply, life-through-time geohistorical artistic portrayals were in vogue with a contemporary *zeitgeist*.

As paleontologist Stephen Jay Gould stated, elucidating the chronology of Earth's past eons, periods, and epochs has been geology's "major triumph," an achievement that took many decades to properly refine. (This remains a protean process continuing in the present day, although scientific emphasis has shifted in the "dinosaur renaissance" era![34]) Certainly, ever since the mid–19th century, culture has reflected this most intriguing geological aspiration through popular books (e.g., Robert Chambers's *Vestiges of Creation*, Jules Verne's *Journey to the Center of the Earth*, Charles R. Knight's *Before the Dawn of History*, etc.), museum displays and a creative variety of life-through-time iconography. Readers and aficionados of Karel Zeman's film *Journey to the Beginning of Time* may identify with this time-honored theme. Perhaps the heyday of projecting life-through-time portrayals was during the late 1920s through the mid–20th century, especially when Charles R. Knight dominated the prehistoric animal restoration field, arguably culminating with exhibition of Rudolph F. Zallinger's triumphant mural *Age of Reptiles*, still displayed at Yale University's Peabody Museum. This was the cultural heyday when the idea of the "evolutionary epic," encompassing galactic history through Man's exalted ascendancy, reached its pinnacle. In formulating *Mountains of Madness* and later *Shadow Out of Time*, Lovecraft couldn't have been shielded from this inexorable paleontologically oriented wave of inspiration either. Yet—and here's the main thing—in his world view, *unlike* the common perspective at that time, or even that endorsed by contemporary paleontologists such as Osborn, mankind was clearly not a pinnacle of galactic, let alone terrestrial, history. For, as explained in *Shadow Out of Time*, mankind would be replaced by mere *beetles*!

Whether or not he was influenced by Lovecraft's *Mountains of Madness*, John Campbell—writing under the pseudonym "Don A. Stuart"—wrote his own Antarctic horror tale, titled "Who Goes There?," which, thanks to Hollywood, has become far better known as *The Thing from Another World*, or more simply *The Thing*. The 1951 version, considered the classic, is loosely adapted from Campbell's novella (*Astounding Science Fiction*, June 1938), as compared to 1982's (arguably better) version starring Kurt Russell—more faithfully conveying Campbell's literary plot and themes. RKO's original 1951 film—starring James Arness as the alien monster and although staged in the Arctic rather than Antarctica—set precedent for a number of filmic scares involving the solemn southern pack ice setting. Most recently, audiences have thrilled to 2004's *Alien vs. Predator*, and an *X-Files* adaptation, *Fight the Future* (1998), for example.

Through a variety of means, other imaginative souls offered homage to Lovecraft's *At the Mountains of Madness*—for instance, in fan-ish fiction such as Colin Wilson's "The Tomb of the Old Ones" (1999) or Arthur C. Clarke's slapstick "At the Mountains of Murkiness" (1973). (When you think about it, even *2001: A Space Odyssey* dabbles in Lovecraftian themes!) I'd be remiss not to mention James Rollins's 1999 novel *Subterranean*. Another entry is Tim Curran's 2005 novel, *Hive*. In this context, however, possibly of more particular interest would be Marc Cerasini's *Godzilla at World's End* (1998).[35]

Perhaps unrecognized by many Godzi-fans, Cerasini's 1998 novel is an ode to Lovecraft. Key climatic events occur on and within Antarctica, especially after the "William Dyer Geological Research Facility" plunges into a gigantic maw, opening into the Earth's interior. Nicholas Roerich's name appears in the text too. A teenage girl named Zoe who falls into the icy cavern reaches the crystalline city of the "Ancient Ones," builders of a now dormant half-billion-year-old civilization. Zoe mysteriously survives, albeit in reassimilated form. She reassembles computer equipment salvaged from wreckage used to cause a worldwide blackout; she controls giant evil monsters invading Earth's major cities. Zoe intends to cause mankind's extinction and revegetate the surface of the world—soon to be covered with a giant plant-monster fusion, Biollante's roots and branches.

As in Burroughs's 1929–1930 novel *Tarzan at the Earth's Core,*[36] in Cerasini's novel a band of heroes fly an airship into the south polar opening in a chapter aptly titled "Journey to the Center of the Earth," although (as in Verne's novel), they never reach the Earth's true center. Then, while the heroes battle Zoe's mind-enslaved, insect-like "Kamakites," Godzilla arrives in time to dispatch Biollante. But with cavern walls crumbling around the heroes as they triumphantly emerge from the opening, Godzilla becomes buried at the Earth's "center." Meanwhile, the Ancient Ones reawaken; they bequeath the planet to mankind and then return to the stars, stating, "Once this was our world ... now it is yours .... Take care of it."[37]

There are also sound and filmic productions founded at least partially upon, or poignantly paying tribute to, *Mountains of Madness*'s central setting and plot. The best of these is a 71-minute faux radio adaptation of the story, superbly produced by the H.P. Lovecraft Historical Society's Sean Branney and Andrew Leman. This Dark Adventures Radio Theater adaptation begins with Professor William Dyer's (played by Branney) broadcast interview, a warning for the Starkweather-Moore party to desist, before it's too late! Before Dyer explains to the audience what he and Danforth pledged never to reveal, a narrator recounts and plays back the stream of Worldwide Wireless News Antarctic broadcasts, leading to Lake's discovery of the star-headed, barrel-shaped Elder Things and matching 600-million-year-old fossil footprints. Dyer clarifies that the fossil discoveries challenged "everything we know about life on the planet." Throughout, with wireless static crackling ominously, we thrill to the icy howling winds drowning out the doomed Lake's reports, and to the hum of airplane engines straining to surmount the world's tallest mountains, and we chuckle at radio cigarette advertisements: "Smoke Fleurs-de-Lys, then leave them—*if you can.*"

By the time in this engaging audio version when Danforth and Dyer enter the "cyclopean city of obscene proportions," there is speculation that poor Gedney, whose body was missing from Lake's slaughtered encampment, may have gone insane, himself conducting the dissections, the bloodshed ... all this "madness." Eventually, from interpreting alien artwork and carvings, as Dyer explains to the interviewer, they realize that over the course of millions of years, the Shoggoth slaves evolved higher intelligence and then rebelled against the Elder Things. But of course, instead it was the awakened star-headed, curiously minded crinoidal creatures who destroyed Lake's party, Gedney included, only to die themselves within the walls of their ancient city when a slimy, "fetid black iridescence" emerged—the Shoggoth. Here is a crisp, intelligently scripted and orchestrated, atmospheric theatrical performance. (And Dark Adventure Radio Theater's CD comes with "authentic" newspaper clipping concerning Lake's discovery, as well as Dyer's field sketches and photos.

Another faux exploration of the southern continent, in itself a loose "sequel" of sorts,

Fig 6-1: Movie still for *The Land Unknown* (1957), concerning an expedition to the bowels of Antarctica (also the eerie setting for Lovecraft's earlier novella, *At the Mountains of Madness*). In *Land Unknown*, intrepid explorers encounter a strange Mesozoic jungle ecosystem, including a tyrannosaur clearly inspired by Rudolph Zallinger's mural *The Age of Reptiles*.

in part, to Lovecraft's masterpiece was filmed under the title *The Land Unknown* (1957), produced by William Alland and directed by Virgil Vogel. (See Figure 6-1.) Once more founded on the premise of an Admiral Byrd expedition (his real 1946–1947 exploration), the story involves a naval team that sets out by helicopter to investigate a "warm water oasis" discovered in Antarctica. Prophetically, geophysicist Alan Roberts (Jock Mahoney) speculates about whether this mysterious polar oasis is the "beginning of a new heat wave or the tail end of a million-year-old cooling-off process." When a pterodactyl collision impairs their antenna and rotor assembly, the helicopter loses power, rapidly descending through a steamy volcanic shaft, 2,500 feet below sea level into a prehistoric lost world jungle valley! Here they encounter an assortment of dinosaurs, most notably a gigantic suitmation *Tyrannosaurus* (whose pot-bellied appearance shows influences of Zallinger's *Age of Reptiles* mural—as do the scenic panoramic sets and matte paintings showing an ancient "Mesozoic" landscape), and an aquatic, long-necked *Elasmosaurus*. Gazing at prehistoric foliage, Roberts utters, "Climatic change, one of the main causes of evolution, doesn't exist here." While the valley is still in a Mesozoic stage, there are no aliens or ancient cities in this movie.

So, perhaps not fully recognized by Lovecraftian scholars, I would place the impetus behind *Mountains of Madness* not so much on any particular facet of Lovecraft's output (e.g., an elaboration of the Cthulhu mythos), event (i.e., the Byrd expedition), or story (e.g., Verne, Burroughs, Roof, Taine, etc.), although certainly Byrd's Antarctic expeditions framed the setting and means of accessing the cyclopean city ruins, but rather on the paleontological *zeitgeist* of the times—establishing life-through-time orderliness—even if it was a cosmically crazed version. It just all dovetailed in Lovecraft's magnificent tale. Lovecraft was clearly taking vast liberties with what scores of paleontologists, science popularizers and paleoartists had been elucidating for over a century, turning the entire geological spectrum on its head. Those paleontologists had been all so wrong after all! Instead, only those "mad" scientists like Dyer and Danforth verging on the brink of insanity would speak with clarity!

And what of that shadowy "Nameless Thing" beyond the mountains of madness that caused poor Danforth to lose his sanity? Better left unsaid here, lest we too go mad.

PART II

Doomsday Dinosaurs

At World War II's end, a war-torn globe lurched toward an uncertain future. Detonation of two fission bombs and numerous fire-bombings had been ordered to weaken the enemy. Red-scare paranoia and the threat of communism arose from the ashes of Hitler's ill-fated, racially founded Third Reich. The paleontological sciences and the intricacies of its inner evolutionary meanings in popular culture—*dinosaurs* having become emblematic cornerstones of prehistory and hence acquiring a totemic essence—certainly took a back seat during this tragic, angst-filled period in human history. It seemed relatively useless and impractical to dwell upon the deep past when instead one must deal with the shambles of the present day. Yet the symbolic value of the dinosaur springs eternal, and soon, having reassimilated man's enlivened concerns and fears, woven into its scaly hide, it rose again in a spectacular, more imposing guise. Life-through-time geological considerations now were relegated to secondary importance as the new, fiercer, filmic, increasingly metaphorical and allegorical giant dino-monsters of Cold War time manifested in public consciousness, spawned in the nuclear fires of war, presaging extinction.

By the 1950s, extinctions of dinosaurs and (therefore metaphorically) mankind were scientifically wedded to devastating volcanic eruptions. Their polluting exhalations were likened to the worsening environmental corruption caused by humans around the globe. Volcanoes were an early familiar if not eerie *symbol* of extinction, especially thanks to Rudolph Zallinger's extraordinary 1947 life-through-time mural, *The Age of Reptiles*. Particularly, the Cretaceous terminus of this mural showed a smoldering volcano marking the great extinction boundary at the end of the dinosaur's reign on Earth, while a mighty, imperious *Tyrannosaurus rex* (painted to impressively large proportions) surveys its domain. As stated in *Paleoimagery*, the grim countenance of Zallinger's post-atomic "Lordly Rex" also optimistically represents how North America's tyrannosaurs of the "atomic age ... seemed majestic ... because they reflected America's might and authority as a world power" at the conclusion of World War II.[1]

Indeed, decades earlier, Yale University paleontologists had reconciled the extinction of dinosaurs with the possibility of climatic-shifting, era-ending volcanism. For example, in their 1907 paper on horned dinosaur evolution and probable causes of extinction, after considering the possibility that increasing ranks of early warm-blooded (and therefore supposedly "superior") mammals (known as "multituberculates") had eaten dinosaur eggs, thus causing their Late Cretaceous demise, authors John Bell Hatcher (1861–1904), Othniel C. Marsh (1831–1899) and Richard Swann Lull (1867–1957) stressed the significance of rapidly changing climatic conditions stoked by intensified rates of volcanic eruption.[2]

However, the life-through-time paleontological format was yielding to a refocusing upon man's precarious existence on Earth, with dinosaurs offering one powerful means of visualizing the inevitable. Cemented by the horrors and atrocities of two world wars, increasingly, there was a confluence of two disparate ideas: recognition from the rock record of Earth's past ages of Cuverian mass exterminations of major life forms was becoming melded with the prospect of man's pending self-annihilation via a variety of potential means. Mankind's unnatural wielding of industrial prowess and armaments seemed tantamount to a (natural) geological force—with longer-term, adverse consequences perhaps as mighty and devastating as an alleged era-ending phase of volcanism!

Meanwhile, the menacing power of nuclear radiation had already become widely recognized, becoming more affiliated with the hydrogen bomb by the mid–1950s. In this Part, two period stories focusing on the shapeless, psychological horror of radiation exposures may be contrasted: the pre–World War II *Dr. Cyclops* (1940), and *The Incredible Shrinking Man* from the Cold War era (1957). This will help place the origin of the 1954 film *Gojira* in context. During the 1950s and 1960s, perhaps of all the dinosaurs known to the general populace, including familiar, recognizable genera such as "Brontosaurus," *Stegosaurus, Triceratops,* and *Tyrannosaurus,* Godzilla's pseudo-dinosaurian visage became most hauntingly familiar. During the height of the Cold War (the early 1950s through the mid–1960s), daily harrowing headlines and geopolitical circumstances only deepened the trend toward taking the old, tired life-through-geological-time theme for granted. The majestic pageant of life through time as portrayed in popular books and museums must have seemed not quite as majestic, when it might have appeared to the frightened masses that civilization could simply extinguish itself tomorrow!

Astonishingly, by the mid–1950s, the dinosaurs' (now loosely including Godzilla among their most familiar ranks) role in popular culture had shifted irreversibly. In the mainstream, they no longer functioned principally as ambassadors of the life-through-time idea. Dinosaurs' fading scientific relevancy became challenged, as the discipline of geology transformed and fractionated into newer arenas of intrigue (spearheaded in programs such as geophysics, plate tectonics and paleoclimatology). As opposed to their familiar functions as life-through-time signposts, or "guides," dinosaurs' popular culture roles shifted dramatically, significantly![3]

The most popular dinosaurs were conceptually "evolving" into mutated dino-creatures, metaphors for the hydrogen bomb, symbolizing what could happen to mankind unless we alter our wayward path.[4] The idea of extinction, alarmingly including its foreboding human social context, was outpacing that of the traditionalized life-through-time theme, with dinosaurs as a familiar totem. The "oxygen destroyer" device is the key weapon used to destroy Godzilla at the somber end of *Gojira* (1954). This weapon is judged to be more powerful than any other thus far invented, and therefore is another symbol of the hydrogen bomb. Throughout life's long history, however, several episodes of oceanic anoxia, recorded in the rock record and interrelated with past phases of global warming, are now known to have exterminated marine life and terrestrial species, causing mass extinctions. Thus, metaphor takes on a semblance of reality awaiting mankind if the pace of human-caused global warming cannot be curbed.

Although in the 1961 film, *Gorgo,* a giant dinosaurian ravages London, much of the haunting message of the scripted tale isn't conveyed quite so admirably as in Carson Bingham's 1960 novelization from the script. Furthermore, a series of comic books from the time—

Gorgo, issued by Charlton—portray the titular dino-monster as a gigantic form of dinosauroid (even before Godzilla had been adapted for analogous "savior" roles). Nukes are a steady theme in the comic series, as they're detonated with near reckless abandon (whereas in Toho's *Gojira* and its "Showa" sequels, one never notices a mushroom cloud).

Perhaps it all began with Ray Bradbury's moving and ecologically minded short stories, "The Beast from 20,000 Fathoms" (later, "The Fog Horn") and "A Sound of Thunder," but concerns about radiation from nuclear tests evolved and extrapolated much further, overtly into environmental and ecological matters during the 1960s and 1970s, at the same time that a "dinosaur renaissance" movement was dawning in America. A curious breed of increasingly anthropomorphized dino-critters and monsters were thus recruited, warning mankind of his folly during the expanding environmental movement, fostering awareness that the fate of the planet literally rests in human hands, a geological age now referred to as "Anthropocene."

Chapter Seven

Dinosaur Extinctions II

Volcanoes Presage Environmental Apocalypse

As if it were the dawning of a new geological epoch, in Grant Allen's gripping 1897 short story, "The Thames Valley Catastrophe," one bright August day, fiery basaltic lava erupts from enormous 12-mile-wide fissures, flooding London, roasting many citizens, forcing the few survivors to flee. Allen (1848–1899), who also authored many essays on evolutionary natural history, didn't relate such geological events with mass extinctions in his writings—yet his startling "observations" of a fictional Thames Valley catastrophe presaged the interest geologists would place on such events a century later.[1]

By the 1950s, the life-through-time paleontological format was giving way to a refocus upon man's precarious existence, with dinosaurs offering one powerful means of visualizing the inevitable. Either in its original glory at Yale University's Peabody Museum or in some replicated form, Rudolph Zallinger's mural *The Age of Reptiles* (1947) simply captivates our imagination. The 110-foot-long painting represents an idealized panorama of terrestrial (although principally reptilian or vegetative) life posed in presumed naturalistic, idealized settings, restored from fossils. Whereas the mural is perhaps intended to be observed from right (Devonian) end to left (Late Cretaceous), our eyes first feast on the huge Cretaceous dinosaurs—a pot-bellied *Tyrannosaurus* and its traditional adversary, *Triceratops.* But ominously in the background we also see three lofty, smoldering volcanic cones, the largest and most dangerous (closest to the viewer) is situated nearest the left edge of the visual timeline. What killed off the dinosaurian clan? From observation of this mesmerizing mural, aren't we tempted to say—obviously, as visually emphasized by Zallinger—volcanoes, that is, at least in North America? (See Figure 7-1.) Or are early mammals likely suspects?

Paleontologist Michael Benton, who considered theories of dinosaur extinctions historically, divides the numerous and assorted ideas, speculations and theories into three phases: the "nonquestion phase (1825–1920)"; the "dilettante phase (1920–1970)"; and the "professional phase (1970 onward)."[2] And in this vein, geologist Peter Vogt is generally credited as originating the dinosaur extinction—volcanic activity tie. However, to see the breadth of Vogt's considerations, it would be illustrative to probe further into his 1972 paper, dating from the early stages of Benton's "professional phase," which was also the dawning of the so-called "dinosaur renaissance."[3]

In a 1972 paper, Vogt, who specialized in marine geology and occurrences of basaltic plume discharge from hypothetical mantle plume "hotspots," applied evidence, observations

Fig 7-1: Schematic illustration showing Late Cretaceous pending extinction scene, inspired by Zallinger's mural *The Age of Reptiles*, with smoldering volcanic cones signaling the end of Nature's most vaunted geological era, thus symbolically ushering in the possibility of Cold War era extinctions as well (illustration by *Prehistoric Times* editor and artist, Mike Fredericks, used with permission).

and knowledge to the seafloor-spreading question. He suspected that three of the most voluminous basaltic plume discharges (including India's Deccan Traps from the Earth's mantle, penetrating through the crust) were essentially synchronous with the Mesozoic-Cenozoic transition, outpouring in "geologically brief intervals, perhaps no more than 5 million years."[4] Vogt hypothesized that heightened episodes of mantle plume convection would reshape Earth's crust, resulting in extensive plume volcanism—such as the Deccan Traps. Volcanic exhalations (trace metals, particularly) would poison the biosphere. Vogt didn't specifically mention "dinosaurs" in this paper, but concluded that the Late Cretaceous "faunal crisis" may be explained in context of flood basalt eruptions, introducing voluminous quantities of metal pollutants into the atmosphere. "It therefore seems admissible that the low pelagic sedimentation rates of the Late Cretaceous/Early Tertiary reflect greatly reduced ... biologic productivity in the world ocean, and that volcanogenic trace metals delivered in toxic doses by increased plume-generated volcanism or volcanic exhalations at this time were responsible for driving diverse genera ... to outright extinction."[5]

Citing toxic trace metals, Vogt appealed to a "promising avenue" of research published in 1959 by paleontologist Preston Cloud (1912–1991).[6] Cloud, in turn somewhat borrowing from predecessors, had suggested a causal mechanism of "chemical extinctions" for the Late Permian and Late Cretaceous faunal crises. Cloud didn't implicate volcanic sources, yet suggested that dissolution and mobility of trace metals such as copper would inhibit contemporary invertebrate organisms, threatening extinctions for those with increased sensitivities to such poisonous trace elements. Herbivorous dinosaurs, which Cloud considered swamp-dwelling, as then conventionalized, would have ingested vegetation tainted with increased concentrations of metals (such as selenium and molybdenum), leading to their doom.

Commenting on this idea over a decade later, extinctions maven Norman D. Newell (1909–2005) dissented, proclaiming that Cloud's idea was categorically unfalsifiable, and therefore should be disregarded.[7] But Vogt resurrected key aspects of Cloud's idea in a more compelling format, founded upon the emerging (if not by then triumphant) theory of plate tectonics and attendant volcanic episodes. After all, volcanoes, especially those of basaltic nature, are known to emit doses of toxic heavy metals, such that would confound and poison organic biochemical and physiological pathways. (Yes!—including iridium, although occurrences of that element at the Cretaceous-Paleogene (K-Pg) boundary (formerly known as the "K-T" Cretaceous-Tertiary transition) wouldn't be of scholarly concern until 8 years later.) If plume activity was prolonged, geologically speaking, extinctions would be expected to occur with greatest severity at the onset or climax of plume volcanism.

With trace metals as a possible culprit, Vogt examined the tectonic mechanism that could issue these toxic elements, comparing evidence at suspect geological boundaries in light of competing factors, such as (1) frequency of geomagnetic reversals, (2) orogenic episodes, (3) periods of continental glaciation, and (4) habitat-destroying reduction in sea level.

In 1963, for example, regarding Vogt's first point, Robert J. Uffen (1923–2009) proposed that during relatively brief episodes of times of geomagnetic reversal—a manifestation of instability within the Earth's convection system—cosmic radiation would penetrate to the Earth's surface, causing increased occurrences of organismic mutations with consequent effects on the evolution of life.[8] Vogt therefore assessed the relative timing of geomagnetic reversal rates, noting there appeared to be *lack* of good correlation between timed pulses of heightened reversal rate and mass extinctions. Years later, paleontologist David M. Raup differed on the alleged lack of correlation, while acknowledging that the "question of magnetic periodicity is a mess. We don't know whether the fine structure of the magnetic record shows periodicity or not, and even if it does, we don't know whether the reversals are related to biological extinction or to large-body impact or both."[9]

Orogenic episodes (i.e., "mountain building"—often extensive *belts* of mountain ranges) are not necessarily equated with periods of voluminous basaltic plume eruption. In fact, by the mid–20th century, geologists had concluded that periods of orogenesis do not correspond to mass extinctions episodes. For example, there was no known periodicity in such worldwide events, although an "average interval" between seemed to be on the order of 200 to 300 million years.[10] Vogt also rejected continental glaciation as an extinctions cause. Because the Permo-Carboniferous and Plio-Pleistocene ice ages "were not associated with great extinctions, it is difficult to believe that continentality and cold alone adequately explain the faunal crises."[11]

For several years, it seemed settled that lowered sea levels caused extinctions through reduction in shallow water habitat area bordering continental margins. These hypotheses generally proved popular through the mid–1970s, that is, until they became swamped by the asteroid theory's overwhelming popularity. (See Chapter Sixteen.)

Vogt rejected Newell's concept, stating that "it seems unlikely that such habitat destruction could have been thorough enough." However, Vogt concluded, "The trace element hypothesis ... provides a geologically rapid, global mechanism." Thereafter, Thomas Schopf, who in his 1974 paper[12] did not cite Vogt, yet referred to the question of deciphering mass extinctions as "Paleontology's outstanding dilemma."[13] In referring to Schopf's "solution," Stephen Jay Gould wrote approvingly, "When a problem has proved intractable for more than one hundred years, it is not likely to yield to more data collected in the old way.... Theoretical ecology allowed us to ask the right questions and plate tectonics provided the right earth upon which to pose them."[14]

Had Schopf's data and conclusions been available a little earlier, Vogt might have concurred on the seafloor-spreading aspect. Yet Vogt had already suspected plume eruption-causing toxic element emissions as a primary factor in, not only the Late Cretaceous extinctions, but, contrary to Schopf and Gould, *also* the Late Permian's "great dying," as the Permo-Triassic extinction boundary (when more than 90 percent of species succumbed) became ominously known.

Vogt's Permian-Triassic evidence—higher concentrations of trace metals detected in Germany's extensive and thick Kupferschiefer shallow water stratigraphic beds (conventionally regarded as Upper Permian in age)—seemed suggestive of volcanic activity. As Cloud noted,[15] since 1912, paleontologists had considered that "abrupt influxes" of copper, silver and zinc to the ancient Kupferschiefer sea might have caused widespread fish kills, as evident in the fossil record. "If then, abnormally large amounts of copper or other potentially lethal metal ions or complexes were supplied to and diffused through the Permian seas ... this might help to explain: (1) Permian extinctions, (2) anomalies in the pattern of extinction and evolution, and (3) ... any mass extinction...."[16]

Was pollution the solution to extinction?

Vogt perceived episodicity in the geological record with respect to mantle plume events which "fall close to geologic period boundaries ... marked (partly by definition) by faunal crises of greater or lesser extent."[17] Particularly, basaltic plume (non-orogenic) events were markedly and distinctively discharged about 50 to 70 million years ago; 110 to 130 million years ago; 160 to 170 million years ago; 190 to 200 million years ago; and 220 to 240 million years ago. They seemed recurrent with an average "megacycle" period of approximately 50 to 60 million years that Vogt referred to as a "basic Earth spot cycle" characterizing mantle convection at least since the Precambrian. Given the uncertainties in radiometric age dating then (e.g., the K-Pg boundary was then "variously dated at 63 to 70 million years ago"), compared to today's precision and accuracy, Vogt's suggested Earth spot rhythm is remarkably aligned with (redated) events presented in a recent popular book, Vincent Courtillot's *Evolutionary Catastrophes*.[18] Here, Courtillot rather convincingly correlated ages of volcanic traps with timing of major extinction events.

Vogt also noted that for the last four geological period transitions (cited above) accelerated mantle plume convection and resulting volcanism correlated with reduced sea levels. He also solemnly suggested that "Earth is approaching another 'period boundary' ... geologically speaking, just around the corner."[19] Grant Allen would have been delighted. Humphry Davy would have been so intrigued!

Scientists rarely work in a vacuum, and Vogt, who relied on Cloud's pollutant chemical exposures model, was no exception. Linkage of dinosaurs with chemically caused, atmospherically controlled extinctions began rather sedately, if not unconvincingly. Cloud referred to the then recent published work of Albert Schatz.[20] Schatz had considered biochemical and physiological factors leading to pituitary disorders in dinosaurs caused not by excessive carbon dioxide, but by increased atmospheric oxygen levels. Therefore, Schatz surprisingly claimed that excessive rates of photosynthesis resulted in dinosaurian extinctions. Then, in 1967, N.C. Koch conjectured that dinosaurs had expired from exposures to a trace element, selenium, emitted from volcanic emissions, and later dissolved and weathered into soil where it was absorbed into vegetation ingested by herbivorous dinosaurs.[21] And in 1970, A. Lee McAlester rather precociously considered how "periodic episodes of animal extinction were caused by environmental stresses that selectively eliminated animals having high rates of energy utilization. Past variation in the concentration of atmospheric oxygen appears to be among the most probable environmental changes that could be expected to produce such an effect."[22] Interestingly, decades prior to the onset of Benton's "professional phase" in the investigation of dinosaur extinctions, in 1928, one L. Muller attributed dinosaur extinctions to "sudden volcanism."[23]

It is intriguing that, while Vogt also considered a *geophysical* possibility that heightened mantle plume discharge could decrease global temperatures because of the incremental increases of atmospheric sun-shielding volcanic dust, as well as increasing a cooling "continentality of climate" caused by "epeirogenic doming under continents," instead he emphasized a chemical poisoning *environmental* factor instead.[24] By this time, however, in the streets and in the press, America's environmental movement was already underway.

Although scientists of many persuasions and in many nations have expressed academic interest in ecology and environmental studies, in America, the environmental movement of the 1960s and '70s was arguably spawned from growing 1950s awareness about the hazards of human exposures to radioactive byproducts spread through the atmosphere by nuclear weapons testing. From the days of biochemist Linus Pauling (1901–1994) to Rachel Carson, and beyond, now earth scientists—including paleontologists—have heightened comprehension of paleoenvironments considered in relation to the success of contemporary fauna and flora. Curiously, the most widely publicized and rather controversial dinosaur extinctions theories of the late 1960s through the 1970s were those involving radiation exposure (e.g., supernovae). These gradually gave way to a host of environmentally oriented catastrophe theories. In fact, Luis Alvarez's (1911–1988) asteroid theory essentially outlined an *environmental* catastrophe, including a cataclysmic multi-season "impact winter," leading to dinosaurian extinctions.[25]

As with the human plight, nearly in parallel, dinosaurian extinction theories have progressed with a profound sense of urgency stemming from radiation causal factors toward chemical environmental disasters (e.g., extreme greenhouse atmospheric conditions and "Strangelove" sterile or anoxic oceans).[26] Just as the cause underlying Heinrich Erben's (1921–1997) theory of dinosaurian eggshell-thinning was attributed in 1972 to volcanic emissions during the Late Cretaceous, by 1962, Rachel Carson (1907–1964) linked eggshell thinning in a flock of modern dinosaurian evolutionary descendants—e.g., raptor birds—to the spread of pesticides such as DDT throughout the biosphere.[27]

And, perhaps inspired during a time when stark implications of mankind's alteration of the atmosphere with resulting greenhouse effects were becoming realized, Dewey M. McLean formulated a dinosaur extinctions theory founded on buildup of carbon dioxide in the ocean-atmosphere system.[28] In retrospect, McLean did not account for feedback buffering capacity of the oceans, which would have diminished the severity of his imagined volcanic greenhouse. Yet, he also did not account for heightened releases of methane gas issued from depositional environments, which (when combined with carbon dioxide volcanic emissions) would have considerably amplified the greenhouse condition. McLean's 1978 paper was prepared nearly coincidentally with another by B.W. Oelofsen, who also considered the reproductive success of egg-laying, presumably endothermic species and, therefore, dinosaurian extinctions.[29]

And in 1972, Vogt certainly had his finger on the pulse of modernity when he predicted, "In addition to the environmental havoc that is man's handiwork on this planet, a 'natural' faunal crisis might be, geologically speaking, just around the corner."[30] Within two decades, other geologists had more or less vindicated Vogt's mantle plume convection cycle idea, especially with regard to Deccan Traps basaltic flood volcanism.[31]

Since the 1970s (the onset of Benton's professional theoretical phase), dinosaur and mass extinctions theories have increasingly acquired environmental and ecological ambiance, emphasizing biogeochemical (as opposed to purely geophysical) factors. Rather presciently, Peter Vogt not only founded his 1972 volcanically caused chemical theory of recurrent mass extinctions on the emerging plate tectonics paradigm, but also upon new understandings of ecological havoc caused by toxic chemicals released profusely to the biosphere.

Vogt certainly went much further with his volcanic extinctions theory than did Humphry Davy with his chemical-volcanic concept of Earth geohistory. In consideration of dinosaur extinctions, volcanoes were very much in vogue (thanks to Vogt) then, as is the case today.

Geology underwent not less than two ideological revolutions over the past 60 years—one involving acceptance of plate tectonics, and another (perhaps more significantly) yielding acceptance of mass extinctions in the fossil record—regardless of how they are caused and unfold. Debate over the possibility of extraterrestrial mechanisms for wiping out ancient flora and fauna during the Cretaceous-Paleogene transition 66 million years ago entered mainstream popular culture, galvanizing mid–1980s intrigue over the mysteries of paleontology and, especially, the riddle of the dinosaurs. While certain scientists were heralded and championed for their far-reaching insights and theories, others were ostracized for expressing less outlandish, opposing views. One of the "victims" was Dewey M. McLean, a biologist and micro-paleontologist (Ph.D. Stanford, later affiliated with Virginia Polytechnic University), who had the fortune (or misfortune) of delving into the K-Pg question during the late 1960s and '70s, publishing a thought-provoking paper on the demise of dinosaurs in 1978 (while others who would arrive at quite different answers were also investigating the question as well).

McLean's theory for extinctions actually melds geology's two 20th-century ideological paradigms (plate tectonics with the most investigated mass extinction, the K-Pg). In retrospect, rereading some of the rationally written papers and books supporting the volcanic theory, McLean seems to have received a raw deal. No wonder text on his Web site sounds just a bit jaded.[32]

McLean diligently developed his case for Late Cretaceous greenhouse-caused extinctions. While other researchers (e.g., the team led by Luis Alvarez) would blame impact of cosmic debris for dinosaurian extinctions (resulting from a prolonged episode of asteroid impact-caused "winter"), instead McLean identified terrestrial causes that would have increased concentrations of carbon dioxide in the ocean-atmosphere system to critical levels. In "Terminal Mesozoic 'Greenhouse': Lessons from the Past," McLean outlined interrelated (biogeochemical) processes that would have conspired to cause extreme warming in the Late Maastrichtian (i.e., uppermost Cretaceous) age.[33] Evidence such as apparent dissolution of marine carbonates dating from this stage, and stable oxygen and carbon isotopic data, suggested a geologically "sudden" onset of climatic warming (which could mean an interval of perhaps less than approximately 100,000 years). While during the 20 million years prior to the Late Maastrichtian, global temperatures had *gradually* fallen, vertebrate animals already adapted to such conditions wouldn't have been capable of evolving suddenly to harsher (warmer) climatic conditions.

The longer-term Cretaceous cooling trend was related to regression of seas off the continents; significantly, extinction of marine calcareous algal phytoplankton (i.e., coccolithophorids) was coincident with climatic changes. Presumably as shallow seas withdrew, the coccolithophorids were deprived of land-derived nutrients (although in his 1978 paper McLean did not conclude what caused their extinction). Then, with calcareous phytoplankton in crisis, final extinctions on land and sea ensued over a relatively brief 100,000- to 1-million-year interval (or, alternatively, as dinosaur paleontologist Dale Russell had concluded in 1976, even more suddenly—possibly in less than a century).

McLean's mechanism for extinctions was novel for its time, even though by then he hadn't isolated the primary causal factor capable of triggering a greenhouse catastrophe. In 1978, McLean focused on the role of carbon dioxide in driving extinctions. Calcareous marine floras underwent extinctions; they no longer (photosynthetically) absorbed atmospheric carbon dioxide into their shelly fortresses. Consequently, excess carbon dioxide wasn't absorbed into organic matter which was later deposited into rock-forming sediment on the ocean floor, but instead dissolved within ocean waters. Such increasing carbon dioxide concentrations acidified the ocean, further leading to dissolution of carbonates on the ocean floor and possibly hampering reproductive success of other carbonate-secreting organisms as well. Meanwhile, on land, extinction of terrestrial vegetation meant less carbon dioxide was being pumped from the atmosphere into plant tissues. With unsuppressed levels of carbon dioxide steadily building in the atmosphere, climate grew hotter because (as we all know) carbon dioxide is one of several atmospheric-heating greenhouse gases (as also are H_2O and methane).

For vertebrates—dinosaurs and large reptiles especially—this became a hothouse nightmare, leading to their extinction! Noting that smaller terrestrial animals would have been more capable of surviving modest temperature increases than those with larger bodies (because of their lower body surface-area-to-volume ratio), McLean proposed that animals such as dinosaurs and marine reptiles would have been among the first to succumb.

During the late 1930s, the University of California at Los Angeles's Raymond B. Cowles (1896–1975) proposed during a meeting held at Chicago's Field Museum, "Heat, not cold, killed off dinosaurs."[34] Cowles had conducted experiments on desert-dwelling reptiles, in which exposure to heat was tolerated less effectively than suboptimal temperatures. Noting that the Late Cretaceous was a time of global warmth, Cowles (rather counterintuitively) suggested that, therefore, it was probably heat that caused the dinosaurian demise. He even suggested that some of the larger reptiles, "which preserved themselves, developed hair at this time to reflect the heat of the sun, thus keeping their body temperatures closer to optimum."[35] For its time, Cowles's idea clearly ran against consensus, which preached that dinosaurs died out in declining (colder) climatic conditions. Later, during the mid–1940s, he and Edwin H. Colbert (1905–2001) joined forces to see how live alligators would react to prolonged heat exposures. They discovered that temperatures in the bodies of larger specimens changed more slowly than in smaller gators. However, only a slight temperature rise above the optimum proved fatal to one large alligator.[36]

Therefore, because during the K-Pg transition, only terrestrial animals smaller than house cats survived, it seemed to McLean that excessive heat (not cold) must have been the culprit. During the gradual 20-million-year cool-down phase in the upper Cretaceous (prior to the postulated Late Maastrichtian greenhouse condition), dinosaurs attained their large sizes, which, according to "Bergmann's principle," would have proven advantageous in surviving colder/declining climate.[37] But large body sizes would have been an impediment to survival under a sudden flash of global warmth, and here's why—according to McLean.

Yes, heat stroke could have occurred in the case of individual dinosaurs, as Cowles and Colbert had noted. More significantly, however, McLean also noted that under temperatures straying more modestly yet continually above the optimum for dinosaurs and other large reptiles, male spermatogenesis would have been impaired. Dinosaurs wouldn't have been able to shed excess body heat effectively, and hence wouldn't have been able to reproduce. "Thus, Late Maestrichtian [*sic*] extinctions of reptiles and other vertebrates may have been generated by a temperature increase of such modest magnitude that evidence for it has been subtly hidden in the rock record."[38] Unfortunately, with now invisible dinosaur sperm at the crux, this isn't a theory that can be easily falsified. (Although not stated in his article, herpetologists realize that the sex of reptile hatchlings is dependent upon incubation temperature. So, extrapolating a bit, it is possible that the last generation of dinosaur species were all of the same sex—male or female—and hence could not reproduce. Meanwhile, dinosaur egg data—discussed below—indicated that in the Late Cretaceous no offspring of either sex would have been possible.)

Furthermore, McLean cited conclusions by Heinrich Erben published in 1972, indicating that Late Maastrichtian dinosaur eggs (possibly *Hypselosaurus*) were thin-shelled, extremely fragile. Coming on the heels of Rachel Carson's 1962 bestseller, *Silent Spring*, exposing the perils of insecticides (e.g., DDT) to birds and the ecosphere, concluding that K-Pg dinosaurs were stressed or that their "hormonal systems (were) hopelessly out of tune" was certainly in vogue with the environmentally conscious times.[39] Erben claimed the record of egg-thinning was geologically rapid. In his 1978 paper, McLean cited studies indicating that chickens exposed to high concentrations of carbon dioxide in breathing air (5 percent) suffered from lowered (i.e., more acid) blood pH; accordingly, hens laid sterile, thin-shelled eggs. McLean, referring to Adrian J. Desmond's 1975 presentation of Erben's data, concluded, "This stress was probably due to elevated environmental temperatures." However, more recently Kenneth Carpenter rather whimsically dismantled Erben's rationale and interpretations of this egg data in *Eggs, Nests, and Baby Dinosaurs: A Look at Dinosaur Reproduction*.[40]

While failure of calcareous phytoplankton was critical to his theory, as of 1978, McLean lacked a viable mechanism that would *cause* extinctions of K-Pg transition coccolithophorids. He would soon find his cause in the volcanic Deccan Traps of India. He presented his idea during the 147th National Meeting of the American Association for the Advancement of Science (AAAS) held in Toronto, January 3–8, 1981. McLean's abstract "Terminal Cretaceous Extinctions and Volcanism: A Link," was published in *Abstracts of Papers*.[41] In retrospect, McLean's insights would have seemed an elegant solution to the problem. However, by this point proponents of the forceful Alvarez asteroid impact team had surged to the forefront of the fray with a far more glitzy theory, which by then had galvanized paleontological popular culture!

McLean went farther than Vogt[42] in suggesting a mechanism with supporting evidence for Late Maastrichtian extinctions. In his 1981 abstract and presentation, McLean accounted for enhancement of siderophile elements (e.g., iridium) in K-Pg boundary clay, the origin and nature of the clay itself and stable isotopic evidence for warming of the oceans—all in terms of India's substantially voluminous Deccan Traps basaltic flow eruption, coincidentally dating from the K-Pg transition. The ecological result was a greenhouse of sufficient magnitude to cause worldwide extinctions both on land and at sea.[43] McLean even had the audacity to debate Luis Alvarez at the 1981 AAAS meeting, thus incurring the latter's wrath forevermore. So, symbolically and metaphorically, physics triumphed over geological and environmental sciences that day, even though geology, which often thrives on a consilience of factors and variables, sometimes rather than decimal-place exactitude, was at stake.

Then in 1985, McLean published a definitive account of his theory, "Deccan Traps Mantle Degassing in the Terminal Cretaceous Marine Extinctions."[44] Here, McLean sized up the volume of the gaseous volcanic carbon dioxide emissions, noting (with calculations) the resulting geochemical imbalances and probable adverse effects on the biosphere. The Deccan Traps basaltic flood volcanism was caused by motion of the northerly moving Indian Plate over a mantle hot spot, and timing of the vast outpouring seemed synchronous with that of the K-Pg mass extinctions themselves! In short—according to McLean—no need for an asteroid impact, after all. McLean proclaimed that after the extinctions (and using a peculiar term coined by Wallace Broecker and Kenneth Hsu), a near-sterile "Strangelove Ocean" prevailed.[45]

For his "audacity," things didn't get immediately better for McLean, even though he continued investigating and publishing papers. Charles Officer (writing with Jake Page in *The Great Dinosaur Extinction Controversy*, noted, "As a result of his work, McLean charged, Alvarez's allies had made an attempt to undermine his career...."[46] Furthermore, in 1988, Luis Alvarez characterized McLean as a "weak sister. I thought he'd been knocked out of the ball game and had disappeared, because nobody invites him to conferences anymore." To him, McLean was "publishing scientific nonsense."[47] Nonsense? McLean made several valid points, offering an objective solution that did not involve a merely postulated solar companion "Nemesis" star, for instance. And at the time, credible evidence for a K-Pg impact crater of sufficient dimensions was lacking.

The volcanism suggested in Zallinger's mural *The Age of Reptiles* (i.e., North America's Laramide Orogeny—formerly "Revolution") was not equated with McLean's volcanic causal factor for Late Cretaceous upheaval, which instead took place on the drifting Indian Plate. Today, the remnant, eroded Deccan Traps cover ⅙ area of the Indian subcontinent and range up to over 6,000 feet in thickness! More recently, Vincent Courtillot and colleagues have radiometrically zeroed in on the Deccan event, finding it to be essentially synchronous with mass extinctions recorded in the K-Pg fossil record. However, as Charles Officer noted, the Deccan was only one of several volcanic contributors then (besides the Laramide): "At its peak, K-T [as the K-Pg transition was formerly referred to] volcanism may have been a hundred times greater than what we experience today—that is, it would be something like a Mount St. Helen's (or bigger) happening every day of the year."[48] Except the Deccan superplume continued erupting for an interminable 100,000 to 200,000 years!

More recently, paleontologists accept that in the aftermath of mega-volcanic pulse, oceans would not have gone completely sterile (as in a Strangelove condition), although they would have been chemically altered. (Terms like "Canfield Ocean" and Anoxic Ocean are now in use.[49]) Charles Officer believes changes in ocean chemistry occurring approximately 66 million years ago had a devastating impact on phytoplankton, although terrestrial animals were relatively unscathed by heightened volcanism; to him, the already waning dinosaurs went extinct for other (more mundane) reasons prior to the K-Pg transition. But with Luis Alvarez's (who died in 1988) daunting persona out of the picture, McLean later attributed dinosaur extinctions to a carbon dioxide enhanced greenhouse effect, exacerbated by calamitous ocean chemistry resulting from failure of the coccolithophorids—in turn, ultimately caused by the Deccan Traps mantle superplume eruption.

In a 1995 paper, "K-T Transition Greenhouse and Embryogenesis Dysfunction in the Dinosaurian Extinctions," posted on his Web site, McLean speculated:

> Females experiencing warming suffered reduced blood flow to the uterine tract, damaging eggs and embryos and killing them in numbers to reduce population sizes to the point of extinction.... Greenhouse warming during the K-T transition accounts for the final phase of the dinosaurian extinctions. Dinosaurs that were adapting to long-duration Late Cretaceous climatic cooling would have literally gone into a greenhouse heat thermal wall. Large female ectothermic dinosaurs attempting to survive in a hot new world would have increasingly shunted blood supply to the skin, reducing blood supply to the uterine tract where conception takes place, and where embryos must develop. Climate-induced reduction of uterine blood flow would have killed increasing numbers of dinosaur embryos, reducing population numbers until the dinosaurs finally dwindled away into oblivion.[50]

With volcanoes blamed, climate change was the culprit.

By this time, however, McLean finally acknowledged that a large asteroid or comet impact event could have also contributed to greenhouse warming. Furthermore, by the mid–1990s, the various factors elegantly structured into his theory of K-Pg reproductive failure has, to him (rather pompously), attained status as no less than a "*law of nature* [*sic*] linking greenhouse climate change associated with mantle plume volcanism, impacts ... to bioevolution and extinctions."[51] (Shades of Osborn!) In his 2002 book *Evolutionary Catastrophes*, Vincent Courtillot stated, "If McLean's style seems rather daringly self-assured in view of the data he had at the time, this no doubt partly reflects the aggressive atmosphere in which he was trying to defend his ideas."[52]

As of the 2000s, greenhouse-caused extinctions in the fossil record remain in vogue as a mechanism of great dying. However, McLean's name is rarely mentioned in popular treatments, such as Peter D. Ward's *Under a Green Sky* (2007).[53] As Ward notes—summarizing recently compiled biogeochemical, paleontological and paleo-oceanographic data—other factors were in play during extinction events, not anticipated by McLean in 1978. Based on the work of Lee Kump and colleagues at Pennsylvania State University, Ward suggests that, while there was a major cosmic impact driving K-Pg extinctions 66 million years ago, nine other geological horizons—planetary greenhouse conditions—are instead principally characterized by oceanic anoxia with buildup of toxic hydrogen sulfide gases in the atmosphere. Rotten eggs![54] And Douglas H. Erwin, esteemed investigator of the Permian-Triassic crisis, suggests that Siberian flood basalt eruption, with resulting greenhouse-induced extinctions, was a principal factor in the puzzling "Great Dying" that took place approximately 251 million years ago.[55] During the Permo-Triassic transition, carbon dioxide levels may have soared to nearly 15 times higher than today's atmospheric level.

So, while in retrospect, McLean may have selected the wrong geological boundary upon which to build his case for greenhouse-caused extinctions, he may deserve credit for recognizing the potential role of such conditions in causing prehistoric biotic upheaval. Although correct in gross outlines but not fine detail (rather analogous to Alfred Wegener's early considerations of continental drift), McLean's 1978 theory lacked sufficient evidence and a viable mechanism to pass modern scientific scrutiny. And at the time, his ideas were overwhelmed by what must have seemed to proponents of volcanic alternatives, the asteroid theory frenzy and contagion.

It would seem that expansive volcanic eruption lasting continuously for geologically prolonged periods, such as occurred during the Permo-Triassic boundary, contribute mightily to oceanic acidification, global warming, and atmospheric toxification—and hence mass extinctions.[56] With growing recognition of the devastating effects caused by or potentially attributable to natural, volcanic pollution, as well as that stemming from mankind's persistent spread of industrial waste byproducts—resulting in atmospheric smog—and that of toxic, cancer-causing radionuclides blown into and throughout our atmosphere decades ago via rampant nuclear bomb testing, citizens were developing a fearful global awareness.

Chapter Eight

Sizing up Radiation's Unnatural Cold War Dangers

By the early 1940s, a cloud of metaphorical "fallout" was wending its way through American consciousness—concerns which had grown supremely ominous by the mid–1950s. From the ultra-small, and seemingly inconsequential atomic scale, huge and awful dangers could arise that threatened the entire globe! Through a peculiar catharsis, public concerns and angst were projected through a litany of contemporary movies, science fiction stories and television shows. But while such fare at times could be laughable at the drive-ins, the inherent underlying dangers—the subliminal messages—were authentic, founded in cold-sweat reality. It is at this juncture that the imagery of what people generally considered a "dinosaur" suddenly mutated, much as humans would when exposed to the deadly rays of a hydrogen bomb, or when faced with sickening symptoms caused by unrelenting chemical pollution spewed by industrial nations.

The new, unnatural shape-shifting dinosaur, genera unknown to science, reflecting mankind's innermost fears of self-annihilation, took refuge in newly found antagonistic roles—the bane of civilization, a stern warning! No longer simply a familiar, friendly marker or "guide" to the ages of prehistory, these anachronistic pseudo-dinosaurs had been resurrected into our awful, war-torn present, ready to strike vicious blows at those who, relying on cold-hearted equations of physics and chemistry, in Frankensteinian or Faustian fashion, had not merely conjured weapons of mass destruction, but more so conceivably had developed weapons of utter *mass extinction* (with a projected outcome not unlike that of the real dinosaurs' then popularly presumed volcanic demise 66 million years ago).

But before we delve into how the dinosaurian lesson plan diverted from life-through-time guidance, toward mirroring man's Cold War plight, it would be instructive to see how the phenomenon of radiation was viewed, publicly, both in the period just prior to development of an atomic (fission) bomb, and then contrasted with the view following invention of the hydrogen (fusion) bomb. The commonality here is that in both instances, humans found themselves shrinking helplessly into insignificance. But whereas hope dawned eternal even during the pre-atomic bomb case, following the hydrogen bomb's development man seemed destined, uncontrollably, hopelessly, to oblivion.

Among our favored monster, horror and sci-fi films, *Dr. Cyclops* (Paramount Pictures, 1940) wouldn't rank among the upper echelon in popularity. True—it's rather neglected today, perhaps unfairly so. Original in its time, the film reflected embryonic fears of natural phenomena that would shortly escalate into world-sweeping events. So let's not "shrink" from this exercise. Instead, let's use this opportunity to take a second look at this remarkable movie, in fact the first science fiction film to be produced in Technicolor. First, let's focus on salient plot elements.

Given that Ernest B. Schoedsack, who had produced *King Kong* seven years earlier, was involved, it's rather unsurprising that a scientific expedition to a mysterious jungle setting was also central to *Dr. Cyclops*. Dr. Alexander Thorkel (played by Albert Dekker), who regards himself (as do several of his colleagues) as the world's greatest living biologist, is conducting clandestine experiments in Peru's Amazon jungle in the shadow of Inca ruins. He peers at slides through a microscope. A radiant source casts an eerie greenish glow, in which he's enveloped. We soon realize he's utterly mad, in fact, one of the earliest and most sadistic filmic monster-scientists!

An associate, Dr. Mendoza, is upset, ruing the day he (Mendoza) exposed Thorkel to the knowledge of an enriched radium deposit. For now Thorkel isn't using the radium for investigating desired healing properties. Instead, Thorkel is tinkering with the "cosmic force of creation. We can shape life, take it apart ... put it together ... mold it like putty." Mendoza accuses Thorkel of tampering with powers reserved for God. Contemptuously forbidding Thorkel to continue his "evil" radium researches, Mendoza is murdered—exposed fully to the radium source.

Biologists Mary Robinson (Janice Logan) and Rupert Bulfinch (Charles Halton) and geologist Bill Stockton (Thomas Coley) are now wending their way to visit Thorkel, who has summoned the party. Robinson heralds Thorkel as an authority on "organic molecular structure." While Thorkel may be arrogant, Bulfinch, his old scientific rival, is pompous and rather eccentric too. Meanwhile, we see Thorkel wearing a radiation suit, shielded from an eerie greenish radiant glow, observing strange phenomena (as yet hidden from the audience) through a window that provides him a view into a sealed laboratory. Upon the arrival of the scientific team, Stockton quickly identifies the presence of iron crystals in the microscope slides, thus proving Thorkel's (as yet mysterious) theory. The crystals *were* there all along. It's just that Thorkel's exceedingly poor vision prevented him from observing them. And so Thorkel rudely banishes Robinson, Bulfinch and Stockton from the premises, back to civilization. He only needed their "trained sight" to complete his "most absorbing" research. Having been treated like an "errand boy," Bulfinch is indignant!

Another of the visiting party, a local named Steve Baker (Victor Kilian), discovers the radium mine shaft upon which Thorkel's experiments rely, spying on the megalomaniac as he elevates the piston ray concentrator from a cavity in the earth. (Please don't snicker, but this is clearly a phallic symbol penetrating Earth's womb, raping the planet. We'll return to this concept later on.) Baker collects ore samples, which are found to be enriched in uranium (and radium) isotopes, suddenly realizing that they have self-serving reasons for not leaving, despite Dr. Thorkel's demand. But then ashamed for briefly attempting to double-cross each other, now they're firmly allied, even more curious to uncover the nature of Thorkel's experiments.

The party invades his office. Following a brief tussle, wary Thorkel decides to cater to their curiosity, allowing Bulfinch to examine his notes, divulging more top secret researches. Leading them into a trap—the laboratory room emitting the greenish glow—he shows them his "condenser" which "concentrates the radioactive force of nature itself." Yes, he's even "drawing cosmic force from the bosom of the earth." Thorkel claims this device is similar to those used in hospitals to treat cancer patients, although now he's learned how to focus the powerful rays far more precisely. Then he locks the door with the infiltrators inside. Quickly donning a radiation helmet, he exposes the party to the rays which reduce them in size to a mere 12 inches tall! In particular, Satanas, the black cat, seems wickedly interested in the outcome of Dr. Thorkel's experiments.

"Why does Providence permit the existence of such a monstrosity?" a diminutive Bulfinch blusters after awakening from the ordeal. But Thorkel can only exult in the fact that they're the first specimens to survive by more than a few hours. Yes, it was the identification of those key iron crystals that led to his success. Thanks to Stockton especially, "Now I can control life, absolutely," sighs Thorkel as he drifts off to sleep. It's still not at all clear what the science is behind those iron crystals, or how one may "control life, absolutely" with a radium condenser, but clearly the movie producer was doing his darnedest to suspend disbelief with more than a mere tad of comic-bookish "science speak" here.

"Strange, how absorbed man has always been in the size of things," muses Dr. Alexander Thorkel in *Dr. Cyclops*. True, size is relative, except when physics comes into play. Escaping to the outside from the living quarters, Bulfinch denounces Thorkel's theory, proclaiming, "A radioactive field cannot be channelized," or just a bit more science-speak. An amused Thorkel retorts sardonically that, well, perhaps Bulfinch is right after all, and rather than members of the visiting party having been shrunk, it is he, Thorkel, who has grown to a towering height!

The movie title is now further explained. It is only in part a reference to Dr. Thorkel's poor vision (a circumstance that will become important shortly), but more so instead to Homer's *The Odyssey*, in which Odysseus (aka Ulysses) and his men become prisoners, trapped within the cave of the one-eyed Cyclops. Whereas the gigantic Cyclops was superior in strength, the brute was also relatively ignorant; the diminutive Ulysses (likened to Bulfinch) possessed greater acumen than Cyclops. But in the end, Bulfinch's superior mind doesn't spare him, as Thorkel determines the effects of the radium ray are wearing off, causing his human specimens to steadily grow at an accelerated rate. Thorkel is stricken with hubris. It isn't he who has erred. No, "Nature is making the mistake." The "mistake" seems to be that his test subjects won't remain small, permanently. And because the party must not interfere with his work once they've reattained full size, Bulfinch is the first to go—suffocated in the clutches of this mad "cyclops."

The rest of the party escapes the enraged Thorkel, out into the jungle, where they find a raft adjacent to the river. When an alligator swims over to them, they seek refuge inside atop a cliff "cave." Our refugees appear as cave people defending their territory.[1]

Eventually, the party (minus poor miniaturized Pedro, who was killed heroically defending his comrades), seeks temporary refuge in Thorkel's specimen bag, and unbeknownst to the giant, are carried back to his jungle outpost. They're intent on killing the mad doctor, in the process debilitating him by smashing every pair of Thorkel's glasses. The last pair, however, retains only one good lens. "Now you can call me Cyclops," a demented Thorkel bellows as he dons these half broken spectacles, "because I have *one* good eye!" Chasing them outside toward the mine shaft, symbolically, Thorkel plunges to his death, downward into the nether region he dared penetrate while probing Nature's forbidden secrets. Many weeks later, back in civilization, the survivors—mule hand/miner Baker, geologist Stockton and biologist

Robinson—vow never to divulge what happened back there ... they'd all be committed (or possibly even accused of murdering the world's greatest no-longer-living biologist).

Two samples of published literature resulted evidently from Tom Kilpatrick's (and an uncredited Malcolm Stuart Boylan's) movie script. One was a scientifiction "novelette of men in miniature" by Henry Kuttner (1915–1958), appearing in *Thrilling Wonder Stories* (1940).[2] Howard V. Brown supplied the issue's classic cover painting. The editor (at this juncture, either Leo Margulies or Mort Weisinger) commented on Brown's artistry. Kuttner suggested a painted "scene showing miniature pygmy men and women in the hands of a scientist?" After all, as Kuttner related during a meeting, this was a key element "from this yarn ... the story I came here to deliver. *Dr. Cyclops*. It's based on the story you assigned me to write.... Why when I watched them make *Dr. Cyclops* in Hollywood, I saw them produce that shot via trick photography."[3] The editor added, "Brown exhibited the sketch he had been discussing with us. It was the exact scene Kuttner had selected.... Brown did as perfect justice to the idea as Kuttner did to the story...."[4]

In Kuttner's tale, Dr. Mary Robinson's name was shifted to "Dr. Phillips." And Kuttner added interesting details that were original, unclear or omitted from the film. For instance, Baker's interest in joining the scientific expedition is so that he can find the whereabouts of his friend, Mira, who became Thorkel's housekeeper. Evidently, she was used as a test subject in one of the earlier failed experiments (before Thorkel learned about the presence of the iron crystals), and didn't survive. There is more on Pedro's shrunken equine too. And Thorkel's dark irony transcends to a line where he decides Dr. Bulfinch and team may "assist" after all in his experiments, although being exposed to the miniaturizing ray isn't what they bargained for.

Most significantly, given that this is a sci-fi story, we finally learn what the devil is going on here, well, more or less. Kuttner (through Thorkel) explains, "All my energies have been devoted to the problem of atomic shrinkage—compression. Perhaps, in time, I can find the antidote, the ray that will turn men into giants. But it will take months of research and experiment—perhaps years." Then shortly, Thorkel divulges his ultimate, insidious aim. Readers must recall that by 1940, war-mongering Germany had already demonstrated its belligerency in Europe. And so, how chilling to read that Thorkel is "conducting an experiment for Germany—my fatherland. If my reduction method proves successful, we will be able to reduce our armies to miniature size. Our men will be able to steal into enemy territory, sabotage industrial centers. And no one will suspect the destruction to—men in miniature."[5]

For most of the rest of the written story, Stockton, Baker and Phillips believe that *only Thorkel* might be capable of restoring them to normal size without realizing that it might occur naturally. So they have a difficult decision to make. If they kill him, they'll be doomed to living as tiny, vulnerable people in the savage Amazonian jungle, but perhaps not for long. After all, they're nearly devoured by a lizard (not an alligator in the short story), which seems like a huge dino-monster compared to them. "Only a lizard—but to Thorkel's victims it was like a triceratops, a dinosaur out of Earth's ferocious past!" Humorously, when they seek water, Stockton remarks, "No use to boil it.... If there's any germs in the water, we can see 'em without a microscope." Eventually they begin to return to normal size, although they deduce this themselves without Thorkel's menacing banter. Mary states, "Once the compressive force of radium power is removed, we expand—slowly but elastically. The electrons swing back to their normal orbits. The energy we absorbed under the ray will be liberated in quanta."[6] Well, such science-speak doesn't hold water today and quantum mechanics wasn't as prevalent in popular culture then as it is today. Mary just meant to say they're growing larger.

As alluded to previously, another note near the back of the 1940 *Thrilling Wonder Stories* issue (pp. 125–126) indicates that Kuttner was able to attend production stages of the *Dr. Cyclops* state of the art "scientifilm" then in the making. Kuttner wrote:

> Writing a fictionization of a photoplay is not always an easy task. However, *Dr. Cyclops* held a special interest for me, for several reasons. First, I had seen it in production at the studio, and thus realized quite vividly the extremely difficult technical problems the story presented to its markers [*sic*]. Ever since the days of *The Cabinet of Dr. Caligari* and the first French surrealistic films, fantasy has held, from time to time, the attention of the movie-makers. *The Girl in the Moon, The Golem, Metropolis, Alraune,* the first European picturization of *Dracula, The Lost World,* down through *King Kong* and the amazing *Eternal Mask*—all these are sign-posts on the road. The technicians are growing more and more skilful as time goes on and their experiments progress. Certainly fantasy can be one of the most effective themes in motion pictures. For this we must thank those technicians, who create sheer magic with their deft double-exposure and special effects and shots. It is difficult to forget the first glimpse of the colossal super-plane in *Things to Come,* or the vast bulk of Kong rising from the jungle. The creation of the robot in *Metropolis* and the breathtaking vistas of the future city in the same picture, are truly powerful. And now we have *Dr. Cyclops.* Basically, the scientific theme is not new. Folk-lore tells of the Little People; Ray Cummings and others have written of dwarfed human beings. But the idea has seldom been transcribed to the screen. The technical difficulties were too tremendous. In one of the Dracula pictures [*sic; Bride of Frankenstein,* 1935], we had a glimpse of the homunculi—miniature, artificial people; but only a glimpse. Now in *Dr. Cyclops,* tiny people are seen on the screen with colossal giants. And this is a picture worth seeing. Not only for the entertainment value and interest of the film alone, but for the significance every good science-fictional "flicker" must have. *Dr. Cyclops* points the way to the movies of the future, in which the triumph of the technicians will be even more apparent. In itself, it is a dramatic and effective piece of work—and certainly everyone connected with it gave their best efforts in producing the picture. I know. I saw it made.[7]

While Kuttner rhapsodized about the advanced technical aspects of the filmmaking process in *Dr. Cyclops,* he didn't delve into the futuristic meaning and stark undertones reflected in the film, most likely because it was simply too early for anyone—even an esteemed sci-fi writer such as himself—to extrapolate fully as to how circumstances associated with radioactivity were about to completely transform world culture and geopolitical affairs.

Kuttner's story was published about 3 weeks following the film's release. But interestingly, his wasn't the only published version of the story. For another writer, Will Garth (possibly a pseudonym for writer Alexander Samalman (1904–1956), who became *Thrilling Wonder Stories'* editor in 1954), is credited with publication of a full-length novel also titled *Dr. Cyclops* (1940).[8] From online sources it seems that "Garth's" book is a novelization from the script. However, the novel is written so masterfully that one may legitimately wonder whether the script may have instead been extracted from the pre-existing novel. (It's peculiar that both Samalman's and Thorkel's first names are "Alexander.") The expertly written novel fills in many aspects of the film that would appear to have been glossed over. It answers many questions and aptly develops characters, especially the relationship between Mary "Phillips" and Bill Stockton. Bulfinch and Pedro are more courageously depicted in the novel. While the novel is more closely aligned with the movie script than Kuttner's "novelette," curiously, there are a few places where the printed dialogue is nearly identical, such as the aforementioned quotation uttered by Mary concerning those relaxing electrons and quanta. In contrast to

Kuttner's take, Garth didn't claim Thorkel's aim was to reduce Nazi armies to miniature size, however.

Several scenes in the novel more fully clarify or substantiate plot elements in the movie. For example, the matter of Bulfinch's blustering reluctance to be so rudely brushed off and peremptorily dismissed after Thorkel is satisfied with Stockton's identification of the iron crystals is more fully fleshed out in the novel. There's also more effective buildup as to evidence and clues leading to the truth about Thorkel's misdeeds. The diminutive bones of Mira the housekeeper, who disappeared and became an unfortunate test subject, are discovered along with bones of "*Dicotylinae bulfinchi*," the 4-inch-long pig, of course shrunken by Thorkel's radium ray. Pinto, Pedro's horse, who was earlier seen to be only 8 inches tall, is later spied at "colt-size" frolicking in the jungle with Paco the dog, allowing the tiny scientists to deduce that they will slowly return to normal size as effects of the ray steadily wear off. There is an added scene in which Thorkel convinces Stockton that he has a malignant, tropical contagion, which is the "real reason" why he wants the scientists to leave his premises as quickly as possible. Feeling protective of Mary, Stockton sides with Thorkel, urging everyone to leave at once. But the ruse is divulged, as the affliction turns out to be a noncontagious yet nasty radiation burn on Thorkel's forearm instead.

Disbelief-suspending dialogue in the novel, analogously expressed in a movie scene in which Thorkel explains his "contractor" device—that is, the probe descending into the mine shaft—to the overly curious scientists, is particularly effective. Here, Thorkel likens his work to that of the early experimentalists, stating of an experiment that helped to inspire Mary Shelley's *Frankenstein*, "Once Benjamin Franklin drew lightning out of the sky with a kite in an electrical storm. In my crude way I am likewise drawing cosmic force out of the bosom of the earth."[9] Yes, he did say "bosom." And, shockingly, Mary bares all, shedding her toga robe on two occasions, scenes which would not have been permitted in a 1940 film.

Later, after the well-meaning intruders are reduced to one foot tall, Thorkel's damning pride is evident, as if *he* has created a new form of life. Dr. Thorkel would seem another in the long line of demented, delusional mad scientists such as Dr. Frankenstein and Dr. Moreau, afflicted with visions of grandeur, while conducting their work in secrecy, in remote settings. That bald bastion of blasphemous biology, Dr. Thorkel (whose name begins with the first 4 letters of element thorium), has no hair—perhaps a symptom of being overexposed to green ("kryptonitic") radiation. He rather resembles Glenn Manning, the famous Colossal Man of 15 years later, who projected further angst about the human plight. Radiation from isotopes was certainly a hot topic during the late 1930s, highly woven into popular culture then.

To gain a deeper sense of how the promise, if not hopefulness of radioactivity was viewed during the turn of the 20th century as well as in the waning years of the pre-atomic bomb era, consider another period film, *Madame Curie* (1942). After the identity of radium is cleverly deduced, Pierre Curie claims exuberantly that now they can "look into the secret of life itself deeper than ever before in the history of the world." With their detection of radium rays, they have discovered a "new concept of the universe." Perhaps it is no small coincidence that actor Walter Pidgeon appears prominently both in this film (as Marie Curie's husband, Pierre Curie), as well as in the iconic role of Doctor Morbius in 1956's *Forbidden Planet*. In both films, scientists played by Pidgeon, probe mysterious powers locked within the atom and hence planets, in the latter case via probing deeply within the forbidden Altair-4—seeking to learn what led to the doom of the former Krell race (as well as Morbius himself). Atom-powered "Monsters from the Id" indeed! "*Curie*-ously," because the Curies were French national scientific heroes (although Marie Sklodowska Curie was Polish), few "visions of radioactive monsters" were concocted in French sci-fi lore and popular culture.

Certainly, through the centuries, the intriguing idea of giants has profoundly delighted human imagination. Adrienne Mayor has demonstrated that the ancient Greeks and Romans may have based their ideologies of gigantic gods and enormous mythical creatures upon the evidence of genuine fossil bones and skulls of large Cenozoic beasts, such as prehistoric elephants, found scattered throughout the Mediterranean region.[10] Although Ulysses's mythical Cyclops is one of the earliest huge humanoid monsters conceived by man, the concept of real giants in modern literature was vastly promoted through Jonathan Swift's ever popular and satirical *Gulliver's Travels* (1726), which has been adapted to film several times. Gulliver not only plays the role of a giant in the land of Lilliput, but is himself dwarfed by giants as well on his voyage to Brobdingnag. In fact, one of the most spectacular, and earliest non-cartoon movies this writer ever saw at a theater was *The 3 Worlds of Gulliver* (1960), starring Kerwin Matthews as Gulliver, featuring the stop-motion animation talents of Ray Harryhausen. Therein we see Gulliver battling a gigantic Brobdingnag crocodile to the death. This marvelously executed footage certainly recalls similar aforementioned scenes involving gator-monsters, such as witnessed in *Dr. Cyclops.*

Whenever one shrinks people to miniature sizes using rays or other strange technological devices, then in the company of normal sized humans, the miniaturized humans would seem to have encountered "giants." And of course, "giants" and giant-size creatures in the relativistic sense have appeared in so many films and programs since *Dr. Cyclops*. In particular, we've thrilled at sight of Dr. Pretorius's "homunculi" from Universal's *Bride of Frankenstein* (1935); Scott Carey's (Grant Williams) awful, progressive "Kafkaesque" (i.e., recalling *The Metamorphosis*) transformation in *The Incredible Shrinking Man* (1957), adapted from Richard Matheson's 1956 novel, *The Shrinking Man*; righteously vengeful doll-sized humans resulting from Mr. Franz's (John Hoyt's) miniaturizing invention in 1958's *Attack of the Puppet People*; and critters and characters inadvertently reduced through wild experimentation of a mad scientist played by Rick Moranis in *Honey, I Shrunk the Kids* (1989).

Usually, the giant-sized people or manifestations are regarded as "evil," while the smaller, tormented protagonists are cast as "good." This is because we have an inherent, psychological fear of uncanny hugeness, which may represent a colossal sense of something-out-of-controlness. And so, consequently we've enjoyed other films emerging in popular culture, mass entertainment such as Bert I. Gordon's *The Amazing Colossal Man* (1957), *War of the Colossal Beast* (1958), and 1957's *The Cyclops* (entirely unrelated to Dr. Thorkel), as well as *Attack of the 50 Foot Woman* (1958), *Village of the Giants* (1965) and television series *World of Giants* (1959) and Irwin Allen's late 1960s *Land of the Giants*. In the earlier cases, hugeness was associated with exposure to radiation of some nature. Even gigantic, radioactive Godzilla was played by a human actor inside a dino-monster costume. Of course, when tortured by the atom, both giants and shrunken humans alike could be sympathetically viewed as "victims."

Dr. Cyclops (novel, novelette and film) may be contrasted with Richard Matheson's outstanding 1956 novel, *The Shrinking Man,* and Universal's fantastic *The Incredible Shrinking Man* (1957).[11] A key difference between *Dr. Cyclops* vs. "Shrinking Man" is that in the former, we see the mad scientist who tampers with Nature, instigating trouble in the Amazonian jungle with repercussions for the world. In *Shrinking Man,* however, phenomena triggering Scott Carey's anguish (and later reawakening) remain largely undefined and at most suggested. While onboard a boat, Scott is exposed to a warm cloud of "glittering spray." (See Chapter 8–1.) Significantly, we never see or know exactly who created or discharged this cloud. Much later, in attempting to decipher what might have caused his body to shrink, Scott ponders with his doctors whether it might have been a toxin, an insecticide he was once exposed to, or more likely a "spray impregnated with radiation. And that was it; ... An insect spray hideously altered by radiation. A one-in-a-million chance. Just that amount of insecticide coupled with just that amount of radiation, received by his system in just that sequence and with just that timing; the radiation dissipating quickly, becoming unnoticeable. Only the poison left."[12] The substance horrifically alters his pituitary gland. Pollution mixed with radiation! Unlike the case with *Dr. Cyclops*'s Alexander Thorkel, however, Scott Carey's plaguing "monster" lacks an exact, identifying face.

Who or what is the true monster, then? *Shrinking Man* was written at a time when the world most feared radioactive dust blasted from test detonation of hydrogen bombs (as well

Fig 8-1: An early scene in 1957's *The Incredible Shrinking Man,* based on Richard Matheson's seminal 1956 novel, showing a menacing toxic cloud approaching doomed Scott Carey while at sea, not unlike the radioactive cloud of ash actually experienced by Japanese sailors three years earlier aboard *The Lucky Dragon No. 5* following a U.S. hydrogen bomb test. Man's reception to radiation had clearly altered, relative to the period when an earlier sci-fi film, *Dr. Cyclops*—also involving humans who were transformed to diminutive sizes adversely, using radiation technology—appeared in 1940, becoming unfavorable.

as the prospect of global thermonuclear annihilation). Radioactive dust clouds billowed high into the atmosphere and could descend literally anywhere, traveling on the winds of chaos. "Fallout" was a new term added to popular lexicon. Virtually anyone or everyone on the planet could be exposed to harmful radiation. As many scientists, citizens and activists then surmised, radiation threatened cancer. This is quite unlike more hopeful, promising circumstances expressed from a quarter of a century earlier (e.g., fully in *Madame Curie,* and alluded to in *Dr. Cyclops*) when beneficial aspects of radiation were sought experimentally as a *cure* to cancer. Also, scientists such as Rachel Carson were beginning to question health hazards associated with exposure to sprayed insecticides such as DDT. But by the mid–1950s, radiation remained the primary concern, and by then *those who wielded* such absolute power (e.g., "ruthless" military strategists, government scientists, evil industrialists—collectively embodying the essence of the traditional mad scientist or engineer) were more recondite. In such a world, innocent ordinary men couldn't expect to be much more than guinea pigs or "victims" of faceless power-hungry officials encumbered with doubtful states of mind. To Richard Matheson, afflicting "everyman" Scott Carey with a double-dose whammy of insecticide and radiation, an exposure for which there is no "antitoxin," was the most awful, disquieting combination of all.

Matheson's novel follows Scott's "final" week, leading to a spiritualistic Sunday, as a conventional human. He's losing $\frac{1}{7}$ of an inch per day, already reduced to an inch in height, on a mad countdown to oblivion. The story is mainly about his relationship to the "giant" spider, viewed as "immortal [as] ... every unknown terror in the world fused into a wriggling, poison-jawed horror. It was every anxiety, insecurity, and fear in his life given a hideous, night-black form."[13] So, while he's trapped of all places in a dank, scary basement, the spider is a psychological translation symbolizing those faceless, power-hungry officials who are doing unspeakable things to the planet. Meanwhile, Scott likens himself to a meaningless, Kafkaesque bug himself: "Much better if he could have concluded life as a true bug instead of being fully conscious each hideous, downward step of the way."[14] Later he realizes that to his wife, Lou, now a towering giant, he is a mere insect. What happens to Scott, and his experience of the transition, is aligned with how many cancer patients suffer. Underscoring his dreadful predicament, persevering physically and psychologically like a patient stricken with a cancer, Scott's body shrivels away while relatives become inured to the inevitable—with no hope of a cure. Yet his mind and intellect remain intact.

Another significant aspect of Scott's relentless slide concerns his descent into life as a "cave man." During the early 20th century, a spate of pre–Hiroshima "scientifiction" published stories, expressing fears of total annihilation caused by Man's ultimate warfare and invention of super weapons (including atomic, atom-splitting, radiation-emitting death rays and bombs), depicted the depressing world inherited by the few unlucky survivors. In many such stories, civilization as we know it has ended, transitioning into a precarious New Stone Age kind of existence. (A 1958 film, *Teenage Caveman,* starring Robert Vaughn, vividly captures the essence of these early 20th century sci-fi stories. Hollywood usually lags 2 to 3 decades behind literature, when it comes to science fiction and fantasy.) We saw this ideology previously reflected in *Dr. Cyclops* when the radium-zapped, diminutive test subjects—dressed as primeval people—escaped into the primitive jungle. Eventually, they wield a "giant" half-scissors and fork as "spears" to defend their "cliff-top cave" and hurl firebrands against a gigantic invading, dino-monster alligator. We see this caveman persona theme in *Shrinking Man* as well, as author Matheson describes the "cliff-like" basement stairs, Scott's shaggy beard and near-nakedness, and his inhabited "cave" dwelling. He uses a sewing pin as his "spear" to subdue the spider. Scott not only reduces in size, he also slips backward deep into time, so to speak, living "Cro-Magnon" style.

True—the contamination he was exposed to hasn't afflicted the entire human race (yet!). However, by witnessing Scott Carey's plight, we not only see how it affects one ordinary individual, but also see reflections of those early and dreadful 20th century sci-fi visions exemplifying civilization's breakdown. Eventually, as he reduces further in size approaching the wee atomic realm, Scott finally attains a state of personal salvation, living *within* the very substance (atomic realm) that triggered his anguish. For him, now there's a prospect of true existence, hope and continued intelligence. Perhaps by now he has learned the secret of the Higgs boson. And of course, whereas three of Dr. Thorkel's human victims are restored to normal size—a happy ending—there is no rational *Wizard of Oz*–ish means of "going back" for Scott Carey, who will only continue to shrink. Likewise, by the 1950s, Man as a species had already trespassed *too far* with invention of nuclear devices; there simply was no going back for humanity! Perhaps Matheson was saying, "Look, if *this* goes on and civilization crumbles to hell, we'll all end up like Scott Carey, cowering in scary basements of our minds (perhaps then metaphorical for bomb shelters), plagued by ineffable terrors, manifested with otherwise unexplainable and incurable medical afflictions."

In the classic 1957 film, the protagonist is Robert Scott Carey (played by Grant Williams) and is married to Louise (played by Randy Stuart). In the screenplay, written by Matheson himself (and Richard Alan Simmons—uncredited), things move quickly along. The meaning of the story is more subtle, say, than in *The Amazing Colossal Man*, that is as far as projecting inchoate fears and angst then gripping the world populace and nation over the hydrogen bomb scare and fears of exposure to radioactive nuclear fallout from test detonations or possibly an impending thermonuclear world war. Also photographic projection is much more enhanced and effective. Scenes showing Scott and the spider, for example, do not appear translucent or superimposed as in many other low-budget contemporary sci-fi movies.

Scott gets covered in a glittery substance deposited from a white misty cloud, as described in the novel, and things begin to unravel from there. Six months later, he notices that his clothes no longer fit properly. A doctor claims there has been a "rearrangement of molecular cells in his body ... not cancer but a diminution." This is attributed to that noxious combo of insecticide and cloud mist Scott has been exposed to—just as described in the novel. An antitoxin slows down the rate of progress for a while, but then this remission phase ceases. Basically, the essentialities of the novel are woven into the film, although the producer obviously had to skip passages in the novel concerning Scott's gnawing sexual hunger.

The house cat scene is subdued in the novel, relative to the film, in which the huge animal becomes a frightening monster played up to then state-of-the-art special effects. In the film, the cat becomes the reason for how he ends up trapped in the basement (whereas in the novel there are other factors more "at large"). The idea to "enlarge" the cat's role in the movie may have been somewhat inspired by analogous sequences involving "Satanas" as projected in *Dr. Cyclops*. The cat toys with Scott, as it would a mouse, and in fact later Scott pries a chunk of moldy cheese from a mousetrap in the basement, although with an unsuccessful outcome. Of course everyone suspects that Scott was devoured by the cat. And so that seems to conclude reporting of the "most fantastic ailment in the annals of medicine." One that someday may afflict us all.

When half-inch (or so) Scott surveys his new cellar kingdom, he regards it as a "vast primeval plane." The giant props are extremely well done and effective. Besides the mousetrap, we see a giant scissors, a drain, a pencil and even convincingly enlarged grainy texture in wooden 2" by 4" boards on the stairs. But of course the most effective "prop" is Tamara the tarantula spider, who also performed in Universal's 1955 film *Tarantula*. At first Scott considers the spider his enemy, "the most terrifying beheld by human eyes.... My enemy seemed immortal, more than a spider—it was every unknown terror in the world. Every fear fused into one night black horror." But he also learns not to feel hatred toward the spider. So he is drawn to the death struggle, the means of which contrasts considerably from how Scott dispatches the spider in the novel.

In the end, as he shrinks to a further degree, he symbolically leaves his prison, stepping through interstices of a window screen, thus entering the outdoors with an "ecstasy of elation." He wonders whether he still is a human being or a "man of the future," for surely other bursts of radiation and drifting clouds may contaminate other men who would follow him into this "vast new world." Matheson indeed wrote another screenplay wherein Louise likewise begins to shrink. The uplifting, spiritual ending, as a transcendent Scott surveys the heavens above, finding his infinitesimal self melded to the infinite, actually wasn't written by Matheson. For example, the line, "To God, there is no zero; I still exist" doesn't appear in the novel. This soliloquy was added by director Jack Arnold.

In early (e.g., 19th-century) fantastic fiction, chemists and their predecessor alchemists were the scientific group who were most often mistrusted. They were the ones always prying into the secret of life, delving into things that man should not know, dastardly interfering with Nature's course. Thus we have the early invention of the idea of the reckless "mad scientist," overweening in nature and of misguided authority, a "Faustian who trespasses ethical boundaries in order to gain forbidden knowledge and fame."[15] In her most famous novel, Mary Shelley's character Victor Frankenstein himself was a chemist utilizing dark arts, infusing a monster with the "spark of being,"[16] only to loathe and abandon his creation.

Statistics reveal that Hollywood is most prone to assimilate chemists and chemistry themes within the horror and science fiction movie genre. In fact, "a major factor in the continuing appeal of the alchemist narrative is its ability to evoke perennially convincing patterns of horror, mystery, and evil. Horror continues to fascinate us. Even though most of the examples from past centuries ... focus on graveyards and charnel houses, corpses, ghosts and monsters have ceased to frighten us, many elements of the Frankenstein narrative remain perpetually relevant as symbols of changing technology, if not that technology itself."[17]

Radioactivity was in fact at first recognized by some as a wonderfully true manifestation of the ancient alchemical dream of "transmutation," perhaps representing the beginning of civilization's new golden era. As the nuclear age dawned, however, and chemists such as Marie Curie and others inaugurated the field of radiochemistry with its dire consequences for life and civilization, that is, when wielded by the wrong hands, the scientific group then most mistrusted (at least during the mid–20th century) increasingly became those reviled nuclear physicists! (Of course, by the mid–1950s, as fears of pollution caused by industrial chemical wastes emerged, "evil-minded" chemists certainly weren't off the hook.)

Spencer R. Weart has meticulously researched the imagery of the nuclear age, concluding that throughout history the Earth has been viewed as "maternal" and that man's attempts to unlock her forbidden secrets have taken on sexual, metaphorical meaning. Thus, Dr. Thorkel's probing of the mine shaft projects rapacious undertones: "Dr. Thorkel's cylindrical ray generator rising and falling in the radium mine shaft in the 1940 horror movie had something in common with 1960s missiles in silos within the earth. The phallic significance of such devices was never a secret, least of all to military officers, who joked about 'emasculating' the enemy by destroying his missiles."[18] Even underground bomb shelters built during the 1950s and '60s Cold War scares have been symbolically likened to seeking shelter within Earth's nurturing womb. The concept of harmful "death rays" of varying nature also is a time-honored theme, not only in science fiction but psychologically long before, in cultures dating back to ancient times. He who dared wield such ominous, cosmic and potentially world-destroying forces could rightfully be viewed as a madman, or even a monster.

So by the time *Shrinking Man* left its impact, but not long after musty old men such as Henry F. Osborn pondered "orthogenesis" (see Chapter Four) as a programmed, predestined pathway leading to "naturalistic" extinction of species, "new meanings were creeping into the old idea of extinction. Up to the mid–1950s, despite dire warnings from some scientists and journalists, it had seemed no more than a theoretical possibility for some distant and hazy future. But as the number of hydrogen bombs mounted into the thousands, citizens began to suspect that the end of humanity was something that a leader like Kennedy could actually bring about, and soon."[19]

Transmutation of flesh! Total control of life! These were the ambitions of soulless Dr. Thorkel. Scott Carey's tragic case comes at an even darker time in civilization, only a few strokes closer to midnight. We cringe at a mind-paralyzing, psychological horror—the giant spider skittering along relentlessly toward us—yet then the monster's true stormy face is hidden. What countenance would be reflected, if only it would peer into the mirror? For you see, although both tales involve miniaturized people, it is easier to understand *Dr. Cyclops* when contrasted with *The Shrinking Man*. By the time of Shrinking Man's fictional calamity, mankind had surely entered into a darker, far more precarious (or a "pre–*Carey*-ous") reality, one that would reset the clockwork of evolution backward by millions of years!

Before we leave this Lilliputian province of woe, twin, twelve-inch-tall, diminutive girls, familiar to all fans of the Godzilla movie series—the "Peanuts," first appearing in 1961's *Mothra*—live on Infant Island in the Pacific, once ravaged by nuclear bomb testing. Although the other islanders appear to be of normal proportions, presumably the Peanuts' (played by Emi and Yumi Ito) lack of physical growth is a mutation caused by radioactivity. In a movie sequel, *Godzilla vs. the Thing* (1964), otherwise known as *Godzilla vs. Mothra,* a reporter played by Akira Takarada, his photographer and a scientist visit the island to plead with the island chieftain for the huge moth's facilitation in battling Godzilla, who is ravaging Japan once again (and threatening Mothra's giant egg, torn loose from the island in a typhoon). Upon arrival, looking around at the stark, visible devastation, they're ashamed for the actions of mankind, even though it wasn't the Japanese who committed such widespread ecological atrocities.

In the English version of the 1964 movie, Takarada's character (Ichiro Sakai) states, "It's so desolate it's hard to believe [the island] is inhabited." His photographer Junko Nakanishi (played by Yuriko Hoshi) replies, "And this is the result of atomic tests?" Professor Muira (Hiroshi Koizumi) adds as his Geiger counter begins clicking erratically, "Once this island was a beautiful green island. As a scientist I feel partly responsible for this." Junko says, "All of mankind is responsible," prompting Muira to proclaim, "It's like the end of the world here." Sakai concludes, providing the scene's message, "This island alone is good reason to end nuclear testing. Those who think of war should see this, eh?"

During the 1950s mankind's plight, physically altered, disfigured and mutated through radiation, became more poignant through such vehicles as *The Amazing Colossal Man,* and Toho's *H-Man* (with the capital H meaning the elemental shorthand term for "hydrogen"). While *Colossal Man* is perhaps better known to American viewers, the Japanese version of *H-Man*'s climactic scene (not involving a major alteration in bodily size, but instead a horrifically altered physical manifestation) merits consideration. The Japanese original version of this 1958 film opens with a visual of a bomb detonation, resulting in a mushroom cloud. As the story develops we learn that radioactive fallout from this blast (at Bikini Atoll) has contaminated the crew of a fishing vessel at sea, causing them to mutate into protoplasmic "melting men." In Tokyo, a persistent rain, polluted with strontium-90 and cesium-137 radioactive isotopes, permits these creatures to rove about melting other people, who are likewise then concealed from human detection in the steady pouring rain.

These blue-greenish wraiths are always seen emerging from rain water in urban scenes, looking like a translucent flowing gelatin. The film ends as a firestorm is used to supposedly eradicate the wraiths in a sewer system, while this prophetic statement is offered: "H-man is gone.... But we cannot guarantee there will never be another H-man again.... If this Earth were covered in radioactive fallout ... and humanity faced extinction ... the next species to rule the Earth could very well be the H-man." But rain also cleanses the Earth in another period film set in a post-apocalyptical time, *The Day the World Ended* (1956). Three-eyed monsters, mutated from normal people exposed to radiation, cannot live in the radiation-free rain, and so perish when exposed to gentle (uncontaminated) rain. In this American tale, rain is optimistically viewed as purifying, while in Toho's film, rain is devastatingly, pessimistically contaminated.

The occurrence of rain in a post-apocalyptical setting carries some additional significance, for in an American short story, Ray Bradbury's 1950 somber tale, "There Will Come Soft Rains," later added to his classic collection titled *The Martian Chronicles* (1950), Bradbury paints the final hours of a house situated on a typical suburban street.[20] There are no living people, only silhouettes of several family members eerily seared into the outside walls, incinerated (like those humans whose shadows were imprinted in pavement at Hiroshima) when the nuclear bombs ignited the city. This happens to be a "smart" computer-controlled house, programmed to go about all its daily functions in the year 2026 ... even in the absence of people, or after man. However, when a fire inadvertently starts, the house burns. There is no actual rainfall occurring in the story, other than alluded to in the title, which is a line from a 1920 poem by Sara Teasdale (1884–1933), published on the horrific heels of World War I. One line in this poem—Bradbury borrowed the complete short poem, inserted within his short story—remarks how if mankind were to perish "utterly" that no one, not even the singing birds, would mind. Neither would anyone know of, nor care about the war that spelled doom for so many. For, as Teasdale suggests, when soft spring rains eventually come, our kind would not be missed ... forgotten. Bradbury often wrote about the horror of oppressing rain, as in another 1950 tale, "The Long Rain." (And let us not forget that in *Shrinking Man,* a shower of water cascading from the broken hot water heater nearly washes Scott Carey into the sewer drain.)

Fig 8-2: A detail showing the disease-carrying dino-monster, Rhedosaurus, unleashed by a hydrogen bomb test conducted in the Arctic region, from Ray Harryhausen's 1953 movie, *The Beast from 20,000 Fathoms.*

With news of the anticipated fusion bomb on the airwaves, stirring dark thoughts in public consciousness, Bradbury's 1951 short story, "The Beast from 20,000 Fathoms" (later renamed "The Fog Horn") was extrapolated into a foreboding film, 1953's *The Beast from 20,000 Fathoms* (Warner Bros.), directed by Eugene Lourie, featuring Ray Harryhausen's amazing stop-motion special effects of a gigantic quadrupedal dinosaurian named Rhedosaurus.[21] (See Figure 8-2.)

This movie begins with a nuclear bomb test named "Operation Experiment" conducted in an icy Arctic region. For all practical purposes the drama and intrigue surrounding the buildup toward the fictional test could even be tantamount to that of a pending "super" or hydrogen bomb blast observation. There is an air of utter desperation within the control room. Paul Christian's character, nuclear physicist Dr. Nesbitt, states, "When energy of that magnitude is released it's never over ... what the cumulative effects of all these explosions and atomic tests will be, only time can tell." His colleague, Prof. George Ritchie (played by Ross Elliott) replies, "You know, every time one of these things goes off, I feel like we're helping to write the first chapter of a new Genesis." Nesbitt remarks prophetically, "Let's hope we don't find ourselves writing the last chapter of the old one." It's obvious both men are scared.

Rhedosaurus, unleashed from the ice, emerging from Operation Experiment's enveloping mushroom cloud, thus became allegorical for the new, more powerful bombs being tested then in the American west and the Pacific islands. To a limited extent, its rampage through New York City anticipates what *might* happen to man if the mad scientist metaphorical roller coaster ride doesn't stop, before things go too far, taking us over the brink. But soon, genuine unfortunate events transpiring in stark reality would spawn an even more frightening, gigantic monster—merely a costume worn by a human actor, yet which when projected onto film appeared proportionally as large as mad Dr. Cyclops with respect to his miniaturized specimens as an ordinary human being would be in relation to the filmic, allegorical super pseudo-saurian.[22]

How did this groundbreaking, powerhouse creation, a prophetic symbol of the nuclear age, come to be? Before turning to the true story of Godzilla's distinctively dinosaurian origin, let's delve into what happened at sea back in the spring of 1954.

Chapter Nine

Nuclear Dragon

Godzilla and the Cold War—1954

"It is still an unending source of surprise for me to see how a few scribbles on a blackboard or on a sheet of paper could change the course of human affairs."—Physicist Stanlislaw Ulam, quoted in Richard Rhodes's *The Making of the Atomic Bomb,* 1986[1]

"But for the accident of the *Lucky Dragon* the world might still be in the dark about the nature of this revolutionary new weapon and its meaning for all men."—Nuclear physicist Richard E. Lapp, *The Voyage of the Lucky Dragon,* 1958[2]

Yes, perhaps circumstances leading to *Gojira* were indeed ... *inevitable.*[3]

Ever notice that daikaiju films and their dino-monsters (here including Ray Harryhausen's Rhedosaurus) proliferated after invention of the hydrogen bomb (or "H-Bomb"), more so than following the atomic bomb's wartime demonstration? Ever notice that while the Godzilla movie series and many other sci-fi films are adjoined to psychological fears concerning radiation and nuclear blasts, that it is the H-Bomb which mostly inspired them, shifting the world's perspective on the likelihood for our long-term survival?

Events unfolding during the late winter of 1954, when the U.S. Atomic Energy Commission's Operation Castle detonated one of its hydrogen bombs at the Bikini Atoll, in a test known as "Bravo" conducted 2,500 miles southwest of Honolulu, were destined to become influential upon contemporary film makers. The film *Gojira* clearly borrows elements from the plight of a very real Japanese fishing trawler, the 93-foot-long *Fukuryu Maru,* or in its English translation, the *Lucky Dragon No. 5,* and its unfortunate crew, underscoring hazards posed by radiation and nuclear fallout exposures, thus wagging a finger to the (obvious) perpetrators (without directly placing blame). Oddly enough, physicist Richard E. Lapp notes that the ship would have been named the *Lucky Dragon No. 4,* yet because the Japanese word for "No. 4" is pronounced like their word for death, the ship builders skipped to "No. 5."

The *Lucky Dragon* incident became a focal point, publicly testifying how nuclear bomb fallout was indeed very dangerous, and in fact would kill. Radioactive debris was strewn over 7,000 square miles of the Pacific, enveloping the deck of the *Lucky Dragon,* then trawling for tuna 75 miles east of Bikini (i.e., 87 nautical miles from the atoll center) at blast time. And while most of us obeisantly and reverently acknowledge how this remorselessly unlucky chain of events represents another significant American stepping stone (besides predecessor filmic influences *King Kong* and *The Beast from 20,000 Fathoms*) leading toward Godzilla's origin, few really understand what happened there on March 1, 1954, the circumstances, or why.

Other contemporary science fiction films invoke elements of the *Lucky Dragon* story as well. Consider the mysterious glittering spray that character Scott Carey experiences while on board a boat at sea in *The Incredible Shrinking Man* (1957), triggering his incessant diminutization to oblivion. In Toho's *H-Man* (1959), seamen from a fishing vessel board another ship drifting at sea, recently exposed to hydrogen bomb test fallout, only to discover that one member of its crew has mutated into pulsing radioactive gelatin. Then in Toho's *Matango* (1963), starving vacationers shipwrecked on a mysterious island eat indigenous mushrooms, transforming into "mushroom people." Mushrooms of course trigger thoughts of the proverbial "mushroom cloud." What's this all about? Doomed vessels at sea, tranquil Pacific isles suddenly subjected to earth-shattering events, harmful exposures to mysterious substances with resulting tragedy cloaked in governmental secrecy ... hallmarks of a real historical episode that shook the world!

As Ed Godziszewski suggested in 2004, "Strangely enough, [*Gojira*] may never have come into being if not for a strange confluence of events in the arena of international politics."[4] His first reason, the subject of this essay, happens to be testing of a hydrogen bomb—known to the U.S. military as "Bravo," fitted with a core lithium-deuteride test device known as "Shrimp," detonated at the Bikini Atoll. The Hiroshima atomic bomb was a mere puffball by comparison. Belying its nickname, Shrimp spawned something quite huge!

Gojira's opening scene reflects contemporary political angst, as we see a doomed fishing vessel, no doubt standing in for the *Lucky Dragon*. By May 12, 1954, Japanese science fiction and mystery writer Shigeru Kayama began developing a story treatment for the movie, completed in just 11 days. His intention was clear, for, following a prologue concerning a hydrogen bomb explosion in March 1954 using a new, more powerful experimental type, he wrote somberly (as translated by Mr. Godziszewski): "Early one evening in the Japan Sea, shortly after sunset a ship sails through a thick fog. Suddenly, a giant shape rises from the sea and there is an intense flash of light—the mysterious form emits a glowing ray which destroys the unsuspecting ship. Shortly thereafter, a second ship drifts into the same fog bank and also meets the same untimely fate. A lone survivor of the second ship manages to escape death...."[5]

As noted by Steve Ryfle, "The opening scene of *Gojira* must have been particularly chilling for Japanese moviegoers in 1954.... Godzilla was born in the mushroom clouds of World War II but the tragedy of *The Lucky Dragon*, an incident now reduced to a footnote in most history books if it is included at all, stirred his anger."[6]

We're so poignantly familiar with these scenes as filmed, evoking real historical terror associated with America's bomb. Small Japanese vessel at sea. Sailors setting to their tasks, methodically. Suddenly, something unknown but hideous attracts their attention toward the horizon, as they're exposed to a brilliant light. The ship is enveloped in an undersea conflagration. Shortly after, another vessel is similarly engulfed in a mysterious wall of flame; the wreckage is dispatched to the sea depths. What is the cause of such wanton destruction? Could it be, metaphorically ... the United States? Well, are you surprised? Yes, Godzilla's "ray" is Bikini's nuclear flame incarnate.

One might legitimately claim that Japan was subjected to not two, but *three* nuclear attacks during the mid–20th century. The first two atomic bomb strikes in Hiroshima and Nagasaki resulted in a rapid end to World War II's Pacific Theater (in August 1945). And although exploded during a time of peace between our nations, the third, inadvertent "attack" in March 1954, in a sense, is remembered as the first publicized instance of a hydrogen (fusion) bomb or "H-Bomb" detonation documented to have resulted in a relatively immediate human casualty—due to exposure to fallout radiation. As most science fiction fans are aware, this last (and hopefully final such) episode led to the fantastic Godzilla movie franchise. Despite how unsettling the *Lucky Dragon No. 5* incident became, matters during the height of the Cold War could have been far, far worse!

The hydrogen fusion bomb, the "super" or, more familiarly, the "H-Bomb," changed everything. As physicist J. Robert Oppenheimer (1904–1967), "father of the *atomic* [i.e., fission] bomb," disturbingly stated: "It is a profound and necessary truth that the deep things in science are not found because they are useful; they are found because it was possible to find them."[7] Atomic bomb weaponry had proven frightful indeed. Each single detonation unleashing raw atomic power was capable of annihilating entire metropolises and, regionally, killing hundreds of thousands—perhaps millions—in one devastating blow. Understandably, Americans found imagery of the atomic bomb, such as published photos of Hiroshima and artist Chesley Bonestell's paintings showing fictional World War III atomic bombings of New York City for 1948 and 1950 issues of *Collier's* magazine, extremely unsettling. After all, for both of the last two world wars, the vast majority of the fighting and destruction had taken place not on the North American continent, but "over there."

Atomic bombs carried the overall destructiveness of several city fire-bombings conducted by the U.S. Air Force during World War II, both in Germany and Japan, but with added radiation. True—the notion of an atomic bomb was awful enough for mankind's psyche. But the vastly more powerful "H-Bombs," if wielded in an all-out war, threatened Man's very existence with plausible extinction. As Spencer R. Weart remarked, "It turned out that a hydrogen bomb could kill people not only nearby, but hundreds of miles away. This fact opened the way for a dismaying idea that had long been buried within nuclear imagery to come into the open: the idea that releasing nuclear energy was a blasphemous violation of the entire planet."[8]

People, in their disquietude, were now realizing that scientists had invented explosive devices of unprecedented, horrific potentiality, which when triggered could affect parts of the planet and its ecosystems even far distant from where they were deployed. Had we really gone too far this time, creating reality out of seemingly science fictional affairs, delving into a forbidden realm where only God should reign?

I was born in the year of the *Lucky Dragon* incident, the year of *Gojira*. Eventually, by the early 1960s, scientists had devised H-Bombs that *incredibly* were 4 times more powerful than H-bombs tested at the Bikini Atoll (which resulted in 1954's *Lucky Dragon* incident). This must have been an angst-filled period for almost anyone who even casually regarded global affairs then, especially our menacing relationship with the Soviet Union and, later, Red China; during my youth both countries were developing imposing nuclear arsenals. And as we'll shortly see, we (i.e., then, the "establishment" of "civilized" American people), given just cause, were prepared to launch nuclear Armageddon, flirting with the possibility of nearly triggering our extinction (or at least killing billions) on several rare occasions, such as during the Cuban Missile Crisis in October 1962.

Meanwhile, within our borders, American citizens were being continually exposed to radioactive fallout from nuclear test explosions of varying magnitude, which after spreading westward through the stratosphere became deposited over North America ... and elsewhere. But also, on a daily basis we confronted scores of sci-fi films and television shows and pulp novels and stories, reflecting and highlighting our deepest, ineffable nuclear fears. What might be the aftermath of such a nuclear holocaust? Writers of fantastic fiction and movie producers offered dire impressions, but at that time, when I was a young naïve person, what was most instilled in me were reflections symbolically conveyed through *Planet of the Apes* (1968), in which Charlton Heston's character Taylor recognizes the Statue of Liberty buried in the sand. This startling climax mirrored circumstances I had read in an English class, in a post-apocalyptical short story, "By the Waters of Babylon," written much earlier by Stephen Vincent Benet. And of course among many other fine examples of such fare, there was Eugene Burdick's and Harvey Wheeler's gripping novel *Fail-Safe*, produced as a movie starring Henry Fonda. During October 1962, *Fail-Safe* was serialized in the *Saturday Evening Post* just as John F. Kennedy and Nikita Khrushchev were cautiously seeking means of averting thermonuclear war. (See Figure 9-1.)

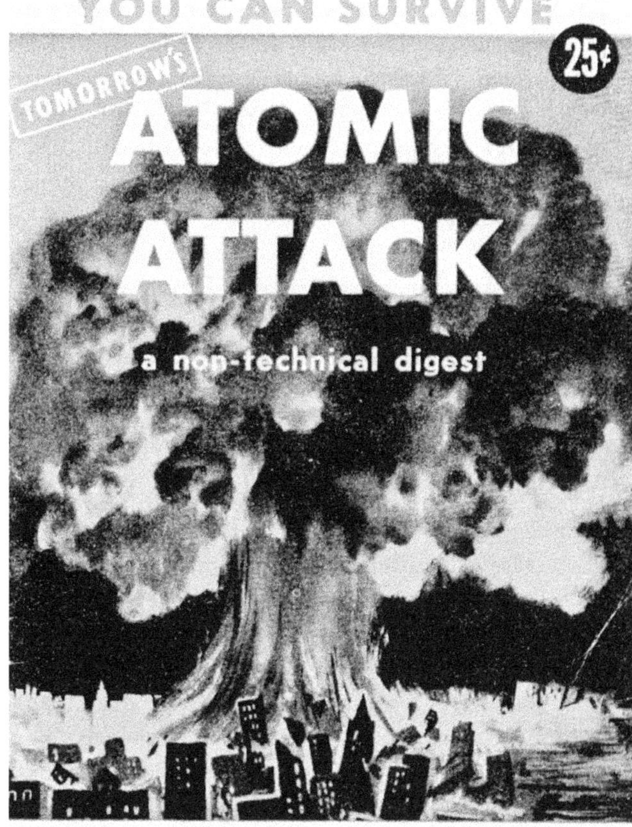

Fig 9-1: During the 1950s, Americans were provided with a sense of false hope as to how many of us would be able to "most likely" survive nuclear attacks in the event of thermonuclear warfare. The indirect consequences of hydrogen bomb testing in the Pacific, such as divulged via the *Lucky Dragon* incident, belied such a possibility.

But a decade earlier, why was there a *Lucky Dragon* incident, and how did this publicized affair pertain to geopolitical circumstances of the time? Here, I shall briefly attempt to put this seminal aspect of *Gojira*'s real, horrific origin within historical context.

U.S. military leadership believed that atomic bombs were conceivably useful not only in war, but as a "deterrent" to prevent future conflict, and indeed intrinsic fear of them had just resulted in Japan's quick surrender. However, when the Soviet Union successfully tested its first atomic fission warhead in 1949, top U.S. military brass sought something far more powerful, to regain advantage in the arms race. U.S. experts now debated whether a "super" fusion bomb, whose theoretical explosive capacities had been understood since May 1941, should be developed too. Today, physicists Edward Teller (1908–2003) and Stanislaw Ulam (1909–1984) are considered chief inventors of America's fusion or H-bomb.

However, fusion bombs, given their unlimited theoretical capacity for destruction, were quickly viewed by several prominent physicists and special committee members as evil, Frankensteinian. Notably, however, Teller insisted on their necessity. So President Harry Truman green-lighted the highly complex, controversial engineering project in January 1950—six months before the Korean War broke out—citing that such a super-weapon was needed for "bargaining purposes with the Russians.... It'll be like poison gas (never used again)."[9] Various insidious poison gas formulae had of course killed many thousands of troops during World War I.

Yes—a deterrent to gain both technological as well as psychological advantage over our political arch-nemesis, the Soviet Union! Or perhaps a devastating, humbling, preemptive first strike, offering no chance for counterattack? The prospective need for such overwhelming, superior force was underscored during the height of the Korean War, when American officials were certainly *tempted* to use atomic bombs against North Korean, Chinese and even possibly Soviet armies. Were it not for measured restraint, this would have resulted in the Asian theater's *second* atomic-bombing (with Japan being the first in 1945), which under the complex, intense political circumstances reigning then might have catalyzed global nuclear conflagration.

Meanwhile, Teller calculated that there is no limit to the fusion bomb's destructiveness. After all, the Sun itself is a self-sustaining gigantic thermonuclear gas "bomb," that will sustain for billions of years beyond its already 4.5-billion-year history, only shining more brightly in time. However, the obsessed Teller speculated that with an explosion of 100 megatons (100 million tons of TNT equivalent), or approximately 10,000 times as energetic as the Hiroshima A-bomb, "it would simply lift a chunk of atmosphere—ten miles in diameter, something of that kind—lift it into space. Then you could make it a thousand times bigger still.... You lift the same chunk into space with thirty times the velocity."[10] By 1984, the most explosive H-Bomb tested, a Soviet device, packed a 60-megaton wallop, or akin to approximately 4,000 Hiroshima bombs!

The U.S. surmounted many difficult engineering hurdles before they could properly simulate and model, let alone actually construct their first H-bomb. For one thing, a super digital computer had to be invented (by mathematics genius John von Neumann) that was capable of calculating how elemental components (liquid deuterium, plutonium, etc., with radiation field compression) would combust as a plasma in a fusion reaction, given the bomb chamber's configurations and features. The first H-bomb was ignited by an atomic bomb fission explosion, thus relying on a sophisticated system for triggering the vastly more potent fusion chain reaction. Sort of like first striking a match to ignite the lighter fluid in a grill.

The first highly monitored American H-bomb test, tagged "Mike," took place at the Pacific Eniwetok Atoll on November 1, 1952, yielding 10.4 megatons of energy, or the equivalent of nearly 1,000 Hiroshima atomic bombs and with a neutron density "10-million times greater than a supernova."[11] The thermonuclear detonation left a one-mile-wide, 200-foot deep crater imprinted in the lagoon, laced with highly radioactive mud. The mushroom cloud canopy ascended to 100,000 feet before spreading outward. Most people didn't realize it at that moment, but world history had just shifted irrevocably toward a highly uncertain future. This should have been that moment when Klaatu and Gort arrived in their flying saucer with a climactic warning. But no such imposing force stopped us.

Yet soon the balance of power would be restored by the Soviets. For no sooner did Americans believe they were safe once more (meaning ahead in the arms race and with respect to national security), than the Soviets followed suit with their first H-bomb test, nicknamed "Joe 4," on August 12, 1953, a much smaller 400-kiloton yield (0.4 megatons), or roughly equivalent to "only" 31 Hiroshima A-bombs. Whereas the USA's "Mike" shot surprised the Soviets, "Joe 4" frightened U.S. military officials even more because it was now clear that the "United States has no monopoly in the production of the hydrogen bomb either."[12] The Soviets were clearly much farther advanced in their bomb-making, developmental capabilities, belying U.S. intelligence. Yet their rapid pace turned out to be the result of, and benefiting from, espionage. That is, in pseudo-James Bond-ish fashion, spies had been stealing American and British bomb-making secrets for over a decade, transmitting numerous classified documents to a crack Soviet scientific and engineering weapons-building team. The spy ring's achievements greatly aided Soviet scientists who were ordered by the Kremlin to first develop an atomic bomb (successfully tested in 1949) ... and now this! Too late to turn back.

An installation constructed at Chelyabinsk served as the Soviet laboratory research center, bomb-making facility and eventually the site of their first test nuclear chain reactor (in December 1946). (In case that city name sounds vaguely familiar, this is the region where a 60-foot-wide meteor blasted its way through the atmosphere on February 15, 2013. The meteor's main fireball upper atmospheric detonation packed a 90-kiloton punch, or about the equivalent of 6 to 8 Hiroshima A-bombs.) Russia's first (1953) H-bomb explosion, "Joe-4," was demonstrated in southeast Kazakhstan, near the Chinese border.

By September 1954 (as divulged to the U.S. in 1991), while preparing for nuclear warfare, the Soviets tested a Hiroshima-sized atomic atmospheric test over a 45,000 man army (with thousands of nearby civilians), used as guinea pigs to determine how efficiently troops exposed to blast debris and fallout radiation could perform routine maneuvers. Later, the USSR's *Sputnik* orbital satellite was launched in 1957, thus gaining a militaristic, outer-space edge over us—literally—that for a time must have seemed insurmountable. The Cold War, persisting until 1989, was in full swing.

And so with this backdrop, America's "Castle" H-bomb test series—8 tests in all—began on March 1, 1954, at the Bikini Atoll (ending on May 12). If Eniwetok represented a foreboding reality to author J.G. Ballard's "terminal beach," then indeed, to many, Bikini represented a veritable beginning of the end.

In the first test, coded "Bravo," a 23,500-pound "Shrimp" lithium-deuteride device was detonated. The lithium was 40 percent enriched in lithium 6 and 60 percent lithium 7. It was designed to release "only" 5 megatons, but something went haywire. Evidently, for the Castle series, scientists hadn't worked all the bugs out of the nuclear engineering details yet. For Shrimp yielded a record-setting 15 megatons, or approximately 1,000 times more powerful than the Hiroshima bomb—more powerful than the combined weapons of war fired throughout history! This over-efficiency resulted from miscalculating an isotopic nuclear "cross section," misjudged by the designers who didn't predict that two—rather than one—neutrons would be emitted upon fusion of the lithium 7, thus significantly accelerating and intensifying the chain reaction.[13]

Castle Bravo (i.e., Shrimp's) fireball swelled to 4 miles in diameter. Thirty miles away, much closer than the *Lucky Dragon*'s position then, physicist Marshall Rosenbluth observed from his U.S. navy vessel, "[W]e had this horrible white stuff raining out on us. I got 10 rads of radiation from it [i.e., about the equivalent of 10 chest x-rays].... It was pretty frightening. There was a huge fireball with these turbulent rolls going in and out. The thing was glowing.

It looked to me like a diseased brain up in the sky. It spread until the edge of it looked as if it was almost directly overhead. It was a much more awesome sight than a puny little atomic bomb."[14] Rosenbluth's "horrible white stuff" was calcium rock powder pulverized from atoll coral to which minute grains of highly radioactive isotopes had affixed. This time the H-bomb gouged a crater 250 feet deep and 6,500 feet in diameter—over a mile wide.

Enter Godzilla lore. On March 1, against darkness in the calm, serene predawn, at 6:45 a.m., crewman Shinzo Suzuki aboard *Lucky Dragon No. 5* was astonished to see the sun rising in the west along the horizon! A "great flare of whitish, yellow light ... changed to a yellow red and then to a flaming orange red."[15] As Lapp recorded from interviews, five (or more likely, according to the captain, six to seven) minutes thereafter there came a "great sound wave," and two concussions "like rifle shots." Oishi Matashichi recalls, "The rumbling sound engulfed the sea, came up from the ocean floor like an earthquake."[16] From these observations, 39-year-old Aikichi Kuboyama, the ship's radioman—long remembered as a kind, intelligent soul who had keen interest in scientific matters—estimated that the explosion had taken place approximately 87 miles away. Although Lapp states in his book that, according to crew members he interviewed, a mushroom cloud was not discernible at such a great distance, immediately there was concern that the crew had witnessed a "pikadon," or an atomic blast.[17] Well—not quite, although much worse. Shortly, a "snowstorm" of white ash began swirling over the deck of the *Lucky Dragon*. Kuboyama doubted they had seen a volcanic eruption.

Within 24 hours, the crew began feeling sick, consumed with symptoms of what was later diagnosed as whole-body radiation sickness. Hair fell out in clumps and their skin appeared deeply scorched or sunburned. Now the crew was driven by a fear that if they were spotted at sea they would be detained by the Americans for questioning.[18] Another Japanese vessel sailing in the Marshall Islands region had indeed mysteriously disappeared in 1952. Worried about atom exposures, the vessel returned to port at Yaizu after 51 days at sea—following two weeks of added, continual exposure to radioactive ash deposited onto the *Lucky Dragon*. Exposed to radioactive ash filtering down from the sky, the seamen rapidly developed acute signs of radiation sickness: nausea, dark sores appearing on their neck and fingers. The boat returned to a Japanese port 2 weeks later on March 14.

Twenty-three crewmen on board *Lucky Dragon No. 5* unfortunately had been exposed to the radioactive fallout, as well as islanders on the nearby Marshall islands, especially on inhabited Rongelap Atoll, 75 miles from Bikini, as well as Rongerik and Utirik Atolls. In 2004, a Marshall island elder recalled how on the morning of March 1, 1954, "the sound that came afterward was just enormous. The earth trembled with a boom ... trees around him shaking.... Later lots of white powder fell to the ground and piled up an inch deep."[19] Within 3 days following the 15-megaton test, Rongelap islanders were evacuated to nearby Kwajalein. Then in 1957, the U.S. declared that Rongelap was sufficiently safe for the islanders to return, yet it wasn't—as medical issues persisted. So another emergency evacuation ensued in 1985; by 1996 the U.S. paid for a costly cleanup of Atoll surface debris, which the islanders were forced to perform themselves.

Only *afterward*, on March 2, 1954, did Admiral Lewis Strauss, head of the United States' Atomic Energy Commission (AEC), issue an official statement concerning its bomb test. There was no official prior warning. Although straying close, the Japanese had deliberately avoided a prior designated danger area around Eniwetok, an atoll 300 miles to the west where, before March 1954, nuclear testing had been most recently conducted. (Bikini Atoll, whose inhabitants had been relocated prior to any testing, hadn't been utilized for nuclear-atomic testing since 1946.)

The *Lucky Dragon* incident transpired during a shift in public attitude in general toward nuclear bombs. You see, fallout from bombs had become a regular occurrence in Nevada during 1953; concerned citizens began questioning the associated risks of exposure to dust churned up and spread by mushroom clouds. According to Spencer R. Weart, there was so much fallout that "Songwriter Tom Lehrer suggested that visitors to the Wild West should bring along lead underwear."[20] But the Atomic Energy Commission wasn't duly informing the public how to protect from fallout. In fact, they insidiously insisted there wasn't any real danger to "downwinders," as Walter Cronkite even echoed during a 1953 broadcast. Don't worry, Cronkite trustingly assured, referring to televised footage of a mushroom cloud swelling from an atmospheric test blast in the desert, "It's not dangerous."[21] In Japan, however, radiation sickness resulting from fallout ("ashes of death" or " shi no hai") was a new phenomenon. Even Hiroshima victims hadn't been exposed to fallout such as the *Lucky Dragon* crew had been exposed because the Hiroshima event was an air burst; there, debris didn't fall from the sky. (Shrimp had been detonated close to the ground surface atop a 50-foot tower, not dropped from a high-altitude plane. So it churned up considerable debris, generating vast volumes of propelling steam.) As opposed to the Hiroshima victims, *Lucky Dragon No. 5*'s crew had become afflicted with radiation *within* their bodies caused by ingestion of radioactive particles—an acute form of *whole-body* radiation sickness.

The *Lucky Dragon* story broke into the press by March 16, but by then crewmen had already been admitted to hospitals for treatment of their atomic affliction, which was at first rather mystifying because symptoms differed in certain, significant respects from ailments suffered by survivors of the Hiroshima A-bomb. A March 16, 1954, headline appearing in the *Yomiuru* newspaper read, "Japanese Fishermen Encountered Atomic Bomb Test at Bikini; 23 men suffering from atomic disease; one diagnosed serious by Tokyo University Hospital; H-Bomb?"[22] Yes, an "H-Bomb." When scientists visited the boat searching for samples, a Geiger counter they carried for the investigation startlingly began clicking *100 feet distant from the boat*!

Kuboyama suffered considerably, then died 6 months afterward on September 23, 1954. To the press, he pleaded that governments would ensure that he would be the "last victim" of the nuclear bomb.[23] His widow received a check for approximately $2,500 from the U.S. government. And we cringe when we learn that Edward Teller (intrepid H-bomb inventor) later stated, "It's unreasonable to make such a big deal over the death of a fisherman."[24] Each of the 22 surviving crew members received $5,500 in compensation out of the $2 million awarded to the Japanese fisheries on "ex gratia" basis—meaning that the U.S. assumed no responsibility for the incident and resulting damages. (By 1997 ten additional crew members died from latent liver illnesses apparently related to H-bomb exposures, similar to that suffered by Kuboyama.)

Men aboard other Japanese vessels were also exposed to the deadly ash, but Kuboyama's publicized death evoked a firestorm of public outcry over America's "ashes of death." As the U.S. Castle series testing proceeded with seven additional H-bomb tests, white radioactive ash began falling out over Japan in April 1954; rain and snow were found to be highly contaminated. Rain falling over Osaka on May 17 registered 24,000 counts per minute! Then, "Almost overnight, the Japanese revived a buried interest in their own nuclear victims. For the first time in nearly a decade, the condition of the survivors of Hiroshima became a national preoccupation. The protests quickly became international. . . ."[25] And there was a cover-up—of sorts, not only here but evidently as well in Japan.

First of all, it seems that the Japanese government had political incentive then in "kow-towing" to or politically placating the U.S. government, thus accepting an inferior settlement for damages caused by the H-bomb. By quickly concluding a deal in January 1955 via monetary compensation, pro-communist antagonism and international condemnation directed toward the U.S. government might be quelled, permitting prolonged American presence in Japan. Many Japanese individuals at the time believed that the compensation package was unacceptable because citizens' human rights had been ignored.[26] Little wonder then, perhaps, that Godzilla is seen as "defiantly" smashing through the Diet Building in *Gojira*.

Although Kuboyama's organs revealed radiation poisoning as the cause of death, American officials claimed instead that he'd died from hepatitis, caused by frequent blood transfusions. It is true that he died from "secondary causes of infection," albeit triggered by radiation exposure. But liver disorder may have been resultant of over-exposure to radioactive ash. The U.S. did at least offer medical radiation specialists to aid the sickened sailors.

Amidst the prevailing murky, shady domain of espionage, diplomatic secrecy became the new byword as authorities attempted to mitigate the international outcome. American statesmen, including Admiral Lewis Strauss, suggested crewmen aboard the *Lucky Dragon* incongruously belonged to a "Red spy outfit" that was "well within the danger area." Meanwhile, American propagandists billed the new weapon as a "humanitarian bomb ... clean."[27] While in such an instance it may have been difficult to anticipate safe vs. dangerous areas, their nautical position at the time of the explosion was documented and obviously they were "endangered."[28] However, there were some discrepancies as to the exact nautical position in ship logbooks, which have since gone missing. So, for example, if it took only approximately 6 minutes for the blast sound to reach the *Lucky Dragon No. 5*, then they may have been just within a designated danger zone; but they were outside the zone if it took as long as 7 minutes.[29] Strauss, whose official statement about the test came only after it was conducted, also denied that the Bravo Shrimp test was ever out of control. Yet, ever cautiously (if not suspiciously), on March 19, the U.S. expanded the restricted zone around Bikini Atoll by a factor of 8 times. Philosophically, in such an instance, how is "danger zone" truly defined? It certainly must extend beyond the range needed to prevent immediate human exposure, as "unfavorable winds" wafted and oceanic currents drifted contaminants widely across the Pacific, irradiating numerous life forms, including the tuna *Lucky Dragon No. 5* had set out to catch.

A primary reason for the United States' disavowal of responsibility, for concealing facts concerning this particular H-bomb explosion, including fallout content—information that might have facilitated medical treatment of the afflicted at an earlier time during their convalescence—pertained to America's objective to prevent the Soviets from learning that the Shrimp bomb had been designed using lithium-deuteride (then a technological breakthrough in H-bomb manufacture). So it was left to Japanese scientists to determine the true nature of the afflicting radioactivity. As Dr. Mituo Taketani of St. Paul University of Tokyo was able to deduce by May 1954, uranium-237 was a telltale, unnatural byproduct of a particular design for a triple-staged, fission trigger-fusion-fission H-bomb.[30] Left to their own tech-savvy and intuition to identify isotopes in samples collected from the *Lucky Dragon*, however, Japanese scientists were able to accurately reconstruct how Bravo's H-bomb was formulated with its particular components and A-bomb trigger. At the time, Soviet radiochemical detection of these substances would have yielded a significant arms race edge. The Japanese also discovered the presence of strontium-90, a deadly radioisotope with a half-life of 28 years, which can graft itself into human and fish bone. From half-life data they were able to back-calculate how much radiation the *Lucky Dragon* crew had been initially exposed to before radioactive decay, eventually publishing their findings. Soon, everyone who cared to know about H-bomb design could simply consult the literature.

Moreover, in time radioactive isotopes became biomagnified up the food chain (a phenomenon later seized upon by the producers of 1959's giant dino-monster film, *The Giant Behemoth*). Using sensitive Geiger counters and detection methods, Japanese scientists were able to trace the origin of the tainted tuna to U.S. nuclear testing "for thousands of miles through the wandering currents of the Pacific."[31] Affected fish causing Geiger counters to click rapidly came to be known as "weeping fish." When it was later determined that tuna reaching Japanese markets were radioactive, as William Tsutsui stated: "Millions of Japanese (including the emperor) refused to eat fish, the tabloids proclaimed the incident yet another U.S. atomic attack on Japan, and strident antinuclear peace movements sprouted around the country. That *Gojira* emerged from this environment suggests not only the canny opportunism (or, as some at the time complained, bald cynicism) of its creators, but also the extent to which the film and its message engaged with the most profound, contentious, and chilling issues of the day."[32] To the Japanese, carp represent stamina and perseverance. Now think of Serizawa's symbolic fish tank in *Gojira* and the fish exposed to his "oxygen destroyer."

It was as if a bubonic plague had broken out. To our chagrin, the U.S. was covertly, yet obstinately unwilling to divulge details to Japanese biophysicists, chemists or physicians concerning the nature of radioactivity contaminating the fish. Admiral Strauss flatly denied that U.S. tests had contaminated any fish. Attitudes toward the U.S. swiftly turned negative. When U.S. Ambassador John M. Allison sounded skeptical and unsympathetic as to the Japanese plight, Professor Mituo Taketani of Tokyo's St. Paul University quipped, "Let's send the highly contaminated fish to Mr. Allison and have him eat it."[33] A total of 683 tuna boats were affected by the radiation, carrying tuna exceeding a designated "safe level" of radiation, which had to be discarded. Decades later the Japanese erected a "Tuna Memorial" to the 914,000 pounds of contaminated tuna that were dumped. The intended message was: "Don't contaminate the all-important ocean with radiation."[34]

The deeply wounding cultural aspect of this circumstance would be as if Americans could not eat any beef due to radioactive contamination. Imagine that—no McDonald's or Burger King hamburgers at your lunch table! The *Lucky Dragon* incident not only fostered the allegorical *Gojira*; it shockingly demonstrated in plain public view how a single human act—a bomb test—could have an adverse impact on the environment not just locally, but widespread over the planet. And who or what nation dared claim it had any right to contaminate international waters across thousands of square miles? Or an entire oceanic ecosystem?

Throughout the stormy political period leading up to the H-bomb's invention, there was considerable controversy among America's scientific team. While many distinguished scientists had previously supported America's invention of the atomic bomb to prevent the Nazis from gaining an edge during World War II, the vastly more powerful H-bomb was another proposition entirely. (During the early war years, Japan was also contemplating a nuclear weapon; in fact, it was a Japanese physicist, Tokutaro Higiwara, who first conceived the notion of a staged hydrogen thermonuclear bomb.) Yet, for humanitarian reasons, weren't there certain technological devices and discoveries that, despite his masterful inquisitive ingenuity, man should refrain from creating or investigating, even if it remained possible to do so? For physicist Oppenheimer, the H-bomb fell into such a dire category.

However, when Oppenheimer was reprimanded for later conscientiously opposing the H-bomb project, opinions that allegedly appeared to be of a pro-communist nature, he was branded a security risk. Was he a martyr, or a traitor—as Edward Teller might have opined? Regardless, there was good reason for nuclear paranoia. Public distrust of those invisible, policy-making guys in charge of the Atomic Energy Commission escalated into a furor over how and whether America's innovative technology was being properly controlled, especially with respect to public safety. (Thus, a beginning of a socio-cultural wave carrying down toward and through America's environmental movement of the 1970s and 1980s.) By then, the U.S. was indeed deceptively subjecting over 9,000 civilians, experimentally, to radiation exposures and, of course, to fallout, although while suppressing "evidence of long-range fallout problems as they became more evident by the mid-1950s."[35]

According to Donald Richie and Mick Broderick, while to the Western world the 1945 atomic bombings could be viewed as an "atrocity" (albeit—politically—a necessary one to truncate a bloody war), to the Japanese people such events cut more like a tragic "act of God"—among many natural phenomena such as typhoons and earthquakes, conflated with occupational guilt. And as Richie comments, during the immediate post–*Lucky Dragon* period, the unpopular H-bomb became "a favorite weapon of Communist propagandists."[36] It didn't help matters when American doctors at Hiroshima's Atomic Bomb Casualty Commission wouldn't offer proper medical assistance to the *Lucky Dragon* crew. The ABCC wasn't a hospital, however, and had been established only to study and research A-bomb victims, not *treat* them (let alone H-bomb victims, who were left hanging, as will be noted). This circumstance certainly fostered the belief (especially seized upon by the Communist Party) that America coldly regarded irradiated victims merely as guinea pigs available for study.

Many sci-fi films of the 1950s and early 1960s represent thinly veiled "what-if" scenarios illustrating war then so keenly threatened between America and the Soviets. While it is possible to chuckle at some of these movies today, it's soberly frightening to learn how close we actually came to conducting thermonuclear war then. America had wisely refrained from use of atomic bombs during the Korean War—in fact, their utility in wartime became seriously questioned. By the mid–1950s, however, stepping beyond the bounds of mere deterrence, U.S. General Curtis LeMay (1906–1990) yearned to destroy the Soviet Union with a single blast. So when it came to overall destructiveness, the H-bomb was right up his alley. LeMay even wanted to *provoke* Russia into war, by prodding their airspace with spy planes and reconnaissance flights. His rationale was that because the U.S. then possessed a more advanced and deliverable nuclear arsenal, such a war could have been readily won then, or so he believed. In May 1954, while *Gojira* was in production, LeMay stated chillingly, "[M]aybe if we do this overflight right, we can get World War III started."[37] As opposed to what Oppenheimer believed, LeMay felt we should attack while we retained an edge.

After 1954—referred to by Richard Rhodes as "the year of maximum danger"[38] (yes, how fitting this is the year I was born!)—when it became realized that a winning preemptive strike could still bring considerable retaliatory nuclear damage to U.S. cities, such antagonistic talk generally quieted down ... for a time. However, with harrowing circumstances ranging throughout the globe (e.g., conflicts over Egypt, 1956; China, 1958; Berlin, 1961; Cuba, 1962, etc.), nuclear diplomacy became resorted to more commonly.[39] For the first and only time ever, the U.S. went to "DefCon 2" on October 24, 1962! At that time, given the primitive controls in place then, there was even reasonable chance of an *unauthorized* strike against the Soviets over Cuba. By the 1980s, using sophisticated computers, a team of scientists including Carl Sagan had modeled what the aftermath of a nuclear World War III would be. Such a war would threaten mankind with extinction in a freezing "cold and dark," analogous to how the last of the dinosaurs expired 66 million years ago.[40]

Certainly the two atomic bomb attacks of 1945 later spawned a cinematic tradition in Japan, known as "Hibakusha cinema," or as Donald Richie stated, a psychological outcome of the "Japanese failure to come to terms with Hiroshima."[41] Many survivors of the atomic bombings, known as the "hibakusha," or the "atom-bomb-affected-people" (survivors), fatalistically presumed they were in an odd way selected to become rather like guinea pigs for American experimentation, an idea cynically reflected by a Nick Adams scene in 1965's *Frankenstein Conquers the World*, as well as another (non-kaiju) film, director Hideo Sekigawa's *Hiroshima* (1953).

"Hibakusha" films, several in the Godzilla series included, have lately become of scholarly concern. Not surprisingly, one of these films, directed by Kaneto Shindo in 1958 and titled *Daigo fukuryu* (*Lucky Dragon No. 5*), concerned the plight of the *Lucky Dragon*, of course focusing on Japan's infamous "third" nuclear attack, rather than Hiroshima. Also, the plight of *Lucky Dragon* incident victims is framed in director Fumio Kamei's *Still, It's Good to be Alive* (*Ikite Ite Yokatta*, 1956). In Shindo's film, there was considerable artistic license applied for spectacle. For instance, "the director thought it necessary to place the fishing vessel much closer to the bomb test than it actually was...."[42] For decades, H-bomb victims were discriminated against as being apart from A-bomb victims. Peculiarly, according to many commentators, radiation-afflicted crewmen of the *Lucky Dragon No. 5* were not considered *hibakusha*.

For a time after proper decontamination, *Lucky Dragon No. 5* was used as a training vessel, although renamed as the *Hayabusa Maru*, or the *Dark Falcon*. Then she was scrapped, but with a nod to history, following its removal from interment in landfill sludge, and restoration in 1976, the *Lucky Dragon* was placed on permanent display at Tokyo's Metropolitan Daigo Fukuryu Maru Exhibition Hall. It remains there for thoughtful men to ponder history, what might have happened, and how to avert what could someday result. In time, rather ironically, Japan reconciled itself to the introduction of nuclear energy reactors accepted for peaceful purposes from the United States to help rebuild a postwar nation, permitting continued U.S. military authority and presence in the western Pacific region.

The *Lucky Dragon* incident is rarely discussed in today's tumultuous times, and is usually not foremost on the minds of Godzilla fans. Yet, as journalist Togo Shighhiko stated, the *Lucky Dragon*'s voyage became "a parable for the nuclear age."[43] In a sense, as noted by Ralph E. Lapp, like Columbus's three fabled ships sailing to a mysterious new world, so did the crew of the *Lucky Dragon* during the spring of 1954 tread waters of an uncertain, ominous future. Without the *Lucky Dragon No. 5* incident, would *Gojira* have been quite the same, or left such generational impact?

But isn't there more here than meets the eye? Weaving *Gojira*'s Dr. Serizawa into the frame, can't we see how the Western world's prototypical mad scientist, sinister Dr. Frankenstein, chose the irresponsible path, living in denial of his godless deeds, whereas heroic, deeply anguished Serizawa, in the end, did the right thing? Is this a cultural east vs. west outcome played out in fantasy literature and film (although we see traces of an arguably "righteous" decision committed at *Fail-Safe*'s dramatic conclusion, atoning for computer-caused disaster)? Shouldn't the very existence of our Frankensteinian creation, the H-bomb (i.e., allegorical Godzilla), have had more reasonable justification for its calling into being than simply "deterrence"? Instead, militaristic and geopolitical circumstances prevented a cautious Serizawa type, perhaps a more influential Oppenheimer (or another thoughtful, foresighted soul like Danish physicist Niels Bohr), from somehow prolonging (or otherwise effectively stalling) the H-bomb's "inevitable" path from the curse of discovery to invention.[44]

With the monster created, we must not now shrink from our responsibilities.

Chapter Ten

Godzilla's Dinosaurian Origins

So whence did we glean the extravagant idea of Godzilla as an authentic dino-monster?

There are those among us who would deemphasize Godzilla's undeniable dinosaurian roots. That Godzilla might have formerly been a *dinosaur*, per se, horribly scarred by radiation from detonation of a nuclear bomb, is far secondary to Godzilla's heroic persona and cool, filmic "monster-ness," and quite apart from any lore or intrigue over dubious dinosaurian origins. So, in the context of the latest G-films, it matters little, then, whether Godzilla is a dinosaur (or dino-monster) any more so than many of his clearly non-dinosaurian kaiju foes.

First, we'll focus on the prototypical Godzilla suit design itself. As much as I believe in biological evolution as fact, I also am committed to Godzilla's intended *dinosaurian* origin. Secondly, pseudoscientific attempts to explain origins of Godzilla and nemesis Anguirus within "Showa" films from *Gojira* (1954) through and including *King Kong vs. Godzilla* (1963) shall be outlined.[1]

According to canonical wisdom, Godzilla was inspired by three real dinosaur genera—a *Tyrannosaurus*, an *Iguanodon*, and a plated *Stegosaurus*. But by 1954, numerous restorations of these dinosaurs had been published and it might be of some interest to know whose paleoimagery, in particular, was selected as possibly being most influential toward the original Godzilla suit design.

During original design stages, Godzilla was conceived by its creators as a mutated dinosaur, emblematic as an apocalyptical, living form of radiation. After all, *Gojira* was in essence an antinuclear film. Visionaries Tomoyuki Tanaka and Eiji Tsubuyara were highly influenced by Ray Harryhausen's *The Beast from 20,000 Fathoms* and RKO's *King Kong*. Furthermore, unfortunate circumstances resulting from the explosion of a hydrogen bomb tested near the Bikini Atoll on March 1, 1954, dovetailed toward a working title for Toho's film—*The Giant Monster from 20,000 Miles Beneath the Sea*. The title was later abbreviated to simply Project "G." Japanese sci-fi novelist Shigeru Kayama penned the story. As Steve Ryfle claims, "Kayama was one of the most prominent mystery writers in postwar Japan, and because his stories sometimes involved mutant reptiles and fish and other monsters, Tanaka felt he was the ideal choice." And we learn from Donald Glut's *Classic Movie Monsters*: "An authorized Godzilla novel based on the first two movies and written by Shigeru Kayama was published in Japan."[2] Because Tsubuyara realized that America's expert stop-motion animation techniques couldn't be duplicated for their picture, it was absolutely essential that Project "G's" plot, story and special effects would be top-notch.

From the outset, Kayama was of the persuasion that the monster, soon named "Gojira" (later anglicized to "Godzilla"), would be some kind of sea monster, or a cross between a gorilla and a whale. Later, in 1963's *King Kong vs. Godzilla,* Godzilla was "explained" on the basis of fossils resembling Godzilla discovered in Japan by a "Dr. Johnson" as a 97- to 125-million-year-old tyrannosaur-stegosaur hybrid that was preserved somehow in suspended animation until its reawakening, vaguely implying some sort of evolutionary, genetic tie between the two real dinosaurs. This "theory" contrasts with the prior 1954 concept of Godzilla's transformation, caused by nuclear radiation—resultant of a sudden mutation of an otherwise normal dinosaur, slumbering until recently in the deeps. Kayama swiftly composed a 50-page manuscript while Gojira's conceptual form was shifting rapidly, from a giant octopus into a giant reptile. A storyboarded script was created, then revised and refined into the final screenplay.

Most fascinating, however, is a photograph presented in Ed Godziszewski's short 13-minute film documentary, *Making of the Godzilla Suit,* conveniently available on YouTube (also included in the authoritative 2006 ClassicMedia 2-disc collector's edition, *Gojira*). Here, we see Toho's design team studiously situated at a planning table. On the table, at right, artist Kazuoshi Abe's head drawings for the monster are visible—sort of a stubby, gorilla-like, if not mushroom cloud–shaped facial rendering. A discernible fold-out page—what appears to be a poster—is held in the hands of two individuals.[3] The illustration in this hand-held sheet is readily recognizable and significant for our present purposes. For this sheet held in the hands of the two designers was published in the September 7, 1953, issue of *Life* magazine for a feature titled "Pageant of Life." One of Toho's team members is pointing suggestively to a figure prominently emblazoned within this fold-out page, a creature fondly referred to by dinosaur aficionados as the "pot-bellied" *Tyrannosaurus.* Yes, the painting shown in the poster is titled *The Age of Reptiles.*[4]

This Toho file photo reflects perhaps a pivotal moment in Godzilla history. It would appear that Abe's "humanoid" designs are on the bubble, so to speak, being superseded and evidently rejected in favor of master paleoartist Rudolph F. Zallinger's (1919–1995) magnificent *Age of Reptiles*! An "Ah hah!" moment, perhaps? An enlightened individual is apparently suggesting that the form of America's bipedal *Tyrannosaurus* should somehow be melded into the monster suit design. (Although the file photo appears undated, by this time, due to temporal and financial constraints, Tsuburaya may have already decided most regrettably that Project G's filmic creature should be a man-sized suit instead of a stop-motion puppet.)

Zallinger had completed his colorful, 110-foot-long, 16-foot-high mural *Age of Reptiles,* a life-through-time emblem of modernity, spanning 300 million years of geological time for Yale University's Peabody Museum in the years 1943 to 1947. The mural depicts idealized scenes of then accurate-looking dinosaurs and other prehistoric life representative of the major geological periods, from the Devonian to the Late Cretaceous. Trees and foliage representative of each successive transition and smoldering volcanoes subtly subdivide "ages" evident in this mural. Dinosaurs and reptiles inhabiting the mural do not seem active, as "renaissance" dinosaurs have been lately depicted, but stand as solemn, statuesque titans attesting to their former grandeur. In the original captivating mural, Time's immensity moves from right to left, opposite to how time flows in the *Life* poster under deliberation by Toho's design team.

Zallinger's monumental dinosaurs appear sculptural, like majestic mythic gods. The poster version being examined by Toho technicians in the photo, however, is not the original

1947 mural, but rather a smaller-scale (82½ inches by 12⅛ inches) test painting or "cartoon," noticeably differing in detail from the large mural. Until recently it was not possible to photograph the entire, huge mural, so for *Life* magazine's spread in 1953, a photograph of the cartoon was substituted instead—although reproduced from the negative in reverse, in left to right fashion, so as to flow with other life-through-time pictorial segments of Lincoln Barnett's "Pageant of Life" article feature.[5]

Unlike other by then famous smooth-backed *T. rexes,* such as painted by Charles R. Knight, intriguingly, Zallinger's tyrannosaur was painted with a series of short, triangular scales adorning the vertebral column and tail. Toho's technicians perhaps perceived these as conceivably vestigial for Godzilla's huge dorsal fins—expanded in size and ostentatious variety even beyond those evident in *Stegosaurus,* resultant of irradiation. The charcoal gray coloration of the early Godzilla suits is not a far cry from the darkish blue-gray hue in Zallinger's pot-bellied tyrannosaur as published in *Life.* And in his painting, Zallinger's tyrannosaur stands in between two other quadrupedal, Late Cretaceous dinosaurs, three-horned *Triceratops* and armored *Ankylosaurus.* These two, when "morphed" together, essentially became a prototype for Toho's second fictional dinosaur resurrected by the hydrogen bomb–Anguirus. Soaring in the skies over the tyrannosaur's shoulder we spy a *Pteranodon,* an obvious basis for design of Toho's third dino-monster, Rodan. They're all there together in the Late Cretaceous segment of Zallinger's painting. And in the Jurassic portion of Zallinger's painting we see another key quadrupedal dinosaur, *Stegosaurus,* while two bipedal, carnivorous allosaurs (both sporting those short, triangular spinal scales—same as the tyrannosaur) go about their predatory business.

So is Godzilla really just a "pseudotyrannosaurus'? Well, in Godzilla's progenitor case, so far we've accounted for the major *Tyrannosaurus* ingredient, the *sine qua non,* and quite possibly the added element of *Stegosaurus* plates as well, which interestingly *also* appear, albeit in diminutive form, on the tyrannosaur. Yet there is no *Iguanodon* visible in Zallinger's *Age of Reptiles.* So, to complete the canonical tale of the dinosaurian triumvirate—*Tyrannosaurus, Iguanodon, Stegosaurus*—one asks, "Which inspirational visual was used for the third bipedal dinosaur genus, complementary to Godzilla's original design?" Once again, Godziszewski illustriously directs to a definitive answer!

In another photograph shown in his film documentary *Making of the Godzilla Suit,* we see an unidentified person regarding a picture of a herbivorous dinosaur, *Iguanodon,* in an opened book. The *Iguanodon* painting as shown was made, not by Zallinger, but by Czech artist Zdeněk Burian (1905–1981). Although not visible in the Toho photo, this particular painting is dated 1941. I cannot tell which of *several* books including Burian's restorations is shown in this photo. But at a young age I was introduced to a lavish volume that made quite a splash in England in 1960, titled *Prehistoric Animals,* featuring 60 of Burian's magnificent plates arranged in a life-through-time tour, with text written by paleontologist Josef Augusta. Burian's *Iguanodon* appears as Plate 27 in my copy. Shortly thereafter, Augusta and Burian teamed toward publication of other eye-dazzling books published in English during the 1960s. So the book shown in the Toho file photo must have been printed prior to 1954. In his documentary, Godziszewski refers to this book as a children's dinosaur encyclopedia. However, based on my 1990s discussions with Donald F. Glut, no dinosaur dictionaries or encyclopedias had been published prior to the 1960s (at least in English). According to Burian researcher Thomas Kovacs,[6] Augusta and Burian worked on at least 6 other outstanding collaborations during the 1940s that dealt with a prehistoric life theme. Four of these titles were (English translations): *Life Long Gone* (1941), *Prehistoric Wonders* (1942), *Lost World* (1948), and *From the Prehistoric Deep* (1949)—the latter which sounds as if it may have been a template of sorts for the Augusta/Burian English 1964 volume *Prehistoric Sea Monsters.*

The artistically prolific Burian, who reportedly made over 20,000 illustrations during his brilliant career according to some accounts, made several *Iguanodon* images, at least two additional, undated examples of which may be found on the Internet. One fine example, appearing highly derivative of his iconic 1941 restoration, was published in Zdeněk V. Spinar's 1981 volume, *Life Before Man,*[7] which also reproduces many images previously compiled in *Prehistoric Animals.*

Furthermore, in this second Toho file photo, showing Burian's *Iguanodon* at upper left, we see a Toho artist sketching a bipedal, carnivorous-looking, fin-backed dinosaur adorned with a single series of triangular dorsal plates, although considerably enlarged relative to *Iguanodon*'s scales. Burian's 1941 *Iguanodon* is bipedal, accurate-looking according to contemporary standards, and like Zallinger's tyrannosaur has a suggestive series of short, triangular spines or scales adorning the vertebral column. Unlike Zallinger's tyrannosaur, however, the *Iguanodon*'s considerably longer arms must have seemed more appealing to Toho's artists because they more effectively approximated the length of the monster suit actor's arms. Proportionally, *Tyrannosaurus* only had diminutive arms and hands, wholly un-*suit*-able for the Godzilla actor(s).[8]

Like Zallinger's pot-bellied tyrannosaur, Burian's *Iguanodon* was faithfully reproduced, circa 1961, as a small hard rubber toy, including visible dorsal scales, by the Louis Marx Company. Over two decades after Burian completed his *Iguanodon* restoration, Zallinger completed a very similar-looking restoration for Jane Werner Watson's *Dinosaurs and Other Prehistoric Reptiles: A Giant Golden Book* (1965), although by this time, Zallinger had all but dispensed with the short vertebral scales in his dinosaur restorations.[9]

Based on these two fascinating Toho file photographs presented by Godziszewski, my hunch is that Godzilla's prominent, symmetrical triple row of pointy, ostentatious osteoderms are more immediately derived or perhaps mutatedly transformed from dorsal scales appearing on Burian's *Iguanodon* as well as Zallinger's pot-bellied *Tyrannosaurus,* maybe equally or more so than being swiped from any particular *Stegosaurus* restoration. By then, America's world-famous plated dinosaur was presumed to have a staggered (non-symmetrical) double row of osteoderms.

However, we do catch a long glimpse of a (single-row-plated) *Stegosaurus* skeletal reconstruction in that angst-filled *Gojira* scene, which oddly has held me spellbound since early 1960s childhood, where paleontologist Dr. Yamane contemplates in his study the fate of Japan in light of mankind's self-created monstrous, radioactive engine of mass destruction. Here, inclusion of a real dinosaur image may intend to suspend disbelief as to what is transpiring in the movie, with such symbolism indicating that Godzilla is somehow organismically related to or derived from a genuine *Stegosaurus,* due to the vertebral plate series shared by both genera. As shall be shortly outlined, the theme of showing reconstructions, drawings and restorations of real or imagined dinosaurs already known to paleo-science, as the reawakened dino-monster attacks civilized centers, was a common filmic theme during the 1950s and early 1960s, in movies from 1953's *The Beast from 20,000 Fathoms* to *Gorgo* (1961) and *Reptilicus* (1962). Toho's inclusion of a *Stegosaurus* skeleton in this scene underscores the plated dinosaur's significance, in an uncertain way, but possibly—contrary to my hunch as stated above—toward the Godzilla suit design.

According to Ryfle and Godziszewski, consulted paleoart, concept art and design sketches led to three clay model versions sculpted by Teizo Tushimitsu working under direction of artist Akira Watanabe, one of which was selected for costume fabrication. These three, approximately 40-centimeter-tall model versions became known as the "sea-monster," "warty," and "alligator" Godzillas. The sea-monster version had a wider head and serpentine scales, while the warty version's head was reduced proportionally but otherwise bulked up in the torso. The latter's skin texture was pebbly, perhaps borrowing somewhat from Burian's 1941 *Iguanodon* restoration. Both of these models were rejected in favor of the alligator version, whose skin texture possessed small, irregular, linear scars, representing disfigurement suffered by the monster during the nuclear bomb explosion. From there a prototypical, human-sized costume was made, yet as Godziszewski relates (rather amusingly) in his documentary film, *Making of the Godzilla Suit*, this first suit was so stiff due to the use of off-spec latex, which cured improperly, that once inside the actor could hardly move. This necessitated making a second version, only permitting "restricted performance," which added to the creature's dinosaurian-like (as opposed to humanoid) movement. Godziszewski states, "[S]ince Godzilla was supposed to be a dinosaur, it should not walk like a human ... [which] ... was all but impossible in this suit." Toho succeeded admirably in this endeavor. (See Figure 10-1.)

Elsewhere, I've referred to Zallinger's pot-bellied *Tyrannosaurus rex* as representing the apotheosis of the "middle age" of Rex iconography, which I've dubbed the age of "Lordly Rex." (The first and last ages then are those of "Savage Rex" and "Renaissance Rex," respectively.) Zallinger's Rex sets an atomic age, Cold War precedent for then contemporary appearances—restorations and reconstructions—of America's greatest and most symbolic dinosaur.[10] How curious and bitterly ironic, then, that Toho selected this particular symbol for its metaphorical monster, "the Japanese Godzilla, a new dinosaur that originates in the 1950s as a by-product of the American atomic bomb, a genetic mutation produced by radioactivity."[11] In part, it is Zallinger's American Lordly Rex, albeit a mutant variety, that pounds through a fiery Tokyo in *Gojira*. Within 20 years, during the so-called dinosaur renaissance, tyrannosaurid anatomy was under reassessment; the upright, bipedal stance was eventually judged inaccurate. Rather than slow-moving, tail-dragging, lethargic "lizards," renaissance Rexes were reinvented as hot-blooded, speedy predators. Likewise, iguanodont anatomy was reconsidered, undergoing analogous contortions and conversions.

In sources I've consulted, only August Ragone *briefly* references Zallinger and Burian.[12] Here, based on the two Toho file photos, presented in Godziszewski's 2006 documentary, I've striven to fill in some of the likely background details regarding the influential western and European paleoart. To dinophiles interested in paleoimagery, however, it is intriguing that Toho's costume designers were evidently not as influenced by Charles R. Knight's (1874–1953) acclaimed artwork toward Godzilla's prototypical creation. For half a century, Knight was considered the world's master paleoartist. In particular, his iconic paintings showing *Tyrannosaurus* about to engage three-horned *Triceratops* in bloody combat, completed for Chicago's Field Museum (circa 1926 to 1930) and New York's American Museum (1906), are perhaps *the* 20th century's most famous dinosaur paintings. Yet, Knight's *Tyrannosaurus rex* vs. *Triceratops* theme *is* most definitely reflected in the Toho Godzilla series—not in

Fig 10-1: These three plastic Marx toy dinosaurs created during the late 1950s and early 1960s are equivalent to and represent Godzilla's dinosaurian roots. (Left to right—*Tyrannosaurus, Stegosaurus, Iguanodon*) The *Tyrannosaurus* and *Stegosaurus* were influenced by figures in Zallinger's mural *The Age of Reptiles*, while the *Iguanodon* toy was inspired by Zdeněk Burian's restoration (Debus collection).

Gojira, but instead in the Americanized 1959 sequel, *Gigantis the Fire Monster*. Although the monster Anguirus resembles a porcupiney ankylosaur, closer examination of its head reveals a ceratopsian-like flared crest or frill along its neck replete with an array of recurved, forward-facing horns, with a short nasal horn more so than *Triceratops*, this facial apparition would appear ultimately founded upon Charles R. Knight's 1897 painted restoration of a conjectural (poorly known) horned dinosaur named the "Agathaumas." So, it's not too much of a stretch to declare Anguirus as a mutated horned dinosaur. "Pseudoankylotops"? Gigantis battling the Anguirus (also known as Angilas), then, is a filmic manifestation of the most revered Knightian dinosaurian theme.

In Toho's original 1955 version of the sequel, *Godzilla Raids Again*, Anguirus is suggested to be not a horned dinosaur variety, but an armored ankylosaur. Dinosaur imagery shown in a segment where scientists discuss Anguirus's probable origins, juxtaposes images of a redrawn Zallinger *Age of Reptiles*–derived tyrannosaur (facing to the left as in the 1953 *Life* magazine spread), a *Triceratops*, and an armored "Paleoscincus," painted in a mural by Knight for the Field Museum, among others on a table before the new monster is identified in a book written by a "Dr. Preterry Hawdon" of Poland as a living example of the "Anguilasaurus." Its picture was even embedded into Hawdon's alleged book. Analogous to how plated *Stegosaurus* was considered then, the Anguirus had not just two, but (in *Gigantis*'s case) at least *three* sets of brains. Unlike the herbivorous *Ankylosaurus*, the allegedly 70- to 150-million-year-old Anguirus was deemed carnivorous, aggressive and strangely if not conveniently destined to reawaken from hibernation when irradiated with fallout from a hydrogen bomb. In other words, Anguirus is not so much a dinosaur mutated by the hydrogen bomb, but one supposedly based on fossils—as in the aforementioned Dr. Johnson's faux explanation of Godzilla in *King Kong vs. Godzilla*. Paleoimagery inspiring the Anguirus monster suit isn't quite as clear today or as well documented as in Godzilla's case, but it would appear to be somewhat founded in the *Ankylosaurus* seen in Zallinger's *Age of Reptiles* painting in *Life*, coupled with

Charles R. Knight's influential restorations and themes—particularly his popular "Agathaumas" restoration.

Thus, in the current heyday of spectacular "Godzimagery" appearing in every *G-Fan* magazine issue, as well as ubiquitously elsewhere, it's rather encouraging to see that master paleoartists Rudolph Zallinger, Zdeněk Burian and Charles R. Knight are in an odd sense honorary, albeit unwitting, Godzimagery pioneers. It is also fitting that Godzilla's essential, morphological components should comprise the first dinosaur to be described with any embryonic sense of diligence and exactitude (i.e., *Iguanodon*), the 20th century's mightiest symbolic carnivorous dinosaur (i.e., *Tyrannosaurus*), and arguably the most distinctive real dinosaur—due to its characteristic osteoderms—of them all (i.e., *Stegosaurus*).

Beyond the suit itself, how did Toho underscore the idea of Godzilla's (and Anguirus's) dinosaurian origins? Actually, they employed a "trick" first used three decades earlier in a silent film. What was the trick and why was it used to fool us?

Because much of the surface of our planet was still relatively unexplored by 1912, the premise of Arthur Conan Doyle's novel *The Lost World* (i.e., dinosaurs still living in a remote corner of the world) might have seemed rather more in the realm of, at best, well ... *possibly* possible at the time it was written. Yet he introduced a trick to suspend disbelief, one replicated by subsequent authors and directors through the next half century, one which in slightly different vein was introduced by Jules Verne 50 years earlier in his *Journey to the Center of the Earth* (1864). A trick?

Yes, and a rather simple yet suggestive one. In Conan Doyle's serialized 1912 novel, we learn that the first modern explorer to ascend the "lost" plateau in the Amazon is Maple White, whose notebook was retrieved during a subsequent mission conducted by Professor Challenger. Within this notebook are sketches of supposedly living animals Maple White witnessed on the plateau summit, including plated dinosaur *Stegosaurus.* A facsimile of the notebook drawing, showing the dinosaur staring at Maple White, was reproduced in *The Strand Magazine,* drawn for the issue by artist Harry Rountree, although signed for authenticity in the lower right corner by Maple White. Seeing is believing, and contemporary readers of the novel would have had no recourse but to be tempted to believe there was a person named Maple White who was actually on the plateau where he saw this living animal! Well, at least seeing the drawing published adjacent to Conan Doyle's remarkable words facilitated imaginative fancy. As in politics, or rather like FBI Agent Mulder of *The X-Files,* we're overly prone or conditioned to accept information confirming what we wish to believe, even when faced by raw, opposing facts. Why? Because, deep down, don't we want to believe?

A dozen years later, First National Pictures filmed an adaptation from the novel as a silent movie, *The Lost World* (First National Pictures, 1925), starring Wallace Beery as Professor Challenger.[13] Notably, director Harry O. Hoyt included scenes where viewers not only glimpsed Maple White's drawings in the notebook, but also witnessed mounted prehistoric animal skeletons in London's Zoological Hall. These scenes are visual extrapolations of passages selected from the novel, where Conan Doyle's Challenger presents physical evidence proving to *Daily Gazette* reporter Edward Malone, as well as intrigued page-turning novel readers, the veracity of Maple White's observations. Both Conan Doyle and Hoyt suspended disbelief sufficiently, so as to lure us in, hook, line and sinker. At this point, we really want to thumb our noses at those fools who scoff at Challenger, an esteemed scientist who wields powerful conviction on this point. Buttressed by "evidence" presented by Conan Doyle and

Hoyt through fictional Challenger, we simply prefer to believe that dinosaurs still live on the plateau, and so we shall.

Incidentally, Jules Verne did something similar in his *Journey to the Center of the Earth* novel, describing real fossils embedded in the walls of labyrinthine underground caverns, before these frightening prehistoria come alive! First National's suggestive use of *Lost World*'s genuine fossils wasn't the first time dinosaur skeletons served as movie props in motion pictures (i.e., *Adam's Rib*, 1923)—nor would it be the last. There's another innovation heralded by First National; namely, eye-catching promotional poster artwork featuring a giant theropodous dinosaur smashing elements of a modern city underfoot.

Next, we see the trick magnificently employed in 1953's *The Beast from 20,000 Fathoms*, involving the release of a giant dino-monster from glacial ice following a nuclear warhead test detonation in the Arctic. Although following the blast, physicist Dr. Nesbitt (Paul Christian) sees a living giant monster moments before becoming injured in a snowy avalanche, medical personnel believe he's suffering from "traumatic hallucination." Nesbitt also claims that because he's a scientist his observations should override any psychological evaluation—but to no avail. There were no monster footprints left near where Nesbitt was rescued (although these could have quickly become covered in the snowstorm). Soon the medical staff at least partly convinces Nesbitt that he was delirious at the time.

That is, until a ship, the *Fortune*, sinks at sea, with crew claiming they spied a sea serpent just before the wreck, an incident which Nesbitt reads in a newspaper account. So he's quickly off to see Dr. Thurgood Elson (Cecil Kellaway) who is the "foremost paleontologist in the world" at the Department of Paleontology. Elson's researches are facilitated by his pretty assistant, Miss Lee Hunter (Paula Raymond). Immediately, the scene entices audiences; we see the mounted skeleton of some kind of sauropod (i.e., "brontosaur-like") animal, and a large image of the American Museum *Tyrannosaurus rex* skeleton (suggested to be in some kind of panel mount) in shots behind Nesbitt. If you melded the skull of the Rex with the body of the sauropod, you'd essentially have the resurrected body of the Rhedosaurus that Nesbitt saw in the Arctic.

In this scene infused with paleo-ambiance, Dr. Elson pooh-poohs Nesbitt's sighting of the monster and doubts his idea that such a creature might have hibernated like a bear for over 100 million years, until the heat from detonation of the bomb (presumably a fusion variety) melted the entombing ice. It's too unlikely that an animal could survive on its tissues for such an incredibly long time. Lee Hunter chimes in, offering the story about the "dead mastodons" frozen in Siberia (although so far, no frozen mastodons have been discovered anywhere—only mammoths). She considers that Nesbitt's theory could have merit, especially because she's a "sympathetic bystander who has a deep abiding faith in the work of scientists; otherwise she wouldn't be one herself." Nesbitt's intriguing story seems worthy of investigating further, in her apartment.

Hunter has gathered together "all the sketches of the known prehistoric animals" for Nesbitt to examine. So the ability to define what the creature is (which by now has destroyed two ships and shortly a lighthouse tower), depends on deciphering paleoart. Ironically, as we'll see shortly, the unrecognized answer to the riddle existed plain as day in Dr. Elson's museum hall all of the time. Sifting through the pictures, Nesbitt remarks that he didn't realize there were so many kinds of prehistoric animals, to which Hunter replies that they haven't even reached the Cretaceous Period yet. This is incorrect, however, because Nesbitt has already sorted through two Charles R. Knight painted restorations of "Trachodon" and *Tyrannosaurus* engaging a *Triceratops* family in battle, which are all Cretaceous animals. Probably few audience viewers saw that only a subset of the pictures Nesbitt pages through are "established" samples of paleoart, as opposed to having been prepared for the movie by production artists and staff.

Then, suddenly, he finds a picture that resembles the animal he saw; Hunter quickly shows him another which is strikingly even more so like the monster he witnessed! They've found it. Now the monster at large can be named—it's the Rhedosaurus. Of course, this is a drawing made for the purposes of the film by production staff. Now Hunter and Nesbitt reason that if one of the sailors who survived the sea serpent sinking can also pick out the same picture (even though they've only seen the monster in the water with its legs submerged), they could prove to Dr. Elson that such a monster lives and that Nesbitt's outlandish theory is correct after all. When shipwrecked sailor Jacob Bowman (Jack Pennick) dramatically identifies the same picture, the concurrence is too uncanny. "What further proof do you need?" Nesbitt implores. Elson, chuckling at the thought that a Mesozoic animal could be alive today, is suddenly convinced, doing a 180-degree turnabout. Furthermore, Elson declares the monster is 100 million years old and a "direct ancestor" of the mounted pseudo-sauropod skeleton displayed before them.

With the monster identified and named, they begin planning how to stop it, leading to its inevitable destruction. But first Elson must witness the creature firsthand, in its natural habitat—the submerged canyons, where its only fossils have been found. (One wonders how the fossils were found and excavated from such a deep underwater deposit, an unlikely and expensive proposition.) So in a later scene, Elson enters a diving bell. Upon spying the creature below the waves, we further learn that it is a "Paleolithic survival," that its "dorsal is singular, not bilateral," and that the "capital suspension appears to be cantileveric. But the most astonishing thing about it is that…." And just at that moment poor Elson expires.

Clearly, use of dinosaur imagery—some real, some concocted for the occasion of the film—facilitated Nesbitt's recognition of the Rhedosaurus, the critical first step needed in a sci-fi flick before the offending beast can be exterminated. The mounted skeleton of the Rhedosaurus's direct ancestor is not a real dinosaur known to science. But it looks sufficiently like dino-skeletons, which many people in the audience would have seen examples of in natural history museums, to pass for a genuine dino-monster. (And incidentally, there was an Australian dinosaur sauropod genus named the "Rhoetosaurus," a name which was pronounced much like Harryhausen's invention.)

So, just how gullible are we?

Conan Doyle's strategy, the trick, was further employed in the decade's most pivotal, heartfelt, tightly wound and powerful giant dino-monster movie, Toho's *Gojira* (1954). Movie-wise, *Gojira* was inspired both by RKO's *King Kong* and also *The Beast from 20,000 Fathoms*. But it was instilled with much originality as well, derived from Japanese wartime and postwar experiences with nuclear bombs. Let us examine how the paleontologist in this story, Dr. Yamane (Takashi Shimura), identifies the sea monster that becomes known to the world as Godzilla. First, there is a backdrop to this film, stated and accepted by the audience. Godzilla claims status as a legendary sea creature of the "old days," when women were sacrificed to appease it, inhabiting Odo Island's coastal waters. The creature is also briefly witnessed by sailors on doomed freighters which have suddenly burst into flame, the first of which is named the *Eiko-maru*.

But can the sinkings instead more logically be resultant of an undersea volcanic eruption? That idea is quickly dismissed. The islanders put things together—as the fishermen aren't catching anything lately, it must be some animal causing this. Ceremonial exorcism of the beast only seems to stir things up, as one eyewitness, Shinkichi, sees a huge animal that night storming through their village. Following the destruction by the "hurricane," and given the local shipping catastrophes, Dr. Yamane is summoned to conduct a thorough investigation of the island. But while addressing officials before embarking for Odo, Yamane prophetically cites the case of alleged Snowman footprints of the Himalayas as examples of what Nature has hidden from us: "After all, Earth has many deep abyssal pockets that may contain secrets."

When the investigation commences, Yamane quickly takes note of groundwater contaminated with radiation on the same side of the island where a huge footprint is found, as well as a trilobite embedded within this footprint. Trilobites became extinct 250 million years ago, but strangely this specimen is not fossilized. Startlingly, it's fresh! Then the monster appears, but comes ashore on the other side of the island, where it is witnessed by dozens of people, including Yamane, who now has its photograph. Afterward, an enormous trackway is seen along the shore leading back to the sea. This is a bipedal monster, unlike the Rhedosaurus. So it would seem that the monster's existence has been very well documented during this visit to Odo Island.

But there is still the pressing matter of explaining how such a creature could be alive today. Yamane is tasked with the job of suspending disbelief concerning this remarkable creature for the viewing audience. True—we've all seen the monster, but how could this be accepted as a plausible prehistoric beast? Much of what we need to know comes in the next pivotal sequence, where Yamane lectures to worried officials back in Japan. The news is grim, and what he has to say is bolstered by paleoart—once again, images of prehistoric life.

In a darkened room, Yamane shows slides of prehistoric animals; first a crudely drawn "Brontosaurus," and then—significantly—a painting showing two animals clearly borrowed or swiped from Rudolph Zallinger's *Age of Reptiles*. Here amidst a volcanic field, we see a striped *Plateosaurus* of the Triassic Period, and more importantly the bipedal, pot-bellied *Tyrannosaurus rex*, dating from the Cretaceous Period—one of the principal creatures whose anatomical features were borrowed for creating the Godzilla suit. These dinosaurs were presumably redrawn from Zallinger's painting by a Toho company artist. Dr. Yamane suggests, however, that like Godzilla, these creatures stem from the Jurassic Period, only two million years ago. Yamane needs to consult his geological timetable, however, as the Jurassic Period is defined by rocks dating from between 205 and 144 million years old. While refinements in this chart have occurred since 1954, even then the Late Jurassic was set around 150 million years ago.

Zallinger's *Tyrannosaurus* also has a single subdued row of integumentary, triangular scales situated along its spinal column, not unlike those seen on the Rhedosaurus. As an aside, note that in Dr. Elson's aforementioned reference to the "singular, not bilateral dorsal" feature may be in reference to the Rhedosaur's low ridge of triangular spinal scales that became far more prominent, jagged and ostentatious a year later in *Gojira*'s Godzilla. Also, it is interesting that the ancestral sauropod-ish skeleton on display in Elson's museum has no bony, stegosaurian osteoderms along its backbone. So Rhedosaur's (possibly derived) dorsal feature may be integumentary, or may be resultant of sexual dimorphism.

Next, Yamane theorizes how this creature came to be. He doesn't have any fossils belonging to this species, but suspects that during and after the Jurassic a creature "somewhere between" marine and terrestrial reptiles evolved, a transitional "intermediate" form. Okay, but why is this animal alive today?

Yamane continues, after accepting its folkloric name of "Godzilla," and estimating from the photo that it is "approximately 50 meters" (about 150 feet) tall, which would defy bounds set by gravity. Yamane suspects that it was disturbed from its particular marine niche following recent hydrogen bomb testing in the Pacific. This conclusion is supported by "strong evidence," such as the trilobite (which he claims has been extinct for only two million years), and the radioactive sandy sediment found in its shell. Also, Geiger counter readings show presence of strontium 90, a product of nuclear bomb detonation. The sand that came from Godzilla, which is characteristic of Jurassic "red clay" marine deposits, absorbed an immense of radiation. Therefore, Godzilla must have absorbed this radiation as well. To metaphorically cap his summary, in a later scene we see Yamane contemplating the folly and fate of mankind in his study adjacent to the miniature *Stegosaurus* skeleton model—the dinosaur that had plates along its spine (in this case shown incorrectly as a single row). Showing an image of a real dinosaur with plates arranged along its spinal column would fortify audience belief in a fictional creature, Godzilla, which has several rows of plates on its spine. This skeleton also foreshadows that of Godzilla's (plated) skeleton briefly witnessed on the seabed after Dr. Serizawa's (Akihiko Hirata) oxygen-destroyer has been successfully deployed.

Now Japan proceeds to destroy the monster, although Yamane would prefer to study its resistance to radioactivity. Yamane concludes the film prophetically, warning of other formidable Godzillas that could be stirred up if mankind continues conducting nuclear tests.

How good a job has Yamane done in explaining the monster? Has he suspended disbelief sufficiently? Well, Godzilla is even larger than the Rhedosaurus, and its enormous, bipedal proportions simply defy the laws of physics. Yamane didn't explain any of that. After the monster begins breathing fire over the city, this curious adaptation is never explained by our resident paleontologist either. If the transitionally evolved Godzilla species is a direct mutation from the hydrogen bomb, he didn't say so explicitly. How does a marine creature like this breathe so efficiently on land as well as underwater? No traces of gills can be seen. But, while he also cannot explain how such a creature could survive in spite of its high degree of radioactivity, to his credit, Yamane did offer to study this death-defying characteristic. Even though Yamane was able to establish the monster's origins, he remains powerless to suggest how it may be destroyed, a task left to Dr. Serizawa. Scenes where Tokyo is destroyed by the horrible reptile visually absorb and mentally engage audiences to such high degree that there is no need for further suspension of disbelief that might be ordinarily achieved through continued pseudoscientific lecturing, prattling, etc., of how such a creature may live yet defy physical laws. By now, *Gojira* has transformed into a frightful monster movie, a grim reflection of our plight. Recalling Hiroshima's arresting scenes of destruction, we simply must accept.

The 1956 Americanized version of the film, *Godzilla, King of the Monsters*, casting Raymond Burr in a spliced-in role as reporter Steve Martin, is not nearly as good. And the science supporting "belief" in the monster is much watered down, if not worse. For instance, Yamane declares that Godzilla is 400 feet tall, making it that much more of an impossible beast! Much of the rest repeats what is learned in the Japanese version (including its presentation of "real" dinosaur imagery intended to bolster belief in the "reel" monster), although maybe some things were lost in translation. But this time a dubbed-in Yamane voice states that Godzilla was "resurrected" due to repeated hydrogen bomb experiments, which can be interpreted to mean anything from mutation to simple (re)awakening from beneath the waves following a disturbing blast (after "some rare phenonemom" [*sic*] of nature allowed the species to "reproduce itself," presumably while submerged, through geological ages until the present day). Or did he imply some sort of supernatural process? Then at the film's conclusion, Steve Martin remarks that the menace was over without suggesting Yamane's angst over what might happen if nuclear bomb testing were to continue (which of course happened).

The very nature of sequels is that the need for proving the existence of the monster is minimized (because we've already seen it alive). Also, explaining the background science of the monsters can be presented much earlier in the film, instead of having the usual big, convoluted buildup deciphering the scientific mystery. Usually in such cases the focus hinges on addressing why it is alive (again!), and above all, how may it be destroyed (again). So in Toho's *Godzilla Raids Again* (1955), there isn't too much emphasis placed on explaining the nature of a second Godzilla. This is indeed a second specimen, as we can see from the more buck-toothed fangs and the slightly different sounding growl. There is added intrigue over a new dino-monster which Godzilla battles to the death. But if audiences already accept that a Godzilla once appeared (i.e., in *Gojira*), then the appearance of a second Godzilla *and* another species of giant dino-monster adversary is much easier to swallow.

So this time, instead, to properly interpret a pairing of dino-monsters, it takes two paleontologists (Drs. Yamane and Tadokoro), who now especially consider the new adversarial creature, Anguirus, which has been reported. It has been witnessed on a small Pacific island (sparring with the second Godzilla) by two pilots, who share their observations with a scientific team. The pilots are shown dinosaur drawings, a pile of paleo-pictures (yes—including another rendition of Zallinger's *Age of Reptiles Tyrannosaurus*), and they flip through pages in "Dr. Preterry Hawdon's" illustrated dinosaur book. And then one of the pilots excitedly finds a picture of the quadruped Anguirus, spliced into the book, which, as Dr. Tadokoro (Masao Shimizu) explains, is an "ankylosaur" that was/is 150 to 200 feet tall, a geological contemporary of Godzilla. It would be unbecoming of me to challenge a true expert such as Dr. Hawdon in such affairs, but note this height would have made Anguirus as tall or taller than the first Godzilla. So either the new live specimen is smaller than its discovered fossilized specimens, or Hawdon meant 150 to 200 feet "long" instead of "tall." Also, borrowing from a prevalent former idea concerning the American plated *Stegosaurus*, Anguirus allegedly contains two brains (*Stegosaurus* was formerly thought to have had two, one in the lumbar region), adding to its aggressive nature. So this time, most of the explanation on logically explaining the beast(s) addresses the new monster, Anguirus. Where has it been hiding? In undersea caves in the ocean abyss, created by geological upheaval.

Both species supposedly lived 70 to 150 million years ago, when most representatives of their species became extinct. However, Dr. Tadokoro claims that hydrogen bomb testing that woke Godzilla also "awakened the ankylosaur." Dr. Yamane, sounding despondent and depressed, adds that Godzilla is "sensitive" to light, presumably due to "memories" of the hydrogen bomb testing exposure. This light sensitivity trait becomes a key plot element later on, when the second Godzilla is attracted to the coast by ignited gasoline tanks. Meanwhile, Anguirus seems relatively invulnerable to Godzilla's fiery breath. Yes, once more Japan is under a greater threat than the prospect of nuclear weapons.

As was the case with *Gojira*, *Godzilla Raids Again* was modified for American audiences, being released as 1959's *Gigantis the Fire Monster.* "Are there darker and more sinister secrets on Earth?" a narrator asks rhetorically. Apparently! Much of the film proceeds as before, although here, Dr. Tadokoro's dubbed-in voice expounds in a slightly different and rather more convoluted vein. The new dino-monster is also referred to a "gigantis" variety of dinosaur, also known as an "anguilosaurus," or the Anguiris, "killer of the living." And strangely enough, it may "come alive after years of hibernation due to radioactive fallout," Tadokoro reads from the children's dinosaur book. Also, it says the Anguirus could wipe out the human race singlehandedly, a curious remark to be found in a dinosaur book. Perhaps most importantly for what is to follow, the Anguirus (now stated to have had at least 3 brains) happens to stem from a breed of "fire monsters," with emphasis on the aspect of fire.

Now, in the American version, Dr. Yamane shows a 1:40-long film showing the provenance of the two fire monsters, emphasizing their fiery nature. (Incidentally, to date, the source of the stop-motion animated dinosaur footage in this clip remains a mystery.) This is essentially a "life through geological time" clip which has been developed "as science has been able to reconstruct it." This strange video purportedly explains why these monsters have a common *fire* derivation, underscoring the picture's Americanized title. Unfortunately, this addition to the American version of the film makes Dr. Yamane look rather feckless. Since paleontology's infancy two centuries ago, the time-honored means of conveying knowledge of the geological past in books, dioramas and natural history museums was through conveying imagery showing life through time. This was how people in the western world generally came to understand what past geological ages were like and what life they contained. The aforementioned *Age of Reptiles* mural by Zallinger, for example, was the 20th century's most magnificent example of a life-through-time portrayal. So it is perhaps not too surprising that in an Americanized version of a Japanese dino-monster movie, in which scientists are striving to put the rational spin on two otherwise distorted and impossible creatures, the traditional way of explaining where such beasts came from would be in deference to the standard for portraying the geological past, as in a life-through-geological-time presentation.

And so the film clip (and we do not know if it was made to match already scripted dialogue or whether the script was tweaked to align with stock footage sequences), focuses on the significance of fire in the creation of the titular "fire monsters." There is a heightened emphasis on explaining the provenance of so-called "fire monsters." The narrator of the film clip discusses the Earth's fiery origins, boiling gases resulting in hotter and more primitive forms of life that were born, adapted to fiery matter. Indeed, "their very existence was based upon the element of fire." Now the science is sounding alchemical, or medieval. Anyway, dinosaurian creatures were evolving that breathed and apparently survived in fire. Indeed, "fire was a part of their organic makeup." Cosmic rays bombarded the Earth, causing extinctions and forcing the fire-adapted monsters to go underground to survive. Then the Earth went through major upheavals; volcanic disturbances occurred and lava issued from the Earth's core. When the monsters "came out of hiding" after nuclear bomb tests filled the atmosphere with radiation, because they were conditioned to being exposed to fire, they were practically indestructible. Well, once reanimated in Japan, one fire monster kills the other, and the survivor (i.e., the second Godzilla) later becomes encased in glacial ice. So ice prevails over fire ... (until *King Kong vs. Godzilla* when the second—or a third?—Godzilla melts his way out of an iceberg).

The films addressed here cover the Cold War period when such giant dino-monsters and assorted species of prehistoria were still taken seriously on one level or another. These movies came with stark messages for mankind. Early on, producers thought such movies were proper vehicles for delivering stern messages, and the formula stuck. At best such creatures are faux-prehistoric, or "prehistoric anachronisms" because they're living in modernity—so they can't be "prehistoric" in the now. All of them are biologically impossible according to natural laws. No known vertebrate animal could hibernate for millions of years. The Japanese variety are too huge and would collapse under their own weight, or their organs wouldn't properly function. Radioactive monsters couldn't possibly live, even if mutated.[14]

By the mid–1960s, real dinosaurs had attained a new unprecedented level of popularity among the masses, which escalated throughout the next half-century. It just wasn't necessary to introduce or explain what a dinosaur was anymore, or to suggest or imply using assorted paleoimagery spliced into the film that if real dinosaurs existed, then something else (a dinosaurian mimic) could also exist that was genetically *allied to* real prehistoric dinosaurs, yet was unlike any real kind of prehistoric animal known to science.[15]

During the Cold War, movie producers and directors recognized the value of presenting examples of real paleoimagery (dinosaur skeletons and paleoart drawings) on screen to help "prove" the "what-if" metaphorical reality of the giant fictional dino-monsters that would soon plunder civilization. Relying on genuine dinosaur anatomy, such as prehistoric monsters restored in museum displays, murals and paintings as visualized by revered contemporary paleoartists (working in concert with professional paleontologists), chimeric, filmic paleomonsters could be designed either as stop-motion puppets or human-sized costumes that would seem more a bit more believable to attentive audiences who comprehended their inner horrific meaning, if only on a subliminal level. And note that, as in the Americanized "Gigantis" fire monster 1959 case, how prevalent, persistent and perhaps soothing remained a dollop of traditional life-through-time messaging, even in the face of stark Cold War reality.

Chapter Eleven

Oxygen Destroyers

When Oceans Die

It seems so silly now, but I remember first fearing for the oceans. In the spring of 1969, a freshman high school science class friend informed me of "polywater," an alleged super-dense phase of water otherwise purported to have physical properties anomalous to ordinary water. Most frighteningly, veritably like something out of a mad scientist/sci-fi flick, this polymeric water could "grow at the expense of normal water under any conditions found in the environment." Yes, my friend nervously sighed, Earth's oceans might solidify like epoxy, inevitably causing life's extinction. Well, as scientists continued to investigate the phenomenon, polywater was falsified, leading to a 1970 *Science* journal letter titled, "Polywater is hard to swallow."[1] But no sooner had this dire global crisis been resolved, than suddenly another more serious issue arose—a proposal for the fate of our growing stock of nuclear reactor wastes, which, according to a contemporary *Time* magazine article, would be best buried at sea in deep subduction zone conveyer belt trenches where, through the course of geological time, the hot rad-waste would descend miles underneath the continents.[2] It only took scant knowledge of giant monster movies to realize what might happen if any hi-rad wastes leaked from those (allegedly) hermetically sealed canisters into seawater. Radiation levels would escalate, at first along Pacific coastlines, but once more resulting in global extinctions. By then, as a budding real scientist, I began to realize that if the oceans were ever to die, so would all life.

Of course, there was also filmdom's ultimate super-weapon—Dr. Serizawa's (played by Akihito Hirata) fictional "oxygen destroyer" device introduced in Toho's *Gojira* (1954) that I first witnessed in the Americanized *Godzilla, King of the Monsters* (1956), with which the first Godzilla, a living radioactive manifestation of the hydrogen bomb, was destroyed in a most curious fashion. As we'll soon see, when it comes to destroying oceanic systems, anoxia (or the lack of oxygen) is a time-honored, naturalistic mechanism, but in the annals of science fiction, the "oxygen destroyer" was unique! Of course this device was a metaphorical invention. Theoretical principles underlying how the oxygen destroyer should work are never clarified for audiences as in the conventions of chemical reaction formulae. Presumably the device somehow vigorously catalyzes splitting of aqueous oxygen into highly reactive oxy-radicals, thus depriving any aquatic organism from aerobically sustaining itself. (No, this couldn't be an elemental fissioning of the oxygen nucleus, which would result in an unlikely nuclear explosion.)

From Serizawa's demonstration in a fish tank, there appears to be rapid and vigorous aqueous oxidation/combustion happening. According to Godzilla maven William Tsutsui, the oxygen destroyer "disintegrates the oxygen in water, asphyxiating the organisms."[3] It seems as if the key component of the oxygen destroyer itself *may* be a powdery substance that Serizawa holds within a crucible. But then the substance is exposed to water, causing bubbles to form, dissolving flesh from fish bone. And as we eventually see when a full scale oxygen-destroying device is used, Godzilla liquefies, leaving its skeleton on the seabed, which in turn disappears. (Presumably, at *Gojira*'s climax, Serizawa's tissues dissolve as well, as do many aquatic organisms through surrounding fathoms and many cubic feet of sea water.)

So conscientiously, Serizawa, who wears the laboratory smock and eye patch symbol of a true mad scientist, wants to keep this awful invention a secret. For if other, belligerent nations of the world authorized widespread use of such a weapon in war, analogous to the Cold War's proliferation of nuclear bombs—especially the hydrogen bomb—well, then, conceivably mankind would either deliberately or perhaps inadvertently sterilize oceanic life, which (making a logical leap not fully divulged or well explained in *Gojira*) would ultimately spell doomsday. In Toho's successful efforts to suspend disbelief, Serizawa's oxygen destroyer is considered more deadly than even a hydrogen bomb. Nevertheless, judging from his dialog, Dr. Serizawa doesn't seem to have a keen grasp on how his invention actually works.

After dropping a small pellet of his substance into the fish tank for its first demonstration—a pellet that dramatically opens, releasing bubbles—Serizawa states that "the oxygen destroyer splits atoms into fluids." One wonders why it doesn't also destroy room air oxygen too, asphyxiating himself, Emiko, or later Ogata. After all, oxygen is more highly concentrated in room air than in the fish tank. Yet despite such hazards, Serizawa describes the device in terms that place it on a par or even above the deadly workings of the hydrogen bomb when he declares that he stumbled "across an unknown form of energy … a powerful force that scared me beyond words … ." These are words that could have been uttered by physicists witnessing the Trinity test explosion (i.e., the first atomic bomb test conducted in 1945), or those who pondered the hydrogen bomb's devastating potentiality. Then, of course, holding a crucible, Serizawa goes on to say, "A little piece of this dropped into the water could turn the entire Tokyo Bay into a graveyard…. Used as a weapon, this would be as powerful as a nuclear bomb. It could totally destroy humankind!"

Intriguingly, whereas it required considerable man-years of research, engineering, testing and calculations for both the U.S. and other countries to first develop atomic bombs, followed several years later by fusion bomb arsenals, Serizawa has created something superior in power and energy all by himself, in his basement laboratory, unbeknownst to others. This suggests that Serizawa's a virtuoso among mad scientists! And ultimately, the oxygen destroyer prevails over the 20th century's most horrific apparition—Godzilla, the allegorical radioactive product of the hydrogen bomb.

As stated, the oxygen destroyer is unique to science fiction. Ordinarily, in such filmic fare—yet not exclusively—when oceanic systems are plagued by terrible inventions, radiation is at the heart of the matter, reflecting compelling Cold War fears of exposure to radiation from bomb testing, the nuclear reactor industry, and of course the totality of thermonuclear war. Eventually, by the early 1960s, as concerns over improper management of industrial wastes and liberal application of toxic chemicals mounted, fears naturally segued from the radioactive arena toward exposures to chemical pollutants while sci-fi creators had a field day mirroring these concerns in many fantastic forms. And sometimes imaginative writers spun frightening "what if?" scenarios, combining radioactive with chemical exposures, a sort of melding of the H-bomb with Rachel Carson's *Silent Spring* (or her *The Edge of the Sea*, if you will) ... such as in a comic book story, "Creatures of the Deep," featured in *Nightmare* no. 5, August 1971.[4]

In this harrowing tale (scripted by Chuck McNaughton; pencil by Jack Katz; inked by Jack Abel), set in a then slightly futuristic setting (i.e., 1978), a team of marine biologists aspire to save the "waters of a world dying of pollution." Already the "water of the world is almost dead—stagnant," with very little life as a result of the dumping and leaking of industrial wastes and defoliants. On the basis of scanty evidence, the solution seems to be in applying a "radioactive protoplasm" invented by the Russians, which initially acts like "penicillin" for seawater. Three days later the ocean is rejuvenated with life forms, although these are horribly mutated, gigantic monstrosities, some of which amble ashore, attacking cities! To destroy the mutant creatures, the Russians nuke the oceans, only worsening the already dire circumstances. With a second armada of fishy-looking monsters gestating below the waves, an awful result of human consumption of contaminated water is divulged; now human newborns exposed to the water mutate into gill-men! Don't just blame the Russians, for we all had skin in this horrendous game. Without healthy oceans, man cannot live. In taking the waters of the world for granted, we caused the oceans to spawn what shall doom mankind. (See Figure 11-1.)

Several other Cold War films and stories were inspired by radioactive polluting of the oceans from nuclear weapons testing, rad-waste dumping and other awful possibilities, although in these cases sparing the oceans was never the primary theme. First, in another comic book, Charlton's *Gorgo* (no. 16, December 1963), a bomb test unleashes a "denser field of radiation," causing kelp (seaweed) to mutate, enlarge and become ambulatory. Only the aquatic dino-monster Gorgo with his mother are able to festoon the fetid foliage, converting it into giant monster salad.[5] And in 1955's *It Came from Beneath the Sea*, a 200-foot-long octopus (having only 5 arms due to the film's modest budget), turned radioactive due to hydrogen bomb explosions in the Pacific Ocean, attacks San Francisco. The implications for the world are dire, yet the oceans of the world (especially the Pacific, where all the H-bomb testing occurred) are not in immediate danger. The U.S. military doesn't invent anything as dastardly as an oxygen destroyer to defeat the menace and does not fear the possible danger of further organismal attacks from the undersea realm. It's as if by defeating this one giant radioactive monster, the true menace was over and done with, even though our guard was down. Yet we're unable to conceive what still might happen, afterward.

And in *The Giant Behemoth* (1958), biomagnification of radiological components in the oceans spawns a gigantic radioactive dino-monster known as the "Paleosaurus" that attacks London. The more conventional dino-monster-as-allegory-for-the-Bomb theme is reflected here, at the expense of how dumping of nuclear waste and bomb testing may actually *transform* the oceans into uninhabitable environments. *The Horror of Party Beach* (1964) surveyed the nuclear waste dumping theme as well, although this time the hideous creatures emerging from the sea are peculiar gill-men. This picture combined the popular beach cult movie theme with then prevalent monster mania. The party-crashing creatures are spawned when radwaste oozing out of drums dumped into the sea secretes onto a human skull, transforming it into beach babe-murdering, blood-sucking, zombie-like jellyfish, "kept alive through radioactive

Fig 11-1: An undersea amphibious dino-monster spawned in the hellish destruction of the oceans, as recounted graphically in *Nightmare* no. 5, "Creatures of the Deep" (illustration by *Prehistoric Times* editor and artist Mike Fredericks, used with permission).

decay." They're destroyed with sodium metal; oceans and marine ecology are left feeling a little exploited, but are otherwise unharmed.

And (using imagery of Serizawa's killed laboratory fish as a segue), in 1964's *The Flesh Eaters*, a mad scientist self-exiled to a deserted island manically intends to rule the world with a dangerous microbe synthesized by Nazi technology during World War II. The flesh-eating microbe, unleashed from a test tube that fortuitously opened at sea long after the war ended, is proliferating in a rather uncontrollable manner, destroying schools of fish and humans, dissolving tissues, leaving only skeletons (and blood). This portends to be an oceanic and therefore world-ending scenario, were it not for a heroic pair of Americans who satisfy us all with another filmic happy ending after they discover that the enlarged and mutated creatures are sensitive to blood hemoglobin.

By the 1970s, however, as may be gleaned from the aforementioned *Nightmare* comic book tale, human angst segued from radiological concerns toward chemical pollution of the globe (or really a merging of the two). This is evident in two British productions, both titled *Doomwatch*. In one episode of the televised BBC program (broadcast 1970–72, comprising a total of 38 episodes covering numerous sci-fi themes), dumping of radioactive wastes causes monstrous creatures to emerge from the sea. Or as Spencer R. Weart noted in his *The Rise of Nuclear Fear* (2012), "Fish grew to a great size while the fisherfolk became shambling monsters with a penchant for insane violence."[6] In the 1972 movie version, however, the cause of monstrous mutations (an affliction known as acromegaly) is dumping of non-radioactive, chemical wastes (i.e., from an oil tanker spill).

Yet with the exception of the menace posed by Dr. Serizawa's haunting invention or perhaps the *Flesh Eaters* circumstance if left unattended, in such cases the oceans were never overtly in danger of *completely* dying, as if stricken with a universal polywater condition, subjected to a globally afflicting oxygen destroyer device or something much worse. Even the most dire episodes of the television series *Voyage to the Bottom of the Sea* (1964–68), or the antecedent 1961 film, never quite hit this theme fully on the noggin. The seas themselves just always seemed to be there and somehow eternal, unchanging, that is, unless our oceans were to be completely absconded by fascist alien reptiloids as in A.C. Crispin's 1984 novel, *V*—based on the popular television series—leaving our planet as desolate as the surface of Mars. H.G. Wells's Martians presumably aimed to exploit this resource, and pillaging our oceans remains a common sci-fi premise today, as in recent films such as *Battle: Los Angeles* and *Oblivion*. In J.G. Ballard's short story "Deep End," it is mankind who has drained the oceans, reducing the ocean basins to mere lakes, in order to electrolytically extract oxygen with which atmospheres of alien worlds could become oxygenated and terraformed.[7]

Serizawa doesn't quite fit the mold of a traditional "mad scientist" because he dies honorably and, in the end, we do find ourselves *trusting* him to save Japan and the planet, and to prevent man from ever going too far with his self-developed, unwieldy weapon of mass destruction. Serizawa destroys his notes and sacrifices himself, thus allowing the secret of the oxygen destroyer to die with him. He does what seems necessary to avoid a very dark moment in future history. Yet it is entirely within man's genetic constitution to tinker and create that which might destroy. The Frankenstein complex, if you will!

The means of oxygen-destroying is rediscovered in 1995's *Godzilla vs. Destoroyah*. This time, another scientist with good, practical intentions aims to resolve worldwide food shortages using "micro-oxygen," which, according to Emiko Yamane, turns out to be "almost identical to Serizawa's invention." Soon Japan and a Godzilla suffering from nuclear overheating, rapidly trending toward a world-shattering critical mass meltdown, experience how toxic are the mutating effects of an oxygen-destroying device on ancient micro-organisms. Fish are killed in a public aquarium, then the resultant reptilian-crustaceans mount an attack. The new, giant crab-like winged creature, Destoroyah, is a manifestation of an oxygen-destroyer. As Steve Ryfle notes in his *Japan's Favorite Mon-star*, like Godzilla, Destoroyah raises "questions about the long-term effects of man's mass-destruction weapons."[8]

Yes, Serizawa had burned his notes, but mankind is wickedly resourceful when it comes to inventions. So, in a *science fictional* vein, isn't it tempting to consider how all that is happening might have come long before? It would seem that inevitably, once any human (or humanoid, or "reptiloid") discovers how to control fire, that someday down the road he is destined to also master nuclear energy, and then, in turn, possibly also discover the means of creating an allegorical oxygen destroyer. Please consider!

Perhaps many of you regard the oceans of our planet as having always been there, sort of like in that ending to Karel Zeman's *Journey to the Beginning of Time* (1955/1966). But the oceans, as we know them today, have certainly not been eternal. They have an origin as well as a distinctive geological/geochemical history. (And so does the composition of our atmosphere.) As our planet testifies, oceans really can "sicken" or even die. Mass extinctions of both oceanic and terrestrial life are the result. Such events have happened in the deep geological past. For example, during the publicized, terminal Mesozoic event 66 million years ago, non-avian dinosaurs and many other marine species became extinct. That infamous "K-Pg" (Cretaceous-Paleogene) episode resulted in a near-sterilized "Strangelove Ocean" of geologically abbreviated duration, triggered by an asteroid impact (but exacerbated by intensive volcanic basaltic flow activity as well).[9] The oceans also were entirely frozen over (perhaps more than twice) too, during the much earlier Precambrian Era.

But, icy conditions aside, it is exceedingly warm, prolonged greenhouse conditions that have most often imperiled our world's oceans of the geological past—creating anoxia (an absence of oxygen). As stated previously, when it comes to destroying oceanic systems, although Serizawa couldn't have known it then, anoxia *is* the time-honored, naturalistic mechanism. In fact, the most prominent greenhouse extinction event (the Permian-Triassic) in which over 95 percent of all marine species suffered extinction 251 million years ago, and at least seven more "minor" mass extinctions episodes (occurring 490, 360, 201, 190, 135, 100 and 58 million years ago) are characterized by an extreme *oxygen deficiency*—anoxia—recorded in marine deposits in the form of blackened deposits, each episode lasting several million years! Under these conditions, anaerobic bacteria (which cannot tolerate oxygen) that are usually confined to the deepest oceanic layers by shallower, circulating oxygenated water, rose to the surface, proliferated and emitted lethal hydrogen sulfide gas, poisoning the upper depths of the seas and atmosphere.[10] These sulfide bacteria are in fact Nature's "real" Destoroyah!

And just what is mankind doing to the atmosphere today? Will human-caused greenhouse conditions ultimately trigger yet another ice-free, mass extinction episode characterized by deadly oceanic anoxia? Are we inadvertently performing what Serizawa vowed should never happen? Are we now, metaphorically, like Serizawa, unwittingly unleashing a "powerful force" even mightier and far more lethal than the hydrogen bomb that will not only harm oceanic but also terrestrial life?

A prevalent sci-fi literary "personification" device that has become especially prevalent since the 1950s is using intelligent dinosaurs (or "dinosauroids") of various constitution (including Godzilla) to reflect the human plight, sometimes humorously, but often ominously. After all, dinosaurs went extinct, so if they could warn us today surely they just might have some useful advice for us to right the course, before it's too late. Right? So it's tempting to speculate even further here, about the meaning of those repeated periods of anoxia recorded in geological time. Bear with me on this little mind-bender for a bit longer. (We'll return to this avenue of thought in Chapter Eighteen.)

Those repeated cases of prolonged oceanic anoxia ... well, what if they had been caused by prehistoric creatures that rose to intelligence, attaining civilization and wielding technology? (Not too crazy—this is a turn of events that sci-fi writers have often rejoiced speculating about.[11]) After fire is harnessed, in time, nuclear power beckons, as it always would to any technological species. A natural consequence might have been that they also discovered how to exploit nuclear energy, building ever-more-powerful hydrogen bombs that at first threatened to doom their species and the planet.

Could there have been previous cases of "Godzillas" mutated by these radioactive weapons when tested, which then could have been destroyed only by ancient, say, conscientious although "reptiloid" versions of Serizawa? And then might have the oxygen-destroyer been discovered, rediscovered and ultimately utilized by belligerent governments, first eliminating the Godzillean threats, but eventually *misused* (Serizawa's greatest fear!), thus killing the oceans successively (i.e., 251 million years ago, 201 million years ago, 190 million years ago, 135 million years ago, 100 million years ago, etc.), while causing extinctions of contemporary higher life forms? Traces of their ancient "reptiloid" civilizations would have long ago weathered and eroded into lifeless seas (as those of modern civilization will in only a few millennia—after people).

Oxygen-destroyers! Is it possible that what could have happened now (if only in a science fictional vein) *already happened before*? And is destined to happen again?

I'm just saying....

Chapter Twelve

"After and Before": *Gorgo's Alternate Adventures*

MGM's *Gorgo,* based on an original story by Eugene Lourie and Daniel Hyatt, debuted in the U.S. on March 29, 1961; Carson Bingham's novelization of the script was published many months earlier, in July of the previous year. Within a few months following release of the filmic blockbuster, Charlton Comics published the first in a series of comic books featuring the two Gorgos appearing in the movie. The first issue, recounting key events transpiring in the film, was published on May 1, 1961. The series would cease in September 1965 ("Land of Long Ago"), concluding a print run of 23 issues, with 3 additional books highlighting both the "return" and "revenge" of the titular monster released between 1962 and 1964. While Toho Godzilla's many heroic and sometimes outlandish adventures ran to considerably longer duration, spanning from 1954 through the early 2000s, along the way spawning late 1970s television episodes and comic books, by comparison Gorgo's adventures were more immediate to the date of MGM's King Brothers film release and quite compressed in time.

By the time Gorgo's final adventure hit the comic book racks, Toho's *Ghidrah: The Three-Headed Monster* was about to be released in America, featuring Godzilla's first encounter with an outer space monster. Yet, by then, in the comic book arena, the two Gorgos seemingly did all that and more and in much faster turn-around than Toho's Godzilla. Toho's Godzilla series eventually covered many themes and "bases" already analogously dealt with by Charlton's creative team.

For ease of convention, the offspring dino-monster will hereafter be referred to as "Gorgo," while the larger mother dino-monster shall be named "Ogra." Or occasionally I will refer to the *pair* of roving monsters as "Ogras." These monikers are consistent with terminology found in the comic book series as well as the tie-in 1960 pulp novel, which we'll also come to.

Yes, even before the movie was released, a pulp writer had published a tie-in novel that probably had moviegoers expecting far more than they actually witnessed in the film's plot. Carson Bingham's 1960 novel, *Gorgo,* is a crisply written, well-kept secret. It's competent, highly satisfying, paced fluently and keeps readers on the edge (even if you've seen the film, which is remarkably different from the book). A case of pulp fiction masterfully rendered; to me, the novel is better than the 1961 MGM film. Why? It's just a more poignant story, one mirroring the early post-nuclear age and Cold War angst far better than does the movie script, yet reminiscent of the Godzilla's original meaning. Plus—in the third main section of the book, titled "Armageddon," you'll read of more intense "daikaiju" urban destruction and abject mayhem than in any other such novel to date. (See Figure 12-1.)

Here, we'll address the novel after considering the comic book series (which rather counterintuitively required more time and personal resources to examine). Perhaps, too, it's just more appropriate to outline the suite of stories comprising the comic book series that are intended for a more general or adolescent audience, before delving into more adult themes, as exploited in the novel.

Fig 12-1: Cover to Carson Bingham's 1960 novel *Gorgo*, detailing a far more harrowing human plight than in the 1961 film.

In the summer of 2011, I became curious about Gorgo's comic book adventures, which until then I only had faint knowledge of. What *else* had happened to Gorgo after the dino-monsters retreated to the Thames River? So I began collecting original copies of the books at the most affordable prices until I achieved a complete collection.[1] Yet beyond idle curiosity concerning Gorgo's two dozen additional adventures, it was inviting to consider—to what extent did Gorgo's numerous experiences mirror what Godzilla would later do or encounter? To what extent is Cold War nuclear angst and fear of radiation reflected therein—as it most certainly was in the early Godzilla film series? More specifically, to what extent did Gorgo's monster rally pattern form a template for Godzilla's films of the later 1960s and beyond? Did Gorgo become a "superhero" icon in the comics before Godzilla did in the movies, and to what extent may Gorgo's comic book persona have influenced Toho?

Furthermore, were aliens, outer space adventures and undersea civilizations in vogue in the Gorgo comic book series even before they were introduced in the Toho Godzilla series? To what extent were Gorgo's probable dinosaurian and prehistoric nature exploited after Godzilla's loose ties with dinosaurs were "explained" in 1954, 1955 and 1963? How does the introduction of villains and mad scientists in Charlton's Gorgo comic book series relate to those slimeball characters in the Godzilla film series? Is Gorgo more of a kaiju in the comic book series than in the 1960 novel or 1961 film, and how does Gorgo's possible kaiju-ness compare to Godzilla's over the same (1961 to 1965) interval? Also of interest—how does Gorgo's relationship with a winged Reptilicus in issue #12 (issue date May 1, 1963) presage Godzilla's later teaming with winged Rodan?

And so with such questions in mind, first, I'll emphasize those books in the series of 26, more thematically hinging upon or exploiting Cold War nuclear angst or environmental fears. (Contents of other books conveying these messages to a lesser extent will be relegated sequentially to accompanying footnotes.) As we'll soon note, Gorgo in the comics and tie-in novel bore overt nuclear and ecological messages that were unapparent in the 1961 film. (See Figure 12-2.)

Fig 12-2: A stylistic recent illustration prepared especially for this book, capturing the essence and action of the *Gorgo* comic book series (illustration by Jason Croghan [2015], used with permission).

Gorgo was "spewed up" from the "bottomless depths" by a volcanic eruption in issue #1 (job #6673).[2] Gorgo would teach mankind that his greed was his/our worst nature, a trait that would surely destroy us someday. Perceived as a "2 million year old" monster (which would place the Ogras' provenance within the Late Pliocene epoch, not during the Mesozoic Era), it isn't satisfactorily explained exactly how Gorgo and its mother survived undersea undetected for so long. Predictably, the comic book is essentially a reprisal of the movie (and not so much the novel). Although known to the inhabitants of Nara Island as the mythical "Ogra," the captured youngster is renamed "Gorgo—the 8th Wonder of the World" by Dorkin's London Circus executives. The juvenile dino-monster is to be exploited, displayed in Battersea Park. Money will be made hand over fist!

Then, fueled by sheer maternal instinct, the considerably larger mother "Ogra" (who is not named a "Gorgo" in the books, although in the 1960 novel, "Ogra" is a norse god affiliated with their appearance) vengefully seeks her offspring, tracing its scent by sea all the way to London, smashing Nara Island along the route. At this time, the Prime Minister judges that "Atomic weapons are out of the question [in the city's] heavily populated area...." Rather, tanks, jet planes and missiles assail mother Ogra, failing to stop the "prehistoric creature." Gasoline is pumped into the Thames, ignited but also to no avail. "Fire was used ... millions of volts of electricity ... nothing availed! Mama and Monster were heading for home...." Young Gorgo is rescued by the mother, picked up and carried back to the sea. In short, this book is a well-done, colorful summarization of the movie.

In issue #2 (August 1961, job #A-457), "Gorgo's Return,"[3] America receives its first taste of giant dino-monster cataclysm since Ray Harryhausen's Rhedosaur pummeled New York City in 1953. This time, we learn that following the devastating London attack, the British have charged the Irish Sea with 10 billion volts of electricity to ward off any future attacks from the Ogras. Certainly not an ecologically friendly preventative or security measure. But Ogra—mother and (presumed) son Gorgo—are resting 30,000 feet down on the sea bed, far removed from where the torturous voltage is being applied. However, they have inadvertently damaged the Trans-Atlantic cable, prompting a repair mission that awakens the young slumbering giant. An air force pilot fires upon Gorgo, enraging the beast, which swims to New York Harbor. Mindful of how London was razed beforehand, the Navy and military land forces are called out to drive the monster back to sea, unsuccessfully. In a panel reminiscent of an amazing scene in *Gojira*, 500,000 volts of electricity applied through high tension wires "doesn't seem to bother him at all!" Meanwhile, the mother Ogra awakens on the sea floor, only to find herself alone.

On land, engineers devise an ingenious way of entrapping Gorgo in a huge sand pit (which later analogously happened to Godzilla in *King Kong vs. Godzilla*). Then one character wonders prophetically, "Have any of you thought ... of Gorgo's mother? We know she exists! She smashed London, remember! Where is she now?" Things get harrowing indeed, as the mother Ogra surfaces, storming ashore. When fire doesn't turn back the beast, the president orders a *hydrogen bomb* strike. (Shades of 2008's *Cloverfield*!) Sirens warn citizens away from the site of impending doom to shelters, while mother Ogra relentlessly advances. The hydrogen bomb is deployed. The dino-monster is engulfed in a fiery blast. Astoundingly, mother Ogra is unfazed, plowing forth through the United Nations Building, onward to the interior of Manhattan Island. What's nearly as strange—New York's buildings remain intact, still available for added dino-monster destruction! And then, while a city broadcast wails reassuringly to any human survivors, "Do not panic, the authorities are in complete control," next, Ogra smashes the Empire State Building. It's evident the book writers vastly underestimated the power unleashed in a fusion bomb chain reaction, as well as the consequences of detonating one in an urban area.

With blatant disregard for radioactivity that must have permeated the region, military personnel track the inevitable path of dino-monster destruction. Only then do they realize the only way to halt Ogra's advance and rid themselves of their plight will be to free young Gorgo from the entrapping sand, such that mother Ogra can escort her son back to the sea. And so, ultimately they "were back where they belonged, miles below the surface. The giant reptiles were able to rest! To sleep!, and perhaps, survive ... and revive again in one year or a century! No man knows ... but we can hope she does not return with her terrible offspring in our lifetime!"

But due to popular demand, the Ogras *did* return, and only a mere month later.

Besides dread of a nuclear attack within our territory, events of the time were wending their way into the Gorgo story continuum. Issue #3, "The Return of Gorgo" (September 1961, job #A-661),[4] concerned a thinly disguised Latin dictator, "Astro," named for a Cuban despot who gained infamy during the Cold War. Not content with ruling just his poverty-stricken island nation, this power-mad terrorist is hellbent on ruling the world—using Gorgo as his invulnerable ally. And he has the scientific backing and wherewithal to serve his awful ambition. Astro's chief zoologist, Dr. Valzo, believes that the Ogra species "did not survive because they could not adjust to changing conditions!" If they had instead been equipped with man's brain they'd be "ruling" our world today. Valzo's statement triggers thoughts of realizing his aspiration for world conquest. Now demented Astro orders Valzo to use fear to condition Gorgo's mind, such that the dino-monster will obey his every spoken command, which of course involves military encroachment upon border nations.

Valzo, fearing punishment, first captures Gorgo (who is peacefully snoozing on the sea bottom alongside his mother), then uses a 1-million-volt wand to prod Gorgo, training the dino-monster to follow orders. This device or weapon would seem rather wimpy compared to the extreme electrical forces Gorgo was already subjected to in issue #2—but comic books *are* quite fanciful, often defying consistency, or bending scientific logic to expediently satisfy plot lines. Plus, younger readers' memory is often short, or forgiving.

Eventually, to avoid pain inflicted from the insidiously charged rod, Gorgo learns to obey Valzo's spoken commands, and hence Astro. Astro augments his military forces with the invincible Gorgo, hence conquering a neighboring country. But the prospect of invincible power and world domination proves contagious. Surprisingly, power-lusting Valzo stages a coup d'etat, seizing control of the island nation itself and also of Gorgo. The tale ends after Gorgo, in the midst of battle, rebels against his master, destroying the volt-carrying rod and dethroning the now helpless Valzo.

And so in issue #4, "Gorgo in Home-Coming" (November 1961, job #A-810),[5] Gorgo becomes something more of a heroic figure, aiding astronaut Major Dunne's return from splashdown in the ocean. While the eye-catching cover of this issue suggests major combat waged between Ogra and mankind, with missiles, jet planes engaging, fiery flames, collapsing buildings and bridges, etc., etc. ... none of this happens in #4's storyline. But first, both Ogras innocently get in the way of U.S. atomic bomb weapons testing; five atomic bombs are detonated in a Navy drill, disturbing their peaceful underwater habitat. So the Ogras are driven southward to a rocky island in a "deserted ocean." Following Major Dunne's successful space orbital mission, his capsule coincidentally parachutes down near the rocky island. Gorgo playfully toys with Dunne's capsule, endangering the astronaut. Dunne eventually befriends Gorgo, even soothing him with a song—"When Irish Eyes Are Smiling"! By sitting on the dino-monster's huge head, Dunne learns how to "ride" Gorgo, like a cowboy would a horse—by kicking the side of his head to coax him into turning in particular directions. In so doing, Dunne directs Gorgo back to New York, where he dismounts and Gorgo submerges, returning to his mother unscathed. Interestingly, other stories were featured within issues of Charlton's Gorgo comics. Issue #4 ends ominously with a short story titled "If you were—," with a civilian answering his son's question ("Dad? Who's our greatest natural enemy?"), to which the father replies, "We have many ... germs and the elements and poisonous snakes and insects ... but man's worst enemy is man himself."[6]

Issue #5, "The Day Manhattan Died," was issued in January 1962 (job #A-969).[7] The cover shows an Ogra battling a strange, gigantic seaweedy-looking organism with a huge eyeball. This time, we gain further "scientific" knowledge concerning the Ogras' origins. Professor Henry Stoddard, who wants to study the creatures, theorizes, "All saurians are sea creatures ... millions, billions of years ago, I think a great upheaval of nature occurred in the sea and the saurians crawled onto land to survive! Thus began the age of the reptiles! But many of the sea creatures were trapped in the water, crusts formed on the sea bottom, preventing them from reaching land," where they survived entombed and concealed *below* the ocean floor. Then during the age of man, atomic testing shattered portions of the sub-oceanic crust, allowing Ogras to venture forth, emerging to the upper sea. But, despite his thirst for knowledge, the military doesn't want Professor Stoddard snooping around to find the Ogras, stirring up more trouble for mankind. So Stoddard furtively charters a boat out to sea anyway.

Stoddard succeeds in his endeavor, locating the Ogras, but while Gorgo's mother slumbers in an undersea cavern, the military attacks, firing at the young dino-monster. Gorgo, "bewildered," heads for shore, soon followed by his mother, who has been awakened by nuclear depth charges. Next, a creature from beneath the "crusts," fractured by the nuclear bomb—as theorized by Stoddard—emerges. This new, tentacular creature is a "living nightmare, a creature of the ancient seas, as old as time itself!" Think of it as sort of a *Cloverfield*-ish entity. The slimy thing heads for Manhattan, where the Ogras are already smashing their regular quota of buildings. The monsters converge, resulting in "abysmal combat, like an nightmare torn from the bloody scenes of the Earth's youth! The thunder of horror of that awful conflict will always remain like a tinge of madness on the brain of every human who witnessed it!" Gorgo's parent dispatches the monster, and New York is spared further damage. Stoddard is elated that his theory was substantiated, admonishing that maybe next time "they will listen" to him. One panel on the final page shows a military coordinator stating through a microphone, "All right! Call in all units! We owe Gorgo and his mother something for killing that other nightmare...." So the Ogras are becoming increasingly "heroic," even though they've been grossly, tragically mistreated by mankind. Shades of Godzilla's 1971 battles with Hedorah—the "Smog Monster."

By the issuance of *Gorgo* #6, "And the Sea Spewed Death" (job #A-1134)[8] in April 1962, the booklet price had leaped from a dime to 12 cents. This time Dr. Stoddard has intriguingly theorized that mythical Atlantis was a genuine continent that slowly sank into the depths. Accordingly, its inhabitants gradually evolved into an advanced race of marine creatures, "pseudo-humans" capable of living underwater. Stoddard wants to find the lost Atlantean cities and civilization. It just so happens that while Stoddard is trying to convince military brass that his new theory is correct, the Ogras have settled into an undersea cave, which is really the mouth leading to what remains of Atlantis! And, unknown to man, the Atlanteans, who communicate via telepathy, are plotting to take back the terrestrial world: "We shall ... rule as Kings! The humans that crawl the Earth shall be helpless against us and our weapons!"

But the sleeping Ogras are blocking their only means of entering the upper ocean, at the cave mouth. Using "*atomic* handguns" to move the beasts proves ineffectual, as the Ogras are only irritated by the disturbance. Consequently, Gorgo and his mother battle the Atlanteans backward through the cave, invading their city, which is razed even more quickly than London and New York were before by our titular "wrecking crew" duo. When the

Atlanteans unleash their giant crabs, dramatically, a battle begins, "such as the deep had never before witnessed! Creatures that should never have lived, never have been born, spawn of the ages, of the devil sea, locked in abysmal combat with death as the prize!" But in the end, the Atlanteans, even aided by giant crab monsters, are no match for the Ogras, who destroy the huge city cavern, burying it under rocky rubble. It's the end of Atlantis, but humans will never realize that Gorgo and his mother defended mankind, however inadvertently, from certain subjugation at the hands of a race technologically superior to man. Meanwhile ... the military continues to view the Ogras as our greatest menace.

In the midst of atomic weaponry testing, the ocean lair was becoming problematic as well as "political" for the Ogras, as we find in issue #7, titled "Menace from the Sea" (June 1962, job #A-1310).[9] Whereas previously Charlton introduced a strangely familiar Latin dictator, this time a certain contemporary Russian communist leader resembling Kruschev menaces both the Ogras as well as the U.S. This unscrupulous leader plans to launch atomic and hydrogen bombs from atomic submarines that will be relatively undetected on radar ... until too late! And so a "mighty armada" of atomic subs sets course to "obliterate the free world." But Gorgo and his mother stand in the way of their plans for conquest. In an underwater assault, they smash the submarines before they're able to launch the deadly missiles. Then they climb ashore and go berserk, attacking and pulverizing the secret communist base. In the end, the Ogras have been so thorough in their eradication of the enemy that the U.S. never catches on to what a close call this actually was. Unaware to the U.S. military, the Ogras allowed the free world to dodge a most deadly "bullet."[10]

In "Return from the Deep," #9 (October 1962, job #A-1679), threat of communist attack menaces mankind once more.[11] As Arctic chill descends upon the Ogras, still residing in the northern polar region, both dino-monsters become frozen into the ice like so many other great reptilians of the past "when the Ice Age had suddenly come down from the North ... trapping and killing the monster dinosaurs that had been kings of the Earth." (And as Gigantis the "fire monster" had been preserved within an icy avalanche.) But really they're held in a kind of suspended animation (unlike those other monster reptiles of the past which evidently were all truly dead.) Meanwhile (this is a comic book, remember, where "meanwhile" is a common word), Red China has established a military base near the Pole. And they've tested a nuclear device—a new kind of hydrogen bomb—that is "more compact and deadly than any means of destruction yet tested by Man." And we learn that the Chinese insidiously intend to launch a missile strike against the "free world," yet carried out surreptitiously, so that it will be blamed on the Soviets instead. So when Russia is wiped out in retaliatory doomsday strikes, China can take over the world.

Of course the nuclear explosion frees the Ogras from icy entombment, awakening them once more. So when U.S. pilot Keith Maynard flies an observation run over the area, his jet is swatted down by Gorgo. Parachuting safely, he's captured by the Chinese.

Untangling himself from underwater nets, Gorgo goes on a rampage. Meanwhile, Maynard escapes his captors, radioing the dire circumstances to U.S. military intelligence. The Reds fire one of their new "unstable" hydrogen bombs from a submarine at mother Gorgo, obliterating their base. On a flyover, U.S. pilots notice Maynard only a mile from ground zero, lying on the ice unconscious. He is rescued, but now ungratefully the U.S. planes begin to shell the Ogras. The book concludes ominously, "Nothing more had been heard from the terrifying creatures that had arisen ... they were presumed to be dead! Were they? Or did

Gorgo and his monstrous mother still live, licking their wounds and gathering their strength somewhere in the darkness of the deeps?"[12]

Aliens make a most impressionable appearance in issue #10 (December 1962), titled "The Venusian Terror" (job # A-1850). As mentioned in a previous *G-Fan* article,[13] Venusian monsters were favored outer space monsters through the early 1960s. (So were Martians, but unlike Venusians, these remain popular even today.) Ray Harryhausen's dino-monster "Ymir" had ravaged Earth only a few years prior in 1957's *Twenty Million Miles to Earth,* possibly an indirect source of inspiration for the outer space monsters featured in Gorgo #10. The opening finds Gorgo and his mother cavorting and snoozing, this time (conveniently) having migrated to south Pacific waters. Meanwhile, a huge flying saucer craft hurtles toward Australia, whooshing over Melbourne at 50,000 miles per hour. When an air force jet is caught on a tentacle extending from the saucer, an all-out interplanetary battle ensues. Although Gorgo mistakes the flying saucer for one of mankind's abusive devices, he's also attracted to the chaos and smoky cataclysm. What is happening? Man's nuclear weapons only minimally impact the saucer. Yet, while the gigantic, horned, cyclopean Venusians render minor repairs to their craft, they order the landing party to "destroy all creatures on this planet."

So the giant monsters wreak havoc on Australian cities while Gorgo approaches, drawn by idle curiosity. But soon the struggling monsters are locked in titanic struggle. Although outnumbered by cyclopeans, Gorgo is heroically winning—until a red death ray is fired from the space vessel, stunning our would-be savior. Gorgo's roar of agony awakens his mother, who swims defiantly to shore. With buildings toppling to and fro, Gorgo comes to, furiously wrestling the evil Venusians ... to the death. Now Gorgo is impervious to the ray, and the Venusians begin to fear. As Gorgo's mother approaches, the military settles back, permitting the pair of dino-monsters to lead Earth's defenses. Having expended their alien arsenal, the Venusians have no recourse but to flee the wrath of our mightiest dino-monsters. The damaged space ship departs from Earth's atmosphere. Human survivors remark that Gorgo and his mother are "gentle creatures."[14]

Gorgo #12, "Monsters Rendezvous" (April 1963), introduces an interesting monster character, the winged Reptisaurus, into the series.[15] Yet this is a rather complex story, with too many plot elements and dimensions to weave together successfully in a short comic book. The intended story theme is founded on Jack Finney's *Invasion of the Body Snatchers,* capitalizing on 1950s communist Red scare menace and paranoia.[16] In "Monsters Rendezvous," yet another race of aquatic Venusians invades Earth, although more surreptitiously. These aren't the same species encountered in issue #10, but a more diminutive variety whose plans for world conquest rely on enslaved, "strange" generic globs of matter that will take the form of humans, replacing us.

After capturing an FBI agent and a scientist, the Ogras inadvertently chase some of the Venusians underwater, mistaking them for octopi-like food. While Gorgo decides the "octopi" (i.e., Venusians) are "alien ... foul things" after all, the U.S. military locates their once hidden, domed alien base. The battle is on! Ogras to the rescue! Facilitating Earth's inevitable victory, "another creature from the dawn of time sensed the aliens and hated them immediately! Reptisaurus, the monster from the past, rose into the air on beating leathery wings ...." Allied with winged Reptisaurus, which appears in a mere 3 panels as well as on the cover, the Venusians prove no match for Earth's mighty defenses. With dying breath, the crippled Venusian leader signals to his planet to always "avoid Earth" because of our superior secret weapons ... "huge beasts."

Besides the regular series of Gorgo comic books, Charlton issued three Special Edition books featuring Gorgo. These, reflecting popularity of the Gorgo series, were issued as "Gorgo's Revenge" (January 1962), "The Return of Gorgo" (Summer 1963), and "The Return of Gorgo" (Fall 1964).[17] The latter two were flagged "no. 2" and "no. 3," respectively, constituting a short recurring trilogy. Two of these dealt with prevalent nuclear Cold War themes. We should survey these productions before returning to the regular sequence.

In "Gorgo's Revenge" (job #A-1642), titled "Sign of the Dragon," communist China menaces the world once again, striving to achieve atomic power and the "big bomb." Unwittingly, Gorgo and his doting mother become incarnate draconic entities of the symbolic Chinese dragon. When Gorgo is caught in a Chinese fishing trawler's netting, mother Ogra rescues him. But inadvertently, the boat is sunk. Shipwreck survivors glimpse Gorgo, one superstitious soul claiming, "It is the dragon our ancestors worshipped. It is angry with us for adopting the ways of the foreigners." The authorities silence him before this "dragon" sighting creates furor among the reactionary peasant class—who are employed in constructing a huge generator, supervised by Russian engineers, that will harness energy from sea tides. When Gorgo's mother is caught in one of the intake valves to the generator, the vengeful "dragon" is revealed to the peasants, who revolt against the military authorities. Clamoring for freedom, the peasants yearn to return to Taiwan, where "the old China still lives in the hearts of our leaders."[18]

Fearful for his mother, who is still entrapped in the inlet valve, Gorgo goes on a rampage on the shore. Artillery shells are useless, but this time a million volts of electricity from high tension wires repels him back into the sea. A Russian destroyer dumps depth charges, but Gorgo rattles the ship, crippling it ... and then returns to shore, where he is once more mistaken as the Chinese dragon vengefully leading the charge against tyranny. Gorgo's mother Ogra has freed herself from the underwater suction. Now, not even jet fighter planes can stop them. And so now the two dino-monsters wage war against evil men who (from their dinosaurian mindset) have harmed them time and again. The great city "created by totalitarianism" is reduced to rubble and the people freed.

In "The Return of Gorgo, no. 2" (job #A-2851), titled "The Creature from Corpus III," a 15-foot-tall, ambitious and aquatic alien plans to subjugate and deliver Earth into the hands of his leaders. The alien is an amphibious biped named "Koorii" who has piloted his spaceship here from a world in another galaxy, where its twin dying suns have all but evaporated the seas. The frog-like being maniacally plans to subjugate our planet by himself, rather than more sensibly calling in reinforcements—superior invasion forces to ensure the job is handily done. This way he alone will greedily reap rewards and laurels. He would be immortally remembered for his extermination of the Earthlings, allowing his people to populate our world, thereafter rejoicing in its vast, bountiful oceans. But only two things evidently stand in his path to world domination—yes, Gorgo and mother Ogra.

Meanwhile, American zoologist Dr. Emory Mason and his pretty assistant, who has the hots for her older mentor, plans to rediscover and nobly study the dino-monster pair in order to "remove the veil of time," providing "intimate knowledge of the ages and the creatures that existed before time began on Earth." But Red China prepares for yet another nuclear bomb test on a deserted island, which just so happens to be in proximity to where Gorgo and his mother are swimming right at that moment. Koorii cautiously observes the incident, somewhat alarmed by the Earthlings' nuclear capabilities, but far more impressed with the invincibility of Gorgo and his mother to the blast and other weapons of mankind. Because the two dino-monsters are sea denizens, akin to his own amphibious race, Koorii therefore decides to militarily recruit Gorgo and his mother in a strike against the Earth. Koorii haughtily muses, "All they need is direction by my super intelligence!"

Once again—"meanwhile," Dr. Mason and his assistant arrive in a sailing ship near the scene where the book's climax will take place. Donning a deep-sea diving suit, Mason prepares to search for the dino-monsters underwater. He observes the pair in their natural habitat, theorizing that the two are "of a species long extinct when the dinosaurs appeared on the land.... This species could be the link between the dinosaurs and the creatures of the sea. Perhaps it was the ancestors of Gorgo who first crawled from the bottom of the sea to land, and from them came the age of reptiles on earth." Well, he just may be on to something with this train of logic, but, ivory tower science aside, look out—here comes Koorii ... and trouble!

Mason observes Koorii swimming fervently, attempting to communicate telepathically with Gorgo and mother Ogra, striving to convince them to facilitate his conquest by eradicating Earthlings so that *he* will be revered as his people's "greatest legend." (You can almost hear the maniacal laughter, can't you?) Gorgo cannot decipher telepathic signals, yet remains curious about Koorii, who has Mason in his clutches. Gorgo's great paw snatches Koorii up—who in turn spasmodically releases Mason's diving suit from his grasp. Mason ascends safely to the surface, now realizing his love for the pretty assistant, while Koorii (and likewise any impending alien invasion) is squashed by Gorgo's mighty fist. "The End."

Now, having outlined two of the Gorgo "Special Editions," we return to the regular Gorgo book series, no. 13, titled "Gorgo Captured" (June 1963, job #A-2454) begins where issue #11 (not #12) left off, with Gorgo nibbling on the submarine "toy" carrying the movie producer and his crew away from the island of head-hunters.[19] The resulting film, *Gorgo's Triumph*, attracts the attention of "famed zoologist, Professor Carl Carlson," who with his pretty assistant Dr. Jan Blake, wants to capture Gorgo for the Bronx Zoo. Furthermore, in this fashion "we could learn of the prehistoric beasts and the age of reptiles before the coming of Man, by study of a real, live monster from that ancient time!" A zoo veterinarian who has eyes for Dr. Blake explains how Gorgo could be made suitably groggy for capture using a hypodermic anesthetic fired from long range. But the Russkys are jealous and suddenly motivated, because, if America successfully captured Gorgo in midst of the ongoing space race, which was heightening at that time, this result would nullify impact of the Soviet "space triumphs." So, not unlike the former race to land a man on the Moon, the race is now on to capture Gorgo first. Who will "win," the Soviet Union or the U.S.?

Essentially, the plan is for mysterious frogmen, who are really communist agents, to infiltrate the crew of the ship carrying Carlson, Blake and the veterinarian to the site where Gorgo and his mother were last sighted. After the offspring's capture, then the frogmen will insidiously claim Gorgo for the Soviets instead. At first, things go well for Carlson, as Gorgo is caught in a sturdy net. But then the agents waste no time in revealing themselves and their plot, springing their trap—only to be thwarted by the heroic veterinarian, who saves the day! But America's plan to exhibit Gorgo isn't viable. For after they deliver Gorgo to the Bronx Zoo, shackling him, of course, mother Ogra readily comes to the rescue, although this time without all the collateral damage witnessed in the first book (or in the novel or 1960 film).

In Gorgo #14 (August 1963), titled "Deadlier Than Man" (job #A-2627), the fate of man hangs in the balance once more.[20] The Russians are transporting atomic warheads and "germ rockets" to a certain island off the coast of Florida, ruled by a man resembling a famous bearded, cigar-smoking dictator. Yes, this tale was clearly founded upon what has become known in history as the Cuban Missile Crisis. Except few historians have ever realized Gorgo's heroic contributions in this near globally disastrous affair.

The Russian convoy arrives at its destination and deadly cargo is offloaded from the vessels. But meanwhile, two political prisoners on the island escape, spy the enemy missile launch site, and radio their observations to the U.S. military. The American president (who resembles one "JFK") accuses the Russian leader of this treachery while the world waits with bated breath. But curious Gorgo surfaces beside the Russian ships, prompting frightened soldiers to fire atomic rockets at him. Cannons onboard Russian ships even shoot Gorgo in the back as he's stomping toward the shore. There is surprisingly little surrounding damage caused from these massive megaton explosions. But, as before, "nothing can stop him!" Then Gorgo's mother emerges and tramples the fleet. Cuban-flown military planes dive in for the attack, although mother Ogra fists them from the sky. Gorgo smashes the launching site. One escapee who observed Gorgo's triumph over tyranny muses that the dino-monsters' (daikaiju-like) actions happened "almost as if fate wanted man to go on ... not to kill his race in foolish atomic war, but to go on to a more glorious future!" And his pretty partner adds, "[F]ate used those monsters to work her strange ends! Now the threat to world peace is over!" Well, perhaps JFK never knew the complete story, but now you know what "really" happened during that fateful episode.[21]

By December 1963, when Gorgo #16 was issued, JFK had been assassinated, while Gorgo battled menacing plant life from the deep, once again sparing mankind utter extermination. Gorgo #16, "Menace from the Deep" (job #A-3185), begins like many others in the series, with another "routine" atomic bomb test in the South Seas.[22] On this occasion, however, the scientific team monitoring the explosion records a much "denser field of radiation," which is rather unusual considering that radiation itself is rarely referred to in the Gorgo book series—that is, despite all the nuclear detonations Gorgo and man become exposed to. But this extra-intense radiation causes kelp to mutate in the ocean depths, forming a quickly growing "fetid horror" which, once shorn of its roots, becomes bipedal. While Gorgo and mother Ogra suffer another aerial attack from military planes, the voracious, bipedal mutant plants come ashore. These plants are referred to as "Chloryllfids," most certainly in homage to a great 1963 sci-fi film, *The Day of the Triffids* (based on John Wyndham's 1951 novel).[23] The Chloryllfids attack south sea islanders and a local missionary, who all manage to flee just in the nick of time.

At first, nobody believes the missionary's crazy story concerning giant walking plants. Meanwhile, one Senator Brockton campaigns politically on the premise that Gorgo and his mother are a menace to mankind. These uncontrollable dino-monsters must be destroyed, Brockton asserts. Then one scientist who (conveniently) had been testing undersea plants and jellyfish, exposing them to gamma rays, accepts the missionary's wild tale. So he accompanies the missionary (and his pretty daughter) back to the island where the Chloryllfids first emerged. They douse the Chloryllfids—which are seeding themselves, increasing their numbers at an alarming rate—with flame throwers, but this isn't enough. The scientist, missionary and daughter suddenly find themselves in dire straits, surrounded by the lethal plants, when Gorgo and mother Ogra storm the beach. It turns out they find the Chloryllfids quite tasty, and so they gobble up every last trace of this peculiar "salad"! To further accentuate our happy ending, the young scientist and the missionary's pretty daughter fall in love. And meanwhile, benighted Senator Brockton continues to denounce the monstrous lizards who menace mankind. An ecological nightmare subverted.

By February 1964, with release of Gorgo #17, titled "Secret Destroyer" (job #A-3218), Gorgo's facial appearance had changed for the better, improving artistically.[24] It seems there is no safe haven for Gorgo and mother Ogra in this tempestuous, deadly world of Man. For in "Secret Destroyer," Gorgo returns to the Caribbean, where a Russian submarine carrying nuclear torpedoes disturbs the tranquil waters. Cuba continues to be a hotbed of iniquity for the U.S. in this new episode. The American president, who now resembles "LBJ," is concerned that Gorgo might instigate a "fiendish prank," which could trigger World War III.

Innocently chasing a huge squid, Gorgo inadvertently enters a great undersea cave where Russian missile silos have been constructed within a natural domed chamber. When the Russians fire guns and grenades upon Gorgo—here referred to by one Muscovite soldier as a "capitalist monster"—the great dino-monster runs amok, knocking all the missiles down, then mauling the Russian submarine. Surfacing, Gorgo and mother Ogra suffer further indignities, coming under fire from U.S. military planes, an attack rendered ineffectually. But the Russians, led by one "Nikita," are conspiring with that certain bearded, cigar-smoking Latin fellow once more, and so far Gorgo has destroyed only one of *several* military bases and launch sites scattered around the island. With the Kremlin accusing America for the "insult" already unleashed by Gorgo, a Russian vessel retaliates, dropping atomic depth charges upon the roving dino-monster. Of course, these never work, and Gorgo and mother Ogra rampage again, destroying the other atomic missile launch sites. In the end, the Russians tire of the Cuban leader, while Gorgo and mother Ogra can *finally* rest peacefully, basking in the warm sunshine. Or can they?

The title of Gorgo # 18, "The Day Earth Gave Up" (May 1964, job #A-3471), suggests Gorgo has now become recognized as a world defender![25] (The story is subtly set in the "future," possibly the 1980s, although leaders resembling "LBJ" and "Nikita" still command their nations.) This time another giant, alien horde—robotic-looking invaders with metallic faces resembling Gort from *The Day the Earth Stood Still*—targets major Earth cities, that is, until Gorgo thwarts their plans for conquest. Also, by issue #18, Gorgo's single row of dorsal fins are clearly more pronounced, rounded (not jagged), yet unlike the large warty dorsal tubercles on the dino-monster's backs and tails evident in movie suitmation (*Gorgo*, 1961).

Given the alien's 5,000-foot-long spaceships' arsenal of "ardra-bursts," "heat tube weapons," and "vibra-rays," it would seem mankind has no chance. To counterattack, the U.S. merely has an outer space rocket resembling the 1960s X-15. The aliens nuke Los Angeles, Moscow and Johannesburg. Time to surrender? Well, apparently the aliens feel threatened by Gorgo's massive size, and the fact that he seems invulnerable to their weapons is also concerning. And so, Gorgo attacks one of their ships, causing a tactical retreat to their home base. Now, following their encounter with Gorgo, the aliens merely want mankind to surrender. A return to Earth results in one of the very few instances where Japan is ever mentioned in the Gorgo comic book series, as alien "Space Scourger 5" is shown "knocking Japanese fighters out of the air!"

Hand-to-hand ... or, rather, claw-to-tentacle combat now ensues between Gorgo and one of the giant aliens who is as tall as Gorgo! Gorgo succumbs to "nerve vapor" while faraway mother Ogra senses her offspring is once more in trouble. Ogra destroys Space Scourger 2 on her deadly path toward Gorgo. Ultimately, the two furious dino-monsters smash the rest of the invading fleet and defeat the giant aliens in close fighting. One alien expresses, "It looked easy when we got here ... it's no use ... save yourself if you can!" The two remaining alien rockets are so damaged, however, that the alien survivors can't lift off ... until Gorgo and mother Ogra rather ludicrously give each ship a swift kick in the pattooties (like angrily kicking those old television sets to make them work), which causes their launch mechanisms to fire![26]

Gorgo #20 (October 1964, job #A-3953), titled "Monsters for the Moon," introduces two new plot elements later materializing or realized in the Godzilla film series as well.[27] First, Gorgo makes a space trip, in this case to the Moon, to save Earth by fighting space aliens. Secondly, Gorgo is cloned into a robot, or a faux "Mecha-Gorgo." Following an abbreviated, more or less prosaic sea adventure leading to a battle near the Rock of Gibraltar, hounded Gorgo—characterized as an endearing "youngster ... a puppy, so to speak [who] ... thrived not on vengeance," heads north toward Russian soil. It turns out, during the height of the 1960s historical "space race," that the Russians are readying their first space mission to land a man on the Moon before America does, just when Gorgo trespasses onto their launch site. The Russians are contemplating launching armed men, and realize that aliens already occupy the Moon. But now they want to send Gorgo along as well!

The Russians knock Gorgo out with a chemical potion and then decide to replicate the monster. And just how is this brilliant feat accomplished? "Duplicator rays focused on Gorgo ... molecular structure was recorded ... gradually an atom-by-atom computer blueprint was put together ... until at last it was done!" While the original Gorgo "carcass" will be disposed of, the clone, presumably under complete Russian control, will be sent to the Moon. Fortunately, the Russians have already built a space rocket sufficiently large to carry such an enormous payload! And while the Russians intend to make a second clone, the original Gorgo rouses from slumber and seeks shelter ... inside one of the Russian rockets—one which on the following day blasts off the Moon! So two Gorgos (one real, the other "Mecha") arrive on the Moon, which fortunately, yet contrary to scientific knowledge, has sufficient atmosphere for Gorgo to breathe without a space suit.

Meanwhile, the Americans are also proceeding to the Moon, led by one astronaut who resembles a young John Glenn. And of course a space battle ensues between the furry-looking "Viking"-headed aliens and man. The Gorgo robot gives the Russians an edge, but when the second giant rocket arrives, the original flesh-and-blood Gorgo steps out onto the lunar regolith, "blazing mad." The real Gorgo is a wild card, unable to be controlled by the frightened Russians. Things wind down quickly! Gorgo scares the aliens off into space, while afterward the American astronauts take sympathy on him. They manage to return to the original Gorgo to Earth. The Russians return to Moscow while a single U.S. astronaut remains on the Moon with the Gorgo mecha-facsimile, hoping that the next contact with aliens will be of a more friendly nature. "Thanks to the monster for the Moon program, Earth will survive in the battle of the stars!"

From the depths of space to the oceanic abyss, Gorgo #21 (December 1964, job #4226) concerns "The Nation Beneath the Sea."[28] A Russian citadel, secretively constructed close to American waters and protected by atomic submarines, is discovered by Gorgo. The subs fire an atomic torpedo at Gorgo, who like always emerges unharmed by the blast. But, next, an

American pilot doing a flyover spots Gorgo carrying a Russian missile in his paw. Nibbling on the missile inadvertently ignites this "snack" and poor Gorgo is blasted again! U.S. officials wonder where the Russian bombs might have come from, and shortly a U.S. atomic submarine commander detects the underwater Russian stronghold. With the two great superpowers poised once again "on the verge of extinction," Gorgo's intervention saves the day by neutralizing the Russians' military strength. Gorgo seizes all the Russian missiles and torpedoes, casting them downward into the "unplumbed depths" of a great oceanic chasm. It turns out, rather incongruously, that the chief aim of the Russian facility is to perform aquacultural operations, deriving food from the oceans. And so now the "population bomb,"[29] as it was once referred to, is being addressed in the Gorgo comic book series. Both the Russians and Americans nobly and cooperatively seek to relieve world poverty, farming the sea for food that will aid the world's starving nations! "One day the ocean floors will have shining cities...."

Incidentally, issues no. 20 and 21 are the first in which Gorgo's mother does not triumphantly appear. She is usually relegated to a reinforcement role, but Gorgo is on his own in these two stories. However, in issue #21, the featured Gorgo is referred to as a "she." Throughout the series, my impression, and perhaps that of many readers at the time, was that our playful "puppy" was a male. Possibly the reference to the female gender in issue #21 is an error, or maybe the writers decided to convert the mother Ogra into the Gorgo dino-monster.

With the book series quickly winding down, in Gorgo #22, "Might of General Thung" (February 1965, job #A-4495), Gorgo once again is challenged by warmongering "communist Asia."[30] To a certain extent, this story reprises the original Gojira *Lucky Dragon* theme. Gorgo, snoozing at "ground zero" on the Bikini Atoll, is rudely awakened when U.S. bomber drops a nuclear warhead. The island is vaporized. Gorgo is badly scarred this time and there is even one frame showing the reddened, blistered, overheated monster—referred to by the pilot as a "dragon"—breathing radioactive flames from his maw! Here, Gorgo rather resembles Godzilla as seen near the conclusion of 1995's *Godzilla vs. Destoroyah*. Then shortly, spying Gorgo at sea—cooling off in the waters—a U.S. aircraft carrier admiral identifies the monster, claiming, "It is the policy of the Joint Chiefs of Staff that this animal has done more for the Free World and all mankind than he has against man so he is not to be considered hostile." Well, it took 25 Gorgo books (so far) to reach this more satisfying conclusion! By early 1965, while still "dangerous," Gorgo is clearly viewed as an ally. A "capitalist monster," protected when needed by his mother Ogra!

Then there's another "meanwhile," in which Washington intelligence officers worriedly contemplate the buildup of communist armies, millions of troops and armored divisions amassed on the "Asian mainland." Communist Asia (think of a symbolic melding of Red China, North Korea and North Vietnam) is ready to strike at General Thung's command, even though "Nikita doesn't know" of Thung's evil intentions. As Thung gloats, the "small nations to the south" will not be able to resist their relentless forces. Armageddon draws ever closer.

Then Gorgo attacks their expansive oil-producing fields and "impregnable fortifications." Thung clambers into a jet fighter, whose pilot bombs Gorgo from above—to no avail! And the dino-monster instinctively ravages the communist war facilities, reducing them to ashes and twisted steel. The U.S. is poised to live up to its commitments to protect those smaller nations that were promised "immunity" from communist invasion. But only Gorgo can become the equalizing factor, as he somehow senses in his great reptilian mind that General Thung is the root of the problem. And so when Thung arranges a great parade exhibiting the splendor of his mighty forces, invincible Gorgo essentially rains mightily on his boastful parade. Gorgo chases Thung, scattering the troops in undignified fashion and ultimately forcing dictator Thung to suffer a nervous breakdown, weeping in terror. Gorgo leaves following this well-timed victory over tyranny, even chuckling at the humiliated Thung. Gorgo strides heavily, not triumphantly, but "disgusted with the race of man once more ... Gorgo ... seemed destined to find disappointment and pain instead of the hand of man extended in friendship!"

With communism soundly defeated once and for all, Gorgo was sent on a journey backward in time in the final segment (issue #23) of his adventures of long ago, aptly titled "Land of Long Ago" (September 1965, job #A-4713).[31] Artwork on the cover of this book shows Gorgo poised in an RKO Kong–like setting atop a cliff, smacking a winged dino-monster—the scene reminiscent of that in *King Kong* in which Kong battles the giant *Pteranodon* with Fay Wray in its clutches. At this juncture, Dr. Hobart Howarth is trying to help Gorgo by more or less sending him out to pasture—a sort of well-deserved "retirement." Howarth empathizes that the many nuclear bombs and considerable antagonism directed toward the monster, while perhaps not scarring the monster physically, had certainly wounded its heavy heart and soul. Mankind has ruthlessly hounded and continually exploited Gorgo, despite the monster's helpfulness, heroic nature, and uncanny sense of right and justice, coupled with the fact that the dino-monster has not willingly or unnecessarily killed humans. So Howarth plans to send Gorgo "back into his own era in the stream of time!," because "he is an anachronism ... in his own time he would be in harmony with his surroundings." This is the first kind gesture any human has extended toward Gorgo since the beginning of the series. Howarth has built a time machine, relying on the principle of "time-reversing radiation" that will (hopefully) do the job. But of course, things never go exactly as planned.

Howarth becomes inadvertently trapped in the time-reversal field along with Gorgo, and so both of them are directed backward in time to the Late Jurassic Period. Together, Gorgo and Howarth dispatch a horned, ceratosaur-like dinosaur, which is as powerful as Gorgo. Howarth courageously stabs the ceratosaur with a quickly fashioned spear. Their slim victory over the huge dinosaurian forges their friendship. Howarth is permitted to ride on Gorgo's huge head as they stride about viewing and fighting red in tooth and claw against ancient, long extinct wildlife. But as Howarth realizes, time-reversal radiation eventually dissipates, causing the two to steadily move incrementally forward in time—back to the future, in an abbreviated "life-through-time" series adventure. So they successively pass through an early glacial ice age of extinction, and a 19th century European conflict, before returning to their proper time. Gorgo's "retirement" turns out to be nothing more than a vacation from the present, although into a formidable past.

And in the final frame, a general overseeing the project thankfully exclaims, "Well, the experiment didn't work, Howarth ... and I'm sort of glad because I'm getting used to Gorgo! I'm going to advise the Pentagon to quit trying to kill him off!" Well, too bad, because just as we were "getting used" to having Gorgo around in the comics, he went completely off the radar screen. Perhaps the general's suggestion was finally taken to heart because, well, has anybody heard of our military bombing Gorgo (or his mother) lately?

In a second story published in Gorgo #23, "A Visit to Earth," a final caption states prophetically, "Storms batter the surface! Thin, cool crust shifts, crumbles, heals itself, breaks ... and ... Man clings unsteadily to his precarious thin surface and tells himself that this is his world, he knows all about it, he has tamed his environment ... and all the while he is uneasily aware of how shaky his tenure on this unstable orb can really be!"[32]

To my knowledge, Gorgo made only one more foray into the world of comic bookdom, this time in 1991, although under the alias name "Kegor." This Canadian book was merely a reprint of Gorgo books nos. 1 and 3, published in black and white. The book, produced by A+ Comics, was titled *Attack of the Mutant Monsters.*[33] Otherwise, tales and artwork were identical to the original versions printed 3 decades before. Gorgo's name had simply been inked over, substituting "Kegor"—containing the same number of letters, instead.

So, before moving on to Carson Bingham's novel, let's consider Gorgo's appearances in the Charlton series; what sort of conclusions may be made?

Gorgo's monster persona transformed over the first dozen adventures outlined herein (much more so than his mother's, who is relegated to the role of monstrous reinforcement). While in filmdom, Gigantis had already led the charge against a second gigantic pseudo-dinosaurian foe, Anguirus, Gorgo analogously settled into a similar role, engaging and defeating other giant monsters, such as the cyclopean Venusians, a tentacular "nightmare" from below the oceanic "crusts," and giant crab monsters. But when Reptisaurus mysteriously appears, rather than fighting this new monster, Gorgo (with his mother) forms an alliance (like Godzilla eventually did with Rodan).

Most noticeably (as in Carson Bingham's prior 1960 novel), Gorgo's existence symbolizes the threat of nuclear Armageddon. However, while in the 1961 film, nuclear warheads were never launched, in the comic book series, we see nuclear bombs detonated with reckless abandon, mirroring unsettling circumstances with all too prevalent and contemporary atomic and hydrogen bomb testing. Even though radiation is rarely discussed or viewed as a significant hazard, it's disturbing to witness nuking of cities and several attempts by our enemies behind the "iron curtain" to exterminate the "free world." Fortunately, sometimes in behind-the-scenes mode, Gorgo and his mother are capable of thwarting these near disasters, as well as fending off similar attacks from the Atlanteans and two alien Venusian invasions. That thinly disguised Latin dictator also suffers an awful fate.

While at first feared by mankind, eventually, humans come to see some good in Gorgo. This is not unlike how Toho's Godzilla persona transforms between the Gigantis and Ghidrah films, although the latter film was released in the U.S. after Charlton's Gorgo series had already ended. However, much of Gorgo's "heroism" goes unacknowledged or unheralded by man. By issue #12, Gorgo and his mother have become staunch world defenders, perhaps the original dinosaur "superheroes" of the comic book realm. By comparison at this juncture, dino-monster Godzilla's roles remained rather conventionally antagonistic, or "classic" in nature.

When Gorgo #12 appeared, Godzilla's blockbuster battle with a huge ape, Kong, was about to be released to American theaters (debut date June 26, 1963). Interestingly, Charlton had also been synchronously running a series based on the titular 1961 film, *Konga,* another filmic giant ape. While Konga did battle giant monster dinosaurians (e.g., a huge tyrannosaur—issue #2, and a pair of legendary, fire-breathing and finbacked "Uuang-Ni"—issue #23), Gorgo's first appearance would later be reprinted alongside, or "versus," *Konga* #1 in a special Charlton feature named *Fantastic Giants* (September 1966).[34]

There is no compelling evidence that *Gorgo* was overtly influenced by the first two entries in the Godzilla film series. According to Eugene Lourie (1903–1991) as explained in his *My Work in Films* (1984), *Gorgo* was conceived as a "dino-derivation" or an offshoot of his prior dino-monster projects, *The Beast from 20,000 Fathoms* (1953) and *The Giant Behemoth* (1958). (In turn, *Gojira* (1954) was partly influenced by the very successful *Beast From 20,000 Fathoms* and 1933's *King Kong*.) Unlike *Beast* and *Behemoth*, which used stop-motion animation special effects, Lourie elected to rely principally on suitmation for the *Gorgo* project. Lourie mentions that for this picture, "Novel approaches to the saga of a dinosaur confronting the cruel, civilized world" were realized. Also, in "keeping a promise" Lourie made to his daughter, "the monsters were not killed but retreated majestically back to the deep sea."[35]

Rather in keeping with *Gorgo*'s filmic sense of independence and originality (except possibly in the instance of issue #22), the Gorgo comic book series *also* doesn't pay obeisance or homage to Toho's landmark dino-monster. So it's perhaps unsurprising that Japan is rarely mentioned throughout the comic book run. There is nary a mention of World War II's Pacific theater or the 1945 Japan nuclear bombings, or the *Lucky Dragon* incident. Assuredly everyone knew of that history, but Charlton's writers clearly sought a fresh, independent and creative path for their Gorgo series, one that hadn't been trod before in film or other media.

Out of the 26 Gorgo comic book tales, 11 dealt *principally* with a Cold War/nukes theme; 5 may be categorized as an alien/outer-space attack theme; 4 were staged principally as "giant monster battles"; 4 sampled the undersea realm theme, and 2 were not associated with any of the above. (Of course, there is thematic overlap, tinged with metaphor.) However, Charlton's focus clearly was on Cold War matters escalating during this harrowing historical period. And so, 21 of the 26 books at least faintly projected or mirrored contemporary Cold War or burgeoning ecological themes. But in the comic book series, Gorgo is neither characterized as an outright manifestation of the bomb (as Godzilla was in its 1954 debut), nor later as a *product* of the bomb (as Godzilla later became).[36]

Gorgo isn't a mutated dino-monster like Godzilla, and doesn't originate from or through an atomic detonation. Instead, following the movie script, in the comic series Gorgo and his mother Ogra are unleashed from a mighty volcanic eruption in the sea. And Gorgo #1, aligned with the movie script, is the only book in the comic series where humans rightly exercise caution in electing *not* to attack Gorgo with a nuclear bomb.

Although well documented by then, both scientifically and medically, the specter of radiation scarring and genetic mutations is barely touched upon in the Gorgo book series. This series was intended for younger people and the horrors of exposure to atomic fallout—addressed in *Gojira* and Lourie's prior dino-monster projects—must have been considered unsuitable for such an impressionable audience. And yet, ironically, this happened to be the heyday of Marvel Comics' heralded superheroes such as Spider-Man, the Hulk, the X-Men and the Fantastic Four—whose powers resulted from exposure to radiation of one kind or another! Even DC Comics' Superman suffered the emanations of green Kryptonite. Furthermore, in the movies, how odd that while mankind emphatically chooses time and again not to attack Godzilla, Rhedosaurus, Paleosaurus (or Gorgo and mother Ogra in the 1961 film) with atomic weapons, in the Gorgo comic book series nuclear bombs are frequently detonated, deliberately fired at Gorgo and his mother on numerous occasions! (Decades later, the *Cloverfield* monster—representing 9/11-style terrorism—was nuked in New York City!)

To a large degree, Gorgo's comic book writers evidently kept abreast of and reflected current geopolitical events and contemporary Cold War fears in their stories. Considerable American paranoia is reflected here. The Gorgo series (novel, film and comic book series—appearing in that order) thus became a vehicle for expressing such relevant concerns independent from Toho's creations, which in their time had their own distinctive agenda. Godzilla's symbolism for contemporary 1950s Japanese viewers has been subjected to considerable scholarly scrutiny, but here it is apparent that Gorgo's meaning in the comic book series was entirely Americanized (at a minimum, from issue no. 2 onward). In short, Gorgo (i.e., in the comics) may be a monster, but at least he was "our" idealized capitalist dino-monster.

Gorgo's appearance brings out mankind's worst nature (arguably more so than in the contemporary Godzilla films). Frightening circumstances, dread over the possibility of nuclear war and detonation of atomic bombs in American cities, are played out in the series. Taken retrospectively, the Gorgo series perhaps was a catharsis for young readers of the time, those who worried about what *could* happen in the real, threatening grownup world.

Charlton's series ran during that angst-laden historical era when those "east vs. west, chest-pounding" atomic and hydrogen bomb tests occurred with more alarming regularity than ever before. Following a short moratorium (1958–1961) on U.S. atomic weapons testing, from 1961 to October 1963 the U.S. alone exploded over a hundred nuclear weapons dramatically in the atmosphere, polluting locations in the Pacific and Nevada. Particularly during this period, the U.S., Russia and other nations contributed to increasing radioactivity levels in Earth's ocean-atmosphere system. Concerns over exposure to radioactive dust and fallout led to the Partial Nuclear Test Ban Treaty; after October 10, 1963, atomic weapons testing could only be conducted underground.

Gorgo, then, may be seen as a mysterious child of nature, so unfairly attacked by mankind, particularly a victim of our continual misuse of atomic weapons. Gorgo and his mother Ogra take the brunt of these nuclear detonations so that civilization won't have to. They are planetary symbols of what is at stake, harmed or jeopardized during atmospheric testing.

Did Gorgo's adventures in the comic books have an impact on Godzilla's Toho continuation? Unless someone can present proper documentation indicating that Toho executives avidly read Gorgo comics, taking notes studiously while they were published, it would be impossible to claim that Toho was swiping from or influenced by Charlton's Gorgo series. Comic books are easier to produce than major motion pictures loaded with special effects, but clearly by the spring of 1963, Godzilla had a long way to go in "catching up" to where Gorgo had already been and was quickly heading. While it may be the case that Charlton's illustration and writing team (often notably comprising Steve Ditko and Joe Gill) may have borrowed or even been inspired by Toho's science fiction and Godzilla series, today it is impossible to prove that Toho in turn was ever aware of Charlton's Gorgo series. However, curious analogies may be made! Gorgo fought giant alien monsters, traveled into outer space, battled monstrous defenders of Atlantean civilizations, teamed with a giant winged dino-monster against alien invaders, was cloned as a Mecha-Gorgo and became a heroic dino-figure for mankind in the war against communist tyranny and abuse of nuclear weapons long before Godzilla was put through similar or analogous paces. Most likely, Charlton's Gorgo and Toho's Godzilla instead represent a case of ideological parallel evolution.

Is Gorgo *daikaiju* in the comics? Arguably in the 1961 film, Gorgo and his mother Ogra might not seem as full-fledged "kaiju" in the sense that their intelligence may be judged not much above that of basal animalistic, instinctual tendencies. However, there is a glimmer of "daikaiju-ness" dawning in later installments of the Gorgo comic book series. Gorgo always seems to have a sixth sense for being in the right place at the right time, maybe more so than his mother Ogra. While Ogra's actions would appear merely instinctual, that of motherly concern and protection for her son, Gorgo always has a heightened cognitive ability to go after the "bad guys" of the particular moment, disrupting their activities before things go too far, which in that period meant a potential for all-out thermonuclear holocaust! So, all things considered, Gorgo in the comics is clearly *daikaiju*.[37] (Also see the Epilogue.)

Astonishingly, Charlton's rarely cited Gorgo series is quite different from the Gorgo we've come to know in the 1961 movie. Through Charlton's creative writing and artistic team, comprising many individuals, their version of Gorgo evolved into our protective, capitalist dino-monster. But such a persona wasn't evident in the brilliant 1960s novelization, *Gorgo*, which preceded both the comic book run and the film.

"Carson Bingham" is a pseudonym for Bruce Cassiday (1920–2005). In the "Author's Profile" to the novel *Gorgo*, we learn Cassiday is "a well known writer who has published several novels under his own name. He is a graduate of U.C.L.A. and after college served in the U.S. Air Force during World War II in Tunisia, Algeria, Italy and Puerto Rico. He has been a radio announcer, a radio script writer and a newsreel caption writer and is presently fiction editor of a large national men's magazine. He now lives in Stamford, Connecticut with his wife and two children."[38] How curious that over half a century later, while few may recall Cassiday's other works, the name "Gorgo" still resounds. Someday, perhaps, another Gorgo film should be produced, although next time using "Bingham's" novel as the basis for a screenplay instead. Not that there's too much wrong with the first film. It's just that one based on the novel could conceivably be so much better.

Unfortunately, that cited Author's Profile doesn't really cut it; Cassiday's long pulp-fiction writing career merits further consideration. For in his delightful, if not hilarious Guest of Honor speech titled "My Life in the Pulps," given at Pulpcon #23, Cassiday recounted many early experiences leading to his prolific writing career.[39] After graduating college with a journalism degree, Bruce served in the U.S. Army for five years, in Africa and Italy, returning stateside in 1946. Most of his very early career was spent in writing blurbs—those "little teases on the title page"—and in editing scores of stories for Old Wild West magazines. It was an eye-opener learning how to sling the lingo and get the formula just right so his hooks would have maximal appeal to readers. Later he got into editing formulaic detective and mystery stories as well, often infused with, for the time, saucy or spicy passages. Eventually his boss enlisted him into writing original copy and stories when commissioned lead stories expected from other writers weren't up to expectations. But then he had to write on exceedingly close deadlines, often working from rather nebulous blurbs, such as "Chain-Gang Gun Doll," coming up with stories from scratch to wrap around the blurb with only a caffeine-fueled weekend to produce the entire tale! Cassiday refers this to his "'title-before-the-story' odyssey down Pulp Paper Lane."[40] *Gorgo* is merely one of Cassiday's numerous published books and stories (the first of which appeared in 1948). Besides his fiction, Cassiday produced over 50 ghost-written celebrity biographies. And besides "Carson Bingham," he had several pseudonyms, one of which was "Robert Faraday," the author of one of the first and most enjoyable "chapter books" I ever read, *The Anytime Rings* (1963), a science fictional tale for children involving prehistoric time travel.[41]

Complete credit for the *Gorgo* novelization as given on the title page follows with "Based on an original story by Eugene Lourie, screenplay by John Loring and David Hyatt." The Hyatt moniker was probably another of Daniel James's pseudonyms (besides "Daniel Hyatt"). As previously noted, Lourie, the film's director (notable for also 1953's *Beast From 20,000 Fathoms* and 1959's *The Giant Behemoth*), vowed to make a picture this time, per his daughter's wishes, in which the monsters weren't killed off, but survive. In Hyatt's early version of the script, titled *Kuru Island,* it was intended for the monster story to be told, as originating from a Pacific Island atoll. But there were numerous and damaging changes made to the script, scrapping the Japanese element, thus possibly explaining why the *Gorgo* novel differs so significantly from the movie. Lourie later described changes made to his story as "embarrassing developments."[42]

The 1960 novel charts the destruction of Nara Island in the Irish Sea followed by London's devastation by a giant, 200-foot-tall dino-monster. (See Figure 12-3.) But there is far more symbolism in the novel than is conveyed in the simple movie plot, which emphasizes family ties. Whereas King Kong was a tragic symbol, *Gorgo*'s dino-monsters are demonic manifestations, near-supernatural warnings to mankind that we not veer from our path, which will lead to the "end of the world," a phrase uttered several times by characters in the novel.[43] The primary difference in the novel is ravishing lady Moira, a red-haired Irish beauty who is the sister of the young boy, Sean (who *does* appear as a character in the movie). Moira is also quite flirty and has roll-in-the-hay adventures with Sam Slade (i.e., the novel's narrative voice) and his partner Joe Ryan, captain of the salvage vessel *Triton,* creating a love triangle.

However, Slade is the story's protagonist, from whose point of view the tale is told. But more importantly, Moira strikes one as a

Fig 12-3: Back cover to Carson Bingham's 1960 novel *Gorgo*.

prophetess who subliminally "knows" when the monster will come and who understands its terrible portent (as does Sean). Meanwhile, the young dino-monster named Gorgo (also dubbed the "sea-spirit") and its mother—both known from wooden prows carved into gargoyles as recovered from old Irish and Viking shipwrecks as "Ogra"—represent demonic manifestations of Nature striking back at our accursed civilization for mankind's hubris. Yes, this is much, much more than a simple (yet prototypical) tale about a protective mother monster vengefully retrieving her kidnapped son, while wreaking havoc upon mankind. No, Ogra isn't the real enemy. Ogra is a vengeful "Gaia" (or perhaps "Medea") incarnate, evincing our inability to project a reverence toward Nature.[44]

In fact, things not only end, but *begin* cataclysmically; the book's tone is ominous from the get-go. For, at first, the *Triton* is subjected to a volcanic convulsion at sea. A superstitious crew, dark storm on the horizon, volcanic clouds mushrooming menacingly—foreshadowing the fiery smoke London shall soon be smothered within—all project a sense of utter gloom and doom. The volcanic explosion and resultant tidal wave at sea—described as "bearing down like the supernatural agency of a malignant sea devil"—may be reminiscent of the 1954's *Lucky Dragon* incident.[45] Then strange fish appear, all dead and floating by the *Triton*. A pervading, supernatural element, which science never fully explains throughout, seizes our consciousness as, after the *Triton* anchors at Nara Island's fog-enshrouded harbor, we are introduced to a mythical "Ogra." Not what will be known as the titular dino-monster—no, not yet—but a mythical gargoyle carved into a salvaged ship's prow, a "personification of some ancient sea monster with fierce eyes, a small mouth and lashing tongue, and with a frightening supernatural look about it."[46]

Rather like as in the 1961 film, after a local diver expires from fright during a dive, Sam Slade and Joe descend beneath the waves in their frog suits, witnessing a "maritime graveyard. Imbedded between rocky formations, the stripped wooden ribs of ancient ships loomed up like reconstructions of dinosaur skeletons."[47] Then they spy something frighteningly huge, hovering over them that readily dispatches an Orca—killer whale. This is their first sighting of Nara Island's sea monsters. During their dive, Sam notices an old sunken Viking shipwreck brandishing a gargoyle prow of "Ogra" similar to an Irish version Sean had showed them earlier in his father's storeroom.

And then there's bewitching temptress Moira, apparently gifted with powers of "knowing" and foresight; she seems mysteriously tied to the dino-monsters' appearances. In a sense, is she also a "bride" of the monster? Moira may perhaps be compared to *King Kong*'s Ann Darrow given her apparent comprehension concerning the nature of the monsters soon to be confronted. Still grieving the tragic drowning of her mother, whose lover was killed by the monster in a diving incident, now Moira wants to flee the island in order to locate her stepmother—that is, Sean's mother. Moira somehow understands the creature's portent better than anyone. Following the seismic marine disturbance, the juvenile is stirred from the depths—lumbering ashore. It is described as a 20-foot-tall "prehistoric saurian, a giant marine lizard of some kind left over from the Mesozoic Era ... certainly never seen ... [in] any textbook."[48] Young Sean is delighted to witness this manifestation of "Ogra." Later this particular beast will be dubbed the titular "Gorgo" named after the Greek monster, the Gorgon, "the mere sight of which could turn a man to stone!"[49]

Moira pleads with Sam and Joe *not* to catch the juvenile, despite the deal they just have struck with Kevin McCartin—the local archaeologist who illegally profits from salvaging booty from undersea wrecks. McCartin must rid his profitable waters of the creature, before his frightened divers will risk their lives on further salvage attempts. But when Joe admits he doesn't understand her hesitancy, Moira exclaims in her native brogue, "'Tis a manifestation of evil.... Don't you see? 'Tis the monster of the devil, making its appearance on earth to warn us all of the cataclysm.... Leave well enough alone. Heed the warning. Do not tempt the devil." For if they capture the monster, "it will be the death of us all. Mark my words."[50]

Sam descends in the bathysphere only to witness Gorgo, attracted to this device, who is likened to a puppy attempting to gnaw on a tennis ball that's too round to fit inside its mouth. A cute scene, yet Sam nearly perishes until the juvenile is caught in lowered shark netting. The film *Gorgo* borrowed certain elements from other films that came before, such as in this particular scene; another dino-monster vs. bathysphere scene was first witnessed in 1953's *The Beast from 20,000 Fathoms*. And so once the monster is caught, then the door is opened for sober scientific inquiry and speculation to explain and comprehend, thus countering Moira's supernaturally founded fears of inherent evil. Gorgo's provenance is suggested in a news broadcast, fueled by interviews from two Irish paleontologists who haven't even yet examined the creature: "Headlines of the entire world are being monopolized today by news of the capture of a fantastic sea monster, seemingly of prehistoric origin, off the coast of Ireland.... Puzzled scientists are already speculating that the monster may have been released from some vast sub-oceanic cavern far beneath the earth's crust by unprecedented volcanic eruptions which occurred in the area recently."[51]

While Moira views juvenile Gorgo, to her an Ogra incarnate, as a "sea god," Sam only sees a possible "prehistoric link between the dinosaur age and ours."[52] Later when the juvenile Ogra, or "Gorgo," becomes a prospective specimen and a short-lived scientific symbol, Moira chastises prophetically. "Science!" snorted Moira, "The beast is death. 'Tis like catching the devil by the tail."[53]

Two Dublin paleontologists, professors Marius Flaherty and Desmond O'Brien, arrive by government seaplane to examine the juvenile from every angle, noting its scales and green luminescent color. They take copious notes, then congratulate Joe on his extraordinary catch, which they naturally, yet naively presume will be sent shortly to the University of Dublin, due to its substantial scientific value, for proper study. But science becomes an unwitting partner in the eventual destruction of London. Because it is Flaherty who recommends continually keeping the amphibious monster's skin wet, resulting in a steady spilling of Gorgo's "luminescence" into the ocean ... thus presenting a scent marker for its mother to later follow. Of course, as we know, Gorgo isn't destined to travel to Dublin, because Joe Ryan isn't by any means a patron of science, despite Sean's insistence that man cannot hold an Ogra in captivity. (How does Sean know? Possibly this trait runs in the family.) But whereas Moira is the main prophetess, Joe intends to become the chief profiteer. Readers want to know where Sam Slade stands, poised in the midst of this peculiar love triangle. For starters, feeling empathy and melded with Moira's warnings about mankind's curse, Slade is torn—already considering freeing the beast, somehow. Rather like the Ogra bound on deck, Slade is also trapped in a torturous, metaphorical prison concerning what is the righteous thing to do.

Two paleontologists appear later in the novel in important London scenes, after the juvenile has been delivered to Dorkin's Circus billed as "The Eighth Wonder of the World," reminiscent of Kong's prior status in New York. This time, Professor Flaherty is instead accompanied by the British Museum's Dr. Leroy Hendricks. They're both outraged at the untrustworthy Americans. Flaherty is especially angry because it will no longer be possible to study the dino-monster, thus depriving "science of a creature unique in evolutionary biology."[54] Gorgo is destined to become a circus freak. Unfortunately for everyone involved, Gorgo will turn out not to be "unique," as the paleontologists soon surmise. Flaherty condemns their plan (here, borrowing from one of *Beast from 20,000 Fathoms'* plot lines—later reused in *Cloverfield*), suggesting that the creature might be harboring unknown parasites or disease-carrying bacteria, thus exposing the populace to possible contagion. Then the two paleontologists realize, based on fossil evidence and from their rough measurements, that Gorgo is merely a juvenile, implying that its parent(s) may be alive, roaming somewhere, if they weren't destroyed in the recent volcanic upheaval. Not only that, but extrapolating from the comparative anatomy of dinosaur skeletons known to science, an adult-sized "Ogra" must grow up to 200 feet tall, which at the time topped presumed Godzilla's height! In fact, such an astounding proportion dwarfs a museum "Brontosaurus" skeleton standing within the Dinosaur Hall.[55] Believing the paleontologists' conclusions, Slade bolts back to Nara Island to be with Moira again.

In another scene, borrowing partly from *King Kong* while anticipating the later *The Valley of Gwangi* (1969), a cameraman's flashbulb rouses Gorgo, who goes on a rampage at Dorkin's, shortly after its steel netting's been severed.[56] In this extended scene, Gorgo attacks a circus elephant, killing it. It's understandable why this gory, published sequence did not appear in the more soulful 1961 film. Bingham pulls out all the stops in his novel, including this next scene when in a sense, Moira's sexual exertions on the beach with Slade conjure mother Ogra. Clasping one another in the "age-old position,"[57] they watch the 200-foot-tall Ogra emerge from the sea, topple a lighthouse with a single talon (either an homage to, or a borrowing from Ray Bradbury's 1951 short story "The Fog Horn"). This new terrifying creature looms over the startled pair of lovers, "like some avenging demon, its fiery red eyes focused on us."[58] Ogra smashes through the village, which is decimated in a scene reminiscent of Godzilla's nighttime stomp across Odo Island in a rainstorm.

The final third of the novel focuses on London's destruction, offering rationale for this awful outcome. It carries far more disturbing symbolism and implications than can be mended by simply reuniting separated (abducted) family members (although this is a theme of both the film and novelization). If Gorgo is merely a warning, then mother Ogra symbolizes the "end of the world" that Moira has spoken of. And at least it would seem Ogra's appearance then literally means the end of London (for starters), unless mankind rights or mends the circumstances (at least temporarily). Joe opines emphatically, "What's the matter.... This is the twentieth century! There must be a way to handle an overgrown lizard!"[59] Apparently not, though. For Ogra destroys a navy battleship, snatches a war plane out of the sky, and relentlessly weaves a path of destruction up the Thames River estuary.

Unlike circumstances within the comic book series, military officials decline to use nuclear missiles against the beast, due to the densely populated areas at stake. (This would not be the case in *Cloverfield*, 48 years later.) Then with a "fiendish grin," its "grotesque" form topples Tower Bridge (an architectural symbol of London, analogous to New York's Empire State Building). This is Armageddon, or at least a real nasty taste of what is to come! But who is good and righteous, and who are the evil ones?

Terrified Londoners seek safety and salvation in an underground station; the "crowd became a huge, coiling reptilian beast itself...."[60] Then, as did Kong in the 1933 film, Ogra destroys an approaching train, its huge claw smashing downward from the labyrinthine ceiling. Jets launch conventional missiles toward Ogra as she nears the large clock tower Big Ben, but Moira mysteriously knows the attempt will be futile. Rather like in 1954's *Gojira*, high tension wires strung across tall pylons carrying four million volts are intended to divert Ogra from the "cursed" circus area where Gorgo resides. To no avail. "No one said a word. People about me were frozen into immobility by this amazing and titanic struggle of animal power against electric power.... Flames from the burning London gas tanks in the distance silhouetted the whole scene in an eerie red glow."[61]

And the final, dire message is repeated. Earlier Slade contemplates, "Manifestation of evil? ... Or maybe a manifestation of man's evil to man? Maybe it was a warning, warning of destruction and disaster to come...."[62] Ultimately, Moira reflects, "This visitation must be heeded, or there will be worse to come." Slade offers the final grim outlook: "H Bombs. A Bombs. Infinity. Space exploration. Unlocking the secret of life. I wondered if mankind would heed the warning. I doubted it. Man has a way of facing up to even the toughest challenges of the universe—and of life itself."[63] In other words, although Man would be punished for his unrestrained Frankensteinian sins, we might still persevere. If *this* (i.e., Bingham's) version of the tale had been produced on film, no doubt Gorgo would today be viewed as the undisputed western Godzilla.

The Gorgo publications (comic books and novel) came as public concerns and reactions over environmental pollution (not just radiation fallout, but also careless and thoughtless dispersion of toxic industrial chemicals and wastes), leading to a conceivable Armageddon, were dawning and becoming widely understood. In a large sense, Gorgo's alternate adventures presaged the environmental movement of the 1960s and 1970s. By this time it is apparent how the most familiar giant dino-monsters of film and pulp literature were become increasingly associated and integrated with mankind's symbolic global cold-blooded cold war—waged not only against fellow man, but Nature itself.[64]

Chapter Thirteen

Prehistoric Life Spawns an Environmental Movement

Although generally unknown today, scientists actually had been investigating widespread environmental disasters, ecological upheavals, and revolutionary global climate shifts decades *before* the onset of America's much publicized and heavily politicized environmental movement of the 1970s (and beyond). At first, lacking scientific tools and conceptual knowledge wielded by modern investigators, early forays into comprehending natural processes active throughout deep prehistory resulted in data and theoretical notions that facilitated understanding of how life changed from one distinct geological epoch to the next. Yet, other than showing the evolutionary path leading to the present, such knowledge and discoveries could be deemed largely irrelevant to man's current, exalted status on planet Earth. The deep past was, of course, interesting to many during the latter 19th century, but theories of Earth's prehistory didn't address man's present course: generating industrial wastes with reckless abandon, or geographic conquests leading to his rapidly increasing usurpation and exploitation of Nature. Organisms were commonly regarded either as resources, or pests for man to manage and control. And at the pinnacle of life's long evolutionary journey, everlasting man was poised, predestined to rule over God's creations. A wide gulf separated us from the animal species, or so it may have seemed to those who reviled Charles Darwin's materialistic and secular process of random trait variation, enacted upon by natural selection.

By the early 1950s, before Godzilla's invention, writer Ray Bradbury (1920–2012) was among the first to link dinosaurs with man's rapid plundering of Nature in two of his most endearing ecologically-themed stories, "The Fog Horn" (1951) and "A Sound of Thunder" (1952).[1] Published in the aftermath of World War II, and on the cusp of the fusion bomb's development, Bradbury's pairing of stories may be viewed as early, allegorical warnings into how the prehistoric can presage what may be in store for modern man unless we veer from our worsening course. True—they're just marvelous stories as is, without need of any interpretation. But the ecological messages remain nonetheless.

In "The Fog Horn," a lonely, last pseudo-dinosaur is called from the mysterious oceanic deeps, by the melancholy "voice" of a lighthouse fog horn. The forlorn call attracts the gigantic creature—a dinosaur—possibly the last of its kind, yet millions of years old. This monster is one that is "alone, all alone in a world not made for you, a world where you have to hide," in the sea depths, waiting for "insanity of time" for a companion.[2] Ultimately, emerging from the concrete rubble of the shattered lighthouse tower, the two human survivors understand that the monster has "gone back to the Deeps. It's learned that you can't love anything too much in this world.... Ah, the poor thing! Waiting out there, and waiting out there, while man comes and goes on this pitiful little planet. Waiting and waiting."[3] Unlike the dinosaur, the human race would seem *unnatural*, "impossible. *It's* like it always was ten million years ago. *It* hasn't changed. It's *us* and the land that have changed, become impossible. *Us!*"[4] If actually alive, Bradbury's last dinosaur would have been the object of a crusade for conservationists.

Bradbury's ecological message rings out louder and clearer, however, in "A Sound of Thunder" (the tale that so poignantly illustrated the meaning of "the butterfly effect"). Essentially, the message is that mankind should not stray from the "path," for to do so will only harm Nature, ultimately resulting in the most adverse backlash consequences imaginable. Basically—look, but don't touch; contemplate, but don't interfere; and all costs, don't veer from the *path*! "A Sound of Thunder" is foremost an ecological story.

In Bradbury's tale, big game hunters commission a time-travel trip back to the Cretaceous Period to hunt the most terrifying creature of all—*Tyrannosaurus rex*. But Time is tricky to deal with, and so the time-safari guide always exercises extreme caution in planning safaris. Upon their arrival in the Cretaceous, the hunters (each individual isolated from the environment in specially designed suits), must remain on a time-stabilizing, metal stasis path, firing guns at the tyrannosaur only just before the exact moment of its natural death, so the consequences for upsetting the future would be infinitesimal. No trophy may be collected; even the bullets must be removed from the corpse. But as the monstrous carnivore approaches, in abject fear a hunter named Eckels does slip off the path, inadvertently crushing a butterfly, symbolic of Nature's fragility, thus completely altering the future course of history, ending their world as they knew it, casting them into an adverse parallel universe, when they move forward in time![5]

Bradbury didn't have a reputation as a writer of "hard" science fiction. Instead he relished and luxuriated in metaphor. Thus his dinosaurs, conceived during the Cold War period, seem emblematic of a harsh dawning age when mankind increasingly tampered with near-incomprehensible, "impossible" technological things, threatening to alter the future course of civilization, casting us all down the wrong path.[6]

Yet over a century prior to Bradbury, one controversial scientist, whose incorrect evolutionary ideology proved influential for over a century, precociously suggested similar ideas—that man's very existence threatened our future course. This view was expressed at a time when man was generally viewed as the apotheosis of Nature, optimistically buoyed by his waxing technological industrial feats and geographical conquests. But perhaps in this particular instance, the scientist was right and most everyone else, his contemporaries, were wrong.

Jean Baptiste Lamarck (1744–1829), the French naturalist who is most often associated with the outmoded evolutionary theory of the "inheritance of acquired characteristics," was also able to consider mankind's impact on the natural world. In a passage of his *Philosophie Zoologique* (1809), Lamarck suggested that man may yet cause his own extinction. This is remarkable, given that he was regarded as *the* most prominent scientist of the day who denounced the possibility of biological extinction. This is what he wrote, as translated by Curt Teichert[7]:

> Man, because of his egotism, pays little attention to his own real interests because of his tendency to exploit his environment; in other words, because he has no consideration for the future and for his fellow man, he seems to neglect and disregard the necessity of conservation, thus bringing about the destruction of even his own species. By destroying the protecting plant cover of the soil, in order to satisfy his momentary needs of the moment, he causes the drying up of springs, ignoring the animals which rely on them for their subsistence; and transforms large parts of the earth, once fertile and populated, into barren, sterile, uninhabitable deserts. Forever refusing to learn from experience, thinking only of his immediate wants, he is always at war with his fellow men, everywhere and under any pretext, so that once great peoples become increasingly impoverished. One may say that he is destined to destroy himself by rendering the earth uninhabitable.[8]

As Teichert concluded, "If Lamarck's ghost were with us here, we might hear him murmur: I told you so!"[9]

By the mid– to late–19th century, during a time when "green" terms such as "environmental" and "ecological" did not have a common, interconnected parlance,[10] in fact implying contradictory matters, certainly human-caused pollution *was* evident throughout Europe and Great Britain, especially in the most heavily populated urban districts. We see this mirrored in popular fiction of the time. Dense industrial smog from coal burning, for example, forms part of the opening setting for Charles Dickens's *Bleak House* (published in installments, 1851 to 1852), as we read in its opening paragraphs, wherein the imaginary presence of a dinosaur, a *Megalosaurus,* is woven into the scene. (Twelve decades later, one giant dino-monster would battle the symbolic, titular "Smog Monster" in a Toho film. See Chapter Fourteen.) Dickens observes: "Implacable November weather. As much mud in the streets as if the waters had but newly retired from the face of the earth and it would not be wonderful to meet a Megalosaurus, forty feet long or so, waddling like an elephantine lizard up Holburn Hill. Smoke lowering down from chimney pots, making a soft black drizzle, with flakes in it as big as ... snowflakes.... Fog everywhere ... fog down the river, where it rolls defiled among the tiers of shipping and the waterside pollution of a great (and dirty) city."

Thus, rather unwittingly thanks to Dickens's perceptive mind, we have one of the earliest literary associations between man's polluting tendencies with a prehistoric monster, the most savage then known to man.

Although the aforementioned Lamarck's opinions on mankind's darkest tendencies and possible pending extinction went largely ignored, instead it was his incipient views on transmutation of species which became so controversial, directly countering those who were discovering that Earth really had an organic "history" involving wholesale extinction of entire fauna characteristic to particular ages or epochs.

In order to comprehend the idea of extinction properly, one must first demonstrate that (despite contemporary theological claims) certain species have indeed disappeared from the planet in past ages. For without solid, properly interpreted evidence of extinctions, or even that of more intensified mass extinction "boundaries," so difficult to conceive then, it becomes difficult proving that Earth has had a progressive history—whether regarded as evolutionary, geological, mystically preordained (e.g., "orthogenesis" coupled with "racial senescence" in species "predestined" to be waning), or otherwise in nature. And so the course of historical events shifted subtly during the early 19th century, so that prehistoric vertebrates, dinosaurs included, would form the most solid, influential and dramatic evidence for the reality of prior extinction events in the fossil record. This was a hard pill for many to swallow!

Although Lamarck, a recognized expert on invertebrates and mollusks, promoted species "transmutation," his ideology prevented Earth's having had any kind of a "true history."[11] His conviction was founded upon the premise that, given sufficient geological time, myriad environmental shifts could produce new species and fauna from preexisting matter. "For Lamarck combined an endless cycle of environmental change with a process through which extremely simple forms of life ... were continuously being generated 'spontaneously' from nonliving matter and thereafter slowly transformed into ever more complex forms. Such a model necessarily implied that at no point would the system be distinctive or characteristic *of that time*."[12] Furthermore, Lamarck denounced ideas of his chief nemesis, fellow countryman Baron Georges Cuvier—that Earth has experienced a number of revolutionary "catastrophes" resulting in widespread extinction events—because "a universal upheaval, which necessarily regularizes nothing, and confuses and disperses everything, is a highly convenient means for those naturalists who want to explain everything, and who take no trouble at all to observe and study the course that nature follows...."[13] So according to Lamarck, not only was the process of extinction precluded, but furthermore there was no evidence for past geological upheavals, which according to Cuvier could have caused or contributed to mass extinctions.

But, as the mounting numbers of discovered fossil species proved, Earth and its living organisms did have a "history" that some viewed as "directional,"[14] although several influential geologists of the day continued to deny it. Charles Lyell, for one, refuted any sort of revolutionary catastrophes as having been part of the Earth's record, and remained suspicious of any claims leaning toward species transmutation—even after colleague and ally Charles Darwin approached him with his concerns over his vexing "species question." Nevertheless, much like Lamarck, Lyell also couldn't accept that Earth had a "true" *life* history, the dominant faunal and floral components in any epoch rather being a function of prevailing climate and environment, factors which were endlessly recyclable, given a sufficient immensity of time.[15]

Compared with natural history popularizer Robert Chambers, author of *Vestiges* (see Chapter Two), Lamarck was "materialist" in his evolutionary leanings, whereas Chambers "presented transmutation as the expression of a divine plan."[16] Although Lamarck was rejected by Lyell, Cuvier, Richard Owen, and later Charles Darwin, and eventually disproved scientifically, he was the 19th century's staunchest and most heralded, if not most controversial defender of organic evolution, until Charles Darwin. Quite apart from fading from the mainstream, however, Lamarck's ideas persisted through the latter 19th century and (as we've already seen in Osborn's case) well into the early 20th, although by then fostering a socially distorted, anti–Darwinian campaign known as "neo–Lamarckism."[17]

Meanwhile, the disturbing reality of *extinctions* was becoming fully documented and realized. At first, scientists of the day attempted to define such occurrences with great geological events. For instance, that curious line cited from Dickens's *Bleak House*, "as if the waters had but newly retired from the face of the earth," remains a tacit reminder of the great, contemporary geological debates that once rankled the major halls of science, hinging on investigations of the causes, agencies and environmental changes involved in prehistoric, biological extinction.

Although extinction in the fossil record was acknowledged long before the concept became popularized, simply entertaining such ideology remained risky because the very idea ran afoul of prevailing religious precepts. Robert Hooke (1635–1703) was one early scientist, a genius many would proclaim today for his work in physics, who declared that "there have been many Species and Creatures in former ages, of which we can find none at present; and that 'tis not unlikely also but that there may be divers new kinds now, which have not been from the beginning."[18] Hooke invoked a catastrophic shifting in Earth's axis occurring in the remote past which caused earthquakes resulting in movements of waters and land surfaces, thus adversely impacting contemporary biota, driving some to extinction. As noted by Stephen Inwood, "Hooke was not a seventeenth century Darwin, but his suggestion that species developed and disappeared in response to changing climatic and environmental conditions has a very modern ring to it, and showed that he was prepared to suggest possibilities that very few of his contemporaries would consider ... [however] ... it was not until the middle of the eighteenth century that most geologists accepted the ideas that Hooke had proposed in the 1660s. And by this time, of course, they had forgotten all about Hooke."[19]

Two 18th-century scientists' careers would become intertwined with the possibility of past extinctions, and of planetary and geological *history*, trending toward one of the brightest academic minds ever to reign over sketchy reconstructions of Earth's remote and poorly documented past. The pace of scholarly pursuits of past ages of geological time would certainly pick up once it was clear that fascinating prehistoric vertebrates and monsters were in the thick of it, forming a vast percentage of the overall intrigue, especially in a popular vein!

One French scientist, Georges Leclerc, comte de Buffon (1707–1788), whose works later became slighted by a fellow countryman, went on record with evolutionary views of the Earth's prehistory, permitting biological extinctions under circumstances of climatic or environmental change.[20] To Buffon, Earth's matter had been ejected from the Sun, resultant of a collision with a passing comet, then forming Earth at first in a molten state; gradual cooling over a postulated 70,000 years effected environmentally-directed migration patterns among the vertebrates, such as mammoths and mastodons, roving from polar to equatorial regions through time. Buffon suggested there were seven progressive "epochs of nature" (thus cautiously aligning his prehistory with that of the seven days of creation). By the early 19th century, however, the younger Cuvier summarily dismissed Buffon's "epochs" as unfounded, flighty cosmic romance.

Another individual who contributed to our knowledge of a succession of geological ages was German geologist and mineralogist, Abraham Gottlob Werner (1749–1817), whose views became misconstrued with the concept of a universal biblical flood.[21] While others of his time clung to the notion of a continually recycling, yet "ahistorical" planet, Werner perceived successional differentiation in rock formations, with the oldest crystalline Primary rocks succeeded by Secondary and Tertiary formations resulting from erosion and weathering of the Primary type. Werner's theory, which relied on seawater from which he thought Primary rock units precipitated, instead of having a volcanic or "plutonic" origin—hence his ranking among the "neptunists"—was later disproved. However, the "Wernerians' 'formations' were the basis for the geological periods we recognize today. Earlier historians failed to recognize this because their attention had been focused on a handful of ... Neptunists who used the theory to revive interest in the story of Noah's flood."[22]

It is far beyond the scope and purpose of this chapter to delve into the numerous physical theories of Earth geohistory that were contemplated and published during the 18th through the mid–20th centuries.[23] Over time, there were men (and back then this arena *was* male-dominated; although not a theoretician, Mary Anning (1799–1847) is one lady who made significant contributions to the collection of fossil specimens) whom historians have cited as "heroes" of the time for their seeming prescience in scientific matters, and perceived "villains"—scourges whose dim insights plagued science, holding back knowledge and scientific progress in the earth sciences for decades. Today, much of the reliance upon old folk tales and misplaced idolatry concerning certain individuals has diminished, as researchers reexamine their former, foundational contributions made, in light of modern scientific understanding, coupled with more objective historical approaches.

One formerly chastised individual, however, whose contributions have been largely vindicated (if not in detail then at least conceptually) is Baron Georges Cuvier. In light of documenting the reality of extinctions and processes causing such phenomena, it is Cuvier, a brilliant anatomist of his time, whose good name weathered over a century's worth of criticism for his dramatic views on extinction of prehistoric vertebrates, who today merits proper reconsideration. Fortunately, there is a munificence of recent scholarship concerning Cuvier, particularly through the researches of historian of science and paleontologist Martin J.S. Rudwick.[24] For our present purposes, however, and at risk of oversimplifying, three of Cuvier's discoveries loom. First, he proved the reality of vertebrate extinction as recorded in the fossil record. Second, Cuvier proposed violent catastrophes or "revolutions of the globe" as having been responsible for these (perceived as sudden environmental) faunal changes. Thirdly, based on the distinctive kinds of vertebrates disinterred from successive periods and epochs framing Werner's major geological formations, "Secondary" and "Tertiary" deposits, the fossil record certainly appeared progressive, yet punctuated at several geological boundaries by mysterious mass extinction events. On all three counts, conceptually, Cuvier would eventually be vindicated. Furthermore, Cuvier's publications created a bit of a stir among the educated classes, thus popularizing the controversial, disquieting tenet of organic extinction, in the wake of violent environmental upheaval.[25]

By 1796, Cuvier, who opposed species "transformism," usually then purported to Lamarckian "speciation," had established important anatomical differences between modern elephants and the extinct mammoth, thus proving the "existence of a world previous to ours," a finding that shook the scientific community.[26] Cuvier questioned of this initially discovered age, "But what was this primitive earth? What was the nature that was not subject to man's dominion? And what revolution was able to wipe it out, to the point of leaving no trace of it except some half-decomposed bones?"[27] By 1800 Cuvier's list of "lost species," distinct from known living species, had expanded to 23. At this preliminary stage he realized they didn't represent the same, single geological horizon.[28]

Furthermore, the geological condition of the very formations and strata from which fossils were found testified that "life on earth has often been disturbed by terrible events: calamities which initially perhaps shook the entire crust of the earth to a great depth.... Living organisms without number have been the victims of these catastrophes."[29] Following the examination of fossil reptile bones discovered in Secondary (i.e., Mesozoic) rocks, geologists acknowledged there had been a great former saurian age, inhabited by creatures such as the *Mosasaurus, Pterodactylus, Plesiosaurus, Iguanodon, Megalosaurus, Teleosaurus,* and *Ichthyosaurus,* antecedent to that of the Tertiary, when mammals predominated.[30] Organic "progress" was absolutely defined in the fossil record (although as yet no fossils attributable to man had been found). Cuvier didn't regard the most recent mass extinction episode—the most obvious and evident catastrophe—as biblical (e.g., a Noachian deluge), although in England, a liberal translation of his work by Scottish mineralogist Robert Jameson (1774–1854) infused theological elements, invoking the Flood.[31]

By 1826, Cuvier's younger colleague, paleo-botanist Adolphe Brongniart (1801–1876), documented that "abrupt floral discontinuities" existed in between each of the "four distinct periods" that were then evident in the fossil plant record.[32] Furthermore, plants of the Carboniferous (i.e., "Coal Age") Period were tropical in nature, suggesting that during this phase of geohistory, Earth's environment had been much like that of the present tropics. Coal Age forests may have thrived during a time of elevated atmospheric carbon dioxide concentrations. After the Coal Age forests died and coal deposits formed, from the morphology of plant life as recorded in the rocks, Brongniart concluded, Earth's global temperature diminished. However, once carbon in fossil wood had been sequestered within those coal-bearing deposits, atmospheric oxygen content gradually rose, thus allowing successively "higher" classes of organisms to proliferate. Accordingly, this pattern of earth systems acting in concert offered a rudimentary biogeochemical explanation of how and why air-breathing reptiles preceded mammalian genera.[33] "Whatever the merits of Brongniart's arguments ... his theory exemplifies the concern of scientists in the 1820s to integrate the results of geological and palaeontological research. Both fields seemed to converge towards a concept of the history of the Earth and of life that was above all *directional* in character."[34]

By 1842, Richard Owen (1804–1892) "invented" the breed of prehistoric vertebrates now referred to as dinosaurs, which he considered gigantic advanced (yet cold-blooded) super-reptiles, the "crown of reptilian creation,"[35]analogous to today's (warm-blooded) elephants and rhinos. In contrast to today's oxygen-invigorated atmosphere, Owen thought, the warm, late Mesozoic world still remained relatively deprived of oxygen, thus prohibiting mammalian types from thriving then. The religious Owen believed that the Creator had providentially equipped dinosaurs with the most advanced anatomical and physiological characteristics permissible under these prevailing environmental circumstances. As Adrian J. Desmond stated in 1975, Owen's position was that "the extraordinary prevalence of giant cold-blooded creatures can only imply that there was less oxygen available."[36] But this ideology exposed a flaw in Lamarck's (objectionable) evolutionist thinking. For Lamarck had envisioned and allowed for a gradual increase in species' overall structural organization and complexity evinced among certain classes of organisms through time. In the present day, reptiles were "lowly," having attained their apparent apotheosis in prehistory ("Secondary Period"). This meant that as a group, reptiles had instead "degenerated" (not advanced) since then, through geological time. Therefore, Owen was able to pronounce with alacrity, Lamarck's views on species transformism, invoking an "innate drive towards complexity," were wrong.[37]

It was during this period as well that Earth's inherent, balancing geochemical controls on the chemical composition of the atmosphere were first being considered, perhaps now viewed as an early precursor of the "Gaia" hypothesis that would follow over a century later. One such precocious individual was J.J. Ebelman, who in 1845 correctly detected, using chemical formulae, the macroscopic relationship between global content of carbonate, silica, calcium silicates and carbon dioxide in the environment. As Robert A. Berner stated in 2004, Ebelman, "more than 100 years ahead of his time, deduced correctly almost all of the major long-term processes affecting atmospheric CO_2 and O_2, including volcanism, the role of plants in weathering, the weathering and burial of organic matter and pyrite, and the weathering of basalt."[38]

However, as the rock record indicated, our prehistoric planet was not only *not* always tropical: there were also times during which savage cold and enduring ice settled in for long wintry spells! And the most recent phase of widespread glaciation seemed to have been intrinsically linked with the most recent geological catastrophe.

Okay—think back again to that passage from *Bleak House*—the quotation about the waters retreating from the Earth's surface along Holburn Hill where the imaginary megalosaur trod. During the early 19th century, "diluvial" formations representing what was scientifically, by 1837, documented to have been evidence of a former Great Ice Age, were often misinterpreted popularly as evidence of Noah's Flood.[39] Swiss geologist Louis Agassiz (1807–1873) laid considerable groundwork toward documenting the glacial period, characterized by a catastrophic temperature decline, with concomitant extinction of *all life*. Agassiz's presumptions began permeating into popular books of the time, such as Isabella Duncan's *Pre-Adamite Man* (1860), which featured a geological time diagram including a "panorama of the modern 'Adamitic' world separated by the lifeless Ice Age from the 'Pre-Adamitic' world of the Tertiary mammals and Secondary reptiles."[40]

However, as additional evidence was brought forward, theories abounded as to what had caused such a phase of planetary history; or phases, when it became realized that glacial times were recurrent, impacting contemporary paleo-fauna. By the 1860s, the most promising avenue for reliable causal explanations seemed to be astronomical in nature,[41] although even by then, educated men still clung to the old idea of deluges to explain the most recent, puzzling paleoclimatology stages and respective geological formations.

So while in 1864, Scottish physicist James Croll (1821–1890) advanced his astronomical theory of ice ages, French popular writer Louis Figuier (1819–1894) was editing editions of his highly circulated, theologically inclined life-through-geological-time "dinosaur book," one which had great influence on Jules Verne's writing of *Journey to the Center of the Earth*.[42] The English edition of Figuier's book was revealingly, and perhaps atavistically, titled *The World Before the Deluge*.[43] Figuier recognized a late near-glacial period, resulting in the "annihilation of organic life in these countries,"[44] while instead emphasizing the significance of three cataclysmic deluges forming the "diluvial" deposits. Two northern European deluges were surmised to have preceded the glacial period. The last of these naturalistic events (yet having a providential purpose), known as the "Asiatic Deluge," was associated with the historical, biblical flood.[45]

But, Figuier's popularized contemplations aside, which would have appealed to scriptural geologists, floods—scientifically—were old hat, generally disregarded by geologists nearly four decades earlier.[46] Secular astronomical regularities in planetary orbit and rotation, coupled with cyclic timing of axis wobbling, more successfully explained why Earth's fauna were subjected episodically to prolonged ages of ice, followed by warmer interglacial periods.[47] By the late 1970s, it also appeared as if varying atmospheric carbon dioxide levels represented an important complicating, contributing factor![48] Understanding carbon dioxide's significant role was long in coming. During the late 19th century, Irish physicist John Tyndall (1820–1893) and Swedish chemist Svante Arrhenius (1859–1927) independently grew interested in how ice ages originated. In particular, Arrhenius reasoned that a *reduction* in atmospheric carbon dioxide, which at sufficiently high atmospheric levels could provide a blanketing, warming effect (known as a "greenhouse effect"), theoretically also contributed to global cooling. At a time when the world's population was only around one billion with considerably less atmospheric pollution occurring annually, relative to today, Arrhenius, who lived in frigid Sweden, actually thought global warming might be beneficial for mankind. Neither Tyndall nor Arrhenius could have anticipated that decades later, global warming would seem on the verge of running out of control, adversely impacting weather patterns, melting icecaps, increasing oceanic levels, marginalizing resource availability, and destabilizing the ecological web of life.[49]

During the 1920s, earth scientists made further strides toward unraveling the riddle of the ice ages. Yugoslav engineer Milutin Milankovitch (1879–1958) made many refinements to the astronomical theory (updating Croll's assumptions), producing a mathematically elegant explanation. Meteorologist Alfred Wegener (1880–1930) not only considered paleoclimatology matters, but also pioneered a new highly controversial concept for how continents might drift around the globe over the Earth's mantle, which would have effected past climate conditions. Around this time as well, Earth's true age, and durations of each of the major geological periods of the Phanerozoic (life-bearing) Eras, was becoming more accurately defined, due to new techniques relying upon naturally occurring radioactive isotopes.[50] Besides advances in geophysics, from 1875 on, the year that geologist Edward Suess (1831–1914) coined the term "biosphere," there was a growing tendency to regard Earth and its inhabitants as an integrated "holistic" biogeochemical system, with geological forces forged with a host of reinforcing organic entities, evolving in tandem through time.[51] During the 1980s, especially, this became construed in the popular organismic hypothesis known as "Gaia," which by the early 1990s acquired something of a cultish flavor.[52]

Prevalence of "Lamarckism" during the first half of the 20th century blinded anti–Darwinians to the significance of environmental changes acting on and impacting life's history. This faction tried to separate inherent biological orthogenetic "trends" leading to extinction, independently, or *apart from (Darwinian) environmental factors*.[53] And because of the prevalence of Lamarckism, supported by men such as the influential Osborn, it wasn't until the introduction of population genetics studies (often founded on laboratory experimentation which Osborn belittled) that support for neo–Lamarckism faded.[54] In popular light, the Darwinian paleontologist George Gaylord Simpson (1902–1984) condemned orthogenesis and its misguided theoretical underpinnings, successfully appealing to the masses in his *Life of the Past: An Introduction to Paleontology* (1953), which went through 11 printings by 1976.[55] In the consideration of prehistoric life through geological time, shifting environmental conditions *were* important!

Meanwhile, a nascent trend in America during the late 1800s and early 1900s was for the establishment of major museum institutions presenting samples of natural history from around the world to the public. Of course museums and museum "cabinets" were already a tradition in Britain and Europe, dating back to the late 1700s in some cases, and Charles Wilson Peale's (1741–1827) museum in Philadelphia opened to patrons during the early 1800s, but essentially for the first time, now fairly complete dinosaur skeletons could be displayed for the public to wonder at in utter awe.[56] Osborn became a major instigator behind the American Museum's paleontology-edifying exhibits in New York, for example.[57] Such august institutions represented man's dominance over the planet, triumphantly placing Nature's subjugation prominently on display. By erecting dinosaur or other magnificent fossil vertebrate exhibits (e.g., "titanotheres," or mammoths), essentially viewed by many as paleotrophies, man was not only self-servingly symbolizing his dominion over Nature, but also signifying, as well as justifying his (predestined) self-righteous conquering capacity. For in that survival-of-the-fittest war with Nature—blood-red in tooth and claw—modern civilized man was most fit.

And so when industrialist steel magnate Andrew Carnegie (1835–1919) ordered casts of his fabulous 87-foot-long sauropod dinosaur, *Diplodocus carnegii*, made from molds, and shipped to several museums around the world (i.e., in Paris, Frankfurt, London, Vienna, La Plata, Mexico City), then each assembled, sometimes under his supervision or that of his chief paleontologists, the underlying message permeated worldwide.[58] Not only was man the ultimate ruler of his environment, surmounting the mighty dinosaurian breed weeded out by Nature (via natural selection) eons ago, but Carnegie's gifting also underscored that America's distinctive, prehistoric reptilians reigned supreme over those of foreign nations! "When displayed in the great cities of the east, and in the capitals of Europe, the larger dinosaurs seemed to confirm the superiority of modern industrial society by showing how the world had been conquered both in space and time." Modern civilized man—the white race especially—was thus entitled to exploit the globe and its inhabitants.[59] In fact, a theme of the lauded movie *King Kong* (RKO, 1933) may be interpreted as blatantly exploitative, with the huge (racially "backward") prehistoric ape subjugated and felled by a cruel modern industrial society.[60]

During the 1930s, climatic degradation became more closely interwoven with theories of dinosaur extinction (including ice ages), although more dramatic theories of dinosaur extinction will be further explored in Chapter Sixteen. (But also see Chapter Seven, note 34.) Although "fear of environmental degradation began in the mid–nineteenth century," such concerns did not "become a major concern for most people until the latter decades of the twentieth."[61] Since the 1950s, "the demand that we should *protect* Nature has grown from a minority position to a major factor in the debate."[62] Since the 1970s onward, practically every day, we're incessantly exposed to (sometimes assaulted by) the latest environmental and ecological news stories, transmitted via any variety of media. Fear of environmental conditions worsening in one way or another has unfortunately become part of modern popular culture.

Quite apart from prevalent concerns over a potential thermonuclear war erupting between the superpowers, the pace of recognizing industrial chemical hazards impacting mankind, and the immediacy of expressing public fears over our pollution of the environment, redoubled during the mid–1950s, accelerating through the early 21st century. At the outset, thick atmospheric haze and smog, radiation exposures from nuclear test fallout, and proliferation of pesticides in the environment swiftly fueled public anger and angst.[63] Lead in gasoline was being spewed over roadsides from the exhaust of internal combustion engines. Later, scientists documented how the protective ozone layer was being degraded by synthetic aerosols; acidified rain was harming natural water systems and aquatic biota. Waste dumps and leaky landfills threatening human health were more commonly encountered, materializing in people's proverbial backyards. Scientists warned of dangers of overpopulating the globe, the world's population now swollen to 7 billion! And in the context of their stories, pseudo-dinosaurs of sci-fi and film reflected our fears, urging us to steer from our (or rather Bradbury's metaphorical) self-destructive "path." One giant dino-monster—Godzilla, in particular—looms mightily here, although there were several notable characters.[64]

The 1957 film (American version), *Rodan, the Flying Monster*, involving the giant mutated pterosaurs, opens with a hydrogen bomb test, concluding with the monsters dying in an erupting volcano. The film's message concerns man's harmful exploitation of nature (i.e., a doomed mining operation with its concomitant pollution), and the fact that only Nature itself (symbolized by the volcano) can destroy one of Nature's mightiest products—the two giant pterosaurs. *Rodan* also presaged mankind's later preoccupation with global warming. For in one scene, a mining chief comments on how hot it is becoming. A brief exchange with a coworker elicits the opinion, "The earth is getting hotter.... If the snow at North and South poles melts, the earth will flood all over." Similar, anomalous "heat wave" concerns were also raised in 1965's *Ghidrah, the Three-headed Monster* (as Toho's outer-space dino-monster—or "exo-dinosaur"—King Ghidorah was first known to American audiences). Another fundamental conservation necessity, properly appreciating our life-giving waters—particularly the oceans—is tangentially addressed in Toho's *Monster Zero* (U.S. release 1970). Here technologically superior aliens from Planet X plan to steal our most valuable resource, the oceans, using the exo-dinosauroid Ghidrah, while enlisting Godzilla and Rodan to facilitate their subterfuge.[65] Eventually Godzilla and Rodan team up to destroy Ghidrah and the Earth is spared from an awful calamity.

Then in 1969's *Son of Godzilla*, clandestine experimentation with global weather patterns is conducted on a remote South Pacific island, with the noble aspiration that uncultivated, desert areas of the planet can be made green and fertile. If so, crops may be grown in these lands to avert human mass starvation. This is a "green theme" that became prevalent in later Godzilla films. Also, we're introduced in this film to Godzilla's "son" Minya, a distinctly anthropomorphized dino-monster character. Taking on human guise will be an increasingly common trait of the shape-shifting, Cold War–era dinosaur. (See Chapters Seventeen through the Epilogue.) Ultimately, the experiment dramatically backfires. Temperature rise goes awry, causing giant bugs to become inadvertently hatched on the island. Radiation-laced rain is emitted, before the scientists find a way to wisely place the island in deep-freeze.

The most notable (and memorable) Toho film in this context, however, is 1971's *Godzilla versus the Smog Monster.* Now, Godzilla is not just Earth-defender; he actively wages war against pollution incarnate! As Mark Justice stated in his excellent 2011 *G-Fan* article, "The most obvious allegory about the dangers of pollution, *Godzilla vs. the Smog Monster,* does more than simply incorporate pollution as part of its plot. Pollution becomes Godzilla's very literal adversary, and by extension, the world's."[66] A song titled "Save the Earth" is featured in this film, in which concerns about smog and heavy metal poisoning of the seas are expressed in lyrics. The entity that grows into Hedorah, the titular Smog Monster, begins as a tadpole-like marine creature. But as it grows, it evolves, thriving on water pollution, feeding on foul exhaust from bong-like smokestacks while in its terrestrial phase, and later evolving a flying capability, spewing out toxic air on the cowering populace below. Hedorah represents a serious global threat. "Hedorah personifies pollution in a most literal and animated form. Hedorah's graphic attacks on the cities of Japan are symbolic representations of pollution's attack on the entirety of the Earth."[67] No longer simply warning mankind about the dangers we face, this time Godzilla must actively step up and battle the (symbolic) nightmarish manifestation. This time Godzilla (ironically itself a byproduct of extreme radioactivity exposures) does save the Earth from its chemical pollution adversary.[68] But the somber conclusion suggests that the war is far from over and may even be impossible to ultimately win. *Smog Monster* "simply asks, 'when will the next environmental disaster happen?'"[69]

Foul smog seems everywhere in another dinosaur-related period piece concerning man's depressing pollution of the planet, Steven Utley's 1976 short story, "Getting Away." Here, protagonist Bruce Holt suffers from an affliction known as "temporal dislodgment."[70] During his uncontrollable "chronopathic flashabacks," his mind wanders into the primeval past—an extreme form of escapism from the awful, world-polluted present. Holt's malady is "triggered by despair, ... due to an overwhelming sense of hopeless oppression in a worsening environment."[71] Not unlike so many who have lost hope for the future, Holt naively yearns for simpler preindustrial times when the Earth was young, before mankind began exploiting the planet. A peculiar symptom of Holt's disease is that his mind forces him back way, way before the advent of man and the stink of 1960s and 1970s socioculture and politics. For brief moments he actually becomes part of prehistory, witnessing events through the eyes of long-dead organisms, including dinosaurs and winged pterosaurs. In these moments he returns to pristine times when "the smell of extinction was not in the air."[72]

During the 1980s, in light of disasters such as Cherbonyl and Three Mile Island, plus the reinvigorated threat of thermonuclear war with the Soviets, protestors railed against the construction of new nuclear reactors and the economically robust industrial-scientific-military complex. There was growing concern over threats to biodiversity, eradication of tropical rain forests, global warming with consequent rising sea levels, while we pondered civilization straining at the brink of sustainability limits. Spencer R. Weart describes the general broadening trend from concerns over radioactivity and thermonuclear holocaust into the "environmentalism" of the 1960s and 1970s:

> People were noticing that new technologies such as offshore drilling and strip-mining could harm broad regions, and they began to protest.... First was a sense of dire crisis, a fear that humanity was headed for self-imposed catastrophe ... a concern with whole systems, with the ways in which pollution could affect ecological relationships around the globe.... These themes—dismay with technological authorities and with systems that seemed about to doom the world—had first been thrust upon the public by hydrogen bombs.... Popular environmentalism had really started with a book attacking chemical pesticides, *Silent Spring*, begun by Rachel Carson in 1958.... It was radioactive fallout, she said, that had killed [her faith in Nature's stability and invulnerability]. Her book, published in 1962, opened with a fable of a town dying from a white chemical powder that snowed down from the sky, a powder that Carson likened to fallout.... Nuclear fear was only one of many forces behind the environmental movement, but it held a special place.[73]

During the early 21st century, scientists began referring to a "sixth" mass extinction, resultant of our term on Earth.[74] Meanwhile, dino-creatures and their giant monstrous brethren were enlivened, divulging mankind's folly, while cathartically and vividly defeating our symbolic polluting nemeses on screen.

So, by the late 1990s, Toho's giant insectoid monster, Mothra, an ecologically righteous protector of Earth, opposed to environmental degradation, became a symbol of natural conservation and green power. Mothra battled a pair of giant, winged dinosaurian creatures, Desghidorah and Dagahara, respectively, in *Rebirth of Mothra* (1996), and *Rebirth of Mothra II: Battle Beneath the Sea* (1997). These films are eco-themed, as the unscrupulous logging of natural forest land unleashes the mighty Desghidorah, which had arrived on Earth 65 million years ago after devastating Mars. The environmentalists are aided by a victorious Mothra, yet ultimately questions linger as to mankind's proper role in managing the Earth's precious resources. And in the 1997 sequel, the ocean becomes an environmental locus, where wanton pollution causes toxic, aggressive starfish-like creatures called Barem to proliferate, resulting in the oceans' demise. It turns out than an ancient race had created a dinosaurian creature—named the Dagahara—to consume oceanic pollutants. Dagahara has been resurrected and, although unnoticed, is doing its job. But an exceedingly nasty byproduct is being formed from the assimilated garbage and contaminants. Then it is divulged that Dagahara is programmed to transform oceanic pollution is into the Barem, which, "Like a red-tide ... cover the ocean's surface, threatening every living thing with which they come into contact."[75] This is an ecological nightmare that only Mothra can mitigate by dispatching Dagahara in a titanic battle.[76]

Then in 1998, in the film *Gargantua*, horrified citizens of a Pacific isle are threatened by a 60-foot-long, mutated, horned male salamander, resembling one of those vaunted Japanese giant monsters, which the military seems helpless against.[77] (See Figure 13-1.) This prehistoric-looking creature and smaller specimens comprising a family unit are the result of exposure to leaking DDT-containing canisters, dumped during the 1960s into a nearby oceanic ridge. This cryptozoological clan was created (unwittingly, although it's clear we should have known better!) by man's reckless pollution of the environment and disruption of oceanic ecology. The youngest member of the monster family trio is a human-child-sized juvenile critter, nicknamed "Casey" when he's caught, who eats junk food. Casey illustrates writers' and producers' efforts to project an appealing *anthropomorphized* dinosaurian-aspect character. As we'll note later, this trend had been evident and building since the 1950s, yet in a popular vein was mounting considerably during the 1990s.[78] Movies such as *Gargantua* and the pairing of the *Return of Mothra* films appealed especially to younger audiences, who after witnessing the impact of pollution personified in the form of giant monsters, may perhaps have been somewhat encouraged to become involved in, or at least be cognizant of, the significance of new millennial environmentalism. (Also, TriStar's contemporary *Godzilla* (1998), and an accompanying novelization tie-in written by Stephen Molstad, underscored the pervading overpopulation theme, as hundreds of baby Gojiras hatch from eggs in Madison Square Garden, threatening Man's symbolic extinction.)

Fig 13-1: The amphibious Gargantua is a giant dino-lizard, a mutated salamander resultant of toxic waste leakage into the Pacific Ocean (illustration by Lisa Szilagyi, with permission).

During the early 1990s, the Disney situation comedy TV series, *Dinosaurs*, carried the anthropomorphic concept to a further extreme. This half-hour program concerned the "Sinclair" family of dinosaurs, headed by a Megalosaur (as in *Bleak House*'s manifestation) father named Earl. Different family members were represented by actors wearing suits based on other dino-genera. For example, Earl's boss is a bullish faux-Triceratops character. Costumes worn by actors were the mastery of Jim Henson (famed creator of the Muppets). The show featured plots and story lines exposing the folly and fallacies faced by mankind in everyday (mirroring present day) life and society.

Fig 13-2: Mike Magee suggested sardonically in his 1994 book *Who Lies Sleeping?* not only that dinosaurs are genetically tied to humans, but that (like humans are doing now) the dinosaurs may have polluted their environment through a number of means, thus resulting in their extinction. Rather facetiously, then, was the elongated nasal structure of the *Parasaurolophus* really a special adaptation to filter pollutants and toxic particulates, such as from coal-burning smokestacks at right, from the Cretaceous atmosphere? Furthermore, after harnessing nuclear energy, in Magee's stark vision, the most anthropocentric dinosaur genera of the time (labeled "Anthroposaurs"—see the Epilogue) released radioactive isotopes, adding to the destruction of their world (illustration based on Magee's original ideas and imagery by *Prehistoric Times* editor and artist Mike Fredericks, used with permission).

As noted by paleontologist Jose Luis Sanz, "The series pays great attention to environmental problems: father Sinclair's company fells forests to build apartment blocks. The dinosaurs are irreversibly damaging their environment, which will lead to their extinction."[79] Here, dino-anthropomorphism becomes as visually right "in your face" about the ecological problems we face, globally, as can be expected or tolerated by viewing audiences. (See Figure 13-2.)

Men into pseudo-dinosaurs; dinosaurs into men. One and the same? Convinced?

These new-wave dino-monster characters mirror a sociocultural outcome of the dinosaur renaissance, a changing landscape. And so, just as the dinosaurs have their own age—the Mesozoic—a newly recognized geological age was recently termed and named, either in our honor, or more likely to our chagrin, casting deserved blame—the "Anthropocene."[80] Thus, thanks to dinosaurs and a host of those other prehistoric organisms, stirrings of a protracted environmental movement began over two centuries ago, gaining momentum during the 1960s, when fearsome dino-monsters—symbolizing extinction—forewarned yet another doomsday.

Where will it all lead?

Chapter Fourteen

Beyond the Smog Monster

Godzilla in the Anthropocene

Introduction

"[T]he old paradox remained in force: doom was still supposed to be staved off by the nightmare image of doom itself."—Spencer R. Weart, *The Rise of Nuclear Fear*[1]

Long a maligned monster film, *Godzilla vs. The Smog Monster* (1971) finally attained status as a scholarly concern through Sean Rhoads's magisterial analysis! This feature film's relevancy may have faded in passing decades. Yet, as we turn to our precarious future looming into the 21st century and beyond, the titular Smog Monster—former "mascot" of human-inflicted atmospheric pollution—alongside its adversary, an evolving "*totemic*" Godzilla, together acting as harbingers of doom, we question: "Have circumstances changed since 40 years ago?" As mankind suffers further, continual environmental and nuclear challenges of greater magnitude, may Godzilla retain chief iconic status warning of doomsday?

Sean Rhoads noted how "industrial pollution, through Hedorah, should be considered equivalent to the earlier nuclear fears exhibited in *Godzilla*" (i.e., *Gojira*). Furthermore, Mark Justice astutely noted that "Godzilla is the realization of every ecologically-threatening phenomenon ... the recurring embodiment of scientific hubris in the wake of the split atom, the lingering effects of fallout from fission ... the entire planet's ecological survival.... The implication is simple in cautionary message: science and technology are more than the cause of dire ecological conditions than the cure. The appearances of monsters such as Godzilla are warning enough of the prospective threats that await if humanity continues on its current path of ecological self-destruction."[2] (See Figure 14-1.)

But beyond Toho's Godzilla filmography, our famous monster may be viewed in a broader context, which may be well illustrated by coalescing ideas of three cultural historians. For Godzilla is an evolving part of a continuum whose visage originated in Rudolph Zallinger's famous *Tyrannosaurus rex* restoration, featured in his 1947 mural *Age of Reptiles*. Godzilla's spirit or "totem" lives on in the guise of increasingly intelligent science fictional dinosauroids, which also warn, reinforcing the idea of our possible extinction.

And so, here, with Rhoads's and Mark Justice's illustrative observations serving as inspiration, from a cultural historian's perspective, further insights are offered concerning pseudo-dinosaurs as symbolic "doomsday prophets." The foreboding, post-modernistic environmental/extinction theme of catastrophe has become universal and provocative.

Fig 14-1: A model confrontation, perhaps metaphorically representing the plight of mankind, waged between (at left) Gfantis, sculpted by Allen A. Debus in 2012, and (at right) the giant mother Gorgo smashing city buildings in its wake, produced and distributed by Monarch. Gfantis is a fictional dino-monster conceived by J.D. Lees for his edited fanzine, *G-Fan* (models from the Debus collection).

Enter Doomsday Dinosauroid Iconology

As Susan Sontag related half a century ago, "Science fiction films are not about science. They are about disaster, which is one of the oldest subjects of art." Furthermore, through such "sensuous elaboration ... one can participate in the fantasy of living through one's own death and more, the death of cities, ... destruction of humanity itself.... It is in the imagery of destruction that the core of a good science fiction film lies." Watching others perish ... yes, a veritable train wreck, but it's impossible to look away. Schadenfreude in its most piquant state! Furthermore, as Spencer R. Weart commented, "[W]hen people vicariously experience something by seeing it in a movie, or even just by hearing it in a story, they may viscerally accept it as factual, almost as if they were witnessing it in person."[3]

While Sontag notes how older sci-fi films bear an "innocent relation to disaster," modernity (i.e., since the 1950s) has imposed a grim, dispassionate dosage of reality upon the often moralistic imagination of disaster, especially fear of future nuclear war and exposure to radiation. Oddly, since the 1950s, mankind has become psychologically acclimated to the specter of his instant annihilation and extinction, or at the very least, dehumanization, anxieties which modern science fiction films convey, yet in the final analysis often allay with traditional happy endings.

Embodiment of dinosaur images within a science fictional "doomsday" context was an unexpected outcome of the "dinosaur renaissance." Through the first 150 years of advanced paleontological vertebrate researches (i.e., since Cuvier's late–18th century researches), a sense of life-through-time transformist processes, yielding to evolution, characterized paleoimagery's broad brush. Then, out of a time when dinosaurs and prehistoric life may have seemed culturally irrelevant, geopolitical machinations gradually transformed the most vaunted prehistoric menagerie—dinosaurs and other Mesozoic reptiles—into reluctant symbols of catastrophe.

Following World War II and during the tumultuous 1960s and '70s, the dire prospect of self-inflicted human annihilation and extinction escalated. Social concerns progressively reflected dinosaurian symbolism, especially when paleontologists reconsidered extinction causes in geological history. Anachronistic pseudo-dinosauria of filmdom became allegorical for the fusion hydrogen bomb, although in time their meaning would broaden in light of other recognized threats to civilization and the natural order. Since the mid–1970s flowering of the so-called "dinosaur renaissance," prehistoric life, emphasizing a popular dinosaurian visage, has increasingly reflected the human plight, perceived as worsening. Particular kinds of fictional dinosaurs and "reptiloids" imbued with intelligence, became metaphorically assimilated with, or melded into, human guise. How did prehistoric life, as instruments of popular culture, enter such a disturbing arena from a state of utter irrelevancy? Why did certain kinds of dinosaurs and pseudo-reptilians become emblematic of catastrophe in our tumultuous post-modernistic world?

Imagetext portraying fictional disaster proved immensely satisfying throughout the past century and even escalated during the early years of the 21st century. For example, think of all those History Channel "what if" documentaries on apocalyptical mega-disasters, covering everything from viral pandemics, Nostradamus and supernovas, or those concerning Earth after man's inevitable extinction. Recently, cultural historians Max Page (*The City's End: Two Centuries of Fantasies, Fears, and Premonitions of New York's Destruction*, 2008), Spencer R. Weart (*Nuclear Fear: A History of Images*, 1988), and (tangentially—only in certain passages) W.J.T. Mitchell (*The Last Dinosaur Book: The Life and Times of a Cultural Icon*, 1998), each dealt with the subject of images reflecting mankind's psychological fears of impending doom. Collectively, the spectrum of imagery considered is an often stereotypical admixture, enveloping films, paintings, novels, science fiction stories, advertising emblems, corporate logos, graphical displays, museum restorations, protest signs, cartoons and psychological impressions. "All seeing involves metaphor" and imagination, claims Mitchell.[4] Such imagetext—composite imagetext or "visual-verbal-tactile (theoretical yet artificial) construction"—incorporates many manifestations available in contemporary popular culture of which the public (here emphasizing English-speaking peoples) may have been consciously aware or subconsciously attuned to.

But for our immediate purposes, let's see how their researches into iconology bear impact on our angst-filled age—Godzillean times, that is, during what has been dubbed the "Anthropocene." What do these authors offer in this regard? How do their ideas first independently, then collectively fit into the overall doomsday equation? Here we see that emblematically, Max Page provocatively presents the image of the crumbling city tower, or the "mangled skyscraper." Spencer R. Weart conjures the harrowing symbol of the mushroom cloud, while W.J.T. Mitchell exposes dinosaur images as a complex and malleable, polysemous "totem" for modernity. And how do these ideas merge with five pop-cultural "publicized pulses of dread," to be outlined later?

The social urgency of these visual messages escalated following World War II's invention of nuclear weapons and, subsequently, atomic power. An apocalyptical movement (considered broadly) recruited curious yet ineluctable means of broadcasting and receiving the message. In particular, we find that especially during the dinosaur renaissance, prehistoric life played a significant although as yet unheralded role in the projection of doom. Why have creatures expiring millennia ago prospered as harrowing agents of *our*—as perceived by prophets—pending cataclysm? While disaster imagery (imagined or documenting real episodes) predates association with paleo-monsters, during the 1950s and especially thereafter during the "dinosaur renaissance" (whose origins usually are allied to the late 1960s discovery and description of the North American Cretaceous raptor dinosaur *Deinonychus*), certain dinosaur images inexorably transformed, becoming more closely allied to the idea of global catastrophe. How and why this happened is a topic rarely touched upon.

Mangled Skyscraper

Why this preoccupation and fascination with civilization's doom? In the case of symbolic New York City, Page suggests that its envisioned destruction resonates

> ... with some of the most long-standing themes in American history: the ambivalence toward cities, the troubled reaction to immigrants and racial diversity, the fear of technology's impact, and the apocalyptic strain in American religious life. Furthermore, these visions of the city's end have paralleled the city's economic, political, racial, and physical transformations.... Each era in New York's modern history has produced its own apocalyptic imagery that explores, exploits, and seeks to resolve contemporary cultural tensions and fears.... Artists and writers of every era—each with their own world of cultural and social concerns—returned to New York, to destroy it, to entertain their audiences, and to define their stances on the social concerns of the day.[5]

Page cites the psychological roller coaster thrill ride provided by such fare as disaster porn, the rush of immediate, palpable terror, the "panoramic view" of the devastating aftermath, followed by "expansive relief" when panic subsides. Perhaps we are an inherently sick species that way, but the malady is no less cerebrally ingrained than other worse tendencies.

True—although Page emphasizes social factors, giant paleo-monsters have routinely had their way with New York, most memorably beginning with a prehistoric ape's resolute climb to the top of a modern skyscraper, clasping Hollywood's first bona fide scream queen within his hairy fingers. In RKO's *King Kong* (1933), the iconic stop-motion animated Kong causes some collateral damage, before being unceremoniously dispatched by a squadron of military biplanes. The tragic, exploited "monster" is subdued not only by "Beauty," but also by the fierce city itself. Kong reappeared in a far less successful 1976 film, and later was featured in a 2005, CGI-animated blockbuster in which the mighty dinosaur-killer succumbs to the wiles of a far more sympathetic Ann Darrow. A Rhedosaurus awakened in the Arctic by a nuclear bomb blast attacks New York City in 1953's *The Beast from 20,000 Fathoms*. As Page remarks, this beast is viewed as the living manifestation of powerfully destructive forces, unleashed at a time of post–hydrogen bomb, Cold War paranoia and when Hitler's invading forces were still in public consciousness. New York is besieged by a twofold menace. For after exposing inhabitants with a deadly plague germ issued from its wounds, the destructive beast can only be annihilated with a "good" isotope (which somehow neutralizes toxic isotopes spawning the nightmare). "Atoms for Peace" vs. Nuclear Dread!

A heroic Godzilla, temporarily subjected to adverse mind control, attacks New York in Toho's *Destroy All Monsters* (U.S. release 1968), and then reappears in different guise (aka "GINO," or Godzilla In Name Only) in an oft-maligned 1998 remake. While aliens are the figurative menace in Toho's version, in TriStar's effort we see more of a mixed bag of thematic inspiration, perhaps emphasizing overpopulation of the globe as we worry what may happen to the planet and mankind if those raptor-like baby godzillas were to escape Madison Square Garden. Finally, playing on modern terrorist fears, a quasi-prehistoric monster of genuinely mysterious provenance attacks New York in 2008's *Cloverfield*. This time the invading creature presumably meets a fiery end when the city is nuked.

However, besides monstrous prehistoria, Page discusses a variety of disasters and catastrophes contrived by authors and imagineers delving back into the 19th century, both man-made and naturalistic, plaguing New York in art, fiction, and fact. He thus wends his way toward current popular culture with modern society's perceived zombie-apocalyptical scenarios, as well as a host of menacing environmental and terrorist threats. Yes—clearly, before the advent of monstrous assaults on Tokyo, we were fearfully confronted with New York City's magnificently mangled skyscrapers! Regardless, nationwide, the 20th century's most disturbing and prolonged, genuine source of civil anxiety concerned … the Bomb.

Mushroom Cloud

> "The figures of mushroom clouds are the visual creation that symbolizes this [i.e., 20th] century, overwhelming all other artistic creation of the time."—Chinese-American artist, Chi Guo-Qiang[6]

Spencer R. Weart's 1988 "history of images," *Nuclear Fear*, traces how the idea of elemental *transmutation* swiftly evolved from crucibles of alchemical idealism to sociopolitical strife concerning nuclear power plants and angst concerning the possibility of global thermonuclear war. Weart extends his vision by incorporating "inarticulate pictures" and even "emotional patterns," confiding, "Associations already in the mind can creep into the picture that people think they perceive.... Much the same kind of study can be made for nuclear energy."[7] History records how pioneering radiochemists conjured potent yet arcane transmutationist formulae and symbolism, at first promising a boundless energy source with mankind's subsequent leap into a new Golden Age. But like metals melded within alchemical crucibles of the Middle Ages, according to tradition, many perceived that in order to attain the new exalted state of civilization the world must first (prophetically) pass through conflagration. Radium's energetic storehouse was thus viewed as a double-edged sword. And so, during the years leading up to World War II, scientists viewed as "mad" abounded in science fiction literature and low-budget films. Science fiction writers had a field day destroying civilization with their bombs or death rays emanating from advanced super-weapons, capable of destroying entire cities. In the wrong hands, horrific detonation perceived even on a planetary scale was not considered unlikely.

A melding of doomsday with modern science had already been forged in popular culture during the early 19th century. This association became enlivened following the discovery of atomic energy with attendant imagetext. However, at first this conditioning had no ties to or basis in paleontology. A century ago, when radium was discovered, dinosaurs represented modern (American) industrialism and our vaunted subjugation of the planet. But by the mid–1930s, dinosaurs were side-railed, merely considered emblematic of *non-nuclear* petroleum-based power. Even worse, they were becoming a popular media circus and, during the heyday of neo–Lamarckism, even losing theoretical importance.

Quoting Hindu scripture (*Bhagavad Gita*), physicist J. Robert Oppenheimer remorsefully stated in a July 1945 interview following Trinity, the first atomic bomb test detonation, "I am become death, the destroyer of worlds." Following Hiroshima and Nagasaki in early August 1945, "the whole tangle of fantastic nuclear imagery, mingled with the very few facts then available, was a significant part of the mental equipment of everyone within reach of a radio."[8] Invention of the "super" or hydrogen bomb changed everything irrevocably. Citizens worried whether man might lose control over the atom, unleashing a golem, an allegorical monster of Frankensteinian proportions bent on destroying its creator—Man. Stereotypical mad scientist and monster were conjoined, metaphorically mirroring anxieties over the awful capabilities and consequences of nuclear physics. It seemed the irrational, overweening technology-driven class would willingly destroy those with more rational, righteous-minded emotions.

Citizen-activists whose minds and opinions were fueled with dark primordial visions conjured by writers and artists seemingly "in the know" protested against radioactive fallout and pollution, and the horror of a total modern war fought *without* security or, after the bombs, worthwhile survival. By the mid–1950s, to many frightened citizens, "Nuclear energy violated the order of nature."[9] *Contamination* and *pollution* became bywords of the wary and fearful. Radioactivity not only could be viewed as a "disease" of "debased and crumbling atoms,"[10] but it also caused cancer and death. At a psychological level, public fear of contamination and pollution increasingly merged nuclear with burgeoning (non-nuclear) environmental concerns. In her classic *Silent Spring* (1962), Rachel Carson even referred to agricultural application of pesticides as white snowy powder descending from the sky and killing a town, thus conjuring images of radioactive fallout. Death *rays* still abounded in science fiction tales, perpetuated in Toho sci-fi 1960s films. However, public fear and the stimulus for many contemporary stories and movies (including *Gojira* following the *Lucky Dragon* incident) yielded to "death *dust*" dread, a resultant phenomenon of H-bomb testing that the U.S. government at first tried unsuccessfully to conceal from public attention. Not our finest hour.

The Soviet *Sputnik* launch in October 1957 triggered hysteria in America, heightening paranoia. Stephen A. Norwick observed, "Clearly, the race to the Moon seemed to be about space, but it was really a competition for control of the ionosphere for prosecuting nuclear war."[11] Would the civilized world become a sterilized, post-war "Hiroshima," photographs of which were pessimistically imprinted on human imagination? A planet eerily glowing in the dark, inherited by hardy, rad-resistant cockroaches? Eventually a slogan, "nuclear freeze," segued into "nuclear winter." "The immediate issue now was the survival of nations or even the whole human race." It is little recognized how during this most disquieting period, dinosaurs and generally paleoimagery became more complexly interwoven with doomsday imagetext.

As Weart confesses, "[I]mages do not always stay quietly within the mind."[12] Or, one might add, the soul. Soon, as people nervously imagined, the threat of nuclear catastrophe seemed less related to political intrigue, as opposed to climactic technological breakdown, such as a "fail safe" malfunction. Evoking the Cold War's most terrifying image and our deepest fear, George W. Bush stated in early 2003 on the impending Iraq invasion, "The smoking gun may come in the form of a mushroom cloud." One never sees a mushroom cloud in *Gojira*, yet it is implicit that phenomena causing Tokyo's destruction, including annihilation of several vessels, are indirectly resultant of America's bomb. Weart acknowledges the towering white mushroom cloud, somber symbol of the nuclear age, a shape that even represented the essence of "transmutation" as in life arising from death.[13]

In a sense, Godzilla and his monstrous radioactive cohorts were created in Chicago, where under the football stadium in 1942, Enrico Fermi conducted the first human-controlled fission chain reaction. Sculptor Henry Moore's rendering of *Nuclear Energy* (1966) commemorated Fermi's triumph. Viewing his sculpture today, one may comprehend Moore's interpretation: "The upper part is very much connected with the mushroom cloud of an atomic explosion, but also it has the shape and eye sockets of a skull." Weart claims this melding of death's head with atomic cloud was already a "visual cliché" by then.[14] Nuclear dino-monster imagery became increasingly familiar and prevalent during the 1950s as well as in many other science fiction stories and films. The trendsetter was perhaps1953's *The Beast from 20,000 Fathoms,* oddly inspired by a nostalgic (non-nuclear themed) short story by Ray Bradbury, yet conveyed most potently in *Gojira*. In fact, during stages of designing the original Godzilla suit, artist Kazuyoshi Abe proposed a monster head bearing simian qualities, but symbolically having a *mushroom cloud shape*. According to Ed Godziszewski "Being a bit far-fetched as a dinosaurian image, the design was discarded."[15]

Totemic Dinosauroid

To this trifold formula of envisioning doomsday via common images, in his *The Last Dinosaur Book* (1998), W.J.T. Mitchell adds an astute observation that by the early 20th century, dinosaurs were becoming our "totem animal of modernity," not merely a symbol, "uniting modern science with mass culture."[16] And the dinosaur is a "creature that no one understands fully—least of all the paleontologists."[17] What? Yes, he declares, dinosaurs and their ubiquitous, shape-shifting "schizosaur" images and familiar accompanying narrative opportunistically convey a highly diverse, seemingly paradoxical and often disparate array of meanings, metaphors and ideas, ceaselessly "read into" and "mined for significance." Their significance shifts in time with historical/cultural and mass media events.[18] They're simply "there," everywhere and available, ready to be recruited into a dizzying variety of sociopolitical causes, but to certain audiences during the mid– to late 20th century, their meaning rapidly matured, attaining poignancy. Indeed, alien "dinosauroids" conceivably visiting Earth in the far-flung future presumably after Man's demise might observe from our relics and ruins that the "greatest epidemic of dinosaur images occurs in the late twentieth century, just at the moment when widespread public awareness of ecological catastrophe is dawning, and the possibility of irreversible extinction is becoming widely evident."[19]

Our late 20th- and early 21st century dinosaurs have become personified for valid, psychological reasons. Mitchell recognized, "Our basis for human fascination with dinosaurs, the most universally recognizable animal of our era and the focus of distinctively modern rituals of resurrection and consumption,"[20] is anatomical and ecological similarity, that is, their stature and status. Dinosaurs are "both our twin and our antagonist ... 'monstrous doubles' of human beings, with many of them resembling us in their erect, bipedal stature and in their status as 'rulers of the earth' in the Age of Reptiles."[21] (Note the sly reference to Zallinger's 1947 mural *Age of Reptiles.*) However, while a generalized, pop-cultural dinosaur "breed" has become significant today, arguably, such a lapse into anthropomorphism didn't manifest itself or become fully realized, ratified or appreciated until during later phases of the dinosaur renaissance period.

Like radiation and atomic secrets which physicists pried from Earth's womb, dinosaurs also traditionally yet mysteriously represented Nature's deepest secrets, although usually of an evolutionary, survival-of-the-fittest, or extinction variety. Long considered the epitome of extinction, today—because dinosaurs are essentially a modernistic invention, poised at the crossroads of scientific interpretation and contemporary culture—their status in natural history could be accentuated and exploited in novel ways. Or as Mitchell professes, while "real dinosaurs" exist as fossils in the Earth's womb or as museum displays, dinosaur *images* have "escaped into every dimension of cultural space, evolving new species, colonizing new habitats."[22] During the height of our catastrophic age, dinosaurs of every persuasion inform and warn us of our plight, Godzilla being the mid–20th century's most familiar spokesman.

Indeed, scholars such as Chon A. Noriega have noted that through a half-century stream of Toho films, one pseudo-dinosaur in particular, Godzilla, also has evolved, representing a host of global threats beyond the prevalent, ever-present nuclear one. However, beyond Mitchell's more general assertion, my contention here is that the *most* significant aspect of the most important grouping of dinosaurs' post-modernistic, meteoric and metaphoric rise is that they've come to represent Man's repressed fear of extinction—our own![23]

Curiously, while Mitchell elaborated on the multiplicative meanings of our totemic, modern dinosaur, he doesn't seem to have such a clear perspective on Godzilla's range of meaning(s). Godzilla is a flame-breathing "dragodinosauroid" (a term coined by paleontologist Jose Luis Sanz) dino-monster (yet actually a suit worn by human actors enhanced with special effects). According to film scholars Chon A. Noriega and William Tsutsui, Godzilla's meaning is as highly malleable or polysemous (if not more so) than any other dinosaur image. Godzilla imbues and radiates far more symbolism, thought and universal meaning than (simply) the H-bomb, so splendidly projected through 1954's *Gojira*, or a psychedelic war on industrial pollution via his exertions versus the Smog Monster.

I have divided paleoimagery's broad history into three generalized periods, or categories. First—a traditional "life through time" emphasis phase, leading to a fierce Cold War mutated variety, followed by the modern "dinosaur renaissance" period in which pop-cultural science dinosaurs increasingly take on human characteristics, qualities, and of course, intelligence.[24] During this latter period, in literature and film, dinosaurs began representing and "speaking" for us, for better or worse. Why do they? Because, psychologically, we're comforted when they do.[25] I place the paleoimagery period timeline "boundary" at 1947, corresponding to completion of the mural *Age of Reptiles*. It was also in 1947 that the hydrogen bomb's inventor, Edward Teller, devised the infamous "clock of doom," reset from seven minutes to "two minutes to midnight" in 1953 after the first successful fusion (hydrogen) bomb tests.

The centrality of Zallinger's Late Cretaceous segment in his mural merits contemplation. In fact, it was Zallinger's great mural, with its wonderful yet ominous Late Cretaceous scene, incorporating North America's "lordly" *Tyrannosaurus rex* presiding over the prehistoric world, a key image inspiring the Godzilla suit design, which catapulted dinosaurs into our postwar world. What transpired since then is something Mitchell didn't quite grasp or at least fully elaborate in his book, so please allow me to carry the ball further. It seems mankind has anointed dinosaurs—that is, particular groupings of dinosaurs, including entirely fictional types blessed with quasi-human intelligence and analogous posture—to be elevated to special prominence. I believe this is the true "totemic" aspect of Mitchell's argument—grafting "dinosauroids" into modern popular culture in light of our threatening, harrowing times (i.e., mangled skyscrapers and mushroom clouds alike).

Here, I've taken vast liberties with the term "dinosauroid," designating it to mean any of a bewildering array of smart sci-fi dinosaurs, when it originally referred only to a 1981 sculptural rendering of a "dinosaur-man" proposed by paleontologist Dale Russell, an intelligent species which might have evolved had the 6-mile-diameter asteroid not impacted Earth 66 million years ago. (Also see the Epilogue.) The annals of science fiction are rife with the ranks of strange reptile/dino-people and smart dino-monsters, going back to H.G. Wells's and Edgar Rice Burroughs's heyday. Yet, perhaps understandably, these dinosauroids (representing the already extinct) began "speaking" for and preaching to mankind during our darkest hour, the mid–1950s, following the hydrogen bomb's invention. (In the gladiatorial arena of life and death, it's as if they're saying, "We who are already dead salute you!") Later, thanks especially to the success of the 1980 asteroid theory of dinosaur extinctions, sci-fi pulp zines and films began churning dinosauroid varieties out in short order.[26] Evidently the new, smarty-pants breed of dinos won't shut up until we listen. "Hey—look, dude, extinction can (and will) happen to you too!"

Godzilla is a significant part of this evolutionary transcendence among pop-cultural dinosaurians. But Godzilla's personal transformation, especially in Toho's Showa series accentuated by an evolving suitmation design, forms only a part of the big picture. From the mid–1960s onward, becoming a heroic creature capable of communicating in "monster talk" while representing Nature, Godzilla becomes more fully represented as a humanoid monster or a "dinosauroid," of sorts, like many others having "evolved" in our post–dinosaur renaissance era's literature and film, such as the titular creature in Mark Jacobson's 1991 novel, *Gojiro*. You see, Mitchell claims a conflated, generic kind of "dinosaur" as the modern totem. But more exactly, I believe it is imagetext associated with the "dinosauroid" (admittedly a loosely used term here, but including certain representations of daikaiju like Godzilla), which has become totemic, a symbol of our precarious age—the Anthropocene. For the science fictional dinosaurs *are* us, sharing a dystopian fate—a most insecure horror.

Post-World War Apocalyptical Waves of Peril

We live in a catastrophic age, so well publicized and exactingly documented—from Krakatoa's 1883 eruption, 1912's *Titanic* disaster, through New York City's World Trade Center Towers 9/11 terrorist strike, a Great Wave triggering Japan's Fukushima Dai-chi nuclear plant meltdown in 2011, disastrous hurricanes, global economic collapse, etc., etc., and who knows what else marching boldly beyond, onward toward the next apocalypse! We're nearly beyond the state of panic, over-exposed to horrific, "in-your-face," mind-numbing stimuli.

Since the end of World War II, one may discern *five* publicized pulses of perceived dread in which dinosaur imagetext became successively slotted into pop-cultural niches, each representing (then) newly identified forms of worldwide peril, yet always introduced by and entrenched in science. These may be dubbed the volcanic, radiation, ecological, asteroid/comet, and greenhouse phases, each over time having had cumulative psychologically oppressing impact. During the past 65 years, dinosaurs and dinosauroids—Godzilla included—have been associated with imagery of each of the five listed groups. (Of course, the reducible common theme or overarching umbrella associated with these is environmental pollution.) However, of particular interest to Godzilla fans may be the most recent greenhouse (aka climate change) phase of publicized concern.

During the early 1980s, Late Cretaceous dinosaur extinctions were ineffectually allied by paleontologist Dewey McLean to atmospheric greenhouse conditions. Paleontologist Peter Ward outlined in a popular 2007 book (*Under a Green Sky*) how several extinctions of the Late Permian and Mesozoic Era may indeed be tied to global warming with resulting anoxia in the oceans. More recently, geologists concluded that massive volcanic episodes dating to the end of the Triassic Period (201 million years ago), associated with plate tectonics opening the North Atlantic Ocean, are responsible for an intense global warming phase. In fact, dinosaurs like the later *Tyrannosaurus* may owe their existence to a global greenhouse condition that exterminated their non-dinosaurian rivals and ecological competitors, as well as considerable marine species, yet allowing dinosaur ancestors to ultimately prevail. (This was also a time of reduced atmospheric oxygen levels, favoring the early dinosaurs' supposedly derived-advanced physiological systems.)

Also, scientists have claimed that dinosaur methane-containing flatulence, especially from those gassy, vegetation-fermenting, long-necked sauropods, may have contributed substantially to global temperature rise, which conceivably could have in turn contributed to greenhouse extinction episodes.[27] And although politicians debate whether man's global carbon dioxide emissions are rising to harmful levels, in his 2010 M.A. thesis, Sean Rhoads noted that Toho film director Banno Yoshimitsu planned to direct a sequel to *Godzilla vs. the Smog Monster* possibly focusing on the global warming threat and "the continuing problems of pollution. Unfortunately, because of creative disagreement between Banno and Tanaka Tomoyuki over *Godzilla vs. Hedorah*, the film was never made."[28] Nuclear threats, industrial pollution and climate change: all now intertwined in modern society.

Not even survivalists can prepare for paroxysmal earthquakes and polluting supervolcanic episodes whenever they may uncontrollably happen. Or, for that matter, are we quite ready to deflect an asteroid from impacting Earth? Fortunately, these days most space bolides miss. (As science fiction author Larry Niven remarked, dinosaurs became extinct due to lack of a space program. Think about it!) Likewise, we'd be toast if a supernova were to happen near our solar system, as occurred during the Late Ordovician (approximately 430 million years ago).[29] These are events that would seemingly occur instantaneously, without much prior notice. But menacing ecological/environmental consequences closely interrelated to man's industrial (waste-producing) prowess as well as our astonishing tendency to overpopulate the globe—thereby depleting natural resources at an ever accelerating pace, with resulting greenhouse climate change conditions—always seem remotely far off in time or place.

By mid-century we'll have more power-hungry, nuclear-tipped nations to worry about than was the case a half-century ago. Today or tomorrow, without warning, nuclear missiles could stream out of the sky, blindsiding us, spewing radiation and death to billions around the globe. Perhaps this is one reason why we fear the mushroom-cloaked, radioactive visage of doom more so than those drawn-out, yet hotly contested environmental concerns. Why? We're a species that has perfected denial. Because that fateful tipping point, when ocean levels shall rapidly rise or when unstable (positive feedback) atmosphere-warming methane hydrate deposits will billow forth uncontrollably from the sea floor, always seems impossibly far off, as long as the politicians say so. However, while suicidal *action* of some kind would prompt nuclear Armageddon or a holocaust, only through *inaction* will ocean levels rise and global temperatures soar.[30]

Geologists have recently proposed that the modern "era" be termed the "Anthropocene" (or the "Age of Man") because of civilization's obvious planetary impacts, so vastly accelerating in magnitude since the early 1800s. We have effectively driven the planet out of the Holocene epoch into a "much less climatically stable age." The impacts of our industry, technology, declining biodiversity and our wastes and pollution will leave an inescapable imprint in the rock record. Scientists claim that one of several useful geochemical markers for setting the boundary of this new Anthropocene age would be 1945, corresponding to the introduction of certain radioactive isotopes into the atmosphere, deposited as sediments, fallout from the first atomic bomb tests (occurring during the time Zallinger was painting his famous mural at Yale).[31]

Ever since the late 1940s, through film, stories, art and a variety of other imagetext, dinosaurians, Godzilla, and imagery of intelligent dinosauroids have become enlisted toward this ultimate cause—helping to define and remind through their words and deeds what abominable modes of peril threaten mankind. Or in some cases instructing how we may avoid impending doomsday. Over a century, dimwitted science fictional amphibioid gill-men, unintelligent dino-monsters and morphologically ostentatious drago-dinosauroids of the silver screen (such as Toho's Godzilla) evolved, shape-shifted or coalesced into more diminutive and smart, technologically adept dinosauroid, reptiloid/dinosaur "men." As Toho's Showa series waned, Godzilla became accustomed to his role as friendly Earth-defender. A few years later, the famous 1980 Dinosauroid sculpture was completed by artist Ron Seguin, under Dale Russell's advisement. Human-like dinosaurs became more ubiquitous in film, sci-fi stories, television, etc., from then on, in many ways mocking us while representing and mirroring the human dilemma. Yes, the dinosaurs not only *are* us, but metaphorically we have become Godzilla. Jacobson's 1991 titular character Gojiro (to be addressed in Chapter Nineteen) assimilated Godzilla fully into the dinosauroid realm, thus completing his transformation into human guise (although in a way most readers might not be familiar with, or would view with apprehension).

If procrastinating mankind were not in such a state of utter denial, would we exercise better judgment and mastery over bomb radiation, ecological and greenhouse peril, where we may exert beneficial judgment and control? Can we diminish our footprint, carbon or otherwise (much larger than Godzilla's) in our self-imposed Anthropocene Age? Godzilla and fellow dinosaurians have played significant, nudging roles throughout, which explains our heightened obsession with these harmful yet sometimes benevolent creatures. Through them we visualize our inevitable fate. In the end will doomsday dinosaurs prevail in the absence of man?

Is this the end?[32]

Part III

Man and Dinosaur as One

There are three "ages" of popular interest in dinosaurs, that is, emphasizing the messages society has received, gleaned or expected from our reliance upon dinosaurs and those pesky other prehistoric animals, as witnessed and conveyed in museum displays, via books and films or other media (e.g., commercial advertising—not considered herein). First, we considered the traditional life-through-time phase of emphasis, roughly 1800 to World War II's aftermath—a plausible beginning of the Anthropocene epoch. The second phase became instilled with inner turmoil, triggered by living with the hydrogen bomb during the 1950s and the dawning realization that mankind might create its own extinction—gone like the dinosaurs (which then "returned" during the 1950s to warn us of our folly in various imposing guises) in a puff of smoke. As we've just seen, giant dino-monsters of the 1950s and beyond (as portrayed in films, novels, comic books) assumed a more visceral meaning than ever before.

In Chapter Two of one of my previous books, *Dinosaur Sculpting: A Complete Guide* (2013), I referred to Paleoimagery's *two* phases of expression, a "First traditionalized phase—life-through-time," and a "Second sweeping phase—Dinosaur Renaissance."[1] I stated, "According to this analysis, broader popularized components of paleoimagery's growth and development since the 1850s—shortly after which the profession (i.e., practice) is said to have 'matured'—will be characterized as a two-stroke engine cycle fueled by man's visionary expectations, and, ultimately, global concerns."[2] While the underlying criteria and rationale for the two phases are well explained therein, remaining valid, I've since split the dinosaur renaissance phase further, as outlined in Parts Two and Three of this book. Part III emphasizes when dinosaurs assumed a more humanoid guise and configuration, thus enhancing their ability to directly *forewarn* (not simply through metaphor) but also by relying on their majesty, innate language and intelligence to remind us of what happened to them.

From a popular culture perspective, the 1980s may be regarded as a "Decade of the Dinosaur," like none other before. From what facets did this popular enthusiasm stem? As already noted, much of the matter may be related to mankind's increasing understanding that our presence on Earth, like that of the extinct dinosaurs, is precarious and that we bear the potential to destroy our present world and its inhabitants. The expanding environmental movement, coupled with heightened tensions with the Soviet Union and new discoveries concerning how the dinosaurian reign really ended, fostered this pre–*Jurassic Park* phase of dino-mania. The 1980s craze over the asteroid impact theory of dinosaurian mass extinctions (addressed in Chapter Sixteen) certainly fostered the invention of the idea of the intelligent dinosauroid, spawned in the theme of evolutionary contingency. But there were simply many things "dinosaur" ongoing then in the news as well, keeping dinosaurology alive and well during this time, summarized in Chapter Fifteen's trip down memory lane.

An ever-increasing manifestation of anthropomorphized dinosaurs in sci-fi and film became evident, especially those stemming from an early 1980s scientific hypothesis. True—anthropomorphized gill-men, reptiloids and dino-monsters have an enduring science fictional presence. In particular, science fictional amphibioid "gill-men" have been with us since the dawn of the 20th century, persisting into the 1950s Cold War era. But for reasons to be explained, gill-men began to be supplanted by humanoid reptiloids during the height of the Cold War, proliferating most vibrantly during the 1980s and early 1990s. The heyday of the gill-men, pinpointing the symbolic transitional film's quite unexpectedly leading to the introduction of the more serious-minded, purposeful reptile-dinosaur men of science fiction, will be addressed in Chapter Seventeen. As we'll see, the "dinosauroid" phenomenon ripens during the Dinosaur Renaissance era.

We have blindly sought ourselves in traces of former races. For centuries, and before the advent of Charles Darwin's researches, or the 1848 discovery of a Neandertal Man skull from Gibraltar, we've inadvertently beguiled ourselves into noticing gross human affinities in fossils actually belonging to other extinct species. For example, in Chapter Two we learned of the "Cheirotherium," or those fossilized human handprints, later ascribed to the amphibian *Labyrinthodon*. But along the way, there were many others, formerly ascribed to humans or humanoid giants, long before any genuine traces of hominid-anthropoid fossils had been discovered in geological formations.[3] Such "authentic" identifications were mistakenly assigned and eventually corrected via the ways and means of scientific method. Modern day science fiction writers and imagineers have different perspectives, often concocting a host of peculiar (if not horrific and sometimes symbolic) sentient saurian life-forms for their protagonists to wrangle with. But it is highly unusual for professional paleontologists to let their imaginations run away to a similar, influential degree that resulted in invention of the Dinosauroid, as will be outlined in Chapter Eighteen.

The satiric 1990 novel *Gojiro* is an exemplary case of a "talking dinosauroid" with its main cantankerous character taking on a host of humanity's folly and woes. This may be compared with another novel from the 1950s Cold War period, *A Case of Conscience*. Both stories end in their own way, cataclysmically. So, then, what are the various kinds of "dinosauroids" and what is their real purpose? Why do we listen and pay them attention? Are they caricatures, dino-doppelgangers, harbingers of an ensuing Cold War II, another (sixth) mass extinction, or represent a decrepit society? If they're all teaching us something, what have we learned? Although you may not like the answers—sometimes looking into the mirror is difficult—such matters will be discussed in Chapter Nineteen and the Epilogue.

Chapter Fifteen

Decade of the Dinosaur

In late September of 1985, I attended author and celebrated dinosaur enthusiast Donald F. Glut's seminar "Fantasy Dinosaurs of the Movies" at the Field Museum of Natural History in Chicago. He related how, about ten years earlier, while laboring on a revision of his *Dinosaur Dictionary* (a popular general reference on dinosaur names and classification), he was asked by a consulting paleontologist, "Why bother? Everything that could ever possibly be written about dinosaurs has already been published." That obviously wasn't true then, and today, certainly following four successive, spirited decades of discovery, nothing could be further from the truth! Regardless, the decade of the 1980s turned out to be most exciting, rife with fresh, publicized discoveries as well as new interpretations resurrecting our favorite dead animals—dinosaurs.[1] This was *the* decade when paleontology suddenly and rather astonishingly became (more so then ever before) "relevant."

Yes—there's an ulterior reason for the dinosaurs' sudden relevancy during this period. And so without further ado, these were the headliners: here's the gist of 1980s "paleo-news."

Seemingly, for decades, dinosaurs enjoyed widespread commercial appeal, but not until the 1980s did their popularity escalate in an out-of-control fashion. Whether we liked it or not, during the 1980s, Americans everywhere became acquainted with paleontology via dinosaurs. For some, this was merely an introduction. For others, it was a reunification. Some thought the whole blasted thing was a nuisance, while others merely tolerated the Mesozoic invasion. Many of us found the time to reaffirm our love for those everlasting Lords of the Mesozoic. (See Figure 15-1.)

It's truly remarkable how prevalent dinosaur imagery became during the 1980s, in books, toys, games, household as well as scientific and pseudoscientific discourse, popular literature, and art. In the 1980s, paleontology was marked by controversy over the right to collect fossil specimens on public lands. Terms like "dino-phile," and "dinosaurologist" became fashionable, and a new forensic science of dinosaurian pathology became established.[2] The fact is that media attention afforded to dinosaurs probably won't end for many decades to come.

Dinosaurs have fascinated many past generations, extending back to their first discovery and recognition as a distinct grouping of ancient animals in the mid–19th century (1841–1842). When the first dinosaur remains were being studied by 19th-century naturalists, savants, and those who would later be known as paleontologists, the table had already been set. By then fossils had been pondered for many centuries. But it really wasn't until the late 18th century that fossil vertebrates attracted a widespread popular interest, principally through the work of Cuvier. Amateurs agreed that fossil collecting was fun and profitable, as well as

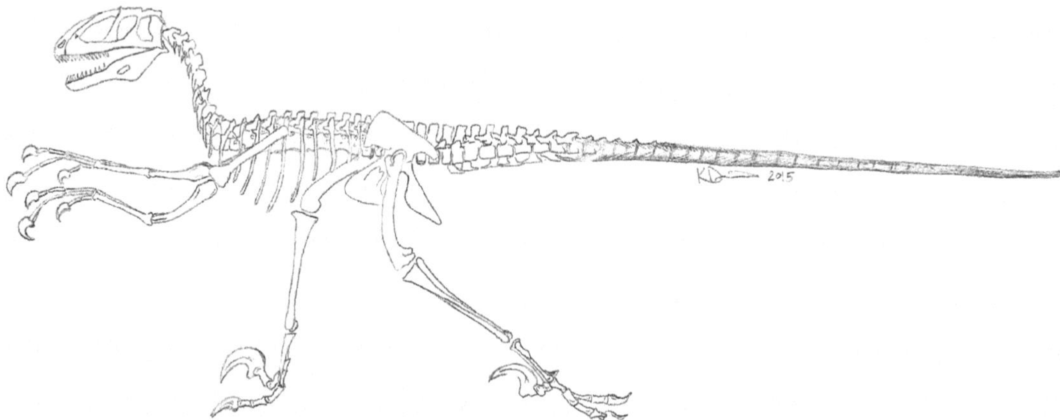

Fig 15-1: The 8-foot-long, slender dinosaur *Deinonychus*, evidently vigorously active in life, discovered in 1964 and described scientifically in 1969, heralded the burgeoning dinosaur renaissance as well as a heightened decade of never-before-attained popular intrigue in dinosaurology during the 1980s (skeletal reconstruction by Kristen L. Dennis, PhD, based partly on an earlier illustration by Robert T. Bakker).

edifying. And controversies surrounding the nature of fossils and the once-living creatures they represented inspired further intrigue.

So it is rather unsurprising to learn that discovery and study of dinosaur remains became one special facet of a popular interest or fad in paleontology, vaulting to stratospheric levels during the late 20th century. I know because I lived through it all, witnessing the developments, while held in rapt attention and collecting numerous representative mementos. And even though scientific study of dinosaurs has been said to have stagnated for short periods, such as during the period of America's Great Depression and World War II, public interest has never truly subsided. That's the way it was, is now, and probably shall continue, *ad infinitum*. Face it, they have returned from oblivion—after 66 million years of extinction—to haunt us, to vex us, but many of us really don't mind at all.

Nevertheless, public fervor over dinosaurs during the decade of the 1980s was nothing short of astonishing. Never before had any group of prehistoric animals captivated human imagination on such a grand scale. Here (as if time itself were a "place"), in one neat little decade, we find all the elements of the initiation of a cult-level fascination with dinosaurs. Fueled by repeated field and laboratory discoveries, media hype, controversial publications, and (then) outrageous or heretical theoretical speculations (especially those concerning mass extinctions and warm-blooded versus cold-blooded dinosaurs), and outstanding museum exhibits strongly appealing to our visual and imaginative senses—dinosaurs of all kinds, shapes, and sizes were on the minds of many youngsters who were first becoming acquainted with the science of paleontology, as well as older charter members of the "cult."

It is not my purpose in this chapter to discuss technical details of scientific advances made by paleontologists during the 1980s. Rather, I am outlining the reaction to their work at the popular level. In so doing, I'll recapitulate the scientific occurrences which, as future historians may perhaps conclude, have had the most noticeable impact on America's public-interest level in dinosaurs.

Before turning back the clock to more specific entries in the dino-highlights of the 1980s, a quick survey of the extreme, obscure, and unusual heralds that this was no ordinary decade with respect to dinosaurs. There was heightened interest in the history of dinosaur paleontology. There were more dinosaur postage stamps and stickers available to collectors than ever before. There was enlivened interest among "creation scientists" over the nature of dinosaurs, and during the height of nuclear tensions with the Soviets, a famous fantasy dinosaur (Godzilla) made a triumphant return to the motion picture screen. There were dinosaur records and songs for children amidst the myriad dinosaur toys, games and coloring books—don't forget those colorful dinosaur posters, postcards and calendars—and of course there were many televised shows on the subject of dinosaurs for young and old alike. (See Figure 15-2.) We enjoyed those peculiar dinosaur Halloween costumes.[3] And while scientists really searched for a live Mesozoic saurian in Loch Ness and the African Congo, opportunities opened for dino-aficionados to actually participate on genuine dinosaur digs with professionally trained scientists.

Late Cretaceous dinosaurs were discovered in Australia and on the Alaskan North Slope in 1985, and in Antarctica in 1986. The new genera were immediately enlisted in the lively mass-extinction controversy. Conceivably some dinosaurs could have already been adapted to low temperatures and might have been capable of surviving a prolonged cold snap brought

Fig 15-2: In 1989, the United States issued a block of four postage stamps featuring three famous North American dinosaurs and a pterosaur (*Tyrannosaurus, Pteranodon,* "Brontosaurus" or *Apatosaurus,* and *Stegosaurus*). These restorations were the handiwork of paleoartist John Gurche (Debus collection).

on by an impacting asteroid. (See Chapter Sixteen for more on this episode.) By the end of the decade, scientists were associating a 180-mile-wide impact crater discovered beneath sediments in the southern Gulf of Mexico off the coast of Yucatan with Late Cretaceous extinctions. Was this *the* long-awaited "smoking gun"? Well, rather than dwelling morbidly on how dinosaurs may have died, several 1980s dino-gurus preferred instead to ponder how dinosaurs lived their extraordinary lives so long ago.[4]

Those loveable Dinamation creations toured every nook and cranny of the U.S., appearing at many shopping malls, museums and carnivals. During the 1980s, the Dinamation International Corporation was headed by Chris Mays. Mays first began importing robotocized (animatronic) dinosaurs from a Japanese company (Kokoro) in 1982, although their accuracy was questioned. When museum curators encouraged him to improve the appearance of his robots, Mays left the Japanese company, founding his first U.S. Dinamation plant in 1986. Thereafter, a collective of American vertebrate paleontologists, including George Callison and Robert Bakker, served as consultants in the construction of Dinamation models. They advised on the proper reconstruction of bones, muscles, skin and probably movement and sound for each of the restored creatures. Artists began with scale drawings, proceeding from miniature clay models to full-scale clay models, the latter of which were used as molds to form the foam-rubber Dinamation skin covering the mechanical, computerized robot skeletons. Artists also consulted experts during the final touch-up painting step. Each newly competed design—a year in the making—cost about $100,000 to build. As of July 1990, there were about 350 Dinamation prehistoric creatures touring the world, although not all of the prehistoria were technically dinosaurs. (See Figure 15-3.)

During the 1980s, scientists' and paleoartists' interests were also directed to reconstructions and restorations of newly discovered dinosaurs, or of new (and sometimes controversial) restorations of old favorites. The historical progression of shifting scientific views of dinosaurs was reflected in trend-setting traveling exhibitions originating at the Los Angeles County Museum of Natural History. One, titled "Dinosaurs, Mammoths and Cavemen: The Art of Charles R. Knight," reached Chicago in late 1985; another, "Dinosaurs Past and Present," arrived at Chicago's Field Museum of Natural History in late 1989. Still another traveling exhibition was titled "Dinosaurs: A Global View." If readers missed these wonderful exhibitions while on the road, there were informative spinoff books resulting from the associated symposia.[5]

Many new dinosaur discoveries were made during this period, but only a handful brought fame to their discoverers. One sensational story concerned the greatest dinosaur of them all, *Tyrannosaurus rex*. Excavation team leader Patrick Leiggi of the Museum of the Rockies claimed after its discovery that the 65-million-year-old beast was the nicest specimen he'd ever seen. This was because, then, this particular 40-foot long specimen was thought to have been the most complete *T. rex* ever found, and only the third reasonably complete one then known. Of particular importance was the fact that its puny front limbs were complete. Preliminary investigations now indicate that *T. rex* used its very muscular arms as hoists capable of lifting up to 400 pounds of prey.

Another predatory dinosaur was unearthed from London clay in 1983. The discovery of a one-foot-long, curved claw seized headlines in both the U.S. and Great Britain. Paleontologists realized that the 115-million-year-old dinosaur represented a new genus, and described it under the name *Baryonyx walkeri*. Alan Charig (1927–1997) of the British

Fig 15-3: During the 1980s, animatronic Dinamation prehistoria such as these four dinosaurs—left to right, *Parasaurolophus, Pachycephalosaurus, Allosaurus and Diplodocus*—toured museums and other venues across the country and abroad (photograph by Allen A. Debus, circa 1990, taken at the Chicago Academy of Sciences).

Museum boasted at the time that it seemed to be the very finest find of the century, although not a missing link—rather, a separate evolutionary line. Michael Brett-Surman noted the mélange of both primitive and advanced skeletal characteristics. Paleoartist Gregory S. Paul emphasized the crocodilian-like snout, suggesting a fish-eating niche for spinosaurid dinosaurs.

Not all dinosaur discoveries are made outdoors. Sometimes reexaminations of previously collected bones in the laboratory or museum drawer can lead to reinterpretations that are equally exciting as finding a brand-new specimen in the field. That is what happened in the case of *Nanotyrannus lancensis*, a carnivore possibly allied to *Albertosaurus*, which seized attention for Robert Bakker in 1988 after he, Michael Williams, and Phil Currie reexamined a skull at the Cleveland Museum of Natural History. Back in 1942, Charles Gilmore (1874–1945) had identified the two-foot-long skull as a juvenile *Gorgosaurus*. The skull, dating from the Late Cretaceous, does share some very advanced traits with its larger cousin, *Tyrannosaurus*. For instance, Bakker noted the powerful neck musculature, and a sophisticated pneumatic canal system interwoven throughout the skull. Such air pockets heightened oxygenation circulation into the lungs. Therefore, according to Bakker, *Nanotyrannus*, like his larger cousin *T. rex*, was labeled an "airhead." Furthermore, the 16-foot-long, 600-pound creature initially appeared to support the theory that modern birds have dinosaurian ancestry.

Then, during the summer of 1989, Bakker divulged his discovery of "*Epanterias*," tagged as the Monster of Masonville, a Jurassic carnivore, considerably larger than its evolutionary cousin, the more familiar *Allosaurus*. This dinosaur was found in the fossiliferous Morrison Formation near the town of Masonville, Colorado. *Epanterias*'s remains had been discovered twice before, in 1877 and 1934, although due to their fragmentary nature, little was known about the genus. Bakker suggested that the 130-million-year-old beast may have grown to 50 feet in length, and weighed about 8,000 pounds in life. *Epanterias* may have been capable of swallowing animals the size of a 1,400-pound cow in a single gulp! The remains of a *Camarasaurus* discovered near the *Epanterias* site indicated its preference for dining fare.

For comparison, *Allosaurus* only weighed half as much and may have been 15 feet shorter than *Epanterias*. Because the latter lived at a later time than did *Allosaurus*, Bakker suggested that the genus was distinct, providing indication that there was an evolutionary tendency for large Mesozoic carnivores to rapidly attain even greater sizes through geological time, perhaps culminating in beasts like *Tyrannosaurus*. *Epanterias*, Bakker claimed, may have been favored through natural selection due to success as a predator, disease resistance, or sexual preferences toward larger size. Of the discovery, Bakker noted (rather in neo–Lamarckian fashion) that, usually, while animals' trending toward larger sizes results in extinction, the large size of his new dinosaur may have resulted from an evolutionary arms race.[6] (By the early 1990s, *Epanterias* was no longer considered a valid generic name, however.)

Two other predators were also discovered during the 1980s, the theropod *Carnotaurus* of the South American Cretaceous, described in 1985, and the Triassic rauisuchian *Postosuchus*, discovered in 1983. The 30-foot-long, immaculately preserved *Carnotaurus* was unearthed by Jose Bonaparte and paleosculptor Stephen Czerkas (1951–2015) from a site in Patagonia. What made the find particularly exciting is that some skin impressions were preserved on fossilized bone. The armor-like skin of *Carnotaurus* appeared roughened, having scaly clusters rising from an eighth to two and half inches above the skin surface. The skin was very much unlike the smoother, flat-scaled skin impressions of a "duckbill mummy" on display at the American Museum of Natural History in New York. *Carnotaurus*'s exotic-looking skull had impressive horns above the eyes, possibly utilized for combat during displays of aggression while competing for mates. The teeth and the slender lower jaw are not as powerful as one would have anticipated after studying its compact, robust skull.

Postosuchus, discovered by Sankar Chatterjee in the 200-million-year-old Dockum Formation of west Texas, allegedly represented the roots of the carnivore lineage leading to the fearsome tyrannosaurs, 135 million years later. *Postosuchus* was about 13 feet long and in life may have weighed about 600 pounds. Its skeleton was said to resemble a diminutive *Tyrannosaurus*. With its 2- to 3-inch long saber-like teeth, curved claws, and bony crest extending from the powerful skull to the tip of its tail, *Postosuchus* was billed as the most formidable predator of its time. Was *Postosuchus* in fact the "oldest dinosaur," as initially billed? Or did it have rivals to the title? Oldest, fiercest, most immense ... when it came to dinosaurs, such claims were often made during the heady days of the 1980s. Further study of *Postosuchus*, however, revealed it to be a large thecodont, not a dinosaur at all.

In August 1984, Bryan Small, then a Texas Tech graduate student, came to Holbrook, Arizona, in search of fossils. Small doubted he would find anything of importance or value and certainly never gambled on making a significant dinosaur discovery. But near Chinde Point in the Petrified Forest National Park and Painted Desert area, he uncovered what was then thought possibly to be the oldest dinosaur skeleton ever to be discovered in the Northern Hemisphere. Since it was late in the season, full extraction was delayed until 1985. Then, for weeks, the fossils—including a complete leg, ribs, vertebrae, and several other additional fragments, were carefully covered in a plaster burlap bandage.

The dig became an exciting tourist attraction, which boosted the number of visitors to the Petrified Forest National Park over the one-million mark for the first time since 1978. The entire slab, weighing an estimated 1,500 pounds, was airlifted by helicopter from its rocky tomb (capturing social interest news headlines) on the morning of Thursday, June 6, 1985, to its destination at the University of California, Berkeley. Dr. Timothy Rowe, chief investigator of the primitive dinosaur described in 1989 as *Chindesaurus bryansmalli* (or "Bryan Small's ghost lizard") dubbed the excavation locale as the "Olduvai Gorge of dinosaurs," due to its early Mesozoic vintage.[7] *Chindesaurus* was characterized as an herbivorous creature that in life approximated the size of a large German shepherd dog, although with a longer tail and neck. Scientists agreed that *Chindesaurus* was probably bipedal, having slender, agile legs, a long tail, and five-fingered hands. Initially it was believed to have been related to the prosauropods such as *Plateosaurus*, on the lineage leading to giant sauropods like *Apatosaurus* and *Diplodocus*. Later, paleontologists came to believe that *Chindesaurus* may be too "primitive" to be classified with the prosauropods, so it was grouped with another dinosaurian family known as the herrerasaurids.

Perhaps a better candidate for the title of "oldest dinosaur" was found a few years later, in 1988, by University of Chicago paleontologist Paul Sereno (who was later named one of *People Magazine's* "50 Most Beautiful People" in 1997). The 230-million-year-old dinosaur from Argentina, known as *Herrerasaurus*, was originally described over 40 years ago from fragmentary remains. Sereno's newer specimen was far more complete. The bipedal carnivore weighed only 300 pounds in life. Concerning the oldest dinosaur claim, Sereno stated philosophically that it was close to the earliest evolutionary branching point. *Herrerasaurus* was certainly not the common ancestor of all dinosaurs; however, some considered the dinosaur to be too primitive to be readily classified with either the saurischian or ornithischian orders.

A new ceratopsian called *Avaceratops*, or "Ava horned face" after the discoverer's wife, represented the first new type of horned dinosaur described in 35 years! It was found on the Lammers family's Careless Creek Ranch near the town of Shawmut, Montana, in 1986. An excavation team headed by paleontologist Peter Dodson later exhumed the 75-million-year-old skeleton from Late Cretaceous deposits of the Judith River Formation. Dodson determined that in life the individual was three feet tall, eight feet long, and weighed about 400 pounds. It had three horns on the skull, two short ones over the eye sockets and another over the snout area. It also had a short, bony, fan-shaped frill protecting its neck. The frill is the oldest such feature noted in the horned dinosaur lineage to be completely solid. Although there is some speculation as to whether this *Avaceratops* specimen represented a juvenile, one cannot deny that it resembled a miniature *Triceratops*. In fact, Dodson then claimed, *Avaceratops* could even be a direct ancestor of the larger genus, *Triceratops*.

Another remarkable announcement concerned a new dinosaur of truly gigantic proportions: *Seismosaurus*, the "earth-shaking lizard," which was discovered all "hush-hush" in 1979 at a locality about 60 miles northwest of Albuquerque, New Mexico. This enormous creature, tentatively estimated to have been 100 to 120 feet long with a body weight of 160,000 to 200,000 pounds in life (about the same as an adult blue whale), was found by amateur fossil collectors Arthur Loy, Frank Walker, Jan Cummings and Bill Norlander. Excavation of the

150-million-year-old dinosaur, beginning at the tail end, didn't commence until 1985. The long-necked *Seismosaurus* was very similar structurally to the more familiar *Diplodocus*.

And some of the new discoveries were, well, for the birds. For a handful of fossil birds were in the news too. They're mentioned here because at the time, a majority of paleontologists were realizing that birds are really dinosaurs, in disguise. This notion had been championed in the latter half of the nineteenth century by Thomas H. Huxley (1825–1895), but was an idea that had fallen out of favor in the years since. The least-popularized, yet still significant discovery concerned a 120- to 130-million-year-old bird, *Iberomesornis*, discovered by Jose Luis Sanz and J.F. Bonaparte in the Las Hoyes Limestone of Cuenca, Spain. No skull was found, although other skeletal features indicated that this new genus was intermediate in form between the 150-million-year-old *Archaeopteryx* and later birds, combining primitive with more advanced characters. Such features, including a bird-like shoulder blade, are thought to have evolved due to adaptational flight demands.

A "new" *Archaeopteryx* fossil was discovered in 1987. This, only the sixth known skeletal specimen and the largest found to date, measured about 16 inches on its limestone slab. It is believed that this Upper Jurassic specimen was collected in the Solnhofen German deposits of the Eichstatt area long ago (sometime between 1877 and 1951), although no records were kept detailing where, by whom, or exactly when it was found. For many years the fossil resided in the private collection of a former mayor of Solnhofen, Friedrich Muller. The skeleton was mistakenly identified as a dinosaur fossil, *Compsognathus*, until subtle feather impressions were eventually recognized.

Controversy erupted during the 1980s when British astronomer Sir Frederick Hoyle (1915–2001) claimed the British Museum's *Archaeopteryx* specimen was a forgery. Hoyle stated that the feather impressions were not genuine records of a feathered wing, but rather represented "artistic" sculpting efforts of a 19th century perpetrator (possibly Sir Richard Owen), seeking somehow to undermine Charles Darwin's theory of evolution through natural selection. The allegation prompted Stephen Jay Gould (1941–2002) to resoundingly denounce Hoyle's accusation.[8] However, so as not to throw any shadow of doubt on the authenticity of the famous Eichstatt specimen discovered in 1877, the feather impressions (preserved only on the left wing) were examined using a low angle illumination technique allowing researchers to conclude that they were indeed genuine.

In 1986, we received word of the alleged paleobird found by Sankar Chatterjee in 1983, who had also discovered some new Late Triassic vertebrates in the Dockum Formation of western Texas, including *Postosuchus*. Incredibly, the new 225-million-year-old paleobird fossil (represented by remains of two partially preserved individuals, known unofficially as "Protoavis," is 75 million years older than *Archaeopteryx*! However, not all paleontologists agreed with Chatterjee's determination that the pigeon-sized creature was avian. First, there are no fossilized feather impressions, but rather an enlarged breastbone which may have been used to anchor flight muscles. Also, there are tiny bumps on "Protoavis's" forelimbs that may have served as attachment sites for wing feathers. (Chatterjee believed that "Protoavis" was capable of rudimentary flight.) The fossil had a relatively large brain case for its size, wide eye sockets and a bird-like jaw lacking teeth. Furthermore, openings in the pelvic bones and skull, along with a fused rather than swiveled ankle assembly, suggested avian affinities. Chatterjee found himself in the midst of scientific controversy, challenging ideas about evolutionary relationships between dinosaurs and birds established during the 1970s. The iconoclastic

Robert Bakker supported the "Protoavis"-as-bird ancestor interpretation. Meanwhile, Chatterjee apologetically requested that enough time be granted so that a satisfyingly correct interpretation may result.

Did dinosaurs experiment with flight on their own, independently of the early birds? Was "Protoavis" only a bird "mimic" or a failed experiment on the lineage leading to later, more advanced dinosaurs? Or did we then see in "Protoavis" the true beginnings of avian evolution, the earliest known ancestor of *Archaeopteryx* and, possibly, all later avian forms? Many intriguing questions were posed by little "Protoavis."

Then on October 12, 1990, Paul Sereno and his Chinese colleague Chen-gang Rao presented their case for a startling new avian fossil at the 50th annual meeting of the Society of Vertebrate Paleontology held in Lawrence, Kansas. Their analysis of a fossil vertebrate named *Sinornis*, found by amateur fossil hunters in an area northeast of Beijing in 1987 (in what used to be a stagnant lake 135 million years ago), revealed that flight adaptations had fully developed in the sparrow-sized creature only 10 million years after the evolution of the more familiar, and more controversial, genus *Archaeopteryx*! And yet, many dinosaurian skeletal features were still retained in *Sinornis*.

No matter how intriguing the mounting evidence for the bird-dinosaur connection may have seemed (See Figure 15-4), one sensational little dinosaur stole the show during the 1980s. Announcement of little "Maia," the embryonic hadrosaur, belonging to the genus *Maiasaura peeblesorum*, discovered inside a fossilized egg by John Horner and Robert Makela, came with considerable fanfare. Paleontologists had known about the now-famous dinosaur

Fig 15-4: Dougal Dixon's 20-inch-long sculpture (2015) of the 20-foot-long, possibly feathered Late Jurassic theropod tyrannosauroid dinosaur, *Juratyrant*, captured the essence of one significant direction of where the dinosaur renaissance had led intellectually, when it came to issues pertaining to the evolution of dinosaurs and close relationships between certain genera of dinosaurs (e.g., avetheropods) to modern birds (illustration by noted paleo-author and artist Dougal Dixon, used with permission).

nest egg site near Bozeman, Montana, since 1978, although the embryo discovery was made in 1983. Certainly, *Maiasaura peeblesorum*, or the "good mother lizard," well symbolized the 1980s dinosaur craze, becoming an early mascot of the dinosaur renaissance.

There were numerous reports of the discoveries of nestlings, nesting sites, and fossil eggs belonging to other dinosaur genera. In 1984, then Soviet scientists found thousands of 105-million-year-old Asian dinosaur eggs and a possible breeding ground in the Fergana Mountains. A fossil egg, possibly belonging to an *Apatosaurus*, was found by an amateur collector in 1986. The discovery threatened to undermine Robert Bakker's theory of live birthing in sauropods. Phil Currie made news for his 1988 discovery of six Late Cretaceous baby armored dinosaur individuals, genus *Pinacosaurus*, in Mongolia. A year earlier Currie had discovered Cretaceous *Hypacrosaurus* embryos, eggs, and nests at Devils Coulee in Dinosaur Provincial Park, Alberta. (Three other fossil mass grave "bonebeds" belonging to horned dinosaurs, *Centrosaurus, Styracosaurus,* and *Pachyrhinosaurus*, were found in Dinosaur Provincial Park as well.)

In 1989, a fossil egg, possibly belonging to *Allosaurus*, was discovered at the Cleveland-Lloyd Dinosaur Quarry in east-central Utah. Investigators were quite certain that the egg contained an embryo. A 1986 highlight concerned discovery of an early Triassic vertebrate assemblage at a 200-million-year-old site in Nova Scotia. Paleontologists related these fossil occurrences to the meteorite impact event responsible for the crater at Manicouagan Lake in Quebec, Canada, which may have formed contemporaneously.

Dinosaurs from Asia entered the limelight during the 1980s. Surely there were political and socioeconomic factors at play, as during the mid–1980s Japan and the United States were basking in a decade of economic prosperity, and China became increasingly exposed to western culture. Perhaps stemming from that ageless Chinese tradition of dragon symbolism and lore, dinosaur popularity was on the rise there and elsewhere in eastern Asia. American sculptor David Thomas made full-size dinosaur models of the North American *Tyrannosaurus* and *Pentaceratops* for a natural history museum in Taiwan.

Godzilla had already been popular among the Japanese for three decades, but during the 1980s, plans were already underway to build what may have been the world's largest dinosaur theme park, Tokorozawa, ambitiously "inhabited" by over 250 animatronic life-sized prehistoric animal models. Dong Zhiming's popular dinosaur book, *Dinosaurs from China* (British Museum, English translation, 1988)[9] was available, and reconstructed Mesozoic vertebrates and skeletons of Asian dinosaurs were loaned to the American Museum of Natural History between 1985 and 1988. Dissemination of knowledge concerning the numerous Asian dinosaur genera to a welcoming American public set the pace for what was to come during the latter 1990s, when the feathered dinosaur revolution was in full swing.

During the early 1970s, about the same time that the strikingly close relationships between modern birds and dinosaurs were being reassessed, a major revolution in our understanding of the pterosaurs was "on the wing" as well. Advances made during this period greatly aided those faced with the task of reconstructing a gigantic life-sized pterosaur from Texas, named *Quetzalcoatlus*. Over a decade following the genus's 1971 discovery, engineers and scientists strove to establish how such a large (presumably 140-pound) creature flew. The Smithsonian backed a half-million-dollar project, financially aided by Johnson Wax, to get old *Quetzalcoatlus* flying again, with a test flight conducted in May 1986. A half-scale, 18-foot-wingspan, computer-controlled, battery-powered restoration was built by aerodynamicist

Paul MacCready (1925–2007).[10] (MacCready did consider building a life-sized version, with a 36-foot wingspan.)

Publicity generated by the project stimulated an enlivened national interest in prehistoric animals. MacCready stated, "I'm trying to combine the good features of a museum and a Zoo. The Zoo has only the present day creatures. The museum shows old ones, but they're dead.... You put a giant pterodactyl on the television screen or in the newspaper, and it's so exciting that people can't help but be interested in finding out more."[11]

Museums also enjoyed a period of growth during the 1980s, in no small part due to the increased appeal of dinosaurs, as funding was made available for the establishment of new institutions housing paleontological displays. For instance, the Witte Museum of San Antonio, Texas, revamped its dinosaur hall in 1983. The venerable Philadelphia Academy of Sciences modernized its dinosaur exhibits in early 1986. New museums dedicated to dino-displays, discoveries and science materialized in Great Britain, notably the Dinosaur Museum of Dorchester and the Museum of Paleontology located at Silver End in Essex. (It would have been unheard of over half a century before to institute a museum solely dedicated to dinosaur paleontology.) The Royal Tyrrell Museum of Palaeontology, located in Drumheller, Alberta, placed an incredible dinosaur and fossil exhibition on display in 1985. China's Zigong Dinosaur Museum in southeast Sichuan Province also opened to the public in 1987.

Bear in mind that many other important contributions and controversies in the field of paleontology—outside the realm of dinosaurs—were made during the same decade (e.g., paleoanthropology, molecular biology, cladistics,[12] and the discovery of many other extinct fossil invertebrate organisms). Nevertheless, this decade should be nostalgically recalled from a pop-cultural perspective, as attempted here. By the end of the decade, 1980s dino-philes looked forward to the forthcoming 150th anniversary of Richard Owen's "invention" of the idea of the dinosaur, and as if they hadn't experienced enough already, diehards were avidly saving their dinosaur collectibles—toys, books, news clippings, posters, etc.—for enjoyment and posterity. Then in the fall of 1990, Michael Crichton's novel *Jurassic Park* invaded bookstore shelves, but that's another story beyond our present scope. (However, see my *Dinosaurs in Fantastic Fiction* for more on the *Jurassic Park* novels.)

Undoubtedly, however, the *central* science news story of the decade concerning (though not exclusively limited to) dinosaurs was the sensational mass extinction advanced by Walter and Luis Alvarez, Helen Michel, and Frank Asaro in early 1980. Their theory that a six-mile-wide asteroid collided with our planet in the Late Cretaceous, throwing up a sunlight-blocking dust cloud into the stratosphere—which cooled temperatures globally for a geologically brief episode, leading to ecological devastation and extinctions of many marine and terrestrial organisms—seemed "heretical" at the time, but was actually a sound falsifiable theory, offering workable scientific predictions. The controversial theory was founded on a body of carefully scrutinized evidence.

By early 1984, other researchers offered further hypotheses that global mass extinctions were periodic or perhaps quasi-periodic, resulting from recurring celestial phenomena once every 26 to 33 million years. *Time* magazine even featured a cover story on the debate over whether celestial factors caused the great dinosaur extinctions: for its May 5, 1985, cover illustration by Braldt Bralds, a *Tyrannosaurus* was shown snarling at a hurtling, incoming, eruption-causing comet, emblazoned below the words "Did Comets Kill the Dinosaurs?—A New Theory About Mass Extinctions." The overwhelming impact of this well-publicized controversy on scientific discourse leaking into the public realm, popular opinion, human philosophy and its daily influence on human imagination cannot be overstated. Then on January 30, 1986, came the dramatic announcement that a 70-kilometer-diameter, 215-million-year-old impact crater in Nova Scotia (Lake Manicouagan) could be correlated to an evolutionary turnover of Late Triassic tetrapods, thus yielding way to the Jurassic Period dinosaurian explosion. Future science historians may well have reason to view this episode as a revolution in earth science on par with the discovery of plate tectonics some two decades before.

According to journalist Ian Warden and (independently) geologist Curt Teichert, associating astronomical catastrophes with extinctions has contributed substantially to the rising popularity of dinosaurian paleontology. One important extrapolation stemming from these 1980s theories was the invention of a "dinosaur man," a resultant of natural contingency dubbed the Dinosauroid, which will become a prominent figure in forthcoming chapters of this book. Developments emerging during the 1980s intrigue over the new, engaging scope of dinosaur science was superbly summarized in a major four-part Arts and Entertainment network television documentary, *Dinosaur!*—now a historic "time capsule," if you will, showcasing contemporary knowledge, hosted by Walter Cronkite (1916–2009). This program was initially broadcast from September 11 through September 14, 1991.[13]

By the late 1980s, inspired by the fervor over dinosaurs and their world, two trendsetting curiosities appeared: Barney, the purple anthropomorphic talking and singing tyrannosaur, which debuted via a direct-to-video feature titled *Barney & the Backyard Gang* (1988); and 1988's animated feature, *The Land Before Time*, directed by Don Bluth. *Land Before Time* was the first full-length motion picture involving dinosaurian characters and perhaps the first to employ talking dinosaurs, for which great efforts were made to enhance their accuracy. Both Barney and the loveable characters in *Land Before Time* greatly appealed to youngsters, thus inculcating impressionable minds subliminally with the notion that we share an intimate association with those strangely absorbing primevals, who could indeed tell us such interesting things ... about ourselves.

Dinosaur popularity will bloom and wane somewhat with the vicissitudes of worldwide affairs. We may wonder how the imaginations of late–21st century dinosaur enthusiasts (not simply scientists) will be fired by the fossil remains of ancient saurians. I suspect that, although the repertoire of knowledge may be quite different by then, the thrill and romanticism one senses in learning about dinosaurs, at least at an impressionable age, will be inherently similar.

From a popular culture perspective, the 1980s may be regarded as a "Decade of the Dinosaur," like none other before. Much of the matter may be related to mankind's increasing understanding that our presence on Earth, like that of the extinct dinosaurs, is precarious and that we bear the potential to destroy our present world, increasingly viewed as fragile. The expanding environmental movement, coupled with early-1980s heightened tension with the Soviet Union, and new discoveries concerning how the dinosaurian reign really ended, fostered such an intriguing and, to me, unforgettable, pre–*Jurassic Park* phase of dino-mania.[14]

Chapter Sixteen

Dinosaur Extinctions III

Warning from Space! Science Fiction Becomes Scientific

"The earth is one great tomb of life."—Ignatius Donnelly, *Ragnarok: The Age of Fire and Gravel*, 1883[1]

"Dinosaurs, it seems, are no longer simply a synonym for obsolescence or the dead-and-gone; their doom is increasingly recalled as a cautionary metaphor for the fate that could befall mankind, if we are not careful. We may never know what really happened to the dinosaurs, but we already know enough to wonder if it could happen to us. If it was a sudden catastrophe that did in the dinosaurs, we think of nuclear war, and shudder."—John Noble Wilford, *The Riddle of the Dinosaur*, 1986[2]

There's a little-known bronze and cement sculpture displayed outdoors in Chicago titled *Ruins III*. I often walked, admiringly, past this statue. Although no doubt interpreted differently by artists in-the-know, to me *Ruins III* represented civilization's twilight with a distinctive science fictional *Martian Chronicles*–esque mystique. That's how it struck me, anyway, eliciting the greatest compliment to the artist—that is, simply because I enjoyed looking at and thinking about the gravity of this visual art. *Ruins III* is a work of prescient truth, of disturbing inevitability and irony; how foreboding its placement in the midst of a vast modern metropolis, one that will not last forever!

Civilizations and cultures afar and across the centuries extending back to biblical times have speculated on the means and outcome of cosmic cataclysm, leading to our total annihilation. Psychologically, fears of planetary destruction are closely allied, perhaps even genetically linked, to causes of mass mortality and urban annihilation. And the more spectacular the inspirational urban setting at stake (e.g., Pompeii, Atlantis, New York, London, Tokyo), the more prone are writers, artists and maliciously minded imaginers to intricately convey visions of the next *ultimate* catastrophe. If there's one thing science has taught us, it's that our species won't perpetuate in this hostile universe. And so, safely from our easy chairs, we vicariously consider twisted wreckage, toppled buildings, immense tidal waves and cities aflame, speculating how, like the great races of the past, our civilization and possibly even our planet will be extinguished.

Yet, long before the heyday of filmmaker Irwin Allen (1916–1991), America's celebrated "master of disaster," there were numerous disaster stories, art, radio and television shows, and movies. Many are science fictional in nature, often technically complex, artistically metaphorical—intended to thrill audiences and the populace, leaving deep impressions about ourselves, our plight and fear in our darkest hour. Such fare, sometimes referred to by cultural historians as disaster porn, reflects genuine public angst in consequence to pervading sociocultural or geopolitical circumstances, or perhaps the latest grim scientific findings advanced on many fronts, illustrating our precarious existence here on fragile planet Earth. Perhaps unsurprisingly, these books, stories and movies have been immensely popular for decades, and if anything (judging from the excitement generated by 2009's action-packed movie, *2012*) are even more so today. More poignantly than any *symbolic* monster, many lives have been shattered by disasters—hurricanes, earthquakes and terrorist attacks. In 2010, for instance, our attention was riveted to news of the uncontrolled Deepwater Horizon BP crude oil spillage into Gulf coastal waters: what if that leak *never* ceased? Or unexpectedly re-erupts? Not to make light of that deplorable situation, but have we spawned ... Gulf-Zilla?

In the realm of popular culture, topically and theatrically, disaster porn's range is broad, reflecting contemporary fears of imminent invasion, global war, terrorism, proliferation of super weapons (such as nuclear bombs), economic and ecological disaster, extreme climate change, and even geological or *astronomical* catastrophe. It is the latter category that I shall turn to here, particularly with respect to two fantastical Japanese films, Daiei's *The Mysterious Satellite* (1956, also known as *Warning from Space*) and Toho's *Gorath* (1962).

Although centuries ago early scientists speculated on geological effects of celestial bodies such as comets influencing affairs on Earth, impacting or staging a near-collision, such ideas were usually pooh-poohed by more "serious"-minded scientists as silly "cosmic romances."[3] Nevertheless, although their ideas were downplayed by the scientific establishment imaginative writers couldn't quite help themselves from considering possibilities of cosmic disaster! One gripping science fictional example is Robert Duncan Milne's 1882 short story, "Into the Sun," about the collision of a comet with our Sun, causing its sudden eruptive illumination and a resulting soon to be molten Earth.[4] However, perhaps *the* writer who explored the outer space disaster theme more engagingly than any writer of this early period was Herbert George Wells (1866–1946), who wrote both "The Star" (1887) and a novel, *In the Days of the Comet* (1906).

A Wikipedia entry on "The Star" proclaims that "the story can be credited with having created a science fiction sub-genre depicting a planet or star colliding, or near-colliding with Earth ... ."[5] A large planetary body observed on the fringe of the solar system first sweeps up Neptune, then ominously glows with increasing intensity in skies above. Jupiter's gravitational field alters its motion as the star converges with Earth's orbit. The story is told in a coldly objective, matter-of-fact tone. The narrator describes the ensuing enormous tides, earthquakes and massive volcanic eruptions, withering heat and melting of polar ice dooming millions. Wells also anticipated the first destruction of Japan in fantastic fiction and, curiously, also mentions Martians malevolently observing Earth's ordeal. Their sinister regard reflected the author's disaffiliated philosophy, "which only shows how small the vastest of human catastrophes may seem, at a distance of a few million miles."[6] Those same Martians were perhaps already preparing their cataclysmic attack on Earth a decade later, dramatically documented in Wells's *The War of the Worlds* (1898)! Perhaps in homage to Wells, Arthur C. Clarke penned a brilliant short story also titled "The Star" (1955), in which a priest rationalizes torturously why the supernova signaling Christ's birth in Bethlehem destroyed a benevolent civilization, superior to our own, on a planet orbiting that doomed star.[7]

Wells's lesser-known *In the Days of the Comet* is mainly about sociological changes, tending toward a utopian society, arising when a comet approaches the Earth. Astronomers and shamans alike have long predicted bad consequences for Earth upon the close approach of comets. For instance, in 1872, a Professor Plantamour's comet was predicted to collide with the Earth; that date was scaled back to 2011, when instead the Earth's surface was predicted to have become frozen. Then, upon the celebrated passing of Halley's Comet in 1910, asphyxiation from poison gases (cyanogen) became a chief concern (perhaps reflecting public fears over mounting supplies of stockpiled chemical warfare weaponry in mounting pre–World War I Europe). Accordingly, in *Days of the Comet,* Wells's ironic twist involves gases emanating from the comet that only become poisonous to symptomatic strains of human enzymes and germ-plasm giving rise to our violent tendencies, which are conveniently eliminated. Karel Zeman's 1970 film *On the Comet*—only loosely based on Wells's 1906 novel—incorporated little-known scenes of rampaging animated alien dino-monsters attacking a city and fort ... that is, while on the comet.

Others too, such as astronomer Garrett P. Serviss, dreamed up catastrophic tales involving the heavens above influencing Earth. Serviss's *The Second Deluge* (1911), for example, told of a watery end to our civilization caused when Earth's orbit plunges through a cosmic spiral nebula—thought to be composed of water molecules, which will gravitate to the surface of our planet, creating a six-mile-deep worldwide ocean. "Then," according to Cosmo Versal, the chief character in the novel, "quintillions of tons of water will condense on the earth and cover it like a universal cloudburst. And then goodbye to the human race—unless—I ... inspired by science, can save a remnant to re-people the planet after the catastrophe."[8] And so with biblical overtones, given that such an occurrence in the past may have also caused the Noachian Deluge, a giant ark is built to save a few people who sail around the globe. Serviss's novel is a legitimate conceptual progenitor for what was to come two decades later, although involving quite a different sort of ark.

By the early 1930s, when the nature and reality of large meteorite impacts (such as Arizona's famous Meteor Crater) were gaining acceptance among formerly skeptical yet still serious geologists, writers Philip Wylie and Edwin Balmer coauthored the most influential novel featuring Earth's total destruction caused by an interstellar invader, *When Worlds Collide* (first serialized in *Blue Book,* 1932).[9] The novel is vastly superior to George Pal's 1951 film of the same title. Wylie and Balmer convey how a team of heroic scientists and engineers resignedly face humanity's twilight and inevitable predicted destruction of Earth resultant of the rapid approach of two orbiting planets, named "Bronson alpha and beta." Their sequel, *After Worlds Collide* (1933), in which the interplanetary survivors investigate their strange, rapidly thawing, and formerly populated new world, Bronson beta, isn't quite as good.

The 1951 movie *When Worlds Collide,* which according to astronomer Gerrit L. Verschur may have been in part "inspired" by the identification of Icarus, "an Earth-crossing asteroid that made headline news" during the early 1950s,[10] became the template or yardstick against which all such others since produced (including the highly publicized 1998 films, *Armageddon* and *Deep Impact*) are compared. (See Figure 16-1.) Despite differences in detail relative to the successful novel, *When Worlds Collide* relates the story unfolding when astronomical data transported by stalwart, trustworthy David Randall (Richard Derr) from a South African observatory allows North American scientists led by Dr. Hendron (Larry Keating) to confirm calculations that Earth will indeed be destroyed upon passage of a double-orbiting pair of bodies, a star and a planet, entering the solar system. The planet's ("Zyra's") early passing will cause high-magnitude earthquakes, tsunamis and other widespread devastation on Earth. Nineteen days later, the much larger star ("Bellus") will collide with and thus destroy the Earth. Dr. Hendron is planning to ship about 40 lucky passengers aboard a 1950s-style rocket ship to Zyra, where if Providence should allow, they might find an earthlike atmosphere, suitable vegetation and water. Their fuel exhausted, they survive a crash landing. Fortunately, the planet's surface is breathable, cute puppies are born onboard the rocket ship, and the crew looks forward to a new beginning in solar orbit. The budget wasn't so huge and many of the key disaster scenes were conveyed either through artist Chesley Bonestell's (1888–1986) matte paintings or by splicing in stock footage.

In *Warning from Space* (aka *The Mysterious Satellite*), the premise is that a race of shape-shifting, technologically advanced starfish people live on the planet Paira, which is in the same orbit as Earth's, although opposite to us behind the Sun, which is why we've never detected them. Their "warning" to us is essentially twofold. First and foremost, there's a runaway "Planet R" that has entered the Solar System "from another galaxy" on a collision course with Earth. If Planet R collides with Earth, there would be awful consequences for Paira, also on its course around the Sun. So this is sort of a melding of American sci-fi movie themes (i.e., *The Day the Earth Stood Still* and *When Worlds Collide*), coupled with contemporary fascination for UFOs. Furthermore, a kindly Dr. Matsuda's theoretical knowledge of a new energetic compound known as "Urium 101" could threaten far more destruction than any nuclear arsenal: "By comparison the H-bomb is only a toy." After the World Congress's salvo of nuclear missiles aimed at Planet R proves ineffective, the Pairans' emissary to Earth—

Fig 16-1: Detail from an advertising poster for the 1951 film *When Worlds Collide*, in a way presaging the direction dinosaur extinction theories would soon be headed. Notice the destroyed buildings and structures indicative of mankind's fragility in the face of certain natural disaster.

who has transmuted into synthetic human guise, appearing essentially identical to a popular actress named Aozora—offers to help the Earth using Matsuda's Urium 101 formula.

As Planet R glows in the heavens, the world's temperatures soar, earthquakes devastate Tokyo, and tidal waves wash away signs of civilization. Planet R manifests itself as a reddish glowing star, white hot at the center, scorching the Earth. Then Planet R is blown to smithereens just in the nick of time. Curiously, Planet R's approach has no apparent consequences for our Moon. No meteoritic debris is seen raining down on Earth following Planet R's destruction, either. Ultimately, as animals come out of hiding and the world returns to normalcy, on the Pairon spaceship above, helpful faux Aozora psychedelically transmutes back into her starfish-like body.[11] In my opinion, *Warning from Space* conveys the "message" more effectively than 1951's *When Worlds Collide* (and the former's special effects are arguably better). However, both films carry considerable nostalgic charm.

Warning from Space is also the forerunner of later stories about the spirit of cooperation needed when dealing with ultimate crisis and dire calamity faced by all humanity. After understanding the Pairans' message, Japan seeks facilitation from the World Congress, yet initially—even in the face of utter doom—the World Congress refuses assistance. Japan must save the planet on its own. Later, however, after Planet R appears in telescopic view—then growing larger in skies above as it relentlessly approaches—the World Congress consents to a united missile launch. Only after that fails do the Pairans offer technology to process Urium 101 as well as equipment for delivering it to the interstellar intruder's fiery surface. Such international spirit of cooperation is later a central theme of the 1979 U.S. film *Meteor*, starring Sean Connery and Natalie Wood.

During the 1950s through mid–1960s, western civilization, especially, was introduced to crazy science over asteroid impacts and wild astronomy that rooted itself in popular culture. For this is the wacky period dominated by Immanuel Velikovsky (1895–1979), labeled a crackpot following publication of his hot-selling 1950 book, *Worlds in Collision*. He claimed that Venus had been ejected from planet Jupiter. Later passing closely to the Sun, Venus heated to extreme temperatures. Along its eventful journey, Venus also streaked across the heavens as a comet and was involved in two grazing collisions with Earth before eventually colliding with Mars. This commotion resulted in Venus's current orbit. This pattern of astronomical billiards was allegedly responsible for catastrophes recorded in myths and Scripture. Velikovsky continued his assault on 20th-century science through other entertaining publications such as *Earth in Upheaval* (1955).[12] I'm not suggesting that Velikovsky fueled Japanese and American filmic fervor and popular interest in astronomical catastrophe during this early period. But clearly Velikovsky should be at least factored into the overall equation. Ultimately, although I cannot prove this, the role of *When Worlds Collide* (i.e., the novel) role cannot be de-emphasized for all that came afterward—perhaps including Velikovsky's erroneous speculations.

Intrigued men began tying evidence of small planetary impact to great events in the fossil record. For instance, astronomer David Baldwin in 1949 speculated:

> The calculated meteoritic diameters bring forcibly to mind such names as Apollo, Hermes, Amor, Adonis, and Albert; names of tiny asteroids which in recent years have paid fleeting visits to our neighborhood; tiny asteroids, each of which could, in some future year, entirely devastate an American state or a European country; tiny asteroids which might wipe out local species of flora and fauna. Sudden disappearance of long-established groups of contemporary life may have been recorded in past geologic history. Is it not possible that the causes of these occurrences were meteoritic impacts?[13]

Of course the unstated yet implied 800-pound gorilla in the room in Baldwin's outrageous speculation is "dinosaur."

While Velikovsky was kept busy slinging planetoids around the inner Solar System, finding ways of accounting for mass extinction occurrences of the recent fossil record, Allen O. Kelly and Frank Dachille resorted to similar tactics of explaining not only recent geological events but also the death of the dinosaurs in their rarely cited *Target: EARTH* (1953). They attributed nearly every geological feature of the American west and much elsewhere (much of which today would be understood more correctly in terms of plate tectonics) to repeated cataclysmic impact events, causing shifts in axis of rotation due to slippage of Earth's crustal shell, with resultant tidal waves scouring continental surfaces. This was named the "collision flood theory." Later, another non-specialist, René Gallant (1906–1985), published a more popular, yet analogous and highly speculative volume titled *Bombarded Earth* (1964), concerning how our planet's geological history has been largely warped by asteroid and meteorite collisions.[14]

Thanks to the scholars involved and the avenues (or sometimes alleyways) they pursued, science was becoming more science fictional in tone. But then, as we shall see, so were developments within the geosciences. However, scientifically, this mid–20th century period corresponds to the apex of Michael Benton's "dilettante phase" of pondering how dinosaurs—by then the most celebrated prehistoric animal group—disappeared. This phase proved attractive to many scientists because, although "mass extinctions were of little importance to a serious paleontologist ... the whole approach was apparently so easy and such fun that everyone felt they had the opportunity" to offer theories. "A large number of the theories" made by a number of scientists often operating beyond their own fields of expertise, "show a remarkable relaxation of scientific standards. It was as if, at the mere mention of 'dinosaur extinction,' scientists breathed a sigh of relief and felt freed from the straitjacket of normal scientific hypothesis-testing."[15]

Beyond pseudoscience or more scientifically-minded efforts of edification, during this period the prospect of astronomical catastrophe proved increasingly captivating to writers of fantastic fiction and artists. In 1947, space artist Chesley Bonestell, for example, painted a horrific scene showing the aftermath of a meteor having gouged a mile-wide crater in Manhattan. And Rod Serling's famous *Twilight Zone* episode, "The Midnight Sun," first aired on November 17, 1961 (directed by Anton Leader), told of nightmarish conditions resulting when the Earth is dislodged from its orbit, now hurtling toward the Sun. In actuality, however, and unknown to audiences until after a woman awakens from her coma and the broiling solar flare of a nightmare forged in her fever-filled mind, we learn that Earth really is moving out of orbit, yet *away* from the Sun. In fact, ironically, Earth will soon be frozen solid. Fritz Lieber's 1964 novel *The Wanderer* also trumpeted the interplanetary collision theme elegantly. Lieber earned sci-fi's coveted 1965 Hugo Award for this masterful account.[16] On a considerably lesser note, *Battle of the Worlds* (released in Italy in 1961; USA 1963), starring Claude Rains, was a low-budget feature about a stray "unknown planet" threatening Earth with collision, seemingly derivative of *Warning from Space. This Island Earth* (1955) extends the theme.

By the 1960s, the gateway to speculative, astronomically founded tales of Earth's destruction had been flung wide open! While NASA scientists paved America's way to the Moon, instead, movie producers luxuriated in crazy science ... delving in their own brand of lunacy.

Gorath (1962), a Toho production fortified by Eiji Tsuburaya's (1901–1970) special effects, quite masterful for the time, extended the popular runaway-celestial-object-heading-right-for-Earth theme. This time a white dwarf star named "Gorath," smaller than Earth in radius ("¾ size") yet initially measured as 6,000 times more massive, is the interloper. A team of scientists aboard rocket ship *JX-1* is sucked in by Gorath's enormous gravitational field, yet not before transmitting vital data back to Earth. As Gorath closes in, its mass increases to 6,200 times the Earth's because it continues to absorb other objects along its destructive path—such as the rings of Saturn, comets and later the Moon. Japanese scientists appeal to the United Nations, this time with a curious strategy for salvation. This incredible plan involves setting up a propulsion base in Antarctica where 6.6 billion megatons of fusion bombs would be detonated in a controlled fashion from numerous thrusters, in order to slide the Earth's orbit out of Gorath's trajectory. (Fortunately, Japanese scientists have solved the problem of radioactive decontamination!) Although nations initially balk at the outlandish and expensive proposal, eventually they see light of day.

Turning the Earth into a giant rocket-powered vessel works, as direct collision with Gorath is averted. But if Gorath passes within 200,000 kilometers, then Earth's oceans and atmosphere would be pulled into space. Also, Mt. Fuji would become a "killer volcano." Fortunately, Gorath misses the Earth by twice that distance; however, due to its continually growing mass, Gorath's near passage still causes considerable destruction: immense tidal waves submerge Tokyo. These scenes are better engineered than any analogous scenes in *When Worlds Collide*. Also, the outer-space footage is state of the art for its time: space ships are not NASA-like, but still convincing. Beauty is in the details and, accordingly, launch pads and miniature bases on Antarctica look nothing short of spectacular.

Far less successful are scenes of the giant prehistoric walrus (named "Magma" in Japan but whimsically nicknamed "Wally the Walrus" in the U.S.), freed from Antarctic ice as a result of melting caused by nearby fusion burners. The creature, Magma, threatens to destroy the thrusters, which have necessarily been shut down due to the monster's awakening. Hence, Magma is killed by laser ray after not much more than a cameo in the Japanese movie version.[17]

One of the Japanese astronauts (Kanai, played by Akira Kubo) suffers amnesia upon close encounter with Gorath. Yet his memory is restored just as Gorath reaches its perihelion point with Earth. Earth is spared! Following this triumph, in wake of dangerous Gorath's passing, the world's nations are more obliged toward mutual international cooperation. Furthermore, the world's scientists wisely intend to reset the Earth's orbit back onto its original trajectory. The film ends on a positive, conciliatory tone—from now on, why can't we just all get along? Of the three major films outlined here, *Gorath* is the best and most thought-provoking.

Yet for further philosophical filmic reflection, many Godzilla fans are mindful that in 1965's *Ghidrah, the Three-headed Monster*, the world's destruction seems imminent with the onslaught of a giant winged exodinosaur, Ghidrah, arriving from outer space in the form of a large meteorite, impacting Earth. As Ghidrah transforms from the meteorite in a dazzling fiery display, subconsciously, the bolide as a planetary destroyer and the most powerful species of dino-monster in the known universe become inextricably linked.

For those of us who have grown up watching Japanese science fiction and monster movies, it would seem that places in Japan like Tokyo are the most monster-molested cities of all. Yet, other urban targets have suffered more in the movies (or fantastic literature), perhaps New York City more so than all the rest. In a sense, using a term coined by Max Page (author of *The City's End*, 2008), *Gojira* (1954) is one of the earliest Japanese "disaster porn" movies. We are horrified, utterly aghast, yet cannot turn away! Historically, however, western cities like London and New York had been targeted by monsters, geological upheavals, aliens and evil mad scientists for decades before Tokyo fell under Godzilla's stomping feet. Today, even in the wake of 9/11, there would appear no end in sight for New York's continual destruction at the hands of demented movie producers and special effects masters. As is the case with Tokyo! While before 1980, cosmological disaster scenarios such as portrayed in *Gorath* and *When Worlds Collide* were relegated to "crazy science," following physicist Luis Alvarez's publication of a sobering hypothesis for the dinosaurs' ultimate extinction 66 million years ago as a result of a 6-mile diameter asteroid (or ten-mile-diameter comet) impact, such crazy concepts were eventually vaulted into *mainstream* science.

As of 1964, on the eve of the dinosaur renaissance, yet during the waning of Michael Benton's "dilettante phase" of intellectual questioning on how dinosaurs became extinct, paleontologist Glenn L. Jepsen (1903–1974) generalized myriad theories proposed for their extinction. Reading this list today, it would seem that even then there was nothing new to explore under a suspect Sun:

> Authors with varying competence have suggested that dinosaurs disappeared because the climate deteriorated (became suddenly or slowly too hot or cold or dry or wet), or that their diet did (with too much food or not enough of such substances as fern oil; from poisons in water or plants or ingested minerals; by bankruptcy of calcium or other necessary elements). Other writers have put the blame on disease, parasites, wars, anatomical or metabolic disorders (slipped vertebral discs, malfunction or imbalance of hormone and endocrine systems, dwindling brain and consequent stupidity, heat sterilization, effects of being warm-blooded in the Mesozoic world), racial old age, evolutionary drift into senescent overspecialization, changes in the pressure of composition of the atmosphere, poison gases, volcanic dust, excessive oxygen from plants, meteorites, comets, gene pool drainage by little mammalian egg-eaters, overkill capacity by predators, fluctuation of gravitational constants, development of psychotic suicidal factors, entropy, cosmic radiation, shift of Earth's rotational poles, floods, continental drift, extraction of the moon from the Pacific Basin, drainage of swamp and lake environments, sunspots, God's will, mountain building, raids by little green hunters in flying saucers, lack of even standing room in Noah's Ark and paleoweltschmerz.[18]

Or perhaps, as Will Cuppy (1884–1949) humorously stated that same year, "The Age of Reptiles ended because it had gone on long enough and it was all a mistake in the first place."[19] But clearly, as Benton's dilettante phase wound down, leading toward his categorical "professional phase" of investigating dinosaur extinctions (from ca. 1970 onward), one notices enhanced communication of scientific ideas to a receptive public sector. Oddly, the more outlandish, controversial or science-fictional in tone the theory (provided that dinosaurs were somehow involved), the more popular it became, instilled beyond scientific literature into popular culture. How and why did this happen, and what dramatic impact did the most vaunted and successful theories have on public perception of dinosaurs and their mysterious fate, especially given their curious association to man?

At a time when the eminent vertebrate paleontologist Edwin H. Colbert (1905–2001) was diplomatically downplaying the importance of catastrophes in Earth history, especially as pertaining to dinosaur extinctions, change was rapidly afoot.[20] Although geological "neo-catastrophism" was a fitting term coined by paleontologist Otto H. Schindewolf (1896–1971), referring to "turning points, or faunal discontinuities" in the fossil record, it took several years for the concept to enter mainstream popular culture. Modern neocatastrophism was distinguished from Cuvier's views in that Cuvier's catastrophism assumed "complete, worldwide destruction of entire life systems followed by new creations."[21] Since 1950, Schindewolf had been a proponent of the possibility that "sharp fluctuations in the high-energy cosmic radiation reaching the Earth should be considered" as a means of causing "twofold mutagenic activity," or proximate cause of extinction.[22] In the following two decades, additional radiation causative theories of mass extinction would appear in the scientific literature, eventually reaching the popular press by 1968.[23]

Thus, two disparate scientific waves emerged from the 1950s onward, making headlines pertaining to the ultimate extinction of dinosaurs during the dinosaur renaissance period, one essentially preceding the other in terms of popularity and public reaction. The first wave entertained an intriguing notion that dinosaurs may have been extinguished by radiation emanating from space, particularly from a star undergoing a supernova explosion that then would have been situated within a critical distance from our Solar System. At a time when the United States and the Soviets were testing nuclear bombs of ever greater capacity, with a populace frightened by trending consequences, it perhaps is of little wonder that geologists began considering the possible effects of ionizing radiation not only upon biota other than man, but also including plausible, "what-if" scenarios applied to past markers of geological mass extinction. Furthermore, it is thought that such theories "probably did prepare the way for the asteroid theory."[24] The supernova theory gained press in several popular articles beginning in the late 1960s.[25] But while public knowledge concerning supernova-cosmic radiation theories was disseminated (although largely dismissed by most geologists), these theories made a far lesser splash compared with what was to come in 1980.

Secondly came the (eventually) far more scientifically successful category of asteroid impact and comet-showering models, the most significant of which was published in 1980, gaining general acceptance by many scientists (due to a conceptually simplistic scenario and the fact that it offered many predictions that could be tested—or falsified—scientifically), as well as approval by a concerned, if not utterly fascinated, reading public. Beyond controversial science and quarreling paleontologists, these theories viscerally *meant* things to philosophically-minded men, and those who kept abreast of worsening contemporary world affairs. After fringe support for the supernova theory subsided (when it became elegantly falsified as of 1979),[26] instead, the impact scenario's chief competition evolved into a hypothesis of cataclysmic volcano-triggered mass extinctions (discussed previously in Chapter Seven).[27]

Historian of science William Glen estimated that between 1980 and 1993, more than 2,500 papers and books had been published on aspects of the mass extinctions theory, as stirred up by the Alvarez-Berkeley team, a weighty number, far more than can be well summarized or encompassed within a single chapter of this book.[28] As Benton proclaimed in 1990, much "spice" was added to the controversy: "From its rather modest image only 20 years or so ago, the extinction of the dinosaurs has now become one of the most studied unique events in the history of life.... [N]ew topics are spawned—nuclear winter, periodicity, comet showers—which keep public interest alive, and which keep levels of funding for research at record levels."[29] So there are far, far too many papers and books to be recounted here; nor will it be possible to fully address the broad scope of this revolutionary episode in the earth sciences. However, let's first briefly examine the pivotal publication which lit a 1980s firestorm of scientific intrigue and controversy that rapidly permeated into the popular realm.

On the surface or to the uninitiated, it may have all seemed like another outbreak of crackpot science, like in a Toho film. But this time it wasn't. At Berkeley University, Nobel laureate physicist Luis Alvarez (1911–1988), his son, geologist Walter Alvarez, and nuclear chemists Frank Asaro and Helen V. Michel were using sophisticated methods to determine the sedimentation rate of transition and faunal turnover at the K-Pg boundary, as denoted by a thin clay layer found at three geological sections, representing marine deposits, in which iridium of presumed meteoritic origin had been determined. They had assumed that a more or less steady stream of ordinary shooting stars ablating in the atmosphere would, over geologic time, contribute to the iridium signal. However, their work led to a riveting, spectacular set of conclusions, relying on extreme habitat destruction as a proximate extinction cause, which they viewed as an "extension of the meteorite hypothesis," developed by previous workers such as Ernst Opik (1893–1985) and Harold Urey (1893–1981). "In brief, our hypothesis suggests that an asteroid struck the earth, formed an impact crater, and some of the dust-sized material ejected from the crater reached the stratosphere and was spread around the globe. This dust effectively prevented sunlight from reaching the surface for a period of several years, until the dust settled to earth. Loss of sunlight suppressed photosynthesis, and as a result most food chains collapsed and the extinctions resulted."[30]

A diameter for the alleged impacting body was calculated at 10 kilometers; this bolide would have an impact velocity of 25 kilometers per second, capable of forming a 200-kilometer diameter crater. The impact would have detonated with the explosive equivalent of 10^8 megatons of TNT—also equivalent to the simultaneous detonation of 10,000 *times* the (then) combined Soviet and U.S. nuclear arsenals. A state of utter ecological disequilibrium would result; only "lucky" species would survive. (Although the extinctions pattern also did favor smaller, and often less specialized vertebrates.) At sea, an enduring "Strangelove" anoxic ocean would have resulted. (See Chapter Eleven.)

Meanwhile, scientists noted such a cataclysmic event may not have been singular in the Phanerozoic Era's geohistory (i.e., over the past 541 million years), as Luis Alvarez and colleagues further speculated that other mass extinctions recorded in the fossil record could have also been triggered by impacts of large meteorites, asteroids or comets, which would be expected to happen with an average recurrence time of roughly every 30 to 100 million years. The theory's immediate success stemmed from its openness to falsification, as it offered many testable predictions.[31] So what would be the consequences—hypothetical, fictional or otherwise?

Interestingly, numerous science fictional short stories and novels, inspired by the idea of a cometary or asteroid dinosaurian demise, quickly appeared. One of the most intriguing and particularly detailed entries, Will Hubbell's 2002 novel *Cretaceous Sea*, offered firsthand witness accounts of human time travelers stranded at the time of the collision, braving the nightmarish horrors in its wake.[32]

During the writing of a paper with Jack Sepkoski (1948–1999) concerning mass extinctions evident throughout geological history, David M. Raup (1933–2015) noted something remarkable. While there were five large extinctions noted (corresponding to the Late Ordovician, Late Devonian, Late Triassic, Late Permian, and Late Cretaceous Periods), now popularly known as the "Big Five" with rates of extinctions far exceeding background or "ordinary" average rates of extinction for marine organisms, several others of lesser magnitude could also be observed in the statistical data—a total of twelve peaks, or "events." This prompted a fated conversation as recounted by Sepkoski: "Do you see it?" Dave asked me. I stared but didn't. "They're regularly spaced in time."[33] This led to a landmark paper, titled "Periodicity of extinctions in the geologic past,"[34] in which they claimed, backed with significant 95 percent statistical confidence using a high-powered, time-series analysis, that for the past 250 million years, twelve major extinction events have recurred with a 26-million-year regularity, concluding, "Although the causes of the periodicity are unknown, it is possible that they are related to extraterrestrial forces (solar, solar system, or galactic)."[35] Their paper triggered a wave of *ad hoc* theories and postulated mechanisms generating 26- and 32-million-year astronomical cycles having propensity to "shower" comets toward Earth during these fated times of havoc. The most famous of these theories involved "Nemesis," dubbed the Death Star.

Although this 26-million-year mass extinctions theory was far more "science-fictiony" in tone than the Alvarez team's 1980 focus on the K-Pg transition, periodicity didn't lend itself as readily to science fiction stories, films or themes. But it did prompt the scientific wheel of fortune with many new papers being churned out at a never-before-seen pace, beginning in 1984, with articles suitable for laymen circulating into the popular press.

One thought-provoking science fiction novel, Robert Silverberg's *At Winter's End* (1988), borrowed from the periodic impact theories. The story's premise, set many millions of years in the future, is structured around the future of Man and his capability of surviving the icy, calamitous episodes (hundreds of thousands of years in duration) wrought by instances of periodically recurring impact cratering on Earth. Future Man (an intelligent species, yet who appear quite simian on artist Michael Whelan's book jacket) has extensive competition from other evolutionary biological products which have opportunistically profited from the evolutionary sweepstakes following numerous catastrophes. Impact cratering has recurred and a central theme in the story concerns Future Man's philosophical search for understanding of why this should be so, and why Man instinctively aspires to repopulate the world and reestablish civilization after every instance. "Am I to understand from what you say that the death-stars that destroyed the Great World were not the first that came to the world?" states a prominent character, Hresh, who in a sense may be viewed as our world's future pioneering geologist. Wise old Noum om Beng replies, "That is so. Millions of years go by between each visit of the death-star swarms. This I know, boy. This knowledge comes to me from the ancient ones. The death-stars fell upon the Great World, and they fell upon the world that existed before the Great World ever was. And upon the world before that."[36] The Great World represents a time of Mankind to come, though deep in their past.

Interestingly, although lacking evidence that would be forthcoming, W.M. Napier and S.V.M. Clube strangely anticipated the scope of dinosaur extinctions theories that were to come over the next few years in a November 1979 paper titled "A theory of terrestrial catastrophism." They suggested that terrestrial catastrophes, randomly distributed in geological time, but recurring about once every 50 million years, are effected by the passage of the Solar System through interstellar clouds having masses far exceeding that of our Sun, within the spiral arms of the Milky Way galaxy. During these periods, recurring cyclically approximately every 100 to 200 million years, planetesimals in the interstellar medium are captured by the Sun, forming a temporarily bound cloud of cosmic debris. This material is eventually either ejected by the Sun, or destroyed during collision with planets of the Solar System.[37] Nevertheless, despite all the excitement and furor of the prior decade, with mass extinctions-causing comet swarms streaking in from the heavens, by the mid–1990s, researches into mass extinctions *periodicity* had slowed to a "virtual standstill."[38]

News of revamped, rapidly evolving mass extinctions theories reached the public sector, dark stormy waves of contention emanating from the hot-zone halls of academia. Besides the standard news media accounts that could hardly keep up, Isaac Asimov (1920–1992) diplomatically took up the cause in his monthly *Magazine of Fantasy and Science Fiction* column, as well as did Jeff Hecht in *Analog*.[39] Stephen Jay Gould, a proponent of stasis in species, followed by rapid "punctuated equilibria" evolutionary processes in the fossil record, offered stalwart support through lectures, his highly regarded *Natural History* column and other popular writings. Capturing the spirit of these heady times, Ian Warden, writing in the *Canberra Times* (May 20, 1984), stated, "To connect the dinosaurs, creatures of interest to everyone but the veriest dullard, with a spectacular extraterrestrial event like the deluge of meteors ... seems a little like one of those plots that a clever publisher might concoct to guarantee enormous sales. All the Alvarez-Raup theories lack is some sex and the involvement of the Royal family and the whole world would be paying attention to them."[40] Imagery showing unwitting, doomed dinosaurs glancing into the heavens at a streaking comet tail, and other envisioned scenes of the frightening terminal Cretaceous event—on the verge of "impact winter"—were often encountered in popular books and magazine articles.[41]

Although Alvarez's and Raup's peculiar, insightful notions were subjected to myriad nuances and levels of hesitation and denial, the principle reason for *why* authors of such papers (and many that would follow) would be so decried is that, to many, the asteroid impact theory represented an attack on conventional, comforting textbook Darwinian evolutionary gradualism and Lyellian geological uniformitarianism.[42] Both Darwin and Lyell underscored during their 19th century careers that—opposed to Cuvier—because catastrophes are not observable in nature, therefore, geologic and natural processes occurring in the past must have been gradual, limited in tempo and intensity. For instance, Kenneth J. Hsu has estimated that, based on information Lyell had access to in his time, although using modern radiometric dating methods, Lyell's estimate for the duration of the Cretaceous-Tertiary transition itself (as represented by boundary clay), would have lasted 72 million years. Hsu noted that uniformitarian geologists "had no clock to measure geologic time, yet they were sufficiently arrogant to believe that what is not observable cannot have happened, forgetting the brevity of human life compared to the course of Earth history."[43] Instead, however, now Alvarez and colleagues were suggesting it may have taken place essentially overnight, because of a nearly unimaginable cataclysm! (Other modern estimates founded upon the impact theory suggested the boundary transition took place anywhere from between a few months or years up to 100,000 years.) The group of scientists most vehemently opposed to the impact theory was, curiously, the dinosaur paleontologists (with rare exception of Dale Russell).[44] Robert Bakker, for example, who gained more than his fair share of media time during the 1980s and 1990s, had this to say: "The arrogance of those people is simply unbelievable. They know next to nothing about how real animals evolve, live, and become extinct. But despite their ignorance, the geochemists feel that all you have to do is crank up some fancy machine and you've revolutionized science."[45] As if in retaliation, of the paleontological community in general, Luis Alvarez unfairly complained, "I don't like to say bad things about paleontologists, but they're really not good scientists. They're more like stamp collectors."[46]

A key question concerning the impact hypothesis became, rather obviously, "So where is the huge crater that should have formed?"—or as it was popularly called, the "smoking gun"? As early as 1948, science fiction editors found the idea inviting; one speculative piece printed in *Fantastic Adventures* by A. Morris and James B. Settles, April 1948, titled "The Bomb Out of Space," suggested that the asteroid which created Arizona's famous tourist attraction, the Meteor Crater, 30,000 years ago, instead may have impacted 100 million years ago, thus causing many of the ancient reptiles to perish.[47] Settles's dramatic painting, appearing on the issue's back cover under the words "Impossible ... but True," showing dinosaurs writhing in the tremendous, fiery impact, certainly underscored this (impossible) notion. Then in 1981, astronomer Fred Whipple (1906-2004) suggested the impact zone must have been in the North Atlantic, possibly situated where volcanic Iceland is today. His pronouncement was popularized through Asimov's writings as well as in a NOVA science documentary buttressed by Gould's fervent commentary, titled "The Asteroid and the Dinosaur," televised on March 10, 1981. Strangely, the real site of the impact had *already* been discovered, although this wouldn't be proven until nearly another decade had passed.

Meanwhile, exciting news of a plausible crater site came in 1989, with the announcement of an impact crater discovered buried under Ice Age glacial drift in central Iowa, near the town of Manson, surprisingly so, because odds were that the impact occurred in the ocean. This Manson crater had a diameter of 35 kilometers and a presumed age of 66 million years. Such a crater dimension was almost only one-tenth that predicted by the Alvarez-Berkeley team, as deemed necessary to raise enough havoc to cause extinctions worldwide. However, further analysis divulged that this crater was older than the K-Pg boundary—74 million years. "I don't know if the collision killed all the dinosaurs on Earth," claimed the Manson crater's discoverer, geologist Ray Anderson, "but it certainly wiped them out in Iowa."[48] Eventually, however, by the early 1990s, the genuine smoking-gun crater was identified to most everybody's satisfaction (well, many supporters of volcano catastrophe continued to vehemently disagree). The culprit became known as the Chicxulub Crater, situated partly off the Yucatan coast, correctly dated at 66 million years, with a diameter estimated between 200 to 300 kilometers. All associated rock and geochemical deposits fingered this impact as the fabled dinosaur killer.[49] By 2003, however, paleontologist Sankar Chatterjee recognized what he believed is a crater off the Indian continental shelf, near the Deccan Traps, in the Indian Ocean west of Mumbai. Its age is approximately 66 million years, and the diameter of this disputed teardrop-shaped crater is 600 kilometers by 400 kilometers. *If* confirmed as an impact crater, it would have been formed by the collision of a *25-mile diameter* asteroid which may have caused concomitant Deccan Traps volcanism, collectively sufficient to have caused the end of the dinosaur's reign on Earth.

During the early 1980s, geopolitical tensions between the United States and the Soviet Union vastly escalated, concerning nuclear weapons deployment in Europe and, particularly, the arms race, spiraling out of control. Upon his election in 1980, President Ronald Reagan appeared likely to launch and seemed intent to "win" a nuclear war against the Soviets.[50] As of 1983, with 50,000 nuclear warheads manufactured for the world's arsenal, carrying a deadly total potential punch of 15,000 megaton TNT-equivalent, based on opinion polls, public fears over the matter expectedly rose as well, back to 1950s levels. Reagan sought to address America's (falsely proclaimed) "window of vulnerability" with a Strategic Defense Initiative, involving invention of a death-ray engineered missile defense network deployed in orbit, rendering nuclear weapons "impotent and obsolete," an escapade which was mockingly referred to in the press and by skeptics as "Star Wars." But the Cold War was far from over then. For according to Spencer R. Weart, Reagan's "anti–Soviet speeches and arms buildup had been taken in dead earnest in the Kremlin. A 1983 NATO war games exercise had particularly frightened Soviet premier Leonid Brezhnev and his colleagues, for it looked to them like preparation for a First Strike—which they were ill prepared to counter. They put their entire military on alert. Some historians have suggested that (unknown to the public and much later) the world came nearly as close to nuclear war, purely by accident, as during the Cuban missile crisis."[51]

Influential during that angst-ridden era, imagery is reflective of that time. Science fiction films such as 1983's *Wargames* (about a Defense Department computer gone mad) and 1984's acclaimed *Terminator*, certainly mirrored public concerns. One of several bone-chilling, realistically portrayed televised features broadcast between 1981 and 1983, *The Day After* (ABC, 1983), "became the most famous nuclear show ever. Heavily promoted as a news event, its television premier gave 100 million citizens their first look at what a real nuclear war might look like, complete with terrifying explosions and corpses."[52] The dire political ramifications trickled into sports as well, not only in a famous Olympics hockey game that pitted the U.S. vs. the Soviet Union, but even in the symbolic 1985's *Rocky IV*, starring Sylvester Stallone, in which the titular hero faces a huge Russian opponent in the ring. As if to ineffectually allay fears, the administration openly began contemplating use of "cleaner" neutron bombs that would potentially limit the radioactive fallout surrounding a devastated target zone.

By the early 1980s, then, scientists, laypersons and journalists were able to intellectually meld concepts of catastrophic dinosaurian extinctions with those conceivably pending for mankind. They could be imagined as equally horrific, in each case striking down the dominant, ruling species of their respective eras. "Extinction" became a byword, although now often coupled with the word "mass." Essentially, buttressed by detailed scientific modeling, and in a large sense fueled by horrific imagery of the prospect of nuclear war with the art of paleocatastrophe (which became prominent following the Alvarez team's 1980s *Science* paper), Alvarez's hypothetical "impact winter" would be equated with what would be encompassed in a Soviet-U.S. thermonuclear conflict, "nuclear winter."[53]

Popular science books of the time, such as Carl Sagan's (1934–1996) and Ann Druyan's *Comet* (1985), made such connections wherein the authors noted, "The Cretaceous extinctions thus seem to have a cause very similar to the possible consequence of modern warfare known as Nuclear Winter. Through the dust excavated by nuclear groundbursts, and smoke from the burning of 'strategic targets' in and around cities, we humans can generate our own climatic catastrophe, perhaps adequate to bring about massive extinctions in our age as in the Cretaceous. The principal difference is that the dinosaurs did not contrive their own extinction." Then the authors concluded philosophically, "It seems likely that had not a comet or asteroid hit the Earth 66 million years ago (or subsequently), the dinosaurs would still be here, and we would not."[54] In his acclaimed *Riddle of the Dinosaur,* intended for laypersons, science journalist John Noble Wilford also associated the probable outcome of all-out thermonuclear war with predictions of the asteroid collision theory; prominent scientists of the time and savvy readers alike could understand the stark connections. Wilford concluded, "In our exploration of time, we have driven down a highway and searched under the junipers for some dinosaur bones and come face to face with ourselves."[55]

Perhaps rather predictably then, Godzilla resurfaced in a 1985 film (released in Japan

Fig 16-2: No matter whether the (non-avian) dinosaurs were selected for extinction because of a nearby supernova blast (as formerly considered—represented at left in the sky), or via an asteroid or comet collision with Earth 66 million years ago—represented in the middle figure in the sky, an outcome of the contingent extinction episode stimulated much philosophical thinking during the early years of the dinosaur renaissance. One such thought experiment was the possibility of a Dinosauroid, in a parallel universe where the supernova hadn't occurred, or the comet or 6-mile-diameter asteroid hadn't collided. Or, on a more science fictional (sardonic) plane, did the dinosaurs evolve heightened intelligence and then eliminate traces of their industry in a thermonuclear war—represented by the figure at right shown in the sky (illustration by *Prehistoric Times* editor and artist Mike Fredericks, used with permission)?

in December 1984). While the newly revamped *Godzilla*'s storyline wasn't "necessitated" by contemporary rising east-west tensions, it clearly borrowed from prevailing geopolitical circumstances, leading to consequences many feared could transpire. As William Tsutsui noted in 2004, "Drawing on public insecurity in the wake of the Three Mile Island accident [i.e., in 1979] and global edginess over Reagan-era superpower confrontations, the new Godzilla was intended as a cinematic wake-up call."[56] Naturally, the story emphasized a nuclear exchange between America and the Soviets, with radiation from the Soviet missile reviving the famed dinosaurian, just when mankind most needed its monstrous cathartic metaphor.

Explosion of the Soviet nuclear reactor at Cherbonyl in 1986 exemplified how catastrophic contamination from radiation fallout could be, an unfortunate consequence, yet at least having a side benefit of ultimately helping to ease Cold War tensions.

Harking back to *When Worlds Collide* and those aforementioned, entertaining mid-century Japanese films, if the idea of giant, impacting, era-ending planetoids and comets smashing into Earth seems too outrageous, well, think again. The latest theory of Solar System formation not only involves a wandering planet Jupiter that eons ago migrated inward to the Sun, at the distance Mars is today, but also focuses on the probability of celestial encounters. Tunguska and Chelyabinsk-magnitude events ought to happen *twice* a century according to revised statistical, astronomical calculations. And the odds are 1 percent over the next billion years that "Venus could collide with Earth, or Earth could go careening off on a totally new orbit, sterilizing the planet."[57] This may smack of Velikovsky, or perhaps more like those doomed characters in *The Twilight Zone*'s 1961 episode, "The Midnight Sun." But it's consistent with the newest model of Solar System origin, while factoring in perceived instability of planetary orbits in a chaotic universe. Furthermore, geologists have considered that if any "relatively small" impacts were to happen today, these could set off the two enormous volcanic magma domes in the American west. One of these is the immense dome at Yellowstone National Park. Another is at Crater Lake, Oregon.[58] So, ultimately, random celestial *chaos* may not have only done in the dinosaurs, but, philosophically, our world civilization might also succumb someday to such outrageously bad luck, like what happened to the dinosaurs.

Today, most paleontologists embrace a renewed condition of "neo-uniformitarianism," in that large-scale, cataclysmic events never before witnessed or recorded by man, even originating in outer space, could occasionally impact or otherwise influence Earth. And while modern geochemists might declare that such perturbations (natural or self-imposed) are, or would be, relatively short-lived, with carbon, oxygen, nitrogen, sulfur and silicate cycles being restored to (Gaian) equilibrium in the geological wink of an eye, in the aftermath the immediate ecological and evolutionary consequences would be severe and everlasting. Such things have happened and will happen again. The only real question is—next time, unlike the dinosaurs 66 million years ago, will *we* be willing and prepared to survive?

After considering their warm-bloodedness, and possible gregarious habits, dinosaurs now seem less alien, and analogies made with birds and mammals somehow seem more fitting than was the case during the mid–20th century. Dinosaurs no longer symbolize the deceased, extinct or defunct. They were, as a group perhaps, the most successful of all terrestrial vertebrates, representing a verdant, youthful era of earth history.[59] In fact, we see ourselves in the history and possible fate of the dinosaurs.[60] (See Figure 16-2.)

Chapter Seventeen

Shadow of Our Past

Evolution of the Beast

"There's something almost primal about a creature that looks human, but is not quite."—Don Mancini, creator of the movie character "Chucky"[1]

In the Minnesota Senatorial election staged between Democrat Al Franken and Republican Norm Coleman in November 2008, one demented soul voted for "Lizard People" as a write-in. Now the real question is ... why not have voted instead for Lovecraftian "Gill People"? A sign of the times and current science fictional affairs perhaps? Who is winning such an odd metaphorical race?

Amphibioid science fictional "gill-men" have persisted since the dawn of the 20th century, reaching their pinnacle during the 1950s Cold War era. Rapid decline ensued thereafter, with gill-men symbolically bowing to their more highly evolved "reptiloid" cousins. Beginning with this chapter, and extending into the next, an overall genre trend may be charted, leading from our fascination with amphibioid monsters of manlike mien and, through the decades, "evolving" into humanoids of more reptilian bearing, including the most important intellectual and instructive group—dinosauroids. And so here I shall outline gill-men's former pop-cultural prominence, culminating in the low-budget, transitional 1958 film presaging the eventual significance of science fictional reptile-dinosaur men.

Few appreciate that decades prior to the current dinosaur age of pop culture, there was an "age of amphibians." While this latter term was in common parlance by the 1930s, used in textbooks such as Charles Schuchert's *Outlines of Historical Geology* (1931), the term "age of amphibians" quite possibly has 19th-century origins, as it appears in Joseph Le Conte's *Elements of Geology* (5th ed. 1903).[2] The term memorializes a progressive ladder-like upward trend noted by 19th-century geologists, that there were successive "ages" of (vertebrate) life recorded in the fossil record; prior to the amphibian age, there was an "age of fishes"; the age of amphibians then evolved into an "age of reptiles." As mentioned in Chapter Two, perhaps the earliest speculation of man possibly having had an amphibious, frog-like ancestor came from early 19th-century naturalists who described Lower Triassic fossil footprints that seemed strangely human-shaped. By 1836, such fossil trackways were named separately as "Cheirotherium." These were eventually attributed to a creature known as the "Labyrinthodon," a large quadrupedal frog amphibian. Despite the consensus, marked by a social and scientific opposition to species transmutation then, the stark similarity of the fossil prints to human handprints inspired one gentlemanly scientist to suggest that "Man had descended from a large frog, which had subsequently become extinct."[3]

Indeed, paleontologists recognized that during the middle Paleozoic Era, fishes were adapting into semi-amphibious species, conquering the land after learning how to breathe air directly from the atmosphere with lungs instead of using gills to extract oxygen through a watery medium.

During the 1950s, Universal Studios introduced the last of their great movie monsters—the Gill Man, in *Creature from the Black Lagoon* (1954). Scientists, preparing only to dig for its fossils from rock deposits in the Amazon, were startled by a live specimen of this "missing link," a living fossil amphibious anthropoid. This was a horror film featuring a monster like none of the prior 1930s–'40s Universal icons suffused with supernaturalism (e.g., werewolves, vampires, mummies reborn via mystical incantations). In tackling evolutionary themes—such speculations having a then half-century tradition in fantasy *literature*, thanks especially to H.G. Wells and Edgar Rice Burroughs—the *filmic* Gill Man theme was distinctively science fictional. In relatively short order, the Gill Man ("half man, half fish") became an "indelible cinematic icon."[4] So let's immerse ourselves in the Gill Man's trilogy of tales, further exploring this creature's origins and what stories it inspired, in turn.

Just how original was Universal's Gill Man and what does he symbolize?

In a 1929 feature film, very loosely adapted from Jules Verne's 1875 novel *The Mysterious Island*, a search for man's aquatic "missing link" spurs scientists aboard a submarine onward into the oceanic deeps. From bony fragment clues detected, eventually an undersea realm is discovered inhabited by peculiar, tool-using undersea people whose appearance strangely anticipates that of science fiction's most famous amphibioid "missing link" of all! Charles Darwin aside, the fishy, axe-wielding creatures of 1929 underscore how intriguing if not utterly horrific the outlandish possibility of man's amphibian (as opposed to simian or reptilian) genetic evolutionary heritage must have seemed a century ago. (See Figure 17-1.)

Perhaps the most hideous and famous filmic fictional anthropoid of all, however, hinting at mankind's most ineffable, recessed evolutionary origins, was the Gill Man, featured in *Creature from the Black Lagoon* (1954) as well as two sequels. Paleo-scientists have prominent roles in *Creature*, in which a living fossil anthropoidal Gill Man is discovered in the Amazon. (Indeed, perhaps the Black Lagoon lies in the vicinity of Arthur Conan Doyle's fabled Lost World land of Curupuri!) While scientists suggest a Devonian (400-million-year-old) origin for the Gill Man, they also speculate that its fossils date from 150 million years ago (which would be the Jurassic Period instead)! Ichthyologist Dr. Reed (played by Richard Carlson) believes, idealistically, that we should study the Gill Man: not only would such knowledge contribute to our understanding of how life evolved on Earth, but it would also offer clues as to how man may eventually adapt to other worlds in outer space having different surface and atmospheric conditions. To suspend disbelief, zoological comparisons are made to the Amazonian Kumonga lungfish, physically unchanged since the Devonian—mysteriously like the Gill Man.

According to monster movie lore, the idea for the Gill Man sprang from Director William Alland's recollection of "an obscure South American legend about a mysterious creature that was reputed to be extant in the swamps and jungles of that continent."[5] Vincent Di Fate adds that "the idea for this new film grew out of a dinner conversation that Alland had ... with Latin American filmmaker Gabriel Figueroa at the home of Orson Welles ... sometime in 1941.... In a memo written in early October 1952, Alland recounted Welles's dinner party and the fantastic story he'd heard of a race of creatures—half man, half fish—that purportedly lived in a remote region along the Amazon River. Maintaining that his story was true, Figueroa further claimed to have financed an expedition to the location in search of the creature."[6] Yes, but there *were* other contemporary, pop-cultural influences at large. (See Figure 17-2.)

Fig 17-1: A humanoid gill man from an oceanic floor civilization appearing in the 1929 film *Mysterious Island*.

Only sixteen years earlier, news headlines had made quite a splash, reporting the sensational discovery of a veritable evolutionary "missing link" between marine and terrestrial vertebrates (or fish and humans!)—the *living* Coelacanth fish, thought to have gone extinct during the Mesozoic Era. As Samantha Weinberg suggests, "Hollywood latched on: *The Creature from the Black Lagoon,* featuring a finned monster that emerged from the sea, apparently was inspired by the discovery."[7] This elusive natural history discovery proved every bit as significant for its time, and duly heralded, as was W. Douglas Burden's mid–1920s observations of the "prehistoric" Komodo Dragons leading to *King Kong*'s genesis. Reptiles *versus* amphibians! The battle for limelight supremacy was already on.

Intriguingly, aquatic anthropoidal amphibian monsters had been anticipated by others. In fantastic literature, we find the idea of undersea anthropoids is traditional. It predates Universal's Gill Man! For instance, Edgar Allan Poe wrote a poem titled "The City in the Sea" (1831–1845), describing the submerged mysterious turrets and domes of a former civilization, which may (or not) have been human. From a proud, "Babylon-like" tower, "Death looks gigantically down."[8]

Then in 1896, H.G. Wells's short story, "In the Abyss," recounted circumstances of Elstead's expedition to the ocean floor in a diving bell. Through thick observation glass, Elstead observes a "strange vertebrated animal.

Its dark purple head was dimly suggestive of a chameleon, but it had a high forehead and such a braincase as no reptile ever displayed.... The vertical pitch of its face gave it a most extraordinary resemblance to a

Fig 17-2: Detail from an advertising poster for the 1955 film, *Revenge of the Creature*, showing the famous Gill Man suit. Although there were many "gill men" of science fiction dreamed up over the years, in popular culture, the "Creature" became the most famous Gill Man of all that may also be considered as the most remotely related "cave man ancestor."

> human being. Two large and protruding eyes projected from sockets in chameleon fashion, and it had a broad reptilian mouth with horny lips beneath its little nostrils. In the position of the ears were two huge gill-covers, and out of these floated a branching tree of coralline filaments, almost like the tree-like gills that very young rays and sharks possess. But the humanity of the face was not the most extraordinary thing about the creature. It was a biped; its almost globular body was poised on a tripod of two frog-like legs and a long thick tail, and its forelimbs ... grotesquely caricatured the human hand....[9]

These undersea denizens are considered "descendants like ourselves of the great Theriomorpha of the New Red Sandstone age." In other words, they're evolutionary cousins to bestial forms of the Permo-Triassic, startlingly related to us! Minus the tail, Wells's description approximates the Gill Man design refined by Milicent Patrick *half a century* later.

Something "fishy."

A few years later, we learn of Irvin S. Cobb's disturbing "Fishhead," a story resoundingly rejected by editors before first appearing in *The Cavalier* (January 11, 1913).[10] We know Lovecraft knew of it, because in his article, "Supernatural Horror in Literature," he stated "'Fishhead' [is] an early achievement ... banefully effective in its portrayal of unnatural affinities between a hybrid idiot and the strange fish of an isolated lake, which at the last avenge their biped kinsmen's murder."[11] As mentioned in S.T. Joshi's *I Am Providence: The Life and Times of H.P. Lovecraft*, connections—which do seem rather obvious—between "Fishhead" and Lovecraft's novella *The Shadow Over Innsmouth* have been suspected since 1986.[12]

"Fishhead" is set in Reelfoot Lake, which mysteriously emerged in a semi-science fictional vein following the New Madrid earthquake of 1811. The primitive creatures thriving within this creepy lacustrine system are like none other, especially its huge catfish—"monstrous creatures ... scaleless, slick things, with corpsy, dead eyes and poisonous fins"! Seemingly related to the catfish is a "human monstrosity, the veritable embodiment of a nightmare," known to the locals as "Fishhead." His titular facial features resemble a catfish, although Fishhead is said to have been spawned from an Afro-American father and a half-breed Indian mother—thus reflecting contemporary miscegenation fears. The primitive Fishhead also has "splay feet with ... prehensile toes," reminiscent of prehistoric men.[13] However, it would seem instead that primitive Fishhead has closer genetic ties to Reelfoot Lake's aquatic denizens!

Fishhead is described as "almost amphibious." According to folklore, for recreation and sustenance he literally swims with the fishes, something which the two murderous (Caucasian) Baxter brothers intend to make happen in a more metaphorical sense. Following their evil deed, Fishhead's catfish "relatives" rise from the depths to the occasion, vengefully drowning and mutilating the Baxter brothers within their cavernous maws. Overall a most curious story, especially for its time, and from an author most widely known not as a writer of the weird, but instead as a humorist and journalist.[14]

Although it's surely a far stretch to suggest that Cobb's "Fishhead" was in the least a template for Universal's Gillman, a few analogies may be noted. In both stories we have the forbidding, ancient lake (or lagoon) setting, inhabited by an isolated, primitive, bipedal, last-of-its-kind amphibious anthropoid that is savagely attacked and left for dead by misguided, culpable humans. However, while Gill Man, who had pretty ladies to cavort with onscreen, became an icon, "Fishhead" faded into relative obscurity—until recently.[15] "Fishhead" dates from the period when sci-fi amphibioid men were considered as weird as they come, although as we shall see, recently, writers of fantastic fiction have found more fertile ground in the menacing form and dealings of reptiloids.

Next, Howard P. Lovecraft's (1890–1937) horrific *The Shadow Over Innsmouth* (1936) concerned a New England coastal colony, whose "people" in adulthood steadily transform into piscine, anthropoidal varieties from the "Palaeogean." As Stephen King mentions, the Gill Man is "remarkably like Lovecraft's half-breed, degenerate aberrations—the crazed and blasphemous results of liaisons between gods and human women."[16] Few *Creature* movie fans realize that prior to his more famous *Shadow Over Innsmouth*, in 1923, Lovecraft had published a short story, "Dagon" (1923), concerning a marine race of anthropoidal men with webbed feet and hands, bulging eyes and "other features less pleasant to recall," foreshadowing dire things to come.[17] "Dagon" may be considered a precursor of sorts to his novella, *The Shadow Over Innsmouth*. Dagon is a "fish-god," while the protagonist of Lovecraft's titular tale dreams of that terrifying day when "nameless things," amphibioid fish-men, "may rise above the billows to drag down in their reeking talons the remnants of puny, war-exhausted mankind—of a day when the land shall sink, and the dark ocean floor shall ascend amidst universal pandemonium."[18] (This passage also presages Karel Čapek's *War with the Newts*, 1936, to be discussed shortly.)

Lovecraft's better-known novella *Shadow* concerns a race of scaly, bipedal anthropoids which have lived since "Palaeogean" times (at least 80,000 years ago), inhabiting coastal waters along the northeast Atlantic. They're fish-headed, with bulging eyes, palpitating gills and long-webbed claws, resembling Universal's Gill Man. These prehistoric, "blasphemous fish-frogs" miscegenate with mankind.[19] To his despair, after escaping the appropriately named Gilman House hotel, the story's "human" protagonist discovers that as he ages, like many others belonging (i.e., in the genetic blood line) to the Innsmouth "family"–through a peculiar kind of biological degeneration, he takes on physical characteristics of Innsmouth's shadow folk. The most ontogenetically "advanced" forms *hop* (like frogs) rather than walk. Lovecraft once wrote, "All my stories are based on the fundamental legend that this world was at one time inhabited by another race. For practicing black magic, they lost their foothold and were expelled."[20] In *Shadow*, reflecting Lovecraft's "fear of tainted ancestry," connections are subtly made to his supernatural, alien Cthulhu mythos.[21]

Richard Tooker's *Inland Deep* (1936), a little-known novel originally published as *Tomb of Time* in the March 1933 *Amazing Stories*, offered further perspective on the literary (and filmic) "evolution" of amphibioid-men into reptiloid men.[22] For the primeval, underground setting, Tooker's tale borrows from Jules Verne's *A Journey to the Center of the Earth*, although in Tooker's case, encounters with intelligent, humanoid beings deep within the Earth's crust are genuinely "real" (not imagined).

Scientist-protagonist Bob Langtree, with his supervisor Roger Anson and his daughter Willa (whom Bob has taken quite a shine for), descend into a cave labyrinth within the Colorado Rockies to investigate recent reports of a strange human-like fossil footprint (yet replete with claws and a webbing impression) discovered therein. Frightening screams were also noted historically by prior spelunking witnesses, 500 years prior, within a portion of the cave system. Once the Anson/Langtree expedition is underway, and after trudging through miles of Stygian darkness walled by "Subcarboniferous" limestone, aided by lamps, they find the footprint. Bob remarks that, given "the shape of the heel combined with the webbed claws it may represent the human species in a reptilian stage of evolution."[23] But Roger then refers to the hypothetical creature as a "Frog man," suggesting a peculiar amphibious tie instead. Bob further speculates that the creatures may have been extinct since the Mesozoic Era (which he claims ended one million years ago). But then, startlingly, our explorers hear a live specimen's voice, sounds emanating from just beyond their tunnel!

So after blasting a hollow wall of their shaft with dynamite, they emerge into another gallery; soon fresh, muddy "Frog man" footprints are witnessed along the flooring. Finding that they've carelessly avalanched themselves in with no clear route of escape into daylight above, instead they beat a swift path leading to a vast underground lake or sea within a gigantic cavern, encircled by a sandy shore with verdant foliage, characteristic of a prehistoric age. The tableau is strangely lit by a phosphorescent glow, a "ghastly luminescence" emanating from lofty granitic deposits! This light source is also described as "radium-like excretions." Yes, radioactivity illuminates this interior realm with its radiance, wherein "some freak of stratification had entombed a remnant of an ancient world."[24] However, one wouldn't proclaim that the radioactivity is somehow responsible, causatively, for the primeval environment or the condition of its soon-to-be-encountered inhabitants.

They reach the shore of this remarkable lake (also referred to as a "sunken sea"[25]), only to spy a "sauranodon" from the Mesozoic swimming by. Mimicking newsworthy statements made by contemporary paleontologists to the press then, Bob reasons they had "indeed discovered an unturned leaf in the evolution of the earth." Roger calls it "the greatest wonderland of science ever known to mankind!"[26] Shortly, a winged beast, half-pterodactyl, half-*Archaeopteryx*, threatens the group. And then a contingent of live Frog Men arrives, who were "physically similar to gigantic frogs, standing on their hind legs ... there was a finlike appendage outside the calves, like half a fish tail."[27] But we humans do have an inherent, xenophobic hostile streak, and so soon their guns spray bullets among the amphibious welcoming party. Bob and Roger then surmise and observe that the Frog men must be intelligent. Also, as things develop, they *really* like Willa—a human female! By the middle of the book, Bob is referring to the semi-amphibious creatures as "half-ape, half-reptile savages,"[28] as if they've made an upward literary evolutionary leap. Later, they're judged as a "mongrel species of anthropoids,"[29] thus seemingly moving further up the evolutionary "ladder."

In the meantime the explorers dodge tyrannosaurs which, as in Conan Doyle's *Lost World*, hop about in kangaroo fashion. The giant dinosaurs battle pterodactyls for supremacy in this primeval setting. And a one-hundred-foot-long brontosaur struts along the beach. They decide to build a raft, naming it the *Rambler*, to explore the coastline. But the explorers are ever wary now because they realize the arch-cunning Frog men have uncovered the body of their dead comrade from its sandy grave. So basically, the explorers wantonly kill Frog men, who trail them continually now, or whenever it is convenient to do so with bullets and sticks of dynamite. Eventually, after the explorers discover an active volcano under the dome of this primeval world, the Frog men capture Willa, holding her for some special although unrealized purpose.

In a final fit of fury, war with the Frog men ensuing, Roger and Bob set off an eruption that sends steam-heated water up a fumarole, conveniently and rather predictably leading them back to the surface! Of course, they've essentially lost any evidence of their discoveries that would convince any of their colleagues. Yes—this tale is a little like *Journey to the Center of the Earth*, melded with elements from *The Lost World*, while also anticipating *Creature from the Black Lagoon* (which wouldn't be released by Universal for another two decades).

Although Tooker's story doesn't explain or rationalize the Frog men's existence in terms of the radiation they're continually exposed to in their underground lair, it is certainly suggested (as in the case of many other stories published prior to 1960) that there is a scaly, semi-amphibious humanoid creature lurking invisibly within our genetic and ancestral makeup. Underscoring this idea is a further poorly fleshed-out, yet implicit tie-in that the ancient Frog men may have evolved into local populations of Native Americans, one of whose remains is found within the cave.[30]

Karel Čapek's (1890–1938) *Válka s Mloky* (Czech, 1936; first published in USA, 1937)[31] satirically chronicled the marine, anthropoidal Newts' decisive military triumph over the human race. The Newts are described as almost black, having tails reminiscently fishlike, who can live out of water for no longer than three hours. They are highly intelligent and soon learn English. In Čapek's brilliant novel, translated into English as *War with the Newts*, prehistoric descendants of a Miocene marine anthropoid-amphibian race soon conquer the world, once mankind has afforded them with weapons and technology. Following the Newts' victory over humans, they turn their arms against one another, repeating mankind's terrible mistakes. In *War*, Čapek (who coined the term "robot" in 1921) mocked the rising Nazi regime.

And additionally, for the April 1940 issue of *Unknown*, L. Ron Hubbard, writing as

"René Lafayette," wrote a lighthearted tale about warring undersea factions of "gill-men." One spear-wielding warrior is described as having a fluked tail with short muscular arms and webbed fingers: "[H]is mouth opened and shut constantly and as it was very wide ... his ears were scarcely ears for they were backward and fanned continually in time to his mouth, evidently functioning as gills; of a nose there was no sign; his eyes were glassy and white-lidded like a shark's and abnormally large."[32] Then there's Clark Ashton Smith's short story, "Mother of Toads" (1938),[33] but by now you probably get the overall idea....

Universal's creation of another kind of "gill man" imbued with a "prehistoric" persona, reflecting human nature's raw, or "webbed," side, heightened popularity of the studio's latest monster. The first 1954 *Creature* entry perhaps owes its essence to Conan Doyle's *Lost World.* In the 1955 sequel, *Revenge of the Creature,* mirroring King Kong's second perilous wave of adventures in Manhattan following his capture, Gill Man is subjected to painful physiological testing, suffering the indignities of being placed mockingly on public display. In this entry, Gill Man pursues Helen Dobson (played by Lori Nelson). In a curious parallel, both Kong and Gill Man appear to be the last of their mysterious kind—each in peculiar ways anthropologically related to *Homo sapiens.* In both cases, and in classic monster movie tradition, it is apparent how our primitive animalistic tendencies reside barely under civilization's veneer. Or as Dr. Morgan (played by Rex Reason) metaphorically professes in *The Creature Walks Among Us,* "It's the jungle or the stars." This second *Creature* sequel (1956) may be likened to a morphing of cruel "Frankensteinic" and Wellsian *Island of Dr. Moreau* themes. And so let us consider each, thematically, in further depth.

In Universal's *Creature from the Black Lagoon* (1954), the tragic Gill Man character stalks a human female, Kay Lawrence, played by pretty "Julia" (now Julie) Adams, and even develops a fascination for her startling beauty—much like Kong did with Fay Wray two decades earlier. As Don Glut suggests, the Gill Man is "aroused" by her invasion of its waters.[34] John Baxter has stated of their underwater "ritual":

> Gliding beneath her, twisting lasciviously in a stylized representation of sexual intercourse, the creature, his movements brutally masculine and powerful, contemplates his ritual bride, though his passion does not reach its peak until the girl performs some underwater ballet movements, explicitly erotic poses that excite the Gill Man to reach out and clutch at her murmuring legs.[35]

In his *Classic Movie Monsters,* Glut also notes, "Though the Gill Man should be indifferent to a female of an alien species, he is most definitely attracted on the physical level to Kay. The implication is that there is a human being awaiting birth underneath the green scales and fins, even though he might not surface until the next 500 million years."[36] In other words, Gill Man is a terrifying manifestation of mankind's most remote evolutionary past, analogous to, yet far more prehistoric than, any species of cave man known to science. Instilled genetically, mankind has a lurid "gill man" past, leading in non-Darwinian "ladder-like" fashion directly to ourselves. In fact, a "living fossil" state is evil. For, as explained by Captain Lucas (Nestor Paiva) in *Revenge of the Creature* (1955), "The Beast exists because it is stronger than—than the thing you call evolution. In it is some force of life, a demon, driving it through millions of centuries. It does not surrender so easily to weaklings like you or me."

This idea is reinforced in the series' concluding, Dr. Moreau-like entry, *The Creature Walks Among Us* (1956). Here, scientists conclude that Gill Man has human-like, underlying tissues that may be accentuated, as one mad scientist (played by Jeff Morrow) suggests, bypassing hundreds of millions of years of intervening (contingent) evolutionary steps as recorded in the fossil record. Or as Glut states, "[W]ith some careful surgery, the Gill Man might be evolved to the next step on the scale of life."[37] Yet, like all monstrous cave men, Gill Man (although now sans gills) retains an objectionable (e.g., to us) infatuation for the beautiful Mrs. Marcia Barton (played by Leigh Snowden)! Gill Man is the most primordial "cave man" imaginable. (See Figure 17-3.)

The Gill Man quickly escalated to iconic status following its 1954 debut. Soon thinly disguised, cheaper yet interesting "copycat" movies were on the loose, such as *The She Creature* (1957); a Mexican entry, *El castillo de los monstruos* (*The Castle of the Monsters,* 1957); *The Monster of Piedras Blancas* (1959); and, although involving reptiloids rather than gill-people, *The Alligator People* (1959).[38] Other films involving aquatic humanoids of one sort of another—too numerous to mention here—continued to be made through the ensuing three decades. Presumably, if Universal ever releases its anticipated remake of *Creature from the Black Lagoon,* there will be another onslaught of filmic derivatives as well.

But besides the spate of "creature features," interestingly, there were novelizations founded on Gill Man lore. One ultra-rare collectible sought after by those who prefer such "creature comforts" is the first edition of Vargo Statten's *Creature from the Black Lagoon* (A Dragon Publication, 1954).[39] An original first edition hardcover copy was auctioned at Christie's in 2006 for $6,000!

Statten's novel begins rather conventionally in theological overtones with Earth's Creation leading to life's development, followed by a quick life-through-time summary of planetary prehistory briefly emphasizing forms of prehistoric amphibians, "some of them to be classified by future man, and some of them to remain forever unidentified."[40] Yet, if any man retains the skill and capacity to reconstruct the appearance of an extinct fossil species, surely it would be paleontologist Dr. Carl Maia, who studied deposits held within the Amazonian jungle. Maia's field assistant Tomas then finds the fossilized hand of a saurian type of man, perhaps eight feet tall, evidently of the Devonian Age. "A human bull-frog?"[41] But of course, while Maia ponders the anthropological possibilities, a living descendant of the "saurian-man" is covertly observing the team from adjacent river shallows. This part of the Amazonian jungle is later considered "Devonian" in nature.

In this, arguably the best *Creature* novelization, at one point, Statten even appears to have set things up for a (different sort of) prehistoric sequel, when Dr. Thompson muses, "I don't exactly enjoy probing around in the Devonian era. There might be *other things* besides gill-men to contend with.... It seems logical to me that if weird fishes and a gill-man can be spawned in this prehistoric area, then *anything else* is possible."[42]

The Gill Man must be seen as a modern cave-man throwback. When Kay is captured, literally swept off her feet from the deck of the *Rita* while they're trying to escape, Gill Man swims her to his grotto—an enormous volcanic cavern, in a scene that clearly takes on "cave man" ambiance. Gill Man has already killed the obsessed Mark, so Dave is its only rival. But Dave , now battling emotions over his *second* male rival, has murder on his mind; now it's a matter of "civilized" man vs. Devonian fish-man, to the death. Kay and Gill Man are able to communicate vocally, crudely, and he even brings her food, the grisly limb of some poor animal. The rescue scene, including Dave's final battle with the Gill Man, is an extended affair as detailed in the novel, well worth reading. Rocks and stones are hurled. In fact, Kay's struggle with the Creature is critical to their survival, as she wounds Gill Man with a tree branch club.

Fig 17-3: In 1956's *The Creature Walks Among Us,* Gill Man's inherent genetics permitted surgery to accentuate its more humaniform features, allowing it to breathe air directly from the atmosphere. But although the amphibious gill creature came closest to becoming human in this film, transformation of science fictional gill-creatures would never approximate the human condition or our intelligence as clearly as would later the reptiloid and dinosauroid variety of sci-fi characters. Here actor Dan Megowan wears the monster suit, and Leigh Snowden is the lady menaced, but now the object of desire.

But in the end, while Dave conscientiously calls a halt to Gill Man's immediate destruction, the monster's thoughts are of Kay: "[As] he staggered towards the edge of the Lagoon, the gill-man looked back over his shoulder. It was hard to judge his expression in the fading light. It could have been a desire for help, a look of unspeakable pain, or even a glance of wistfulness that they failed to understand each other's point of view."[43]

Additionally, several books and printed stories have appeared in fantasy fiction over the years, borrowing on the Gill Man mystique; here's a sampling of the most notable or prominent entries.

A distinctly *dinosaurian* Gillman variant slashed its way through Carl Dreadstone's *Creature from the Black Lagoon* (1977).[44] This page-turner *inspired by* the classic film (based on a story by Maurice Zimm) doesn't follow the movie script by any means, although the Amazonian setting is familiar. After spying the gigantic creature, which is 30 feet tall and has a powerful tail, scientists onboard the *Rita* debate whether the animal is prehistorical (e.g., descendant from plesiosaur or diplodocine stock), a creature from outer space, or an atomic mutant. Theories abound! Does it represent our distant future or the past? Although they name the monster *Mutantus giganticus,* its reptilian-amphibian characteristics seem predominant. Yet it defies zoological classification because it has a "tail like an ocean-going kangaroo.... The monster has two completely separate but complementary circulatory systems, one cold blooded, one hot."[45] (Recall, the mid–1970s was the height of the scientific debate over hot- versus cold-blooded dinosaur metabolism, introducing the dinosaur renaissance period, reflected in Dreadstone's novel.) Plus, *Mutantus* is highly intelligent, and in tragic, Kong- or Creature-like fashion holds strange, deadly reverence for the expedition's sole female, Kay. In the end, after the immensely strong creature has been subdued by a no less than a torpedo, Kay stares at its severed head lying on the ship's deck. "Looking down at the eye, Kay screamed repeatedly, for the eye was accusing her, reproving her. The eye was the eye of a betrayed friend."[46] Nature betrayed?

The "alien-ness" of gill-men, perhaps first entertained by Lovecraft and later merely suggested in Universal's trilogy, was further explored in a number of sci-fi publications. Here, Gill Man, not mankind nor a reptiloid-humaniform, finally vaulted from the jungle to the stars!

Fantastic Four issue nos. 97, 124 to 125 (April 1970, July–August 1972), featuring Stan Lee's "The Monster From the Lost Lagoon!,"[47] "The Return of the Monster," and "The Monster's Secret," were about a shape-shifting, alien Gill Man who crash-landed on Earth, possessing the power to convert into human form. This Gill Man is intent on protecting its mate; yet in *Fantastic Four* issue 124, the Gill Man abducts the Invisible Girl, Sue Storm, as part of a plot to rid its presumably "female" mate (Gill Woman) of a virus.

Guy N. Smith's *The Slime Beast* relates the tale of a mad scientist-archaeologist seeking King John's treasure, who instead disinters the titular, loathsome slime beast from the stars; it goes on a killing spree in the British Isles. The science fictional premise is: "[W]ell, the Russians experimented with monkeys in space, didn't they? Imagine an alien race, amphibians possibly on a distant planet, a world of mud and water. Perhaps their planet is drying up. They need to look for another. Earth has more than its fair share of the type of terrain they require to live in, so they sent the old Slime Beast as an experiment. But something went wrong, and the ship caught fire and crash-landed on the marshes ... burying its occupant in the mud.... Miraculously it's still alive."[48]

And in award-winning sci-fi author Paul Di Filippo's 2006 novel, *Creature from the Black Lagoon: Time's Black Lagoon,* scientists intent on splicing genes from legendary, although now extinct, amphibious Gill-men rely on a compact time machine to travel back into the Devonian Period, where they encounter living specimens.[49] Facing our own impending extinction due to atmospheric pollution-caused global warming, scientists realize how adapting amphibious traits—i.e., Gill-Man characteristics—would benefit descendant generations of humans surviving on a future, flooded planet after the melting of the Greenland and Antarctic icecaps. A surprise is that Di Filippo's Gill-Men originated on another planet, crash-landing on Earth during the Devonian; they're civilized and peaceful beings. However, a terrestrial viral affliction converts the colony into aggressive beasts, like the monstrous living fossil observed in the Amazon (linking to the 1954 Universal film). Soon the scientists find themselves fending off an invasion through a time portal from the Devonian directly onto the University of Rhode Island campus. Ultimately, a female tragically infected with the virus transforms into a Gill-*woman*, who for her very survival must be time-projected back into the Devonian.

Notice how familiar themes and motifs resurface, however subliminally, in one gill-man story to the next over the years? Furthermore, the *Creature*'s evolutionary flavor (perhaps secondary to the more prominent "beauty and the beast" replayed theme, with Gill Man carrying off a succession of beautiful Hollywood starlets) is distinctively modern, even though evolutionary themes have longer standing tradition in fantasy fiction (compared to film). What is more noteworthy, and until now not documented (or at least stated), however, is how compellingly amphibious humanoids became superseded, especially after the dinosaur renaissance was in full swing, during the latter 1970s.

True—the idea of "*reptile*-men" had been around at least since the 1930s; Burroughs's race of "Horibs" encountered in *Tarzan at the Earth's Core* (1930) may represent fantastic literature's inaugural example. Yet among the pantheon of famous and classic monsters, the "hideous" sun demon generally receives short shrift. The 1959 film, *The Hideous Sun Demon*, stems from a time when Hollywood producers and science fantasy writers had us inclined to believe that deep within our mysterious evolutionary past, mankind had a scaly, bipedal human-wannabe sort of ancestor. By the 1950s, as if an apish (Darwinian) ancestry wasn't unsettling enough to many, an additional assortment of scaly, long-clawed amphibious gill-men and reptiloids assaulting us from pages of the pulps or the silver screen simply held us spellbound in abject fear. But when (and why) did the popular transformation from gill-men into reptilian-men become essentially complete in sci-fi film? Perhaps part of the answer is reflected in the riddle of the Sun Demon's horrific, yet iconic countenance.

The "what if" fantastic notion that primeval beings, primitive humans and other semi-civilized classes of "humanoids" may reside within our planet's interior is a time-honored, "charter member" sci-fi theme. Therefore, to find our ancestors, long extinct on the surface world, one need "only" find the right geological shaft, perilously leading into prehistory. But what if even far closer genetic ties could be established between modern humans and the oldest ancestral lineage, say, within a laboratory setting—without having to explore deep, dark recesses of the planetary interior? How could the beast lurking within become manifested and unleashed? Biochemical tinkering and unlocking the secret of the gene might pose one promising, yet tedious direction. But isn't there another means of *suddenly* unveiling the beast, shown shockingly to be much more ancient and horrific than even our fossil apish cousins?

Although the theme of radiation increasingly became a staple of science fiction after the 1930s, it wasn't a key feature of Tooker's story, and in terms of scaly humanoid evolutionary monsters, wouldn't be optimally incorporated until *The Hideous Sun Demon* emerged in 1959. *Sun Demon* is surprisingly well scripted and acted. This old black and white remains a first-flight cult fright flick, quite intelligently conceived. It also borrows from true classics of the genre. Yes, it is a bit derivative in nature.

The titular Sun Demon creature is the opposite of a werewolf, that is, as it transforms from human into a monster (or "demon") only when exposed to the Sun's rays (as opposed to the full Moon's illumination). And the tragic character Dr. Gil McKenna (played convincingly by Robert Clarke) is also analogous to Robert Louis Stevenson's Dr. Jekyll, whose appearance and mentality become altered (essentially reverting to a lower, more base type of human) after he concocts (and unwisely samples) a chemical elixir, thus reverting into the abominable Mr. Hyde. Dr. McKenna's propensity to change by the Sun's catalyzing rays is enhanced after he is exposed to another kind of "elixir"—a strange new isotope "that never existed in nature before." (This poses a new radiation hazard from the Sun "even more dangerous than cosmic rays.") Then, not unlike King Kong, McKenna—fully transformed into a hideous Sun Demon—climbs upward atop a tall oil gas tank, from which he plummets hundreds of feet below after being shot by a policeman's bullet. (See Figure 17-4.)

But most significant for our present purposes is the underlying reason for the Sun Demon's hideous transformation, entrenched in evolutionary biology. Exposure to the new isotope's radioactivity makes possible a retro-kind of somatic evolution, *within Gil himself*. The Sun's rays then trigger a temporary transformation that becomes more permanent with each subsequent change. In other words, mad scientist McKenna's body begins to evolve backwards into a representative primeval reptilian, as man once was (or may have been). There are three devices used to suspend disbelief here. One is Dr. Stern's references to embryology. True—during the 19th century, several biologists ascribed to a (since discredited) organic evolutionary principle (deduced from study of embryos of various species at various stages of development) known as the Biogenetic Law,

Fig 17-4: In 1958's *The Hideous Sun Demon*, audiences were treated to an early glimpse of a representative of a human retro-transformed into a genetically tied reptilian precursor, as a result of exposure to radioactivity. Here Robert Clarke wears the monster suit, while menacing Nan Peterson.

in which ontogeny recapitulates phylogeny. You know ... fish into man, evolutionary ladder stuff! (Evolutionary science has moved on considerably since then!)

As an aside, utilization of the biogenetic law impacting individuals had been done before in the sci-fi pulps. Edgar Rice Burroughs employed elements of the biogenetic law in his three 1918 novels, *The Land That Time Forgot*, *The People That Time Forgot*, and *Out of Time's Abyss*. And Edmond Hamilton proceeded similarly in his 1940 short story, "The Isle of Changing Life."[50] In the case of Burroughs's stories, radiation isn't invoked as a causal factor for the rapid evolutionary changes observed on the insular Caspak. But in Hamilton's story, radium is indicated as a "brake" on the course of evolution of the organisms existing on the obscure island. But when the "most powerful radium chloride ever found"[51] is removed and depleted by human mining prospectors, evolution suddenly is allowed a chance to really take off practically overnight, like gangbusters, from jelly-like protoplasm into cave men! "In other words," one character hypothesizes, "... this island has suddenly started to catch up with the rest of the world in evolution."[52] In neither case, however, are the rapid evolutionary processes observed to be *retrograde*, as in the Sun Demon's circumstance.

A second disbelief-suspending device in *The Hideous Sun Demon* concerns a set of photographs showing mutations resulting in modern insects when subjected to extreme doses of X-rays and gamma radiation. They appear more hairy and primitive. Finally, so as to better comprehend his plight, Gil McKenna is shown browsing through an encyclopedia, particularly an illustrated entry on fossil reptiles from the Permo-Triassic through the Mesozoic Era. McKenna invokes Charles Darwin, muttering, "Darwin never even scratched the surface ... evolution backwards to the age of reptiles, half-human, half-lizard." Despairing, he realizes that unwittingly he's become a guinea pig to science. So are you totally convinced now that Gil could indeed become a hideous Sun Demon? Well, such reinforcing, substantiating material shown in the movie was as state of the art scientifically as could be mustered for such a film then (regardless of the operating budget).[53]

McKenna's unfortunate demise stems from a laboratory accident he suffered after spilling of the new isotope from its protective lead liner. He's also victimized by alcoholism. He gets involved with a floozy barfly named Trudy (played by Marilyn Monroe lookalike Nan Peterson) and gets into fist fights with an unsavory mob-type crowd. Perhaps, given his character flaws, he's had this sense of doom coming for a long time. But (like Lawrence Talbot's plight) doesn't Gil's ultimate penance seem far beyond what mortal man should have to endure?

By the 2000s, we've become quite accustomed to seeing these scaly-looking, reptilian fellows. For instance, think of *Star Trek*'s "Gorn," *Land of the Lost*'s "Sleestaks," *Dr. Who*'s "Silurians"(as presented in Malcolm Hulke's 1974 novel, *Doctor Who and the Cave-Monsters*), or scores of other intelligent "dinosauroids" so prevalent in post–1980s contemporary fiction and film.[54] What happened, and why were the amphibious gill-men eclipsed? Quite simply, a resultant of the escalating 1980s dinosaur craze was that intelligent, monster "dinosauroids" became more trendy relative to the older breed of shuffling, air-gulping gill-men monsters they supplanted. Reptile-founded stories now just seemed fresher—plus, outer space connections, only alluded to in Gill Man movies, would now (in the "space age") be fully exploited in printed fiction. It's as if gill-men had emblematically evolved into conquering, star-roving dinosaur-men. Perhaps we simply needed this transformation to happen when it did.

But the trend was already set in motion decades ago. Lovecraft (with Kenneth J. Sterling), for example, published "In the Walls of Eryx" (1939),[55] in which a colonial (human) explorer is insidiously trapped in a transparent man-killing maze, constructed for amusement by Venusian reptiloids. Later, encouraged by Carl Sagan's 1977 thought experiment,[56] paleontologist Dale Russell and sculptor Ron Seguin created an idealized, hypothetical image of a quintessential "Dinosauroid"—which conceivably could have been the dominant, technology-wielding life form on Earth today, were it not for the contingent dinosaur-killing asteroid (or comet) impact. But read on to the next chapter for more on this phenomenon.

Things had been going, well, "swimmingly" for gill-men through the 1970s. Both gill men and dinosauroids were hypothetical constructs—stimulated by evolutionary precepts. Yet, suffice it to say that as the 1980s unfolded, gill-men could not stem the rising pop-cultural tide of intrigue over (more) intelligent dinosaurs (so suffused with fascinating evolutionary implications and bearing complex messages for mankind). Increasingly, gill-people were being relegated to the backwaters by more demonic sea monsters, such as Peter Benchley's *Jaws* (1975) or Steve Alten's *Meg* (1997), concerning a giant prehistoric shark. Meanwhile a plethora of dinosauroid "lizard people" fictionally conquered outer space, either in our prehistory, or in parallel universes. By 1988, when L. Sprague de Camp and Catherine Crook de Camp published their novel *The Stones of Nomuru*, with its "stolid, single-minded, and coldly unsentimental 'Kooks,' ... what our Terran dinosaurs might have become if the Cretaceous catastrophe hadn't wiped them out,"[57] the idea of intelligent, yet sometimes monstrous and alien "dinosaur-men" had become quite standard.

Dinosauroids were projected on a more intriguing, objective (Darwinian) level, founded on the intriguing premise of (extinction/evolutionary) "contingency"[58] then pervading pop-culture on so many fronts during the 1980s. Conversely, Gill Man's simpler, more mysterious genetic ties to humanity seemed somehow more disconnected and less intellectual, if even on a hypothetical basis. According to the (non-Darwinian) conceptual ladder of evolution, dinosauroids were a "rung" above less-evolved gill-men. And so in the pop-cultural arena, dinosauroids emerged victorious.

Chapter Eighteen

That *First* Intelligence

Man and Dinosaur—forever as one!

Near the conclusion of the four-part 1991 televised Arts and Entertainment network documentary *Dinosaur!* hosted by Walter Cronkite,[1] in what nearly appears as a segment of the Syfy Channel's *Face Off* program gone out of control, a most peculiar, science fictional-looking creature fills the screen. We are startled to see a genuine Dinosauroid in-the-flesh, telling us in an ironic twist via a Dinosaur TV broadcast how it was humans who took Earth for granted, allowing dinosaur descendants to inherit the planet. Speaking in Cronkite's dubbed-in voice, the Dinosauroid is played by actress Emma Norman, donning a costume made by Peter Minister.[2] The green-skinned, three-fingered, relatively tailless, brainy reptiloid explains how millions of years ago, even "after investigating dinosaur extinctions, those clever humans were unable to see their own downfall." (See Figure 18-1.) Humans fatefully fought nuclear wars, and polluted the environment, which led to uncontrolled global warming. Feathered dinosaurs—birds—survived the human-caused catastrophe by fleeing to polar regions, eventually losing their feathers, evolving into dinosauroids, while learning the most "humble truth ... our [i.e., be it dinosaur species' or man's] existence is but a flicker on Earth." The message broadcast during this eye-opening, thought-provoking Dinosaur TV "episode" differs rather from the intent of the Dinosauroid as originally conceived in 1981 via "informed speculation."[3] Yet the televised broadcast, expressed as science fictional allegory, splendidly conjures our next topic.

To the uninitiated, there are perhaps two principal, distinctive, yet disparate forms of intelligent science fictional dinosaurs, having emerged since the early 1980s. Imagetext variety no. 1 is that of the now classic, tailless Dinosauroid. Imagetext variety no. 2 is illustrated as a militaristic raptor or deinonychid-like creature, with a tail, adorned with body armor while clutching weaponry.[4] Stories usually associated with respective imagery contrast, although in both cases descriptions are wedded to evolutionary thought experiments (sans corroborating evidence). Both imagetext varieties mirror mankind's harrowing condition, the state of our environment and civilization. Between and beyond the two generic science fictional prototypes exist myriad entertaining cases, with distinctive "natural histories," further exemplifying the human plight. Accordingly, the pop-cultural impact of intelligent dinosaurs of every persuasion has not been concisely addressed, until now.

Today, through exposures to such film fare as *Jurassic Park* (1993), most do appreciate that certain dinosaurs, particularly the smaller, sharp-taloned, carnivorous variety, could be insidiously smart. For example, think of the character Muldoon's key line in that movie, as the *Velociraptors* close in on him for the kill—"Clever girl." By then, through a remarkable dawning of scientific endeavor, popularly known as the "dinosaur renaissance" (c. 1965 to the present day), it was understood that many species of dinosaurs were not sluggish, dumb, cold-blooded brutes. However, a fascinating, if not iconic Dinosauroid unveiled in 1981, became a rather satisfying embarrassment for its designer, Dr. Dale Russell. Today, the Dinosauroid is rarely mentioned in standard dinosaur books, texts, encyclopedias, etc. Yet its haunting visage remains firmly established among the dinophile community. For proper historical context, the nature of intelligent, bipedal dino-critters emerging onto the public scene, especially in sci-fi literature, prior to the Dinosauroid's launching, should be quickly summarized.

Fig 18-1: If the 6-mile-asteroid had missed Earth, 65 million years ago, perhaps a dinosaurian descendant might have tuned in to watch this visage via special "Dinosaur TV" broadcast. This is a suitmation representation (here faithfully captured in a charcoal drawing) of the Dinosauroid imagined and sculpted by Ron Seguin for Dale Russell, created for the 1991 televised series *Dinosaur!*, hosted by Walter Cronkite (illustration by Mike Fredericks, used with permission).

One questions the originality of the bewildering technological dinosaur, reptiloid and dinosauroid array, today so prevalent within the annals of science fiction. Hasn't this all been done before? Whence spawned such menacing crypto-prehistoric creatures? Through uncanny literary convergence, the purpose of these often formidable creatures has surely evolved. As noted in Chapter Seventeen, many science fictional varieties of both scaly reptile men and web-toed amphibian men have plagued mankind since the 19th century. However, while the latter category reigned until the 1950s—having reached a pinnacle with Universal Studio's celebrated "Gill Man" filmic trilogy, beginning with *Creature from the Black Lagoon* (1954)—during the 1980s, the popularity of reptile men competitors eclipsed that of their amphibioid cousins.

Yet, in sci-fi literature (and later film), cold-blooded reptile men have been with us since at least H.G. Wells's heyday, as in his 1896 short story, "In the Abyss."[5] Here, explorers in a diving bell discover a living amphibious, undersea city–dwelling descendant form of Permo-Triassic "Theriomorpha." Then, for example, from Edgar Rice Burroughs's pterodactlyoid Mahars (*At the Earth's Core*, 1914) and bipedal Horribs (*Tarzan at the Earth's Core*, 1930), H.P. Lovecraft's alligator people described in his 1921 short story "The Nameless City," lizardmen described in A. Merritt's *The Face in the Abyss* (1931), *Dr. Who*'s 1970s "Silurians," and Frederick D. Gottfried's space-faring, fateful "Homosaurus" ("Hermes to the Ages," *Analog*, January 1980) and beyond to Harry Harrison's "Yilane" (mosasaur descendant antagonists in his trilogy of novels beginning with 1984's *West of Eden*), we witness a mounting succession of endogenous reptile or reptiloid species on the vanguard, akin to conventional dinosaurs, which are evidently intelligent to boot.[6] There are also the evidently exogenous[7] (not-of-this-Earth) varieties, which we'll come to shortly as well. Intriguingly, Burroughs foreshadowed this strange horizon, describing the origin of Horibs in his 1930 novel. "Nor did it seem to ... [Tarzan], after reflection, any more remarkable that a man-like reptile might evolve from reptiles than that birds should have done so...."[8]

Meeting Plato's definition of a man, "a biped without feathers,"[9] there was a flowering in multiplicity of intelligent "dinosaur men" (both endogenous-terrestrial and exogenous) during the 1980s, arguably because of the Dinosauroid. Why? One possibility is that dinosauroids were projected on a more intriguing, objective (Darwinian) level, founded on the premise of (extinction/evolutionary) contingency pervading pop culture on so many fronts during the 1980s. Conversely, the Universal Pictures Gill Man's simpler, more mysterious genetic ties to humanity seemed somehow less intellectual, if even on a hypothetical basis. According to the (non-Darwinian) conceptual ladder of evolution, dinosauroids were a rung above less-evolved gill-men. And so in pop-cultural arena, dinosauroids prevailed. But for present discussion, this explanation may be too simplistic.

As to the intellectual origins of the scientifically conventional Dinosauroid precursor, by 1975 we find Adrian J. Desmond writing in *The Hot-Blooded Dinosaurs*:

> The most intriguing Late Cretaceous inhabitants were the intelligent "mimics," unearthed in recent years, wide-eyed ostrich dinosaurs, and dromaeosaurids like *Deinonychus* and *Sauronithoides*, with stereo-vision functionally mated to opposable thumbs. These dinosaurs, capable of more skillful behavioural feats than any land animal hitherto, were separated from other dinosaurs by a gulf comparable to that dividing men from cows; the disparity in brain size is staggering. The potential inherent in dromaeosaurs and coelurosaurs for an explosive evolution as the Tertiary dawned cannot be doubted—who knows what new peaks the sophisticated "bird-mimics" would have attained had they survived the "Age of Mammals"? Yet, apparently, not a single breeding population of these beautiful, alert dinosaurs outlived the comparatively cumbersome and dim-witted giants.[10]

In a popular vein, Desmond's sheer "what if?" speculation paved the way to fruitful "thought experiments," composed by Carl Sagan and, later, Dale Russell.

Invoking the no-longer-supported supernova theory (which at the time Russell advocated) for Maastrichtian mass extinctions, in 1977, Sagan contemplated what the most considerably intelligent dinosaurs (i.e., "Saurornithoides"—now *Troodon*) might have evolved into had its kind not suffered extinction. Then Sagan eloquently speculated, "If the dinosaurs had not all been mysteriously extinguished some sixty-five million years ago, would the *Saurornithoides* have continued to evolve into increasingly intelligent forms? Would they have learned to hunt large mammals collectively and thus perhaps have prevented the great proliferation of mammals that followed the end of the Mesozoic Age? If it had not been for the extinction of the dinosaurs, would the dominant life forms on Earth today be descendants of *Saurornithoides*, writing and reading books, speculating on what would have happened had the mammals prevailed?"[11] Furthermore, wouldn't they have vaulted to the stars and other planets by now, millions of years before NASA's inventions? (Long before Gill Man would ever have.)

According to science fiction master Dr. Brian Stableford, "[C]ertain difficulties stand in the way of the ever popular lizard-men who figure so frequently as science fictional villains. Reptiles, having no internal temperature control, are rather limited in the amount of brain activity they can indulge in...."[12] However, the Dinosauroid's invention provided scientific authenticity for such villains to challenge human supremacy both on Earth and in Space.

No—in themselves, Sagan's musings didn't redouble the ranks of science fictional lizard/dinosaur-men. However, in 1980, an overthrowing of the supernova extinction theory certainly paved the way to heightened acceptance of such creatures.

Like none before, the 1980 asteroid impact theory proposed in *Science* by Luis and Walter Alvarez, Frank Asaro and Helen V. Michel galvanized the arena of mass extinctions science.[13] The intrepid Alvarez team offered testable predictions; their idea was eminently falsifiable. Unlike so many theories proposed prior to 1980, this was good science in the making on a sound footing and it took the media by storm! Stephen Jay Gould supported the Alvarez team, adding a philosophical notion of *contingency* to the scenario—a further "what if?" For what if, through Newtonian, heavenly workings, the impending 6-mile-diameter asteroid had instead *missed* Earth, say, by mere minutes, and the dinosaurs had indeed not perished 66 million years ago? Hardcore, mainstream scientists reinforced scientific aspects of the now proven catastrophic extermination of dinosaurs. Ostensibly, good science had never seemed so science *fictional*! Given the appealing pop-cultural climate and milieu, fascinated followers and dinophiles worldwide became receptive to further speculation and extrapolation. So, thanks to Dale Russell, ideas germinated by Desmond and Sagan resurfaced, although this time more dramatically and in new guise. The startling result was the "life-sized" Dinosauroid "restoration" sculpted by taxidermist Ron Seguin.[14]

While the Alvarez team's revolutionary asteroid theory catalyzed new dinosaur renaissance thinking on the matter, three key biological elements gave pause, invigorating the plausibility of dinosaur men such as a Dinosauroid. Here we may attribute Robert Bakker's spirited embellishment of the warm-blooded dinosaur theory, coupled with the notion that modern birds are evolutionarily derived from (warm-blooded) saurischian dinosaurs. Russell did not support Bakker then. However, in the Dinosauroid's case, Russell opined, "The elevated metabolic requirements of a large brain ... are consistent with the attainment of endothermy and the need for energy-rich food."[15] Furthermore, tailless, bipedal Dinosauroids may have had "bird-like voices," which lent themselves to language; and since their three-fingered hands had opposable thumbs, they could have used tools.

Most significantly, Russell relied upon Harry Jerison's studies of brain evolution. Jerison had introduced a metric known as "encephalization," or a ratio established between a species' brain size and body mass. A higher ratio signals greater potential for "braininess," as in the *Troodon*, or likely in its hypothetical descendant (i.e., the Dinosauroid). In a 1978 American Psychological Association presentation, Jerison commented on the eventual evolution of a hypothetical *Dromiceiomimus* "sapiens" ostrich dinosaur-man, having attained heightened intelligence owing to "useful compulsions."[16] Although Jerison's unpublished paper was then unknown to Russell, in 1982 Russell echoed Sagan: "It would be entertaining to speculate in a qualitative manner on how the descendants of *Stenonychosaurus inequalis* might have appeared had they survived the terminal Mesozoic extinctions, and achieved an encephalization quotient similar to that of *Homo sapiens*... ."[17] According to John Noble Wilford, the 4.5-foot-tall sculptural Dinosauroid resultant was not intended to represent a creature necessarily smarter than modern man,[18] although other related species—also distant descendants of "Stenonychosaurus"—could have been so imbued. Perhaps sounding a tad too "Trekkie," Russell rather controversially suggested that the human form had a "non-negligible probability" of occurring through evolutionary convergence. Intelligence—as defined by high encephalization—may recur in other species.[19] (See Figure 18-2.)

Fig 18-2: A two-part 2012 sculpture by Allen A. Debus, showing (left) a feathered *Troodon*, adjacent to a sculpted Dinosauroid, inspired by the artistry of Ron Seguin.

During the sculpting phase, Russell was tormented with self-doubt: "I was not enthusiastic about the prospect of facing my peers with a model of a highly encephalized bipedal dinosaur. Several times I nearly had it destroyed before it was cast. However Seguin was less disturbed about embarking on a project that might lie within the area of an academic 'taboo' and gave me the courage to see it through."[20] Ultimately, not all paleontologists were pleased with Russell's Dinosauroid researches. Following the Dinosauroid's unveiling, during the summer of 1981, Russell's colleagues critiqued the result, one anonymous reviewer proclaiming, "I do not see much value in the extremely speculative 'dinosauroid' discussion. Dinosaur studies today are already characterized by a prominent science fiction component."[21]

But more scientifically founded objections were also raised. Dougal Dixon stated in *The New Dinosaurs* (1988) that even if the asteroid had missed our planet 66 million years ago, any intelligence attained by a dinosaurian descendant would most likely not be anthropomorphic.[22] He questioned whether the most intelligent dinosaur species living today would be a tool-using, war-mongering animal. Besides, "Intelligence has yet to prove itself as a feature that has any evolutionary advantage at all, let alone representing the ultimate goal of evolutionary development. (The record of *Homo sapiens* as a successful long-term survivor is not good.)"[23] Wouldn't the probability for any intelligent species to have exterminated itself through environmental pollution, or following discovery of nuclear chain reactions, be perilous? In contrast to Dougal Dixon's premise, "new" dinosaurs—those surviving into modernity—may indeed attain heightened intelligence, in fictionalized, cryptozoological settings, as in Joe DeVito's and Brad Strickland's with John Michlig *Kong: King of Skull Island*

(2004).[24] Or think of *Dinotopia's* dino-denizens, and Harry Harrison's Yilane—a Dinosauroid alternative.[25]

While scientists debated such questions at scholarly symposia, sci-fi writers certainly had a field day! The key element, absent during Burroughs's and Lovecraft's heyday, was the concept of contingency, or a rolling of the dice—pure chance. Space and time were melded by the Dinosauroids' haunting visage. While by the 1980s, parallel worlds were conventional sci-fi fare, dinosauroids (term used loosely, this time) became favored denizens of alternate realities. Arguably, interest in habitable sci-fi parallel universes heightened *because of* the Russell/Seguin Dinosauroid.[26] After all, we are but manifestations of myriad probabilities, and "Everything we are or seem is but a dream, within a dream."[27] Yes—even those fascinated with UFO–alien abduction cases were influenced by the Dinosauroid!

So how did Cretaceous-Tertiary "K/T" boundary (now known as the Cretaceous-Paleogene, or K-Pg boundary) researches trigger "-roid rage"? When considering the varieties of post–1980 intelligent saurians, there's a blurring of faunal representation, stemming from terrestrial settings—to the stars. Thus it is important to distinguish the two previously mentioned imagetext varieties, with respect to their science fictional origins. As noted here, imagetext variety no. 1 is the prototypical tailless, official Dinosauroid, as conceived by Dale Russell and Ron Seguin. Imagetext ("warrior deinonychid") variety no. 2 emerged from John C. McLoughlin's brooding imagination. Both symbolic varieties resulted from the introduction of parallel universes where the asteroid (or volcano-caused) mass extinctions didn't happen 66 million years ago. At the level of popular culture, such circumstances invited us to ponder what the dinosaurian fate—however it happened, exactly—implied for man as well. For if mankind could only be encouraged to "think like a dinosaur" (or, more exactly, like a space-faring dinosauroid species most logically wielding technologies beyond man's comprehension and capabilities), as in James Patrick Kelly's 1995 titular short story, then perhaps we might survive.[28] Isn't this the true "riddle of the dinosaur"?[29]

Michael Crichton's *Jurassic Park* (1990) underscored the blight upon Nature caused by man's errant technology.[30] Here, the wielding of genetic power was likened to, yet considered more potent than, atomic power. Meanwhile, paleontologists like Scott D. Sampson proclaim, "My firm belief is that any sustainability in any meaningful form is going to be grounded in a new relationship between humans and nonhuman nature. Although it may seem counter-intuitive, those long-dead dinosaurs may just have an important role to play in forging this relationship."[31] In a world having recently witnessed a voluminous oil spill in the Gulf Coast, concentrated radiation leaking from a Japanese atomic power plant into the Pacific Ocean, on an overpopulated planet where global warming and greenhouse gasses are in everyday conversation and where angst over nuclear winter still looms—Sampson's words *speak* to us like never before.

Catastrophe and its pop-cultural reflection as disaster porn cause inescapable dread and consternation! However, the rational ecological mindset evoked by modern paleontologists, like Sampson, goes back several decades. We may reflect on that curious chain of logic stated by Jeff Goldblum's character, Ian Malcolm, in *Jurassic Park* (1993), "God creates dinosaur, God destroys dinosaur, God creates Man, Man destroys God, *Man creates dinosaur....*" Yes, but for what purpose? In our enlightened dinosaur renaissance, can the dinosaurs truly save us?

W.J.T. Mitchell's caption for a photo of the Russell/Seguin Dinosauroid model, showcased in a chapter titled "Reptilicus erectus" of his *The Last Dinosaur Book* (1998) begins "This is not an alien...."[32] Dale Russell affirms he was not consulted by Steven Spielberg for the special effects design of "E.T."[33] However, the *Encyclopedia of Extraterrestrial Encounters* (2001)—yes, there really is such a thing—contains a revealing entry on "Reptoids."[34] Here the Russell/Seguin Dinosauroid is cited as an influential "alien" design, reminiscent in alleged UFO abduction cases. While too tangential to probe here, the popcultural theme of intelligent beings—aliens vs. "dinosauroids" from outer space, or perhaps out of our remote past—not *exploiting* as in A.C. Crispin's 1984 novel *V*,[35] but *rescuing* mankind from plight, rings parallel, strikingly familiar, and evidently to certain individuals, true.[36]

Why such time-honored intrigue over the K-Pg boundary? Is it because dinosaurs are "us," and their mysterious demise forebodingly projects our precarious juggernaut?[37]

Most viscerally, we *love* dinosaurs because humans *identify* with them psychologically. This curious circumstance has been facilitated especially during the dinosaur renaissance, due to recent discoveries concerning dinosaurian social nature and their extinctions. Accordingly, a spate of intelligent, human-like dinosaurians has invaded sci-fi literature and fantasy film. The trend toward ever smarter pseudo-dinosaur-like creatures became more evident during the 1960s, at a time coincident with America's environmental movement—also synchronous with the early dawn of the dinosaur renaissance. Were, or are, this flock of faux dinosaurs ominously trying to tell us something? If dinosaurs could speak, of what would they forewarn? Well, dinosaurs of the small screen, movies and sci-fi literature have "spoken." And their message, although at times cryptic, is foreboding, looming. Whereas before, when it came to dinosaurs, huge meant *scary*, today, *smart* dinosaurs often are synonymous with scary.

Frederick D. Gottfried's "Hermes to the Ages," published half a year before the Alvarez team's "asteroid theory" appeared in print and prior to invention of the Russell/Seguin Dinosauroid, told of a humaniform, intelligent *Homosaurus* freeze-dried mummy dating from the K-Pg boundary—found on the Moon, and then restored to life! Turns out their species committed biological racial suicide. Resurrected *Homosaurus* may now *judge* us—that *second* intelligence? After all, as Gottfried proclaims, "All intelligence is an aberration."[38]

First, how or what kind of intelligence is evident in these dino-derived creatures, lizardmen? How may we categorize the many examples? Briefly, there are cases where dinosaurs' brains are controlled through transplantation processes by more intelligent human (or alien) minds. Personified dinosaurs (e.g., in the comic strip *Calvin and Hobbes*) also exist in the psyche of children, the demographic who most identify with those ruling reptiles. There are dinosaur genera known to science although depicted in fantasy fiction, displaying natural (often menacing) intelligence astonishingly beyond our expectations! Then there are those strange dinosaurians from outer space or of parallel universes, of ambiguous origin yet perhaps eerily descended from or related to terrestrial ancestors, who pilot spacecraft through the cosmos. And let's not forget that prototypical, if not metaphorical, "man-in-suitasaurus" himself—Godzilla—who after acquiring giant monster language[39] and becoming increasingly anthropomorphic, became mankind's savior just when Japan most needed such a hero's protection from environmental peril. (Yes—another underlying reason is that it's relatively easy to fit an actor inside a human-shaped lizard-man costume for a movie or TV role. Conversely, in the case of Eric Garcia's *Anonymous Rex* (2000),[40] "real" dinosaurs wearing human disguises infiltrate modern society—getting the bad guys.) The annals of post–1980s science fiction and fantasy are rife with such assorted dino-species.

The apparently smartest grouping of ancestral dinosaurs, represented by the infamous raptor breed, especially *Troodon,* catalyzed the dinosaur renaissance intelligent-dinosaur phenomenon. The famous Dinosauroid statue prepared by Dale Russell and Ron Seguin was paired with a life restoration of the "Stenonychosaurus," in a suggested evolutionary relationship difficult to decipher without proper captioning. Yet, the modern intellectual focus on intelligent dinosaurs really began with scientific considerations of *the* dinosaur, *Deinonychus* (the evolutionary cousin of "Stenonychosaurus")—which led the way toward the dinosaur renaissance. Intensified study of such species began during an early period of elevated interest and public reflection concerning Man's impact on the global environment and ecosphere—the mid–1960s and early 1970s. Curious questions naturally arose. What would descendants of such evolutionarily derived dinosaurs have become had they survived the K-Pg boundary? More intriguingly, is it possible that such dinosaurs evolved into even more intelligent, although as yet *undiscovered* genera during the Late Cretaceous, i.e., dinosaur men who indeed suffered yet inevitably succumbed to fate, as faced by Technological Man?

While the Russell/Seguin Dinosauroid was introduced as a benign, gentle and thoughtful species, soon another, yet sinister, bellicose variety of intelligent dinosaur—the *warrior deinonychid*—itself also an intellectual product of K-Pg mass extinctions study, became rooted in dinosaurian lore. Rather emblematic of Man's range of tendencies, the two opposing varieties contrast—perhaps not unlike H.G. Wells's Eloi and Morlocks, or more so Stevenson's psychological study of Jekyll and Hyde! The warrior deinonychid presages man's harrowing future, not unlike Charles Dickens's Ghost of Christmas Future (or, amusingly, like Dr. Seuss's Grinch that stole our Christmas).

For many decades, scholars, artists and laymen alike have wondered whether dinosaur-ruled civilizations could have arisen during the Mesozoic Era. In *Jurassic Park III,* for example, we learn that those devious raptors were capable of language; they were even "smarter than primates." So what else were they capable of—fictionally speaking, of course—yet mirroring alleged "*wise* man"—*Homo sapiens,* our exalted moniker?

Well, for the warrior-type specimen of intelligent dinosaur, we turn to Isaac Asimov, who in 1941 wrote a short story titled "Big Game," about a time traveler who witnesses the dinosaurs' final extermination at the claws of telepathic dinosaurs who killed all the contemporary dino-wildlife, and then using their weapons, self-exterminated.[41] Asimov's original version of the story wasn't printed until 1972, although in the midst of the Cold War he had published a more fleshed-out similar themed tale, "Day of the Hunters" (1950). In "Hunters," Asimov's time traveler utters this revealing, prophetic line: "[W]e're the second intelligence—and how the devil do you think *we're* going to end?"[42] Since then, other authors have expertly explored this theme. For example, readers have been entertained by apocalyptic dino-fiction, such as Barry B. Longyear's *The Homecoming* (1989), S.D. Howe's short story, "Wrench and Claw" (1998), and Thomas P. Hopp's 2000 novel, *Dinosaur Wars.*[43] A more recent entry is Stephen Baxter's "The Hunters of Pangaea" (2002), in which tool-using "orniths" hunt diplodoci for food, until they exhaust their resources. Baxter tantalizes—no, *condemns* with these words, "The whole of the orniths' rise and fall was contained in a few thousand years.... When they were gone, the orniths would leave no trace for human archaeologists to ponder but the puzzle of the great sauropods' abrupt vanishing, an anomalous mass extinction in the middle of the dinosaur era."[44]

Such stories, of course, mirror mankind's peril on our "Pale Blue Dot,"[45] using fictionalized dinosaurian characters and settings. Has our (too) rapidly evolving braininess, ability to (mimetically) record vital tool-making information to pass along such knowledge from one generation to the next, and knack for mastering technology and wielding doomsday weaponry outstripped our capacity and sensibility for our very survival? Do we need smart-aleck, talking dinosaurians like Godzilla or Rodan to symbolically save us from our metaphoric engines of destruction? "Do not look behind the curtain!"—or, rather, inside the dino-monster suit. For after all, what's inside isn't a fin-backed superhero, but merely a man. Can we save ourselves? Do intelligent dinosaurs represent our salvation (or damnation)?

Increasingly, intellectuals ask, "Were there ever any dinosaur civilizations and, if so, what happened to them? How similar were they to human societies?"

Artist and writer John C. McLoughlin, author of books like *Archosauria: A New Look at the Old Dinosaur* (1979) and a sci-fi novel highly relevant to our discussion, *Toolmaker Koan* (1988), tackled such ideas in his 1984 article, another thought experiment, titled "Evolutionary Bioparanoia."[46] Precociously, McLoughlin contemplated the nature of mass extinctions. For instance, in his *Archosauria,* he outlined the essence of the asteroid impact theory prior to publication of the Alvarez team's revolutionary 1980 *Science* paper![47] In "Evolutionary Bioparanoia," McLoughlin influentially depicted the prototypical warrior deinonychid form of intelligent dinosauroid. McLoughlin described "evolutionary bioparanoia" as a psychological affliction, or a "post–Darwin, post–Hiroshima disorder."[48]

Without referring to the Dinosauroid reconstruction, McLoughlin alarmingly noted parallelism between geochemistry of the Late Cretaceous K-Pg event and our modern polluting condition (exposed so meticulously by Rachel Carson and others), bordering on risk of nuclear holocaust. In fact, the great Quaternary extinction—the Sixth Extinction—has already begun. Essentially, if the potential for our self-extermination is so great, isn't it also plausible that former (technological) societies of as-yet unrecognized species of intelligent dinosaurians may have analogously self-annihilated, explaining their abrupt disappearance from the fossil record? True—McLoughlin's essay is a bit "out there," rather facetious and a rather allegorical. But through his treatment of science fictional warrior deinonychids, McLoughlin forces us to think about human peril. Like his postulated technologically competent warrior deinonychids, in a geologically short wink-of-an-eye span of 35,000 years, modern *Homo* could evolve and then abruptly disappear, leaving no direct trace to be found millions of years later! Such an outcome is possible because, while bodily/cellular evolution is Darwinian, eventually—because cultural tool-making knowledge can be handed down through many generations—mental development becomes solemnly Lamarckian. Therefore, in intelligent species, tool and weapon-making capabilities accelerate through the centuries, vastly outstripping the pace of biological evolution and accordant cerebral capacity to righteously control our worst tendencies. Furthermore, "technological progress happens exponentially, not linearly."[49] The result is a distinct mass extinctions *pattern* left for future intelligent species to ponder.

McLoughlin's pessimistic evolutionary bioparanoia is science fictionally oriented, yet not a sci-fi "story," per se. It is an illustrated warning comparing the evidence for K-Pg extinctions to those of the Quaternary. Thus far, everything we have done—save committing nuclear winter–causing self-annihilation—the intelligent, presumably warlike and polluting dinosaurs already did. Those resource-eradicating dinosaurs spared few large contemporary animals, with the exception of their own domesticated cattle—the horned ceratopsids. Telltale atomic fallout elements expected in the aftermath of our nuclear annihilation have been discovered in K-Pg boundary clays. Dinosaurs were just like us, McLoughlin suggests. Don't look in the mirror if you don't like what you see there. Referring to his illustration of a dino-warrior, McLoughlin states, "[T]his hypothetical creature is obviously a cultural toolmaker—and doesn't he look just the sort to meddle with nuclear physics to gain a political advantage?"[50] (See Figure 18-3.)

Fig 18-3: A "Warrior Deinonychid" sculpted by Allen A. Debus in 2012. See text for more on this most menacing, anthropomorphized variety of imagined dino-monsters.

McLoughlin's fascinating sci-fi novel, *Toolmaker Koan*, dramatically illustrates his philosophy.[51] A few decades hence, humans—Earth's *second* intelligence—prepare to destroy the planet in a volley of thermonuclear warheads. But a godlike machine named Charon, masquerading as the Pluto planetoid system, which has been observing our solar system for eons, strives to prevent the conflagration, so similar to what happened before to Earth's *first* intelligence. Meanwhile, we're introduced to a race of technologically competent theropodous (birdlike) dinosaurs named the "whileelin." Whileelin raised herds of ceratopsids like cattle, and trained tyrannosaurs to round 'em up like cattle dogs and cutting horses. Eventually we learn these are the same villainous creatures, that "first intelligence," which self-inflicted K-Pg mass extinctions, 66 million years ago. At that time, then, one crazed political faction aimed to destroy its adversaries by launching the infamous asteroid toward Earth, causing ... oblivion. Charon has preserved specimens of these dangerous dinosaurs in a vast spaceship; following our inevitable nuclear holocaust, they launch an attack on human survivors. Conceptually, McLoughlin's revolutionary warrior-deinonychids, and intellectual dino-derivatives, are allied to *Jurassic Park*'s crafty, "clever girls," *Velociraptors*.

Warrior deinonychid imagery was popularized in other publications, melding the extinct dino-civilization theme with that of intelligent dinosaurs of space and time, incorporating parallel universe settings, such as Harry Harrison's trilogy of novels beginning with 1984's *West of Eden*.[52] Furthermore, we see warrior theropodous dinos in sequel novelizations to Ray Bradbury's classic 1952 short story "A Sound of Thunder" written by Stephen Leigh (i.e.,

Ray Bradbury Presents Dinosaur World, 1992; *Ray Bradbury Presents Dinosaur Planet*, 1993).[53] Also, in a contingent alternate universe, militaristic utahraptor-derived monstrosities menace the Starship *Enterprise* crew in Diane Carey's *First Frontier* (1995).[54] Harry Turtledove's novel *World War: In the Balance* (1994) explored a parallel 1942 World War II setting, where Earth's military forces are attacked by alien dino-lizard invaders.[55]

Imaginative writers, or those proffering fringe ideas, would suggest that if we can't *prove* that dinosaur civilizations *didn't* exist, then indeed they must have existed. But despite appealing to long-term geological processing of sediments and scarcity of organismal preservation, absence of evidence in the fossil record does not validate former existence. In his 1993 book, *Who Lies Sleeping?: The Dinosaur Heritage and the Extinction of Man*, Mike Magee's forceful premise is reminiscent of McLoughlin's, although it seems Magee was unaware of the latter's evolutionary bioparanoia.[56] Like his predecessor, Magee projects environmental angst. Relying on a limited, convoluted chain of circumstantial evidence, Magee invokes the "Anthroposaur sapiens," the creature which caused the K-Pg mass extinctions!

In reconstructing his idea of the intelligent, Late Cretaceous *Anthroposaurus*, Magee takes his cue from Desmond and Sagan, incorporating an image of the Russell/Seguin Dinosauroid, while omitting explicit warrior-deinonychid imagery. Furthermore, Magee's vision of the Anthroposaur is conveniently equated to the famous 1982 Dinosauroid reconstruction: "Russell's conjectures give us a model, not of the impossible but the possible. Not of the hypothetical dinosauroid today but the actual anthroposaur of 66 million years ago."[57] Yet Magee's Anthroposaur is as destructive as McLoughlin's warrior deinonychid. As a result of widespread technological pollution leading to atomic war, Anthroposaurs "could have destroyed much of the life on earth at the end of the Cretaceous.... The meteor never came but the anthroposaurs fooled observers 66 million years later into believing it had, by simulating all its symptoms.... We are no different! ... Have we inherited fatal flaws from our predecessors, the dinosaurs?"[58] Alas, Magee's stimulating account received little fanfare. Is there still time to contemplate the riddle of the dinosaur?

The art, imagery and imagetext of paleocatastrophe portrayal may envelop many curious forms. Hypothetical images featuring intelligent dinosaur people are highly derived extrapolations of this paleoart theme. Arguably, the most profound and provocative paleoimagery, including pictures of the Dinosauroid and strange warrior deinonychids, probes contingent aspects of the K-Pg boundary. Without the 1980 K-Pg asteroid discovery, visual imagery, associated stories and ideas outlined in this chapter are mere fantasy, as opposed to being of harder science fictional constitution. We would think far less about these ideas, were it not for the raging success of the asteroid theory.

Every picture tells a story; the Russell-Seguin Dinosauroid is no exception. The persuasive, rhetorical nature of intelligent dinosaur images is confusing, and associated stories would be undecipherable without proper interpretation of the underlying science. The 1980 asteroid theory concerns a prehistoric environmental-ecological disaster, a theme which perhaps unsurprisingly emerged during the height of the environmental movement. The idea of environmental exploitation at the metaphorical wrath of fictional prehistoric species is not new. When properly interpreted, the dinosaur renaissance is as much about Man as it concerns dinosaurs and other prehistoric organisms and their paleoworlds.

Chapter Nineteen

When Dinosauroids Speak!

This chapter concerns two distinct kinds of dino-monsters, culled from the literary realm, which may be regarded as "dinosauroids," that are indelibly woven with fears of nuclear holocaust.

How curious that physicist Luis Alvarez (1911–1988), who in 1980 intellectually "obliterated" the last dinosaurs with an asteroid, thereby prohibiting their possible evolution into Earth-dominating, technologically proficient intelligent "dinosauroids," also was, in a sense, Godzilla's godfather. Thus, as read today, a rarely cited sci-fi novel, James Blish's *A Case of Conscience* (1958), *metaphorically* melds Alvarez's contributions to science and science fiction in a tale concerning nuclear annihilation of (alien) "dinosauroids."[1] *A Case of Conscience*, published at the height of the Cold War (the first half published in 1953 as a novella), mirrors contemporary America's atom bomb angst. In the end, an entire civilization is destroyed by Man's nuclear folly and greed. Blish's novel reflected dark and somber messages presaging our uncertain future, as mirrored in Toho's *Gojira* (1954). Yet, although inspired during that historical Godzilla-spawning period, the novel is rarely cited.

Abstractly, Luis Alvarez's ideas conceptually and intellectually link the brainy creatures dinosaurs *may have* become had they not been exterminated 66 million years ago by the asteroid (or comet) Alvarez "discovered," with fear of atomic annihilation—symbolized by Godzilla, who later evolved into filmdom's "brainiest" giant dino-monster. Few may realize that Godzilla—stemming from the Cold War monster tradition—is quite indirectly a product of Alvarez's technological prowess.

Luis Alvarez's achievements are outlined in his autobiography, *Alvarez: Adventures of a Physicist* (1987). The brilliant, consummate, Nobel Prize-winning scientist developed an explosive trigger device that allowed both the Trinity (Alamogordo test) and Nagasaki "Fat Man" fission bombs to detonate. He also flew in a B-29 bomber (*Great Artiste*) accompanying the *Enola Gay* on its fateful journey over Hiroshima, where "Little Boy" (relying on a different triggering system) was delivered on August 5, 1945. Alvarez's objective that day was to make measurements and observations of the pressure pulse and shock waves generated upon detonation. Onboard, following Hiroshima's total destruction, Alvarez wrote to his then 4-year-old son, Walter, "A single plane disguised as a friendly transport can now wipe out a city. That means to me that nations will have to get along together in a friendly fashion, or suffer the consequences."[2]

Thus, perhaps inevitably, the age of widespread nuclear bomb testing had begun! Following the two wartime attacks, in March 1954 a third "attack" on Japan occurred, resultant of the USA's hydrogen bomb detonated at Bikini Atoll. (See Chapter Nine.) Radioactive ash falling onto the Japanese fishing trawler, the *Lucky Dragon No. 5*, poisoned seamen. The incident was considered "yet another U.S. atomic attack on Japan.... That *Gojira* emerged from this environment suggests ... the extent to which the film and its message engaged with the most profound, contentious and chilling issues of the day."[3]

A quarter of a century later, Luis Alvarez, with his then geologist son Walter, detected high iridium concentrations distributed globally in 65-million-year-old sediments. They collaborated on a paper concluding that a 6-mile-diameter asteroid impact (also consistent with the possibility of an 8- to 10-mile-diameter comet collision) caused the dinosaur extinctions. Their 1980 *Science* article galvanized the earth and planetary sciences, with reverberations continuing even today. Essentially, they postulated that impact debris would have entered the stratosphere, darkening skies for months if not years, thus blocking photosynthesis and also causing temperatures to plummet during this most unlucky geological interval. Unlike prior doomsday scenarios offering explanations for dinosaur extinction, the Alvarez theory was falsifiable, and shortly came substantiation of their premise.

The trendy asteroid extinction theory also created waves of intrigue and discussion on a popular level, vastly rekindling interest in dinosaurs (and a new Godzilla movie series). But as Carl Sagan noted somberly in 1983, the Alvarez extinction scenario would be highly analogous to what mankind would suffer in the aftermath of global thermonuclear warfare—a dreadful circumstance popularly known as "nuclear winter." Thus, in pop culture, the nuclear winter scenario became interwoven with the asteroid extinction theory: the twilight of dinosaurs conflated with possible extermination of man, both "nuked" to oblivion.

As we've also noted, one curious outcome of scientific discourse over the 1980 asteroid extinction theory was philosophically founded. *What*, scientists like Sagan and paleontologist Dale Russell wondered, would the most intelligent of dinosaurs (especially such as those related to the infamous, crafty "raptor" types from the later *Jurassic Park*) have become if the asteroid or comet hadn't fallen through their fateful skies? Granted another 66 million years of uninterrupted evolution, might they not have eventually developed civilization and acquired technological expertise? Would certain derived, human-sized species—termed Dinosauroids—perhaps now be space-faring?

Technically, not all intelligent dinosaurs are "dinosauroids." In post–1980 science fictional accounts, that term refers strictly to species descended from terrestrial dinosaurs left unscathed, when the Cretaceous-Tertiary boundary asteroid or comet *missed* its target. But, clearly, 30 years before the asteroid theory's publication, writers of fantastic fiction were considering the arena of intelligent dinosaurians, even those hypothetically evolving on other worlds, as fair game. (See Figure 19-1.)

In *A Case of Conscience*, author James Blish precociously melded man's worsening futuristic nuclear plight with "dinosauroidian" destruction—profound ideas which in another light, on foreign soil, led to Godzilla's dark invention (and later re-invention).[4] For all practical purposes, such reptilian creatures—especially those in Blish's novel, known as "Lithians"—may be regarded as, if you will, "precursor" dinosauroids. Lithians resemble bipedal theropodous dinosaurs. Lithians (12 feet tall in adulthood and possessing opposable thumbs) aren't dinosauroids, per stricter definitions. However, although they haven't invented space travel yet, they're still, perhaps, emblematic of and embody all that "proper" Dinosauroids (e.g., of Russell and Sagan) theoretically aspired to be.[5]

The Lithians communicate verbally with their human guests. They're highly logical and

Fig 19-1: Two outer space "dinosauroid" examples of the many varieties, proliferating since the invention of the hydrogen bomb, would include *Star Trek*'s "Gorn" race (at right), and the intelligent dinosaurian (at left—after a painting by Darrell Sweet) from Planet Lithia in James Blish's novel, *A Case of Conscience* (illustration by *Prehistoric Times* editor and artist Mike Fredericks, used with permission).

rational (perhaps not unlike the Vulcans in *Star Trek*), yet they lack religion, a circumstance which in the year 2049 leads protagonist Father Ramon Ruiz-Sanchez to the very odd conclusion that they're satanic beings. Because of their satanic nature, Ruiz-Sanchez, a Jesuit priest who is also a biologist, proclaims that Lithia should be placed under quarantine. Yet, besides its remarkable inhabitants, Planet Lithia is highly strategic for its abundance of the light element lithium. (An intriguing appendix to the novel describes the planet's geological and paleontological history.[6]) So in contrast to Ruiz-Sanchez's preference for planetary quarantine, a colleague named Cleaver counters that, instead, Lithia's enriched lithium ore should be mined. Cleaver supports converting Lithia into a thermonuclear laboratory and production center capable of manufacturing an inexhaustible arsenal of fusion bombs! These weapons would be stockpiled for the eventuality that rogue nations on Earth would rise up in defiance of United Nations precepts.

Later, one Lithian embryo is transported back to Earth, a peculiar "gift" to Ruiz-Sanchez on the interstellar journey home. This organism, deprived of Lithian culture, rapidly grows into an irresponsible, radical-minded demon named Egtverchi. Egtverchi threatens strife and warfare among an already unstable human society that decades before found it necessary to burrow underground, sheltering itself from impending nuclear attack. Riots ensue. In the end, rioting is suppressed, but plans to build the fusion bomb plant on Lithia are not. So, using a technologically advanced super-telescope, Ruiz-Sanchez ultimately observes the allegorical runaway, *planet-wide* chain reaction that destroys Lithia entirely!

Extrapolating, let's briefly consider Luis Alvarez's penchant for engineering *huge* paroxysmal explosions, which in a sense gave rise to both science fictional dinosauroids and, indirectly, to the most intelligent classic giant dino-monster of the silver screen—Godzilla. Throughout, Luis Alvarez's mad brilliance figured prominently, ushering in the nuclear age and later a revolution in the geological sciences.

Arguably, mastermind Luis Alvarez is not unlike the fiend, Joseph Prometheus Brooks, the dark, brooding atomic scientist in Mark Jacobson's 1991 novel, *Gojiro*. Jacobson links the first atom bomb's ground zero in "The Valley of Decision" with the setting where a comet annihilating the dinosaurs impacted (*symbolically* also protagonist Gojiro's birthplace). Consider also that throughout most of Jacobson's novel, loquacious Gojiro (child of the "Heater" or his death ray) appears human-sized—like a dinosauroid. Curiously, then, this stark "Alvarez-ish" reality of nuclear bomb blasts, extinction-causing catastrophes and the prospect of intelligent dino-monsters ("dinosauroids" and such) has been abstractly explored in art, fictionally, both by Blish and Jacobson. Here, art imitates life, or is it vice versa?

Although in Mary Shelley's 1818 novel the monster was most articulate, fluent in languages, most would agree Universal Studios certainly got it right when in their 1931 production of *Frankenstein*, the monster played by Boris Karloff *didn't* speak. And many of us probably cringed when in 1965 we saw, for the first time, giant monsters (Godzilla and Rodan included) "speak" in their native "tongue," in Toho's *Ghidrah the Three-Headed Monster*.[7]

When giant monsters *speak* at the cinema—for example, as translated for us in *Ghidrah* by Mothra's diminutive singing gal pals, the "Peanuts"—we get inside their heads, learning their thoughts, hangups and feelings. For an American audience, there's a danger of intimacy with creatures that we're used to seeing rightfully destroyed. Well, over four decades later, nostalgically, I embrace *Ghidrah* and all the curious doings of its monstrous adversaries therein. And, in retrospect, what proved so abhorrent then—my favorite giant monsters *talking*—is on a far lesser plane than what has happened since, that is, in giant monster literature.[8]

While "monster-speak" scenes have been scripted only to a limited degree in the Godzilla series, there's at least one novel where Godzilla (or at least a faux-Godz named "Gojiro"—notice the "o" at the end instead of "a") is a surly, loquacious protagonist. In Mark Jacobson's rather surrealistic and satirical novel *Gojiro* (1991), the titular, introspective monster lets it all hang out loosely. But rather than feeling chagrined by its verbosity, as I did for the first time witnessing the monster-speak scene in *Ghidrah* decades ago, in an odd sense grumpy Gojiro's discourse deepens our understanding of the misunderstood movie monster, offering yet another personality dimension. This is a highly original take on our monster, congruent, thematically, with the original film series' deepest inspirations—angst over eco-awareness, atomic weaponry, and especially the men who wield such destructive power.

Before we delve into Jacobson's peculiar entry, why not ask what triggered this rather trendy, stylistic shift in giant monster literature? For example, Walter Wager's *My Side by King Kong: As Told to Walter Wager* (1976) offered a comedic "firsthand" perspective on Kong's rearing and what "really" happened during filming of RKO's 1933 classic. A few years prior to Jacobson, William Schoell's intelligent, conversant, shape-shifting "Gigantosaurus" pounded through his 1988 novel, *Saurian*. And a Gorgo-like dinosaur communicates with a much larger, sentient oceanic kraken in Sam Enthoven's fantastic 2008 novel, *Tim: Defender of the Earth*. Yet, we must perhaps hark back to John Gardner's 1971 novel, *Grendel*, named after one of our most time-honored monsters, for the literary origins of giant monster-speak.[9]

The story of Grendel dates from the period, historically, following the fall of Rome under barbarian hordes. Rising to a mere 8 to 9 feet in height, Grendel doesn't exactly qualify as a "giant" monster based on today's *daikaiju* standards[10]—yet the principles of complexly woven monster-speak inherent throughout Gardner's novel seems prerequisite to Jacobson's *Gojiro*, published 20 years later. Grendel narrates the entire novel, like the monster did in several chapters of Mary Shelley's *Frankenstein*. Cynical Grendel converses with human foes and a haughty, ancient and deterministically philosophical winged Dragon who can see throughout all time. Gardner's *Grendel* is an impressive and acclaimed work of literature. This is essentially a modern "My Side" telling of the tale of what happened to the vile, man-eating monster from the mere, originally recorded in the epic Norse poem, *Beowulf*.

Indeed, critics have compared Gardner's monster Grendel to King Kong. For example, Grendel is considered by scholar Joseph Andriano to represent a lesser evolved form of ape-man, or *our* inner bestial self. Grendel's origins are unclear, because his "water hag" mother is a survivor of the deluge; she in turn coupled with "some unknown being—the devil? The dragon? A bear? A man?—to give birth to Grendel." Like Gardner's Grendel, Jacobson's Gojiro is plagued by the fact that he is the only one of his kind. Grendel also becomes the "brute existent by which [humans] learn to define themselves."[11] Likewise, Jacobson's anthropogenic Gojiro mirrors human plight.

Most likely for copyright reasons, Jacobson never uses words like "Gojira" or "Godzilla" in his novel *Gojiro*. Instead, it's as if the rubber suit itself came to life! Yet this Gojiro has a triple ring pattern emblazoned on his chest, branding Jacobson's *daikaiju* one apart from Toho's commercial variety. Names of Toho's other famous monsters—e.g., Rodan, Mothra, Ghidrah—do not appear. Gojiro's sidekick isn't another giant monster, but instead a boy named "Komodo—the Coma boy," who awakened from a prolonged coma following exposure to Hiroshima's nuclear radiation. As Komodo proclaims, "Our fates are intertwined into a common identity. One cannot proceed without the other."[12] While, in the novel, Gojiro is a B movie star, who calls Radiation Island his home, author Jacobson's references to Toho's movieland Godzilla are merely swiping and peripheral. Still, it's pretty obvious who Gojiro—often referring to his "G-fans" as "zard-pards" (i.e., lizard partners)—is supposed to be. If Godzilla were really alive, we read what he might cynically say about his filmic popularity.

Fifty-ton Gojiro, sporting huge "dorsals" and having a "blue-collar" persona, has human intelligence due to the heightened development of his "quadcameral" mind. The quadcameral part of his brain is the "compendium of Life's great march from the days of the reptilian up through the mammalian limbic belt.... The quadcameral was unique among minds. It was the wellspring of Cosmo, the citadel of Evollooic Thought! The Four-Tiered Oracle!"[13] He alters his quadcam perception, though, by getting high ingesting chunks of Uranium 235, or sometimes "rotgut" U-238. Stoned, mentally distorted, or not, Gojiro comments shrewdly on such matters as environmental pollution, mass destruction, nuclear weaponry and the excesses of Hollywood. Editorializing from his unique perspective, Gojiro has a dim view of American society, and is preoccupied with evolution's mystic power.

Besides his powerful "irradi-breath," Gojiro can also shrink himself to human or toy size, and has an extrasensory power of empathetic projection, which he struggles to control, allowing him to connect telepathically with Komodo and others invading the corners of his quadcameral.

Meanwhile, Komodo's mad-scientist leanings often come to the fore, as he dabbles in numerous bioengineering experiments. Utilizing a full-sized, functioning walk-in quadcameral model, not only does he tinker with the interstices of Gojiro's mind, but Komodo also attempts to restock the planet with extinct creatures such as the Dodo, the Quagga and giant ground sloths. The problem with such "reanimation jobs," now surviving in the Zoo of Shame, however, is that their former worlds have passed on and so they're disconnected from the Evolloo's "Beamic" flow. The lesson learned is that mankind is "pro" at causing extinctions, because "that's why people were invented."[14] But when Gojiro attempts to destroy Komodo's unnatural freaks of nature with a fatal blast of irradi-breath, taking proper responsibility for our dismal, unintended creations, Komodo declares, "No ... perhaps we should not have given them life, but it is not our place to destroy them. Their fate is now beyond our hands...."[15]

A key message here is that regardless of origin—unnatural (e.g., mutations, abominations or *Jurassic Park*–like anachronisms caused by human experimentation) vs. natural (i.e., generated in the "Evolloo")—all life has a place! And how can we distinguish what is truly "natural"? Like Frankenstein's tragic monster, Gojiro is still a *product* of sinister human (natural) invention, although now rejected and isolated from the natural world.

For years, Komodo, Gojiro and the Atoms (who are children mutated by radiation who simply "arrive" on the shore), live in relative harmony on Radiation Island. In Twilight-Zonish fashion, Radiation Island is protected from the outer oceanic environs by "Cloudcover," or, "that grayish Astrodome that encased their world like a tarnished platter surrounds a cooked goose. It was nothing solid, no jut of geology with weight and properties. Instead, it was an angry wall of heat, a sheer blare, a space-age Styx. So much had come through that fevered curtain, but nothing had ever gotten out."[16] Under metaphoric Cloudcover's skies, flotsam builds up from afar "whenever the fissions and fusions were busy...."—that is, during heightened periods of atomic weapons testing.

For amusement, Gojiro—ensconced in his bachelor pad underlying the island volcano—watches movies broadcast on his wraparound dish screen. He and pal Komodo also film home movies, which a notorious character, Shig, one of the first "Atoms" to arrive, smuggles to Hollywood and fame. There is much filmic "versus" humor sprinkled throughout the novel, as Gojiro and Komodo make movies with titles such as *Gojiro vs. the Enigmatic-Inking Squid at the Rock of Knowledge*. These became Hollywood movie releases, making Gojiro a B-star, hence Gojiro's celebrity status overseas.

Stylistically, Jacobson explains that one-of-a-kind Gojiro has become suicidal, despite the "Triple Ring Promise," an oath he took with Komodo some years before, essentially meaning that only together shall they seek answers about the world, and that they shall do together whatever they accomplish. Gojiro's anguished because he doesn't remember what exactly happened to him: "Just that I used to be one way, and now I'm like this."[17] Mortified by his awful appearance—the 500-foot-tall, mutated "radioactive cancer" that he has become—Gojiro despairs because he cannot kill himself, because a reflex of the reptilian "zard" part of his brain prevents self-annihilation.

Cathartically concentrating, from the depths of his weary soul and quadcameral mind, Gojiro summons his Muse, Budd Hazard, or the "Cosmo-zard," who "knows the secret of the Endless (evolutionary) Chain ... the present and the past, He knows who be first and who be last. He knows what is green and what is blue, and what goes down in the Evolloo."[18] Drifting into a trance-like projection or séance, with Komodo taking copious notes, Gojiro probes the meaning of existence from these "Budd Hazard sessions." This is how they learn of the "all-encompassing system called the Evolloo," or their understanding of the "Beam," or in other words, the normal stream of life-through-time, evolutionary development—within or from the perspective of which, disturbingly, Gojiro can't reconcile his existence because of his mutated condition. The all-encompassing, yet mystic Evolloo "covers Fate like paper covers rock."[19] Gojiro ponders the Muse's deciphering of the Inviolate Binary, a tendency for "all life to seek its particular identity." And he marvels at the evolutionary chain catalyzed by the energetic "Beam" creating new species (known as the "Bunch"). But the "most central point" of all is "Reprimordialization," the mysterious "'engine of the Evolloo,' a continuous unending series of 'invisible instants' during which Beamic energy cleaved to create new Bunches therefore springing forth 'more life, different and unique.'"[20] Does this have anything to do with the creature Gojiro once was at the invisible instant when irradiated by the Heater?

Gojiro is a child of "The Heater," which is the nuclear furnace created in 1945 by former nemesis, demented fictional nuclear scientist Joseph Prometheus Brooks, in this novel—brainchild of the atom bomb. Gradually, Gojiro learns that Brooks (described as an "apparition in black, set down on the earth by demonic forces to torment the planet"[21]) is responsible for preventing him from attaining Varanid monitor maturity with understanding of self-identity—instead, exposing Gojiro to the radioactive Cloud, and therefore isolating and preventing him from progressing along the "Beamic flow" of the Evoloo. Thus, former "zard-plebe" Gojiro could not advance in the natural order.

Profoundly inspired by the Muse, yet haunted by nightmares conjured by his quadcameral, Gojiro despairs because he doesn't understand *his* origin. He cannot establish his rightful identity, or, as a Child of the Heater, even comprehend the meaning of his existence. Gojiro yearns to understand what happened to him—*he,* the reclusive mutant, who was once a happy 'tile (e.g., reptile) basking on Lavarock in the Pacific sun. He needed to know "how he'd come to be this thing he was." Forlorn Gojiro is "bereft of Beam and Bunch,"[22] as are all of Radiation Island's infinitely mutated recombinate organismic possibilities. And regardless of origin, don't we all commonly seek to understand the *contingency* of our origins and fate?

Gojiro and Komodo have been scarred both physically and psychologically. Now the Triple Ring Promise as originally articulated is no longer sufficient; it must be amended, redirected to the goal of determining "who we are ... where we come from ... what we will be."[23] This is one of our most fundamental human traits, the search for self-identity. So, in penetrating through Cloudcover warp, they begin a quest seeking answers to their fundamental questions. But if they don't find answers within one year—they'll dejectedly end their lives. Once in Hollywood they expect to make a new film titled *Gojiro vs. Joseph Prometheus Brooks in the Valley of Decision,* seemingly central to their quest. And so it will be.

When they arrive in southern California, they encounter a number of peculiar individuals, including Sheila Brooks, daughter of Joseph Prometheus Brooks, who summoned them with her letter. An interesting exchange takes place between Komodo and a film critic during a soiree. They debate Gojiro's intrinsic nature, the critic claiming he is "reptilian. A Moby Dick with scales." Komodo, not about to be outdone, defiantly retorts, "Something like Moby Dick ... but there are differences. For instance, Gojiro is green. Moby Dick was white." Furthermore, this is "not the green of the windswept sea, nor the green of the most fertile lichens growing in the emerald forests, nor the green of the sturdy pine. Just the opposite. The green of Gojiro is the green that is too well known. It is the green of the slick left by a malfunctioning motorcraft in a previously pristine lake. The green of the dacron weave, the green of a garish paint chip in a homemaker's catalog, the curious green of a jungle resurging from defoliation.... His is the color that God never splashed upon the spectrum. His is the green of men. The green we have created. That is the greenness of Gojiro."[24] Anthropomorphic Gojiro is a mirror of mankind's dark and misguided tendencies, as is Godzilla in *Gojira* (1954). Furthermore, in a later passage, Joseph Prometheus Brooks is likened to *Moby-Dick*'s Ahab.

But aside from any comparisons to mythical Moby Dick, Gojiro is symbolically "us," everyman. Shrunken to human child size, Gojiro gets ticked off at reckless drivers in Hollywood, as we would. Witnessing the smog and emptiness of Hollywood, Gojiro's true monster (i.e., Godzillean) persona is prompted: "Be better if this place was smashed flat." He "decided there wasn't anything wrong with the town that a little radicalized urban renewal wouldn't cure." Angrily jostled in his seatbelt, he fantasizes about growing to full size, then smashing the Capitol Records tower, prying stars out of the Walk of Fame, and then triggering a huge earthquake along the San Andreas with a perfectly placed stomp. "A seethe of excitement came over Gojiro. To be bad. To be *really* bad. To show the sapiens once and for all. To ... to stand before them a *true* monster, a destroyer without conscience, a dark shadow across landscapes, dorsals silhouetted in the flaming destruction he wreaked, immune to weapons, beyond the reach of fevered prayers, remorseless, unstoppable. A killing machine, tearing ships from the sea ... ripping bodies between his cutting teeth." In the end, however, he restrains himself after realizing there is no way to destroy the essence of such a diffuse sprawling place, lacking an Empire State Building to climb or an Eiffel Tower to snap—nothing to "break its will with a swift and symbolic act."[25]

Finally arriving in the Encrucijada Valley of Decision, setting of the first atomic test in 1945, it dawns upon Gojiro and Komodo that the site of the initial Heater blast—its birthplace—was strangely *also* where a comet impacted 66 million years ago, this the era-ending, dinosaur extinctions–causing cosmic impact. The uncanny coincidence is enough to send shivers down your dorsals! It is here, in a metaphorical egg-shaped cavern underlying the valley where an in-ground nuclear test occurred, that Gojiro gets really stoned on U-235, then has a magnificent ("beamic") flashback, a "waking dream" whisking him backward through geological time. This psychic Beam melds evolutionary with geological history. Gojiro's desperate search for self-identity propels his mind into Time's abyss. The extended passage is nicely done, and for those of you who have enjoyed Jules Verne's *Journey to the Center of the Earth*, it recalls and pays homage to Axel's magnificent central waking dream.[26] Incidentally, references to eggs and hatching sprinkled throughout the novel foreshadow Gojiro's metaphorical rebirth.

Another curious connection between "Beam" and the Encrucijada Valley is that there is oil underlying the location where the comet crashed ... oil ("blood from the earth") formed by myriad dinosaur deaths so long ago. And as Komodo realizes, the "Beam" that mysteriously drew them and specter-like Joseph Prometheus Brooks (and his weird Vampyra-like daughter Sheila) to the Valley "comes from oil."[27] This is also where the original "Zard" line spawned, whence from "a single pair of cells, a whole new world" arose.[28] Now certain death reigns in the Valley of Decision. But what is to be decided here?

Although propelled via Beamic energies fueled by U-235, enabling him to witness his remote ancestors, Gojiro ultimately despairs. "Sure, he'd spun back through every eon, but ... had he ever felt the succoring commonality of the group? Had he ever—through the nightmare visions of Saurian death, the muggings by furball marauders, or even during the relatively sedate eras of basking and burrowbuilding—felt himself woven into the magnificent tapestry of the Zardic Bunch? ... no. Not for a single moment.... Everything he did was as a loner, a solitary figure.... A Beam for him alone? One of a kind?"[29] At the (nuclear) core of the matter and responsible for his (beamic) isolation is catatonic Joseph Prometheus Brooks, who stands dreadfully in the Valley of Decision.

To Gojiro, Joseph Prometheus Brooks's crime is what mankind was *fated* to do ever since Olduvai. This is our repugnant outcome, our Child—the nature-destroying, Evolloo-stymieing hellish Heater. Mad scientist Komodo, who is an eternal optimist and a kind, emotional person at that, may be contrasted with the irrational Brooks. For decades ago, crazy Brooks willed an even larger explosion on Gojiro's Lavarock, of sufficient *excessive* magnitude such that the scientists could blasphemously witness the face of God! This is tantamount to premeditated murder. Brooks is a mad scientist in the extreme, as we may glean from this horrifying passage. Brooks had failed because he was unable to "make Him look at us. So we might see His face.... There is only one thing we can do to get His attention. We must threaten *all* creation. We must harness the power to extinguish every light, to obliterate every blade of grass. Ultimate destruction is the only path to ultimate redemption. He will show His face when everything is at stake, and only then."[30] And so now, the quixotic B-film possibility that sparked their quest to the Valley of Decision takes on stark reality. For Gojiro—as supreme defender of the Evolloo—must prevail absolutely over Joseph Prometheus Brooks, who has derived a *new* physics equation on his vile blackboard, threatening an irreversible and terminal Crisis of the Evolloo. (In a sense, think of Earth-protector Godzilla beginning with his later 1960s films, although responding to a dark-lord threat vibrant in the *Star Wars* "Force.")

This is the ultimate, near-psychedelic battle of monsters ("King of Monsters" Gojiro vs. "World-shatterer" Brooks) with more at stake for humans and the rest of life on Planet Earth than in any of the Godzilla movies. This is Life vs. Death—total annihilation. For a quantum-cosmological event threatening the "Evolloo" that would amaze even the likes of Stephen Hawking must now be averted! Who will prevail? Will self-loathing Gojiro make the righteous decision? Up on a distant cliff, Shig's movie camera rolls, of course, capturing the intense action for the later-to-be-released blockbuster.

And so, as the monster rears to full height, godlike, looming 500 feet over catatonic Prometheus Brooks in the fated Valley of Decision, at the singular moment of salvation, Gojiro's quadcameral mind saves the day. The Triple Ring Promise binding Komodo and Gojiro is fulfilled. Through a kind of total reprimordialization filtered through Gojiro's quadcameral, there is renewed hope and optimism in the world and no need for despairing suicidal actions after all. And through his heroism, Gojiro's collective "zardic" genetic memory is restored. At last, he comprehends his past and true identity and purpose.

Gojiro, so imbued with self-awareness, on a noble "know thyself" quest (like Gardner's Grendel) differs considerably from other kinds of giant monster sci-fi writings, such as Marc Cerasini's Godzilla novels.[31] According to Nancy Anisfield, *Gojiro* is the "next logical step in the Godzilla series—the evolution of a classic movie monster."[32] Jacobson's personalized and distinctively *American* take on Godzilla's persona is the most original, stylistic *and* insightful you'll probably ever know.

Lesson learned? When dino-monsters and dinosauroids speak, we'd best listen.

Epilogue

"I cringe every time I read that this failed business, or that defeated team, has become a dinosaur in succumbing to progress. *Dinosaur* should be a term of praise, not opprobrium. Dinosaurs reigned for more than 100 million years and died through no fault of their own. *Homo sapiens* is nowhere near a million years old, and has limited prospects, entirely self-imposed, for extended geological longevity."—Stephen Jay Gould, *Dinosaur in a Haystack*, 1995[1]

In this book we've entertained a broad, at times esoteric, spectrum of perspectives on dinosaurian and pseudo-dinosaurian manifestations ultimately derived from a scientific foundation, both from the literary realm and from striking visual elements, covering two centuries of intrigue. Lizard-men and humaniform reptiloids complement this picture, because—in the guise of "dinosauroids"—they're derived from dinosaurian mass extinctions theory. Sometimes I've relied upon classic examples reigning in some capacity throughout popular culture, while at other times resorting to, well, less sophisticated, or even cryptic examples. Such a continuum is welcome here as each example may be regarded as a record of its time.

The resultant remains relevant today because, as W.J.T. Mitchell opined in 1998, "The dinosaur is no longer an exotic, unfamiliar novelty; it is now the most publicized animal image on the planet."[2] Why? Crass, blatant, financially fueled excesses may lie at the core. In recent decades, successful commercial undertakings (dinosaur toys, books, T-shirts, trading cards, etc.) may explain our heightened familiarity with the variety of dinosaur types known to science and moviegoers. But in itself the availability of toys, collectibles and miscellaneous dino-kitsch doesn't explain our apparent psychological "need" for dino-consolation—given our overall similarities—or even an occasional dinosaurian "intervention."

The title of this book, *Dinosaurs Ever Evolving*, is mischievously deceiving; it is not a reference to the three familiar geological periods of the Mesozoic Era (Triassic, Jurassic and Cretaceous). Instead, as we may now surmise, it has everything to do with how dinosaurs (a term used *quite* loosely throughout, given the range of prehistoria considered overall) were perceived principally by the public during successive historical periods spanning two centuries. It's about what dinosaurs mainly "meant" to people during three distinct phases of collective cultural history, as vested within the subconscious, or literal, mind's eye. It's about the dinosaurs' imaginative impact.

During the heyday of the life-through-time age of dinosaurian intrigue, a century ago, the mystery of what dinosaurs were and what they rightfully should represent in the form of magnificent mural restorations and impressive reconstructed museum skeletons in their classic poses was read in social context, and was sufficiently captivating. Dinosaurs were certainly real and successful former biological denizens of our planet, yet it was difficult to pin down how they actually appeared in life and deduce why they vacated their reign on Earth. While they were most certainly scientific objects, by the 1930s, through advertising and other visual cues, their appeal, especially influential to children, was becoming noticed by entrepreneurs. This was also the period when famed writers and movie producers strove to establish and exploit their niche, pop-culturally, in geological time—and in relation to evolution of other paleo-organisms. Thus, there were evolutionary science fiction novels such as Edgar Rice Burroughs's *The Land That Time Forgot* (1918), or Max Fleischer's film documentary *Evolution* (1923), to dwell upon. From there in ensuing decades, "real" dinosaurs moved on to further, more famous filmic roles and became stars in scores of science fictional tales. Meanwhile, trips to see the more scientifically accurate dinosaurs (and other prehistoric animals) represented in local museums will forever satisfy the hearts of young and old.

Until the mid–20th century, the very *idea* of prehistoric animals (eventually showcasing and favoring dinosaurs over paleo-mammals by the mid–1930s) became mainly interwoven with the foreboding, sublime vastness of geological time and evolutionary ideals (or to a lesser extent, catastrophic extinction problems). In the dawning atomic age, Zallinger's 1947 mural *The Age of Reptiles* became the apotheosis of how life through geological time was imagined, with its emphasis on dinosaurs and volcanic doom. Later, in the wake of the early 1950s hydrogen bomb tests with subsequent concerns for man's adverse impact on our environment, extinction matters became increasingly prominent, as the most illustrious faux-dinosaurian mutations of the Cold War period warned us of our folly; tampering with Nature, threatening civilization's fragile fabric. Then, particularly following publication of the most scientifically sensible and robust theory accounting for the dinosaurs' mass extinction, by 1980, intelligent, human-sized, hypothetical dinosaurian extrapolations proliferated throughout a host of science fiction stories and visual media, becoming conventionalized figures—this, just as America's relations with the Soviet Union dimmed and threat of a "nuclear winter" (likened to the K/Pg "impact winter") was looming. Accordingly, in charting the dinosaurian odyssey through the three successive phases, I have selected a disparate range of examples, comprising both imaginative verbal as well as certain visual forms (e.g., movies).

Ralph O'Connor has noted a key difference between more scientifically leaning visual restorations of dinosaurs (reasoning which may also be applied to other kinds of extinct, non-dinosaurian fossil vertebrates) and verbal restorations: "A full-scale pictorial restoration serves up all the visual ingredients, leaving the artist open to criticism from all sides; but a verbal restoration recalls the case of Schrodinger's cat, with the image of the dinosaur floating in a kind of superimposed quantum state, compelling the reader to complete the picture in the mind's eye."[3] Of course, the middle, melded ground is "imagetext," combining the visual with textual information.

Indeed, our perception and image of "real" (e.g., museum) dinosaurs and other genera of prehistoric vertebrates as well, shifts, sometimes in rather a protean fashion, depending upon the latest evidence, as interpreted, and resulting theories. Scientifically, dinosaur renaissance–era prehistoria, for example, do appear quite differently from those perceived during Victorian times.[4] Most paleontologists would view the history of dinosaurian images (in various forms of paleoart, paleoimagery, or other imagetext including verbal restorations and literary descriptions), in a more "purely scientific," threefold linear sense of "progressive evolution."[5] These three stages in dinosaur images include the following (as cited in Mitchell, 1999):

1. The "Victorian" or early modern era (1840–1900), a period of eclecticism inaugurated by (Benjamin Waterhouse) Hawkins's "antediluvian monsters," in which dinosaurs are depicted in a variety of shapes reminiscent of reptiles, lizards, dragons, large mammals, birds, fishes, kangaroos, and amphibians.
2. The period of what Stephen Jay Gould calls "the modern consensus" (1900–1960), when dinosaurs take on their "classic" and still popular image as "swamp-bound monsters of sluggish disposition, plodding with somnolent strides ... dimwitted and unresponsive to change" on a slow path to extinction.
3. The period of the "dinosaur renaissance" since the 1960s, which has transformed the image of the dinosaur into that of a lively, intelligent, agile, birdlike, warm-blooded creature that works in groups to solve problems.[6]

With slight modification, although intending to be *more inclusive* to images of other kinds of extinct organisms besides only dinosaurs, this is essentially the general outline ascribed to in the 2002 volume *Paleoimagery*.[7] But therein I also divided the dinosaur renaissance period into three shorter stages, culminating in the recent, post–1996 "feather revolution."[8]

In 1987, Dale Russell stated, "Artists are the eyes of paleontologists, and paintings are the windows through which nonspecialists can see the dinosaurian world."[9] However, W.J.T. Mitchell disputes whether the mind's eye—*as perceived by paleontologists*—is the most correct, reliable, or objective perspective for framing the meaning of dinosaur images. Mitchell views this complicated, loaded history in dinosaurian iconology differently, countering Russell's claims, in noting that the standard tripartite history excludes significant sociocultural historical elements.

Mitchell also notes that paleoartists are not "eyes," and that paleontologists are human beings, not coldly objective automatons hardwired to resolve scientific questions only via pure logic—like *Star Trek*'s Mr. Spock. (Think of Osborn's odd perspectives and ideals on extinction processes in Chapter Four, for example, a product of his cultural age and exalted social status.) Mitchell further explains that even if the paleo-images conceived by artists working with paleontologists were "'windows through which nonspecialists can see the dinosaurian world' (which they clearly are not), those nonspecialists would also be coming to those windows not with pure, innocent eyes, but with preconceptions, fantasies, and prejudices much like those shared by the scientists and artists."[10] Instead, it is suggested that a history of dinosaur imagetext, which must incorporate both visual portrayals and verbal restorations per O'Connor, cannot properly be considered as disconnected from the history of mankind's woes, triumphs and endeavors throughout the past tumultuous two centuries, the period corresponding to discovery, theoretical treatment and elucidation of those ubiquitous, fascinating, yet mysterious dinosaurs.

In Mitchell's "Schematic History of Dinosaur Images," also referred to as a "historical tableau of the evolution of the dinosaur image,"[11] there are also three "periods," although corresponding to (1) from the American Revolution of the Civil War, (2) from the Gilded Age to the Depression, and (3) from World War II to end of the Cold War. In particular, his third period emphasizes the *Jurassic Park* "chaos theory" phenomenon, while the key "narrative" for his first period—Jules Verne—indeed represents an early life-through-time representation, left unrecognized. Mitchell's three periods evolved through a process of "cultural selection."[12] However, both Mitchell's idea and the standard threefold "progressive evolution" (see above) contrast with the three scientifically founded and technologically/psychologically driven "ages" outlined in this book, instead characterized by punctuated evolutionary transformations in the derivation of new conceptual interpretations of prehistoric monsters and their implicit or stated messaging via paleoimagery, verbal restorations or imagetext. Mitchell's thesis applies principally to dinosaur images, whereas here, consideration of meaning and metaphor within their two-century-old odyssey is not exclusively reliant on images or visual cues that are technically or specifically dinosaurs. For instance, as we have noted in the case of popular culture, published novels and stories concerning giant dino-monsters, other (non-dinosaurian) paleo-monsters and extinction theories are clearly relevant too.

Despite Mitchell's claims, science remains foundational, both toward comprehending the dinosaurian odyssey and in regard to our present dilemma as divulged by the dinosaur. While it has not been my aim to plot such a detailed course of human history in the context of the dinosaur, we have witnessed the result, macroscopically: a rather benign omnipresence throughout their first twelve decades or so of understanding as characterized in scores of, and wide variety in, popular life-through-geological-time portrayals (more than can be represented here), punctuated during wartime development of nuclear weapons and concomitant concerns for the environment when dinosaurs suddenly (yet necessarily) "evolve" into more monstrous or captivating, intelligent humaniform-reptiloid creatures, harbingers of possible forthcoming cataclysm—presaging our fate if *this* goes on.

Irrespective of media type, among the pantheon of dinosaurian "types" encountered throughout their historical reign in popular culture, we find that they correspond to several groupings, thematically. We may chart their first appearances in relation to their three "ages" as assigned here. While the most popular, steadfast theme remains comprehending the science and "correct" restoration of real dinosaurs as they lived during the Mesozoic, today a vastly more provocative theme invokes fictional exploits of a variety of intelligent dinosaur genera. Real dinosaurs' scientific transformation through the recent dinosaur renaissance decades has been dramatic and logically fulfilling to paleontologists and layman enthusiasts alike, presenting rhetorical statements concerning these ancient creatures in relation to prevailing cultural views such as their relevance to human society. Still, such intrigue over proper (theoretical) representation of real dinosaurs known to science may seem prosaic when compared to how hypothetical dino-monsters of science fiction and horror have outstripped and irrevocably shifted perspectives concerning our scaly reptilian cousins. Why? For better or worse, because the latter, deliberately fictionalized grouping especially mimics and mirrors human intentions and inclinations. Thus, moving onward from the real museum dinosaurs known to science, let's consider a plausible classification.

By the early years of the Cold War period, mankind's darkest tendencies, with recognition of where geopolitical matters could lead during our lifetimes, had been exemplified, and so the time was ripe for new, patently different kinds of (mutated) "impossible" dino-creatures, ones that would really get in our face, challenging us and tormenting our psyche—for our own damn good. As discussed in Part II, this was the dawn of the Godzillean era of giant dino-monster movie making, but also incorporating other menacing creatures such as the Rhedosaurus, Rodan, Gorgo and Paleosaurus, to name a few. This is generally familiar territory for monster movie buffs and, as in the case of life-through-time considerations, throughout this book I've highlighted several *relatively unexplored* aspects. But the cinematic variety of dino-monsters merit their own quasi-classification as well.

Accordingly, vertebrate paleontologist Jose Luis Sanz offers a useful, yet loosely applied classification scheme for these famous giant monsters of filmdom in his *Starring T. Rex!* First, there are the already discussed "real dinosaurs," and dinosauroids, a term "proposed for the dinosaurs of cinema whose appearance clearly differs from that suggested by the available scientific knowledge."[13] Sanz further subdivides dinosauroids into three giant-sized categories, which he has named "paradinosauroids," "sauriodinosauroids," and "dragodinosauroids." The quadrupedal, relatively short-necked and carnivorous Rhedosaurus is an example of a paradinosauroid, as is—per its physical description—the titular beast in William Schoell's 1988 novel *Saurian.*[14] Sauriodinosauroids are based upon the general lizard framework—typically created for movies by applying prosthetics such as fins and horns to real reptiles. Dragodinosauroids are typically those draconian, sometimes fire-breathing, invulnerable monsters, such as Godzilla, portrayed by a human actor inside a monster suit, "which have made possible the development of one of the richest and most complex strands of mythology within dinosaur cinema."[15] (However, note my particular spin on the definition of "dinosauroid" per Chapter Eighteen and as further detailed below.)

Many of the dinosauroids as categorized by Sanz are also popularly known as "kaiju," "daikaiju," or "kaiju eiga"—commonly known as mysterious giant monsters and beasts, and usually associated with Japan's Toho and Daiei film studios. Of course we've already explored the pseudo-dinosaurian roots of giant dino-monsters like Godzilla and Anguirus in Chapter Ten, and Gorgo in Chapter Twelve. But what exactly could be regarded as "kaiju," as J.D. Lees suggested in 2007? To Lees, in order to be kaiju, the following three criteria must be met: "(1.) Its size must be beyond the upper limit of natural and enable the entity to destroy buildings. (2.) It must present a menacing aspect. (3.) It must show some degree of purposeful intelligence beyond that of any comparable animal."[16] While not a hard set of criteria (and mainly intended as a basis for further discussion), it would appear that most of Sanz's designated "dinosauroids" fall into the kaiju category. Rhedosaurus from *The Beast from 20,000 Fathoms* and one of Sanz's proclaimed "paradinosauroids," is an exception, however, because according to Lees, its dino-monster intelligence rating and behavior doesn't appear much above that of any ordinary reptilian animal. Oddly, the silicon-based kaiju monsters from 2013's *Pacific Rim,* especially as described in Alex Irvine's novelization from the movie script, are indeed derived from more familiar dino-monsters, and would be nondescript "dinosauroids" per Sanz.[17]

But, to me, Sanz's supra-"dinosauroid" term (or "clade") is rather disappointing and has taken on a variant meaning, quite opposite from implicating any sort of *giant* dino-monster or kaiju. Providing some background, Stephen Jay Gould's fourth "waystation"[18] corresponds to "Postmodern iconography." In 1993, he pronounced the rapidly diversifying field of paleoiconography then as in too great a transitional flux: "Above all, interest in ancient life is now so widespread, and consumer demands for its iconography so great, that the field will not soon lapse again into the general desuetude that limited nearly all available work to one man—even to so great an artist as Charles R. Knight."[19] However, despite questioning how one would portray the "iconography of contingency"[20]—scholarly contemplation which inspired the Russell/Seguin Dinosauroid, given evolution's unpredictable course—Gould did not mention the growing trend in dinosauroids, a significant product of this new age, or waystation. Therefore, what has been far lesser documented than real dinosaurs or their curious Cold War counterparts, are the many human-sized, intelligent dino-creatures and dinosauroids, demarcating the third cultural "age" of the dinosaur, a phenomenon escalating considerably during the 1980s period, corresponding to the dinosaur renaissance, during the mass extinctions controversy. Their meaning, hypothetical existence, plus the anthropomorphic unification of man with dinosaur, spreading like a mad zombie plague, is nothing less than profound.

In 1912, Arthur Conan Doyle likened a flock of pterodactyls nesting atop his fabled "lost world" plateau to wizened old hellish hags: "Their huge membranous wings were closed by folding their fore-arms, so that they sat like gigantic old women, wrapped in hideous web-colored shawls...."[21] Decades later, "Lizardmania" swept the country during the summer of 1988, as related by Lyle Blackburn in his 2013 book, *Lizardman: The True Story of the Bishopville Monster*, following several allegedly true sightings in South Carolina of what was believed to be a swamp-living, 7-foot-tall scaly bipedal creature. Whether it was a hoax or not, Blackburn attributes widespread interest in such "cryptid" creatures to "communal fascination.... Various concepts of 'reptile men' or 'fish men'—whether perceived as actual men or as gods—can be found throughout human history. They are woven into the very fabric of our mythology, religion, and folklore."[22] As Blackburn opines, a number of films such as 1954's *Creature from the Black Lagoon* certainly may have predisposed the locals' perception and "wild reaction to Lizard Man sightings."[23] But as noted here, dinosauroids had essentially prevailed over gill-men in the world of pop culture by the 1980s (although 1954's *Creature from the Black Lagoon* will forever be revered among classic monster movie fans). But another factor remains. Lizardmania may have been founded upon a realistic preconditioned cause, because the sensation erupted, oddly, *during* the dinosauroid heyday. (For the record, however, anatomically and in an evolutionary sense, lizards are much different from dinosaurs.) The Russell/Seguin Dinosauroid, whose arresting visage had appeared in a variety pulp magazines by then, was of course invented as a hypothetical (science fictional) *descendant* of the most skeletally avian forms of Eumaniraptoran theropod dinosaurs. But unless you were "in the know," most individuals wouldn't comprehend this complicated technical backstory (*especially* those who don't accept biological evolution as a true natural occurrence). There may be other deeply rooted, preconditioned factors in play as well.

In his *The Last Dinosaur Book* (1999), Mitchell writes, "[T]he dinosaur may be the most publicized animal in children's lives."[24] And exposure to dinosaurs of every persuasion during the impressionable, formative years (circa 1st-grade level) becomes nearly a modern instructional rite of passage, inculcating concepts of nature, while reinforcing a sense of dinoidentification."[25] This is where it all begins, learning how to accept our saurian doppelganger, so as to become receptive to the more significant messages it may later convey. In our household half a century ago it was Syd Hoff's then latest book, *Danny and the Dinosaur*, that made it seem perhaps not so strange that a young boy could have a live, talking, not-so-imaginary dinosaur to play and interact with, "borrowed" from the local museum. As we all know, there are many "romantic boys who never outgrew their dinomania"; Stephen Jay Gould, who in youth became infatuated with Charles R. Knight's paleoart and the American Museum's *Tyrannosaurus*, and Robert Bakker, whose dino-fascination was inspired by a reproduction of Zallinger's famous painting *Age of Reptiles* in *Life* magazine, are two such outspoken paleo-celebrities.[26] Mitchell cites the "Calvinosaurus" of *Calvin and Hobbes* comic fame, the ravenous dino-monster which young Calvin imaginatively transforms into to satisfy his fantasies of "absolute power."[27]

Clearly, as many youngsters come to understand—especially boys—displaying knowledge of science (e.g., memorizing dinosaur names) is tantamount to possessing special power, thus empowering children to convey *their* dinosaur lessons to adults, if only adults would listen and comprehend.[28] Although it's debatable whether Gould's plausible formula explaining why dinosaurs often prove so attractive to young individuals is due to the fact that dinosaurs generally are "big, fierce, and extinct" is correct, it remains a foundational factor.[29] Meanwhile, in 2015, I was rather pleasantly startled to hear my then 22-month-old grandson already audibly pronouncing the names "Godzilla" and "dinosaur" during a visit to my house—where there are many such visual examples on view. And so the next generational cycle begins.

The anthropomorphism of dinosaurs and unification of dinosaurs with humans is evident on several characteristic levels, and explored using several science fictional tricks, or "devices." Placing the characteristics into a short checklist, in fact, you may qualify as a science fictional dinosauroid, if (1) you are biologically derived from any species of real dinosaur, and now have intelligence or sentience (regardless of your absolute size or form), or (2) are a scaly reptiloid of humanoid form and size (regardless of intelligence quotient), or (3) are such a derived reptiloid having speech capability and self-awareness (thus implying basic intelligence), or (4) are such a derived reptiloid and have the capability of having sex with humans. Science fictional devices in which we see these creatures develop, transform or evolve and permeate into human society include (1) the Frankensteinian human mind transference into a prehistoric animal's or dinosaur's body and mind, (2) such intelligence and humanoid form arising in a derived dinosaurian resulting from Darwinian evolutionary convergence, (3) DNA-genetic "connectivity" between humans and reptiloid-dinosaurians, such as that occurring in "phylosynthesis," (4) dinosaurs applying clever disguises to appear human (or as a very loosely applied definition, vice versa), (5) metaphorical—wearing of dinosaurian costumes, such as suitmation.[30] (See Figure 20-1.)

So although Sanz applies the general term "dinosauroid" for dinosaurians that are not real (and stemming from movies), here I reserve this term for a broader fictional subset, a variety that are *not* necessarily daikaiju, or kaiju eiga (per Lees's definition) and not exclusively filmic (and therefore largely unrecognized). To me, dinosauroids are instead "species" of fictional dinosaurs formulated more upon the anthropic form (and, of lesser importance, absolute size), although reptiloid or possibly avetheropod in nature, while invested with human-level intelligence, powers of communication, and perhaps capable of wielding or at least comprehending advanced technology. (Gojiro, as discussed in the previous chapter, is *both* daikaiju and a dinosauroid, due to his ability to dramatically change size, converting from a human-reptiloid–like creature into a full-fledged, cinematic-type dragodinosauroid.)

Here, it is tempting to envision a dinosaur/dino-monster "cladogram" in which the various kinds of dinosaurs (both real, as known to science, and those imagined by more science fictionally–minded souls) are comparatively represented. At the root base would be the "clade" of real dinosaurians from which later appearing dino-monsters of fiction and filmdom are all derived. Some of these could even be grouped, or lumped together according to Sanz's definitions (i.e., para-, saurio-, and drago-dinosauroid daikaiju), according to similar traits, thus approximating a phylogenetic "bush" founded upon common ancestral anatomical and physical features. At the most recent end of such a diagram would appear the science fictional dinosauroids, subcategorized per their differential proximity to humaniform characteristics.

Fig 20-1: A postcard mailer received from the Burpee Museum in 2012, advertising the traveling "Walking with Dinosaurs" theatrical show, in which humans don dinosaur suits, masquerading as dinosaurs ... or is the configuration of the dinosaur suits rather controlling actions of the human performers? Like Godzilla, Gorgo and many other science fictional varieties, humans meld with dinosaurian forebears in such well-received programs.

Of course, simply because giant dino-monsters and, afterward, more humaniform dinosauroids appeared in popular culture later than did real dinosaurs known to science, would not imply that earlier categories were utterly replaced by those appearing later; they're simply branched off from more ancestral lineages. And so it is today, that we still have "real" dinosaurs curated in our museums, giant dino-monsters like Godzilla still starring in motion pictures, and dinosauroid-type creatures catering to our better interests in various media.

Although numerous examples of dinosauroids were mentioned in my 2006 book, *Dinosaurs in Fantastic Fiction,* as well as elsewhere in Part III of this book, let's consider several others in the context of the dinosaurs' "third" sociocultural age.[31]

In Bob Buckley's intriguing 1978 short story entry, "The Runners," extinction and lucky survival in the face of impending paleo-ecological catastrophe are prominent themes. During the 1970s, the supernova theory of Late Cretaceous mass extinctions remained popular among neo-catastrophist paleontologists. Supporting speculations of Carl Sagan as mentioned in his *Dragons of Eden* (1977), Buckley wonders what if there indeed were highly intelligent dinosaurs that survived into Late Cretaceous time. Would they have evolved to heightened intelligence by now if the mass extinction hadn't happened? And so in Buckley's tale, when a team of humans journeys through space-time into the Late Cretaceous (relying on physics of the "Jovian Twist effect"), they encounter a brooding pair of cave-dwelling, crude tool–using dromaeosaur-like creatures, "the dinosaurian equivalent of Australopithecines"![32]

Beyond *Stenonychosaurus*, the earliest dinosaur "cave men." Pitying their forthcoming supernova fate from a star some 2 light years distant, one of the scientists retrieves two of their eggs for the return leg, back to the future.

By the mid–1990s, in a variety of fiction, smart, tool-wielding dinosauroids (some having long tails, versus those with vestigial tails) populated other worlds in space, or reigned in parallel universe settings, or in obscure locations such as James Gurney's Dinotopia. But in some tales, their appearance shifted slightly too, even acquiring feathery integument in matching the latest theoretical notions and evidence. For instance, in Robert Reed's 1994 story, "Stride," a bird-like dinosaurian interloper, disguised as a human, yet descended from protobirds that survived numerous mass extinctions, terrorizes a human long-distance runner. The creature explains how, after achieving industrial prowess on its planet following an ice age, the avian-dino species exterminated all mammalian populations thousands of centuries ago, and the two race on ... to the bitter end, toward certain death.[33] And a recent crop of novels and stories build on a premise that humans can coalesce into menacing dinosaurians, not simply through clever disguises (such as in that early 2010s stage performance show, BBC's *Walking with Dinosaurs: The Live Experience*), but *biogenetically*—implying how close are the DNA ties between dinosaur and man. Perhaps the most trendy of these concerned humans rendered into reptilian zombies after being exposed to a virus preserved in deep-freeze dinosaurian tissues, afflicting specimens discovered in Antarctica.[34]

Certainly by the dawning of the new millennium, a dinosaur-human connection had become established to an unprecedented degree. A few deftly written passages underscoring this close-knit tie, reflecting the intimacy of our renaissance relationship with dinosaurs, are found in James F. David's space-time warping *Footprints of Thunder* (2005). In a passage in which the author describes the aftermath of a calamitous series of predatory attacks upon two characters, Colter and his girlfriend Petra, a bloody Colter emerges from underneath the corpse of a tyrannosaur, killed by Petra, "Like some bizarre Cesarean-born baby.... " Dinosaur giving "birth" to man! Then after their awful ordeal, as Petra relaxes comfortably with Colter inside their banged-up RV, nestled with friendly, pampered dinosaur hatchlings, we read this droll exchange, "'Well, honey,' Colter said, 'It's been quite a vacation.' 'Yes, dear,' Petra replied. 'But the kids are exhausted.... '"[35] And in case you're wondering, dinosaur-human sexual relations are no longer taboo in the realm of the science fictional/fantasy dinosaur, but let's not go there![36]

Nature itself lies at the core of the prophetic dinosaurian tale, although here man often confuses what is regarded as a predetermined "natural" world versus what is unpredictable reality. Gould noted this in the case of 1993's celebrated film, *Jurassic Park*. Professor Ian Malcolm, played by Jeff Goldblum, an expert on chaos theory, predicts that with so many variables in play, inevitably some factor or circumstance will spiral out of control in billionaire showman John Hammond's Jurassic Park, harboring his fantastic bio-engineered dinosaurs. Malcolm proclaims that dinosaurs had their "shot" but didn't make it, because (predictably), "nature selected them for extinction." But when the crafty, resurrected dinosaurs emerge, gun-toting humans barely measure up, especially to the *Velociraptors*. As Gould states, "How can a chaotician talk about nature's proper course at all? ... You can't have it both ways. If you take dinosaur revisionism seriously, and portray them as smart and capable creatures ... then you can't argue against reviving them by depicting their extinction as both predictable and appointed, as life ratcheted onward to greater complexity."[37] Man doesn't control nature;

we're simply part of it. Furthermore, through the *Jurassic Park* series, we learn that genetic power is more powerful, and perhaps even less controllable, than nuclear power.

The two most prominent, anticipated dino-monster movies of the mid–2010s, *Godzilla* (2014) and *Jurassic World* (2015) shed further light on fictional dinosaurs. Whereas *Jurassic Park*'s Malcolm seems a bit befuddled by nature's course, contemplative Dr. Serizawa (played by Ken Watanabe) in *Godzilla* (2014), views the titular mega-saurian as a balancing natural force, destined to restore (human-dominated) ecological harmony, one that should inevitably triumph over the radiation-absorbing insectoid MUTOs. Whereas not every Godzilla expert acclaimed the 2014 film,[38] Serizawa's beliefs are revealed more clearly in Greg Cox's 2014 novelization. Here we read that, as Serizawa anticipated, "Godzilla destroyed the MUTOs ... as Nature *intended*." (My italics.) Furthermore, "Godzilla was Nature incarnate, eternally resilient and unstoppable."[39] Given his simplified view of a Gaian universe in which Earth's evolutionary processes can properly be restored by introducing a more or less benevolent giant dino-monster, Serizawa is no "chaotician." Resuming a superhero filmic presence (as in the half-century-old Toho films), Godzilla, and human protagonist Ford Brody, deepen their relationship throughout the story, with personified Godzilla increasingly taking on anthropomorphic tendencies.[40]

Then in 2015's *Jurassic World*, traits of four species, including the cunning and voracious *Velociraptor*, are melded genetically to spawn a fictional, diabolical dino-monster dubbed *Indominus rex*. This new "highly intelligent" entity manifests and mirrors man's worst tendencies. Not only is the new monster capable of communicating—"talking"—with raptors in dino-speak, but we learn that the movie's human hero, an ex-Navy animal trainer, is able to communicate with the raptors. The raptor dinosaurs are viewed by the movie's villain as possible subjects for eventual military "weaponizing," breeding a formidable infantry of raptors! In the end, though, the semi-natural (i.e., cloned) variety of "real" dinosaurs (raptors teamed with an enlisted tyrannosaur and ultimately aided by the hungry maw of a marine *Mosasaurus*) triumph over the entirely unnatural, genetic concoction *Indominus rex* (whose characteristics are also coveted for possible weaponizing). So in the end, symbolically, primeval Nature becomes heroic.

Man's precarious existence on Earth has only become realized over recent decades. Nearly two centuries ago, while geologists were hammering out some of the first dinosaur specimens known to science from the rocks, Mary Shelley's then latest novel, her apocalyptical *The Last Man* (1826), received a cool reception from readers, partly for its pervading sense of gloom and "godlessness." According to her biographer, Emily W. Sunstein, writing in 1989, "The concept of the human race ending, which today seems plausible, affronted progressives...."[41] "Progressives" were those who believed, as conveyed to the public by scientists and later by paleoartists, that life through geological time had and was leading "somewhere" providentially, purposefully—toward the ascent of man on our (as then perceived) virtually indestructible planet. Today, however, scientists disparage the most primitive, "reptilian" R-complex of the human brain for many of our social deficiencies and behavior that could lead to doomsday, resultant of aberrant tendencies embedded within the psyche. Monsters unleashed from the Id![42] As Mike Magee suggests, invoking his metaphorical "anthroposaurs" once more, "Do we suffer from the same affliction as the anthroposaurs and perhaps all intelligent life forms—some self-destructive syndrome that is a *sine qua non* of intelligence? If the answer is 'yes' we are doomed. Even if we can see the fault in ourselves, we are powerless to change it. I believe we have a legacy from the dinosaurs. It is part of our psyche. We cannot reject it. It is our dinosaur heritage!"[43]

So today, the critical means leading to our end is often equated with a multitude of flashy "out with a bang" speculative scenarios, several inspired by present knowledge of the dinosaurian demise. And if the pathway leading to cataclysm is natural (an asteroid impact, a nearby supernova or intensive volcanism), versus mass extinctions caused instead by a self-inflicted means (unrestrained thermonuclear warfare resulting from geopolitical strife, uncontrolled nuclear reactor meltdowns, beyond-the-tipping-point depletion of resources with industrial pollution leading to runaway climate change and global warming, or a pandemic leading to extinction caused by unleashing an experimental gene or superbug), then does it really matter how we exit if our fate is already sealed?[44] Yes, it does, for which epitaph would man prefer to have inscribed on his bedrock tombstone, strata-documented for future (presumably non-human) archaeologists to disinter and interpret?

Personally, I'd rather see us go out, unavoidably yet nobly, like the dinosaurs, rather than self-extinguished, victimized by our worse, innate animalistic tendencies. Unlike the dinosaurs, however, that final blow would not befall us quite so unwittingly. Self-awareness and ability to analyze our present circumstances *may* offer a distinct advantage over the real dinosaurs' fate, prolonging our civilization. Although my R-complex wouldn't condone it, let us avoid becoming another "anthroposaur." That would be the ultimate fear and loathing injustice of being a "dinosaur" in post-modernity.[45]

Chapter Notes

Introduction

1. Allen A. Debus and Bob Morales, *Dinosaur Sculpting: A Complete Guide,* 2nd ed. (Jefferson, NC: McFarland, 2013).

2. Jose Luis Sanz, *Starring T. Rex!: Dinosaur Mythology and Popular Culture* (Bloomington: Indiana University Press, 2002), p. 143.

3. Paul D. Brinkman, *The Second Jurassic Dinosaur Rush: Museums and Paleontology in America at the Turn of the Twentieth Century* (Chicago: University of Chicago Press, 2010), p. 3.

4. The early period of this movement is discussed by Martin J.S. Rudwick in *Scenes from Deep Time: Early Pictorial Representations of the Prehistoric World* (Chicago: University of Chicago Press, 1992).

5. Stephen Jay Gould, "Reconstructing (and Deconstructing) the Past," preface to *The Book of Life: An Illustrated History of the Evolution of Life on Earth* (New York: W.W. Norton, 1993), pp. 6–21; W.J.T. Mitchell, *The Last Dinosaur Book* (Chicago: University of Chicago Press, 1998), pp. 101, 104.

6. Furthermore, Jane P. Davidson's *A History of Paleontology Illustration* (Bloomington: Indiana University Press, 2008) doesn't address a threefold historical pattern in paleoimagery, whether linear, abstract, or otherwise. The "three ages of the dinosaur" may partially be perceived as an offshoot of three visual "eras" of scientific restorations evident in *Tyrannosaurus rex,* dubbed as "Savage Rex" (1902–1942), "Lordly Rex" (1947–1979), and "Renaissance Rex" (1979–2000)—although now here extended throughout the whole of dinodom. See Debus and Debus, *Paleoimagery: The Evolution of Dinosaurs in Art* (Jefferson, NC: McFarland, 2002, pp. 158–59), and Debus, *Prehistoric Monsters: The Real and Imagined Creatures of the Past That We Love to Fear* (Jefferson, NC: McFarland, 2010), pp. 171–207. Temporally, and now in retrospect, these three phases in the scientific progression of *T. rex* art do roughly correspond to those outlined in this book.

7. W.J.T. Mitchell, "Dinos R Us," *University of Chicago Magazine* 90, no. 3 (Feb. 1998): pp.16–22. Quote is taken from pp. 17–18.

8. Spencer R. Weart uses the term "human volcano" in his 2003 book, *The Discovery of Global Warming* (Cambridge, MA: Harvard University Press), p. 91.

9. Stephen L. Brusatte, *Dinosaur Paleobiology* (West Sussex: John Wiley & Sons, 2012), p. 257.

10. Jase Short, "Kaiju in Context: Why we create them and what they represent," *G-Fan* 103 (Summer 2013): pp. 20–23. Quote is taken from p. 23.

11. Allen A. Debus, "Giant Dino-Monster 'Theory': Visualizing the *Real* 'Dino' in Dino-Monster Reel," in *Scary Monsters,* no. 88 (June 2013): pp. 107–119.

12. Henry R. Knipe, *Evolution in the Past* (London: Herbert and Daniel, 1912), p. 78.

13. J.D. Lees, "Wardrobe! The Many Suits of Godzilla," in *The Official Godzilla Compendium,* ed. J.D. Lees and Marc Cerasini (New York: Random House, 1998), pp. 96–99.

14. Stephen Jay Gould, "A Biological Homage to Mickey Mouse," in *The Panda's Thumb: More Reflections in Natural History* (New York: W.W. Norton, 1980), pp. 95–107.

15. For instance, occasionally, several lavishly illustrated popular books (i.e., non-textbook variety) published during the Dinosaur Renaissance are organized along the not-to-be-relinquished life-through-time theme. Among the few examples are: Willy Ley, *Worlds of the Past* (New York: Golden Books, Western Publishing Company, Inc., 1971); Richard Moody, *Prehistoric World: The 3400 Million Years Before Modern Man* (Secaucus, NJ: Chartwell Books, Inc., 1980); Zdeněk V. Spinar's *Life Before Man,* illustrated by Zdeněk Burian (New York: Crescent Books, 1981); Carroll Lane Fenton and Mildred Adams Fenton, *The Fossil Book: A Record of Prehistoric Life,* revised and expanded by Patricia Vickers Rich, Thomas Hewitt Rich and Mildred Adams Fenton (New York: Doubleday, 1989); Sylvia J. Czerkas and Stephen A. Czerkas, *Dinosaurs: A Global View* (New York: Mallard Press, 1991); Stephen Jay Gould, ed., *The Book of Life: An Illustrated History of the Evolution of Life on Earth* (New York: W.W. Norton, 1993); John Lanzendorf, *Dinosaur Imagery: The Science of Lost Worlds and Jurassic Art* (London: Academic Press, 2000); and Julius Csotoni and Steve White, *The Paleoart of Julius Csotoni: Dinosaurs, Sabre-tooths and Beyond* (London: Titan Books, 2014). Also during this period, three startling life-through-time themed entries incorporating visuals to a far lesser extent are Stephen Baxter's sci-fi novel, *Evolution* (2003)—offering a highly anthropomorphized evolutionary perspective; Richard Fortey's *Life: A Natural History of the First Four Billion Years of Life on* Earth (New York: Vintage Books, 1999); and paleobiologist Richard Dawkins's popular treatise in evolutionary biology, *The Ancestor's Tale: A Pilgrimage to the Dawn of Evolution* (New York: Houghton Mifflin, 2004). Infrequently, televised documentaries delve into the life-through-time as well. One recent example is the program titled *How the Universe Works,* with its episode "Extinction" (S3; Ep06) first aired on August 13, 2014, on the Science Channel network.

Chapter One

1. Michael Allaby and James Lovelock, *The Great Extinction: The Solution to One of the Great Mysteries of Science—the Disappearance of the Dinosaurs* (New York: Doubleday, 1983), p. 115.
2. David M. Knight, "Humphry Davy," *Dictionary of Scientific Biography*, vol. 3 (New York: Scribner's, 1971), p. 604.
3. James A. Secord, *Victorian Sensation: The Extraordinary Publication, Reception, and Secret Authorship of Vestiges of the Natural History of Creation* (University of Chicago Press, 2000), p. 57. Charles Darwin's grandfather, Erasmus Darwin, was also a major influence on young Mary's writing of *Frankenstein*. For more on both Davy and Darwin in this vein, see also Radu Florescu, *In Search of Frankenstein* (Boston, MA: New York Graphic Society, 1975), pp. 29, 206–209.
4. Robert Siegfried and Robert H. Dott Jr., *Humphry Davy on Geology: The 1805 Lectures for the General Audience* (Madison: University of Wisconsin Press, 1980), p. xliv.
5. Humphry Davy, *Consolations in Travel, or the Last Days of a Philosopher* (Philadelphia: John Grigg, 1830). Davy's *Consolations* went through at least 5 editions, one of which is dated 1851, published in London. To my knowledge none of these were illustrated.
6. Knight, *op. cit.*, pp. 598–604.
7. A lithograph figure of Davy's assistant administrating gas from contained glassware to another assistant (which shows laughing gas blowing out of the latter's rear end, exploding his pants bottom) was recently printed on the cover of *Chemical Heritage* 26, no. 4 (Winter 2008–2009). The cover of this journal, however, doesn't show the entire figure, identified as "Scientific Researches! New Discoveries in Pneumaticks! An Experimental Lecture on the Powers of Air, 1802 -colored etching by James Gillray (1757–1815)." My father owned a copy of this print and the entire figure was reprinted to illustrate an article of mine published in "Humphry Davy's 'Consolations' Prize (Part 1 of 2)," in *Fossil News: Journal of Avocational Paleontology* 12, no. 5 (May 2006): pp.14–17.
8. T.K. Kenyon, "Science and Celebrity: Humphry Davy's Rising Star," *Chemical Heritage* 26, no. 4 (Winter 2008–2009): pp. 30–35 (quote from p. 32).
9. *Ibid.*, p. 31.
10. *Ibid.*
11. *Ibid.*, p. 35.
12. Siegfried and Dott, *op. cit.*
13. *Ibid.*, pp. xiii, 143.
14. Stephen Jay Gould, "The Proof of Lavoisier's Plates," *The Lying Stones of Marrakech: Penultimate Reflections in Natural History* (New York: Harmony Books, 2000), pp. 91–114; Martin J.S. Rudwick, *Bursting the Limits of Time: The Reconstruction of Geohistory in the Age of Revolution* (University of Chicago Press, 2005), pp. 111–115.
15. John Ayrton Paris, *The Life of Sir Humphry Davy*, 2 vols. (London: Henry Colbourn and Richard Bentley, 1831).
16. *Ibid.*, vol. 2, p. 205.
17. *Ibid.*, pp. 203–207. Plutonists generally concurred that basaltic rocks originated via volcanism or deep within the Earth, whereas Neptunists ascribed to an aqueous, marine, depositional origin.
18. *Ibid.*, p. 158.
19. Samples of Davy's poetry were printed in vol. 1 of Paris, *op. cit.*, pp. 25–39.
20. Charles Coulton Gillispie, *Genesis and Geology: The Impact of Scientific Discoveries Upon Religious Beliefs in the Decades Before Darwin* (Cambridge, MA: Harvard University Press, 1951), p. 89.
21. H. Davy, *Consolations, op. cit.*, pp. iii–iv. For more on John Davy (1790–1868), see Robert Siegfried's outline in *Dictionary of Scientific Biography*, vol. 3 (New York: Scribner's, 1971), pp. 604–605.
22. H. Davy, *Consolations, op. cit.*, pp. 128–129.
23. Secord, *op. cit.*, p. 56; H. Davy, *Consolations, op. cit.*, pp. 136–137.
24. H. Davy, *Ibid.*, p. 134.
25. *Ibid.*, pp. 134–135.
26. *Ibid.*, p. 135.
27. *Ibid.*, pp. 135–136.
28. Paris, vol. 1, *op. cit.*, p. 305. More recently, Peter J. Bowler summarized, "The chemist Humphry Davy ... suggested that extensive local heating could be caused where highly reactive metals such as the newly discovered sodium combined with water or oxygen. If the earth had originally contained large underground deposits of such metals, episodes of violent activity would occur from time to time whenever air or water penetrated into the depths to begin the reaction.... The chemical theory was gradually abandoned in favour of the idea that the whole centre of the earth was intensely hot, presumably as a result of the planet having been formed as a molten mass." *The Norton History of the Environmental Sciences* (New York: W.W. Norton, 1992), p. 232.
29. H. Davy, *op. cit.*, p. 138.
30. Paris, vol. 2, op. *cit.*, p. 347.
31. Rachel Laudan, *From Mineralogy to Geology: the Foundations of a Science 1650–1830* (University of Chicago Press, 1987), p. 200.
32. H. Davy, reprinted in Paris, vol. 2, *op. cit.*, p. 347.
33. H. Davy, *Consolations, op. cit.*, pp. 142–143.
34. *Ibid.*, p. 143.
35. Martin J.S. Rudwick, *Bursting the Limits of Time: The Reconstruction of Geohistory in the Age of Revolution* (University of Chicago Press, 2005), p. 592.
36. H. Davy, *Consolations, op. cit.*, pp. 41–42, 144.
37. *Ibid.*, p. 147.
38. Siegfried and Dott, *op. cit.*, pp. xliii, xliv.
39. H. Davy, *Consolations, op. cit.*, pp. 148–149.
40. Paris, vol. 2, *op. cit.*, pp. 295–296.
41. Rudwick, *op. cit.* (2005), pp. 631–632. Rudwick further claims in this passage, "Davy's citation was significant because he clearly recognized the innovative character of what Buckland had done. It was a kind of science unlike his own mainly chemical researches, in that it was concerned not with discovering perennial 'laws of nature' but with reconstructing nature's contingent and unrepeated *history*. Davy, like any savant, took for granted the 'immensity' of geohistory as a whole, but within that vast panorama Buckland had vividly reconstructed one specific moment or 'epoch.' In contrast to Buffon's famous *epoques*, however, this had not been deduced as the necessary consequence of an overarching physical model; he had inferred it from a detailed study of specific historical 'records' left by nature itself. Davy saw that this 'fixed point' in the immediately antediluvian world could act both as an exemplar of how geohistory should be done, and as a point of reference from which it could be extended back into the deeper past towards the primal 'creation.' Other naturalists had already explored this kind of geohistorical approach. Davy's reference to 'the revolutions of the globe,' for ex-

ample, echoes Cuvier's phrase. But there had been no comparable reconstruction of a whole vanished world; landscape, lake, cave, mammoths, hyenas, water rats, and all."

42. Siegfried and Dott, *op. cit.*, pp. xxxvi, 146.
43. *Ibid.*, pp. xiii–xliii.
44. *Ibid.*, p. xlii.
45. Verne's famous life-through-time paleontological journey both begins and ends in volcanoes. Allen A. Debus, "Reframing the Science in Jules Verne's *Journey to the Center of the Earth*," Part 3, in *Science Fiction Studies* 100, vol. 33 (Nov. 2006): pp. 405–420.
46. Second, *op. cit.*, p. 41.

Chapter Two

1. Ralph O'Connor, *The Earth On Show: Fossils and the Poetics of Popular Science, 1802–1856* (Chicago: University of Chicago Press, 2007, p. 187.
2. Susan Shatto, "Byron, Dickens, Tennyson, and the Monstrous Efts," *Yearbook of English Studies* 6 (1976): p. 154.
3. Robert Chambers, *Vestiges of the Natural History of Creation* (London: John Churchill, 1844). The absolute best reference to understanding Chambers's motive for writing *Vestiges*, along with its remarkable success with respect to its time, is James A. Secord's *Victorian Sensation: The Extraordinary Publication, Reception, and Secret Authorship of Vestiges of the Natural History of Creation* (Chicago: University of Chicago Press, 2000).
4. Claude C. Albritton, Jr., *The Abyss of Time* (Los Angeles: Jeremy P. Tarcher, 1986), p. 80.
5. William Buckland, *Geology and Mineralogy Considered with Reference to Natural Theology*, 2 vols. (London: William Pickering, 1836).
6. O'Connor, *op. cit.*, p. 249.
7. Charles Lyell, *Principles of Geology, Being an Attempt to Explain the Former Changes of the Earth's Surface, by Reference to Causes Now in Operation*, 3 vols. (London: John Murray, 1830–1833).
8. Stephen Jay Gould, *Time's Arrow, Time's Cycle* (Cambridge, MA: Harvard University Press, 1987), pp. 98, 137–142.
9. The term "evolutionary epic" is used extensively throughout (e.g., p. 219) Bernard Lightman's *Victorian Popularizers of Science: Designing Nature for New Audiences* (Chicago: University of Chicago Press, 2007). O'Connor, *op. cit.*, p. 416 refers to the term "Panorama of the Ages," in part meaning the pageant of life.
10. Charles C. Gillespie, *Genesis and Geology: A Study in the Relations of Scientific Thought, Natural Theology, and Social Opinion in Great Britain* (Cambridge, MA: Harvard University Press, 1951), p. 162.
11. Robert Chambers, *Explanations: A Sequel to "Vestiges of the Natural History of Creation" by the Author of That Work*, 2nd ed. (London: John Churchill, 1846), p. 151.
12. Lynn C. Barber, *The Heyday of Natural History 1820–1870* (Garden City, NY: Doubleday, 1980), p. 215.
13. Dr. Roget quoted in Robert Chambers's *Vestiges of the Natural History of Creation*, 5th ed. (London: John Churchill, 1846), p. 279.
14. Jane P. Davidson, *A History of Paleontology Illustration* (Bloomington: Indiana University Press, 2008), pp. 59–63; Joseph Augusta, *Prehistoric Animals* (London: Spring Books, 1956), Plate 16.
15. Chambers, *op. cit.*, 1846, p.62, 68. The term "leaves from the stone book" is borrowed from p. 56.
16. *Ibid.*, p. 70.
17. *Ibid.*, pp. 101–103.
18. *Ibid.*, p. 129.
19. *Ibid.*, pp. 132–133.
20. *Ibid.*, p. 137.
21. *Ibid.*, p. 149.
22. O'Connor, *op. cit.*, pp. 195, 236.
23. Secord, *op. cit.*, p. 151.
24. But even the concept of "illustration" was in flux during this time. O'Connor, *op. cit.*, p. 284.
25. Gillespie, *op. cit.*, p. 283.
26. This premise is the core and foundation of O'Connor's book. Hess's reference to "geopoetry" may be found in his 1962 article, "History of Ocean Basins," in A.E.J. Engel, H.L. James, and B.F. Leonards, eds., *Petrologic Studies: A Volume in Honor of A.F. Buddington* (New York: Geological Society of America, 1062), pp. 599–620.
27. O'Connor, *op. cit.*, pp. 366–375.
28. *Ibid.*, p. 385.
29. Hugh Miller (1802–1859) was another vaunted contemporary amateur who also wrote numerous popular books on geology. One of these was in the life-through-time vein, *The Testimony of the Rocks; or, Its Bearing on the Two Theologies, Natural and Revealed* (Edinburgh: Constable, 1857). Miller and Chambers were strongly opposed to one another in their view on life's apparent "progress" as recorded in fossils.
30. O'Connor, pp. 131–132.
31. *Ibid.*, p. 197.
32. Henry Morley, "Our Phantom Ship on an Antediluvian Cruise," 1851, *Household Words* 3, pp. 492–496. The subsequent quote is borrowed from p. 492.
33. Chambers, *op. cit.*, *Explanations*, p. 101; also see Secord, *op. cit.*, pp. 238–239.
34. *Ibid.*, p. 33.
35. *Ibid.*, p. 57.
36. *Ibid.*, p. 118.
37. Chambers, *op. cit.*, *Vestiges*, p. 232.
38. Chambers quoted from *Vestiges*, 1st ed., p. 222, in Secord, *op. cit.*, p. 105.
39. Chambers, *op. cit.*, *Explanations*, p. 162.
40. As summarized by Henry Fairfield Osborn in his *From the Greeks to Darwin: An Outline of the Development of the Evolution Idea*, 2nd ed. (New York: Macmillan, 1899), pp. 217–218.
41. Writing of Chambers in his *From the Greeks to Darwin*, p. 216), Osborn exuberantly stated, "The great sensation which this book caused, and its rapid sale, through ten editions in nine years, is proof that the truth of Evolution was ready to burst forth like a volcano, and that the times were ready for Darwin."
42. Barber, *op. cit.*, p. 265.
43. For further perspective, see Philip Stone and Adrian Rushton, "Charles Darwin, Bartholomew Sullivan, and the geology of the Falkland Islands: unfinished business from an asymmetric partnership," *Earth Sciences History* 32, no. 2 (2013): p. 178.
44. David Page, *The Past and Present Life of the Globe: Being a Sketch in Outline of the World's Life-System* (Edinburgh: William Blackwood and Sons, 1861), p. 209. For more on Page, see Lightman, *op. cit.*, pp. 223–238.
45. David M. Raup and Steven M. Stanley, *Principles of Paleontology*, 2nd ed. (San Francisco: W.H. Freeman, 1978). An early example of the life-through-time geology textbook is James D. Dana's *Textbook of Geology: Designed for Schools and Academics*, 2nd ed. (New York: Ivison, Blakeman, Taylor & Co., 1874; 1st ed. 1861).

46. Edward O. Wilson, *The Social Conquest of Earth* (New York: Liveright, 2012).

Chapter Three

1. Stephen Jay Gould, ed. *The Book of Life: An Illustrated History of the Evolution of Life on Earth* (New York: W.W. Norton, 1993), p. 15.
2. *The Geological Magazine* 5, no. 9 (1918): p. 432. Thanks to Karl Debus for supplying a copy of H.R. Knipe's obituary.
3. Henry R. Knipe, *Nebula to Man* (London: J.M. Dent, 1905).
4. Sorry for ruining it for you already, unless you like that sort of thing. In her 2011 article, Lynne Clos defended the rhyme in *Nebula to Man*. Lynne Clos, "Selected Portion of Knipe's *Nebula to Man* Poem," *Fossil News: Journal of Avocational Paleontology* 17, no. 4 (July/August 2011): pp. 6–7.
5. Knipe, *Nebula to Man, op. cit.*, p. v. Over half a century earlier, Alfred Tennyson (1809–1892) incorporated geological lines within his *In Memoriam* (appearing in 1850), which is thought to have been partly inspired by Chambers's *Vestiges.* Tennyson laid out the Earth's and life's history in his poem, incorporating descriptions of the old dragons of the Mesozoic sea. He also coined the famous phrase, "Nature, red in tooth and claw." For much more on the reasons for Tennyson's composing of *In Memoriam*, see Stephen Jay Gould's "The Tooth and Claw Centennial," in *Dinosaur in a Haystack* (New York: Harmony Books, 1995), pp. 63–75.
6. Bernard Lightman, *Victorian Popularizers of Science: Designing Nature for New Audiences* (Chicago: University of Chicago Press, 2007). Robert Ball is discussed on pp. 406–417.
7. Knipe, *op. cit.*, p. 99.
8. Henry R. Knipe, *Evolution in the Past* (London: Herbert and Daniel, 1912), p. 6.
9. *Ibid.*, p. 2.
10. *Ibid.*, p. xv.
11. *Ibid.*, p. 206.
12. *Ibid.*
13. *Ibid.*, p. 69.
14. *Ibid.*, p. 78.
15. *Ibid.*, pp. 62–64, 80–81.
16. *Ibid.*, p. 81.
17. *Ibid.*, p. 100.
18. *Ibid.*, p. 102.
19. *Ibid.*, p. 103.
20. *Ibid.*, pp. 108–109.
21. *Ibid.*, p. 104.
22. *Ibid.*, p. 115.
23. *Ibid.*, p. 116.
24. *Ibid.*, p. 140.
25. *Ibid.*, pp. 123, 145.
26. *Ibid.*, p. 160.
27. *Ibid.*, p. 181.
28. *Ibid.*, p. 186.
29. *Ibid.*, p. 196.
30. Knipe, *Nebula to Man, op. cit.*, p. v.
31. H.N. Hutchinson, *Extinct Monsters and Creatures of Other Days: A Popular Account of Some of the Larger Forms of Ancient Animal Life* (London: Chapman and Hall, 1910), p. x.
32. For more on Hutchinson, see Lightman, *Victorian Popularizers*, pp. 450–460.
33. H.N. Hutchinson, *op. cit.*, p. xx.
34. Copy of letter in Allen Debus files.
35. Knipe, *Evolution in the Past, op. cit.*, p. 5.
36. Copy of letter in Allen Debus files.
37. W. Maxwell Reed, *The Earth For Sam* (Harcourt, Brace, 1929); Charles R. Knight, *Before the Dawn of History* (New York: McGraw-Hill, 1935).
38. Peter D. Ward, *Out of Thin Air* (Washington, DC: John Henry Press, 2006).

Chapter Four

1. Henry Fairfield Osborn, *The Origin and Evolution of Life* (New York: Scribner's, 1918), p. 146. The best biography on Osborn available is Ronald Rainger's *An Agenda for Antiquity: Henry Fairfield Osborn and Vertebrate Paleontology at the American Museum of Natural History, 1890–1935* (Tuscaloosa: University of Alabama Press, 1991). Osborn, branded today as racist for his views on human evolution, coined an influential evolutionary term and concept, "adaptive radiation." Yet he was not a "Darwinian" evolutionist, at least in the modern sense. He is more closely linked to the much older ideas of Jean Baptiste Lamarck, and therefore counted among the then prevalent anti–Darwinian ranks, known as "neo–Lamarckians." See Peter J. Bowler's *The Norton History of the Environmental Sciences* (New York: W.W. Norton, 1992), pp. 340–344, 440–442, 451–452 on this point.
2. Knipe, *op. cit.*; B. Webster Smith, *The World in the Past: What It Was Like and What It Contained* (London: Frederick Warne, 1930 ed.); Charles Schuchert, *Outlines of History Geology* (New York: John Wiley & Sons, 1931); E. Ray Lankester, *Extinct Animals* (New York: Henry Holt, 1905). Note that while Schuchert's book was intended as a student textbook, Smith's was published in a popular vein. And like Osborn's, Lankester's was a published compilation of public lectures.
3. J. Willard Gibbs (1839–1903) was an American physicist who published extensively on the principles of thermodynamics and phase equilibria, now a cornerstone of modern chemistry and physics.
4. H.F. Osborn, *Cope: Master Naturalist* (Princeton University Press, 1931).
5. Osborn, *The Origin and Evolution of Life, op. cit.*, p. vii.
6. *Ibid.*, p. 283.
7. *Ibid.*, p. 6, 18–23.
8. *Ibid.*, p. 8. Furthermore, Rainger, *op. cit.*, mentions, "Following World War I, Osborn became distressed over the advance of materialism and the demise of old-time religion and old-time Americanism.... Osborn ... signed a statement maintaining that scientific research supported religion. Osborn's evolutionary theory could be reconciled with religion because he maintained that organic change proceeded in definite directions and embodied plan and purpose" (p. 233).
9. Lawrence J. Henderson, *The Fitness of the Environment: An Inquiry into the Biological Significance of the Properties of Matter* (1913; New York: Macmillan, 1958).
10. *Ibid.*, p. 156.
11. John Parascandola, author of entry for Lawrence Henderson, in *Dictionary of Scientific Biography*, vol. 6 (New York: Scribner's, 1972), pp. 260–262, quote from p. 261.
12. Osborn, *op. cit.*, p. 9.
13. *Ibid.*, pp. 15–16.

14. *Ibid.*, p. 20.
15. *Ibid.*, pp. 18–23.
16. *Ibid.*, p. 21.
17. *Ibid.*, p. 38.
18. Relying on his observations of samples from the fossil record as well as the researches of early, contemporary geneticists, Osborn was elevating his own insights to the status of scientific "laws," not unlike or comparable in magnitude to those of modern physics, but within the realm of biology, although surpassing those of Charles Darwin. Over a century later, everyone knows the name "Darwin," while few may have heard of Osborn.
19. Osborn, *op. cit.*, 1918, p. 138.
20. *Ibid.*, pp. 138–140.
21. Osborn quoted in Ronald Rainger, *op. cit.*, p. 127.
22. Osborn, *op. cit.*, 1918, p. 143.
23. Rainger, *op. cit.*, p. 13.
24. Osborn, *op. cit.*, 1918, p. 146.
25. *Ibid.*, p. 151.
26. *Ibid.*, p. 155.
27. *Ibid.*, p. 159.
28. "Dollo's Law" was named after the Belgian paleontologist Louis Dollo (1857–1931), who performed extensive research in reconstructing the dinosaur skeletons of *Iguanodon* during the 1880s. Dollo's Law, essentially a biological restatement of the Second Law of Thermodynamics, simply suggests that in any system, disorder (in this case *genetic* disorder, or DNA "reshuffling") increases through time across generations. Furthermore and therefore, the course of evolution through time is irreversible.
29. Osborn, *op. cit.*, 1918, p. 225.
30. *Ibid.*, p. 233.
31. *Ibid.*, pp. 237–240.
32. *Ibid.*, p. 240.
33. *Ibid.*, p. 242.
34. *Ibid.*
35. *Ibid.*, p. 253.
36. *Ibid.*, p. 117.
37. *Ibid.*, pp. 263–64.
38. *Ibid.*, p. 265.
39. *Ibid.*, p. 269.
40. *Ibid.*, p. 278. In its chewiest passages, Osborn peppered *Origin and Evolution* with statements such as this: "Negatively we may say from palaeontology that there is positive disproof of the existence of an internal perfecting principle or entelechy of any kind which would impel animals to evolve in a given direction regardless of the direct, reversed, or alternating directions taken by the organism in seeking its life environment or physical environment" (pp. 277–278).
41. *Ibid.*, p. 283.
42. George Gaylord Simpson, *Life of the Past* (New Haven: Yale University Press, 1968); Stephen Jay Gould, *Ever Since Darwin* (New York: W.W. Norton, 1977), "The Misnamed, Mistreated and Misunderstood Irish Elk," pp. 79–90; David M. Raup and Steven M. Stanley, *Principles of Paleontology*, 2nd ed. (San Francisco: W.H. Freeman, 1978). A related, outmoded term was "phylogeronty," discussed and soundly denounced in Michael Allaby and James Lovelock, *The Great Extinction: The Solution to One of the Great Mysteries of Science—the Disappearance of the Dinosaurs* (Garden City, NY: Doubleday, 1983), pp. 142–145.
43. Referring to *Gryphaea*, in 1966 to 1967, our family had the good fortune of spending a year in Cambridge, England. My father was doing a research sabbatical; for me this was 7th grade, or "form," at the Perse School for Boys. Following a long trip from Illinois, my brother Rick and I—the young fossil collectors of the Debus clan—most enjoyably found ourselves among tempting piles of flinty, gravel stones lying outside and around the newly constructed apartments or "flats," in the roadbed and parking lot, and also deposited in a huge pile fit for climbing that would later form the base of a nearby chapel. There were so many fossils, all for the picking! We spent hours combing through the rubble, selecting only the best specimens. Many of these were of a strange, coiled shell. We were used to the appearance of Silurian fossils collected from a "Niagaran" age coral reef near Chicago, but these British fossils, which we guessed must be Mesozoic, were very unfamiliar. We identified the tightly coiled bivalve as genus *Gryphaea arcuata*, dating from the Lower Liassic age. (There were also other thick shells but of a less coiled and flatter shape, evidently dating from a later time strewn throughout the pile, the Bajocian. These belonged to the same genus although a different species, *G. sublobata*.) While we avidly collected our assorted specimens, it wasn't until much later that I comprehended *Gryphaea*'s significance in paleontological history. For a modern perspective on Osborn's "titanotheres," see Donald Prothero's *The Eocene-Oligocene Transition: Paradise Lost* (New York: Columbia University Press, 1994).
44. Stephen Jay Gould, ed., *The Evolution of Gryphaea* (New York: Arno Press, 1980).
45. Stephen Jay Gould, *The Structure of Evolutionary Theory* (Cambridge, MA: Belknap Press of Harvard University Press, 2002), p. 365.
46. A.E. Trueman, "The Use of Gryphaea in the Correlation of the Lower Lias," *Geology Magazine* (1922): p. 265, reprinted in Gould, ed., *op. cit.*, 1980.
47. Trueman, 1939 (published as "The meaning of orthogenesis," *Transcriptions of the Geological Society of Glasgow* 20 (1940): pp. 77–95, reprinted in Gould, ed., *op. cit.*, 1980. By 1972, Gould had falsified Trueman's claims, demonstrating that the supposed phyletic gradualistic trends noted were ill-founded (Gould, *op. cit.*, 2002, pp. 762–63, 1040 to 1045). Instead, and as opposed to something caused by mystical, apparently out-of-control, anti–Darwinian trends, the 1970s consensus held that the evident coiling was indeed an *adaptive* shell-stabilizing feature, permitting the animal to keep its aperture from submerging (or rolling over upside down) into muddy substrate, a circumstance that would lead ultimately to its death. Here, Gould used the analogy of the rocker of a hobby horse for describing *Gryphaea*'s life position, resting on its convex, tightly coiled "underside." "Moreover, once the heavy shell is tipped, the animal cannot right itself" (Gould, p. 1043). Furthermore, it was determined that, through geological time, evolutionary descendants of *G. arcuata* became *less* (rather than more tightly) coiled, proportionally. This growth pattern stemming from *G. arcuata*'s heyday may be ascribed to "paedomorphosis" (e.g., neoteny).
48. Michael Benton, "Scientific methodologies in collision: The history of the study of the extinction of the dinosaurs," *Evolutionary Biology* 24 (1990), pp. 371–400.
49. Kenneth J. McNamara, *Shapes of Time: The Evolution of Growth and Development* (Baltimore: Johns Hopkins University Press, 1997), p. 221.
50. Simpson, *Life of the Past*, 1953, *op. cit.*, 1968 ed., p. 119.
51. Raup and Stanley, *op. cit.*, p. 333.

52. First two quotations in this paragraph borrowed from Rainger, *op. cit.*, p. 164.

53. *Ibid.*, p. 166.

54. For a detailed overview of hormonal growth trend terms, peramorphosis and more generally speaking "heterochrony," Kenneth McNamara's book, *The Shapes of Time*, *op. cit.*, 1999, is highly recommended.

55. Paul C. Sereno, Lin Tan, Stephen L. Brusatte, *et. al.*, "Tyrannosaurid Skeletal Design First Evolved at Small Body Size," *Science* 326 (Oct. 16, 2009): p. 421.

56. *Ibid.*, p. 418. When added to other Rex ancestors known to science, including Jurassic genera, the "Rex" lineage (like that of horses, elephants and titanotheres) was "bushy," in an evolutionary sense. Furthermore, characters evident in *Tyrannosaurus* were already in place proportionally, albeit in more diminutive, human-sized form, 60 million years *before* the late Cretaceous. So enormous growth evident in the lineage was not a "trend," per se, and *Tyrannosaurus*'s "features seem first to have evolved as an efficient predatory strategy at relatively small body size" (Sereno, *et. al.*, *op cit.*, p. 421). If retainment of features manifested in *Raptorex* ultimately resulted in the lineage's largest variety, *Tyrannosaurus*, over an extended *60-million-year* time frame, then this growth progression can't rightly be viewed as "peramorphic *acceleration*." In fact, in all its signature features, *T. rex*—even though considerably larger—looks so quaintly yet so faintly like its remote ancestor, *Raptorex*. While the overall body grew larger, hallmark features were retained, conservatively and amazingly over a prolonged 60-million-year interval of time! In his aforementioned *Shapes of Time*, McNamara, p. 217, outlined the now overturned case for Rex growth as a product of peramorphic *acceleration*. There were certainly no Osborn-favored predetermined, orthogenetic forces at large in Rex's evolution.

57. Osborn, *op. cit.*, p. 225.

58. Trueman, *op. cit.*, 1939/1940, p. 86. To Eimer, variation was "directed." And developmental acceleration (successively) tacked on terminal life stages resulting in phylogenetic "trends" described via Ernst Haeckel's Biogenetic Law of recapitulation (i.e., "ontogeny recapitulates phylogeny"). Natural selection and environmental factors merely weeded the less fit, although the prescribed, primary evolutionary direction—the overall "orthogenetic pathway"—is programmed from within the organism. Natural selection was relegated to a secondary role. By 1866, Hyatt (with the Neo-Lamarckian Edward D. Cope) supported the "principle of acceleration" through "terminal addition" of characters. Trends toward larger growth could only result through a speeding up of organic life processes, accreting new life stages onto the end of the last in each successive speciation event. So, in essence and vastly oversimplifying, "acceleration" acted in concert with Haeckel's recapitulation to produce trends macroscopically noted as "orthogenesis." (Cope believed that individual organs would be effected, for instance, via acceleration; Haeckel felt that embryological acceleration applied to the entire organism.)

59. *Ibid.*

60. Stephen Jay Gould distinguished later conceived American "Neo-Lamarckian" versions of evolutionary theory from the older Orthogenetic school in that the former eliminated reliance on predictable "internally programmed series of new stages" (Gould, *op. cit.*, p. 367). Neo-Lamarckians objected to and rejected Darwinian reliance on "randomness" of variation, and "saw themselves as bringers of hope and inspiration," in that Man's vaunted place in nature must be more directed and preordained than Darwin realized: Richard Milner, *The Encyclopedia of Evolution* (New York: Facts On File, 1990), p. 324. They upheld (Jean-Baptiste) Chevalier de Lamarck's basic tenet that environment could influence organismal expression, without claiming to know how this came about. Interestingly, there's a modern breed of "new Lamarckians" not allied to the former neo-Lamarckians, seeking genetic evidence for "acquired characters" through phenomena such as "jumping" or other regulatory genes and retroviruses suggesting that under certain circumstances environment may significantly influence the inherited germ-plasm after all. Whereas Cope aptly saw "retardation" in relative size of body characters as a possible evolutionary outcome (besides growth acceleration, although not as frequently observed as growth resulting from acceleration), Hyatt solely interpreted fossil lineages along lines of internally programmed acceleration. Hyatt's grand idea became popularly known as the "old age" or "racial senescence" theory—an inescapable course leading to extinction. Here, it is understood that an organism has only a finite time in which to live. And so speeding up life stages—all those reflecting its long phylogeny via the Biogenetic Law—would eventually become time-limiting. While Cope viewed acceleration as increased quickening or compression of sequential ontogenetic life stages, Hyatt instead perceived that some of the intermediate stages would not be manifested. So, ultimately, at younger ages individuals of the most "advanced" species would appear already "old" and therefore ripe for extinction. When Hyatt wrote to Charles Darwin, however, outlining the American orthogenetic view, Darwin could only proclaim, "I confess that I have never been able to grasp what you wish to show.... After long reflection I cannot avoid the conviction that no innate tendency to progressive development exists" (Gould, *op. cit.*, 2002, pp. 372–373). Hyatt aspired to understand the mechanisms of evolution to the point where evolutionary pathways would be "as predictable as ontogeny." Gould stated, however: "Charles Darwin, who understood the contingent character of history, could not have disagreed more forcefully (Gould, *op. cit.*, p. 382). Without much further ado over such details and nuances, Gould expertly sorted much of the general confusion over concepts such as "acceleration," "retardation," and so forth in his definitive 1977 book, *Ontogeny and Phylogeny* (Cambridge, MA: Harvard University Press). As modern scholars would agree, Haeckel's "Biogenetic Law," conceived in 1866, has long been discredited. But Haeckel missed the salient points, which were correctly outlined by Gould and others—including McNamara, as in his aforementioned *Shapes of Time*. Instead, *heterochrony* as considered today applies to the science of growth and resulting phylogenetic patterns, therein, referring to the relative rates in growth of body parts, when compared to species thought to be either ancestral or descendant. For more on Haeckel, see Bowler, *op. cit.*, pp. 337–339, 437–438.

61. Rainger, *op. cit.*, p. 132.

62. *Ibid.*, p. 177.

63. Osborn, *The American Naturalist* 29 (May 1895): pp. 418–439, excerpt from p. 439.

64. Jack Horner and James Gorman, *How to Build a Dinosaur: Extinction Doesn't Have to Be Forever* (New York: Dutton, 2009).

65. Osborn, *op. cit.*, p. 153.

66. Peter J. Bowler adds further insight. "As middle-

class and even working-class interests challenged the established social order, science was often employed as a symbolic arena in which to fight ideological battles. Darwinian evolutionism is an example of a theory that was adopted by middle-class thinkers because it portrayed Nature in terms that paralleled their preferred framework of society. Conservative interests sought their own way of picturing the order of Nature, preferring images that admitted change only within the framework of a divinely preordained plan of creation." In terms of social standing, Osborn belonged to the latter category. *The Norton History of the Environmental Sciences* (New York: W.W. Norton, 1992), p. 251.

67. However, Bowler (*op. cit.*) noted that the general public may have been unaware of, or simply misunderstood the underlying intentions of museum displays, substituting more simplistic conceptions. "For most ordinary people, evolution means the rise and fall of the dinosaurs and other prehistoric beasts displayed at their local museum" (p. 447).

Chapter Five

1. For more on Pallenberg, see Allen A. Debus, "Of Prehistoric (Sculpted) Creatures Great & Small: Pallenberg's and Edwards' Monsters of Bygone Ages," *Prehistoric Times* 106 (Summer 2013): pp. 41–44.

2. Mark F. Berry, *The Dinosaur Filmography* (Jefferson, NC: McFarland, 2002), pp. 99, 116.

3. Jeff Rovin, *From the Land Beyond Beyond* (New York: Berkley, 1977), pp. 12–13.

4. *Ibid.*, p. 13.

5. George E. Turner with Orville Goldner, expanded ad revised by Michael H. Price with Douglas Turner, *Spawn of Skull Island* (Baltimore, MD: Luminary Press, 2002), p. 88.

6. Personal E-mail received from Donald F. Glut on Nov. 8, 2010.

7. Stephen Czerkas, "O'Brien vs. Dawley: The First Great Rivalry in Visual Effects," *Cinefex* 138 (July 2014): pp. 13–26. Here, interestingly, Czerkas has documented a considerable body of historical documentation he was able to come across, indicating that O'Brien and Dawley's falling out may have resulted from O'Brien's rather presumptuous actions. Czerkas seeks convincingly to clear Dawley's name in history as a well-intentioned and highly talented stop-motion animator.

8. Steve Archer, *Willis O'Brien: Special Effects Genius* (Jefferson, NC: McFarland, 1993), pp. 5–6.

9. Neil Pettigrew, *The Stop-Motion Filmography* (Jefferson, NC: McFarland, 1999), pp. 273–274.

10. Allen A. Debus, "Skullduggery, a Piltdown 'Elementary' (Parts 1 to 3)," in *Fossil News: Journal of Avocational Paleontology* 10, nos. 3–5 (March–May 2004): pp. 14–18; pp. 14–17; pp. 15–18.

11. Michael Klossner, *Prehistoric Humans in Film and Television* (Jefferson, NC: McFarland, 2006), p. 181.

12. Berry, *op. cit.*, p. 99. Another recognized period film, Disney's *Fantasia* (1940), contains in its "Rite of Spring" segment a brief animated life-through-geological-time sequence, climaxing with demise of the dinosaurs. And although never released, Ray Harryhausen experimented with his own analogous film project, titled *Evolution* (c. 1938–1939). See Berry, *op. cit.*, pp. 99–103, 438, for more on these titles.

13. A rare, 7-minute trade film, *Fifty Million Years Ago* (Service Film Company), first released in July 1925, also explored the paleontological life-through-time theme, utilizing stop-motion animation and two-dimensional graphical techniques. This film begins with the nebular hypothesis of planetary formation, and then briefly presents visual dioramas of life from the Cambrian Period through the Recent Ice Age. Dinosaurs were emphasized, as several of Charles R. Knight's 1897 painted and sculptural restorations were brought to life in realistic-looking dioramas. The film was preserved in 2015 by Colorlab Corp. for the National Film Preservation Foundation (www.filmpreservation.org/preserved-films/screening-room/fifty-million-years-ago-1925). Another period film, *Murders In the Rue Morgue* (1932), starring Bela Lugosi (playing a "Dr. Mirakle"), staged in 1845 Paris, introduces human-ape ancestry, evolutionary themes—dangerous for the time—invoking an illustrated life-through-time sequence seen on a drawn chart in an early scene. Pointing to his time chart showing the succession of life, labeled "The Story of Man," which includes a dinosaurian image, Mirakle proclaims, "From the slime of chaos there was seed that held and grew into the tree of life. Life was motion. Fins changed into wings, wings into ears. Crawling reptiles grew legs. Eons of ages passed. There came a time when a four-legged thing walked upright. Behold the first man." Here, Mirakle points to his murderous gorilla specimen.

14. For more on the concept of "imagetext," a composite melding of visual with textual language, see Allen A. Debus and Diane E. Debus, *Paleoimagery: The Evolution of Dinosaurs in Art* (Jefferson, NC: McFarland, 2002), p. 7; W.J.T. Mitchell, *The Last Dinosaur Book: The Life and Times of a Cultural Icon* (University of Chicago Press, 1998), pp. 52, 287.

15. For more on Zallinger's murals, see Chapter Ten. For considerably more on Verne's and Burroughs's cited novels, see Allen A. Debus, *Dinosaurs in Fantastic Fiction: A Thematic Survey* (Jefferson, NC: McFarland, 2006).

16. BBC Video, *The Complete Walking with Collection* (2006, includes *Walking With Dinosaurs*, 1999).

17. Gary Williams, "Prehistoric Journeys of Karel Zeman," *Dinosaur World* 3 (October 1997): pp. 49–52.

18. Neil Pettigrew, *op. cit.*, pp. 117–124. Also see Berry, *op. cit.*, pp. 142–147.

19. Josef Augusta, *Prehistoric Animals* (London: Spring Books), 1956.

20. Thomas Kovacs's letter printed in in *Dinosaur World* 5 (Oct. 1998): pp. 3–5, as well as Karel Zeman entry online at Wikipedia.

21. Vincent Campbell, "The extinct animal show: the paleoimagery tradition and computer generated imagery in factual television programs," *Public Understanding of Science* 18, no. 2 (2009): pp. 199–213.

22. This term seems an invention of Martin J.S. Rudwick, as in his 1992 book, *Scenes from Deep Time: Early Pictorial Representations of the Prehistoric World* (University of Chicago Press, 1992).

Chapter Six

1. For further perspective on Lovecraft pertaining to this chapter, see "What is the Chthulhu Mythos?" A Panel Discussion, *Lovecraft Studies* 6, no. 14 (Spring 1987): pp. 3–30. Here panel members discuss Lovecraft's "world view," as stated by S.T. Joshi, that "mankind occupies some very tiny, insignificant position in the whole realm of space and time; we are lost atoms in the vortices of infinity" (p.

11); "On *At the Mountains of Madness*: A Panel Discussion," *Lovecraft Studies* 34 (Spring 1996): pp. 2–10.

2. H.P. Lovecraft, *At the Mountains of Madness*, reprinted in *The Antarktos Cycle: At the Mountains of Madness and Other Chilling Tales* (A Chaosium Book, 1999), pp. 307–392. Quote is from p. 335.

3. *Ibid.*

4. *Ibid.*, p. 320.

5. *Ibid.*, p. 321.

6. *Ibid.*, p. 324.

7. Crinoids as known in the real fossil record were stemmed, calcified echinoderms—related to modern sea urchins and starfish—much more abundant in tropical marine settings than today. Their fossil remains are most common in Paleozoic limestone.

8. Lovecraft, *op. cit.*, 1999, p. 346.

9. *Ibid.*, p. 327. Dyer further concludes, astonished by the "sheer appalling antiquity" of the relics, that the strange beings "had built and inhabited ... this monstrous dead city millions of years ago, when man's ancestors were primitive archaic mammals, and vast dinosaurs roamed the tropical steppes of Europe and Asia" (Lovecraft, *op. cit.*, p. 354).

10. Robert M. Price, ed., "Lovecraft's Cosmic History," in *The Antarktos Cycle: At the Mountains of Madness and Other Chilling Tales* (A Chaosium Book, 1999), pp. ix–xiii.

11. *Ibid.*, p. 384.

12. S.T. Joshi, *I Am Providence: The Life and Times of H.P. Lovecraft*, vols. 1 and 2 (New York: Hippocampus Press, 2010). Here Joshi states, "The absurdities and implausibilities in this tale, along with its wildly overheated prose, give it a very low place in the Lovecraft canon" (pp. 382–83). Quotations in this paragraph taken from "The Nameless City" are from an online source, www.hplovecraft.com/writings/texts/fiction/nc.aspx.

13. Joshi, *I Am Providence*, vol. 2, pp. 973–74.

14. *Lovecraft Studies* 34, *op. cit.*, "Panel Discussion," 1996, p. 9.

15. *Ibid.*, p. 2.

16. Donald F. Glut, *The Dinosaur Scrapbook* (Secaucus, NJ: Citadel Press, 1980), pp. 67, 73.

17. Quoted in S.T. Joshi and David E. Schultz, *An H.P. Lovecraft Encyclopedia* (New York: Hippocampus Press, 2004), p. 11; Joshi, *I Am Providence*, vol. 2, p. 783.

18. William H. Goetzmann, *New Lands, New Men: America and the Second Great Age of Discovery* (New York: Viking Penguin, 1986).

19. William Standish, *Hollow Earth* (Cambridge, MA: Da Capo Press, 2006).

20. Joshi, *I Am Providence*, vol. 1, p. 120.

21. Price in *Antarktos Cycle, op. cit.*, 1999, p. 165.

22. John Taine, "The Greatest Adventure," reprinted in *The Antarktos Cycle: At the Mountains of Madness and Other Chilling Tales* (A Chaosium Book, 1999), pp. 167–304. Discussion of the "botched" creatures is found on pp. 208–212.

23. *Ibid.*, pp. 264–268, 295–296.

24. Price in *Antarktos Cycle, op. cit.*, p. 165. Fiction author Lin Carter placed Burroughs's insular Caspak near the Antarctic.

25. Jason C. Eckhardt, "Behind the Mountains of Madness: Lovecraft and the Antarctic in 1930," in *Lovecraft Studies* 6, no. 14 (Spring 1987): pp. 31–38.

26. Joshi, *I Am Providence, op. cit.*, vol. 2, p. 1006; Allen A. Debus, "Really Cool Monsters," *Scary Monsters* no. 44 (Sept. 2002): pp. 29–34.

27. Eckhardt, *op. cit.*, p. 33.

28. *Ibid.*, p. 38.

29. Panel discussion, *Lovecraft Studies* 34, *op. cit.*, 1996, p. 7.

30. See both Standish, *op. cit.*, and Goetzmann, *op. cit.*, for more on Symmes.

31. H.P. Lovecraft, *The Complete Cthulhu Mythos Tales*, "The Shadow Out of Time" (New York: Fall River Press, 2013), pp. 520–573. Quotation borrowed from pp. 542–543.

32. Paul Monteleone, "The Vanity of Existence in 'The Shadow Out of Time,'" in *Lovecraft Studies* 34 (Spring 1996): pp. 32–33.

33. Olaf Stapledon, *Last and First Men and Star Maker: 2 Science-Fiction Novels by Olaf Stapledon* (New York: Dover, 1968).

34. Stephen Jay Gould, ed., "Preface—Reconstructing (and Deconstructing) the Past," *The Book of Life: An Illustrated History of the Evolution of Life on Earth* (New York: W.W. Norton, 1993), p. 15; Bernard Lightman, *Victorian Popularizers of Science: Designing Nature for New Audiences* (University of Chicago Press, 2007).

35. Marc Cerasini, *Godzilla at World's End* (New York: Random House, 1998). *Mad Scientist* editor Martin Arlt, himself a PhD scientist, believes the creatures featured in Legendary's 2014 hit film *Godzilla* bore a "Lovecraftian" aspect. He mentioned this during a July 12 panel discussion at the 2014 G-Fest convention, held in Chicago.

36. Edgar Rice Burroughs, *Tarzan at the Earth's Core*. 1929–30 (New York: Ballantine Books, 1964).

37. Cerasini, *op. cit.*, p. 314.

Part Two

1. Allen A. Debus and Diane E. Debus, *Paleoimagery: The Evolution of Dinosaurs in Art.* (Jefferson, NC: McFarland, 2002), p. 159. Invention of the hydrogen bomb and the horrors of the Korean War would follow shortly after Zallinger completed his Yale masterpiece, thus altering any general sense of national optimism.

2. Hatcher, Marsh and Lull wrote, "By far the most reasonable cause ... seems to be changing climatic conditions and a contracting and draining of the swamp and delta regions caused by the orographic upheavals which occurred toward the close of the Cretaceous. The Ceratopsidae and their nearest allies, the Trachodontidae, both highly specialized plant feeders, were unable to adapt themselves to a profoundly changed environment because of this very specialization, and, as a consequence, perished. That the Ceratopsidae made a gallant struggle for survival seems evident, for they lived through the first series of upheavals at the close of the Laramie and also the second series at the close of the Arapahoe, which were accompanied by great volcanic outbursts in the Colorado region; but the changes accompanying the final upheaval which formed most of the great western mountain chains and closed the Mesozoic era gave the death blow to this remarkable race." John B. Hatcher, O.C. Marsh and R.S. Lull, "The Ceratopsia," *Monographs U.S. Geological Survey* 49 (Washington, DC: 1907), p. 195.

3. Peter J. Bowler, *The Norton History of the Environmental Sciences* (New York: W.W. Norton, 1992), pp. 400–401. Here, Bowler states, "Geologists still use the traditional system to establish the relative age of formations, and the twentieth century has seen notable developments in the precision with which fossils, especially microfossils,

are used to identify strata. But these are refinements of a system that was already established by the 1850s. By the end of the nineteenth century, the theoretical interests of geologists had already switched to the structure of mountains and continents.... The new ideas came from within geophysics, and as a result the earth sciences were reconstituted along a new axis into a subordinate role. On this interpretation, the theoretical confusion of the early twentieth century represents the death-throes of the once-powerful discipline of geology, and the birth-pangs of the modern earth sciences."

4. In this vein, but rather tangential to my premise, are those myriad "last man on Earth" scenarios, perhaps inaugurated with Jean-Baptiste Francois Xavier Cousin de Grainville's 1805 novel, *Le Dernier Homme*, or *The Last Man*. For in his preface to a new English translation, science fiction historian and scholar I.F. Clarke stated Grainville's "singular story was the first tale of the future to consider the death of all human beings and the destruction of the earth—as Last Day acted out in accordance with the will of God. Grainville's tale of global apocalypse was perhaps the first in this genre, but it would be far from the last. One hundred and forty years later, after Hiroshima, the greatest flood of apocalyptic fiction would begin; and throughout the ensuing four decades, a seemingly endless succession of books and films would describe the End of the World as the last act in a chain of human follies." *The Last Man* (Middletown, CT: Wesleyan University Press, New English translation by I.F Clarke and M. Clarke, 2002), p. xviii. See also Clarke's "Introduction," pp. xi–xli. Of course, giant dino-monsters had pivotal roles in this postwar apocalyptical media wave. (Mary Shelley would publish a similar novel in 1826 bearing the same title as Grainville's.) Furthermore, Spencer R. Weart discusses the prevalent "last man" theme in his *Nuclear Fear: A History of Images* (Harvard University Press, 1988), pp. 19, 39, 211, 228. Most recently, followers of AMC's popular television *The Walking Dead* are keenly familiar with this theme in fictional fare. A 2014 novel, David Sakmyster's and Rick Chesler's *Jurassic Dead* (severedpress.com), poignantly melded the zombie-last man theme, reinforcing the dinosaurian/dinosauroid aspect into mainstream. As stated by Paul K. Alkon, "apocalyptic themes in recent fiction are usually not intended to provide a true vision of the future but to raise disturbing questions about the present." *Origins of Futuristic Fiction* (Athens, GA: University of Georgia Press, 1987), p. 59.

Chapter Seven

1. Grant Allen, "The Thames Valley Catastrophe," in *Isaac Asimov Presents the Birth of Science in Fiction: The Best Science Fiction of the 19th Century* (New York: Knightsbridge, 1981), pp. 275–293. For more on Allen's nonfictional pursuits in regard to his "evolutionary epic" writings, see Bernard Lightman's *Victorian Popularizers of Science: Designing Nature for New Audiences* (University of Chicago Press, 2012), Chapter Five.

2. Michael Benton, "Scientific Methodologies in Collision: The History of the Study of the Extinction of the Dinosaurs," *Evolutionary Biology* 24 (1990): pp. 371–400.

3. Peter Vogt, "Evidence for Global Synchronism in Mantle Plume Convection, and Possible Significance for Geology," *Nature* 240 (Dec. 8, 1972): pp. 338–342. The term "dinosaur renaissance" was perhaps first used to celebrate the masses of plastic dinosaur toys being manufactured during the late 1950s, in the July 27, 1958, issue of *This Week Magazine*, p. 9, under a paragraph heading titled "We're in a Dinosaur Renaissance." (Thanks to Jack Arata for providing a Xerox supplying this information.) But the term was later inaugurated in a scientific vein two decades later on the cover of *Scientific American* 232, no. 4 (April 1975), which included an important article by Robert T. Bakker, also having that same title (pp. 58–78). The dawning of a scientific dinosaur renaissance—as far as developments in paleo-science go—may perhaps be traced further back from 1975 to circa 1965, coinciding with Loris Russell's seminal paper, "Body temperature of dinosaurs and its relationship to their extinction," *Journal of Paleontology* 39 (1965): pp. 497–501, in which the consequences of warm-blooded dinosaurs were considered. The summer before, a team of paleontologists led by Prof. John Ostrom discovered the remains of *Deinonychus* in Montana's Lower Cretaceous Cloverly Formation. Elucidation of this dinosaur as disseminated in Ostrom's 1969 paper, "Osteology of *Deinonychus antirrhopus*, an Unusual Theropod from the Lower Cretaceous of Montana," Bulletin 30, Peabody Museum of Natural History—Yale University. "Unusual" proved to be a vast understatement, as the little dinosaur would revolutionize conceptual understanding of dinosaur mobility and probable physiology, triggering a storm of contention enduring through the 1970s and 1980s over presumed dinosaur warm-bloodedness.

4. Vogt, *op. cit.*, p. 340. According to William Glen, following the advent in 1980 of the Alvarez team's theory of mass extinction caused by asteroid impact (of which more will be said in Chapter Sixteen), Vogt readily ascribed to the new hypothesis, overturning his own volcanic model. Glen, *The Mass-Extinction Debates: How Science Works in a Crisis* (Stanford, CA: Stanford University Press, 1994), pp. 30–31.

5. *Ibid.*, p. 341.

6. Preston Cloud, "Paleoecology—Retrospect and prospect," *Journal of Paleontology* 33 (1959): pp. 926–962.

7. Norman D. Newell, "Revolutions in the History of Life," *Geological Society of America Special Paper* 89 (1967): pp. 63–91; N.D. Newell, "Crises in the History of Life," *Scientific American* (Feb. 1963): pp. 77–92.

8. Robert J. Uffen, "Influence of the earth's core on the origin and evolution of life," *Nature* 198 (April 13, 1963): pp. 143–144.

9. David M. Raup, *The Nemesis Affair* (University of Chicago Press, 1986), p. 191.

10. James Gilluly, 1949, cited in Newell, 1967, *op. cit.*, p. 86; Alfred G. Fischer, "The Two Phanerozoic Supercycles," chapter 7 in *Catastrophes and Earth History: The New Uniformitarianism*, W.A. Berggren and John A. Van Couvering, eds. (Princeton University Press, 1984), pp. 129–150.

11. Vogt, *op. cit.*, p. 341.

12. Thomas Schopf, "Permo-Triassic Extinctions: Relation to Sea-Floor Spreading," *Journal of Geology* 82, no. 2 (March 1974): pp. 129–143.

13. *Ibid.*, p. 129.

14. Stephen Jay Gould, *Ever Since Darwin* (New York: W.W. Norton, 1977), p. 138.

15. Cloud, *op. cit.*, p. 954.

16. *Ibid.* However, more recently their Late Permian age has been reassigned to the Late Jurassic instead—*American Geophysical Union Fall Meeting 201, Abstract# GP33-0960*, "Paleomagnetic dating of the copper-zinc-lead Kupferschiefer deposit," Germany, D.T. Symons, *et al.*, found online.

17. Vogt, *op. cit.*, p. 342.

18. Vincent Courtillot, *Evolutionary Catastrophes* (Cambridge: Cambridge University Press, 1999), p. 98.

19. Vogt, *op. cit.*, p. 342.

20. Albert Schatz, "Some Biochemical and Physiological Considerations Regarding the Extinction of the Dinosaurs," *Pennsylvania Academy of Science* 31 (1957): pp. 26–36.

21. Neil C. Koch, "Disappearance of the Dinosaurs," *Journal of Paleontology* 41, no. 4 (July 1967): pp. 970–972. For more on this conceptual matter, see Charles Officer and Jake Page, *The Great Dinosaur Extinction Controversy* (New York: Addison-Wesley, 1996), pp. 174–177.

22. A. Lee McAlester, "Animal Extinctions, Oxygen Consumption, and Atmospheric History," *Journal of Paleontology* 44, no. 3 (May 1970): pp. 405–409.

23. Muller's work cited in Benton, *op. cit.* Muller, "Sind die Dinosaurier durch Vulkanausbruche ausgeratet?" *Unsere Welt* 20 (1928): pp. 144–146. But also see the analogous 1907 contemplations of Hatcher, Marsh and Lull, cited in Note #2, herein the Introduction to Part Two.

24. Vogt, *op. cit.*, p. 340.

25. The quoted term borrowed from Elizateth Kolbert's *The Sixth Extinction: An Unnatural History* (New York: Henry Holt, 2014), p. 87.

26. The quoted term was coined by chemical oceanographer Wallace Broecker, referring to an instance in which all plankton died off in a mass extinction, thus killing the ocean-atmosphere system, such as what was once hypothesized for the post-asteroid impact Late Cretaceous ocean. See Kenneth Hsu, *The Great Dying: Cosmic Catastrophe, Dinosaurs, and the Theory of Evolution* (New York: Harcourt, Brace, Jovanovich, 1986), p. 232. Note that the title to Hsu's book is a bit of a misnomer, as the term "great dying" is usually applied to the much more severe Permo-Triassic extinction, occurring approximately 185 million years earlier.

27. Adrian J. Desmond, *The Hot-Blooded Dinosaurs: A Revolution in Palaeontology* (New York: Dial Press/James Wade, 1976), p. 196; Rachel Carson, *Silent Spring* (New York: Fawcett World Library), 1962.

28. Allen A. Debus, "Dewey McLean's Volcanic Greenhouse Theory," in *Fossil News: Journal of Avocational Paleontology* 17, no. 2 (March–April 2011): pp. 5–9.

29. B.W. Oelofson, "Atmospheric Carbon Dioxide/Oxygen Imbalance in the Late Cretaceous, Hatching of Eggs and the Extinction of Biota," *Palaeontology Afr.* 21 (1978): pp. 45–51. Although not considering extinctions as resultant of global warming, Oelofson attributed diminishing atmospheric oxygen levels at the K-Pg boundary to selective extinctions and survivals among the vertebrates. His root cause was carbon dioxide-laden (kimberlitic) eruptions, with an assist from basaltic plumes—such as India's Deccan Traps.

30. Vogt, *op. cit.*, p. 342.

31. Robert S. White and Dan P. McKenzie, "Volcanism at Rifts," *Scientific American* (July 1989): p. 71.

32. Search online for Dewey Max McLean, "Dinosaur: K-T Transition Greenhouse and Embryogenesis Dysfunction in the Dinosaurian Extinctions" (available for viewing as of late 2010). Filebox.vt.edu/users/dmclean/fileboxmigration/artsci/geology/mclean/Dinosaur_Volcano_Extinction/index.html.

33. Dewey McLean, "Terminal Mesozoic 'Greenhouse': Lessons from the Past," *Science* 201 (Aug. 4, 1978): pp. 401–406.

34. "Heat, Not Cold, Killed Off Dinosaurs, Scientist Holds," Sept. 14, 1939. Newspaper clipping found in Allen G. Debus's dinosaur scrapbook (p. 102). Publication unknown. Note that for several years, it was thought that the dinosaurs had died off when the climate turned too wintry. A cartoon, captioned "Frozen Out," found on p. 241 of astronomer W. Maxwell Read's *The Earth for Sam* (New York: Harcourt, Brace, 1930), a popular book intended for younger, impressionable readers underscores this older idea.

35. *Ibid.*

36. Edwin H. Colbert, *A Fossil-Hunter's Notebook: My Life with Dinosaurs and Other Friends* (New York: E.P. Dutton, 1980), pp. 104, 106–108.

37. Relying on a physics concept, this principle suggests that during conditions of prevailing colder climate, species which tend to grow larger (i.e., greater body mass-per-volume ratio) would be expected to retain and conserve body heat more effectively—a factor that would render them more capable of surviving in freezing conditions.

38. McLean, 1978, *op. cit.*, p. 403.

39. Desmond, *op. cit.*

40. Kenneth Carpenter, in *Eggs, Nests, and Baby Dinosaurs: A Look at Dinosaur Reproduction* (Indiana University Press, 1999), pp. 254–255. For more on egg-laying via reproduction as a possible factor in dinosaurian extinctions, see Michael Allaby and James Lovelock, *The Great Extinction* (Garden City, NY: Doubleday, 1983), pp. 151–154.

41. McLean, "Terminal Cretaceous Extinctions and Volcanism: A Link," was published in *Abstracts of Papers*, p. 128.

42. Peter Vogt was a pioneer in linking volcanoes with mass extinctions. For in 1972, he suggested that intensified episodes of tectonically triggered volcanism may have caused or contributed to mass extinctions recorded in the fossil record. Particularly intense volcanic episodes may have resulted in large-scale pollution and poisoning of the ocean-atmosphere system. Such worldwide episodes were viewed as recurring every 50 to 60 million years (*Nature* 240, p. 338). Some of you recall that much of the contention toward Alfred Wegener's continental drift theory was that he lacked sufficiently convincing evidence, as well as a viable mechanism causing horizontal continental movement. Arguably, McLean apparently had both circumstances in his favor. Yet it wasn't enough to prevail in the hallowed courtroom of science.

43. McLean, "Deccan volcanism and the Cretaceous-Tertiary transition scenario: a unifying causal mechanism," *Syllogeus* 39 (1982): pp. 143–44.

44. McLean, "Deccan Traps Mantle Degassing in the Terminal Cretaceous Marine Extinctions," *Cretaceous Research* 6 (1985): pp. 235–259.

45. *Ibid.*, p. 249; Hsu, *op. cit.*

46. Officer and Page, *op. cit.*, p. 80. McLean's website is a popularly aimed tour-de-force defense of the Deccan Traps as causal factor of K-Pg mass extinctions.

47. Officer and Page, *op. cit.*, p. 81.

48. *Ibid.*, p. 171. As explained by William Glen, "Volcanism theory in its original, post-Alvarez form ... which I termed the 'non-explosive volcanism hypothesis,' did not entail great explosive volcanism but merely a carbon-cycle perturbation of long duration triggered by the Deccan Traps volcanism. And even in its modified form, which I termed the 'explosive volcanism hypothesis,' ... and which included great explosive episodes, volcanism-extinction

theory did not at first have to accommodate the additional problem of providing impact-level shock pressures, because the shocked-quartz evidence for impact was not found until almost a year later [1984]": William Glen, ed., "How Science Works in the Debates," by William Glen, Chapter Two, p. 66, in *Mass- Extinction Debates: How Science Works in a Crisis* (Stanford University Press, 1994).

49. Terms such as Canfield and anoxic oceans are described, for instance, in Peter Ward's 2007 book, *Under A Green Sky* (Smithsonian Books). A Canfield rather simplistically may be viewed as one in which ocean layers are "stratified" with lower, bottom waters depleted of oxygen—resulting in production of poisonous hydrogen sulfide introduced by sulfur bacteria. Anoxia and death of higher organisms within the oceanic realm is a result. Two of the scientists who investigated this phenomenon as recorded in the fossil record are Lee Kump and Don Canfield.

50. McLean, 1995, cited online publication, *op. cit.*

51. *Ibid.*

52. Courtillot, *op. cit.*, p. 60.

53. Ward, *op. cit.* In 1989, geologists John D. O'Keefe and Thomas J. Ahrens suggested that there must have been a carbon dioxide-greenhouse heating of the atmosphere in the aftermath of the K-Pg impact because the host (terrestrial) rock in the target zone was carbonate, which would have immediately volatilized from heat transfer of the impacting body into gaseous CO_2. O'Keefe and Ahrens, "Impact production of CO_2 by the Cretaceous/Tertiary extinction bolide and the resultant heating of the Earth," *Nature* 338 (1989): pp. 247–249. In their prior 1982 paper, they stressed the importance of water vapor, volatilized during a plausible impact, as a greenhouse-reinforcing, geologically short-term global warming factor. John D. O'Keefe and Thomas J. Ahrens, "The interaction of the Cretaceous/Tertiary Extinction Bolide with the atmosphere, ocean and solid Earth," *Geological Society of America*, Special Paper 190, pp. 103–120.

54. *Ibid.*, pp. 137–138.

55. Douglas Erwin, *Extinction: How Life on Earth Nearly Ended 250 Million Years Ago* (Princeton University Press, 2006), p. 216.

56. Without delving into the geochemical equations here, intense volcanic emissions add carbon dioxide to the atmosphere, which then can be dissolved into the uppermost oceanic layers. Dissolution of carbon dioxide forms carbonic acid, contributing to acidification (i.e., a lowering of pH), thus inhibiting species of shelly organisms from forming their calcitic (or aragonitic) shells. Furthermore, heightened atmospheric levels of carbon dioxide contribute to "greenhouse" global warming of the planet, as predicted by chemist Svante Arrhenius in 1896. S. Arrhenius, "On the Influence of Carbon Acid in the Air upon the Temperature of the Ground," *Philosophical Magazine* 41 (1896): p. 237. Also see John Gribbin's *Future Weather and the Greenhouse Effect: A Book about Carbon Dioxide, Climate and Mankind* (New York: A Delta/Eleanor Friede Book, 1982).

Chapter Eight

1. This scene is not unlike a similar one witnessed in *One Million B.C.* (1940); both may have been in some ways inspired by analogous passages penned by Arthur Conan Doyle for chapter fifteen of his 1912 novel *The Lost World*. Also we see similar scenes in Irwin Allen's 1960 *Lost World* remake involving camera-enlarged pseudo-dinosaurs, one fashioned from a live alligator.

2. Henry Kuttner, "Dr. Cyclops," *Thrilling Wonder Stories* 16, no. 3 (June 1940): pp. 14–32.

3. The editor's quoted remark is found on p. 119 of *Thrilling Wonder Stories* (June 1940); Kuttner, *op. cit.*, "Men in Miniature," pp. 125–126.

4. *Ibid.*, p. 119.

5. Kuttner, "Dr. Cyclops," *op. cit.*, p. 23.

6. *Ibid.*, pp. 25, 31.

7. Kuttner, *op. cit.*, pp. 125–126.

8. Will Garth, *Dr. Cyclops* (1940; New York: Centaur Books, 1976 reprint).

9. *Ibid.*, p. 86. For more on the scientific violation of Nature, cast as a female entity, see Spencer R. Weart's *Nuclear Fears: A History of Images* (Cambridge, MA: Harvard University Press, 1988).

10. Adrienne Mayor, *The First Fossil Hunters: Paleontology in Greek and Roman Times* (Princeton University Press, 2000).

11. Richard Matheson, *The Shrinking Man* (New York: Berkley Books, 1979).

12. *Ibid.*, pp. 1, 118–119.

13. *Ibid.*, p. 170.

14. *Ibid.*, p. 108.

15. Peter Weingart, "Chemists and their Craft in Fiction Film," in *The Public Image of Chemistry*, ed. Joachim Schummer, Bernadette Bensaude-Vincent, Brigitte Van Tiggelen (London: World Scientific Publishing, 2007), p. 92.

16. Mary Shelley, *Frankenstein, or the Modern Prometheus.* (1818) (New York: Pyramid Books, 1964), p. 48.

17. Roslynn Haynes, "The Alchemist in Fiction: The Master Narrative," *HYLE—International Journal for Philosophy of Chemistry* 12, no. 1 (2006): pp. 5–29.

18. Spencer R. Weart probes this idea considerably in his *Nuclear Fears, op. cit.* Quote is from p. 148. Of special interest, he proclaims: "Womb symbolism was most explicit in *Rodan*, where scientists went down a tunnel to an underground room and saw a monster emerge from an egg, what the actors called a forbidden sight. If moviegoers did not already associate radioactivity with such primal problems when they sent into the theater, they would do so by the time they came out" (p. 193). Also, Weart discusses man's historical fascination with "death rays" throughout this book. Godzilla, of course, comes equipped with his own unique death "heat ray."

19. *Ibid.*, p. 215.

20. Ray Bradbury, *The Martian Chronicles* (New York: Doubleday, 1950), pp. 166–172. Notably, Bradbury also nuked Chicago in his 1953 novel, *Fahrenheit 451* (New York: Ballantine Books).

21. The background on how Bradbury's "The Fog Horn" led to the 1953 film is given in Chapter Four, "Shadow of Gojira," of my book, *Dinosaurs in Fantastic Fiction* (Jefferson, NC: McFarland, 2006).

22. As noted by David Prus at a July 2014 G-Fest panel discussion, Godzilla makes its very first dramatic "supernatural" appearance on Odo Island during the midst of a (not so gentle or soft) driving *rain* storm! I participated in the G-Fest panel discussion, "Atom Age Connections," organized and chaired by Michael Bogue on July 12, 2014, along with Mark Matzke. David Prus was an attendee at this panel. Steve Ryfle, *Japan's Favorite Mon Star: The Unauthorized Biography of "The Big G"* (Toronto: ECW Press, 1998), p. 35.

Chapter Nine

1. Richard Rhodes, *The Making of the Atomic Bomb* (New York: Simon & Schuster, 1986), p. 11. Interestingly, decades earlier, Mary Shelley dwelled on a similar intonation, as expressed by her father William Godwin (and reflected in her novel *Frankenstein, or the Modern Prometheus*), "What the heart of man is able to conceive, the hand of man is strong enough to perform." Yes, as biographer Emily W. Sunstein notes, "Mary Shelley recognized that what her father trusted as the promise of humankind ... was also its gravest threat." Sunstein, *Mary Shelley: Romance and Reality* (Boston: Little Brown, 1989), p. 132.

2. Ralph E. Lapp, *The Voyage of the Lucky Dragon* (New York: Harper & Brothers Publishers, 1958), p. 185.

3. Rhodes, *op. cit.* (1986), pp. 356, 620; Michihiko Hachiya, M.D., *Hiroshima Diary,* translated by Warner Wells (New York: Avon, 1955).

4. Ed Godziszewski, ed., *Japanese Giants: The Magazine of Japanese Science Fiction and Fantasy* 10 (Sept. 2004): p. 5.

5. *Ibid.*, p. 8.

6. Steve Ryfle, "Godzilla's Footprint," notes included in ClassicMedia's DVD compilation set *Gojira: The Original Japanese Masterpiece*, Toho, p. 2.

7. Rhodes, *op. cit.* (1986), p. 11.

8. Spencer R. Weart, *The Rise of Nuclear Fear* (Harvard University Press, 2012), p. 97.

9. Richard Rhodes, *Dark Sun: The Making of the Hydrogen Bomb* (New York: Simon & Schuster, 1995), pp. 407–408.

10. *Ibid.*, p. 402.

11. *Ibid.*, p. 510.

12. *Ibid.*, p. 524.

13. *Ibid.*, p. 541.

14. *Ibid.*, pp. 541–542.

15. Lapp, *op. cit.*, p. 28.

16. Oishi Matashichi, *The Day the Sun Rose in the West* (University of Hawaii Press, 2011), p. 19.

17. Lapp, *op. cit.*, p. 29. But also see Oishi, p. 19, concerning a contrasting mushroom cloud observation.

18. Oishi, *op. cit.*, p. 20.

19. Oishi, *op. cit.*, p. 157.

20. Weart, *op. cit.*, p. 97.

21. *Ibid.*

22. Oishi, *op. cit.*, pp. 25–26.

23. *Ibid.*, p. 43.

24. Oishi, *op. cit.*, p. 126.

25. Mick Broderick, ed., *Hibakusha Cinema: Hiroshima, Nagasaki and the Nuclear Image in Japanese Film* (London & New York: Kegan Paul International, 1996), pp. 57, 72.

26. Oishi, *op. cit.*, pp. 57–63.

27. Lapp, *op. cit.*, p. 197.

28. Rhodes, *op. cit.* (1995), p. 542; Oishi, *op. cit.*, pp. 27, 35.

29. Oishi, *op. cit.*, p. 102.

30. *Ibid.*, pp. 38–39.

31. Weart, *op. cit.*, p. 98.

32. William Tsutsui, *Godzilla On My Mind: Fifty Years of the King of Monsters* (New York: Palgrave Macmillan, 2004), p. 19.

33. Lapp, *op. cit.*, p. 127.

34. Oishi, *op. cit.*, pp. 126–127, 133.

35. James T. Patterson, *Grand Expectations: The United States, 1945–1974* (Oxford University Press, 1996), pp. 277–278; Broderick, *op. cit.*, p. 18, note 8.

36. Broderick, *op. cit.*, pp. 4, 27.

37. Rhodes, *op. cit.* (1995), p. 566.

38. *Ibid.*, p. 568.

39. *Ibid.*, pp. 444, 569–575.

40. Paul R. Ehrlich, Carl Sagan, Donald Kennedy, Walter Orr Roberts, *The Cold and the Dark: The World after Nuclear War* (W.W. Norton, 1984).

41. Broderick, *op. cit.*, p. 1; Oishi, *op. cit.*, pp. 73–74, 140.

42. Broderick, *op. cit.*, p. 30.

43. Oishi, *op. cit.*, p. 92.

44. Allen A. Debus, "Nuclear Dragon," *G-Fan* no. 105 (2014): pp. 22–29.

Chapter Ten

1. Allen A. Debus, "Godzilla's Roots: The earliest stego-tyrannosaur 'hybrid,'" *G-Fan* 1, no. 67 (Spring 2004): pp. 12–14; Allen A. Debus, "Rise of the Gigantis Imposters," *G-Fan* 1, no. 103, pp. 14–18. The "Showa" series of Godzilla films corresponds to those released between 1954 and 1974, during the reign of Japan's emperor Hirohito.

2. Quotes are from Steve Ryfle, *Japan's Favorite Mon-Star: The Unauthorized Biography of "The big G"* (Toronto: ECW Press, 1999), p. 22, and Donald F. Glut, *Classic Movie Monsters* (Metuchen, NJ: Scarecrow Press, 1978), p. 403. Thus, to a certain extent, the original written story treatment seems to have enveloped action from the first two movies in the series.

3. Also in this photo, another poster is seen affixed to the rear wall of the room, possibly suggesting yet another set of prehistoric animals then under consideration. Figures in this second illustration are not clearly visible, however. In order to make a continual, single-sided copy of the *Life* pictorial *Age of Reptiles* spread, two copies of the magazine, tape and scissors would have been needed. But the poster does not appear to be a second copy of Zallinger's *The Age of Reptiles,* nor would it appear to be a reproduction of Zallinger's *Age of Mammals* life-through-time painting, first published in *Life* magazine's Oct. 19, 1953, issue. Although figures indiscernible within the rearmost picture hanging on the wall in the Toho file photo may not have been quite as influential as Zallinger's pot-bellied tyrannosaur toward designing Godzilla's theropodous attributes, it would be interesting to eventually someday identify this fuzzy-looking picture (which for all we know may not even portray any prehistoric animals).

4. To my knowledge, *Life* actually didn't print *The Age of Reptiles* as a poster then, but as a double-sided set of fold-out pages. But for simplicity here, I'll refer to it simply as a poster.

5. A trip to the Peabody Museum touches a chord. Given the skeletal armatures displayed below Yale's great mural, *The Age of Reptiles* takes on three-dimensional ambiance, as reconstructed bones of many of the painted animals stand erected directly below their restored figures, projected in colorful landscapes (offering even further visual depth, receding into the wall). Seen correctly, *in situ* at Yale University, the mural's perspective uncannily projects into the exhibit hall where observers stand, onto the vividly painted surface and then magically transforms beyond into the wall itself. Toho certainly selected an inspirational masterpiece for its first giant monster! Beginning circa 1955, Zallinger's prehistoric reptile and mammal figures, appearing as *Life* installments and a later volume, *The*

World We Live In (1955), were recreated three-dimensionally by Phil Derham and a team of sculptors, including Joe Ferriot, as small sculptures converted into immensely popular plastic toys sold by the Louis Marx Company. These once ubiquitous toys proved highly influential in fostering love and curiosity for heralded creatures of prehistory among a generation of young dinophiles, coincidentally when Godzilla was gaining popularity in America. The pot-bellied tyrannosaur was molded with characteristic ridged spinal scales. Thanks to Mike Fredericks and Jack Arata for identifying Derham and Ferriot.

6. Josef Augusta, *Prehistoric Animals* (London: Spring Books, 1956). Burian researcher Thomas Kovacs's letter was printed in *Dinosaur World* (Summer/Fall 1998): pp. 3–5.

7. Zdeněk V. Spinar, *Life Before Man* (New York: Crescent Books, 1981), p. 128.

8. I'll stray one step farther with this. The head and snout of the carnivorous "proto–Godzilla" which the artist is seen sketching in this Toho file photo does vaguely resemble the shape of the head in Burian's *Tyrannosaurus* (1938), as seen in *Prehistoric Animals, op. cit.*, Plate 34.

9. Jane Werner Watson, *Dinosaurs and Other Prehistoric Reptiles* (New York: Golden Press, 1960), p. 32.

10. "Cold War era 'Lordly' tyrannosaurids exude a self-confident, battle-hardened, unthreatened demeanor, evidently secure in their role as Mesozoic overlords. If *T. rexes* of the atomic age, painted or sculpted by paleoartists in America seemed majestic, it was because they reflected America's might and authority as a world power." Allen A. Debus and Diane Debus, *op. cit., Paleoimagery*, p. 159.

11. W.J.T. Mitchell, *The Last Dinosaur Book* (University of Chicago Press, 1998), p. 197.

12. August Ragone, *Eiji Tsubuyara: Master of Monsters* (San Francisco: Chronicle Books, 2007), p. 38. Also, see Allen A. Debus, "Triumphant Triumvirate: Godzilla's Dinosaurian 'Progenitors'," in *G-Fan* 1, no. 98 (Winter 2012): pp. 50–56.

13. For considerably more on this movie, the 1960 "remake" and the 1912 novel, see my lead article in "Lost World Revisited" in *Scary Monsters Magazine: Scary Summer Special* no. 4 (2012): pp. 5–19.

14. Note that Arthur Conan Doyle's visual "trick" mentioned in this chapter was also employed in several other period giant dino-monster films—*Rodan, the Flying Monster* (1956), *The Giant Behemoth* (1959), *Gorgo* (1961), and *Reptilicus* (1962). Giant prehistoric monsters Rodan and Reptilicus have wings but are too large to fly. Furthermore, it seems that in the Japanese films, radiation isn't usually the accepted cause or culprit of the dino-monsters' great size, although in the case of Paleosaurus from 1959's *The Giant Behemoth*, and Rhedosaurus, nuclear bombs instigate their appearances and their wrath. The idea that their giant sizes somehow resulted from radiation exposure became grafted into popular culture and general ideology of 1950s giant monster movies through several American directors—like Bert I. Gordon of *Amazing Colossal Man* fame, or David Weisbart, who produced 1954's *Them!* Also, several of the dino-monsters are amphibious, yet lack signs of gills or other aquatic adaptations. Their invulnerability to conventional weapons defies comprehension. Besides Reptilicus's penchant for fresh cows on the hoof, the dietary habits of these giant creatures is left to the imagination. Because aberrations such as Rhedosaurus, Godzilla, Anguirus, Paleosaurus, Rodan, Gorgo and Reptilicus are such flagrantly different sorts of pseudo-dinosaurs, extra emphasis must be placed on explaining their occurrences and unnatural history. In cases of movieland dinosaurs that are "real," that is, more closely aligned with those known to science, as in films like *The Lost World* (1925), *Jurassic Park* (1993), and *King Kong* (1933), fewer pains and concocted stories are needed to explain why these supposedly extinct creatures are still alive. In such cases, the scientific intrigue simplifies to something like this: "Yes—it's a genuine, living tyrannosaur." But then it must be explained how it has (a) survived, or (b) been resurrected into modernity. The answers usually are, "Gosh, we aren't scientists, but we just ever so conveniently found these creatures in a 'lost world' setting, which is naturally where one would expect to find such animals." Or, "Yes, we are scientifically trained people, and so we recreated it in a laboratory using biochemistry."

15. Of course, following 1962's *Reptilicus*, audiences probably had fully wised up to the fact that these giant dino-monsters and those that would soon follow (e.g., Gamera, Gappa and Yongary) clearly were not at all genetically allied to *real* prehistoric animals, such as those appearing in Zallinger's famous mural *Age of Reptiles*. Usually in sci-fi and horror flicks, disbelief in what is about to transpire at the gruesome hands of a mad scientist, whose deranged capabilities are called into question, is satisfactorily suspended by use of apparatus in a la-BOR-a-tory, bedecked with splendorous, electrically sparkling "Strickfaden devices"—created for Universal's *Frankenstein* (1931), or bubbling flasks of chemicals in flasks and glassware, or even physics inventions (e.g., time machines, transportation devices, radiation death ray emitters, etc. But with paleo-themed sci-fi/horror monster movies, circumstances are necessarily different. Here, different pseudoscientific lines of evidence must be called upon to suggest the veracity of what is unfolding before our very eyes. For more on these and related dino-monsters see Allen A. Debus, "Giant Dino-Monster 'Theory': Visualizing the *Real* 'Dino' in Dino-Monster Reel," *Scary Monsters* 88 (June 2013): pp. 107–119.

Chapter Eleven

1. I. Bernard Cohen, *Revolution in Science* (Cambridge, MA: Harvard University Press, 1985), pp. 32–35.

2. Luis W. Alvarez (of whom more shall be said in Chapter Nineteen) was an early proponent of this strategy. See Alvarez's *Alvarez: Adventures of a Physicist* (New York: Basic Books, 1987), p. 65.

3. William Tsutsui, *Godzilla On My Mind: Fifty Years of the King of Monsters* (New York: Palgrave Macmillan, 2004), p. 29.

4. Rachel Carson, *The Edge of the Sea* (New York: Mentor Books, 1955); Rachel Carson, *Silent Spring* (1962; New York: Fawcett Books, 1970); *Nightmare—Creature of the Deep!* 1, no. 5 (August 1971): pp. 36–47.

5. "Menace from the Deep," *Gorgo* 1, no. 16 (Dec. 1963). Because Gorgo was an amphibious dino-monster, as we'll see in the next chapter, logically many of its stories involved marine monsters, threats and cataclysmic disturbances.

6. Spencer R. Weart, *The Rise of Nuclear Fear* (Harvard University Press, 2012), p. 189.

7. J.G. Ballard, *The Terminal Beach* (1962; New York: Carroll & Graf, 1987), "Deep End," pp. 158–170. In "Deep End," Ballard's character Granger states, "In draining them [i.e., the oceans] we deliberately obliterated our own pasts,

to a large extent our own self-identities.... Without the sea ... we become nothing more than the ghosts of memories, blind and homeless, flitting through the dry chambers of a gutted skull" (p. 164); A.C. Crispin, *V: The Terrifying Novel Based on the Full Ten-hour NBC-TV Miniseries* (New York: Pinnacle Books, 1984). Also, an aim of the alien race in Toho's *Monster Zero* (1970 U.S. release) was to seize control of our bountiful oceans.

8. Steve Ryfle, *Japan's Favorite Mon Star: The Unauthorized Biography of "The Big G"* (Toronto: ECW Press, 1998), p. 307.

9. The "Strangelove Ocean" hypothesis was appropriately named after the titular character in the popular 1964 anti-nuclear film, *Dr. Strangelove, Or: How I Learned to Stop Worrying and Love the Bomb.* For more detailed overview on the Strangelove Ocean effect and pertinent geochemical evidence, see pertinent chapters in Kenneth J. Hsu's *The Great Dying: Cosmic Catastrophe, Dinosaurs, and the Theory of Evolution* (New York: Harcourt, Brace, Jovanovich, 1986), and George R. McGhee's *The Late Devonian Mass Extinction: The Frasnian/Famennian Crisis* (New York: Columbia University Press, 1996).

10. The natural "driver" of these past extinctions is thought to be carbon dioxide or methane-greenhouse warmed conditions, perhaps initiated by intensified volcanic activity, hampering how oceanic currents continually replenish the lower layers with fresh oxygenated water. Lack of circulating oxygen in the oceans leads to anoxia. See Peter Ward's *Under A Green Sky* (Smithsonian Books, 2007) and *The Medea Hypothesis: Is Life On Earth Ultimately Self-Destructive?* (Princeton University Press, 2009), for more on this intriguing topic. During heightened volcanic phases, excess carbon dioxide would have acidified the oceans too, killing organisms (but possibly, eventually curbing the activity of the hydrogen sulfide-releasing microbes). Incidentally, over the past half-billion years, atmospheric oxygen levels have fluctuated through geological time, dipping to as low as 13 percent about 200 million years ago. (Today it is 21 percent.) Today, California's Salton Sea is an ecologically perturbed example of "eutrophication" caused by excessive farmland chemical runoff into the waters that has effectively de-oxygenated lower parts of the water column, resulting in a microbial sulfide emission. Millions of years ago, such eutrophication around the globe resulted in formation of today's coal and petroleum deposits. Stanley E. Manahan, *Environmental Chemistry,* 2nd ed. (Boston, MA: Willard Grant Press, 1975), pp. 186–187; Robert A. Berner, *The Phanerozoic Carbon Cycle* (Oxford University Press, 2004); Michael Allaby and James Lovelock, *The Great Extinction: The Solution to One of the Great Mysteries of Science—the Disappearance of the Dinosaurs* (New York: Doubleday, 1983), pp. 130–132.

11. For more on this matter, see *Dinosaurs in Fantastic Fiction: A Thematic Survey* (Jefferson, NC: McFarland, 2006).

Chapter Twelve

1. When I was six years old, my parents never took me to see *Gorgo* (which I finally saw on a local Chicagoland station called "Creature Features" as a teenager about a decade later). Nor were any of those promotional comic books ever purchased for our household, despite my uncanny interest in the monster based on the advertising and the fact that "all my friends" got to see the film. While I patiently purchased most of these from eBay over the course of several months, I paid a small mint for the complete collection. I hope my wife never reads this footnote!

2. *Gorgo* 1, no. 1 (May 1961). A convention I will use only in this chapter is not to state page numbers from each of the "Gorgo" books, although every quote cited in paragraphs concerning a book is borrowed from each respective book as cited. As stated by J.D. Lees in *G-Fan* no. 100 (Fall 2012): p. 45, "The writer of the Charlton Comics series was the prolific Joe Gill. He did most of his work at Charlton, but also wrote some DC comics. In addition to *Gorgo,* he also wrote the *Konga* series. He and Steve Ditko created the hero Captain Atom. Joe Gill died in 2006. Steve Ditko is best known for co-creating Spider-Man with Stan lee. He penciled the first three issues of *Gorgo,* then came back for issues #11 and #13 to #16. He also did the art in *Return of Gorgo* #2 and #3. His work at Marvel Comics prevented him from doing more at Charlton. Ditko, born in 1927, is still working as of this writing. *Gorgo* #5 to #10 were drawn and inked by Joe Sinnott and Vince Coletta, both of whom went on to make names for themselves at Marvel. Art in issues #17 to #23 was by Bill Montes and Ernie Bache."

3. *The Return of Gorgo* 1, no. 2 (August 1961).

4. *Gorgo* 1, no. 3 (Sept. 1961).

5. *Gorgo* 1, no. 4 (Nov. 1961).

6. *Ibid.*

7. *Gorgo* 1, no. 5 (January 1962).

8. *Gorgo* 1, no. 6 (April 1962).

9. *Gorgo* 1, no. 7 (June 1962).

10. In *Gorgo* 1, no. 8 (August 1962, job A-1531), "The Graveyard of Lost Ships," thieves lead a documentary film producer named Hal and his wife Ja, to the legendary Sargasso Sea, where they can cherry-pick treasure all for taking from sunken ships and ancient naval vessels. Meanwhile, the Ogras swim northward to Arctic waters, in order to flee the quarrelsome ways of mankind. Curiously, the northernmost sector of the planet is warm (not frigid) and inhabited by a "lost" race of native Eskimos. The thieves sail to the same polar waters, where they indeed find the treasure of lost ships. Hal and Jan are then stranded, while the thieves to take off with their loot. But the Ogras—Gorgo and mother—end their plans, crunching their fleeing ship to "kindling wood," while Hal and Jan make it safely to shore in a small motorboat. Eventually, thanks to the Ogras, they're rescued and return to civilization, with a wonderful set of film footage documenting their polar adventures in the Sargasso Sea. A second comic book tale appearing in issue #8, titled "The Monster," would seem a curious, low-tech forerunner of Robert Hood's 2007 short story, "Flesh and Bone," published in *Daikaiju! 3: Giant Monsters vs. the World.* A final tale, not involving Gorgo, "The Executioner," spins the tale of a mad scientist who has created a mechanical, pre-Mechagodzilla dino-monster, built to destroy, or rather "execute" a world which had mocked him. The plan is thwarted by a silly, stupid mistake.

11. *Gorgo* 1, no. 9 (October 1962, #A-1679).

12. Obviously by this time in history, the United States had grown an antagonistic stance toward "Red" China and other communist countries of the world, which threatened the U.S. The pattern is highly evident throughout the Charlton series.

13. *Gorgo* 1, no. 10 (December 1962, #A-1850). Also see my article, "Three Giant Venusian Dino-Monsters," in *G-Fan* 1, no. 96 (Summer 2011): pp. 18–22.

14. *Gorgo* 1, no. 11, titled "Gorgo's Triumph!" (Feb. 1963, job # A-2221), is a lighthearted excursion from the Cold War nuclear weapons-flinging business. This tale is about a stereotypical, down-on-his-luck movie director, who decides the perfect way to stage a major comeback would be to make a movie about the dino-monster Ogras, while also featuring fading film stars who can be gotten on the cheap. The setting will be an island populated by natives who vaguely resemble those Skull Islanders in RKO's *King Kong* (1933). Things quickly take turn for the worse, though, as the islanders happen to be headhunters and Gorgo doesn't necessarily want to follow a "script" on camera. Gorgo "toys" with the submarine, carrying away the terrified film crew as it flees. And even the mother Ogra gets into the act. As things turn out, the director has sufficient footage to make his movie, tagged the "most colossal epic ever filmed!" So in the movie, *Gorgo's Triumph!*, the monster who, ironically, originated as a genuine movie monster icon finally becomes a film star of the comic book world. In a sense, this tale presages a premise (but not the somber tone) of Mark Jacobson's 1991 novel, *Gojiro*. The "feel" of Gorgo #11 has a rather fun and humorous spirit, quite a departure from that in earlier issues.

15. *Gorgo* 1, no. 12 (April 1963).

16. Jack Finney, *Invasion of the Body Snatchers*. 1954, *Collier's* (New York: Simon & Schuster, 1978). Stephen King discusses the 1956 film version adapted from Finney's novel in *Danse Macabre* (New York: Berkley Books, 1981), pp. 5–6, with its subliminal "better dead than Red" implication. "They're here already. You're next." Reptisaurus of course was "Reptilicus," which inaugurated its own Charlton book series in August 1961. In Gorgo #12, there is even reference to Reptisaurus' mate, which is peculiar considering how Reptilicus reproduced itself, in carrot- or clone-like fashion, in the 1961 film. The alternative name Reptisaurus was christened with issue #3, printed in January 1962. The "body snatching" story element conveyed in Gorgo #12, although pertaining directly neither to nuclear bomb testing nor the threat of thermonuclear holocaust, reflects yet another important Cold War period theme.

17. *Gorgo's Revenge* (January 1962, #A-1642); *The Return of Gorgo* no. 2 (Summer 1963, #A-2851); *The Return of Gorgo* no. 3 (Fall 1964, #A-4072). By the fall of 1964, *The Return of Gorgo* no. 3 was issued with a feature story titled "Hidden Witness" (job #A-4072). We see a playful, helpful porpoise on the cover, reminding older readers of a popular television series named *Flipper*, which debuted on Sept. 19, 1964—an obvious influence for this particular Gorgo tale. Gorgo's "porpoise"—as stated on the cover—is named Cecil, but is later referred to as a bottle-nosed dolphin named "Clyde" within the book. It turns out that "Clyde" is being trained to communicate with humans by a friendly marine zoologist. When atomic sub USS *Ripper* becomes trapped two miles deep in the Atlantic Ocean abyss under an avalanche of boulders and rocks, the zoologist conveys to Clyde that he should dive as far as possible to see if he can spot the downed submarine. Meanwhile, the Navy also hopes to reach the USS *Ripper* with a man in a bathysphere. Of course Clyde can't dive to such a great depth, so instead attracts the attention of Gorgo, who can. Tugging insistently on his enormous ears, the dolphin/porpoise cajoles Gorgo, who can withstand pressures of the far deeps below, into swimming down to the site of the stricken submarine—before it is too late. Gorgo removes rocks and boulders from the USS *Ripper*'s hull, yet at first doesn't complete the "mission." When weary Gorgo surfaces on a break, military jets unfairly commence firing on him until ordered sternly to cease fire. So next time, Gorgo descends with a manned bathysphere; Gorgo frees the submarine, lifting it safely to shallow waters in his powerful jaws. The story ends with Clyde happily whispering into one of Gorgo's huge ears, perhaps the first instance of interspecies, giant "monster talk" (e.g., as in Toho's later *Ghidrah, the 3-Headed Monster*, U.S. release, Sept. 29, 1965).

18. Aided by the U.S., Taiwan incidentally had been enjoying a rapid period of economic success during the 1950s and early 1960s. Meanwhile, China detonated its first atomic warhead in October 1964—intended as a deterrent against both the U.S. and the former Soviet Union, and later exploded its first hydrogen bomb in 1967, long after Charlton's *Gorgo* series ended. Records document that in 1958, the U.S. considered dropping atomic weapons on China during a dispute over Taiwan.

19. *Gorgo* 1, no. 13 (June 1963, #A-2454).

20. *Gorgo* 1, no. 14 (August 1963, #A-2627).

21. Gorgo visits "The Land That Time Forgot" in issue #15, (*Gorgo* 1, no. 15, October 1963, job #A-2955), borrowing a well-known title from a Edgar Rice Burroughs novel. On the cover we see Gorgo poised to attack a gigantic Tyrannosaur resembling Rudolph F. Zallinger's pot-bellied *T. rex* as printed in a famous 1953 *Life* magazine issue. This Gorgo book begins ominously with these words printed on the splash page: "No one knows what might lie deep in the jungle of the dark continent, in places where mankind has never trod! The ages mask the secrets of those sections of swamp and slime in Africa! Here the past may be the present and the present a macabre horror! Here may live creatures of that frightful era at the Earth's beginning, that spawned Gorgo and his monstrous mother! Strange things can happen ... and strange things do happen in ... The Land That Time Forgot." In an extended prologue, many years ago, the aged curator of the Metropolitan Museum of Natural History yearns to find living dinosaurs rumored to inhabit portions of deepest, darkest Africa. Although he's too old for such a quest, he does inspire a younger associate, zoologist Dr. Carl Engstrom, to give it a shot. (Several such real expeditions have occasionally occurred, since over a century ago.) So, off goes Engstrom with his wife and young daughter Gloria to find living African dinosaurs. At a particular turn in the river, however, their native guides desert Engstrom, leaping from the boat for the shore. It is "taboo" to continue further into the forbidden territory. Three days later, after penetrating farther into dense jungle, they see a "Brontosaurus" munching on foliage. But Engstrom's wife and daughter are captured by savage primitives; tragically, his wife is killed. Engstrom buries his wife's body, but is unable to find his daughter's whereabouts. So he returns to civilization, feeling empty and woefully alone. But meanwhile, Gorgo swims toward Africa. The "odor of creatures of his own kind of the centuries beyond the veil of time" instinctively appeals to him and he wades ashore, searching for his saurian kind. Now the aged Engstrom, who has settled in to teach zoology at a university, meets with John Serviss, a famous younger African explorer. Serviss informs Engstrom about the legend of a "white goddess" who is said to live in the most remote part of Africa. Suspecting this person may be his daughter, Engstrom eagerly sets off for Africa once again, eventually teaming with one of his former students on a return to taboo territory. Engstrom does indeed find the white goddess, who happens to be the

grown-up Gloria, but just as the local tribe is threatened by a vicious tyrannosaur. Now both Engstrom and Gloria are to be sacrificed to this scaly dino-monster! The graduate student arrives, firing his mighty gun at the tyrannosaur, ineffectually. How will they survive this predicament? So here comes Gorgo and his mother Ogra, who dispatch a trio of tyrannosaurs and other prehistoria that abound in this awful, forbidden place. It seems that Gorgo and Ogra, viewed as "amphibians of an earlier era than the saurians," exterminate what remained of the creatures in the land that time forgot.

22. *Gorgo* 1, no. 16 (December 1963, #A-3185).

23. John Wyndham, *The Day of the Triffids* (New York: Doubleday, 1951).

24. *Gorgo* 1, no. 17 (Feb. 1964, #A-3218).

25. *Gorgo* 1, no. 18 (May 1964, #A-3471). Another image that seems to presage the Godzilla series, the cover of the book might strike G-fans with a *Godzilla vs. Jet Jaguar* sort of Toho ambiance.

26. Giant monsters were all the rage by July 1964, when *Gorgo* #19, titled "The World Shaker," was issued (job # A-3632). Curiously, Toho had a project in the offing titled *Frankenstein Conquers the World* (U.S. release, 1966; released in Japan as *Frankenstein vs. Baragon*, 1965), in which a gigantic variant of the Frankenstein monster battles the 150-foot-long reptilian Baragon, whose giant ears remarkably resemble Gorgo's. While, comparatively, the imagery looks similar, it would be difficult to proclaim Charlton's book influenced Toho's then forthcoming film. The giant human clubbing Gorgo with a telephone wire pole on the cover of issue #19 doesn't resemble a Boris Karloff–derived Frankensteinian creature. Yet this gigantic "Dr. Zhunli" is even more deranged than the prototypical Dr. Frankenstein. Dr. Zhunli, one of those unfortunates bullied early in life, maniacally vows vengeance on the world. His warped, yet ingenious mind causes him to study the occult dark arts to control his subordinates, while in his laboratory he invents a serum that causes normal creatures to grow to enormous sizes. His first (indirect) encounter with Gorgo comes when a bee, grown to hugeness and released from Zhunli's lab, stings Gorgo's mother in the rear end, many miles away. This causes Gorgo to laugh and chortle, an early example of giant monster humor! But what Zhunli has in mind is no laughing matter. He intends to culture mass quantities of his serum in a living giant body that can be induced into a state of suspended animation. Of course, this creature turns out to be Gorgo. Meanwhile, Zhunli's assistants mistrust his intentions and sabotage the mad experiment before things go too far. But things do go further awry, as Zhunli inadvertently drinks a full dose of the serum, causing him to suddenly grow exactly to Gorgo's height. What's more, the serum is so potent that even his clothes grow proportionally to huge size (a side benefit not enjoyed by the *Amazing Colossal Man*, who embarrassingly was forced to wear a diaper). Now the well-dressed Zhunli giant bellows, "[A]ll mankind is at my mercy. My detractors shall suffer and die...." Soon Zhunli is smacking fighter jets out of the sky. Abhorred by this outcome, Zhunli's assistants try to rouse Gorgo with caffeine stimulant poured into his open maw. And so great fighting begins! At first, the fighting is even, with no apparent victor, until Gorgo is knocked out when Zhunli tosses a great boulder at the monster's head. (Strange how Gorgo is impervious to hydrogen bomb explosions, yet can be so easily dispatched with a mere boulder! We must bear in mind, however, that this is a *comic book* series, with plot elements and sequences so conveniently arranged by the writers so as to make things work themselves out in the end. There may seemingly be little logic in these stories sometimes, especially when one tries to compare events and occurrences in prior stories with those published later on.) So just when Zhunli is exulting his apparent victory over the great reptile, Gorgo's mother arrives—and she's pretty darn angry! Zhunli swiftly succumbs to her wrath but then reduces to normal human size when the serum wears off, evidently contrite for his former evil ways. When last seen, Gorgo and Ogra are slumbering at the North Pole.

27. *Gorgo* 1, no. 20 (October 1964, #A-3953).

28. *Gorgo* 1, no. 21 (December 1964, #4226).

29. The term "population bomb," intended to alert the world to the threat of human overpopulation, was coined by Paul Ehrlich and Anne Ehrlich (uncredited) originating in their 1968 book, *The Population Bomb* (Sierra Club/Ballantine Books); Arthur N. Strahler and Alan H. Strahler, *Environmental Geoscience: Interaction Between Natural Systems and Man* (Santa Barbara, CA: Hamilton, 1973), p. 478.

30. *Gorgo* 1, no. 22 (February 1965, #A-4495).

31. *Gorgo* 1, no. 23 (Sept. 1965, #A-4713).

32. *Ibid.*

33. *Attack of the Mutant Monsters*, no. 1 (1991).

34. *Fantastic Giants* 2, no. 24 (Sept. 1966, #6932, #6673); *Konga* 1, no. 23 (Nov. 1965, #A-4811). In *Konga* #23, titled "The Creature of Uuang-Ni," the great King Kong-like ape defeats two Uuang-Ni that emerge from a smoldering, lava-belching volcano populated by a tribe of Melanesian islanders, whose thatched huts resemble those on Skull Island. Konga's fire-breathing, dino-monster antagonists, the legendary Uuang-Ni, which sport ceratosaurus-like nasal horns, vaguely resemble the 2nd Godzilla as illustrated in American promotional advertising for 1959's *Gigantis the Fire Monster*. Konga defeats both of the dino-monsters, whose provenance is described as "spawned in the ageless flames of the Earth's core!" Yes, true "fire monsters" indeed! The book features scenes of the giant ape and dino-monsters fighting along the slope of a volcano, not unlike footage seen in Toho's *King Kong vs. Godzilla*, fighting on the slope of Mt. Fuji.

35. Eugene Lourie, *My Work in Films* (San Diego: A Harvest/HBJ Book, 1984), pp. 240–246.

36. Mark Justice, "Save the Earth!" (Part 1 of 2), *G-Fan* no. 94 (Winter 2011): pp. 24–25.

37. J.D. Lees, "What is a Kaiju?" *G-Fan* no. 78 (Fall 2006): pp. 68–71; Mike Field, "What is the Meaning of Kaiju?" *G-Fan* no. 81 (Fall 2007): pp. 38–39.

38. Carson Bingham, *Gorgo* (Derby, CT: Monarch Books, 1960).

39. Bruce Cassiday, "My Life in the Pulps: Guest of Honor Speech, Pulpcon 23," *Pulp Vault* no. 12/13 (Aug. 1996): pp. 17–21; Richard Bleiler, "Bruce Cassiday: A Bio-Bibliography," *Pulp Vault* no. 12/13 (Aug. 1996): pp. 22–26.

40. *Ibid.*, pp. 18–19.

41. Robert Faraday, *The Anytime Rings* (New York: Dell, 1963).

42. Lourie, *op. cit.*, p. 244. Introduction of antagonistic military forces versus the dino-monsters was not his aim.

43. Bingham, 1960, *op. cit.*, *passim*.

44. Peter Ward offered the concept of a "Medean" planet that would willfully use its procreation for deliberate self-destruction (somewhat in contrast to a "Gaian" Earth), in his 2009 book, *The Medea Hypothesis: Is Life on*

Earth Ultimately Self-Destructive? (Princeton University Press). And note that on p. 10 of the 1960 novel *Gorgo*, a crew member utters prophetically yet revealingly, "Just when we get our hooks into something, Mother Nature screws it up for us!"

45. Bingham, 1960, *op. cit.*, p. 12.
46. *Ibid.*, p. 19.
47. *Ibid.*, pp. 31–32.
48. *Ibid.*, p. 42. On p. 58, where Moira mentions that the juvenile beast they've caught is "Ogra, the sea god," there are further dinosaurian connections made. Sam states that rather than the creature being a sea god, instead it "looks to me like some link between the dinosaur age and ours."
49. *Ibid.*, pp. 88–89.
50. *Ibid.*, p. 48.
51. *Ibid.*, p. 53.
52. *Ibid.*, p. 58.
53. *Ibid.*, pp. 66–67.
54. *Ibid.*, p. 90.
55. This exchange occurs on pp. 100–101 of the 1960 novel *Gorgo*. I discussed the use of genuine dinosaur skeletons, restorations and imagetext in giant dino-monster films of the 1950s and early 1960s in an article "Giant Dino-Monster 'Theory': Visualizing the *Real* 'dino' in Dino-Monster Reel," *Scary Monsters* no. 88 (June 2013): pp. 107–119.
56. For more on *The Valley of Gwangi* (1969), see Mark F. Berry's *The Dinosaur Filmography* (Jefferson, NC: McFarland, 2002), pp. 397–406.
57. Bingham, *op. cit.*, p. 105.
58. *Ibid.*, p. 107.
59. *Ibid.*, p. 116, 118.
60. *Ibid.*, p. 130.
61. *Ibid.*, p. 139.
62. *Ibid.*, p. 73.
63. *Ibid.*, p. 141.
64. In this chapter I mentioned that Gorgo in the comics had come to represent, albeit to the rather limited readership of these books, "our" idealized capitalist dino-monster. It may be of further interest that decades prior, the genuine dinosaur *Tyrannosaurus rex* was already representing America's might, as in paleoartist Charles R. Knight's turn-of-the-20th-century artwork, and later as exemplified in Alexander Phillips's 1929 science fiction story "Death of the Moon." See my *Dinosaurs in Fantastic Fiction: A Thematic Survey* (Jefferson, NC: McFarland, 2006), pp. 59–63 for more on this topic. By mid-century, Rudolph Zallinger furthered *T. rex*'s emblematic, nationalistic appeal, as explained here in Chapters Seven and Ten.

Chapter Thirteen

1. Ray Bradbury, *Dinosaur Tales* (New York: Bantam Books, 1983). Bradbury's 1952 story "A Sound of Thunder" may be found on pp. 51–84; his 1951 "The Fog Horn" is reprinted on pp. 93–114.
2. *Ibid.*, p. 106.
3. *Ibid.*, p. 111.
4. *Ibid.*, p. 102.
5. Bradbury's story was later extended through a series of novels written for younger audiences by Stephen Leigh during the early 1990s, such as *Ray Bradbury Presents Dinosaur World* (New York: Avon Books, 1992).
6. Allen A. Debus, "Time Steps Aside: Bradbury's Unsung Safari Legacy," *Prehistoric Times* no. 80 (Winter 2006): pp. 20–22. Other than a prevalent interest and fascination with rockets and rocket ships, Bradbury was not regarded (by Isaac Asimov) as a hard-technology writer of science fiction.
7. Curt Teichert, "Jean-Baptiste de Lamarck—the First Environmentalist," *Earth Sciences History: Journal of the History of the Earth Sciences Society* 7, no. 1 (1988): p. 44.
8. *Ibid.*
9. *Ibid.*
10. Peter J. Bowler, *The Norton History of the Earth Sciences* (New York: W.W. Norton, 1992), pp. 309, 324, 362, 363, 377, 426.
11. Martin J.S. Rudwick, *Bursting the Limits of Time: The Reconstruction of Geohistory in the Age of Revolution* (University of Chicago Press, 2005), p. 390. Geologist Kenneth J. Hsu adds somewhat paradoxically that Lamarck, who was a uniformitarian naturalist like Lyell, "became an evolutionist, because he was a creationist.... There was no extinction, he claimed, only 'pseudoextinction.' None of the older species had died out; all had been converted into new species by slow and gradual changes during the immensity of time since the Creation." Hsu, "Uniformitarianism vs. Catastrophism in the Extinction Debate," in William Glen, ed., *The Mass-Extinction Debates: How Science Works in a Crisis* (Stanford University Press, 1994), pp. 219–220.
12. Rudwick, *op. cit.* (2005), p. 390.
13. *Ibid.*, p. 391.
14. Martin J.S. Rudwick, *The Meaning of Fossils: Episodes in the History of Palaeontology* (University of Chicago Press, 1985), pp. 147–149.
15. Stephen Jay Gould, *Time's Arrow, Time's Cycle: Myth and Metaphor in the Discovery of Geological Time* (Cambridge, MA: Harvard University Press, 1987), pp. 99–180.
16. Bowler, *op. cit.*, p. 293.
17. Bowler *op. cit.*, discusses neo–Lamarckism at length throughout the latter third of his book, but see p. 434 on the adverse environmental aspects of the philosophy, where he states, "Darwinism has been blamed for many modern evils, and its opponents have tended to stress the more humane viewpoint of those who adopted anti-materialist theories such as Lamarckism. Environmentalists have assumed that anyone from the past who shared their perspective must have been on the right side on a whole range of related issues. Those who have made such assumptions may get a nasty shock when the more critical historian points out that many Lamarckians were vicious racists, or that there was an environmental component in Nazi ideology ... bias exists on all sides."
18. Hooke quoted in Charles C. Albritton, *The Abyss of Time* (Los Angeles: Jeremy P. Tarcher, 1986), p. 50. Also see Bowler, *op. cit.*, pp. 118–119.
19. Stephen Inwood, *The Forgotten Genius: The Biography of Robert Hooke 1635–1703* (Denver, CO: MacAdam/Cage), pp. 118–119.
20. Bowler, *op. cit.*, p. 123. Note also that both Albritton, *op. cit.*, and Rudwick, *op. cit.* (2005), offer extensive information on Buffon.
21. Bowler, *op. cit.*, p. 129.
22. *Ibid.*, pp. 128–130.
23. For further interesting information on contemporary theories of the Earth, for example, see Mott T. Greene, *Geology in the Nineteenth Century: Changing Views of a Changing World* (Ithaca: Cornell University Press, 1982); Rachel Laudan, *From Mineralogy to Geology: The Founda-*

tions of a Science, 1650–1830 (University of Chicago Press, 1987); Martin J.S. Rudwick, *Worlds Before Adam* (University of Chicago Press, 2008); Albritton, *op. cit.*; Gould, *op. cit.*; Rudwick, *op. cit.* (2005); Rudwick, *op. cit.* (1985); S. Warren Carey, *Theories of the Earth and Universe: A History of Dogma in the Earth Sciences* (Stanford, CA: Stanford University Press), 1988; Stephen Baxter, *Ages in Chaos: James Hutton and the Discovery of Deep Time* (New York: Forge, Tom Doherty Assoc., 2006).

24. Martin J.S. Rudwick, *Georges Cuvier, Fossil Bones, and Geological Catastrophes: New Translations & Interpretations of the Primary Texts* (University of Chicago Press, 1997).

25. Elizabeth Kolbert stresses Cuvier's abilities as a grand popularizer of the time, having "showman's flair," in her book, *The Sixth Extinction: An Unnatural History* (New York: Henry Holt, 2014), pp. 34, 38, 44. Also see Rudwick, *op. cit.*, pp. 499–512.

26. Quotation borrowed from Martin J.S. Rudwick, *op. cit.* (1997), p. 24. Also see Adrian J. Desmond, *The Hot-Blooded Dinosaurs: A Revolution in Palaeontology* (New York: Warner Books, 1977), p. 12; Rudwick, *op. cit.*, 392, claims "Lamarck in effect denied geohistory: in his geotheory the continents and oceans at any one time would have been the same in general characteristics as those at any other time (though the details of geography might never have been repeated exactly). Cuvier, in sharp contrast, ... was ... claiming that the former world of his extinct mammals was distinctly different from the present world of living species, proving that life on earth had had a history of its own.... This, rather than any catastrophe, was the most important point that Lamarck was rejecting."

27. Rudwick, *op. cit.*, 1997, p. 24.

28. *Ibid.*, pp. 44, 53–58.

29. *Ibid.*, p. 190.

30. Rudwick, *op. cit.* (2005), pp. 501–502. Rudwick states (p. 502) that upon his examination of the first known pterodactyl fossil (an "inhabitant of a world so different from ours," p. 501), that as Cuvier "had suspected since early in his research, the vast span of geohistory that these formations represented seemed to have been an age of reptiles: truly a former world, and one without mammals."

31. *Ibid.*, pp. 596–597, 650; Cuvier, rather like Lamarck, perceived a dim forecast for mankind, warning that "the present era will be reproached if we do not conserve for the future..." Cuvier quoted in Mike Magee's *Who Lies Sleeping? The Dinosaur Heritage and the Extinction of Man* (Selwyn, Frome, England: AskWhy! Publications, 1993), p. 168.

32. Rudwick, *op. cit.* (1985), p. 146.

33. *Ibid.*, pp. 148–149.

34. *Ibid.*, p. 149; Rudwick, *op. cit.* (2008), pp. 430–431. Here, Rudwick states that Brongniart considered that "progressiveness lay not in any greater 'perfection' in the later forms, but in an increasing diversity and the successive addition of' 'higher' kinds of life. And he claimed that this was not the product of any gradual transmutation; somehow or other, new forms of life had been fashioned providentially to suit new environmental conditions as they developed on the ever-changing surface of a slowly cooling planet" (p. 431). Brongniart's notion was therefore in opposition to Lamarck.

35. Desmond, *op. cit.*, p. 16.

36. *Ibid.*, p. 17.

37. Desmond, *op. cit.*, pp. 20–25. Later on, however, Owen's position shifted in light of newer developments (rather adding to conceptual complexity). As noted by Stephen Jay Gould, "Owen was not an anti-evolutionist who rejected the transformation of one species into another by means of natural forces; he simply disagreed with the driving force proposed by Darwin (natural selection). As pointed out by Gould, 'although a fierce anti-Darwinian—[Owen] was also an evolutionist.'" Passage and Gould quote excerpted from Luis M. Chiappe, *Glorified Dinosaurs: The Origin and Early Evolution of Birds* (Hoboken, NJ: John Wiley & Sons, 2007), p. 131.

38. Robert A. Berner, *The Phanerozoic Carbon Cycle* (Oxford University Press, 2004), pp. 7, 126. Stephen Baxter states that decades before Ebelman, Scottish geologist James Hutton (1726–1797) may also have anticipated James Lovelock's and Lynn Margulis's Gaia hypothesis, with its integrated biogeochemical controls coupled with environmental feedback systems. Baxter, *op. cit.*, p. 219. For more on Gaia, see James Lovelock's books, *Gaia: A New Look at Life on Earth* (Oxford University Press, 1979), and *The Ages of Gaia* (New York: W.W. Norton, 1988. Also see Lawrence E. Joseph, *Gaia: The Growth of an Idea* (New York: St. Martin's Press, 1990), and Dorion Sagan's *Biospheres: Reproducing Planet Earth* (New York: Bantam Books, 1990).

39. During the 1820s, William Buckland became a proponent of "scriptural geology." Charles Coulton Gillespie addresses this episode in his 1951 book, *Genesis and Geology: A Study in the Relations of Scientific Thought, Natural Theology, and Social Opinion in Great Britain, 1790–1850* (New York: Harper & Row, 1959). Also see Rudwick, *op. cit.* (2008), pp. 501–539.

40. Martin J.S. Rudwick, *Scenes from Deep Time: Early Pictorial Representations of the Prehistoric World* (University of Chicago Press, 1992), p. 139.

41. John Imbrie and Katherine Palmer Imbrie, *Ice Ages: Solving the Mystery* (Harvard University Press, 1986).

42. John Breyer and William Butcher, "Nothing New under the Earth: The Geology of Jules Verne's *Journey to the Center of the Earth*," *Earth Sciences History* 22, no. 1 (2003): pp. 36–54

43. Louis Figuier, *The World Before the Deluge*, newly edited and revised by H.W. Bristow, F.R.S., F.G.S. (London: Cassell, undated but most likely the 1867 ed.).

44. *Ibid.*, p. 439.

45. Rudwick, *op. cit.* (1992), pp. 204–213.

46. Curiously, however, in the 1920s, geologist J. Harlan Bretz (1882–1981) did indeed find dramatic evidence of a genuine widespread (although localized, not "universal") flood taking place during Pleistocene times in eastern Washington state. Stephen Jay Gould, *The Panda's Thumb: More Reflections in Natural History* (New York: W.W. Norton, 1980), Chapter Nineteen, "The Great Scablands Debate," pp. 194–203. Victor R. Baker and Dag Nummedal, *The Channeled Scabland: A Guide to the Geomorphology of the Columbia Basin* (Washington, DC: Planetary Geology Program, Office of Space Science, 1978).

47. Imbrie and Imbrie, *op. cit.* A startling rival astronomical theory involving a sudden cataclysmic comet collision with the Earth was published by Ignatius Donnelly (1831–1901) in 1883, titled *Ragnarok: The Age of Fire and Gravel* (1970 ed. reprinted by University Books). Donnelly, who rejected the evidence for an "Ice Age" as then and now perceived, was not a scientist, but his books were highly popular for the time. Eventually, by the 1960s, geologists were even turning to the revolution of the Solar

System through our Milky Way galaxy to explain the recurrence of ice ages. See, for example, J. Steiner and E. Grillmair, "Possible Galactic Causes for Periodic and Episodic Glaciations," *Geological Society of America Bulletin* 84 (1973): pp. 1003–1018; Allen A. Debus, "Steiner's (and Grillmair's) Ice Age Theory (Parts 1 to 3)," in *Fossil News: Journal of Avocational Paleontology* 13, nos. 1–3 (Jan. 2007): pp. 6–9; (Feb. 2007): pp. 6–9; (March 2007): pp. 4–7.

48. Imbrie and Imbrie, *op. cit.*, pp. 201–202.

49. Spencer R. Weart, *The Discovery of Global Warming* (Harvard University Press, 2003), pp. 4–9. Here, Weart (p. 8) stresses, "Hardly anyone imagined that human actions, so puny among the vast natural powers, could upset the balance that governed the planet as a whole. This view of Nature—suprahuman, benevolent, and inherently stable—lay deep in most human cultures. It was traditionally tied up with a religious faith in the God-given order of the universe, a flawless and imperturbable harmony. Such was the public belief, and scientists are members of the public, sharing most of the assumptions of their culture."

50. Albritton, *op. cit.*, pp. 200–213; Imbrie and Imbrie, *op. cit.*, pp. 104, 106, 116–117, 197.

51. Besides Seuss, Russian geochemist Vladimir Vernadsky (1863–1945) made major contributions to understanding the earthly biosphere. See Dorion Sagan, *op. cit.*, pp. 42–49, 60.

52. Lawrence E. Joseph, *op. cit.*, pp. 200–252.

53. Bowler, *op. cit.*, pp. 451–452. Bowler mentions that natural selection and "struggle for existence" were perceived as only important in the "end game," using as one example the titanotheres that Osborn had extensively studied.

54. *Ibid.*, pp. 456–459.

55. George Gaylord Simpson, *Life of the Past: An Introduction to Paleontology* (Yale University Press, 1953). My 1968 paperback edition was printed by Bantam Books.

56. Charles Wilson Peale's Museum is discussed on pp. 39–54 of Robert West Howard's *The Dawnseekers: The First History of American Paleontology* (New York: Harcourt, Brace, Jovanovich, 1975). Bowler, *op. cit.*, p. 313, states, "When displayed in the great cities of the east, and in the capitals of Europe, the larger dinosaurs seemed to confirm the superiority of modern industrial society by showing how the world had been conquered both in space and time." In particular, Andrew Carnegie's *Diplodocus* specimen is discussed in Desmond, *op. cit.*, pp. 161–173.

57. Ronald Rainger, *An Agenda for Antiquity: Henry Fairfield Osborn and Vertebrate Paleontology at the American Museum of Natural History, 1890–1935* (Tuscaloosa, AL: University of Alabama Press, 1991), pp. 105–181.

58. Edwin H. Colbert, *Men and Dinosaurs* (Baltimore, MD: Penguin Books, 1968), p. 183.

59. This theme is broadly discussed as a theme of Bowler's 1992 book, *op. cit.* Rather ironically, given the emphasis on life through time during the period when Darwinism was either vehemently opposed, or deliberately misconstrued, during the mid–20th century, "By eliminating the possibility that evolution is driven in a predictable direction by purely biological factors, modern Darwinism has turned biology into a historical science.... But the historical/geographical dimension certainly implies that the course of evolution will be a complex, haphazard process that makes it impossible to get a single species (our own, for instance) as the goal towards which life on earth has been working over millions of years" (Bowler, p. 473). Regardless, even today in the popular realm, "most non-scientists probably continue to think of evolution as the ascent of a ladder towards the high point represented by humankind.... [They] continue to argue against the whole idea of evolution so that they can present their alternatives offering a more purposeful, or at least more romantic, story of our origins" (Bowler, p. 475).

60. Kong's tender human-like qualities (as opposed to simian) accentuate this theme.

61. Bowler, *op. cit.*, p. 504. Furthermore, Bowler discusses natural "conservationism" throughout, such as from its beginnings, as on p. 320.

62. Bowler, *op. cit.*, p. 505.

63. For more on photochemical smog, which became of growing concern since the mid–1950s, see the following references: James L. Pyle, *Chemistry and the Technological Backlash* (Eaglewood Cliffs, NJ: Prentice-Hall, 1974), pp. 53–61; Baldwin H. Ward, ed., *Year*, 1955 edition (New York: Simon & Schuster, and Los Angeles: YEAR, 1955), p. 118, "Smog-New World Worry"; Stanley E. Manahan, *Environmental Chemistry*, 2nd ed. (Boston, MA: Willard Grant Press, 1975), pp. 387–397. A century after Dickens wrote *Bleak House*, smog remained an issue of public health concern in London, as it does even today in certain highly populated Chinese cities.

64. Mark Justice, "Save the Earth!: Ecological Messages in Toho's Giant Monster Movies" (Part 2 of 2), *G-Fan* no. 95 (Spring 2011): pp. 20–29.

65. Justice, *op. cit.*, p. 24. For more on oceanic conservationism considerations, see Chapter Eleven in this book.

66. *Ibid.*, p. 20.

67. *Ibid.*, p. 21.

68. Steve Ryfle mentions, "In the late '60s and early '70s, Japan was plagued by the by-products of its own industrial growth, modernization, and dependence on cheap energy: the heavy pollution of its urban areas, air, and water. Pollution-related illnesses were now considered a serious threat and legislation was enacted to control emissions and dumping. Things were so bad in some cities that oxygen tanks were installed on street corners to prevent pedestrians from passing out, and children went to school wearing face masks to filter out photo-chemical smog." Steve Ryfle, *Japan's Favorite Mon-Star: The Unauthorized Biography of "The Big G"* (Toronto: ECW Press, 1998), p. 162.

69. Justice, *op. cit.*, p. 27.

70. Steven Utley, "Getting Away" (originally published in *Galaxy Science Fiction*, 1976), reprinted in *Dinosaurs!* Edited by Jack Dann and Gardner Dozois (New York: Ace Books, 1990), pp. 68–75. The mental conditioning element in Utley's story seems reminiscent of Jack Finney's classic 1970 novel, *Time and Again*.

71. *Ibid.*, p. 72.

72. *Ibid.*, p. 74.

73. Spencer R. Weart, *The Rise of Nuclear Fear* (Harvard University Press, 2012), pp. 193–195. Bowler, *op. cit.*, adds, "The First World War cast serious doubts on the optimistic philosophy of progress. Perhaps the European powers were morally no better than the savages they had conquered in the name of civilization. For many intellectuals, the moral superiority of Europe had vanished in a cloud of poison gas drifting over the trenches of the Western Front.... Britain, France and America retained the traditional system and continued the exploitation of those parts of the world colonized during the age of imperialism before the war" (pp. 380–381). Following the Second World War, in-

vention of the hydrogen bomb only deepened these psychological concerns. Also see James T. Patterson, *Restless Giant: The United States from Watergate to Bush vs. Gore* (Oxford University Press, 2005), pp. 354–355, touching on latter stage trends in the environmental since the 1970s.

74. For example, see Elizabeth Kolbert's 2014 book titled *The Sixth Extinction: An Unnatural History*. Kolbert discusses man's impact through climate change on many kinds of terrestrial and marine fauna and flora, and the discrete exacerbating factors that have resulted in vastly accelerated extinctions of thousands of species during this warm interglacial period (i.e., since circa 10,000 BCE). Eradication of tropical rain forests, ocean acidification, and extermination of avian fauna on Pacific islands are three of the major culprits. The overall effect is akin to one of the major mass extinctions episodes of geological history, namely the sixth one (i.e., besides those occurring in the Late Ordovician, the Upper Devonian, the End-Permian, the Late Triassic and the Upper Cretaceous periods—now known collectively as the "Big Five"). Note Kolbert's term "unnatural" in her title. By contrast, in their book *The Great Extinction* (Garden City, NY: Doubleday, 1983), pp. 170–174), Michael Allaby and James Lovelock defer to an interesting, yet alternate philosophy, which is that because we are part of the animal kingdom, whatever man does to the planet is still to be regarded as "natural." For example, Earth's microorganisms, especially, are known to have naturally transformed the planetary environment (i.e., ocean-atmosphere system) eons ago. "Many of our environmental fears derive from the observation that human beings modify their environment to make it more hospitable for themselves and for their domesticated plant and animal species" (p. 170). But like man, all species necessarily modify their environments to their ready advantage, so simply because man does so at perhaps an alarming rate today does not mean that "man-made" should be equated with "unnatural." Furthermore, "our power to destroy the world, or even ourselves, is quite imaginary, a product of our own hubris.... The credible threats must come from outside the Earth and the impact of a large planetesimal is the most immediate of them" (p. 173).

75. Justice, *op. cit.*, pp. 22–23. In more recent times, Japan's fishing industry has been plagued by a profusion of jellyfish that, not unlike the noxious Barem, threaten the food supply of that nation.

76. As discussed by Justice, *op. cit.*, two other Toho Godzilla films of more recent vintage, *Godzilla vs. Biollante* (1989) and *Godzilla vs. Mothra* (1992), also dealt tangentially with ecological/green themes.

77. A novelization of the 1998 film from Ronald Parker's teleplay was also published by K. Robert Andreassi, *Gargantua* (New York: Tor, 1998). For more on this novel, see my article, "From Kong to Godzilla—A survey of giant dino-monster 'novelizations' (Part 1 of 2)," *Mad Scientist*, no. 29, pp. 25–39.

78. Included among the more familiar examples best suited for children of anthropomorphized dinosaurs would be that once-ubiquitous kiddies' character, Barney the purple dinosaur, and an assortment of talking dinosaurs such as in James Gurney's *Dinotopia* universe, 1988's *The Land Before Time*, the 2000 Disney film *Dinosaurs*, and a 2012 computer-animated film, also named *Dinosaurs*. The mid-1970s television program *Land of the Lost* incorporated "Sleestaks," who were intelligent insectoid-reptiloid men. And an entertaining 2010s theatrical production, *Walking With Dinosaurs*, featured 15 life-size dinosaurs, elaborate costumes worn by human actors hidden inside. During the new millennial period, there were also several comedic *Ice Age* animated films for children, starring Ray Romano, who provided voice-overs.

79. Jose Luis Sanz, *Starring T. Rex!: Dinosaur Mythology and Popular Culture.* (Bloomington: Indiana University Press, 2002), p. 90. W.K. Stevens stated in 1991, "The actions of an exploding human population are sundering the ecological webs that support life by setting off a worldwide wave of extinctions comparable to the one in which the dinosaurs perished some 65 million years ago" ("Species loss: Crisis or false alarm?" *New York Times*, Aug. 20, 1991, pp. B5-B6).

80. The term "Anthropocene" was coined in 2002 by Paul Crutzen. This is in recognition that "[u]nless there is a global catastrophe—a meteor impact, a world war or pandemic—mankind will remain a major environmental force for many millennia." The boundary for the beginning of the Anthropocene, a new geological epoch, has been debated but may be settled in "practical" terms on the "global spread of radioactive isotopes created by the atomic bomb tests of the 1960s; however, this postdates the major inflection in global human activity. Perhaps the best stratigraphic marker near the beginning of the nineteenth century has a natural cause: the eruption of Mount Tambora in April 1815" (Jan Zalasiewicz *et al.*, p. 7). Thus, volcanoes, nuclear bomb tests, and a major factor instigating Mary Shelley's writing of *Frankenstein* all come into odd, yet somehow pleasing juxtaposition. For more on metaphorical associations between Shelley's Frankenstein monster and Toho's 1954 film, *Gojira*, see my book *Prehistoric Monsters: The Real and Imagined Creatures of the Past That We Love to Fear* (Jefferson, NC: McFarland, 2010), Chapter Nine, titled "Modern Prometheus," pp. 208–230. For more on elucidation of the Anthropocene, also see Paul J. Crutzen, "Geology of Mankind," *Nature* 415 (Jan. 3, 2002): p. 23; Chris D. Thomas, *et al.*, "Extinction risk from climate change," *Nature* 427 (Jan. 8, 2004): pp. 145–148; Jan Zalasiewicz *et al.*, "Are we now living in the Anthropocene?" *GSA Today* 18, no. 2 (Feb. 2008): pp. 4–6; Edward O. Wilson, "Threats to Biodiversity," *Scientific American* (Sept. 1989): pp. 108–115; Pieter Westbroek, *Life as a Geological Force: Dynamics of the Earth* (New York: W.W. Norton, 1992); Carl Sagan, *Billions & Billions: Thoughts on Life and Death at the Brink of the Millennium* (New York: Random House, 1997), pp. 63–135.

Chapter Fourteen

1. Spencer R. Weart, *The Rise of Nuclear Fear* (Harvard University Press, 2012), p. 257.

2. Sean Rhoads, "Godzilla the Social Critic," *G-Fan* no. 98 (Winter 2012): pp. 18–28; Mark Justice, "Save the Earth!: Ecological Messages in Toho's Giant Monster Movies (Part 2)," *G-Fan* no. 95 (Spring 2011): pp. 20–29. Besides Rhoads's and Justice's astute commentary, my contribution, "The Doomsday Dinosaurs: Cold-Blooded Relics," in *G-Fan* 1, no. 61 (March/April 2003), may also be of some interest.

3. The two quotations in this paragraph are from Susan Sontag, "The Imagination of Disaster," reprinted in *Hiba Kusha Cinema: Hiroshima, Nagasaki and the Nuclear Image in Japanese Film*, ed. Mick Broderick (London & New York: Kegan Paul International, 1996), pp. 38–53, and Spencer R. Weart, *op. cit.* (2012), p. 125.

4. W.J.T. Mitchell, *The Last Dinosaur Book: The Life*

and Times of a Cultural Icon (Chicago: University of Chicago Press, 1998), p. 54.

5. Max Page, *The City's End: Two Centuries of Fantasies, Fears, and Premonitions of New York's Destruction* (New Haven: Yale University Press, 2008), pp. 4, 6–7.

6. Quote from Weart, 2012, p. 290.

7. Spencer R. Weart, *Nuclear Fear: A History of Images* (Cambridge: Harvard University Press, 1988), pp. xi, 8, 15.

8. Weart, *op. cit.*, p. 106. (Oppenheimer quote is from p. 101.)

9. *Ibid.*, p. 188.

10. *Ibid.*, p. 189.

11. Norwick, "Dean Chapman's Contributions of Tektite Science," *Earth Sciences History* 31, no. 1 (2012): p. 105. Further cultural evidence of this may be noticed in the 1960 film *The Time Machine* (starring Rod Taylor and Yvette Mimieux). In a then "futuristic" scene staged in 1966, reference is made to an "atomic satellite," visible from the ground, which attacks London with an atomic ray, immediately thereafter triggering a cataclysmic volcanic eruption. The "atomic satellite" must reflect then prevalent fears of the Soviet's satellite *Sputnik*, and what they intended to do with such technology. Stephen King describes the palpable fear that gripped America following the Soviet's successful launching of *Sputnik* on October 4, 1957, in Chapter One of his *Danse Macabre* (New York: Berkley Books, 1981), pp. 1–15.

12. *Weart, op. cit.*, (1988), p. 74.

13. *Ibid.*, pp. 402, 406.

14. *Ibid.*, p. 403.

15. Ed Godziszewski, "The Making of Godzilla," *Japanese Giants* 1, no. 10 (2004): p. 11.

16. Mitchell, *op. cit.*, p. 84.

17. *Ibid.*, pp. 91, 254.

18. *Ibid.*, p. 18.

19. *Ibid.*, p. 19.

20. *Ibid.*, p. 75.

21. *Ibid.*, p. 33.

22. *Ibid.*, pp. 164, 244.

23. "Postmodernism" evidently has several artistic meanings, but you may read further in Mitchell's cited book, p. 217 or in Weart (2012), pp. 261–62. Chon Noriega's article "Godzilla and the Japanese Nightmare: When *Them!* is Us," was published in *Hibakusha Cinema: Hiroshima, Nagasaki and the Nuclear Image in Japanese Film*, pp. 55–74. Also see Susan J. Napier's article, "Panic Sites: The Imagination of Disaster from Godzilla to Akira," in *Journal of Japanese Studies* 19, no. 2 (Summer 1993), pp. 327–351. On p. 340 Napier refers to postmodernistic film as surreal "panic sites." Susan Sontag's article "The Imagination of Disaster" was reprinted in the Broderick compilation (*op. cit.*, pp. 39–53).

24. See Chapter Two, "An Overview of Paleoimagery" by Allen A. Debus, in *Dinosaur Sculpting: A Complete Guide*, 2nd ed. (McFarland, 2013).

25. A similar circumstance rests with hopeful UFO symbology; presumably thoughtful aliens will lead us from the brink to salvation. UFO mystique is yet another source of sci-fi fare which Toho has liberally availed itself of. Weart, *op. cit.*, pp. 398–400.

26. See my article concerning Gorgo as conveyed in the early 1960s Charlton Comics, printed in *G-Fan* nos. 99 and 100. Also see my article, "A Mastermind of Godzillean Proportions," in *G-Fan* 1, no. 94 (Winter 2011): pp. 58–60.

27. Gaseous methane is even more efficient in its greenhouse-causing effect, than carbon dioxide. Trevor Butterworth, "A Mighty Wind: Did flatulent dinosaurs really cause climate change?" *Newsweek*, May 21, 2012, p. 11. Furthermore, greenhouse conditions caused by volatilization of methane (sequestered on the sea floor today in an unstable, chemically hydrated form), may have also contributed to mass extinctions of the past, such as during the Permian-Triassic transition. Release of voluminous amounts of methane "via volcanic heating of the Siberian coal beds" may have been a factor in the event that exterminated up to 96 percent of marine species 250 million years ago: Douglas H. Erwin, *Extinction: How Life on Earth Nearly Ended 250 Million Years Ago* (Princeton University Press, 2006), pp. 172–179). Such an accelerated greenhouse heating from eruption of methane hydrates from the ocean floor could happen in man's future, if global temperatures (and hence seawater temperatures at depth) continue to rise beyond a trigger point.

28. Sean Alexander Rhoads, "Godzilla the Social Critic: Big 'Green' Monsters and Environmental Commentary in Japanese *Kaiju Eiga* of the 1970s" (master's thesis, University of Pennsylvania, 2919), pp. 69, 71–72.

29. Allen A. Debus, "A Cosmic Ice Age Extinction: Learning by 'O-S' mosis (Parts 1 to 2)," in *Fossil News: Journal of Avocational Paleontology* 14, nos. 9–10 (Sept. 2008): pp. 4–8; (Oct. 2008): pp. 6–9.

30. James Poniewozik, "The Ends of the World: How the Apocalypse became mainstream TV," *Time*, Sept. 1, 2014, p. 52. Poniewozik stated, "So where cold war disaster scenarios warned that mankind had become recklessly mighty, these new postapocalypses suggest that we are insignificant, riders on the earth who can be shrugged off like a dog scratching away a flea." Also see Stephen Jay Gould's *Full House* (New York: Three Rivers Press, 1996), and Lawrence E. Joseph's *Gaia: The Growth of an Idea* (New York: St. Martin's Press, 1990).

31. Gaia Vince, "An Epoch Debate," *Science* 334, no. 6052 (Oct. 7, 2011): pp. 32–37; Allen A. Debus, "Triumphant Triumvirate: Godzilla's Dinosaurian 'Progenitors,'" in *G-Fan* 1, no. 98 (Winter 2012): pp. 50–56.

32. There may be one totemic "challenger" to the Dinosauroid, namely the Zombie of modern apocalypse. Zombies attained their peak in popularity during a time in America when unemployment was exceedingly high; they're most popular at a time when people wonder how to survive a genuine apocalypse. Far from merely a "kick-the-can" concern for those future generations, in reality we're already being steadily plagued by adverse ramping-up greenhouse phenomena! Rather ironically, and despite citizens' general widespread fear of the misuse of nuclear energy, James Lovelock, environmentalist and co-inventor of the nurturing planetary scale "Gaia" hypothesis, advocates substitution of nuclear reactors in order to reduce industrial carbon dioxide emissions. Finally, like some sort of odd, out-of-control breeder reactor, to what extent did childhood memories of *Godzilla: King of the Monsters*, *The Beast from 20,000 Fathoms*, and other contemporary dino-monster filmic imagery inspire both worldwide protest within the baby-boomer generation against proliferation of anti-ballistic missile systems, fallout, nuclear reactors and associated buried radioactive wastes, and possibly even inspire the environmental movement?

Part Three

1. Allen A. Debus, Bob Morales, and Diane E. Debus, *Dinosaur Sculpting: A Complete Guide*, 2nd ed. (Jefferson, NC: McFarland, 2013), Chapter Two, pp. 24–52.

2. *Ibid.*, p. 25.

3. Some prior examples of such mistaken identity would include a well-preserved Miocene salamander fossil thought to have been a human relic drowned in the Flood, the *Homo diluvia testis*, and a Megalosaur thigh bone assigned the suggestive name *Scrotum humanum*. For more on the salamander "Flood Witness," see Martin J.S. Rudwick, *Bursting the Limits of Time* (University of Chicago Press, 2005), pp. 500–501, and Allen A. Debus, "Revenge of the Flood Witness," in *Fossil News: Journal of Avocational Paleontology* 15, no. 4 (April 2009): pp. 2–9, 12–13. For more on the *Scrotum humanum*, see Allen A. Debus, *Prehistoric Monsters* (McFarland, 2009), pp. 110, 289; and Jane P. Davidson, *A History of Paleontology Illustration* (Indiana University Press, 2008), pp. 28–30, 35–36. Also see two books by Adrienne Mayor, *The First Fossil Hunters* (Princeton University Press, 2000), and *Fossil Legends of the First Americans* (Princeton University Press, 2005), as well as Chapter One in my *Prehistoric Monsters*, titled "Inventing the Prehistoric Monster." Note that Benjamin Waterhouse Hawkins's *Hadrosaurus foulkii* skeletal reconstruction of 1868 was fabricated with sculpted bone components scaled-up from human bones. See Allen A. Debus and Diane E. Debus, *Paleoimagery: The Evolution of Dinosaurs in Art* (McFarland, 2002), pp. 56–58.

Chapter Fifteen

1. From the late 1970s through the late 1990s, I maintained "Paleo-News" scrapbooks wherein I pasted in newsworthy items from newspaper accounts, popular mainstream magazines, advertising flyers and other paper media concerning a host of paleontological issues as transmitted to the general public. As a young boy, my father had done the same during the mid–1930s. (See Allen A. Debus, "The Original Dinosaur Scrapbooks," *Prehistoric Times* no. 96 (Winter 2011): pp. 29–31.) I heavily relied on these scrapbooks (as well as an assortment of other items salvaged during the 1980s) to write this chapter. Thus, for me, the primary reference material for this chapter is my collection of fifteen dinosaur scrapbooks, which recreated the spirit of the times, featuring highlights from the early dinosaur craze. However, in certain cases as needed, I have cited exact source information. As I was striving to recapture the heady aura of the day, I generally elected to avoid historically updating or critiquing paleo-theories as originally announced or the contemporary interpretations surrounding certain fossil evidence, as since divulged. However, updates on many of the genera discussed here may be found in Donald F. Glut's set *Dinosaurs: The Encyclopedia* (Jefferson, NC: McFarland, 1997–2012).

2. Dinosaurologist generally refers to anyone who studies or is otherwise absorbed with dinosaurs at any level of intrigue—scientifically, avocationally, recreationally, artistically, etc. Another term, "Dinosaurabilia," was coined by master dino-collector Dean Hannotte, in 1980.

3. "During the 1980s a veritable explosion of dinosaur merchandizing swept America, replacing Teddy bears and Disney characters as the most ubiquitous image in popular culture": Richard Milner, *The Encyclopedia of Evolution: Humanity's Search for its Origins* (New York: Facts On File, 1990), p. 133.

4. Paleontologist Jack Horner was a major figure who expressly favored studying how dinosaurs lived, versus involving himself in theories of their extinction.

5. Tie-in books for these three traveling shows are as follows: Sylvia M. Czerkas and Stephen A. Czerkas, *Dinosaurs: A Global View* (New York: Mallard Press, 1991); *Dinosaurs Past and Present*, vols. 1 and 2, eds. Sylvia M. Czerkas and Everett C. Olson (Seattle and London: Natural History Museum of Los Angeles County in association with University of Washington Press, 1987); Sylvia Massey Czerkas and Donald F. Glut, *Dinosaurs, Mammoths and Cavemen: The Art of Charles R. Knight* (New York: E.P. Dutton, 1982). Publishers seized opportunities too, as the 1980s saw an unprecedented number of new dinosaur dictionaries, encyclopedias, books, and magazine articles, many of which were extraordinarily and lavishly illustrated (and far too many to mention here), all fell favorably into public view. In particular, three dinosaur books riding the crest of the wave during this heyday of dino-related publishing, receiving critical acclaim, written principally for laymen, were John Noble Wilford's *The Riddle of the Dinosaur* (New York: Alfred A. Knopf, 1986), and Robert T. Bakker's *The Dinosaur Heresies: New Theories Unlocking the Mystery of the Dinosaurs and Their Extinction* (New York: William Morrow, 1986), and Jack Horner's (with James Gorman) *Digging Dinosaurs* (New York: Workman Publishing, 1988). Quite literally, an entire book could be written simply about the many dinosaur and paleo-books published during this decade! In the still captivating field of paleoanthropology, no book scored more mightily then than Donald Johanson's and Maitland Edey's controversial *Lucy: The Beginnings of Humankind* (New York: Warner Books, 1981).

6. More recent analyses of enlarged body size attained purely as a consequence of natural selection offers rational explanations as to why such larger species may more easily succumb to extinction pressures. See "Cope's Rule, Hypercarnivory, and Extinction in North American Canids," by Blaire Van Valkenburgh, Xiaoming Wang and John Damuth, published in *Science* 306 (Oct. 1, 2004): pp. 101–104.

7. The "Olduvai Gorge" quote is found in James Coates's article, "Hope, hype greet discovery of 'magnificently ancient' dinosaur," *Chicago Tribune*, Sunday, June 2, 1985.

8. For more on Hoyle's misguided claim, see Chapter 8 in Leonard Krishtalka's *Dinosaur Plots and Other Intrigues in Natural History*, titled "The *Archaeopteryx* 'Hoax'" (New York: William Morrow, 1989), pp. 94–102; Allen A. Debus, "Way Out Evolution—OMG!" Parts 1 and 2, in *Fossil News: Journal of Avocational Paleontology* 16, nos. 9 (Nov.–Dec. 2010): pp. 16–19; 17, no. 1 (Jan.–Feb. 2011): pp. 7–11.

9. Dong Zhiming, *Dinosaurs from China* (English text by Angela C. Milner, British Museum (Natural History), China Ocean Press, 1987, 1988).

10. Robert Telleria, "The Rise and Fall of the QN," *Prehistoric Times* 107 (Fall 2013): pp. 48–51. An illustration of a "live" *Quetzalcoatlus* swooping down over city streets graced the cover of the April issue of *Science* 86, heralding Patrick Cooke's feature story, "The Man who launched a dinosaur," pp. 26–35. The magazine cover advertised in bold lettering, "Return of the Pterosaur to fly again after 65 million years."

11. Michael Parrish, "The big guy's back, flying high again and creating a flap," *Smithsonian* (March 1986): pp. 73–81.

12. Cladistics, a means of categorizing relationships among species, attained stormy popularity during the 1980s. It refers to those relationships thought possible and valid in a reconstructed evolutionary history of organisms based on observed differences and similarities ("characters") noted in fossils or other organismic manifestations.

13. The 1991 show was directed by Jim Black and Christopher Rowley. An informative companion book, *Dinosaur!*, was also published, written by British paleontologist David Norman (New York: Prentice Hall, 1991). Furthermore, there were a number of other televised paleo-oriented documentary programs broadcast during the 1980s as well, especially those featuring dinosaurs. One of these, identically titled *Dinosaur!*, was hosted by Christopher Reeve, directed by Robert Guenette. At a running time of 60 minutes, this program (originally broadcast on Nov. 5, 1985) was less ambitious and, due to its mid–1980s release, less comprehensive than that hosted by Cronkite.

14. Although the next cultural phase of dinosaur popularity may be said to have begun with release of the blockbuster 1993 film *Jurassic Park*, it should be noted here that Michael Crichton's 1990 bestseller of same title (New York: Ballantine Books) was itself a product of 1980s dinosaur mania, intrigue and hype. Both the 1980s dino-craze and what followed during the *Jurassic Park* era wouldn't have been possible had it not been for the fact that dinosaurs became revolutionized during their "renaissance" of the 1960s and 1970s. Elizabeth Clemens has researched the impact of the mass extinctions dinosaur controversy during the 1980s on popular culture, science journalism and popular knowledge. She noted in a search of journal titles in the annual *New York Times* index (corresponding to the years 1978 through and inclusive of 1989) that of 230 items "abstracted under the heading 'Paleontology,'" only three categories comprised 56 percent of individual entries. These three subcategories related to the mass extinctions impact debate (32 entries), evolutionary relationships between birds and dinosaurs or prehistoric animals that flew such as pterosaurs (27 individual entries), and 70 entries pertaining to "other dinosaur-related topics." Another ~ 20 percent related to mammoths and mastodons, or fossil whales. "By comparison, a residual category including reptiles other than dinosaurs, marine life, amphibians, invertebrates, insects, plants and algae—in other words, the great bulk of life on Earth—accounts for little more than 12 percent of the total articles covering paleontology during this period." So clearly dinosaurs and their mysterious demise dominated this field, for which reasonable explanation is proffered. Clemens quoted in William Glen, ed., "The Impact Hypothesis and Popular Science: Conditions and Consequences of Interdisciplinary Debate," by Elizabeth S. Clemens, Chapter Three, pp. 98–99, in *Mass-Extinction Debates: How Science Works in a Crisis* (Stanford University Press, 1994).

Chapter Sixteen

1. Ignatius Donnelly, *Ragnarok: The Age of Fire and Gravel* (New York: D. Appleton, 1883), p. 436.

2. John Noble Wilford, *The Riddle of the Dinosaur* (New York: Alfred A. Knopf, 1986), p. 271.

3. For example, corresponding to Michael Benton's "non-question" temporal phase of addressing how dinosaurs became extinct (see Chapter Seven) are five early speculations into comet interactions with Earth, outlined here. William Whiston (1667–1752) published his *A New Theory of the Earth, from its Original to the Consummation of All Things, Wherein the Creation of the World in Six Days, the Universal Deluge, and the General Conflagration, As Laid Down in the Holy Scriptures, Are Shown to Be Perfectly Agreeable to Reason and Philosophy,* in 1696. Here, Whiston proposed that Noah's Flood had been caused by the near approach of a comet. As historian of science John C. Greene summarized concerning Whiston's "new theory," "The Deluge ... might easily have resulted from a comet's approach to the newly formed planet, swamping it with great masses of water the weight of which would expel the underground waters of the planet [i.e., Earth] from their caverns, augmenting the general flood. Such a comet would probably alter the planet's orbit from a circular to a slightly eccentric one": Greene, *The Death of Adam* (Ames: Iowa State University Press, 1959), pp. 30–31. Later theories of comet approaches or collisions roughly coincided with the late 18th century discovery of the fact that species had undergone extinction in the past. Pierre Louis de Maupertius's (1698–1759) "Essay de Cosmologie," in *Les Oeuvres de M. de Mauptertius* (a Dresde, Chez George Conrad Walther, Libraire du Roy, 1752), pp. 35–36, considered the heat emanating from the comet and toxicity of vapors resulting from passage of Earth within its tail. Then in 1761, German astronomer J.H. Lambert (1728–1777) reflected on the possibility of impacts in a remarkably precocious fashion: "When the movement of the comets is considered and we reflect on the laws of gravity, it will be readily perceived that their approach to the Earth might there cause the most woeful events, bring back the universal deluge, or make it perish in a deluge of fire, shatter it into small dust, or at least turn it from its orbit, drive away its Moon, or, still worse, the Earth itself outside the orbit of Saturn, and inflict upon us a winter several centuries long, which neither men or animals would be able to bear. The tails even of comets would not be unimportant phenomena, if the comets in taking their departure left them in whole or in part in our atmosphere." Lambert's quote from Carl Sagan's *Broca's Brain* (New York: Ballantine Books, 1980), p. 95. In 1797, the year Cuvier scientifically demonstrated the reality of vertebrate extinction in the fossil record, French astronomer Pierre Simon de Laplace (1749–1827) published his *System of the World* (English translation by Henry H. Harte, Dublin University Press, 1830), pp. 49–50, in which Laplace proposed that substantial comet impacts would dramatically shift Earth's axial tilt and spin. Oceans would swamp the equator, resulting in extinctions, or killing "the greater part of men and animals." "Laplace proposed that such an impact had caused the ocean to cover the highest mountains (leaving traces of its presence there), cause the extinction of animals and plants in the north that still live in the south, and reduced humanity to such a state that civilization had to begin anew (limiting the age of the earliest mountains to scarcely more than five thousand years old)." Laplace's conviction was based partially on the close passage of Comet Lexell in 1770. "He recognized that on the timescale of a single century, the probability of a comet striking the Earth is very low, but suggested that on longer timescales ('a long succession of ages') the probability of such a collision is great." Quotes from author Steven D'Hondt's "Theories of Terrestrial Mass Extinction by Extraterrestrial Objects," in *Earth Sciences History* 17, no. 2 (1998): pp. 157–173. In 1823, after the discovery and announcement of numerous extinct vertebrates, British geologist William Buckland extrapolated Cuvier's notions on extinction, although briefly comment-

ing on the possibility of the approach of a comet which could have caused the last biblical Deluge. "What this cause was, whether a change in the inclination of the earth's axis, or the near approach of a comet, or any other combination of causes purely astronomical is a question the discussion of which is foreign to the object of this memoir." Buckland quoted in Benton, *op. cit.*, 1990), p. 3. Then, in 1883, Ignatius Donnelly (1831–1901) theorized in his *Ragnarok: The Age of Fire and Gravel* that widespread, geologically recent deposits situated worldwide including glacial Drift clay were not resultant of movement and melting of continental glaciers during previous Ice Ages, but rather debris distributed during the impact of a comet, occurring in the early historical past—as witnessed by early Pleistocene man.

4. Furthermore, astronomer Camille Flammarion (1842–1925), who suggested that Earth's atmosphere might be contaminated by cyanogen gas upon the close passing through a cometary tail, wrote a science fictional tale, *The End of the World*, in 1893, in which we read: "Like a great celestial projectile the solid nucleus of the comet pierced the egg-shell crust of the Earth and buried itself in the semimolten interior.... The Earth was immediately converted into a planetary volcano. Oceans were spilled like thimbles of water ... continents were twisted and torn like paper." Flammarion cited and quoted in *Comet*, by Carl Sagan and Ann Druyan (New York: Random House, 1985), p. 279.

5. Wikipedia entry for "The Star" may be found at "'The Star' (Wells Short Story)."

6. Wells, "The Star," 1887, available online at www.online-literature.com/wellshg/17/

7. Arthur C. Clarke, "The Star," p. 235 in *The Nine Billion Names of God: The Best Short Stories of Arthur C. Clarke* (New York: The New American Library, 1974).

8. Garrett P. Serviss, *The Second Deluge* is available online at www.gutenberg.org/ebooks/9194. Also see Wells's *In the Days of the Comet* (1906), in *The Complete Science Fiction Treasury of H.G. Wells* (New York: Avenel Books, 1978). pp. 689–860.

9. Philip Wylie and Edwin Balmer, *When Worlds Collide* (1933; New York: Warner Books, 1982).

10. Gerrit L. Verschur, "The End of Civilization," *Astronomy* (Sept. 1991): p. 54.

11. Several years ago, when I went in to the hospital for a routine colonoscopy, a nurse sedated me for the procedure with morphine. After being released and ensconced at home, I decided to watch *Warning from Space* (aka *The Mysterious Satellite*). According to my wife, I was still slightly "tripping" even hours after the surgery, a condition which probably piqued my fascination for those none-too-stately starfish people clothed in saggy, sack-like costumes, each with a big, cutesy central eye. Psychedelic, man! In an opening scene, one of them says, "The earthmen must be stopped!" Thanks to the residual morphine in my system, I was really digging this film. But *please*, readers, don't try this exercise on your own.

12. Immanuel Velikovsky, *Earth in Upheaval* (New York: Pocket Books, 1955); Velikovsky, *Worlds in Collision* (New York: Dell, 1950).

13. David Baldwin, *The Face of the Moon* (University of Chicago Press, 1949), p. 155.

14. Allan O. Kelly and Frank Dachille, *Target: EARTH—The Role of Large Meteors in Earth Science* (Carlsbad, CA: Target: Earth, 1953); Rene Gallant, *Bombarded Earth: An Essay on the Geological and Biological Effects of Huge Meteorite Impacts* (London: John Baker, 1964); H.S. Torrens, "'No Impact': Rene Gallant (1906–1985) and his book of 1964," *Earth Sciences History* 17, no. 2 (1998): pp. 174–189. A number of other more scientifically elegant impact collision theories stemming from this period included the following: During the early 20th century, evidence was mounting favoring a conceptually non-uniformitarian view that astronomical events do sometimes have great implications for life's contingent history. For instance, by 1947, Robert S. Dietz (1914–1995) considered evidence of "shatter-cone" deposits found in what he thought were meteorite craters were signatures of impact: Dietz, "Meteorite Impact Suggested by the Orientation of Shatter-Cones at the Kentland, Indiana Disturbance," *Science* 105 (1947): pp. 42–43. A decade later, in 1958, Dietz aberrantly proposed that the Pacific Ocean basin resulted from a giant meteorite impact, a wild theory that he abandoned shortly afterward: Joanne Bourgeois and Steven Koppes, "Robert S. Dietz and the Recognition of Impact Structures on Earth," *Earth Sciences History* 17, no. 2 (1998): pp. 139–156. In 1956, fossil sponge specialist Max W. De Laubenfels (1894–1960) based a theory of dinosaur extinctions upon heat released by the impact of a large 100-meter-diameter meteorite: De Laubenfels, "Dinosaur Extinction: One More Hypothesis," *Journal of Paleontology* 30, no. 1 (1956): pp. 207–218. Also see Allen A. Debus and Diane E. Debus, "Before Alvarez: The Early Dinosaur-Killers," Chapter Thirty-two in *Dinosaur Memories: Dino-Trekking for Beasts of Thunder, Fantastic Saurians, "Paleo-people," "Dinosaurabilia," and other Prehistoria* (New York: Authors Choice Press, 2002), pp. 535–544. In 1958, Ernst J. Opik used similar reasoning to cause catastrophes: Opik, "On the catastrophic effects of collision with celestial bodies," *Irish Astronomical Journal* 5, pp. 34–36. In 1969, highly respected paleontologist Digby McLaren of Ottawa reasoned in his presidential address to the Paleontological Society, titled "Time, Life and Boundaries," that in rocks representing a geological boundary in the Upper Devonian, 365 million years ago, an event occurred that couldn't be suitably explained in traditional terms (e.g., Lyellian philosophy). McLaren boldly suggested that events of such great magnitude, as recorded in the rock record, could possibly be viewed as the outcome of a massive meteorite collision with Earth. "I do not believe that this explanation is far-fetched ... and I have become increasingly convinced that we must look for more than everyday happenings to explain many geological features": Address published in *Journal of Paleontology* 44, no. 5 (1970): pp. 801–815. Few took McLaren's proposal seriously because there was little evidence supporting such a heretical scheme, thus sounding the knell for Benton's "dilettante phase" of inquiry. Furthermore, his proposal was generally ignored, not gaining publicity because it nothing to do with celebrity prehistorians bearing cult status—"dinosaurs"—but primarily with marine shelly organisms. Also, McLaren was "only" a geologist—not a hard-scientist member of science's most exalted ruling class (i.e., physics and chemistry), such as was Nobel laureate Harold Urey. Urey led off Benton's next, subsequent "professional phase of considering what killed the dinosaurs in 1973 with a letter published in *Nature*. Here, Urey expanded on his ideas, originally published between 1957 to 1963, concerning collisions of comets with Earth. Urey suggested that the tremendous collision energy resulting could have been repeatedly responsible for cycles of mass extinctions on Earth. In earlier treatments he had

identified tektites as the glassy remnants of melted debris flung into the atmosphere after collision. In his 1973 paper, Urey correlated radiometric ages of geological boundaries representing the various epochs of the Cenozoic Era, with ages of tektite sequences in the rock record. Urey also considered the cataclysmic after-effects of collision, supporting his notions with geophysical calculations. Although his paper created little sensation, prophetically, Urey did predict that someday, perhaps, tektites corresponding in age to the terminal Cretaceous would be found, possibly establishing a link between impacts and the dinosaur extinctions. "Of course ... land based reptiles, such as alligators, as well as the primitive mammals and birds, survived the Cretaceous into the Paleocene. Such survival could be due to 'good luck'—not all areas were equally affected and some animals and plants took the adverse conditions better than others. But it does seem possible and even probable that a comet collision with the Earth destroyed the dinosaurs and initiated the Tertiary division of geologic time": Urey, "Physical Sciences—Cometary Collisions and Geological Periods," *Nature* 242 (March 2, 1973): pp. 32–33.

15. Michael J. Benton, "Scientific methodologies in collision: the history of the study of the extinction of the dinosaurs." *Evolutionary Biology* 24 (1990): p. 385. (Also available online—http://palaeo.gly.bris.ac.uk/Essays/Dino90.html.)

16. Fritz Leiber, *The Wanderer* (New York: Ballantine Books, 1964).

17. According to author Steve Galbraith IV, "the creature was prominently featured in the original film's advertising and was undoubtedly added to insure its box office success.... Brenco Pictures, the film's U.S. distributor, decided to eliminate the creature after preview audiences laughed at the buck-toothed mammal." See entry for *Gorath* in his *Japanese Science Fiction, Fantasy and Horror Films* (Jefferson, NC: McFarland, 1994).

18. Glenn L. Jepsen, "Riddles of the Terrible Lizards," *American Scientist* 53 (1964): pp. 227–240.

19. Will Cuppy, *How to Become Extinct* (New York: Dover, 1964), quoted in Benton, *op. cit.*

20. Colbert wrote: "[I]t seems logical to look for some great change that took place at the end of Cretaceous times, thereby bringing to an end the multitudes of dinosaurs and other reptiles that then populated the earth. This is not to imply that there was of necessity a great world-wide catastrophe, which by the violence of its expression suddenly wiped out the dinosaurs. Catastrophes are the mainstays of people who have very little knowledge of the natural world; for them the invocation of a catastrophe is an easy way to explain great events. But the modern student of nature is quite aware that the evolution of the earth and the evolution of life upon the earth have not proceeded by catastrophic events, even though local catastrophes—the eruption of a volcano or the sweep of an epidemic—may temporarily affect the progress of nature in some specific area. The history of the earth and of its life have advanced through the ages by a grand succession of events, by the action of forces of immense scope and significance": *Dinosaurs: Their Discovery and Their World* (New York: E.P. Dutton, 1961), pp. 249–259.

21. David M. Raup had this to say about Schindewolf's theories in 1986: "He was certainly the most respected scholar of the fossil record in Germany and perhaps the in the world, widely known for his research on the great mass extinction at the end of the Permian period, 250 million years ago...." In 1963, he published a paper entitled "Neokatastrophismus?" (English translation by V. Axel Firsoff—"Neocatastrophism?," *Catastrophist Geology* no. 2 [1977]: pp. 9–21). "Schindewolf proposed that the Permian mass extinction had been caused by a nearby exploding star, a supernova.... It has been estimated that a supernova explosion within 100 light years may occur on average every 750 million years, and this is a reasonable frequency for an event as unusual as the Permian mass extinction.... Professor Schindewolf had no independent evidence at all for an exploding star in the Permian. He made the proposal because he found the suddenness and intensity of the mass extinction inexplicable in any other way. He could think of no earth-bound process that would explain [the event].... Had this idea come from anyone of lesser experience with the Permian record and paleontology in general, it probably would have been ignored as naïve. As it happened, the proposal caused very little stir: A few papers published over the next few years evaluated the biological effects of high-energy radiation, and that is about all. Also, there was little any of us could do with the proposal because of the lack of any geological trace of a supernova in the Permian": *The Nemesis Affair: A Story of the Death of Dinosaurs and the Ways of Science* (New York: W.W. Norton, 1986), pp. 38–39.

22. Schindewolf, *op. cit.*, p. 19.

23. See Allen A. Debus, "Atomic Age Extinctions," Chapter Nineteen in *Dinosaur Memories: Dino-Trekking for Beasts of Thunder, Fantastic Saurians, "Paleo-people," "Dinosaurabilia," and other Prehistoria* (New York: Authors Choice Press, 2002), pp. 360–368. Other scientists of the late 1950s through the early 1970s introduced variations of the cosmic radiation and supernova theories in Schindewolf's stead. In 1957 Russian astrophysicist Josef Shklovskiy (1917–1985) invoked a supernova emitting "waves of cosmic radiation in proximity to our planetary system" as a potential dino-killer. See Antoni Hoffman, "Changing palaeontological views," in Stephen K. Donovan, ed., *Mass Extinctions: Processes and Evidence* (New York: Columbia University Press, 1989), pp. 4, 15. By 1958, there were unconvincing attempts made to link telltale traces of radioactive elements in key geological transition deposits corresponding to faunal discontinuities. In 1963, Robert Uffen (1923–2009) stated that life couldn't have originated until after the Earth's dynamo generated a magnetic field sufficiently strong to decrease the intensity of sterilizing cosmic radiation reaching the Earth's surface to a non-critical level. Quite possibly, Uffen speculated, geomagnetic field reversals became responsible for higher mutation rates, promoting the evolution of marine organisms: "Influence of the earth's core on the origin and evolution of life," *Nature* 198 (April 13, 1963): pp. 143–144. However, to others, the opposite seemed true. Perhaps Earth's geomagnetic field reversals could be related to the extinction of organisms, especially in the wake of a nearby exploding star. So, for example, in 1966, J F. Simpson proposed that the reduction in magnetic field intensity during a magnetic field reversal would have allowed entry of cosmic rays and other lethal forms of charged particles into the atmosphere. This phenomenon *could have* wiped out the dinosaurs: "Evolutionary pulsations and geomagnetic polarity," *Geological Society of America* 77 (1966): pp. 197–204. In 1964, A.R. Loeblich and H. Tappan ("Foraminiferal facts, fallacies and frontiers," *Geological Society of America* Bulletin 75, pp. 367–392) claimed that mass extinctions of microscopic marine planktonic fauna at the close of the

Mesozoic Era might have resulted from cosmic radiation, stating speculatively that the phenomenon "might be explained by such an increased rate of radiation or chemically induced mutations" (p. 386). C.R. Hatfield and M.J. Camp ("Mass Extinctions correlated with Periodic Galactic Events," *Geological Society of America* 81 (March 1970): pp. 911–914) concluded that mass extinctions, in general, are precipitated by Earth's motion through the Milky Way Galaxy, proposing that mass extinctions of great intensity have a quasi-periodicity of 80 to 90 million years, and exceptionally catastrophic mass extinction events (of which there is only one recorded event, the Permian/Triassic transition—so they claimed) have a frequency of once every 225 to 275 million years. Dale Russell and Wallace H. Tucker ("Supernovae and the extinction of dinosaurs," *Nature* 229 [Feb. 19, 1971]: pp. 553–554) suggested that Upper Cretaceous extinctions were caused by climatic deterioration resulting from the atmospheric irradiation by a nearby supernova. X-rays, cosmic rays and gamma rays would be sufficiently intense to cause global cooling, with decidedly disastrous effects on exposed fauna adapted to more stable and moderate climatic conditions. They rejected a conventional hypothesis that climatic adversity and faunal shifts were caused by global regressions of epicontinental seas. "It does suggest that the extinctions were of unusual magnitude and geological brief duration," occurring within approximately100,000 years. An energy equivalent of 100,000 ten-megaton H-bombs would have been absorbed by the upper atmosphere, destroying the ultraviolet-shielding ozone layer. By 1982, however, Russell recanted his former position ("The Mass Extinctions of the Late Mesozoic," *Scientific American* [Jan. 1982]: pp. 58–65), by then instead embracing the asteroid impact model, as well as its philosophical implications. K.D. Terry and Wallace H. Tucker in "Biological Effects of Supernovae," *Science* 159 (Jan. 26, 1968): pp. 421–423, considered the probability of occurrence of high-atmosphere doses of cosmic radiation from a nearby supernova blast, concluding that a dosage of at least 50 roentgens (or at least 1,700 times normal background) has a probability of occurrence every 50 million years. This frequency supported their belief that mass extinctions recur once every 60 million years. Plant life would be less seriously affected. An increased rate of mutations would lead to increased rates of extinction. Although astrophysicist Malvin Ruderman, "Possible Consequences of Nearby Supernova Explosions for Atmospheric Ozone and Terrestrial Life," *Science* 184 (June 7, 1974): pp. 1079–1081, initially supported similar notions, he later acquiesced, declaring that the Alvarez-Berkeley team was right after all: Richard Muller, *Nemesis: The Death Star* (New York: Weidenfeld & Nicolson, 1988), p. 68. A major problem with many of these ideas as proposed is that there was a great deal of "iffiness" involved, meaning that IF there had been a nearby supernova, then dinosaurs or other prehistoric organisms could have succumbed, despite the lack of evidence for any such supernova.

24. Benton (online), *op. cit.*, p. 16.

25. Isaac Asimov, "Those Dying Lizards," *The Solar System and Back* (New York: Avon Books, 1970), pp. 212–224, originally published in the Sept. 1968 issue of *The Magazine of Fantasy and Science Fiction*; Adrian J. Desmond, *The Hot-Blooded Dinosaurs: A Revolution In Palaeontology* (New York: The Dial Press-James Wade, 1975), pp. 190–193, 195, 209; Daniel Cohen, "The Great Dinosaur Disaster," *Science Digest* 65, no. 3 (March 1969): pp. 45–52; Stephen Jay Gould stated that "Radiation increases the mutation rate and yields a population with more variation. But more variation per se leads neither to extinction by prevalence of monstrosities nor in unusually rapid rates of evolution, because evolutionary tempos seem to be controlled by a different force—natural selection. Ordinary populations possess enough variation ... to permit evolutionary rates so rapid that they appear instantaneous in geologic perspective. Mutation rates so high that they kill animals directly (not through the passage of defective genes to offspring) require supernovae too close to our sun to be plausible, given the spacing of stars in our part of the galaxy": "The Belt of an Asteroid," *Hen's Teeth and Horse's Toes* (New York: W.W. Norton, 1983), pp. 325–326.

26. For details on how the supernova theory was disproved, using elemental isotopic data in 1979, see L.W. Alvarez, W. Alvarez, F. Asaro, and H.V. Michel, "Extraterrestrial causes for the Cretaceous-Tertiary extinction," *Science* 208: 1095–1108, 1980, esp. pp. 1102–1104; Dale Russell, "The Mass Extinctions of the Late Mesozoic," *Scientific American* (January 1982): pp. 61–63; Donovan, *op. cit.*, p. 45. Although support for irradiation theories of mass extinctions had faltered with the wide-sweeping success and high-profile visibility of the controversial Alvarez-Berkeley team's asteroid impact hypothesis of 1980, by the late 1990s on into the 2000s, there was rational resurgence (i.e., new variations on the central theme), in regard both to Late Cretaceous extinctions (i.e., involving a chain of events initiated and accelerated by a supernova) as addressed in David Brez Carlisle's book *Dinosaurs, Diamonds, and Things from Outer Space: The Great Extinction* (Stanford University Press, 1995), and extinctions occurring in the Late Ordovician, 444 million years ago (A.L. Melott, et al., "Did a Gamma-ray Burst Initiate the Late Ordovician Mass Extinction?" *International Journal of Astrobiology* 3, no. 1 (2004): pp. 55–61—and as later sensationalized in a 2007 History Channel *Mega-Disasters* broadcast, "Gamma Ray Bursts—Ordovician Extinction." For more on this broadcast feature, see my article, "A Cosmic Ice Age Extinction: Learning by 'O-S' mosis' (Parts 1 and 2)," in *Fossil News: Journal of Avocational Paleontology* 14, nos. 9 and 10 (Sept. 2008): pp. 4–8; (Oct. 2008): pp. 6–9. And emphasizing alternative causes of the "sixth extinction," Richard Firestone, Allen West and Simon Warwick-Smith prosecute a dramatically presented case for a supernova event transpiring 41,000 years ago in their book *The Cycle of Cosmic Catastrophes: Flood, Fire, and Famine in the History of Civilization* (Rochester, VT: Bear, 2006).

27. William Glen discusses the impact of the vulcanist theories in context of the 1980s mass extinctions debates authoritatively in Chapters 1 and 2 in *Mass-Extinction Debates: How Science Works in a Crisis* (Stanford University Press, 1994), pp. 7–91. Also see *The Great Dinosaur Controversy*, by Charles Officer and Jake Page (New York: Addison-Wesley, 1996).

28. Glen, *op. cit.*, p. 8.

29. Benton (online), *op. cit.*, p. 17.

30. L. Alvarez, 1980, *op. cit.*, p. 1105. Referring to Walter Alvarez's description of the cataclysm as a "Dante's Inferno of appalling environmental disturbances," vertebrate paleontologist William A. Clemens graphically characterized circumstances this way in an interview with William Glen. Clemens added, "In addition to darkness and cold—an 'impact winter'—acid rain, global wildfires, and greenhouse warming after the dust cloud settled were added to

the horrors. The resulting hypothesis is one of a brief period of short-term, catastrophic changes of the global environment": Walter Alvarez quoted by Clemens in Glen, *op. cit.*, 1994, p. 245.

31. Clemens cited in Glen, *op. cit.*, p. 245. An enlightening conversational exchange is documented in Glen's book between Stephen Jay Gould and David M. Raup. Gould states, "I remember Dave calling me up when Alvarez was circulating his preprint and we first learned of it and his saying to me, 'You know this is different from all the other extraterrestrial hypotheses—from Schindewolf to Digby McLaren,' which were just guesses and didn't mean a damn thing. Dave said, 'This is different' and I said, 'Yes, Dave, I understand that. You've got iridium, you've got something you can test for.' What's more, most of the others had been overt speculations" (pp. 256–257). Bruce Bohor's 1984 reported discovery in K-Pg boundary clays of what became referred to as shocked quartz grains—diagnostic of meteoritic impact—also proved particularly significant during early rounds of the ensuing debate, favoring the asteroid collision guild.

32. Will Hubbell, *Cretaceous Sea* (New York: Ace Books, 2002). In his novel *Return to Mars* (New York: HarperCollins, 1999), Ben Bova dramatically offered the intriguing notion that an ancient intelligent Martian civilization had *also* been exterminated by massive bolide bombardment, 65 million years ago (pp. 462–466). This implied a comet "swarm" invading the inner Solar System then, or possibly even a "stepwise extinctions" process. And as many film buffs know, a spate of meteor-collision movies was generated since the 1990s; fanciful movies involving dinosaurs commonly incorporated dramatic, recreated scenes of the impact. Televised dinosaur documentaries, including the aforementioned 1991 A&E Network *Dinosaur*, often included special effects footage of the terminal Cretaceous impact as well.

33. Jack Sepkoski, "What I did with My Research Career," cited in Glen, *op. cit.*, p. 143.

34. David M. Raup and J. John Sepkoski, "Periodicity of extinctions in the geologic past," *Proceedings of the National Academy of Sciences USA* 81 (Feb. 1984): pp. 801–805. Following announcement of the "Death Star" theory, the story really took off.

35. *Ibid.*, p. 801. Also see Raup and Sepkoski, "Mass Extinctions in the Marine Fossil Record," *Science* 215 (March 19, 1982): pp. 1501–1503. For more on these out-of-this-world theories, see Raup's *The Nemesis Affair: A Story of the Death of Dinosaurs and the Ways of Science* (New York: W.W. Norton, 1986), and *Extinction: Bad Genes or Bad Luck?* (New York: W. W. Norton, 1991); Richard Muller, *Nemesis, the Death Star: The Story of a Scientific Revolution* (New York: Weidenfeld & Nicolson, 1988); Donald Goldsmith, *Nemesis: The Death-Star and other Theories of Mass Extinction* (New York: Berkley Books, 1985); Roman Smoluchowski, John N. Bahcall, and Mildred S. Matthews, eds., *The Galaxy and the Solar System* (Tucson: University of Arizona Press, 1986). The astronomical cycle for mass extinctions proposed by Raup and Sepkoski wasn't the first of its kind. Hatfield and Camp's theory was mentioned here previously, as was Napier's and Clube's 1979 proposal. But scientists had long probed for terrestrially driven megacycles as well. One such terrestrially founded example was a 32-million-year cycle, as perceived and published by paleontologists Alfred G. Fischer and Michael A. Arthur in 1977, titled "Secular Variations in the Pelagic Realm," which was soundly dismissed by Raup and Sepkoski; see Raup, *op. cit.*, 1986, pp. 109–110, and Fischer, "The Two Phanerozoic Supercycles," in *Catastrophes and* Earth *History: The New Uniformitarianism*, W.A. Berggren and John A. Van Couvering, eds. (Princeton University Press, 1984), pp. 129–150.

36. Robert Silverberg, *At Winter's End* (New York: Warner Books, 1988), p. 293. (Sadly, this author's novella, *Dolphinian Dynasty*, relying on the 26-million-year cycle never saw the light of day in regards to publishing.) Science fictional stories involving astronomical cycles impacting man, while few and far between, carry inherent appeal. One of the very first in this subcategory, although not involving dinosaurs and substituting archaeology for paleontology, was Isaac Asimov's 1941 "Nightfall," voted as the greatest science fiction short story ever written in 1970. Robert Silverberg, ed., *The Science Fiction Hall of Fame* (New York: Avon Books, 1970), pp. x, 145–182.

37. W.M. Napier, and S.V.M. Clube, "A theory of terrestrial catastrophism," *Nature* 282 (Nov. 29, 1979): pp. 455–459.

38. Glen, *op. cit.*, p. 256. Quite recently, since 2014, physicists have invoked the possibility of dark matter as causing periodicity in mass extinctions on Earth, via (periodic) comet bombardment. See Lisa Randall's *Dark Matter and the Dinosaurs: The Astounding Interconnectedness of the Universe* (New York: HarperCollins, 2015) for more on this intriguing concept.

39. Isaac Asimov, "Yes! With A Bang!" in *Counting the Eons* (New York: Avon Books), 1984 (originally published in the June 1981 issue of *The Magazine of Fantasy and Science Fiction*); Jeff Hecht, "Global Catastrophes and Mass Extinctions," *Analog—Science Fiction, Science Fact* (May 1991): pp. 78–89.

40. Raup, 1986, *op. cit.*, pp. 169–170. Furthermore, Ellen Goodman, columnist for the *Boston Globe*, stated rather astutely, "The latest theories may reflect our own contemporary world view. Surely we are now more sensitive to cosmic catastrophe, to accident. Surely we are more conscious of the shared fate of the whole species.... In that sense, the latest dinosaur theory fits us uncomfortably well. 'Our' dinosaurs died together in some meteoric winter, the victims of a global catastrophe. As humans, we fear a similar shared fate": Goodman, "Musings of a Dinosaur Groupie," *Boston Globe*, Jan. 3, 1984, cited in Raup, 1986 *op. cit.*, pp. 169–170.

41. Allen A. Debus, "Portraying Paleocatastrophe," Chapter 24 in *Paleoimagery: The Evolution of Dinosaurs in Art* (Jefferson, NC: McFarland, 2002), pp. 152–156.

42. Digby J. McLaren, "Impacts and Extinctions: Science or Dogma?" pp. 121–131, in Glen, *op. cit.*; David M. Raup, "The Extinction Debates: A View from the Trenches," pp. 145–151, in Glen, *op. cit.*; Kenneth J. Hsu, "Uniformitarianism vs. Catastrophism in the Extinction Debate," in Glen, *op. cit.*, pp. 217–229.

43. Hsu cited in Glen, *op. cit.*, pp. 222, 229. Also see Stephen Jay Gould's essay, "Jove's Thunderbolts," in *Dinosaur in a Haystack* (New York: Harmony Books, 1995), pp. 159–169.

44. Glen, *op. cit.*, p. 49, 52–53. During the waning years of the "dilettante phase," not all startlingly new or fresh theories of mass extinction invoked catastrophes, or phenomena originating in outer space. Dinosaur paleontologist Loris S. Russell (1904–1998), for example, proposed a non-catastrophic hypothesis that was for its time potentially rather controversial, as it relied on the then outrageous notion of warm-blooded dinosaurs. In presuming a

warm-blooded metabolic condition for dinosaurs, not unlike that which occurs in "reptile-like monotremes of today," Russell hypothesized that declining temperatures during the Late Cretaceous led to their extinction. The dinosaurs, which according to Russell's view lacked external insulation, were left exposed to adverse climatic conditions and eventually suffered extinction when temperatures gradually fell beyond a certain critical level. Russell refuted 1940s theories suggesting rising temperatures killed off the dinosaurs, as all existing evidence pointed to the contrary: Loris S. Russell, "Body Temperature of Dinosaurs and its Relationships to their Extinctions," *Journal of Paleontology* 39, no. 3 (May 1965): pp. 497–501. A characteristic of the dawning professional phase in considering mass extinctions is that, as William Glen noted, languishing terrestrial-oriented, non-catastrophic or uniformitarian, endogenous "(quasi-paradigmatic) hypotheses, such as sea-level changes, climate changes, and plate movements, which had accumulated during the past century ... had generally come to be regarded, singly or multiply, as ineffective or only partially explanatory of mass extinctions," and thus "drifted further from center stage": William Glen, ed., *Mass-Extinction Debates: How Science Works in a Crisis* (Stanford University Press, 1994), Chapter Two by Glen, "How Science Works in the Debates," p. 62. Interestingly, Frederick A. Lucas also conjectured about the possibility of dinosaurian warm-bloodedness in his 1901 book, *Animals of the Past* (New York: American Museum of Natural History), p. 99.

45. *Ibid.*, p. 130 (cited from the *New York Times*, Oct. 29, 1985).

46. L. Alvarez quoted in Glen, *op. cit.*, p. 111.

47. A. Morris and James B. Settles, "The Bomb Out of Space," *Fantastic Adventures* 10, no. 4 (April 1948): p. 177.

48. Teri Randall, "Crater may hold key to dinosaurs' demise," *Chicago Tribune*, July 23, 1989, section 1, p. 14.

49. Walter Alvarez, *T. rex and the Crater of Doom* (Princeton University Press, 1997); James Lawrence Powell, *Night Comes to the Cretaceous: Dinosaur Extinctions and the Transformation of Modern Geology* (New York: W.H. Freeman, 1998); A.R. Hildebrand and W.V. Boynton, "Proximal Cretaceous-Tertiary boundary impact deposits in the Caribbean," *Science* 248 (May 18, 1990): pp. 843–847; A.R. Hildebrand and G.T. Penfield, "A buried 180-kilometer diameter probable impact crater on the Yucatan peninsula, Mexico," *Eos* 71 (1990): p. 1425. Mass extinctions intrigue certainly began reentering mainstream avenues by the fall of 1979, when David M. Raup published data suggesting that up to 96 percent of all marine species could have been exterminated at the end of the Paleozoic Era, a time corresponding to the Permo-Triassic transition, 250 million years ago. This is nearly *all* of marine life! Raup, "Size of the Permo-Triassic Bottleneck and Its Evolutionary Implications," *Science* 206 (Oct. 12, 1979): pp. 217–218. Raup didn't speculate about particular causes, but within a few years, following publication of the Alvarez team's theory, as well as bolstered by statistical data for mass extinctions periodicity, the search was on for evidence of *recurrent* impact cratering, that is, in tune with "cyclic" (as then perceived) mass extinctions boundaries besides the K-Pg, thus (if proven) elevating prominence of the Alvarez hypothesis into a general theory of nature. At first there didn't appear to be definitive evidence of impact cratering during the Permo-Triassic transition. Because a consequence of plate tectonics is that dense ocean floor rock becomes geologically recycled, subducted under less dense continental plate margins (a process causing energetic earthquakes), if an impact took place in ocean basins, the crater may have long disappeared. (The oldest ocean floor remaining is 200 million years old.) Three claims of Permo-Triassic impact structures, since raised as remote possibilities, have not proven persuasive as having causal relationship to this mass extinction event: Douglas H. Erwin, *Extinction: How Life on Earth Nearly Ended 250 Million Years Ago* (Princeton University Press, 2006), pp. 33–35, 206–207. But during the 1980s, other large impact crater structures, corresponding to other extinctions horizons (the Late Devonian, Late Triassic and Late Eocene Epoch) were quickly recruited into the periodicity debate. For more on these (respectively), see George R. McGhee, Jr., *The Late Devonian Mass Extinction: The Frasnian/Famennian Crisis* (New York: Columbia University Press, 1996); P.E. Olson, et al., "New Early Jurassic tetrapod assemblages constrain Triassic-Jurassic tetrapod extinction event," *Science* 237 (Aug. 28, 1987): pp. 1025–1029; C. Wylie Poag, *Chesapeake Invader: Discovering America's Giant Meteorite Crater* (Princeton University Press, 1999). In his 1991 book intended for laypeople, *Extinction: Bad Genes or Bad Luck?*, David Raup introduced his concept of "kill curves," in which impact cratering of particular immensity and statistical frequency of recurrence could be related to expected percentages of extinctions in the fossil record. Raup estimated that the "Big Five" species mass extinctions of ~ 65 percent extinction were on the order of "100 million year events" (New York: W.W. Norton), pp. 85, 171.

Also see Lisa Randall's *Dark Matter and the Dinosaurs* (New York: HarperCollins, 2015), pp. 209–217.

50. Spencer R. Weart, *The Rise of Nuclear Fear* (Harvard University Press, 2012), pp. 231–241.

51. *Ibid.*, p. 238.

52. *Ibid.*, p. 233.

53. As Elizabeth S. Clemens stated in 1994, causal connections linked "both direct and metaphorical," between "nuclear winter" simulations and the proximate causal mechanism of the Late Cretaceous extinctions proposed by the Alvarez team (i.e., extended darkness with elimination of photosynthesis for a prolonged period in the immediate aftermath of impact). "By suggesting the generalizability of climate-mediated extinction—and underscoring the identification of the fate of mankind with that of the giant reptiles who once ruled the earth—these findings heightened the salience of the Alvarez hypothesis for both scientific and general audiences": Clemens, "the Impact Hypothesis and Popular Science: Conditions and Consequences of Interdisciplinary Debate," in Glen, *op. cit.*, p. 113. The term "nuclear winter" was coined in 1983 by a group researching the atmospheric effects resulting from a widespread nuclear war, led by Richard P. Turco, Owen B. Toon, Thomas P. Ackerman, James Pollack and Carl Sagan. Luis Alvarez also recognized that the impact winter scenario for dinosaur extinctions was comparable to the outcome of a large thermonuclear warhead exchange. Meanwhile, Paul J. Crutzen and John W. Birks were also considering ecological consequences of nuclear war, recognizing that extensive fires resulting from bomb detonation would throw up vast quantities of sky-darkening soot and dust, globally. During a 1983 meeting concerning mass extinctions ("Dynamics of Extinction" symposium, held in Flagstaff, Arizona), the event at which David Raup and John Sepkoski announced their data supporting the 26-million-year mass extinctions cycle, not unexpectedly,

this channeled discussion on how mankind might cause catastrophic extinctions through any of a variety of self-imposed means: Wilford, *op. cit.*, pp. 269–272.

54. Carl Sagan and Ann Druyan, *Comet* (New York: Random House, 1985), p. 289. Also, writing in *The Cold and the Dark: The World After Nuclear War*, Paul R. Ehrlich, Carl Sagan, Donald Kennedy, Walter Orr Roberts, eds. (New York: W.W. Norton, 1984), Sagan stated, "It was ... proposed by Alvarez *et al.* that the extinction of the dinosaurs and many other species 65 million years ago, at the boundary of the Cretaceous and Tertiary epochs, was due to the collision with the Earth of an asteroid 10 kilometers across, and the subsequent spewing of enormous quantities of fine dust into the atmosphere. Joined by Richard Turco of R&D Associates in Marina del Ray, California, [James B.] Pollack and [Owen B.] Toon calculated that a severe cooling and darkening event might have been attendant to such an asteroidal collision. I wish to stress, however, that our calculations on the climate consequences of nuclear war do not depend on this interpretation of the Cretaceous/Tertiary extinctions. The dinosaurs could have died of influenza without affecting the validity of our conclusions" (p. 5). Instead of the full-blown "nuclear winter," Weart, *op. cit.*, 2012, clarifies (p. 234): "Later, more-detailed studies showed that a nuclear war would not bring on an ice age; however, the smoke from even a limited war with a few hundred explosions could bring a 'nuclear autumn' that would ruin agriculture around the world, threatening billions with starvation." David Raup has noted, "The interesting point here is that the experiments and computer modeling that went into the dinosaur-extinction problem were soon picked up by Carl Sagan and others and applied to the environmental effects of a major thermonuclear war. And nuclear winter, in its American version, was born": Raup, *op. cit.*, 1986, pp. 21–22.

55. Wilford, *op. cit.*, p. 272.

56. William Tsutsui, *Godzilla On My Mind* (New York: Palgrave Macmillan, 2004), p. 65.

57. Corey S. Powell, "The Madness of the Planets," in *The Best American Science and Nature Writing 2014*, Deborah Blum, ed. (New York: Houghton Mifflin Harcourt, 2014), pp. 222–230. Furthermore, a quarter of a century ago, a 1,000-foot-wide meteorite making a "near-miss" on its close approach to within two Earth-Moon diameters on March 23, 1989, made eye-opening headline news. Upon impact, such a moderately sized space rock would unleash the energy equivalent of up to 2,500 one-megaton hydrogen bombs! Besides comets from the Sun's distant Kuiper Belt and the much more distant Oort Cloud, those asteroid bombs from space continue to lurk out there in what are known as menacing "Earth-crossing orbits."

58. "A Panel Discussion on the Debates," in Glen, *op. cit.*, p. 281.

59. Of course, the fallacy in all this intrigue over the ultimate cause of dinosaur extinctions 65 million years ago is that they really did survive after all. For species of non-avian dinosaurs evolved into the highly successful bird lineage!

60. With the jury still out in some cases, the ultimate, principal causes of each of the "Big Six" mass extinction events would appear to be, respectively: intense cosmic radiation with a concomitant ice age period for the Late Ordovician; multiple (up to six) large meteorite impacts for the Late Devonian; a globally intensified greenhouse condition for the Permian-Triassic transition with volatilization of toxic gases from the sea beds; another global greenhouse condition possibly triggered by intensified volcanism and coupled with one large asteroid impact for the Late Triassic-Early Jurassic boundary; a much larger dinosaur-killer asteroid or comet impact for the Late Cretaceous; and, for the very Late Pleistocene and recent Anthropocene—Man!

Chapter Seventeen

1. Don Mancini commenting during the SyFy Network's program *Face Off*, March 31, 2015, season 8, episode 12.

2. Charles Schuchert, *Outlines of Historical Geology* (New York: John Wiley & Sons, 1931); Joseph Le Conte, *Elements of Geology: A Text-book for Colleges and for the General Reader*, 5th ed. (New York: D. Appleton, 1903), p. 358.

3. Quote is from Lynn Barber, *The Heyday of Natural History, 1820–1870* (Garden City, NY: Doubleday, 1980), p. 279. Also see Chapter Two in this book.

4. Vincent Di Fate, "The Monster Makers," *FilmFax* no. 99–100 (Oct. 2003–Jan. 2004), p. 56.

5. Donald F. Glut, *Classic Movie Monsters* (Metuchen, NJ: Scarecrow Press, 1978), p. 259.

6. Di Fate, *op. cit.*

7. Samantha Weinberg, *A Fish Caught in Time: The Search for he Coelacanth* (New York: HarperCollins, 2001), p. 89.

8. Edgar Allan Poe, "The City in the Sea" (1831–1845), *Great Short Works of Edgar Allan Poe* (New York: Harper & Row, 1970), pp. 63–65.

9. H.G. Wells, "In the Abyss" (1896), Isaac Asimov, ed., *Isaac Asimov Presents: The Best Science Fiction of the 19th Century—The Birth of Science in Fiction* (New York: Knightsbridge, 1981), pp. 257–273.

10. Cobb's 1913 story is available to readers online at http://gaslight.mtroyal.ca/fhshhead.htm.

11. H.P. Lovecraft, "Supernatural Horror in Fiction" in *At the Mountains of Madness* (Modern Library, NY: Random House, 2005), pp. 148–149.

12. S.T. Joshi, *I Am Providence: The Life and Times of H.P. Lovecraft* (New York: Hippocampus Press, 2010), p. 252.

13. Cobb, *op. cit.*

14. For more on Cobb (1876–1944), see Wikipedia entry at http://en.wikipedia.org/wiki/Irvin_S_Cobb.

15. Decades later, *Psycho*'s Robert Bloch rediscovered "Fishhead," praising this tale, which changed his course. Bloch's recommendation lingered in the fertile minds of Lawrence Adam Shell and Michael Price, inspiring a graphic novelization, departing from and elaborating the story beyond where Cobb left matters. Artist Mark Evan Walker illustrated the graphic series, appearing at ComicMix.com. In their updated version, Fishhead is a wretched, fishy, freakish character, exploited at a circus road show. Their creation appeared not long ago in serial format.

16. Stephen King, *Danse Macabre* (New York: Berkley Books, 1981), p. 97.

17. H.P. Lovecraft, "Dagon" (1923), in *100 Creepy Little Creature Stories*, Robert Weinberg, *et al.*, eds. (New York: Barnes & Noble, 1994), pp. 86–90.

18. *Ibid.*, p. 90.

19. H.P. Lovecraft, *The Shadow Over Innsmouth and Other Stories of Horror* (New York: Scholastic Book Service, 1981), pp. 164–255. Quote is from p. 246.

20. *Ibid.*, from A Word to the Reader by Margaret Ronan, p. 7.

21. August Derleth, "H.P. Lovecraft and his Work," in *The Dunwich Horror* (New York: Lancer Books, 1963), pp. 7–21; Joshi, *op. cit.*

22. Richard Tooker, *Inland Deep* (Philadelphia: Penn, 1936).

23. *Ibid.*, p. 48. Tooker's term, Mesozoic "frog man," first appears on p. 49.

24. *Ibid.*, pp. 105–106, 111.

25. *Ibid.*, p. 106.

26. *Ibid.*, p. 115.

27. *Ibid.*, p. 131. Tooker also regards their "manlikeness," and as Willa states, "There's something human about them" (p. 131).

28. *Ibid.*, p. 142.

29. *Ibid.*, p. 167.

30. *Ibid.*, pp. 53–55.

31. Karel Čapek, *War with the Newts* (London: George Allen & Unwin, 1936) (1985 translation by Ewald Osers).

32. L. Ron Hubbard, *The Indigestible Triton*, The L. Ron Hubbard Classic Fiction Series (Hollywood, CA: Author Book Services, 1993), pp. 134–135.

33. Clark Ashton Smith, "Mother of Toads" (1938), in *100 Creepy Little Creature Stories*, Robert Weinberg, *et al.* eds. (New York: Barnes & Noble, 1994), pp. 328–334.

34. Glut, *op. cit.*, p. 264.

35. *Ibid.*, p. 264. (Baxter cited therein.)

36. *Ibid.*, p. 265.

37. *Ibid.*, p. 269.

38. For more perspective on *The Alligator People*, see my article, "Moreau: H. G. Wells' Exercise in Youthful Blasphemy," in *Mad Scientist* no. 21 (Spring 2010): pp. 26–33. Transforming into a humanoid reptile ancestor for drive-in movie scares was one way to entertain monster-loving audiences of the late 1950s and early '60s. Two additional contemporary instances are also rather memorable for the period, 1956's *The She Creature* and *The Alligator People* (1959). The scaly-looking She Creature turns out to be a psychic manifestation or ghost, conjured through past-life hypnosis, of an amphibious humanoid, one which supposedly walked the planet one million years ago. Alligator men were ordinary humans who have reverted to a savage, ancestral "archosaurian" state under the mad-science-gone-awry influence of hormone treatments, initially intended to medically regenerate damaged tissues. However, suggesting to audiences that men's closest genetic ties were to prehistoric reptiloids possessing humanoid qualities (or even similarly anointed aquatic gill men) must have been far trickier and less convincing, rather than conjuring the more obvious ancestral lineage, the "accepted" consensus path leading backward through an assortment of prehistoric primates and cave men.

39. For more on "Vargo Statten," pseudonym for John Russell Fearn, see my articles, "Dino-Monster to the Rescue versus Aliens in 1953," *G-Fan* no. 107 (Fall 2014): pp. 66–68, and "On the Loose Again: Vargo Statten's *Creature from the Black Lagoon* (Dreamhaven redux)," *Mad Scientist* no. 28 (Winter 2014): pp. 41–44.

40. Vargo Statten, *Creature from the Black Lagoon* (1954; Minneapolis, MN: Dreamhaven Books, 2011 reprint), p. 6.

41. *Ibid.*, p. 9.

42. *Ibid.*, p. 124.

43. *Ibid.*, pp. 183–184. Gill Man isn't just another run-of-the-mill monster. Its tragic failure stems from an inability to understand the human world, which he wants part of, that is, at least the desirable Kay. It doesn't understand why humans have both an interest in, as well as hatred for him, or why *their* rules should apply in his primeval paradise. Gil Man's fatal downfall is his sexual naivety, manifested both in a lack of available gill-women consorts and in the inappropriateness of pursuing Kay. While Gill Man comprehends that Kay is female, unlike the hated invading males, he doesn't realize that she is the wrong species for him.

44. Carl Dreadstone, *Creature from the Black Lagoon* (New York: Berkley, 1977).

45. *Ibid.*, p. 42–44.

46. *Ibid.*, p. 194.

47. Glut, *op. cit.*, pp. 273–274.

48. Guy N. Smith, *The Slime Beast* (London: New English Library, 1975), p. 26.

49. Paul Di Filippo, *Creature from the Black Lagoon: Time's Black Lagoon* (Milwaukie, OR: DH Press, 2006).

50. Edmond Hamilton, "The Isle of Changing Life," *Thrilling Wonder Stories* 16 (June 1940): pp. 33–43.

51. *Ibid.*, p. 35.

52. *Ibid.*, p. 37.

53. As recounted by Gary D. Rhodes, back in 1958, adoring teenagers who flocked to see this film "placed it more firmly in the cross-genre of horror-science fiction." Terms like radiation, isotopes, misleading advertising—"Thermodynamic Horror from Outer Space," and "atomic created a modern texture for the film." A "werewolf" flick jazzed with a trendy radiation premise, spawned from Cold War angst, reverberating technological science fictional themes certainly also lent a refreshing air to the aging and by then worn "lost world/hollow Earth" premise leading toward face-to-face encounter with scary primeval monster "props." Plus, there was a refined element to ponder: the scaly raging *prehistoric* beast dwelled, if not ruled, from within. *The Hideous Sun Demon* screenplay, drafted by Phil Hiner (from a story by Hiner and Robert Clarke), was originally titled "Sauros." It was evidently the intention at this preliminary stage to approach makeup artist Jack P. Pierce with the task of creating the monster suit. Further embellishments by E.S. Seeley, Jr., resulted in the final screenplay (final revised shooting script, dated October 17, 1957). Rather than Jack Pierce, the scaly Sun Demon mask and costume instead were the handiwork of Richard Cassarino (costing a mere $500). Many readers may be more familiar with an awful comedic version of the film (*Hideous Sun Demon: The Special Edition*, 1989), for which a second new monster costume was made from a mold owned by Bob Burns. Rhodes quoted in "The Sun Demon: Its Drive-in World Premiere," p. 303, in *Tom Weaver Presents the Scripts from the Crypt Collection: No. 1, The Hideous Sun Demon, the Original Screenplay* (Duncan, OK: BearManor Media, 2011). "Sauros," as well as Seeley's final shooting script, and an intended yet never filmed sequel, Arthur C. Pierce's "Sorceress" (outline dated 1976), are presented in this volume.

54. Lately, annals of recent sci-fi (both film and literature) are rife with species of intelligent reptiloid/dinosauroids. Intelligent CGI-animated reptiloids are commonplace in movies now, most recently featured in a SyFy channel cheapie (*Heatstroke*). Then there's that outer space/parallel universe "quantum connection" to ponder, as intelligent reptiloids now threaten not only from within, but also *beyond*.

55. H.P. Lovecraft, "In the Walls of Eryx" (1939, with

Kenneth I. Sterling), *The Shadow Over Innsmouth and Other Stories of Horror* (New York: Scholastic Book Services, 1971), pp. 110–150.

56. Carl Sagan, *The Dragons of Eden* (New York: Ballantine Books, 1977), p. 144.

57. L. Sprague de Camp's and Catherine Crook de Camp's *The Stones of Nomuru* (New York: Simon & Schuster, 1988), p. 175. Other examples might include Stuart Vaughn Stockton's *Starfire: The Mending*, Book 1 (Marcher Lord Press, 2009). Outer space connections deepened following discovery that a comet or asteroid decimated the dinosaurs 65 million years ago via publication of A.C. Crispin's 1984 novel *V* (based on the NBC miniseries). In particular, the aforementioned pairing of Camps wrote that alien dinos of Nomuru are "closer to our Terran reptiles" (p. 175). Meanwhile, Harry Turtledove launched a series of novels staged within a parallel universe setting in which Earth was attacked by tech-savvy lizards during the 1940s, beginning with his *World War: In the Balance* (New York: Ballantine Books, 1994). These and additional examples will be considered here in Chapter Eighteen.

58. Contingency as Stephen Jay Gould explained in popular books such as *Wonderful Life: The Burgess Shale and the Nature of History* (New York: W.W. Norton, 1989), and as quite opposed to how men such as Osborn perceived life's history as preordained or internally "programmed" within the germ plasm (or DNA genes), so much of the history of life on Earth, and the results of mass extinctions, is due to blind chance.

Chapter Eighteen

1. *Dinosaur!* 1991, hosted by Walter Cronkite, Arts and Entertainment Network. Directed by Jim Black and Christopher Rowley.

2. David Norman, *Dinosaur!: Based on the Acclaimed Four-part Television Series* (New York: Prentice Hall, 1991), p. 187. The general appearance of the televised Dinosauroid is vaguely reminiscent of another kind of "dinosauroid," the "Sleestaks," intelligent insectoid-reptiloid denizens of *Land of the Lost*'s (Krofft Entertainment, BC, 1974–1976) parallel universe, or lizard-men Sleestaks of the "new" *Land of the Lost* program (1991). Intriguingly, the intelligent Sleestaks humanoid-reptiloid race—couple d with the dinosaur-inhabited milieu, cast in an alternate dimension—was dreamed up shortly before Carl Sagan offered speculations concerning his "what-if" scenario, had the dinosaurs not succumbed to extinction. (See Note 11, below.) However, I have no evidence suggesting the eminent Sagan "borrowed" his idea for a hypothetical intelligent "dinosauroid" from a Saturday morning children's show.

3. Phrase in quotes stated by paleoartist Tylor Keillor published in *Wall Street Journal*, "Did Dinosaurs Have Lips? Paleoartist puts on a face on ancient bones," March 20, 2015, p. 1.

4. The published archetype of Imagext variety no. 2 is perhaps as illustrated by John C. McLoughlin in his April–May 1984 article "Evolutionary Bioparanoia," in *Animal Kingdom* (New York Zoological Society), pp. 24–30.

5. H.G. Wells, "In the Abyss" (1896), Isaac Asimov, ed., *Isaac Asimov Presents: The Best Science Fiction of the 19th Century—The Birth of Science in Fiction* (New York: Knightsbridge, 1981), pp. 257–273.

6. Each title mentioned in this paragraph was thoroughly discussed in critical context, accordingly, in my book, *Dinosaurs in Fantastic Fiction: A Thematic Survey* (Jefferson, NC: McFarland, 2006).

7. The term "exogenous" refers to "exodinosaurs," a term referring to fictional dinosaurs of other planets, coined by paleontologist Jose Luis Sanz in his book *Starring T. Rex!* (Bloomington: Indiana University Press, 2002), pp. 69–72.

8. Edgar Rice Burroughs, *Tarzan at the Earth's Core* (1930; New York: Ballantine Books, 1964), p. 150.

9. Henry R. Knipe, *Evolution in the Past* (London: Herbert and Daniel, 1912), p. 78.

10. Adrian J. Desmond, *The Hot-Blooded Dinosaurs: A Revolution in Palaeontology* (New York: Warner Books, 1976), pp. 265–66.

11. Carl Sagan, *The Dragons of Eden: Speculations on the Evolution of Human Intelligence* (New York: Ballantine Books, 1977), p. 144.

12. Brian Stableford cited in Mike Magee's *Who Lies Sleeping?: The Dinosaur Heritage and the Extinction of Man* (Selwyn, Frome, England: AskWhy! Publications, 1993), p. 53.

13. L.W. Alvarez, *et al.*, "Extraterrestrial cause for the Cretaceous-Tertiary extinction," *Science* 208 (June 6, 1980): pp. 1095–1108.

14. Dale A. Russell and Ron Seguin, "Reconstructions of the small Cretaceous theropod *Stenonychosaurus inequalis* and a hypothetical dinosauroid," *Syllogeus* 37 (1982).

15. *Ibid.*, p. 22.

16. Jerison cited in Dale A. Russell, "Models and Paintings of North American Dinosaurs," in *Dinosaurs Past and Present*, vol. 1, eds. Sylvia M. Czerkas and Everett C. Olson (Natural History Museum of Los Angeles County in association with University of Washington Press, Seattle and London, 1987), p. 127.

17. Russell and Seguin, *op. cit.*, p. 22.

18. John Noble Wilford, *The Riddle of the Dinosaur* (New York: Alfred A. Knopf, 1986), p. 267.

19. Russell, *op. cit.*, p. 129–130; Paleoanthropologist C. Owen Lovejoy argued against the probabilistic attainment of heightened intelligence, in that "intelligence is selected against." Lovejoy quoted in "Smart Dinosaurs," by Jeff Hecht and Gurney Williams III in *Omni* 4 (May 1982): p. 54. Also see Dale A. Russell, "Speculations on the Evolution of Intelligence in Multicellular Organisms," in *Life in the Universe* (Cambridge, MA: MIT Press, 1981), pp. 259–275; George Gaylord Simpson, "The Nonprevalence of Humanoids," *Science* 143 (Feb. 21, 1964): pp. 769–775; Allen A. Debus, "A Paleontological 'Parallel'," Chapter Eighteen in Debus and Debus, *Dinosaur Memories* (Lincoln, NE: Authors Choice Press, 2002), pp. 341–352.

20. Russell, *op. cit.*, (1987), p. 125.

21. *Ibid.*, p. 127.

22. Dougal Dixon, *The New Dinosaurs: An Alternative Evolution* (Topsfield, MA: Salem House Publishers, 1988), pp. 111–112.

23. *Ibid.*, p. 112.

24. Joe DeVito, Brad Strickland, John Michlig, *Kong: King of Skull Island* (Milwaukie, OR: DH Press, 2004).

25. James Gurney, *Dinotopia* (Atlanta: Turner, 1992); James Gurney, *Dinotopia: The World Beneath* (New York: HarperCollins, 1995); James Gurney, *Dinotopia: Journey to Chandra* (Kansas City: Andrew McMeel, 2007).

26. For example, Geoffrey A. Landis's 1992 short story "Embracing the Alien," features a Dinosauroid. *Analog Science Fiction and Fact* 112 (November 1992): pp. 10–39.

27. *Ibid.*, p. 33. The poetry as quoted is borrowed and somewhat adapted by Landis from Edgar Allan Poe's "A Dream Within a Dream" (1827–1849).

28. James Patrick Kelly, "Think Like a Dinosaur," *Asimov's Science Fiction* 19 (June 1995): pp. 10–43.

29. The phrase is borrowed from John Noble Wilford's 1986 book title, *op. cit.*

30. Michael Crichton, *Jurassic Park* (New York: Ballantine Books, 1990).

31. Scott D, Sampson, "From Lost Continents to Dinosaur Trains," *Prehistoric Times* no. 92 (Winter 2009): p. 11.

32. W.J.T. Mitchell, *The Last Dinosaur Book: The Life and Times of a Cultural Icon* (University of Chicago Press, 1998), p. 3.

33. Russell, 1987, *op. cit.*, p. 128.

34. Ronald Story, *Encyclopedia of Extraterrestrial Encounters* (NAL Trade, 2001), pp. 488–491.

35. A.C. Crispin, *V* (New York: Pinnacle Books, 1984).

36. But for further perspective or gist of this idea, see the illustrated advertisement in *Prehistoric Times* no. 26 (Sept.–Oct. 1997): p. 21.

37. In the 1991 documentary *Dinosaur!*, Stephen Jay Gould states during an interview that the extinction of the dinosaurs appeals to humans for two primary reasons. First, we do have "enormous parochial interest ... because dinosaurs died and mammals survived and that's why we're here." Secondly, the K-Pg event is the "most recent of the mass extinctions and the evidence is better."

38. Frederick D. Gottfried, "Hermes to the Ages" (1980), in *The Science Fictional Dinosaur*, Robert Silverberg, *et al.*, eds. (New York: Avon Books, 1982), pp. 111–146.

39. This is in reference to the verbal communications expressed by and exchanged between Rodan, Godzilla and the larval Mothra near the conclusion of Toho's *Ghidrah, the Three-headed Monster* (1965).

40. Eric Garcia, *Anonymous Rex* (New York: Popular Library, 2000); Eric Garcia, *Casual Rex* (New York: Villard Books, 2001). I discuss these works in Debus, 2006, *op. cit.*

41. Isaac Asimov, "Big Game" (1941), in *Before the Golden Age*, edited by Isaac Asimov (Garden City, NY: Doubleday, 1974), pp. 810–812.

42. Isaac Asimov, "Day of the Hunters," in *Dinosaurs: Stories by Ray Bradbury, Arthur C. Clarke, Isaac Asimov and Many Others*, Martin H. Greenberg, ed. (New York: Donald I. Fine Books, 1996), pp. 15–25.

43. Barry B. Longyear, *The Homecoming* (New York: Walker, 1989); S.D. Howe, "Wrench and Claw," *Analog Science Fiction & Fact* 68 (Nov. 1998): pp. 60–91; Thomas P. Hopp, *Dinosaur Wars* (Lincoln, NE: Authors Choice Press, 2000).

44. Stephen Baxter, "The Hunters of Pangaea," *Analog Science Fiction & Fact* 122 (Dec. 2002): pp. 76–88.

45. This is a term coined by Carl Sagan, used as the title of his 1994 book, *Pale Blue Dot: A Vision of the Human Future in Space* (New York: Random House). The phrase refers to an image of Earth, taken by the Voyager 1 spacecraft from a distance of 3.7 billion miles, in which Earth appears merely as a seemingly insignificant pale blue spot in the void of space.

46. John C. McLoughlin, "Evolutionary Bioparanoia," *Animal Kingdom* (April–May 1984): pp. 24–30.

47. John C. McLoughlin, *Archosauria: A New Look at the Old Dinosaur* (London: Allen Lane, 1979), pp. 107–108.

48. McLoughlin, 1984, *op. cit.*, p. 25.

49. Lev Grossman, "2045: The Year Man Became Immortal," *Time*, Feb. 21, 2011, p. 46.

50. McLoughlin, 1984, *op. cit.*, p. 30.

51. John McLoughlin, *Toolmaker Koan* (New York: Baen Books, 1988).

52. Harry Harrison, *West of Eden* (New York: Bantam Books, 1984). I discuss Harrison's works in Debus, 2006, *op. cit.*

53. Stephen Leigh, *Ray Bradbury Presents Dinosaur World* (New York: Avon Books, 1992); Stephen Leigh, *Ray Bradbury Presents Dinosaur Planet* (New York: Avon Books, 1993).

54. Diane Carey, Star Trek: *First Frontier* (New York: Pocket Books, 1995).

55. Harry Turtledove, *World War: In the Balance* (New York: Ballantine Books, 1994). There were several published sequels.

56. Magee, *Who Lies Sleeping? The Dinosaur Heritage and the Extinction of Man* (Selwyn, Frome, England, AskWhy! Publications, 1993).

57. *Ibid.*, p. 106.

58. *Ibid.*, pp. 150–151.

Chapter Nineteen

1. James Blish's *A Case of Conscience* (1953; New York: Ballantine Books, 1958).

2. Luis Alvarez and W. Peter Trower, *Discovering Alvarez: Selected Works of Luis W. Alvarez with Commentary by His Students and Colleagues* (University of Chicago Press, 1987), p. 69; Luis Alvarez, *Alvarez: Adventures of a Physicist* (New York: Basic Books, 1987). During the early 1940s as well, Luis Alvarez published significant experimental data, proving that nuclear fusion occurred at "much lower ignition temperatures" than previously thought, thus paving the way for later development of the hydrogen bomb (p. 71).

3. William Tsutsui, *Godzilla on My Mind*, New York: Palgrave Macmillan, 2004, p. 19.

4. Interestingly, the beginning part of Blish's novel was published in *IF Worlds Science Fiction* in 1953—a year before *Gojira*'s release.

5. According to J.D. Lees's definition ("What is a Kaiju?" *G-Fan* no. 78 (Winter 2007): pp. 68–72), besides displaying other characteristics, a true *daikaiju* must display some measure of purposeful intelligence beyond that of a comparable animal. Despite their intelligence, however, Lithians aren't themselves *daikaiju* due to their nominal size. Also see Chapter Eighteen, notes, 11, 14 and 16.

6. Blish, *op. cit.*, pp. 183–188.

7. Imagine my consternation! In spite of all my concerted efforts at the tender age of 11 to be "cool," this insidious, monstrous on-screen conversation only affirmed that I was indeed watching a "kiddie movie"! Mutated bestial beings and dino-monsters simply aren't supposed to talk; speech was reserved only for their helpless, shrieking human victims, or so I had thought.

8. Aside from *monsters*, it will suffice to say that the idea of dinosaurs capable of verbal communication became a more common if not staple phenomenon in fantasy fiction books and other media following the 1980s dinosaur craze.

9. Walter Wager, *My Side by King Kong: As told to Wal-*

ter Wager (New York: Simon & Schuster, 1976); William Schoell, *Saurian* (Book Margins, 1988); Sam Enthoven, *Tim: Defender of the Earth* (London: Doubleday–Random House, 2008); John Gardner, *Grendel* (New York: Vintage Books, 1971).

10. Lees, *op. cit.*

11. Joseph Andriano, *Immortal Monster: Mythological Evolution of the Fantastic Beast in Modern Fiction and Film* (Westport, CT: Greenwood Press, 1999), p. 112.

12. Mark Jacobson, *Gojiro* (New York: Grove Press, 1991), p. 21.

13. *Ibid.*, p. 187.

14. *Ibid.*, p. 14.

15. *Ibid.*, p. 15.

16. *Ibid.*, p. 76.

17. *Ibid.*, p. 27.

18. *Ibid.*, p. 32. "Evolloo," of course, refers to the natural course of evolution.

19. *Ibid.*, p. 68.

20. *Ibid.*, p. 37.

21. *Ibid.*, p. 161.

22. *Ibid.*, pp. 27–28, 35, 236.

23. *Ibid.*, p. 35.

24. *Ibid.*, pp. 109–110, 235.

25. *Ibid.*, pp. 170–171.

26. *Ibid.*, pp. 198, 213–219, 233–244. I discussed the significance of life-through-geological-time "waking dreams" in my *Dinosaurs in Fantastic Fiction: A Thematic Survey* (Jefferson, NC: McFarland, 2006), pp. 27–28, 189.

27. *Ibid.*, p. 325.

28. *Ibid.*, p. 295.

29. *Ibid.*, p. 296.

30. *Ibid.*, p. 266.

31. For example, Marc Cerasini, *Godzilla Returns* (New York: Random House, 1996).

32. Nancy Anisfield, "Godzilla/Gojira: Evolution of the Nuclear Metaphor," *Journal of Popular Culture* 29, no. 3 (1995), p. 53.

Epilogue

1. Stephen Jay Gould, "Dinomania," in *Dinosaur in a Haystack: Reflections in Natural History* (New York: Harmony Books, 1995), p. 50.

2. W.J.T. Mitchell, *The Last Dinosaur Book* (University of Chicago Press, 1998), p. 108.

3. Ralph O'Connor, *The Earth on Show: Fossils and the Poetics of Popular Science, 1802–1856* (University of Chicago Press, 2007), p. 358.

4. This idea was a motif in *Paleoimagery: The Evolution of Dinosaurs in Art* (Jefferson, NC: McFarland, 2002), by Allen A. and Diane E. Debus.

5. Mitchell, *op. cit.*, pp. 103–108.

6. *Ibid.*, p. 104; "Godzimagery," a term used in Chapter Ten of this book, referring to visuals associated with Godzilla, may be viewed as a subset of paleoimagery.

7. Debus and Debus, 2002, *op. cit.*, p. 241.

8. *Ibid.*

9. Dale Russell cited in Mitchell, *op. cit.*, p. 108.

10. *Ibid.*

11. *Ibid.*, p. 100.

12. *Ibid.*, pp. 100, 106–109.

13. Jose Luis Sanz, *Starring T. Rex!: Dinosaur Mythology and Popular Culture* (Bloomington: Indiana University Press, 2002), p. 114.

14. William Schoell, *Saurian* (Book Margins, 1988).

15. Sanz, *op. cit.*, p. 115.

16. J.D. Lees, "What is a Kaiju?" *G-Fan*, no. 78 (Fall 2006): pp. 68–72 (quote from p. 71).

17. Allen A. Debus; "Toward a Unified Theory of Dinosaurian Kaiju: A *Pacific Rim*–inspired, 'what if?'" *G-Fan* no. 108 (Jan.–Feb. 2015): pp. 88–90. Also note Mike Field, "What is the meaning of 'Kaiju'?" *G-Fan* 81 (Fall 2007): pp. 38–39.

18. Stephen Jay Gould, "Reconstructing (and Deconstructing) the Past," preface to *The Book of Life: An Illustrated History of the Evolution of Life on Earth* (New York: W.W. Norton, 1993), pp. 20–21.

19. *Ibid.*, p. 20.

20. *Ibid.*, p. 21.

21. Arthur Conan Doyle, *The Lost World* (New York: A.L. Burt, 1912), p. 167.

22. Lyle Blackburn, *Lizardman: The True Story of the Bishopville Monster* (San Antonio: Anomalist Books, 2013), p. 60.

23. *Ibid.*, p. 63.

24. Mitchell, *op. cit.*, p. 231.

25. *Ibid.*, pp. 234, 238–239.

26. *Ibid.*, pp. 187–198; Gould, *op. cit.* (1995), p. 253.

27. *Ibid.*, p. 249.

28. *Ibid.*, p. 244.

29. *Ibid.*, pp. 9–10; Gould, 1995, *op. cit.*, p. 233. One example of a well-done animated dinosaur movie involving talking dinosaurs that appealed to children is Walt Disney Pictures' *Dinosaur* (2000).

30. A curious example in the "evolutionary convergence" category regards the BBC program *Primeval*, which in episodes 4.3 and 5.5 (2011) incorporated a nasty "Tree Creeper," described as a "humanoid-like species of arboreal raptor from the Cretaceous period" (http://primeval.wikia.com/wiki/Tree_Creeper). Thanks to dinosaur movie expert Mark Berry for this information. "Phylosynthesis" is a term adapted for science fictional consideration of Edgar Rice Burroughs's novels *The Land That Time Forgot* (1918) and *The People That Time Forgot* (1918), by Charles De Paolo, in his book *Human Prehistory in Fiction* (Jefferson, NC: McFarland, 2003), pp. 37–45. Also see Allen A. Debus, *Dinosaurs in Fantastic Fiction: A Thematic Survey* (Jefferson, NC: McFarland, 2006), pp. 46–49.

31. Allen A. Debus, 2006, *op. cit.* Dinosauroids as discussed in *Dinosaurs in Fantastic Fiction* are not addressed quite in the particular vein, as outlined herein. Note that in science fiction, there are multiple kinds of "origination" backstories explaining occurrences of anthropomorphized dinosaurs and intelligent dinosauroids, such as those escaping to outer space during the Mesozoic, or retreating to Earth's interior, inhabiting "lost" continental surfaces such as "Dinotopia" or converging from parallel universes via space-time warps. A much closer association happens when humans share and/or control the mental faculties of the dinosaur itself through mind-transfer (while it lives in its Mesozoic time). Most palpably, however, is the biomolecular connection resulting from DNA-genetic mutations and abnormalities, thus converting humans into dino-reptiloids through a variety of mechanisms. The theme of DNA-genetic connectivity to humans (our closest possible science fictional relationship) became more pronounced during the dinosaur renaissance period. Some science fictional examples illustrating the close-knit genetic tie between humans and fictional dinosaurians and dinosauroids include: from the life-through-time age outlined in Part One of this book, Edgar Rice Burroughs's *The Land That*

Time Forgot and *The People That Time Forgot* (1918), both reprinted by New York: Ace Books (1963); and from the third age, Penelope Banks Kreps' novel *Carnivores* (New York: Kensington, 1993); Michelle M. Sagara's short story, "Shadow of a Change" (1993), reprinted in *Dinosaur Fantastic*, Mike Resnick and Martin H. Greenberg, eds. (New York: Daw Books, 1993), pp. 145–159; Bill Johnson's "The Vaults of Permian Love," *Analog Science Fiction and Fact* 119, no. 5 (May 1999): pp. 72–85; Johnathan Green's *Pax Brittanica: Unnatural History* (Surrey, England: Bookmarque, Abaddonbooks.com, 2007), see especially p. 149.

32. Bob Buckley, "The Runners," *Analog* (April 1978), reprinted in *Dinosaurs!*, Jack Dann and Gardner Dozois, eds. (New York: Ace Books, 1990), pp. 76–96.

33. Robert Reed, "Stride," *Asimov's Science Fiction* (1994), reprinted in *The Dragons of Eden* (Collinsville, IL: Golden Gryphon Press, 1999), pp. 96–128.

34. David Sakmyster and Rick Chesler, *Jurassic Dead* (Severed Press, 2014). Another title in the vein of ill-fated, Frankensteinian DNA transferal is Jeremy Robinson's *Project Nemesis* (Breakneck Media, 2012).

35. James F. David, *Footprints of Thunder* (New York: Tor Books, 1995), pp. 456, 461.

36. For instance, unread by me, are erotic books by Christie Sims, available online as e-books, with titles like *T. Rex Troubles* and *Mating with the Raptor*.

37. Gould, 1995, *op. cit.*, p. 233.

38. For instance, J.D. Lees commented in an editorial in *G-Fan* no. 108 (Jan.–Feb. 2015): p. 5, on how the 2014 film proved lackluster.

39. Greg Cox, *Godzilla* (London: Titan Books, 2014), p. 284, 293–294.

40. Allen A. Debus, "Battle of the Giant Monster Novels: King Kong vs. Godzilla, (Part 2 of 2)," *Mad Scientist* no. 30 (Winter 2015): pp. 35–43.

41. Emily W. Sunstein, *Romance and Reality* (Boston: Little, Brown, 1989), p. 271. For further modern insight on the nature of temporal organismal ordering through geological time, and the matter of (cladistic) evolutionary progress, see Gould's essay, "Evolution by Walking," in his essay collection, *Dinosaur in a Haystack: Reflections in Natural History* (New York: Harmony Books, 1995), pp. 248–259.

42. Carl Sagan, *The Dragons of Eden: Speculations on the Evolution of Human Intelligence* (New York: Ballantine Books, 1977); Mike Magee, *Who Lies Sleeping? The Dinosaur Heritage and the Extinction of Man* (Selwyn, Frome, England: AskWhy! Publications, 1993); Edward O. Wilson, *The Social Conquest of Earth* (New York: Liveright, 2012). In particular, Wilson notes that as humans proliferated during the Pleistocene, "The rest of the living world could not coevolve fast enough to accommodate the onslaught of a spectacular conqueror that seemed to come from nowhere, and it began to crumble from the pressure" (p. 16). Here we learn that man's rapacious, xenophobic, tribalistic, carnivorous tendencies, coupled with warlike practices, may obviate extended survival for modern civilization. Also see "Assessing the Causes of Late Pleistocene Extinctions on the Continents," by Anthony D. Barnosky *et al.*, published in *Science* 306 (Oct. 1, 2004): pp. 70–75.

43. Magee, *op. cit.*, p. 153. Added to the mix are the spate of new millennial disaster films expressing fears and concerns over suspected human-induced climate change, or "cli-fi" flicks, as aptly termed by Lily Rothman in "Nature Bites Back" (*Time*, May 19, 2014), pp. 50–52.

44. Loren Eiseley, *The Invisible Pyramid* (New York: Scribner's, 1970); James Lovelock, *The Revenge of Gaia: Earth's Climate Crisis and the Fate of Humanity* (New York: Basic Books, 2006); James Lovelock, *The Vanishing Face of Gaia: A Final Warning* (New York: Basic Books, 2009). Lovelock now believes that the only handle humankind can get on reducing the threat of adverse climate change this century would be to predominantly switch over to energy sources leaving a minimalistic carbon footprint, such as nuclear power. In 2015, Pope Francis stated in his encyclical, concerning how man must combat climate change, "The earth, our home, is beginning to look more and more like an immense pile of filth" (*Time*, July 6–July 13, 2015, p. 10).

45. Another valid reason for why sci-fi writers and imagineers may prefer anthropomorphized or anthropocentric dinosaurs is that, as indicated in my *Dinosaurs in Fantastic Fiction* (*op. cit.*), it is easier to convey stories via a human(oid) or reptiloid perspective, as opposed to via the more alien-minded cognition of real dinosaurs, creatures which usually function in such stories as monstrous "props." However, Robert T. Bakker splendidly captured the cognitive essence, senses and mindset of Late Cretaceous raptor dinosaurs (the titular Raptor Red being of the genus *Utahraptor*) in his 1995 novel, *Raptor Red* (New York: Bantam Books). Also on Bakker's *Raptor Red*, see Debus, *op. cit.* (2006), pp. 142–143,159–160.

Note added in proof: Lees' kaiju definition delimits what may be considered a giant mysterious beast.

Bibliography

Alvarez, Luis W. *Alvarez: Adventures of a Physicist.* New York: Basic Books, 1987.

______, W. Alvarez, F. Asaro, and H.V. Michel. "Extraterrestrial causes for the Cretaceous-Tertiary extinction." *Science* 208 (1980): pp. 1095–1108.

Alvarez, Walter. *T. rex and the Crater of Doom.* Princeton University Press, 1997.

Bakker, Robert T. *The Dinosaur Heresies.* New York: William Morrow, 1986.

Benton, Michael. "Scientific Methodologies in Collision: The History of the Study of the Extinction of the Dinosaurs." *Evolutionary Biology* 24 (1990): pp. 371–400.

Berry, Mark F. *The Dinosaur Filmography.* Jefferson, NC: McFarland, 2002.

Bingham, Carson. *Gorgo.* Derby, CT: Monarch Books, 1960.

Blish, James. *A Case of Conscience.* New York: Ballantine Books, 1958.

Bowler, Peter J. *The Norton History of the Environmental Sciences.* New York: W.W. Norton, 1992.

Bradbury, Ray. *Dinosaur Tales.* New York: Bantam Books, 1983.

Broderick, Mick, ed., *Hibakusha Cinema: Hiroshima, Nagasaki and the Nuclear Image in Japanese Film.* London & New York: Kegan Paul International, 1996.

Chambers, Robert. *Vestiges of the Natural History of Creation.* London: John Churchill, 1844.

Chiappe, Luis M. *Glorified Dinosaurs: The Origin and Early Evolution of Birds.* Hoboken, NJ: John Wiley & Sons, 2006.

Czerkas, Stephen. "O'Brien vs. Dawley: The First Great Rivalry in Visual Effects." *Cinefex* 138 (July 2014): pp. 13–26.

Czerkas, Sylvia M., and Stephen A. Czerkas. *Dinosaurs: A Global View.* New York: Mallard Press, 1991.

Czerkas, Sylvia M., and Donald F. Glut. *Dinosaurs, Mammoths and Cavemen: The Art of Charles R. Knight.* New York: E.P. Dutton, 1982.

Czerkas, Sylvia M., and Everett C. Olson, eds. *Dinosaurs Past and Present,* vols. 1 and 2. Seattle: Natural History Museum of Los Angeles County in association with University of Washington Press, 1987.

Davy, Humphry. *Consolations in Travel, or the Last Days of a Philosopher.* Philadelphia: John Gregg, 1830.

Debus, Allen A. *Dinosaurs in Fantastic Fiction: A Thematic Survey.* Jefferson, NC: McFarland, 2006.

______, and Diane E. Debus. *Paleoimagery: The Evolution of Dinosaurs in Art.* Jefferson, NC: McFarland, 2002.

Debus, Allen A., Bob Morales, and Diane E. Debus. *Dinosaur Sculpting: A Complete Guide.* 2nd ed. Jefferson, NC: McFarland, 2013. Chapter Two, "An Overview of Paleoimagery," by Allen A. Debus.

Desmond, Adrian J. *The Hot-Blooded Dinosaurs: A Revolution in Palaeontology.* New York: Warner Books, 1975.

Dixon, Dougal. *After Man: A Zoology of the Future.* New York: St. Martin's Press, 1981.

______. *The New Dinosaurs: An Alternative Evolution.* Topsfield, MA: Salem House, 1988.

Erwin, Douglas. *Extinction: How Life on Earth Nearly Ended 250 Million Years Ago.* Princeton University Press, 2006.

Fastovsky, David E., and David B. Weishampel. *The Evolution and Extinction of the Dinosaurs.* 2nd ed. Cambridge: Cambridge University Press, 2005.

Glen, William, ed. *Mass-Extinction Debates: How Science Works in a Crisis.* Stanford University Press, 1994.

Glut, Donald F. *Dinosaurs: The Encyclopedia.* Jefferson, NC: McFarland, 1997.

______. *Dinosaurs: The Encyclopedia—Supplement 1.* Jefferson, NC: McFarland, 2000.

______. *Dinosaurs: The Encyclopedia—Supplement 2.* Jefferson, NC: McFarland, 2002.

______. *Dinosaurs: The Encyclopedia—Supplement 3.* Jefferson, NC: McFarland, 2003.

______. *Dinosaurs: The Encyclopedia—Supplement 4.* Jefferson, NC: McFarland, 2006.

______. *Dinosaurs: The Encyclopedia—Supplement 5.* Jefferson, NC: McFarland, 2008.

______. *Dinosaurs: The Encyclopedia—Supplement 6.* Jefferson, NC: McFarland, 2010.

______. *Dinosaurs: The Encyclopedia—Supplement 7.* Jefferson, NC: McFarland, 2012.

Godziszewski, Ed. "The Making of *Godzilla.*" *Japanese Giants* 1, no. 10 (2004): p. 11.

Gould, Stephen Jay. *Dinosaur in a Haystack: Reflections in Natural History.* New York: Harmony Books, 1995.

______, ed. *The Book of Life: An Illustrated History of the Evolution of Life on Earth.* New York: W.W. Norton, 1993.

Henderson, Lawrence J. *The Fitness of the Environment: An Inquiry into the Biological Significance of the Properties of Matter.* 1913. New York: Macmillan, 1958.

Horner, John R., and Don Lessem. *The Complete T. rex.* New York: Simon & Schuster, 1993.

Jacobson, Mark. *Gojiro.* New York: Grove Press, 1991.

Justice, Mark. "Save the Earth! Environmental and Ecological Messages in Toho's Giant Monster Movies,"

Parts 1 and 2. *G-Fan* nos. 94 (Winter 2011: pp. 24–25; 95 (Spring 2011): pp. 20–29.

Knipe, Henry R. *Evolution in the Past*. London: Herbert and Daniel, 1912.

______. *Nebula to Man*. London: J.M. Dent, 1905.

Kolbert, Elizabeth. *The Sixth Extinction: An Unnatural History*. New York: Henry Holt, 2014.

Lapp, Ralph E. *The Voyage of the Lucky Dragon*. Harper & Brothers, 1958.

Lightman, Bernard. *Victorian Popularizers of Science: Designing Nature for New Audiences*. University of Chicago Press, 2007.

Lovelock, James. *The Vanishing Face of Gaia: A Final Warning*. New York: Basic Books, 2009.

McLean, Dewey. "Terminal Mesozoic 'Greenhouse': Lessons from the Past." *Science* 201 (August 4, 1978): pp. 401–406.

McLoughlin, John C. "Evolutionary Bioparanoia," *Animal Kingdom* (April/May 1984): pp. 24–30.

Magee, Mike. *Who Lies Sleeping? The Dinosaur Heritage and the Extinction of Man*. Selwyn, Frome, England: AskWhy! Publications, 1993.

Matashichi, Oishi. *The Day the Sun Rose in the West*. University of Hawaii Press, 2011.

Mitchell, W.J.T. *The Last Dinosaur Book: The Life and Times of a Cultural Icon*. University of Chicago Press, 1998.

Norman, David. *Dinosaur!: Based on the Acclaimed Four-part Television Series*. New York: Prentice Hall, 1991.

O'Connor, Ralph. *The Earth on Show: Fossils and the Poetics of Popular Science, 1802–1856*. University of Chicago Press, 2007.

Osborn, Henry Fairfield. *The Origin and Evolution of Life*. New York: Scribner's, 1918.

Ostrom, John H. *Osteology of Deinonychus antirrhopus, an Unusual Theropod from the Lower Cretaceous of Montana*. Bulletin 30, Peabody Museum of Natural History, Yale University, July 1969.

Page, Max. *The City's End: Two Centuries of Fantasies, Fears, and Premonitions of New York's Destruction*. New Haven: Yale University Press, 2008.

The Past and Present Life of the Globe: Being a Sketch in Outline of the World's Life-System. Edinburgh: William Blackwood and Sons, 1861.

Powell, James Lawrence. *Night Comes to the Cretaceous: Dinosaur Extinctions and the Transformation of Modern Geology*. New York: W.H. Freeman, 1998.

Ragone, August. *Eiji Tsubuyara: Master of Monsters*. San Francisco: Chronicle Books, 2007.

Rainger, Ronald. *An Agenda for Antiquity: Henry Fairfield Osborn and Vertebrate Paleontology at the American Museum of Natural History*. Tuscaloosa: University of Alabama Press, 1991.

Randall, Lisa. *Dark Matter and the Dinosaurs: The Astounding Interconnectedness of the Universe*. New York: HarperCollins, 2015.

Raup, David M. *The Nemesis Affair: A Story of the Death of the Dinosaurs and the Ways of Science*. University of Chicago Press, 1986.

Rhoads, Sean. "Godzilla the Social Critic." *G-Fan* 98 (Winter 2012): pp. 18–28.

Rhodes, Richard. *Dark Sun: The Making of the Hydrogen Bomb*. New York: Simon & Schuster, 1995.

______. *The Making of the Atomic Bomb*. New York: Simon & Schuster, 1986.

Rovin, Jeff. *From the Land Beyond Beyond*. New York: Berkeley, 1977.

Rudwick, Martin J. S. *Bursting the Limits of Time: The Reconstruction of a Science 1650–1830*. University of Chicago Press, 2005.

______. *Scenes from Deep Time: Early Pictorial Representations of the Prehistoric World*. Chicago: University of Chicago Press, 1992.

______. *Worlds Before Adam: The Reconstruction of Geohistory in the Age of Reform*. University of Chicago Press, 2008.

Russell, Dale A. "Models and Paintings of North American Dinosaurs," in *Dinosaurs Past and Present*, volume 1. Ed. Sylvia J. Czerkas and Everett C. Olson. Seattle and London: Natural History Museum of Los Angeles County in association with University of Washington Press, 1987.

______, and Ron Seguin. "Reconstructions of the small Cretaceous theropod *Stenonychosaurus inequalis* and a hypothetical dinosauroid," *Syllogeus* (1982).

Ryfle, Steve. *Japan's Favorite Mon Star: The Unauthorized Biography of "The Big G."* Toronto: ECW Press, 1998.

Sagan, Carl. *The Dragons of Eden: Speculations on the Evolution of Human Intelligence*. New York: Ballantine Books, 1977.

Sanz, Jose Luis. *Starring T. Rex!: Dinosaur Mythology and Popular Culture*. Bloomington: Indiana University Press, 2002.

Scully, V., R.F. Zallinger, L.J. Hickey, and J.H. Ostrom. *The Age of Reptiles: The Great Dinosaur Mural at Yale*. New Haven: Peabody Museum of Natural History, 1990.

Secord, James A. *Victorian Sensation: The Extraordinary Publication, Reception, and Secret Authorship of Vestiges of the Natural History of Creation*. University of Chicago Press, 2000.

Siegfried, Robert, and Robert H. Dott Jr. *Humphry Davy on Geology: The 1805 Lectures for the General Audience*. Madison: University of Wisconsin Press, 1980.

Simpson, George Gaylord. *Life of the Past*. New Haven: Yale University Press, 1968.

Stout, William, edited by Byron Preiss and narrated by William Service. *The Dinosaurs: A Fantastic New View of a Lost Era*. New York: Mallard Press, 1981.

Tooker, Richard. *Inland Deep*. Philadelphia: Penn, 1936.

Tsutsui, William. *Godzilla on My Mind: Fifty Years of the King of Monsters*. New York: Palgrave Macmillan, 2004.

Vogt, Peter. "Evidence for Global Synchronism in Mantle Plume Convection, and Possible Significance for Geology." *Nature* 240 (December 8, 1972): pp. 338–342.

Ward, Peter. *The Medea Hypothesis: Is Life on Earth Ultimately Self-Destructive?* Princeton University Press, 2009.

______. *Under a Green Sky*. Smithsonian Books, 2007.

Weart, Spencer R. *The Discovery of Global Warming*. Harvard University Press, 2003.

______. *Nuclear Fear: A History of Images*. Harvard University Press, 1988.

Weaver, Tom. *Tom Weaver Presents the Scripts from the Crypt Collection: No. 1, The Hideous Sun Demon, the Original Screenplay*. Duncan, OK: BearManor Media, 2011.

Wilson, Edward O. *The Social Conquest of Earth*. New York: Liveright, 2012.

Index

Numbers in ***bold italics*** refer to pages with photographs.

www.ingramcontent.com/pod-product-compliance
Ingram Content Group UK Ltd.
Pitfield, Milton Keynes, MK11 3LW, UK
UKHW060612180726
13836UKWH00012B/2514